MOON HANDBOOKS®
MAUI

Haleakala, as seen from West Maui looking across Kahului Bay

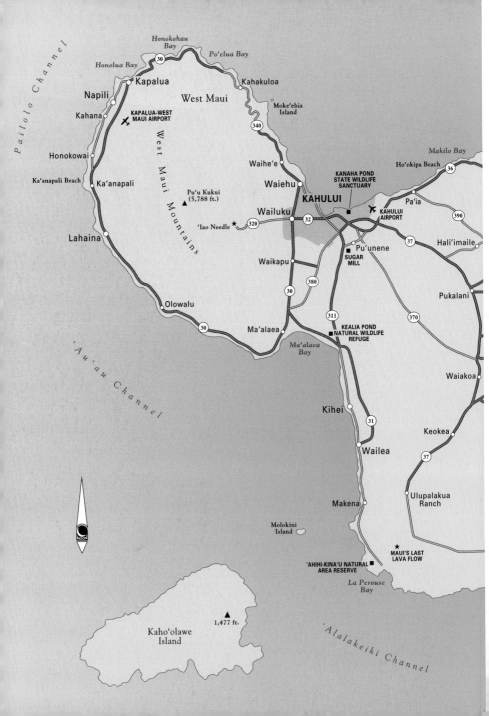

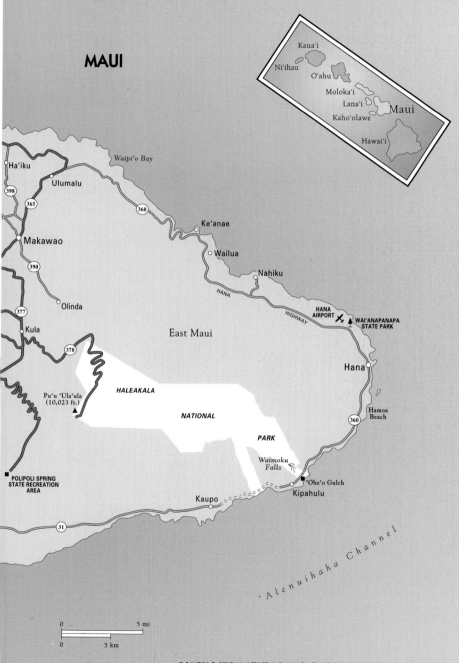

MAUI

Ha'iku

Ulumalu

Makawao

Olinda

Kula

Waipi'o Bay

398

365

360

390

377

378

Ke'anae

Wailua

Nahiku

HANA

HIGHWAY

East Maui

Pu'u 'Ula'ula
(10,023 ft.)
▲

HALEAKALA

NATIONAL

PARK

*Waimoku
Falls*

POLIPOLI SPRING
STATE RECREATION
AREA

Kaupo

31

**HANA
AIRPORT** ✈

**WAI'ANAPANAPA
STATE PARK**

Hana

Hamoa
Beach

360

'Ohe'o Gulch

Kipahulu

Alenuihaha Channel

Kaua'i

Ni'ihau

O'ahu

Moloka'i

Lana'i

Kaho'olawe

Hawai'i

Maui

0   5 mi

0   5 km

sunset at Napili Bay

MOON HANDBOOKS®
MAUI

INCLUDING MOLOKA'I AND LANA'I

SEVENTH EDITION

ROBERT NILSEN

AVALON
TRAVEL

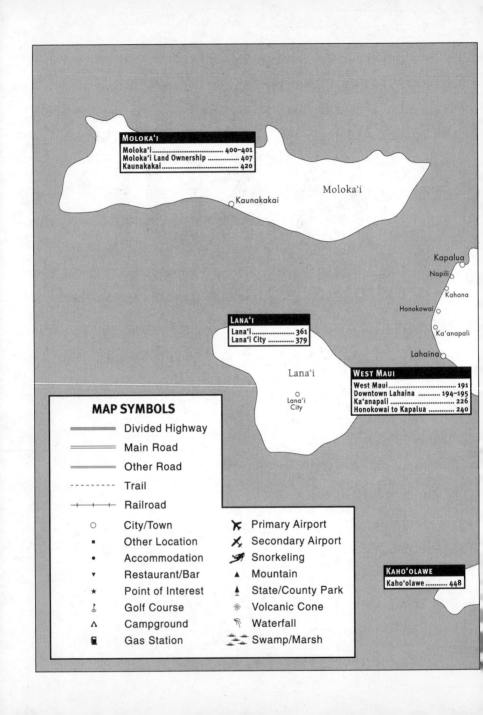

MOLOKA'I

Moloka'i

○ Kaunakakai

Kapalua
Napili ○
○ Kahana
Honokowai ○
○ Ka'anapali
Lahaina ○

LANA'I

Lana'i

○
Lana'i
City

WEST MAUI

MAP SYMBOLS

═══════	Divided Highway
═══════	Main Road
─────	Other Road
- - - - -	Trail
┼──┼──┼	Railroad

○	City/Town	✈	Primary Airport
▪	Other Location	✕	Secondary Airport
•	Accommodation	🤿	Snorkeling
▼	Restaurant/Bar	▲	Mountain
★	Point of Interest	⚑	State/County Park
⚓	Golf Course	✳	Volcanic Cone
⋀	Campground	⫶	Waterfall
⛽	Gas Station	⸎	Swamp/Marsh

KAHO'OLAWE

MAPS

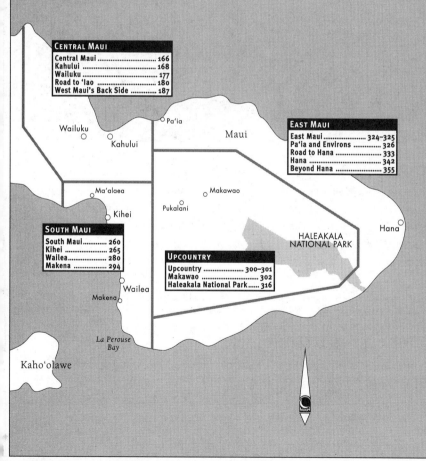

Wailuku
Kahului
Pa'ia
Maui
Ma'alaea
Kihei
Pukalani
Makawao
Hana
HALEAKALA
NATIONAL PARK
Wailea
Makena
La Perouse
Bay
Kaho'olawe

© SANDRA E. BISIGNANI TRUST AND AVALON TRAVEL PUBLISHING, INC.

Contents

ROBERT NILSEN

Central Maui: The Isthmus

Known for the striking monolithic spires of 'Iao Valley, this isthmus between east and west also has deep historical significance. Wailuku, with its 19th-century courthouse and white-steeple church, has been home to both kings and missionaries. This is also where a quarter of the island's population lives, giving these towns a much homier feel than the deluxe resort complexes elsewhere on the island.

West Maui

Busy Lahaina is Maui's center of art, history, fine dining, and nightlife. Nearby, the seemingly endless beach at Ka'anapali stretches uninterrupted for miles. Is it any surprise that gorgeous resorts have become as plentiful in West Maui as the surf and sunshine?

South Maui

The south side offers something for every personality. High-class Wailea boasts jewel-box resorts, 1,450 acres of world-class golf courses, and five sparkling beaches open to the public, while former hippie enclave Makena clings to its free spirit—and the area's last stretch of pristine coastline. Less expensive Kihei suffers from overdevelopment, but still offers unbeatable sun and surf.

Upcountry

All over Maui, people look Upcountry to the muscled mountain of Haleakala. With cool temperatures and fertile soil, this region is ideal for farms, botanical gardens, and cattle—paniolo still ride the ranges of enormous ranches. Art galleries, fine dining, and even wine tasting lend some sophistication, but the cowboy culture lives on—Upcountry is a state of mind.

East Maui

On the long and winding road to Hana, daydreams of paradise come true. It's worth enduring more than 600 rollicking turns and 57 one-lane bridges to experience the most remarkable 50 miles in the world: a journey marked by surfing beaches, sacred pools, tunnels of trees, and glimpses of azure blue.

Lana'i

Known as the "Secluded Island," Lana'i caters to well-to-do travelers seeking peace, quiet, and the perfect beach. Set foot on this little-visited island and you'll also find a well-preserved ancient Hawaiian village, magnificent panoramas along the Munro Trail, and one of the best snorkeling spots in all of Hawaii.

Moloka'i 398

Moloka'i is both sanctuary and tribal homeland, where a primeval world of emerald green waits beyond the farthest reaches of the last road. This once-lonely isle has in recent years become "The Friendly Isle," where visitors can enjoy the white expanse of Papohaku Beach, the state's only continuous barrier reef, and its tallest sea cliffs.

Kaho'olawe 447

Decades ago, this sacred isle was commandeered by the U.S. Navy for target practice. Since its rescue by native-rights organizations, it's begun a long restoration process, and may once again become a place where Hawaiians can go to practice age-old traditions. For now, most visitors must be content to view Kaho'olawe from across the water.

Resources 453

ABOUT THE AUTHOR
Robert Nilsen

ROBERT NILSEN

Robert Nilsen was born and raised in Minnesota. His first major excursion from the Midwest was a two-year stint in South Korea with the Peace Corps. Following that eye-opening service, he stayed on in Korea independently, teaching and traveling, and soaking up as much of its history and culture as he could. Setting his sights on other lands and cultures, he made a two-year trek through Asia before returning home to the United States, and since then has had the good fortune to return to Asia and the Pacific on numerous occasions. Robert has written *Moon Handbooks South Korea* for Avalon Travel Publishing, and has contributed to *Moon Handbooks Indonesia.*

Since the passing of his good friend J.D. Bisignani, he has shouldered full responsibility for the revision of Moon Handbooks' Hawaii series, including *Moon Handbooks Hawaii, Moon Handbooks Kaua'i, Moon Handbooks O'ahu, Moon Handbooks Maui,* and *Moon Handbooks Big Island of Hawai'i.*

It is the many wonderful aspects of the Hawaiian Islands—slack-key guitar, palm-fringed beaches, tropical mountain hikes, the reemergent culture of the Hawaiian people and their friendly *aloha* spirit—that keep Robert heading back each year.

Introduction

The *Kumulipo,* the ancient genealogical chant of the Hawaiians, sings of the demigod Maui, a half-human mythological sorcerer known and revered throughout Polynesia. Maui was a prankster on a grand scale who used guile and humor to create some of the most amazing feats of derring-do ever recorded. A Polynesian combination of Paul Bunyan and Hercules, Maui's adventures were known as "strifes." He served humankind by fishing up the islands of Hawaii from the ocean floor, securing fire from a tricky mud hen, lifting the sky so people could walk upright, and slowing down the sun god by lassoing his genitals with a braided rope of his sister's pubic hair. Maui accomplished this last feat on the summit of the great mountain Haleakala

("House of the Sun"), thus securing more time in the day to fish and to dry tapa. Maui met his just but untimely end between the legs of the great goddess, Hina. This final prank, in which he attempted to crawl into the sleeping goddess's vagina, left his feet and legs dangling out, causing uproarious laughter among his comrades, a band of warrior birds. The noise awakened Hina, who saw no humor in the situation. She unceremoniously squeezed Maui to death. The island of Maui is the only island in Hawaii and throughout Polynesia named after a god. With such a legacy, the island couldn't help but become worthy of the moniker *"Maui no ka ʻoi"* ("Maui is the best!").

In a land of superlatives, it's quite a claim to call your island *the* best, but Maui has a lot to back it

ROBERT NILSEN

sunset at Kaʻanapali

up. Maui has more miles of swimmable beach than any of the other islands. Haleakala, the massive mountain that *is* East Maui, is the largest dormant volcano in the world, and its hardened lava rising over 30,000 feet from the sea floor makes it one of the heaviest concentrated masses on the face of the earth. There are legitimate claims that Maui grows the best onions and potatoes, but the boast of the best *pakalolo* may only be a pipe dream, since all islands have great soil, weather, and many enterprising gardeners. Some even claim that Maui gets more sunshine than the other islands, but that's hard to prove.

West Maui

If you look at the silhouette of Maui on a map, it looks like the head and torso of the mythical demigod bent at the waist and contemplating the uninhabited island of Kahoʻolawe. The head is West Maui, and its profile is that of a wizened old man whose wrinkled brow and cheeks are the West Maui Mountains. The highest peak here is **Puʻu Kukui,** at 5,788 feet, located just about where the ear would be. If you go to the top of the head you'll be at **Kapalua,** a resort community that's been carved from pineapple fields. Fleming Beach begins a string of beaches that continues down over the face, stopping at the chin, and picking up again at the throat, covers the chest, which is South Maui. **Kaʻanapali** is located at the forehead; its massive beach continues almost uninterrupted for four miles, an area that in comparison would take in all of Waikiki, from Diamond Head to Ala Moana. The resorts here are cheek to jowl, but the best are tastefully done with uninterrupted panoramic views and easy and plentiful access to the beach. Between Kapalua and Kaʻanapali, pineapple fields fringe the mountain side of the road, while condos are strung along the shore throughout the communities of **Honokowai, Kahana,** and **Napili.**

Lahaina is located at the Hindu "third eye." This town is where it's "happening" on Maui, with concentrations of craftspeople, artists, museums, historical sites, restaurants, and nightspots. Used in times past by royal Hawaiian *aliʻi* and then by Yankee whalers, Lahaina has always been somewhat of a playground, and the good-times mystique still lingers. It's from Lahaina, across the waters of the ʻAuʻau Channel, better known as the "Lahaina Roads," that people can catch a glimpse of the island of Lanaʻi. At the tip of the nose is **Olowalu,** where a lunatic Yankee trader, Simon Metcalfe, decided to slaughter hundreds of curious Hawaiians paddling toward his ship just to show them he was boss. From Olowalu you can see four islands: Molokaʻi, Lanaʻi, Kahoʻolawe, and a faint hint of Hawaiʻi far to the southeast. The back of Maui's head is little known, but for the mildly adventurous it presents tremendous coastal views and Kahakuloa, a tiny fishing village reported to be a favorite stomping ground of great Maui himself.

Central Maui: The Isthmus

A low, flat isthmus planted primarily in sugarcane is the neck that connects the head of West Maui to the torso of East Maui, which is Haleakala. The Adam's apple is the little port of **Maʻalaea,** which has a good assortment of pleasure and fishing boats as well as the new **Maui Ocean Center.** Maʻalaea provides an up-close look at a working port that is not nearly as frenetic as Lahaina. The nape of the neck is made up of the twin cities of **Wailuku,** the county seat, and **Kahului,** where most visitors arrive at Maui's principal airport. These towns are where the "people" live. Some say the isthmus, dramatically separating east and west, is the reason Maui is called "The Valley Isle." Head into **ʻIao Valley** from Wailuku, where the West Maui Mountains have been worn into incredible peaked monolithic spires. This stunning valley area played a key role in Kamehameha's unification of the Hawaiian Islands, and geologically it seems to be a more fitting reason for Maui's nickname.

East Maui/Haleakala

Once you cross the isthmus you're on the immensity of **Haleakala,** the one mountain that makes up the entire bulging, muscled torso of the island. A continent in microcosm, its geology encompasses alpine terrain, arid scrub desert, moonscape, blazing jungle, pastureland, and lava-encrusted wasteland. The temperature, determined by altitude, ranges from subfreezing to subtropical. If you head east along the spine, you'll find world-class windsurfing beaches, the artist and surfer village of **Pa'ia,** long-forgotten towns, and a few remaining family farms planted in taro. Route 360, the only coastal road, rocks and rolls you over more than 600 curves and shows you more waterfalls and pristine pools than you can count. After crossing more than 50 bridges, you come to **Hana.** Here, the dream Hawaii that people seek still lives. Farther along is **Kipahulu** and **'Ohe'o Guich,** known for its fantastic pools and waterfalls. Close by is where Charles Lindbergh is buried, and many celebrities have chosen the surrounding hillsides for their special retreats and hideaways.

On Haleakala's broad chest is the macho cowboy town of **Makawao,** complete with a Wild West rodeo contrasting with the gentle but riotous colors of carnation and protea farms down the road in **Kula. Polipoli Spring State Recreation Area** is here, a thick forest canopy with more varieties of imported trees than anywhere else in Oceania. A weird cosmic joke places **Kihei** just about where the armpit would be. Kihei is a mega-growth condo area ridiculed as an example of what developers shouldn't be allowed to do. Oddly enough, **Wailea,** just down the road, exemplifies a reasonable and aesthetic planned, although much more exclusive, community and is highly touted as a model development area. Just at the belly button, close to the Kundalini, is **Makena,** long renowned as Maui's alternative beach, but rapidly losing its status as the island's last "free" beach.

Finally, when you make your pilgrimage to the summit of Haleakala, it's as if you've left the planet. It's another world: beautiful, mystical, raw, inspired, and freezing cold. When you're alone on the crater rim with the world below garlanded by the brilliance of sunrise or sunset, you'll know that you have come at last to great Maui's heart.

The Land

The modern geological theory concerning the formation of the Hawaiian Islands is no less fanciful than the Polynesian legends sung about it. Science maintains that 30 million years ago, while the great continents were being geologically tortured into their rudimentary shapes, the Hawaiian Islands were a mere ooze of bubbling magma 20,000 feet below the surface of the primordial sea. For millions of years this molten rock flowed up through fissures in the sea floor. Slowly, layer upon layer of lava was deposited until an island rose above the surface of the sea. The island's great weight then sealed the fissures, whose own colossal forces progressively crept in a southeasterly direction, then burst out again and again to build the chain. At the same time the entire Pacific plate was afloat on the giant sea of molten magma, and it slowly glided to the northwest, carrying the newly formed islands with it.

In the beginning the spewing crack formed Kure and Midway islands in the extreme northwestern sector of the Hawaiian chain. This process continued for eons, and today 132 islands, islets, and shoals make up the Hawaiian Islands, stretching 1,600 miles across an expanse of the North Pacific. Geologists maintain that the "hot spot" now primarily under the Big Island remains relatively stationary and that the 1,600-mile spread of the Hawaiian archipelago is caused by a northwest drifting effect of about 3–5 inches per year. Still, with the center of activity under the Big Island, Mauna Loa and Kilauea volcanoes regularly add more land to the only state in the Union that is literally still growing. About 20 miles southeast of the Big Island is Lo'ihi Seamount, waiting 3,000 feet below the waves. Frequent eruptions bring it closer and closer to the surface; one day it will emerge as the newest Hawaiian island and later, perhaps, merge with the Big Island.

Mountains

After the Big Island of Hawai'i, Maui is the second largest and second youngest of the main Hawaiian Islands. The land was formed from two volcanoes: the **West Maui Mountains** and

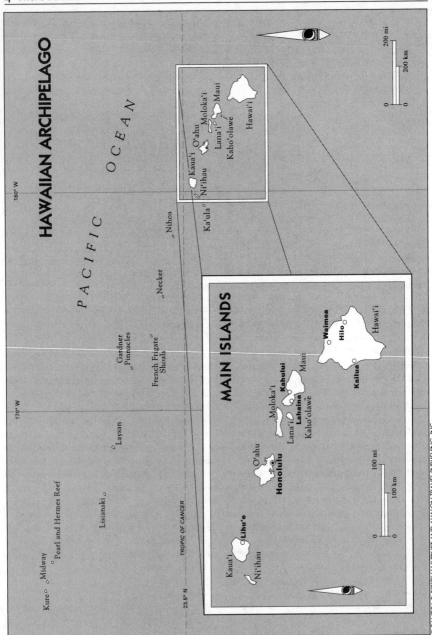

HAWAIIAN ARCHIPELAGO

PACIFIC OCEAN

160° W

170° W

Kure
Midway
Pearl and Hermes Reef

Lisianski

Laysan

Gardner
Pinnacles

French Frigate
Shoals

Necker

Nihoa

Ka'ula

Ni'ihau

Kaua'i

O'ahu
Moloka'i
Lana'i
Kaho'olawe
Maui

Hawai'i

23.5° N
TROPIC OF CANCER

0   200 mi
0   200 km

MAIN ISLANDS

Kaua'i
Lihu'e

Ni'ihau

O'ahu
Honolulu

Moloka'i

Lana'i

Kahului
Lahaina
Kaho'olawe
Maui

Waimea
Hilo

Kailua

Hawai'i

0   100 mi
0   100 km

Haleakala. The West Maui Mountains are geologically much older than Haleakala, but the two were joined by subsequent lava flows that formed a connecting low, flat isthmus. **Pu'u Kukui,** at 5,788 feet, is the tallest peak of the West Maui Mountains. It's the lord of a mountain domain whose old, weathered face has been scarred by a series of deep crags, verdant valleys, and inhospitable gorges. Rising over 30,000 feet from the ocean floor, **Haleakala** is by comparison an adolescent with smooth, rounded features looming 10,023 feet above sea level, with a landmass four times larger than West Maui. The two parts of Maui combine to form 727 square miles of land with 120 linear miles of coastline. At its widest, Maui is 26 miles from north to south and 48 miles east to west. The coastline has the largest number of swimmable beaches in Hawaii, and the interior is a miniature continent with almost every conceivable geological feature evident.

Island Builders

The Hawaiians worshipped Madame Pele, the fire goddess whose name translates equally well as "Volcano," "Fire Pit," or "Eruption of Lava." When she was angry, Madame Pele complained by spitting fire and spewing lava that cooled and formed land. Volcanologists say that the islands are huge mounds of cooled basaltic lava surrounded by billions of polyp skeletons, which have formed coral reefs. Maui, like all the Hawaiian Islands, is in essence a shield volcano that erupted rather gently, creating an elongated dome much like a turtle shell. Once above sea level, its tremendous weight seals the fissure below. Eventually the giant tube that carried lava to the surface sinks in on itself and forms a caldera. Wind and water take over and relentlessly sculpt the raw lava into deep crevices and cuts that become valleys. The once-smooth West Maui Mountains are now a mini-mountain range as a result of this process. Great Haleakala is being chiseled, too, as can be seen in the Kaupo Gap and the valleys of Kipahulu and Ke'anae.

Lava

Lava flows in two distinct types, for which the Hawaiian names have become universal geological terms: 'a'a and pahoehoe. They're easily distinguished in appearance, but chemically they're the same. 'A'a is extremely rough and spiny, and will quickly tear up your shoes if you do much hiking over it. Also, if you have the misfortune to fall down, you'll immediately know why they call it 'a'a. Pahoehoe, a billowy, ropy lava resembling burned pancake batter, can mold into fantastic shapes. Examples of both are encountered on various hikes throughout Maui. Other lava oddities are peridots (green gemlike stones called "Pele's Diamonds"); clear feldsparlike, white cotton candy called "Pele's Hair"; and gray lichen known as "Hawaiian snow" covering the older flows.

Rivers and Lakes

Maui has no navigable rivers, but there are hundreds of streams. Two of the largest are **Palikea Stream,** which runs through Kipahulu Valley forming 'Ohe'o Gulch, and **'Iao Stream,** which has sculpted the amazing monoliths in 'Iao Valley. The longest, at 18 miles, is Kalialinui-Wai'ale Stream, which starts just below the summit of Haleakala, runs through Pukalani, and empties into the ocean near Kahului Airport. A few reservoirs dot the island, but the two largest natural bodies of water are the 41-acre **Kanaha Pond,** on the outskirts of Kahului, and 500-acre **Kealia Pond,** on the southern shore of the isthmus, both major bird and wildlife sanctuaries. Hikers should be aware of the countless streams and rivulets that can quickly turn from trickles to torrents, causing flash floods in valleys that were the height of hospitality only minutes before.

Channels

Each of the Hawaiian islands has a channel of water between it and its neighbor island. Maui County, unlike the other island counties in the state, comprises four islands: Maui, Moloka'i, Lana'i, and Kaho'olawe. Based on its underwater topography and the characteristics of island building, it's assumed that these islands were joined at some time in the distant past, probably when the ocean level was much lower than it is today. The channels between these islands are much shallower than others in the island chain. **Pailolo Channel,** that between Maui and Moloka'i, is 8.8 miles wide and 846 feet deep; **'Au'au Channel,** lying between Maui and Lana'i, is 9 miles wide and only 252 feet deep; between Maui and Kaho'olawe, the **'Alalakeiki Channel** is 6.7 miles wide and 822 feet deep; **Kalohi Channel,** 9.2 miles wide and 540 feet deep, separates Moloka'i and Lana'i; and **Kealaikahiki Channel,** lying between Lana'i and Kaho'olawe, is the widest at 17.8 miles, but it is only a scant 331 feet deep.

Tsunamis

Tsunami is the Japanese word for "tidal wave." It ranks up there with the worst of them in sparking horror in human beings. But if you were to count up all the people in Hawaii who have been swept away by tidal waves in the last 50 years, the toll wouldn't come close to those killed on bicycles in only a few Mainland cities in just five years. A Hawaiian tsunami is actually a seismic sea wave that has been generated by an earthquake or underwater landslide that could easily have originated thousands of miles away in South America or Alaska. Some waves have been clocked at speeds up to 500 mph. The safest place during a tsunami, besides high ground well away from beach areas, is out on the open ocean where even an enormous wave is perceived only as a large swell. A tidal wave is only dangerous when it is opposed by land. The worst tsunami to strike Maui in modern times occurred on April 1, 1946. The Hana coast bore the brunt with a tragic loss of many lives as entire villages were swept away. The same tsunami also struck Halawa Valley on the eastern end of Moloka'i, destroying that valley community.

Earthquakes

These rumblings are also a concern in Hawaii and offer a double threat because they can generate tsunamis. If you ever feel a tremor and are close to a beach, get as far away as fast as possible. Maui rarely experiences earthquakes, but like the other islands it has an elaborate warning system against natural disasters. You will notice loudspeakers high atop poles along many beaches and coastal areas; these warn of tsunamis, hurricanes, and earthquakes. The loudspeakers are tested at 11 A.M. on the first working day of each month. All island telephone books contain a civil defense warning and procedures section with which you should acquaint yourself—note the maps showing which areas traditionally have been inundated by tsunamis and what procedures to follow in case an emergency occurs.

CLIMATE

Maui has similar weather to the rest of the Hawaiian islands, although some aficionados claim that it gets the most sunshine of all. The weather on Maui depends more on where you are than on what season it is. The average daily temperature along the coast is about 78°F (25.5°C) in summer and during winter is about 72°F (22°C). On Haleakala summit, the average is 43–50°F (6–10°C). Nights are usually no more than 10 degrees Fahrenheit cooler than days. Because Haleakala is a main feature on Maui, you should remember that altitude drastically affects the weather. Expect an average drop of three degrees for every 1,000 feet of elevation, so at the top, Haleakala is about 30 degrees cooler than at sea level. The lowest temperature ever recorded on Maui was atop Haleakala in 1961, when the mercury dropped well below freezing to a low, low 11°F. In contrast, sunny Kihei has recorded a blistering 98°F.

Maui has wonderful weather, and because of near-constant breezes, the air is usually clear and clean. Traffic and weather conditions never create smog, but because of burning cane fields, Maui air will at times become smoky, a condition that usually rectifies itself in a day when the winds are blowing. On rarer occasions, a volcanic haze, known as VOG, will filter over the island, blown in from the Big Island. If it's hazy, doesn't smell of smoke, and nothing has been burning, it's probably VOG.

Precipitation

Rain on Maui is as much a factor as it is elsewhere in Hawaii. On any day, somewhere on

MAUI TEMPERATURE AND RAINFALL

Town		Jan.	March	May	June	Sept.	Nov.
Lahaina	high	80	81	82	83	84	82
	low	62	63	68	68	70	65
	rain	3	1	0	0	0	1
Hana	high	79	79	80	80	81	80
	low	60	60	62	63	65	61
	rain	9	7	2	3	5	7
Kahului	high	80	80	84	86	87	83
	low	64	64	67	69	70	68
	rain	4	3	1	0	0	2

Note: Temperature is in degrees Fahrenheit; rainfall in inches.

Maui it's raining, while other areas experience drought. A dramatic example of this phenomenon is a comparison of Lahaina with Pu'u Kukui, both on West Maui and separated by only seven miles. Lahaina, which translates as "Merciless Sun," is hot, arid, and gets only 15 inches of rainfall annually, while Pu'u Kukui can receive close to 400 inches (33 *feet!*) of precipitation. This rivals Mt. Wai'ale'ale on Kaua'i as the wettest spot on earth. Other leeward towns get a comparable amount of rain to Lahaina, but as you move upcountry and around the north coast, the rains become greater. Finally, in Hana, rainfall is about five times as great as on the leeward side, averaging more than 80 inches per year. The windward (wet) side of Maui, outlined by the Hana Road, is the perfect natural hothouse. Here, valleys sweetened with blossoms house idyllic waterfalls and pools that visitors treasure when they happen upon them. On the leeward (dry) side are Maui's best beaches: Kapalua, Ka'anapali, Kihei, Wailea, and Makena. They all sit in Haleakala's rain shadow. If it happens to be raining at one spot, just move a few miles down the road to the next. Anyway, the rains are mostly gentle and the brooding sky, especially at sundown, is even more spectacular than normal.

A consequence of the rains are the gorgeous rainbows. Because it's always raining somewhere on Maui, these arched bands of color can be seen anywhere on the island. Caused by light diffused through raindrops or mist in the air, rainbows are usually seen after or during a rain, but may also be spotted in a waterfall. A few lucky ones may also have the fortune of seeing a full-round rainbow from a helicopter. As lovely as these daytime polychrome bands of color are, nighttime "moonbows," caused by light from the moon, are also attractive but somehow ethereal, a real treat.

"So Good" Weather

The ancient Hawaiians had words to describe climatic specifics such as rain, wind, fog, and even snow, but they didn't have a general word for "weather." The reason is that the weather is just about the same throughout the year and depends more on where you are on any given island than on what season it is. The Hawaiians did distinguish between *kau* (summer, May–Oct.) and *ho'oilo* (winter, Nov.–Apr.), but this distinction included social, religious, and even navigational factors, far beyond a mere distinction of weather variations.

The Trade Winds

Temperatures in the 50th state are both constant and moderate because of the trade winds, a breeze from the northeast that blows at about 5–15 miles per hour. These breezes are so prevailing that the northeast sides of the islands are always referred to as **windward,** regardless of where the wind happens to blow on any given day. You can count on the trades to be blowing on an average of 300 days per year, hardly missing a day during summer and occurring half the time in winter. Although usually calm in the morning, they pick up during the heat of the afternoon, then weaken at night. Just when you need a cooling breeze, there they are, and when the temperature drops at night, it's as if someone turned down a giant fan.

The trade winds are also a factor in keeping down the humidity. They will suddenly disappear, however, usually in winter, and might not resume for a few weeks. The tropic of Cancer runs through the center of Hawaii, yet the latitude's famed oppressively hot and muggy weather is joyfully absent in the islands. Honolulu, on the same latitude as sweaty Hong Kong and Havana, has only a 50–60 percent daily humidity factor.

Kona Winds

Kona means "leeward" in Hawaiian, and when the trades stop blowing, these southerly winds often take over. To anyone from Hawaii, *kona* wind is a euphemism for bad weather because it brings in hot, sticky air. Luckily, *kona* winds are most common Oct.–Apr., when they appear roughly half the time. The temperatures drop slightly during the winter, so these hot winds are tolerable and even useful for moderating the thermometer. In the summer they are awful, but luckily—again—they hardly ever blow during this season.

A *kona* storm is another matter. These subtropical low-pressure storms develop west of the Hawaiian Islands, and as they move east they draw winds up from the south. Usually only occurring in winter, they can cause considerable damage to crops and real estate. There is no real pattern to *kona* storms—some years they come every few weeks, whereas in other years they don't appear at all.

Severe Weather

With all this talk of ideal weather, it might seem as if there isn't any bad. Read on. When a storm does hit an island, conditions can be bleak and miserable. The worst storms occur in

GREEN FLASH

Nearly everyone who has visited a tropical island has heard of the "green flash"—but few have seen it. Some consider the green flash a fable, a made-up story by those more intent on fantasy than reality, but the green flash is real. This phenomenon doesn't just happen on tropical islands; it can happen anywhere around the midriff of the earth where an unobstructed view of the horizon is present, but the clear atmosphere of a tropical island environment does seem to add to its frequency. The green flash is a momentary burst of luminescent green color that happens on the horizon the instant the sun sets into the sea. If you've seen the green flash you definitely know; there is no mistaking it. If you think you saw something that might have been green but just weren't sure, you probably didn't see it. Try again another day.

The green flash requires a day where the atmosphere is very clear and unobstructed by clouds, haze, or air pollutants. Follow the sun as it sinks into the sea. Be careful not to look directly at the sun until it's just about out of sight. If the conditions are right, a green color will linger at the spot where the sun sets for a fraction of a second before it too is gone. This "flash" is not like the flash of a camera, but more a change of color from yellow to green—an intense green—that is instantaneous and momentary.

However romantic and magical, this phenomenon does have a scientific explanation. It seems that the green color is produced as a refraction of the sun's rays by the thick atmosphere at the extreme low angle of the horizon. This bending of the sun's light results in the green spectrum of light being the last seen before the light disappears.

Seeing the green flash is an experience. Keep looking, for no matter how many times you've seen it, each time is still full of wonder and joy.

HURRICANE FACTS

A tropical depression is a low-pressure system or cyclone with winds below 39 mph. A **tropical storm** is a cyclone with winds 39–73 mph. A **hurricane** is a cyclone with winds over 74 mph. These winds are often accompanied by torrential rains, destructive waves, high water, and storm surges.

The National Weather Service issues a **Hurricane Watch** if hurricane conditions are expected in the area within 36 hours. A **Hurricane Warning** is issued when a hurricane is expected to strike within 24 hours. The state of Hawaii has an elaborate warning system against natural disasters. You will notice loudspeakers high atop poles along many beaches and coastal areas; these warn of tsunami, hurricanes, and earthquakes. These sirens are tested briefly at the beginning of each month. As the figures below attest, property damage has been great but the loss of life has, thankfully, been minimal.

Major Hurricanes since 1950

Name	Date	Islands Affected	Damages
Hiki	Aug. 1950	Kaua'i	1 death
Nina	Dec. 1957	Kaua'i	—
Dot	Aug. 1959	Kaua'i	$5.5 million
Fico	July 1978	Big Island	—
'Iwa	Nov. 1982	Kaua'i, O'ahu	1 death; $234 million
Estelle	July 1986	Maui, Big Island	$2 million
'Iniki	Sept. 1992	Kaua'i, O'ahu	8 deaths; $1.9 billion

the fall and winter and often have the warped sense of humor to drop their heaviest rainfalls on areas that are normally quite dry. It's not infrequent for a storm to dump more than three inches of rain per hour; this can go as high as 10, making Hawaiian rainfalls some of the heaviest on earth.

Hawaii has also been hit with some walloping **hurricanes** in the last few decades. There haven't been many, but they have been destructive. Most hurricanes originate far to the southeast off the Pacific coasts of Mexico and Latin America; some, particularly later in the season, start in the midst of the Pacific Ocean near the equator south of Hawaii. Hurricane season is generally considered June–November. Most pass harmlessly south of Hawaii, but some, swept along by *kona* winds, strike the islands. The most recent and destructive was Hurricane 'Iniki, which battered the islands in 1992, killing eight people and causing an estimated $2 billion in damage. It had its greatest effect on Ni'ihau, the Po'ipu Beach area of Kaua'i, and the leeward coast of O'ahu.

Flora and Fauna

THE MYSTERY OF MIGRATION

Anyone who loves a mystery will be intrigued by the speculation about how plants and animals first came to Hawaii. Most people's idea of an island paradise includes swaying palms, dense mysterious jungles ablaze with wildflowers, and luscious fruits just waiting to be plucked. In fact, for millions of years the Hawaiian chain consisted of raw and barren islands where no plants grew and no birds sang. Why? Because they are geological orphans that spontaneously popped up in the middle of the Pacific Ocean. The islands, more than 2,000 miles from any continental landfall, were therefore isolated from the normal ecological spread of plants and animals. Even the most tenacious travelers of the flora and fauna kingdoms would be sorely tried in crossing the mighty Pacific. Those that made it by pure chance found a totally foreign ecosystem. They had to adapt or perish. The survivors evolved quickly, and many plants and birds became so specialized that they were not only limited to specific islands in the chain but to habitats that frequently encompassed a single isolated valley. It was as if after traveling so far, and finding a niche, they never budged again. Luckily, the soil of Hawaii was virgin and rich, the competition from other plants or animals was nonexistent, and the climate was sufficiently varied and nearly perfect for most growing things.

The evolution of plants and animals on the isolated islands was astonishingly rapid. A tremendous change in environment, coupled with a limited gene pool, accelerated natural selection. For example, many plants lost their protective thorns and spines because there were no grazing animals or birds to destroy them. Before settlement, Hawaii had no fruits, vegetables, coconut palms, edible land animals, conifers, mangroves, or banyans. The early Polynesians brought 27 varieties of plants they needed for food and other purposes. About 90 percent of plants on the Hawaiian islands today were introduced after Captain Cook first set foot here. Tropical flowers,

wild and vibrant as we know them today, were relatively few. In a land where thousands of orchids now brighten every corner, there were only four native varieties, the least in any of the 50 states. Today, the indigenous plants and animals have the highest rate of extinction anywhere on earth. By the beginning of the 21st century, native plants growing below 1,500 feet in elevation were almost completely extinct or totally replaced by introduced species. The land and its living things have been greatly transformed by humans and their agriculture. This inexorable process began when Hawaii was the domain of its original Polynesian settlers, then greatly accelerated when the land was inundated by Western peoples.

The indigenous plants and birds of Maui have suffered the same fate as those of the other Hawaiian Islands; they're among the most endangered species on earth and disappearing at an alarming rate. There are some sanctuaries on Maui where native species still live, but they must be vigorously protected. Do your bit to save them; enjoy but do not disturb.

PLANTS, FLOWERS, AND TREES

Hawaii's indigenous and endemic plants, flowers, and trees are both fascinating and beautiful, but unfortunately, like everything else that was native, they are quickly disappearing. Most flora considered exotic by visitors was introduced either by the original Polynesians or by later white settlers. The Polynesians who colonized Hawaii brought foodstuffs, including coconuts, bananas, taro, breadfruit, sweet potatoes, yams, and sugarcane. They also carried along gourds to use as containers, 'awa to make a basic intoxicant, and the ti plant to use for offerings or to string into hula skirts. Non-Hawaiian settlers over the years have brought mangos, papayas, passion fruit, pineapples, and the other tropical fruits and vegetables associated with the islands. Also, most of the flowers, including protea, plumeria, anthuriums, orchids, heliconia, ginger, and most hibiscus, have come from every continent on earth. Tropical America, Asia, Java, India, and China have contributed their most beautiful and delicate blooms. Hawaii is blessed with national and state parks, gardens, undisturbed rainforests, private reserves, and commercial nurseries that offer an exhaustive botanical survey of the island. The following is a sampling of the common native and introduced flora that add dazzling color and exotic tastes to the landscape.

Native Trees

Koa and **'ohi'a** are two indigenous trees still seen on Maui. Both have been greatly reduced by the foraging of introduced cattle and goats, and through logging and forest fires. The koa, a form of acacia, is Hawaii's finest native tree. It can grow to over 70 feet high and has a strong, straight trunk that can measure more than 10 feet in circumference. Koa is a quickly growing legume that fixes nitrogen in the soil. It is believed that the tree originated in Africa, where it was very damp. It then migrated to Australia, where it was very dry, which caused the elimination of leaves so that all that was left were bare stems that could survive in the desert climate. When koa came to the Pacific islands, instead of reverting to the true leaf, it just broadened its leaf stem into sickle-shaped, leaflike foliage that produces an inconspicuous, pale-yellow flower. When the tree is young or damaged it will revert to the original feathery, fernlike leaf that evolved in Africa millions of years ago. Koa does best in well-drained soil in deep forest areas, but scruffy specimens will grow in poorer soil. The Hawaiians used koa as the main log for their dugout canoes, and elaborate ceremonies were performed when a log was cut and dragged to a canoe shed. Koa wood was also preferred for paddles, spears, even surfboards. Today it is still, unfortunately, considered an excellent furniture wood; and although fine specimens can be found in the reserve of Hawaii Volcanoes National Park on the Big Island, loggers elsewhere are harvesting the last of the big trees.

The 'ohi'a is a survivor and therefore the most abundant of all the native Hawaiian trees. Coming in a variety of shapes and sizes, it grows as miniature trees in wet bogs or as 100-foot giants on cool, dark slopes at higher elevations. This tree is often the first life in new lava flows. The 'ohi'a produces a tuftlike flower—usually red, but occasionally orange, yellow, or white, the latter being rare and elusive—that resembles a natural pompon. The flower was considered sacred to Pele; it was said that she would cause a rainstorm if you picked 'ohi'a blossoms without the proper prayers. The flowers were fashioned into lei that resembled feather boas. The strong, hard wood was used to make canoes, poi bowls, and especially temple images. 'Ohi'a logs were also used as railroad ties and shipped to the Mainland from Pahoa. It's believed that the "golden spike" linking rail lines between the U.S. East and West Coasts was driven into a Puna 'ohi'a log when the two railroads came together in Ogden, Utah.

'Ahinahina (Silversword)

Maui's official flower is a tiny pink rose called a *lokelani*. The island's unofficial symbol, however, is the silversword. The Hawaiian name for silversword is *'ahinahina*, which translates as "gray gray," and the English name derives from a silverfish, whose color the plant is said to resemble. The *'ahinahina* belongs to a remarkable plant family that claims 28 members, with five in the specific silversword species. It's kin to the common sunflower, and botanists say the entire family evolved from a single ancestral species. Hypothetically, the members of the *'ahinahina* family can interbreed and produce remarkable hybrids. Some plants are shrubs, while others are climbing vines, and some even become trees. They grow anywhere from desert conditions to steamy jungles. On Maui, the *'ahinahina* is only found on Haleakala, above the 6,000-foot level, and is especially prolific in the crater. Each plant lives from 5–20 years and ends its life by sprouting a gorgeous stalk of hundreds of purplish-red flowers. It then withers from a majestic six-foot plant to a flat, gray skeleton. An endangered species, *'ahinahina* are totally protected. They protect themselves, too, from radiation and lack of moisture, by growing fuzzy hairs all over their swordlike stalks. You can see them along the Haleakala Park Road at Kalahaku Overlook or by hiking along Silversword Loop on the floor of the crater.

Protea

These exotic flowers are from Australia and South Africa. Because they come in almost limitless shapes, sizes, and colors, they captivate everyone who sees them. They are primitive, almost otherworldly in appearance, and they exude a life force more like an animal than a flower. The slopes of leeward Haleakala between 2,000 and 4,000 feet are heaven to protea—the growing conditions could not be more perfect. Here are found the hardiest, highest-quality protea in the world. The days are warm, the nights are cool, and the well-drained volcanic soil has the exact combination of minerals on which protea thrive. Haleakala's crater even helps by creating a natural air flow that produces cloud cover, filters the sun, and protects the flowers. Protea make excellent gifts that can be shipped anywhere. As fresh-cut flowers they are gorgeous, but they have the extra benefit of drying superbly. Just hang them in a dark, dry, well-ventilated area and they do the rest. You can see protea, along with other botanical specialties, at the gardens, flower farms, and gift shops in Kula.

prickly pear cactus

BOB RACE

Carnations

If protea aren't enough to dazzle you, how about fields of carnations? Most Mainlanders think of carnations stuck in a groom's lapel, or perhaps have seen a table dedicated to them in a hothouse, but not fields full of carnations! The Kula area produces carnations that grow outside nonchalantly, in rows, like cabbages. They fill the air with their unmistakable perfume, and they are without doubt a joy to behold. You can see family and commercial plots throughout the upper Kula area.

Prickly Pear Cactus

Interspersed in countless fields and pastures on the windward slope of Haleakala, adding that final nuance to cattle country, are clusters of prickly pear cactus. The Hawaiians call them *panini*, which translates as "very unfriendly," undoubtedly because of the sharp spines covering the flat, thick leaves. These cactus are typical of those found in Mexico and the southwestern United States. They were introduced to Hawaii before 1810 and established themselves, coincidentally, in conjunction with the cattle being brought in at that time. It's assumed that Don Marin, a Spanish advisor to Kamehameha I, was responsible for importing the plant. Perhaps the early *paniolo* felt lonely without them. The *panini* can grow to heights of 15 feet and are now considered a pest, but nonetheless they look as if they belong. They develop small, pear-shaped fruits that are quite delicious. Hikers who decide to pick them should be careful of small yellowish bristles that can burrow under the skin and become very irritating. The fruits turn into beautiful yellow and orange flowers. An attempt is being made to control the cactus in *paniolo* country. *El cosano rojo*, the red worm found in the bottom of Mexican tequila, has been introduced to destroy the plant. It burrows into the cactus and eats the hardwood center, causing the plant to wither and die.

Lobelia

More species of lobelia grow in Hawaii than anywhere else in the world. A common garden flower elsewhere, in Hawaii it grows to tree height. You'll see some unique species covered with hair or with spikes. The lobelia flower is tiny and resembles a miniature orchid with curved and pointed ends, like the beak of the native *'i'iwi*. This bird feeds on the flower's nectar; it's obvious that both evolved in Hawaii together

MAUI BOTANICAL GARDENS

Kula Botanical Gardens, 808/878-1715, has some 2,000 varieties of tropical and semitropical plants, including orchids, bromeliads, fuchsia, protea, *kukui* and sandalwood trees, and numerous ferns, on more than five acres. Located at 3,300 feet near the junction of Routes 377 and 37 at the south end, this privately owned garden is open daily 9 A.M.–4 P.M. for self-guided tours; $5 admission.

Enchanting Floral Gardens, 808/878-2531, is located along Route 37 just south of Pukalani at mile marker 10. This private garden features about 2,000 species of native Hawaiian plants as well as exotic plants from around the world on eight acres. Open daily 9 A.M.–5 P.M. for self-guided tours; $5 admission.

University of Hawaii Experimental Station offers 20 acres of constantly changing, quite beautiful plants, although the grounds are uninspired, scientific, rectangular plots. Located on Mauna Place just off Copp Road above Route 37 in Kula, this garden is open Mon.–Thur. 7:30 A.M.–3:30 P.M., closed for lunch. Although admission is free, visitors should check in with the station manager.

Garden of Eden, along the Hana Highway, is a 26-acre private garden of tropical plants and flowers, many labeled. Open daily 9 A.M.–3 P.M.; $7.50 admission.

Ke'anae Arboretum, above Ke'anae Peninsula on the Hana Highway, is always open with no fee. In a natural setting with walkways, many identifying markers, and mosquitoes, this six-acre arboretum is split into two sections: ornamental tropical plants and Hawaiian domestic plants. The native forest swaths the surrounding hillsides.

Kahanu Gardens, a branch of the Pacific Tropical Botanical Gardens, is located on the rugged lava coast west of Hana at the site of Pi'ilanihale Heiau. In this 123-acre garden, you'll find stands of breadfruit and coconut trees, a pandanus grove, and numerous other tropical plants from throughout Polynesia. Open Mon.–Fri. 10 A.M.–2 P.M. for self-guided tours; $10 admission. Call 808/284-8912 for information.

Maui Nui Botanical Gardens in Keopuolani Park in Kahului is a new garden that focuses on coastal and dryland forest plants from the four islands of Maui County. Open Mon.–Fri. 8 A.M.–4 P.M. and Saturday 9:30 A.M.–2:30 P.M. Free admission. Call 808/249-2798 for information.

Maunalei Arboretum is accessible to guided hikes only. Located above Kapalua, this private botanical garden was started in the 1930s.

While not a botanical garden, **Polipoli Spring State Recreation Area** has some magnificent stands of redwoods, eucalyptus, conifers, ash, cypress, cedar, *sugi* and other pines. Various trails lead through the forest. Always open, but way off the beaten track. Similarly, **Hosmer Grove,** within Haleakala National Park at 6,800 feet in elevation, is an experimental forest project from the early 20th century that has fine examples of introduced trees like cedar, pine, fir, juniper, and *sugi* pine that were originally planted in hopes of finding a commercial, economically marketable wood for Hawaii. A short trail now winds through the no-longer-orderly stands of trees. Hike on your own or take a periodic ranger-guided tour. For recorded park information, call 808/572-4400.

and exhibit the strange phenomenon of nature mimicking nature.

Tropical Rainforests

When it comes to pure and diverse natural beauty, the United States is one of the finest pieces of real estate on earth. As if purple mountains' majesty and fruited plains weren't enough, it even received a tiny, living emerald of tropical rainforest. A tropical rainforest is where the earth takes a breath and exhales pure sweet oxygen through its vibrant green canopy. Located in the territories of Puerto Rico and the Virgin Islands, and in the state of Hawaii, these forests comprise only .5 percent of the world's total, and they must be preserved. The U.S. Congress passed two bills in 1986 designed to protect the unique biological diversity of its tropical areas, but their destruction has continued unabated. The lowland rainforests of Hawaii, populated mostly by native 'ohi'a, are being razed. Landowners slash, burn, and bulldoze them to create more land for cattle and agriculture, and, most distressingly, for wood chips to generate electricity! Introduced wild boar gouge the forest floor, exposing sensitive roots and leaving tiny fetid ponds where mosquito larvae thrive. Feral goats roam the forests like hoofed locusts and strip all vegetation within reach. Rainforests on the higher and steeper slopes of mountains have a better chance because they are harder for humans to reach. One unusual feature of Hawaii's rainforests is that they are "upside down." Most plant and animal species live on the forest floor, rather than in the canopy as in other forests. Maui's Nature Conservancy Preserve in Waikamoi has managed to fence in a speck of this forest, keeping it safe from these animals for the time being. The Waikamoi Preserve is a broad swath of thick forest and arid volcanic land on the north slope of Haleakala that stretches roughly from Olinda to the eastern end of the Haleakala basin rim. The Nature Conservancy of Hawai'i occasionally conducts guided hikes into the Waikamoi Preserve. For information on the preserve or these hikes, call 808/572-7849.

Almost half the birds classified in the United States as endangered live in Hawaii, and almost all of these make their homes in the rainforests. For example, Maui's rainforests have yielded the po'ouli, a new species of bird discovered only in 1974. Another forest survey in 1981 rediscovered the Bishop's 'o'o, a bird thought to be extinct at the turn of the 20th century. We can only lament the passing of the rainforests that have already fallen to ignorance, but if this ill-fated destruction continues on a global level, we will be lamenting our own passing. We must nurture the rainforests that remain, and with simple enlightenment, let them be.

BIRDS

One of the great tragedies of natural history is the continuing demise of Hawaiian bird life. Perhaps only 15 original species of birds remain of the more than 70 native families that thrived before the coming of humans. Since the arrival of Captain Cook in 1778, 23 species have become extinct, with 31 more in danger. And what's not known is how many species were wiped out before the coming of white explorers. Experts believe that the Hawaiians annihilated about 40 species, including seven other species of geese besides the nene, a rare one-legged owl, ibis, lovebirds, sea eagles, and hunting creepers—all gone before Captain Cook arrived. Hawaii's endangered birds account for 40 percent of the birds officially listed as endangered or threatened by the U.S. Fish and Wildlife Service. In the last 200 years, more than four times as many birds have become extinct in Hawaii as in all of North America. These figures unfortunately suggest that a full 40 percent of Hawaii's endemic birds no longer exist. Almost all of O'ahu's native birds are gone, and few indigenous Hawaiian birds can be found on any island below the 3,000-foot level.

Native birds have been reduced in number because of multiple factors. The original Polynesians helped wipe out many species. They altered large areas for farming and used fire to destroy patches of pristine forests. Also, bird feathers were highly prized for making lei, for featherwork in capes and helmets, and for the large kahili fans that indicated rank among the ali'i. Introduced exotic birds and the new diseases they carried are another major reason for reduction of native bird numbers, along with predation by the mongoose and rat, especially on ground-nesting birds. Bird malaria and bird pox were also devastating to the native species. Mosquitoes—unknown in Hawaii until a ship named the *Wellington* introduced them at Lahaina in 1826 through larvae carried in its water barrels—infected most native birds, causing a rapid reduction in birdlife. Feral pigs rooting deep in the rainforests knock over ferns and small trees, creating fetid pools in which mosquito larvae thrive. The most damaging factor by far, however, is the assault on native forests by agriculture and land developers. Most Hawaiian birds evolved into specialists. They lived in only one small area and ate a limited number of plants or insects, which once removed or altered soon killed the birds.

You'll spot birds all over Maui, from the coastal areas to the high mountain slopes. Some are found on other islands as well, but the ones listed as follows are found only or mainly on Maui. Every bird listed is either threatened or endangered.

Maui's Endangered Birds

Maui's native birds are disappearing. The island is the last home of the crested honeycreeper (*'akohekohe*), which lives only on the windward slope of Haleakala from 4,500–6,500 feet. It once lived on Moloka'i, but no longer. It's a rather large bird, averaging over seven inches long, and predominantly black. Its throat and breast are tipped with gray feathers, and it has bright orange on its neck and underbelly. A distinctive fluff of feathers forms a crown. It primarily eats 'ohi'a flowers, and it's believed that the crown feathers gather pollen and help propagate the 'ohi'a.

The parrotbill is another endangered bird, found only on the slopes of Haleakala above 5,000 feet. It has an olive-green back and a yellow body. Its most distinctive feature is its parrotlike bill, which it uses to crack branches and pry out larvae.

Two waterbirds found on Maui are the Hawaiian stilt (*ae'o*) and the Hawaiian coot (*'alae ke'oke'o*). The stilt is about 16 inches tall and lives on Maui at Kanaha and Kealia ponds. Primarily black with a white belly, its sticklike legs are pink. The adults will pretend to be hurt,

putting on an excellent performance of the "broken wing" routine, in order to lure predators away from their nests. The Hawaiian coot is a web-footed waterbird that resembles a duck. It's found on all the main islands but mostly on Maui and Kaua'i. Mostly a dull gray, it has a white bill and tail feathers. It builds a large floating nest and vigorously defends its young.

The dark-rumped petrel is slightly different from other primarily marine birds. This petrel is found around the visitors center at Haleakala Crater about one hour after dusk from May–October. The *'amakihi* and the *'i'iwi* are endemic birds that aren't endangered at the moment. The *'amakihi* is one of the most common native birds. It's yellowish-green, and it frequents the high branches of 'ohi'a, koa, and sandalwood looking for insects, nectar, or fruit. It's less specialized than most other Hawaiian birds, which is the main reason for its continued existence. The *'i'iwi* is a bright red bird with a salmon-colored hooked bill. It's found only on Maui, Hawai'i, and Kaua'i in forests above 2,000 feet. It, too, feeds on a variety of insects and flowers. The *'i'iwi* is known for its harsh voice, which sounds like a squeaking hinge, but it is also capable of a melodious song.

The *po'ouli* is a dark brown, five-inch bird with a black mask and dark brown feet. Its tail is short, and it sports a conical bill. It was saved from extinction through efforts of the Sierra Club and the Audubon Society, who successfully had it listed on the Federal List of Endangered Species. The bird has one remaining stronghold deep in the forests of Maui.

Other indigenous birds found on Maui are the wedge-tailed shearwater, the white-tailed tropic bird, the black noddy, the American plover, and a large variety of escaped exotic birds.

Pueo

This Hawaiian owl is found on all of the main islands, but mostly on Maui, especially in Haleakala Crater. The *pueo* is one of the oldest examples of an *'aumakua* (family-protecting spirit) in Hawaiian mythology. It was an especially benign and helpful guardian. Old Hawaiian stories abound where a *pueo* came to the aid of a warrior in distress or a defeated army, which would head for a tree in which a *pueo* had alighted. Once there, they were safe from their pursuers and were under the protection of "the wings of an owl." There are many introduced barn owls in Hawaii, easily distinguished from a *pueo* by their distinctive heart-shaped faces. The *pueo* is about 15 inches tall with a mixture of brown and white feathers. The eyes are large, round, and yellow, and the legs are heavily feathered, unlike a barn owl. *Pueo* chicks are a distinct yellow color.

Nene

The *nene,* or Hawaiian goose, deserves special mention because it is Hawaii's state bird and is making a comeback from the edge of extinction. The *nene* is found only on the slopes of Mauna Loa, Hualalai, and Mauna Kea on the Big Island, and in Haleakala Crater on Maui. It was extinct on Maui until a few birds were returned

there in 1957, but some experts maintain that the *nene* lived naturally only on the Big Island. *Nene* are raised at the Wildfowl Trust in Slimbridge, England, which placed the first birds at Haleakala, and at the Hawaiian Fish and Game Station at Pohakuloa, along the Saddle Road on Hawai'i. By the 1940s, fewer than 50 birds lived in the wild. Now approximately 125 birds live on Haleakala and 500 on the Big Island. Although the birds can be raised successfully in captivity, their life in the wild is still in question.

The *nene* is believed to be a descendant of the Canada goose, which it resembles. Geese are migratory birds that form strong kinship ties, mating for life. It's speculated that a migrating goose became disabled and, along with its loyal mate, remained in Hawaii. The *nene* is smaller than its Canadian cousin, has lost a great deal of webbing in its feet, and is perfectly at home away from water, foraging and nesting on rugged and bleak lava flows. The *nene* is a perfect symbol of Hawaii: let it be, and it will live.

OTHER HAWAIIAN ANIMALS

Hawaii had only two indigenous mammals: the monk seal, or *'ilio holu i ka uaua* (found throughout the islands), and the hoary bat (found primarily on the Big Island); both are threatened or endangered. Recently, a second species of bat (now extinct) was identified from bone fragments taken from caves on four of the Hawaiian Islands. The remainder of Maui's mammals are transplants. But like anything else, including people, that has been in the islands long enough, they take on characteristics that make them "local." There are no native amphibians or reptiles, ants, termites, or cockroaches. All are imported.

The **Hawaiian hoary bat** *('ope'ape'a)* is a cousin of the Mainland bat, a strong flier that made it to Hawaii eons ago and developed its own species. Its tail has a whitish coloration, hence the name. Small populations of the bat are found on Maui and Kaua'i, but most are on the Big Island. The hoary bat has a 13-inch wingspan and, unlike other bats, is a solitary creature, roosting in trees. It gives birth to

ROBERT NILSEN

The *nene* (Hawaiian goose and the state bird) lives mainly on Haleakala and on the slopes of Mauna Loa and Mauna Kea on the Big Island. Shy but curious, it may be found on roadways and in parking lots. Please leave it alone, take care not to disturb.

twins in early summer and can often be spotted darting over a number of bays just around sundown.

Feral dogs *('ilio)* are found on all the islands but especially on the slopes of Mauna Kea on the Big Island, where packs chase feral sheep. Poisoned and shot by local ranchers, the *'ilio* population is diminishing. Black dogs, thought to be more tender, are still eaten in some Hawaiian and Filipino communities.

Drosophila, the Hawaiian Fly

Most people hardly pay attention to flies, unless one lands on their plate lunch. But geneticists from throughout the world, and especially from the University of Hawaii, make special pilgrimages to the volcano area of the Big Island and to Maui just to study the native Hawaiian drosophila. This critter is related to the fruit fly and housefly, but hundreds of native species are singularly unique—more than one-third of the world's estimated total. The Hawaiian ecosystem is simple and straightforward, so geneticists can trace the evolutionary changes from species to subspecies through mating behavior. The scientists compare the species between the two islands and chart the differences. Major discoveries in evolutionary genetics have been made through these studies.

Coral

Whether you're an avid scuba diver or novice snorkeler, you'll become aware of Maui's underwater coral gardens and grottoes whenever you peer at the fantastic seascapes below the waves. Although there is plenty of it, the coral in Hawaii doesn't do as well as in other more equatorial areas because the water is too wild and it's not quite as warm. Coral looks like a plant fashioned from colorful stone, but it's the skeleton of tiny animals, zoophytes, which need algae in order to live. Coral grows best on the west side of Maui where the water is quite still, the days more sunny, and the algae can thrive. Many of Hawaii's reefs have been dying in the last 20 years, and no one seems to know why. Pesticides, used in agriculture, have been pointed to as a possible cause.

WHALES Nov – May

Perhaps it's their tremendous size and graceful power, coupled with a dancer's delicacy of movement, that render whales so aesthetically and emotionally captivating. In fact, many people claim that they even feel a spirit-bond to these obviously intelligent mammals that at one time shared dry land with us and then re-evolved into creatures of the great seas. Experts often remark that whales exhibit behavior akin to the highest social virtues. For example, whales rely much more on learned behavior than on instinct, the sign of a highly evolved intelligence. Gentle mothers and protective "escort" males join to teach the young to survive. They display loyalty and bravery in times of distress and innate gentleness and curiosity. Their songs, especially those of the humpbacks, fascinate scientists and are considered a unique form of communication in the animal kingdom. Humpback whales migrate to Hawaii every year Nov.–May. Here, they winter, mate, give birth, and nurture their young until returning to food-rich northern waters in the spring. It's hoped that humankind can peacefully share the oceans with these magnificent giants forever. Then, perhaps, we will have taken the first step in saving ourselves.

Evolution and Socialization

Many millions of years ago, for an unknown reason, animals similar to cows were genetically triggered to leave the land and readapt to the sea—their closest land relative is the hippo. Known as cetaceans, this order contains about 80 species of whales, porpoises, and dolphins. Being mammals, cetaceans are warm-blooded and maintain a body temperature of 96°F, only 2.5 degrees lower than humans. After a gestation period of about one year, whales give birth to fully formed young, which usually enter the world tail first. The mother whale spins quickly to snap the umbilical cord, then places herself under the newborn and lifts it to the surface to take its first breath. A whale must be taught to swim or it will drown like any other air-breathing mammal. The baby whale, nourished by its mother's

ROBERT NILSEN

The humpback whale visits Hawaiian waters every year to mate, give birth, and raise its young before its long migration to feed in Alaskan waters.

rich milk, becomes a member of an extended family, or pod, through which it's cared for, socialized, and protected by many "nannies."

Physiology

The best way to spot a whale is to look for its spout, a misty spray forced from a blowhole—really the whale's nostrils, which have moved from its snout to just behind its head. The spray from the spout is not water, but highly compressed air heated by the whale's body and expelled with such force that it condenses into a fine mist. A whale's tail is called a fluke; unlike the vertical tail of fish, a whale's tail is horizontal. The fluke, a marvelous appendage for propelling the whale through the water, is a vestige of the pelvis. It's so powerful that a 40-ton humpback can lift itself completely out of the water with only three strokes of its fluke. A whale's flippers are used to guide it through the water. The bones in the flippers closely resemble those of the human arm and hand; small, delicate bones at the ends of the flippers look like fingers and joints. On a humpback the flippers can be one-third as long as the body and supple enough to bend over its

back, like a human reaching over the shoulder to scratch an itch.

A whale's eyes are functional but very small and not the primary sensors. Instead, the whale has developed keen hearing; the ears are small holes about as big around as the lead of a pencil. They have protective wax plugs that build up over the years. Like the growth rings in a tree, the ear plugs can be counted to determine the age of a whale; its life span is about the same as that of a human being. Because of strong ocean currents, and because of the myriad dangers inherent to being at sea, whales enjoy a very light sleep, more like a rest similar to humans just awakening, a state that is not fully conscious but aware.

Dolphins are the smallest cetaceans and spend only 30 percent of their time feeding, with the rest given to leisure and social activities. They have evolved sleep patterns even further, and they almost *never* sleep. In a constant soothing and revitalizing alpha-wave state, much like meditation, they refresh themselves with only two or three minutes in a 24-hour period of what we would call sleep. And even then, they sleep literally with one eye open, resting the corresponding half of their brain, while the other eye and half of their brain stay alert for danger.

Types of Whales

Although all whales, dolphins, and porpoises are cetaceans, they are arbitrarily divided according to length. Whales are all those animals longer than 30 feet; dolphins range from 6–30 feet; and porpoises are less than six feet long. There are basically two types of whales: toothed, which includes the sperm, killer, and pilot whales, as well as porpoises and dolphins; and baleen, including the blue, minke, right, fin, and humpback.

Toothed whales feed by capturing and tearing their prey with their teeth. The killer whale or orca is the best known of the toothed whales. With its distinctive black-and-white markings and propensity for aquabatics, it's a favorite at marine parks around the world. The orca hunts other cetaceans, often attacking in packs to overcome larger whales. A killer whale in the wild lives about four times as long as one in captivity, even if it is well cared for. A baleen whale eats by gliding through the water with its mouth open, sucking in marine plankton and tiny shrimplike creatures called krill. The whale then expels the water and captures the food in row after row of a prickly, fingernail-like substance called baleen.

Hawaiian Whales and Dolphins

The role of whales and dolphins in Hawaiian culture seems quite limited. Unlike fish, which were intimately known and individually named, only two generic names described whales: *kohola* (humpback whale) and *palaoa* (sperm whale). Dolphins were all lumped together under one name, *nai'a;* Hawaiians were known to harvest dolphins on occasion by herding them onto a beach. Whale jewelry was worn by the *ali'i.* The most coveted ornament came from a sperm whale's tooth, called a *lei niho palaoa,* which was carved into one large, curved pendant. Sperm whales have more than 50 teeth, ranging in size from 4–12 inches and weighing up to two pounds. One whale could provide numerous pendants. The most famous whale in Hawaiian waters

is the humpback, but others often sighted include the sperm, killer, false killer, pilot, Cuvier's, Blainsville, and pygmy killer. There are technically no porpoises, but dolphins include the common, bottlenose, spinner, white-sided, broad- and slender-beaked, and rough-toothed. The mahimahi, a favorite eating fish found on many menus, is commonly referred to as a dolphin but is unrelated and is a true fish, not a cetacean.

The Humpbacks of Maui

Humpbacks get their name from their style of exposing their dorsal fin when they dive, which gives them a humped appearance. Their dorsal fin also puts them into the **rorqual** family. There are about 10,000 humpback whales alive today, down from an estimated 100,000 at the turn of the 20th century. The remaining whales are divided into three separate global populations: North Atlantic, North Pacific, and South Pacific groups. About 3,000 North Pacific humpbacks migrate from coastal Alaska beginning in November. Migration peaks in February, when humpbacks congregate mostly in the waters off Maui, with smaller groups heading for the waters off the other islands. In 1992, the **Hawaiian Islands Humpback Whale National Marine Sanctuary** was designated, encompassing waters off all six major islands. This will hopefully ensure a perpetual safe haven for the whales.

Adult humpbacks average 45 feet long and weigh in at a svelte 40 tons (80,000 pounds) or more. Females come to Hawaii mainly to give birth to 2,000-pound, relatively blubberless calves, most of which are born by the end of January. They nurse their calves for about one year and become impregnated again the next year. While in Hawaiian waters, humpbacks generally don't eat. They wait until returning to Alaska, where they gorge themselves on krill. It's estimated that they can live off their blubber without peril for six months. They have an enormous mouth filled with more than 600 rows of baleen stretching one-third the length of their bodies. Humpbacks have been known to blow air underwater to create giant bubble-nets that help corral krill. They rush in with mouths agape and dine on their catch.

Like other baleen whales, humpbacks feed in relatively shallow waters and sound (dive) for periods lasting a maximum of about 25 minutes. In comparison, sperm whales, toothed bottom-feeders, can stay down for over an hour. On the surface humpbacks will breathe about once every two minutes. They also sleep on the surface or just below it for two hours.

A distinctive feature of the humpback is the flipper, some up to 15 foot long, that it can bend over its back. The flippers and tail flukes have white markings that differ among individuals, much like human fingerprints. These markings are used to identify individual migrating humpbacks. Scientists photograph the distinctive tails and send copies to Seattle, Washington, a center of whale research. There computer analysis is done to identify the individual or to record it as a new specimen. Thereafter, any sightings become part of its life history. The humpback is the most aquabatic of all whales, and it is a thrilling sight to see one of these agile giants leap from the water and create a monumental splash.

The Humpback's Song

Humpbacks have a special ability to sing unlike other whales. They create their melodies by grunting, shrieking, and moaning. No one knows exactly what the songs represent, but it's clear they're a definite form of communication. The singers appear to be escort males that tag along with, and seem to guard, a mother and her calf. Some scientists believe that these are lone males, and perhaps the song is territorial, or a mating call. The songs are exact renditions that last 20 minutes or longer and are repeated for hours. Amazingly, all the whales know and sing the same song, and the song changes from year to year. The notes are so forceful that they can be heard above and below the water for miles. Some of the deep bass notes will even carry underwater for 100 miles.

Whaling History

Humans have known about whales for many thousands of years. A Minoan palace on the island of Crete depicts whales on a 5,000-year-old mural. The first whalers were probably Norwegians who used stone harpoon heads to capture their prey more than 4,000 years ago. Inuit have long engaged in whaling as a means of survival, and for centuries many peoples living along coastal waters have harpooned migrating whales that ventured close to shore. The Basques had a thriving medieval whaling industry in the 12th century centered in the Bay of Biscay, until they wiped out all of the Biscayan right

ENVIRONMENTAL RESOURCE GROUPS

Anyone interested in Hawaii's environmental issues can contact the following for more information:

Earthjustice Legal Defense Fund, 223 S. King St., 4th Fl., Honolulu, HI 96813, 808/599-2436, www.earthjustice.org

Greenpeace, 702 H Street NW, Ste. 300, Washington, DC 20001, 202/462-1177 or 808/263-4388 in Hawaii, www.greenpeace.org

The Nature Conservancy, 923 Nu'uanu Ave., Honolulu, HI 96817, 808/537-4508, www.tnc.org/hawaii

Rainforest Action Network, 221 Pine St., Ste. 500, San Francisco, CA 94104, 415/398-4404, www.ran.org

Sierra Club Hawaii Chapter, P.O. Box 2577,

Honolulu, HI 96803, 808/538-6616, www.hi.sierraclub.org

Earth Trust, 25 Kaneohe Bay Dr., Ste. 205, Kailua, HI 96734, 808/254-2866, www.earthtrust.org

A savvy monthly newsletter that focuses on environmental and political issues facing Hawaii today is *Environment Hawai'i,* 282 Ululani St, 1st Fl., Hilo, HI 96720, 808/934-0115, www.environment-hawaii.org; individual subscription rate $35 per year. The well-researched and concisely written newsletter attempts to be fair to all parties concerned. Short on preaching and long on common sense, *Environment Hawai'i* is an excellent resource for anyone interested in the sociopolitical and environmental issues of the 50th state.

whales. The height of the classic whaling industry that inspired Melville's *Moby Dick* occurred 1820–60. The international whaling capital perfectly situated in the center of the winter whaling grounds was Lahaina, Maui. At that time 900 sailing ships roamed the globe in search of whales. Of these, 700 were American, and they started the trend away from coastal to pelagic whaling by bringing their trypots (blubber pots) aboard ship.

Although the killing was great during these years, every part of the whale was needed and used: blubber, meat, bone, teeth. Whale oil, the main product, was a superior lighting fuel and lubricant unmatched until petroleum came into general use in the mid-19th century. Today, every single whale by-product can be manufactured synthetically, and there's absolutely no primary need to justify slaughtering whales.

During the great whaling days, the whales actually had a fighting chance. After all, they were hunted by men in wooden sailing ships that depended on favorable winds. Once sighted by a sailor perched high in the rigging using a low-powered telescope, a small boat heaved off; after desperate rowing and dangerous maneuvering, the master harpooner threw his shaft by hand. When the whale was dead, the efforts of all able-bodied men were needed to haul it in.

Today, however, modern methods have wiped out every trace of daring and turned the hunt into technologically assisted slaughter. Low-flying aircraft radio the whales' location to huge factory ships that track them with radar and sonar. Once the pod is spotted, super-swift launches tear into them, firing cannon-propelled harpoons with lethal exploding tips. The killer launches keep firing until every whale in the pod is dead, and the huge factory boat follows behind merely scooping up the lifeless carcasses and hauling them aboard with diesel winches.

Many pirate whalers still roam the seas. The worst example perpetrated by these vultures occurred in the Bahamas in 1971. A ship that ironically carried the name of *the* classic conservation group, the *Sierra*, succeeded in wiping out every single humpback whale that wintered in Bahamian waters. Since 1971 not one whale has

been sighted in the Bahamas, and whale-watchers lament that they will never return.

The Last Whalers

Thanks to world opinion, and the efforts of benign but aggressive organizations such as Greenpeace and Earth Trust, the **International Whaling Commission (IWC),** a voluntary group of 49 nations, now sets standards and passes quotas on the number and species of whales that can be killed. Over the last several decades the blue, right, gray, bowhead, and humpback have become totally protected; however, many great whales such as the sperm, minke, sei, and fin are still hunted. Also, the IWC has no power of enforcement except for public opinion and possible voluntary economic sanction.

The Japanese and Norwegians still hunt for whale, their operations often thinly disguised as "research." Native American Inuit and a few other indigenous peoples of the world, like the villagers of Lamalera on Lembata in Indonesia, hunt whale, but the numbers of whales taken from these groups is minuscule. The Japanese technically stay within their quotas, but they hire and outfit these and other nationals to hunt whales for them. Their main argument is that whaling is a traditional industry on which they rely for food and jobs. This is patently false. Hardly more than 100 years old, pelagic whaling is a new industry to the Japanese. Much of the Japanese whale meat becomes pet food anyway, which is mainly exported.

Amazingly, a recent poll taken in Japan by the Whale and Dolphin Society of London found that 69 percent of the people opposed whaling. Finally, through the efforts of the **International Cetacean Education and Research Conference (ICEARCH),** the first pillars of a bridge were laid between Japanese and Western scientists who are dedicated to finding a way for humans and the great whales to live in harmony. On Maui in April 1993, these scientists came together for the first time to discuss the issue.

Whale-Watching

If you're in Hawaii from late November to early May, you have an excellent chance of spotting a humpback. March is perhaps the best month. You can often see whales from a vantage point on land, but this is nowhere near as thrilling as seeing them close-up from a boat. Either way, binoculars are a must. Telephoto and zoom lenses are also useful, and you might even get a nifty photo in the bargain. But don't waste your film unless you have a fairly high-powered zoom: Fixed-lens cameras give pictures with a lot of ocean and a tiny black speck. If you're lucky enough to see a whale breach (jump clear of the water), keep watching because they often repeat this several times. If a whale dives and lifts its fluke high in the air, expect it to be down for at least 15 minutes and not come up in the same spot. Other times they'll dive shallowly, then bob up and down quite often. From shore you're likely to see whales anywhere along Maui's south coast.

If you're staying at any of the hotels or condos along Ka'anapali or Kihei and have an ocean view, you can spot them from your lanai or window. Two good vantage spots are Papawai Point and McGregor Point along Route 30 just west of Ma'alaea. During whale-watching season, a Pacific Whale Foundation naturalist will be at McGregor Point daily from 8:30 A.M.–3:30 P.M. with a display van to help people locate whales and answer questions. Ma'alaea Bay is another favorite nursing ground for female whales and their calves; there you can also see a small working harbor up close. Another excellent viewpoint is Makena Beach, on the spit of land separating Little and Big Beaches. If you time your arrival near sunset, even if you don't see a whale you'll enjoy a mind-boggling light show.

To learn more about whales and the Hawaiian Islands Humpback Whale National Marine Sanctuary, www.hihwnms.nos.noaa.gov, stop by the office at 726 S. Kihei Rd., Kihei, HI 96753, 800/879-2818; open Mon.–Fri. 9 A.M.–3 P.M., grounds open dawn to dusk. In an adjacent building is the sanctuary's Education Center, open 10 A.M.–3 P.M. weekdays, which offers marine life displays, information on all aspects of the sanctuary, and periodic lectures. Another good source of information is the **Pacific Whale Foundation,** at the Ma'alaea Harbor Village in Ma'alaea, 808/249-8811, www.pacificwhale.org. Both of these organizations have plenty of printed information about whales and other marine animals, and the Pacific Whale Foundation prints the free *Outdoor Adventures* tabloid that details other information about these mammals and doings of the foundation.

Additional research on whales and dolphins is undertaken by the **Island Marine Institute,** 658 Front St., Ste. 101, Lahaina, HI 96761, 808/661-8397 or 800/275-6969, www.whalewatch maui.com.

History

THE ROAD FROM TAHITI

Until the 1820s, when New England missionaries began a phonetic rendering of the Hawaiian language, the past was kept vividly alive only by the sonorous voices of special *kahuna* who chanted the sacred *mele*. The chants were beautiful flowing word pictures that captured the essence of every aspect of life. These *mele* praised the land *(mele 'aina),* royalty *(mele ali'i),* and life's tender aspects *(mele aloha).* Chants were dedicated to friendship, hardship, and favorite children. Entire villages sometimes joined together to compose a *mele*—every word was chosen carefully, and the wise old *kahuna* would decide if the words were lucky or unlucky. Some *mele* were bawdy or funny on the surface but contained secret meanings, often bitingly sarcastic, that ridiculed an inept or cruel leader. The most important chants took listeners back into the dim past, even before people lived in Hawaii. From these genealogies *(koihonua)* the *ali'i* derived the right to rule because these chants went back to the gods Wakea and Papa from whom the *ali'i* were directly descended.

The Kumulipo

The great genealogies, finally compiled in the

late 1800s by order of King Kalakaua, were collectively known as *The Kumulipo, A Hawaiian Creation Chant,* basically a Polynesian account of Genesis. Other chants related to the beginning of this world, but *The Kumulipo* sums it all up and is generally considered the best. The chant relates that after the beginning of time, there is a period of darkness. The darkness, however, mysteriously brims with spontaneous life; during this period plants and animals are born, as well as Kumulipo, the man, and Po'ele, the woman. In the eighth chant darkness gives way to light and the gods descend to earth. Wakea is "the sky father" and Papa is "the earth mother," whose union gives birth to the islands of Hawai'i. First born is Hawai'i, followed by Maui, then Kaho'olawe. Apparently, Papa becomes bushed after three consecutive births and decides to vacation in Tahiti. While Papa is away recovering from postpartum depression and working on her tan, Wakea gets lonely and takes Ka'ula as his second wife, who bears him the island-child of Lana'i. Not fully cheered up, but getting the hang of it, Wakea takes a third wife, Hina, who promptly bears the island of Moloka'i. Meanwhile, Papa gets wind of these shenanigans, returns from Polynesia, and retaliates by taking up with Lua, a young and virile god, and soon gives birth to the island of O'ahu. Papa and Wakea finally decide that they really are meant for each other and reconcile to conceive Kaua'i, Ni'ihau, Ka'ula, and Nihoa. These two progenitors are the source from which all the *ali'i* ultimately traced their lineage, and from which they derived their god-ordained power to rule.

Basically, there are two major genealogical families: the Nanaulu, who became the royal *ali'i* of O'ahu and Kaua'i, and the Ulu, who provided the royalty of Maui and Hawai'i. The best sources of information on Hawaiian myth and legend are Martha Beckwith's *Hawaiian Mythol-*

> *The past was kept vividly alive only by the sonorous voices of special* kahuna *who chanted the sacred* mele. *These chants were beautiful flowing word pictures that captured the essence of every aspect of life. Entire villages sometimes joined together to compose a* mele— *every word chosen carefully.*

ogy and the monumental three-volume opus *An Account of the Polynesian Race,* compiled by Abraham Fornander 1878–1885. Fornander, after settling in Hawaii, married an *ali'i* from Moloka'i and had an illustrious career as a newspaper man, Maui circuit judge, and finally Supreme Court justice. For years Fornander sent scribes to every corner of the kingdom to listen to the elder *kupuna*. They returned with the firsthand accounts, which he dutifully recorded.

The Great Navigators

No one knows exactly when the first Polynesians arrived in Hawaii, but the great "deliberate migrations" from the southern islands seem to have taken place A.D. 500–800, although anthropologists keep pushing the date backward in time as new evidence becomes available. Even before that, however, it's reasonable to assume that the first people to set foot on Hawaii were probably fishermen, or perhaps defeated warriors whose canoes were blown hopelessly northward into unfamiliar waters. They arrived by a combination of extraordinary good luck and an uncanny ability to sail and navigate without instruments, using the sun by day and the moon and rising stars by night. They could feel the water and determine direction by swells, tides, and currents. The movements of fish and cloud formations were also utilized to give direction. Because their arrival was probably an accident, they were unprepared to settle on the fertile but uncultivated lands, having no stock animals, plant cuttings, or women. Forced to return southward, undoubtedly many lost their lives at sea, but a few wild-eyed stragglers must have made it home to tell tales of a paradise to the north where land was plentiful and the sea bounteous. This is affirmed by ancient navigational chants from Tahiti, Moorea, and Bora Bora, which passing from father to son revealed how to follow the stars to the "heavenly homeland in the north." Possibly a few migrations followed, but it's known that for centuries there was no real reason for a mass exodus, so the chants alone remained and eventually became shadowy legend.

From Where They Came

It's generally agreed that the first planned migrations were from the violent cannibal islands that Spanish explorers called the Marquesas, 11 islands in extreme eastern Polynesia. The islands are harsh and inhospitable, breeding a toughness into these people that enabled them to withstand the hardships of long, unsure ocean voyages and years of resettlement. Marquesans were a fiercely independent people whose chiefs could

rise from the ranks because of bravery or intelligence. They must also have been a fierce-looking lot. Both men and women tattooed themselves in complex blue patterns from head to foot. The warriors carried massive, intricately designed ironwood war clubs and wore carved whale teeth in slits in their earlobes that eventually stretched to the shoulders. They shaved the sides of their heads with sharks' teeth, tied their hair in two topknots that looked like horns, and rubbed their heavily muscled and tattooed bodies with scented coconut oils. Their cults worshipped mummified ancestors; the bodies of warriors of defeated neighboring tribes were consumed. They were masters at building great double-hulled canoes launched from huge canoe sheds. Two hulls

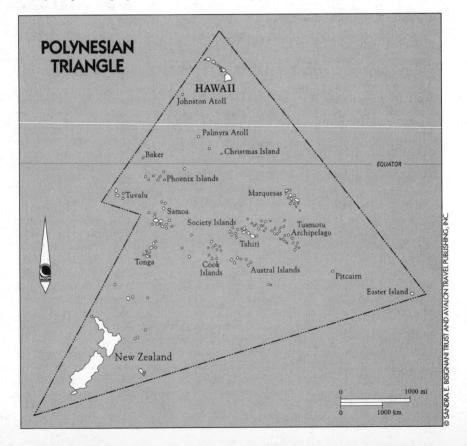

POLYNESIAN TRIANGLE

HAWAII
Johnston Atoll

Palmyra Atoll

Baker
Christmas Island

EQUATOR

Phoenix Islands

Tuvalu
Marquesas

Samoa
Society Islands
Tuamotu Archipelago

Tahiti

Tonga
Cook Islands
Austral Islands
Pitcairn

Easter Island

New Zealand

0   1000 mi
0   1000 km

were fastened together to form a catamaran, and a hut in the center provided shelter in bad weather. The average voyaging canoe was 60–80 feet long and could comfortably hold an extended family of about 30 people. These small family bands carried all the staples they would need in the new lands.

The New Lands

For five centuries the Marquesans settled and lived peacefully on the new land, as if Hawaii's *aloha* spirit overcame most of their fierceness. The tribes coexisted in relative harmony, especially because there was no competition for land. Cannibalism died out. There was much coming and going between Hawaii and Polynesia, and new people came to settle for hundreds of years. Then, it appears that in the 12th century a deliberate exodus of warlike Tahitians arrived and subjugated the settled islanders. They came to conquer. This incursion had a terrific significance on the Hawaiian religious and social system. Oral tradition relates that a Tahitian priest, Pa'ao, found the mana of the Hawaiian chiefs to be low, signifying that their gods were weak. Pa'ao built a *heiau* at Waha'ula on the Big Island, then introduced the warlike god Ku and the rigid *kapu* system through which the new rulers became dominant. Voyages between Tahiti and Hawaii continued for about 100 years, and Tahitian customs, legends, and language became the Hawaiian way of life. Then suddenly, for no recorded or apparent reason, the voyages discontinued and Hawaii returned to total isolation.

The islands remained forgotten for almost 500 years until the indomitable English seaman, Captain James Cook, sighted O'ahu on January 18, 1778, and stepped ashore at Waimea on Kaua'i two days later. At that time Hawaii's isolation was so complete that even the Polynesians had forgotten about it. On an earlier voyage, Tupaia, a high priest from Raiatea, had accompanied Captain Cook as he sailed throughout Polynesia. Tupaia demonstrated his vast knowledge of existing archipelagoes throughout the South Pacific by naming more than 130 islands and drawing a map that included the Tonga group, the Cook Islands, the Marquesas, even tiny Pit-

cairn, a rock in far eastern Polynesia where the mutinous crew of the *Bounty* found solace. In mentioning the Marquesas, Tupaia said, *"He ma'a te ka'ata,"* which equals "Food is man" or simply "Cannibals." But remarkably absent from Tupaia's vast knowledge was the existence of Easter Island, New Zealand, and Hawaii.

The next waves of people to Hawaii would be white, and the Hawaiian world would be changed quickly and forever.

THE WORLD DISCOVERS HAWAII

The late 18th century was an extraordinary time in Hawaiian history. Monumental changes seemed to happen all at once. First, Captain James Cook, a Yorkshire farm boy, fulfilling his destiny as the all-time greatest Pacific explorer, found Hawaii for the rest of the world. For better or worse, it could no longer be an isolated Polynesian homeland. For the first time in Hawaiian history, a charismatic leader, Kamehameha, emerged, and after a long civil war he united all the islands into one centralized kingdom. The death of Captain Cook in Hawaii marked the beginning of a long series of tragic misunderstandings between whites and natives. When Kamehameha died, the old religious system of *kapu* came to an end, leaving the Hawaiians in a spiritual vortex. Many takers arrived to fill the void: missionaries after souls, whalers after their prey, traders and planters after profits and a good time, traders and planters after profits and a home. The islands were opened and devoured like ripe fruit. Powerful nations, including Russia, Great Britain, France, and the United States, yearned to bring this strategic Pacific jewel under their own influence. The 19th century brought the demise of the Hawaiian people as a dominant political force in their own land and with it the end of Hawaii as a sovereign monarchy. An almost bloodless yet bitter military coup followed by a brief Hawaiian Republic ended in annexation by the United States. As the United States became completely entrenched politically and militarily, a new social and economic order was founded on the plantation system. Amazingly rapid population growth occurred with the importation of plantation workers from Asia and Europe, which yielded a unique cosmopolitan blend of races like nowhere else on earth. By the dawning of the 20th century, the face of old Hawaii had been altered forever; the "sacred homeland in the north" was hurled into the modern age. The attack on Pearl Harbor saw a tremendous loss of life and brought Hawaii closer to the United States by a baptism of blood. Finally, on August 21, 1959, after 59 years as a "territory," Hawaii officially became the 50th state of the Union.

Captain Cook Sights Hawaii

In 1776, Captain James Cook set sail for the Pacific from Plymouth, England, on his third and final expedition into this still vastly unexplored region of the world. On a fruitless quest for the fabled Northwest Passage across the North American continent, he sailed down the coast of Africa, rounded the Cape of Good Hope, crossed the Indian Ocean, and traveled past New Zealand, Tasmania, and the Friendly Islands (where an unsuccessful plot was hatched by the "friendly" natives to murder him). On January 18, 1778, Captain Cook's 100-foot flagship HMS *Resolution* and its 90-foot companion HMS *Discovery* sighted O'ahu. Two days later, they sighted Kaua'i and went ashore at the village of Waimea. Although anxious to get on with his mission, Cook decided to make a quick sortie to investigate this new land and reprovision his ships. He did, however, take time to remark in his diary about the close resemblance of these newfound people to others he had encountered as far south as New Zealand, and marveled at their widespread habitation across the Pacific.

The first trade was some brass medals for a mackerel. Cook also stated that he had never before met natives so astonished by a ship, and that they had an amazing fascination for iron, which they called *ko'i*, Hawaiian for "adze." There is even some conjecture that a Spanish ship under one Captain Gaetano had landed in Hawaii as early as the 16th century, trading a few scraps of iron that the Hawaiians valued even more than the Europeans valued gold. It was also noted that the Hawaiian women gave themselves freely

Captain James Cook

COURTESY OF HAWAII STATE ARCHIVES

to the sailors with the apparent good wishes of the island men. This was actually a ploy by the *kahuna* to test if the newcomers were gods or men—gods didn't need women. These sailors proved immediately mortal. Cook, who was also a physician, tried valiantly to keep the 66 men (out of 112) who had measurable cases of venereal disease away from the women. The task proved impossible as women literally swarmed the ships; when Cook returned less than a year later, it was logged that signs of VD were already apparent on some natives' faces.

Cook was impressed with the Hawaiians' swimming ability and with their well-bred manners. They had happy dispositions and sticky fingers, stealing any object made of metal, especially nails. The first item stolen was a butcher's cleaver. An unidentified native grabbed it, plunged overboard, swam to shore, and waved his booty in triumph. The Hawaiians didn't seem to care for beads and were not at all impressed with a mirror. Cook provisioned his ships by trading chisels for hogs, while common sailors gleefully traded nails for sex. Landing parties were sent inland to fill casks with fresh water. On one such excursion a Mr. Williamson, who was eventually drummed out of the Royal Navy for cowardice, unnecessarily shot and killed a native. After a brief stop on Ni'ihau, the ships sailed away, but both groups were indelibly impressed with the memory of each other.

Cook Returns

Almost a year later, when winter weather forced Cook to return from the coast of Alaska, his discovery began to take on far-reaching significance. Cook had named Hawaii the Sandwich Islands in honor of one of his patrons, John Montague, the Earl of Sandwich. On this return voyage, he spotted Maui on November 26, 1778. After eight weeks of seeking a suitable harbor, the ships bypassed it, but not before the coastline was duly drawn by Lieutenant William Bligh, one of Cook's finest and most trusted officers. (Bligh would find his own drama almost 10 years later as commander of the infamous HMS *Bounty.*) The *Discovery* and *Resolution* finally found safe anchorage at Kealakekua Bay on the Kona coast of the Big Island. It is very lucky for history that on board was Mr. Anderson, ship's chronicler, who left a handwritten record of the strange and tragic events that followed. Even more important were the drawings of John Webber, ship's artist, who rendered invaluable impressions in superb drawings and etchings. Other noteworthy men aboard were George Vancouver, who would lead the first British return to Hawaii after Cook's death and introduce many fruits, vegetables, cattle, sheep, and goats, and James Burney, who would become a long-standing leading authority on the Pacific.

By all accounts Cook was a humane and just captain, greatly admired by his men. Unlike the many supremacists of that time, he was known to have a respectful attitude toward any people he encountered, treating them as equals and recognizing the significance of their cultures. Not known as a violent man, he would use his superior weapons against natives only in an absolute case of self-defense. His hardened crew had been at sea facing untold hardship for almost three years; returning to Hawaii was truly like reentering paradise.

A strange series of coincidences sailed with Cook into Kealakekua Bay on January 16, 1779.

It was *makahiki* time, a period of rejoicing and festivity dedicated to the fertility god of the earth, Lono. Normal *kapu* days were suspended, and willing partners freely enjoyed each other sexually, along with dancing, feasting, and the islands' version of Olympic games. It was long held in Hawaiian legend that the great god Lono would return to earth. Lono's image was a small wooden figure perched on a tall mastlike crossbeam; hanging from the crossbeam were long, white sheets of *tapa*. Who else could Cook be but Lono, and what else could his ships with their masts and white sails be but his sacred floating *heiau?* This explained the Hawaiians' previous fascination with his ships, but to add to the remarkable coincidence, Kealakekua Harbor happened to be considered Lono's private sacred harbor. Natives from throughout the land prostrated themselves and paid homage to the returning god. Cook was taken ashore and brought to Lono's sacred temple, where he was afforded the highest respect. The ships badly needed fresh supplies, and the Hawaiians readily gave all they had, stretching their own provisions to the limit. To the sailors' delight, this included full measures of the *aloha* spirit.

The Fatal Misunderstandings

After an uproarious welcome and generous hospitality for over a month, it became obvious that the newcomers were beginning to overstay their welcome. During the interim a seaman named William Watman died, convincing the Hawaiians that the *haole* were indeed mortals, not gods. Watman was buried at Hikiau Heiau, where a plaque commemorates the event to this day. Incidents of petty theft began to increase dramatically. The lesser chiefs indicated it was time to leave by "rubbing the Englishmen's bellies." Inadvertently, many *kapu* were broken by the English, and once-friendly relations became strained. Finally, the ships sailed away on February 4, 1779.

After plying terrible seas for only a week, *Resolution*'s foremast was badly damaged. Cook sailed back into Kealakekua Bay, dragging the mast ashore on February 13. The natives, now totally hostile, hurled rocks at the sailors. Orders were given to load muskets with ball; firearms had previously only been loaded with shot and a light charge. Confrontations increased when some Hawaiians stole a small boat and Cook's men set after them, capturing the fleeing canoe, which held an *ali'i* named Palea. The Englishmen treated him roughly; to the Hawaiians' horror, they even smacked him on the head with a paddle. The Hawaiians then furiously attacked the marines, who abandoned the small boat.

Cook Goes Down

Next the Hawaiians stole a small cutter from the *Discovery* that had been moored to a buoy and partially sunk to protect it from the sun. For the first time, Captain Cook became furious. He ordered Captain Clerk of the *Discovery* to sail to the southeast end of the bay and to stop any canoe trying to leave Kealakekua. Cook then made a fatal error in judgment. He decided to take nine armed marines ashore in an attempt to convince the venerable King Kalani'opu'u to accompany him back aboard ship, where he would hold him for ransom in exchange for the cutter. The old king agreed, but his wife prevailed upon him not to trust the *haole*. Kalani'opu'u sat down on the beach to think while the tension steadily grew.

Meanwhile, a group of marines fired on a canoe trying to leave the bay. A lesser chief, No'okemai, was killed. The crowd around Cook and his men reached an estimated 20,000, and warriors outraged by the killing of the chief armed themselves with clubs and protective straw-mat armor. One bold warrior advanced on Cook and struck him with his *pahoa* (dagger). In retaliation Cook drew a tiny pistol lightly loaded with shot and fired at the warrior. His bullets spent themselves on the straw armor and fell harmlessly to the ground. The Hawaiians went wild. Lieutenant Molesworth Phillips, in charge of the nine marines, began a withering fire; Cook himself slew two natives.

Overpowered by sheer numbers, the marines headed for boats standing offshore, while Lieutenant Phillips lay wounded. It is believed that Captain Cook, the greatest seaman ever to enter the Pacific, stood helplessly in knee-deep water instead of making for the boats because he could not swim! Hopelessly surrounded, he was knocked on the head, then countless warriors passed a knife around and hacked and mutilated his lifeless body. A sad Lieutenant King lamented in his diary, "Thus fell our great and excellent commander."

The Final Chapter

Captain Clerk, now in charge, settled his men and prevailed upon the Hawaiians to return Cook's body. On the morning of February 16 a grisly piece of charred meat was brought aboard: the Hawaiians, according to their custom, had afforded Cook the highest honor by baking his body in an underground oven to remove the flesh from the bones. On February 17, a group of Hawaiians in a canoe taunted the marines by brandishing Cook's hat. The English, strained to the limit and thinking that Cook was being desecrated, finally broke. Foaming with bloodlust, they leveled their cannon and muskets on shore and shot anything that moved. It is believed that Kamehameha the Great was wounded in this flurry, along with four *ali'i*; 25 *maka'ainana* (commoners) were killed. Finally, on February 21, 1779, the bones of Captain James Cook's hands, skull, arms, and legs were returned and tearfully buried at sea. A common seaman, one Mr. Zimmerman, summed up the feelings of all who sailed under Cook when he wrote, ". . . he was our leading star." The English sailed next morning after dropping off their Hawaiian girlfriends who were still aboard.

Captain Clerk, in bad health, carried on with the fruitless search for the Northwest Passage. He died and was buried at the Siberian village of Petropavlovsk. England was at war with upstart colonists in America, so the return of the expedition warranted little fanfare. The *Resolution* was converted into an army transport to fight the pesky Americans; the once-proud *Discovery* was reduced to a convict ship ferrying inmates to Botany Bay, Australia. Mrs. Cook, the great captain's steadfast and chaste wife, lived to the age of 93, surviving all her children. She was given a stipend of 200 pounds per year and finished her days surrounded by Cook's mementos, observing the anniversary of his death to the very end by fasting and reading from the Bible.

THE UNIFICATION OF OLD HAWAII

Hawaii was already in a state of political turmoil and civil war when Cook arrived. In the 1780s the islands were roughly divided into three kingdoms: venerable Kalaniʻopuʻu ruled Hawaiʻi and the Hana district of Maui; wily and ruthless warrior-king Kahekili ruled Maui, Kahoʻolawe, Lanaʻi, and later Oʻahu; and Kaeo, Kahekiliʻs brother, ruled Kauaʻi. War ravaged the land until a remarkable chief, Kamehameha, rose and subjugated all the islands under one rule. Kamehameha initiated a dynasty that would last for about 100 years, until the independent monarchy of Hawaii forever ceased to be. To add a zing to this brewing political stew, Westerners and their technology were beginning to come in ever-increasing numbers. In 1786, Captain Jean de François La Pérouse and his French exploration party landed in what's now La Perouse Bay, near Makena on Maui, foreshadowing European attention to the islands. In 1786 two American captains, Portlock and Dixon, made landfall in Hawaii. Also, it was known that a fortune could be made on the fur trade between the Pacific Northwest and Canton, China; stopping in Hawaii could make it feasible. After this was reported, the fate of Hawaii was sealed.

Hawaii under Kamehameha was ready to enter its "golden age." The social order was medieval, with the *aliʻi* as knights, owing their military allegiance to the king, and the serflike *makaʻainana* paying tribute and working the lands. The priesthood of *kahuna* filled the posts of advisors, sorcerers, navigators, doctors, and historians. This was Polynesian Hawaii at its apex. But like the uniquely Hawaiian silversword, the old culture blossomed, and as soon as it did, it began to wither. Ever since, all that was purely Hawaiian has been supplanted by the relentless foreign influences that began bearing down upon it.

Young Kamehameha

The greatest native son of Hawaii, Kamehameha was born under mysterious circumstances in the Kohala District of the Big Island, probably in 1753. He was royal born to Keoua Kupuapaikalaninui, the chief of Kohala, and Kekuiapoiwa, a chieftess from Kona. Accounts vary, but one claims that before his birth, a *kahuna* prophesied that this child would grow to be a "killer of chiefs." Because of this, the local chiefs conspired to murder the infant. When Kekuiapoiwa's time came, she secretly went to the royal birthing stones near Moʻokini Heiau and delivered Kamehameha. She entrusted her baby to a manservant and instructed him to hide the child. He headed for the rugged and remote coast around Kapaʻau. Here Kamehameha was raised in the mountains, mostly by men. Always alone, he earned the nickname "The Lonely One."

Kamehameha was a man noticed by everyone; there was no doubt he was a force to be reckoned with. He had met Captain Cook when the *Discovery* unsuccessfully tried to land at Hana on Maui. While aboard, he made a lasting impression, distinguishing himself from the multitude of natives swarming the ships by his royal bearing. Lieutenant James King, in a diary entry, remarked that Kamehameha was a fierce-looking man, almost ugly, but that he was obviously intelligent, observant, and very good-natured. Kamehameha received his early military training from his uncle Kalaniʻopuʻu, the great king of Hawaiʻi and Hana, who fought fierce battles against Alapaʻi, the usurper who stole his hereditary lands. After regaining Hawaiʻi, Kalaniʻopuʻu returned to his Hana district and turned his attention to conquering all of Maui. During this period, young Kamehameha distinguished himself as a ferocious warrior and earned the nickname of "the Hard-shelled Crab," even though old Kahekili, Maui's king, almost annihilated Kalaniʻopuʻu's army at the sand hills of Wailuku.

When the old king neared death he passed on the kingdom to his son Kiwalao. He also, however, empowered Kamehameha as the keeper of the family war god Kukaʻilimoku: Ku of the Bloody Red Mouth, Ku the Destroyer. Oddly enough, Kamehameha had been born not 500 yards from Ku's great *heiau* at Kohala and had heard the chanting and observed the ceremonies dedicated to this fierce god from his first breath. Soon after Kalaniʻopuʻu died, Kamehameha found himself in a bitter war that he did not seek against his two cousins, Kiwalao and his brother Keoua, with the island of Hawai'i at stake. The skirmishing lasted nine years, until Kamehameha's armies met the two brothers at Moku'ohai in an indecisive battle in which Kiwalao was killed. The result was a shaky truce with Keoua, a much embittered enemy. During this fighting, Kahekili of Maui conquered O'ahu, where he built a house of the skulls and bones of his adversaries as a reminder of his omnipotence. He also extended his will to Kaua'i by marrying his half-brother to a high-ranking chiefess of that island. A new factor would resolve this stalemate of power—the coming of the *haole*.

The Olowalu Massacre

In 1790 the American merchant ship *Eleanora,* commanded by Yankee captain Simon Metcalfe, was looking for a harbor after its long voyage from the Pacific Northwest. Following a day behind was the *Fair American,* a tiny ship sailed by Metcalfe's son Thomas and a crew of five. Simon Metcalfe, perhaps by necessity, was a stern and humorless man who would broach no interference. While his ship was anchored at Olowalu, a beach area about five miles east of Lahaina, some natives slipped close in their canoes and stole a small boat, killing a seaman in the process. Metcalfe decided to trick the Hawaiians by first negotiating a truce and then unleashing full fury on them. Signaling he was willing to trade, he invited canoes of innocent natives to visit his ship. In the meantime, he ordered that all cannon and muskets be readied with scatter shot. When the canoes were within hailing distance, he ordered his crew to fire at will. Over 100 people were slain; the Hawaiians remembered this killing as "the day of spilled brains." Metcalfe then sailed away to Kealakekua Bay and in an unrelated incident succeeded in insulting Kameiamoku, a ruling chief, who vowed to annihilate the next *haole* ship that he saw.

Fate sent him the *Fair American* and young Thomas Metcalfe. The little ship was entirely overrun by superior forces. In the ensuing battle, the mate, Isaac Davis, so distinguished himself by open acts of bravery that his life alone was spared. Kameiamoku later turned over both Davis and

the ship to Kamehameha. Meanwhile, while harbored at Kealakekua, the senior Metcalfe sent John Young to reconnoiter. Kamehameha, having learned of the capture of the *Fair American,* detained Young so he could not report, and Metcalfe, losing patience, marooned his own man and sailed off to Canton. (Metcalfe never learned of the fate of his son Thomas and was later killed with another son while trading in the South Pacific.) Kamehameha quickly realized the significance of his two captives and the *Fair American* with its brace of small cannons. He appropriated the ship and made Davis and Young trusted advisors, eventually raising them to the rank of chief. They would all play a significant role in the unification of Hawaii.

Kamehameha the Great

Later in 1790, supported by the savvy of Davis and Young and the cannon from the *Fair American,* which he mounted on carts, Kamehameha invaded Maui, using Hana as his power base. The island defenders under Kalanikupule, son of Kahekili who was lingering on O'ahu, were totally demoralized, then driven back into the deathtrap of 'Iao Valley. There, Kamehameha's forces annihilated them. No mercy was expected and none given, although mostly commoners were slain with no significant *ali'i* falling to the victors. So many were killed in this sheer-walled, inescapable valley that the battle was called *"ka pani wai,"* which means "the damming of the waters"—literally with dead bodies.

While Kamehameha was fighting on Maui, his old nemesis Keoua was busy running amok back on Hawai'i, again pillaging Kamehameha's lands. The great warrior returned home flushed with victory, but in two battles could not subdue Keoua. Finally, Kamehameha had a prophetic dream in which he was told that Ku would lead him to victory over all the lands of Hawaii if he would build a *heiau* to the war god at Kawaihae. Even before the temple was finished, old Kahekili attempted to invade Waipi'o, Kamehameha's stronghold. But Kamehameha summoned Davis and Young, and with the *Fair American* and an enormous fleet of war canoes defeated Kahekili at laid on the altar, along with 11 others who were slaughtered and dedicated to Ku, of the Maggot-dripping Mouth.

Increasing Contact

By the time Kamehameha had won the Big Island, Hawaii was becoming a regular stopover for numerous ships seeking the lucrative sandalwood trade with China. In February 1791, Captain George Vancouver, still seeking the Northwest Passage, returned to Kealakekua, where he was greeted by a throng of 30,000. The captain at once recognized Kamehameha, who was wearing a Chinese dressing gown that he had received in tribute from another chief, who in turn had received it directly from the hands of Cook. The diary of a crew member, Thomas Manby, relates that Kamehameha, missing his front teeth, was more fierce-looking than ever as he approached the ship in an elegant double-hulled canoe sporting 46 rowers. The king invited all to a great feast prepared for them on the beach. Kamehameha's appetite matched his tremendous size. It was noted that he ate two sizable fish, a king-size bowl of poi, a small pig, and an entire baked dog. Kamehameha personally entertained the English by putting on a mock battle in which he deftly avoided spears by rolling, tumbling, and catching them in midair, all the while hurling his own spear a great distance. The English reciprocated by firing cannon bursts into the air, creating an impromptu fireworks display. Kamehameha requested from Vancouver a full table setting, with which he was provided, but his request for firearms was prudently denied. Captain Vancouver became a trusted advisor of Kamehameha and told him about the white man's form of worship. He even interceded for Kamehameha with his headstrong queen, Ka'ahumanu, and coaxed her from her hiding place under a rock when she sought refuge at Pu'uhonua O Honaunau. The captain gave gifts of beef cattle, fowl, and breeding stock of sheep and goats. The ship's naturalist, Archibald Menzies, was the first *haole* to climb Mauna Kea; he also introduced a large assortment of fruits and vegetables. The Hawaiians were cheerful and outgoing, and showed remorse when they indicated that the remainder of Cook's

Kamehameha I by Louis Choris

Waimanu. Kahekili had no choice but to accept the indomitable Kamehameha as the king of Maui, although Kahekili remained the administrative head until his death in 1794.

Now only Keoua remained in the way, and he would be defeated not by war, but by the great *mana* of Ku. While Keoua's armies were crossing the desert on the southern slopes of Kilauea, the fire goddess Pele trumpeted her disapproval and sent a huge cloud of poisonous gas and mud-ash into the air. It descended on and instantly killed the middle legions of Keoua's armies and their families. The footprints of this ill-fated army remain to this day outlined in the mud-ash as clearly as if they were deliberately encased in wet cement. Keoua's intuition told him that the victorious *mana* of the gods had swung to Kamehameha and that his own fate was sealed. Kamehameha sent word that he wanted Keoua to meet with him at Ku's newly dedicated temple in Kawaihae. Both knew that Keoua must die. Riding proudly in his canoe, the old nemesis came gloriously outfitted in the red and gold feathered cape and helmet signifying his exalted rank. When he stepped ashore he was felled by Kamehameha's warriors. His body was ceremoniously bones had been buried in a temple close to Kealakekua. John Young, by this time firmly entrenched into Hawaiian society, made no request to sail away with Vancouver. During the next two decades of Kamehameha's rule, the French, Russians, English, and Americans discovered the great whaling waters off Hawaii. Their increasing visits shook and finally tumbled the ancient religion and social order of *kapu*.

Finishing Touches

After Keoua was laid to rest, it was only a matter of time until Kamehameha consolidated his power over all of Hawaii. In 1794 the old warrior Kahekili of Maui died and gave O'ahu to his son Kalanikupule, while Kaua'i and Ni'ihau went to his brother Kaeo. In wars between the two, Kalanikupule was victorious, although he did not possess the grit of his father nor the great *mana* of Kamehameha. He had previously murdered a Captain Brown, who had anchored in Honolulu, and seized his ship, the *Jackall*. With the aid of this ship, Kalanikupule now determined to attack Kamehameha. However, while en route the sailors regained control of their ship and cruised to the Big Island to inform and join with Kamehameha. An army of 16,000 was raised and sailed for Maui, where they met only token resistance, destroyed Lahaina, pillaged the countryside, and vanquished Moloka'i in one bloody battle.

The war canoes next sailed for O'ahu and the final showdown. The great army landed at Waikiki, and although defenders fought bravely, giving up O'ahu by the inch, they were steadily driven into the surrounding mountains. The beleaguered army made its last stand at Nu'uanu Pali, a great precipice in the mountains behind present-day Honolulu. Kamehameha's warriors mercilessly drove the enemy into the great abyss. Kalanikupule, who hid in the mountains, was captured after a few months and sacrificed to Ku, The Snatcher of Lands, thereby ending the struggle for power.

Kamehameha put down a revolt on Hawai'i in 1796, and the king of Kaua'i, Kaumuali'i, accepting the inevitable, recognized Kamehameha as supreme ruler without suffering the ravages of a needless war. Kamehameha, for the first time in Hawaiian history, was the undisputed ruler of all the islands of "the heavenly homeland in the north."

Kamehameha's Rule

Kamehameha was as gentle in victory as he was ferocious in battle. Under his rule, which lasted until his death on May 8, 1819, Hawaii enjoyed a peace unlike any the warring islands had ever known. The king moved his royal court to Lahaina, where in 1803 he built the "Brick Palace," the first permanent building of Hawaii. The benevolent tyrant also enacted the "Law of the Splintered Paddle." This law, which protected the weak from the exploitation of the strong, had its origins in an incident of many years before. A brave defender of a small overwhelmed village had broken a paddle over Kamehameha's head and taught the chief—literally in one stroke—about the nobility of the commoner.

Just as Old Hawaii reached its golden age, however, its demise was at hand. The relentless waves of *haole* both innocently and determinedly battered the old ways into the ground. With the foreign ships came prosperity and fanciful new goods after which the *ali'i* lusted. The *maka'ainana* were worked mercilessly to provide sandalwood for the China trade. This was the first "boom" economy to hit the islands, but it set the standard of exploitation that would follow. Kamehameha built an observation tower in Lahaina to watch for ships, many of which were his own, returning laden with riches from the world at large. In the last years of his life Kamehameha returned to his beloved Kona coast, where he enjoyed the excellent fishing that is renowned there to this day. He had taken Hawaii from the darkness of warfare into the light of peace. He died true to the religious and moral *kapu* of his youth, the only ones he had ever known, and with him died a unique way of life. Two loyal retainers buried his bones after the baked flesh had been ceremoniously stripped away. A secret burial cave was chosen so that no one could desecrate the remains of the great chief, thereby absorbing his *mana*. The tomb's whereabouts remain unknown, and disturbing the dead remains one of the strictest *kapu* to this day. "The Lonely One's" kingdom would pass to his son, Liholiho, but true power would be in the hands of his beloved but feisty wife Ka'ahumanu. As Kamehameha's spirit drifted from this earth, two forces sailing around Cape Horn would forever change Hawaii: the missionaries and the whalers.

MISSIONARIES AND WHALERS

The year 1819 was of the utmost significance in Hawaiian history. It marked the death of Kamehameha, the overthrow of the ancient *kapu* system, the arrival of the first whaler in Lahaina, and the departure of Calvinist missionaries from New England determined to convert the heathen islands. Great changes began to rattle the old order to its foundations. With the *kapu* system and all of the ancient gods abandoned (except for the fire goddess Pele of Kilauea), a great void permeated the souls of the Hawaiians. In the coming decades Hawaii, also coveted by Russia, France, and England, was finally consumed by America. The islands had the first American school, printing press, and newspaper *(The Polynesian)* west of the Mississippi. Lahaina, in its heyday, became the world's greatest whaling port, accommodating more than 500 ships of all types during its peak years.

> *The year 1819 was of the utmost significance in Hawaiian history. It marked the death of Kamehameha, the overthrow of the ancient* kapu *system, the arrival of the first whaler in Lahaina, and the departure of Calvinist missionaries from New England determined to convert the heathen islands.*

The Royal Family

Maui's Hana District provided Hawaii with one of its greatest queens, Ka'ahumanu, born in 1768 in a cave within walking distance of Hana Harbor. At the age of 17 she became the third of Kamehameha's 21 wives and eventually the love of his life. At first she proved to be totally independent and unmanageable, and was known to openly defy her king by taking numerous lovers. Kamehameha placed a *kapu* on her body and

even had her attended by horribly deformed hunchbacks in an effort to curb her carnal appetites, but she continued to flaunt his authority. Young Ka'ahumanu had no love for her great, lumbering, unattractive husband, but in time (even Captain Vancouver was pressed into service as a marriage counselor) she learned to love him dearly. She in turn became his favorite wife, although she remained childless throughout her life. Kamehameha's first wife was the supremely royal Keopuolani, who so outranked even him that the king had to approach her naked and crawling on his belly. Keopuolani produced the royal children Liholiho and Kauikeaouli, who became King Kamehameha II and III, respectively. Just before Kamehameha I died in 1819 he appointed Liholiho his successor, but he also had the wisdom to make Ka'ahumanu the *kuhina nui* or queen regent. Initially, Liholiho was weak and became a drunkard. Later he became a good ruler, but he was always supported by his royal mother, Keopuolani, and by the ever-formidable Ka'ahumanu.

Kapu Is Pau

Ka'ahumanu was greatly loved and respected by the people. On public occasions, she donned Kamehameha's royal cloak and spear and, so attired and infused with the king's *mana*, she demonstrated that she was the real leader of Hawaii. For six months after Kamehameha's death, Ka'ahumanu counseled Liholiho on what he must do. The wise *kuhina nui* knew that the old ways were *pau* (finished) and that Hawaii could not hope to function in a rapidly changing world under the *kapu* system. In November 1819, Ka'ahumanu and Keopuolani prevailed on Liholiho to break two of the oldest and most sacred *kapu* by eating with women and by allowing women to eat previously forbidden foods, such as bananas and certain fish. Heavily fortified with strong drink and attended by other high-ranking chiefs and a handful of foreigners, Ka'ahumanu and Liholiho ate together in public. This feast became known as 'Ai Noa (Free Eating). As the first morsels passed Ka'ahumanu's lips, the ancient gods of Hawaii tumbled. Throughout the land, revered *heiau* were burned and abandoned and the idols knocked to the ground. Now the people had nothing but their weakened inner selves to rely on. Nothing and no one could answer their prayers; their spiritual lives were empty and in shambles.

Missionaries

Into this spiritual vortex sailed the brig *Thaddeus* on April 4, 1820. It had set sail from Boston on October 23, 1819, lured to the Big Island by Henry Opukaha'ia, a local boy born at Napo'opo'o in 1792, who had earlier been taken to New England. Coming ashore in Kailua-Kona, where Liholiho had moved the royal court, the Reverends Bingham and Thurston were granted a one-year, trial missionary period by King Liholiho. They established themselves on Hawai'i and O'ahu and from there began the transformation of Hawaii. The missionaries were men of God but also practical-minded Yankees. They brought education, enterprise, and most important a commitment to stay and build (unlike the transient seafarers). By 1824, the new faith had such a foothold that Chieftess Keopuolani climbed to the firepit atop Kilauea and defied Pele. This was even more striking than the previous breaking of the food *kapu* because the strength of Pele could actually be seen. Keopuolani ate forbidden '*ohelo* berries and cried out, "Jehovah is my God." Over the next decades the governing of Hawaii slipped away from the Big Island and moved to the new port cities of Lahaina on Maui and, later, Honolulu.

Rapid Conversions

The year 1824 also marked the death of Keopuolani, who was given a Christian burial. She had set the standard by accepting Christianity, and several of the ali'i had followed the queen's lead. Liholiho had sailed off to England, where he and his wife contracted measles and died. Their bodies were returned by the British in 1825, on the HMS *Blonde* captained by Lord Byron, cousin of *the* Lord Byron. During these years, Ka'ahumanu allied herself with Reverend Richards, pastor of the first mission in the islands, and together they wrote Hawaii's first code of laws based on the Ten Commandments. Foremost was the condemnation of murder, theft, brawling, and the desecration of the Sabbath by work or play. The early missionaries had the best of intentions, but like all zealots they were blinded by the single-mindedness that was also their greatest ally. They were not surgically selective in their destruction of native beliefs. *Anything* native was felt to be inferior, and they set about wiping out all traces of the old ways. In their rampage they reduced the Hawaiian culture to ashes, plucking self-will and determination from the hearts of a once-proud people. More so than the whalers, they terminated the Hawaiian way of life.

The Early Seamen

A good portion of the common seamen of the early 19th century came from the dregs of the Western world. Many a whoremongering drunkard had awoken from a stupor and found himself on the pitching deck of a ship, discovering to his dismay that he had been "pressed into naval service." These sailors were mostly a filthy, uneducated, lawless rabble. Their present situation was dim, their future hopeless, and they would live to be 30 if they were lucky and didn't die from scurvy or a thousand other miserable fates. They snatched brief pleasure in every port and jumped ship at any opportunity, especially in an easy berth like Lahaina. They displayed the worst elements of Western culture, which the Hawaiians naively mimicked. In exchange for *aloha* they gave drunkenness, sloth, and insidious death by disease. By the 1850s, the population of native Hawaiians tumbled from the estimated 300,000 reported by Captain Cook in 1778 to barely 60,000. Common conditions such as colds, flu, venereal disease, and sometimes smallpox and cholera decimated the Hawaiians, who had no natural immunities to these foreign ailments. By the time the missionaries arrived, *hapa haole* children were common in Lahaina streets.

The earliest merchant ships to the islands were

owned or skippered by lawless opportunists who had come seeking sandalwood after first filling their holds with furs from the Pacific Northwest. Aided by *ali'i* hungry for manufactured goods and Western finery, they raped Hawaiian forests of this fragrant wood so coveted in China. Next, droves of sailors came in search of whales. The whalers, who were decent men at home, left their morals back in the Atlantic and lived by the slogan "no conscience east of the Cape." The delights of Hawaii were just too tempting for most.

Two Worlds Tragically Collide

The 1820s were a time of confusion and soul-searching for the Hawaiians. When Kamehameha II died, the kingdom passed to Kauikeaouli (Kamehameha III), who made his lifelong residence in Lahaina. The young king was only nine years old when the title passed to him, but his power was secure because Ka'ahumanu was still a vibrant *kuhina nui*. The young prince, more so than any other, was raised in the cultural confusion of the times. His childhood was spent during the cusp of the change from old ways to new, and he was often pulled in two directions by vastly differing beliefs. Because he was royal born, according to age-old Hawaiian tradition he must mate and produce an heir with the highest ranking *ali'i* in the kingdom. This mate happened to be his younger sister, the Princess Nahi'ena'ena. To the old Hawaiian advisors, this arrangement was perfectly acceptable and encouraged. To the increasingly influential missionaries, incest was an unimaginable abomination in the eyes of God. The problem was compounded by the fact that Kamehameha III and Nahi'ena'ena were drawn to each other and were deeply in love. The young king could not stand the mental pressure imposed by conflicting worlds. He became a teenage alcoholic too royal to be restrained by anyone in the kingdom, and his bouts of drunkenness and womanizing were both legendary and scandalous.

Meanwhile, Nahi'ena'ena was even more pressured because she was a favorite of the missionaries, baptized into the church at age 12. She too vacillated between the old and the new. At times a pious Christian, at others she drank all night and took numerous lovers. As the prince

and princess grew into their late teens, they became even more attached to each other and hardly made an attempt to keep their relationship from the missionaries. Whenever possible, they lived together in a grass house built for the princess by her father.

In 1832, the great Ka'ahumanu died, leaving the king on his own. In 1833, at the age of 18, Kamehameha III announced that the "regency" was over and that all the lands in Hawaii were his, personally, and that he alone was the ultimate law. Almost immediately, however, he decreed that his half sister Kina'u would be "premier," signifying that he would leave the actual running of the kingdom in her hands. Kamehameha III fell into total drunken confusion, until one night he attempted suicide. After this episode he seemed to straighten up a bit and mostly kept a low profile. In 1836, Princess Nahi'ena'ena was convinced by the missionaries to take a husband. She married Leleiohoku, a chief from the Big Island, but continued to sleep with her brother. It is uncertain who fathered the child, but Nahi'ena'ena gave birth to a baby boy in September 1836. The young prince survived for only a few hours, and Nahi'ena'ena never recovered from her convalescence. She died in December 1836 and was laid to rest in the mausoleum next to her mother, Keopuolani, on the royal island in Mokuhina Pond in Lahaina. After the death of his sister, Kamehameha III became a sober and righteous ruler. Often seen paying his respects at the royal mausoleum, he ruled longer than any other king until his death in 1854.

The Missionaries Prevail

In 1823, the first mission was established in Lahaina, Maui, under the pastorate of Reverend Richards and his wife. Within a few years, many of the notable *ali'i* had been, at least in appearance, converted to Christianity. By 1828 the cornerstones for Waine'e Church, the first stone church on the island, were laid just behind the palace of Kamehameha III. The struggle between missionaries and whalers centered around public drunkenness and the servicing of sailors by local native girls. The normally god-fearing whalers had signed on for perilous duty that lasted up to three years, and when they anchored in Lahaina they demanded their pleasure. The missionaries were instrumental in placing a curfew on sailors and prohibiting native women from boarding ships, which had become customary. These measures certainly did not stop the liaisons between sailor and *wahine,* but it did impose a modicum of social sanction and tolled the end of the wide-open days. The sailors were outraged; in 1825 the crew from the *Daniel* attacked the home of the meddler, Reverend Richards. A year later a similar incident occurred. In 1827, confined and lonely sailors from the whaler *John Palmer* fired their cannon at Reverend Richards' newly built home.

Slowly the tensions eased, and by 1836 many sailors were regulars at the Seamen's Chapel, adjacent to the Baldwin Home. Unfortunately, even the missionaries couldn't stop the pesky mosquito from entering the islands through the port of Lahaina. The mosquitoes arrived from Mexico in 1826 aboard the merchant ship *Wellington.* They were inadvertently carried as larvae in the water barrels and democratically pestered everyone in the islands from that day forward regardless of race, religion, or creed.

Lahaina Becomes a Cultural Center

By 1831, Lahaina was firmly established as a seat of Western influence in Hawaii. That year marked the founding of Lahainaluna School, the first *real* American school west of the Rockies. Virtually a copy of a New England normal school, it attracted the best students, both native and white, from throughout the kingdom. By 1834, Lahainaluna had an operating printing press publishing the islands' first newspaper, *The Torch of Hawaii,* starting a lucrative printing industry centered in Lahaina that dominated not only the islands but also California for many years.

An early native student was David Malo. He was brilliant and well educated, but more importantly, he remembered the "old ways." One of the first Hawaiians to realize his native land was being swallowed up by the newcomers, Malo compiled the first history of precontact Hawaii and the resulting book, *Mo'olelo Hawaii* (Hawaiian Antiquities), became a reference masterpiece

which has yet to be eclipsed. David Malo insisted that the printing be done in Hawaiian, not English. Malo is buried in the mountains above Lahainaluna where, by his own request, he is "high above the tide of foreign invasion." By the 1840s, Lahaina was firmly established as the "Whaling Capital of the World"; the peak year 1846 saw 395 whaling ships anchored here. A census in 1846 reported that Lahaina was home to 3,445 natives, 112 permanent *haole,* 600 sailors, and over 500 dogs. The populace was housed in 882 grass houses, 155 adobe houses, and 59 relatively permanent stone and wooden-framed structures. Lahaina would probably have remained the islands' capital, had Kamehameha III not moved the royal capital to the burgeoning port of Honolulu on the island of O'ahu.

Foreign Influence

By the 1840s, Honolulu was becoming the center of commerce in the islands; when Kamehameha III moved the royal court there from Lahaina, the ascendant fate of the new capital was guaranteed. In 1843, Lord Paulet, commander of the warship *Carysfort,* forced Kamehameha III to sign a treaty ceding Hawaii to the British. London, however, repudiated this act, and Hawaii's independence was restored within a few months when Queen Victoria sent Admiral Thomas as her personal agent of good intentions. The king memorialized the turn of events by a speech in which he uttered the phrase, *"Ua mau ke e'a o ka 'aina i ka pono,"* ("The life of the land is preserved in righteousness"), now Hawaii's motto. The French used similar bullying tactics to force an unfavorable treaty on the Hawaiians in 1839; as part of these heavy-handed negotiations they exacted a payment of $20,000 and the right of Catholics to enjoy religious freedom in the islands. In 1842 the United States recognized and guaranteed Hawaii's independence without a formal treaty, and by 1860 more than 80 percent of the islands' trade was with the United States.

The Great Mahele

In 1840, Kamehameha III ended his autocratic rule and instituted a constitutional monarchy.

This brought about the Hawaiian Bill of Rights, but the most far-reaching change was the transition to private ownership of land. Formerly, all land belonged to the ruling chief, who gave wedge-shaped parcels called *ahupua'a* to lesser chiefs to be worked for him. The commoners did all the real labor, and their produce was heavily taxed by the *ali'i*. The fortunes of war, the death of a chief, or the mere whim of a superior could force a commoner off his land. The Hawaiians, however, could not think in terms of owning land. No one could *possess* land, one could only *use* land, and its ownership was a strange foreign concept. As a result, naive Hawaiians gave up their lands for a song to unscrupulous traders, which remains an integral, unrectified problem to this day. In 1847 Kamehameha III and his advisors separated the lands of Hawaii into three groupings: crown land (belonging to the king), government land (belonging to the chiefs), and the people's land (the largest parcels). In 1848, 245 *ali'i* entered their land claims in the *Mahele Book,* assuring them ownership. In 1850 the commoners were given title in fee simple to the lands they cultivated and lived on as tenants, not including house lots in towns. Commoners without land could buy small *kuleana* (farms) from the government at $.50 per acre. In 1850, foreigners were also allowed to purchase land in fee simple, and the ownership of Hawaii from that day forward slipped steadily from the hands of its indigenous people.

KING SUGAR

It's hard to say just where the sugar industry began in Hawaii. The Koloa Sugar Plantation on the southern coast of Kaua'i successfully refined sugar in 1835. Others tried, and one success was at Hana, Maui, in 1849. A whaler named George Wilfong hauled four blubber pots ashore and set them up on a rocky hill in the middle of 60 acres on which he had planted sugar. A team of oxen turned "crushing rollers," and the cane juice flowed down an open trough into the pots, under which an attending native kept a roaring fire burning. Wilfong's methods of refining were crude, but the resultant high-quality sugar turned a neat profit in Lahaina. The main problem was labor. The Hawaiians, who made excellent whalers, were basically indentured workers. They became extremely disillusioned with their contracts, which could last up to 10 years. Most of their wages were eaten up by manufactured commodities sold at the company store, and it didn't take long for them to realize that they were little more than slaves. At every opportunity they either left the area or just refused to work.

Imported Labor

The **Masters and Servants Act of 1850,** which allowed importation of laborers under the contract system, ostensibly guaranteed an endless supply of cheap labor for the plantations. Chinese laborers were imported but were too enterprising to remain in the fields for a meager $3 per month. They left as soon as opportunity permitted and went into business as small merchants and retailers. In the meantime, Wilfong had sold out, releasing most of the Hawaiians previously held under contract, and his plantation fell into disuse. In 1860, two Danish brothers, August and Oscar Unna, bought land at Hana to raise sugar. They solved the labor problem by importing Japanese laborers, who were extremely hardworking and easily managed. The workday lasted 10 hours, six days a week, for a salary of $20 per month, with housing and medical care thrown in. Plantation life was structured with stringent rules governing even bedtimes and lights out. A worker could be fined for being late or for smoking on the job. Even the Japanese couldn't function under these circumstances, and improvements in benefits and housing were slowly gained.

Sugar Grows

The demand for "Sandwich Island Sugar" grew as California was populated during the gold rush and increased dramatically when the American Civil War required a constant supply. The only sugar plantations on the Mainland were small plots confined to the Confederate states, whose products could hardly be bought by the Union and whose fields were destroyed later in the war. By the 1870s it was clear to the planters, still mainly New Englanders, that the United States was their market; they tried often to gain closer ties and favorable tariffs. The Americans also planted rumors that the British were interested in annexing Hawaii; this put pressure on the U.S. Congress to pass the long-desired **Reciprocity Act,** which would exempt sugar from import duty. It finally passed in 1875, in exchange for U.S. long-term rights to use the strategic naval port of Pearl Harbor, among other concessions. These agreements gave increased political power to a small group of American planters, whose outlooks were similar to the post–Civil War South, where a few powerful whites were the virtual masters of a multitude of dark-skinned laborers. Sugar was now big business, and the Hana District alone exported almost 3,000 tons per year. All of Hawaii would have to reckon with the sugar barons.

Queen Liliʻuokalani

COURTESY OF HAWAII STATE ARCHIVE

Changing Society

The sugar plantation system changed life in Hawaii physically, spiritually, politically, and economically. Now boatloads of workers came not only from Japan but also from Portugal, Germany, and even Russia. The white-skinned workers were most often the field foremen *(luna)*. With the immigrants came new religions, new animals and plants, unique cuisines, and a plantation language known as pidgin, or *daʻkine*. Many Asians, and to a lesser extent the other groups, including the white plantation owners, intermarried with Hawaiians. A new class of people properly termed "cosmopolitan" but more familiarly and aptly known as "locals" was emerging. These were the people of multiple-race backgrounds who couldn't exactly say *what* they were, but it was clear to all just *who* they were. The plantation owners became the new chiefs of Hawaii who would carve up the land and dispense favors. The Hawaiian monarchy was soon eliminated.

A KINGDOM PASSES
The Beginning of the End

Like the Hawaiian people themselves, the Kamehameha dynasty in the mid-1800s was dying from within. King Kamehameha IV (Alexander

Liholiho) ruled 1854–1863; his only child died in 1862. He was succeeded by his older brother Kamehameha V (Lot Kamehameha), who ruled until 1872. With his passing the Kamehameha line ended. William Lunalilo, elected king in 1873 by popular vote, was of royal, but not Kamehameha, lineage. He died after only a year in office, and being a bachelor left no heirs. He was succeeded by David Kalakaua, known far and wide as the "Merrie Monarch," who made a world tour and was well received wherever he went. He built ʻIolani Palace in Honolulu and was personally in favor of closer ties with the United States, helping push through the Reciprocity Act. Kalakaua died in 1891 and was replaced by his sister, Lydia Liliʻuokalani, last of the Hawaiian monarchs.

The Revolution

When Liliʻuokalani took office in 1891, the native population was at a low of 40,000, and she felt that the United States had too much influence over her homeland. She was known to personally favor the English over the Americans. She attempted to replace the liberal constitution of 1887 (adopted by her pro-American brother) with an autocratic mandate in which she would have had much more political and economic control of the islands. When the McKinley Tariff of 1890 brought a decline in sugar profits, she made no attempt to improve the situation. Thus the planters saw her as a political obstacle to their economic growth; most of Hawaii's American planters and merchants were in favor of a rebellion. She would have to go! A central spokesperson and firebrand was Lorrin Thurston, a Honolulu publisher who, with a central core of about 30 men, challenged the Hawaiian monarchy. Although Lili'uokalani rallied some support and had a small military potential in her personal guard, the coup was ridiculously easy—it took only one casualty. Captain John Good shot a Hawaiian policeman in the arm and that did it. Naturally, the conspirators could not have succeeded without some solid assurances from a secret contingent in the U.S. Congress as well as outgoing President Benjamin Harrison, who favored Hawaii's annexation. Marines from the *Boston* went ashore to "protect American lives," and on January 17, 1893, the Hawaiian monarchy came to an end.

The provisional government was headed by Sanford B. Dole, who became president of the Hawaiian Republic. Lili'uokalani surrendered not to the conspirators, but to U.S. Ambassador John Stevens. She believed that the U.S. government, which had assured her of Hawaiian independence, would be outraged by the overthrow and would come to her aid. Incoming President Grover Cleveland *was* outraged, and Hawaii wasn't immediately annexed as expected. When queried about what she would do with the conspirators if she were reinstated, Lili'uokalani said that they would be hung as traitors. The racist press of the times, which portrayed the Hawaiians as half-civilized, bloodthirsty heathens, publicized this widely. Because the conspirators were the leading citizens of the land, the queen's words proved untimely. In January 1895, a small, ill-fated counterrevolution headed by Lili'uokalani

failed, and she was placed under house arrest in 'Iolani Palace. Officials of the Republic insisted that she use her married name (Mrs. John Dominis) to sign the documents forcing her to abdicate her throne. She was also forced to swear allegiance to the new Republic. Lili'uokalani went on to write *Hawaii's Story* and the lyric ballad "Aloha O'e." She never forgave the conspirators and remained queen to the Hawaiians until her death in 1917.

Annexation

An overwhelming majority of Hawaiians opposed annexation and desired to restore the monarchy, but they were prevented from voting by the new Republic because they couldn't meet the imposed property and income qualifications—a transparent ruse by the planters to control the majority. Most *haole* were racist and believed that the common people could not be entrusted with the vote because they were childish and incapable of ruling themselves. The fact that the Hawaiians had existed quite well for 1,000 years before whites even reached Hawaii was never considered. The Philippine theater of the Spanish-American War also prompted annexation. One of the strongest proponents was Alfred Mahon, a brilliant naval strategist who, with support from Theodore Roosevelt, argued that the U.S. military must have Hawaii in order to be a viable force in the Pacific. In addition, Japan, which had been victorious in its recent war with China, protested the American intention to annex, and in so doing prompted even moderates to support annexation in fear that the Japanese coveted the prize. On July 7, 1898, President McKinley signed the annexation agreement, and this tropical fruit was finally put into America's basket.

MODERN TIMES

Hawaii entered the 20th century totally transformed from what it had been. The old Hawaiian language, religion, culture, and leadership were all gone. Western dress, values, education, and recreation were the norm. Native Hawaiians were now unseen citizens who lived in dwindling numbers in remote areas. The plantations, new centers of social order, had a strong Asian flavor; more than 75 percent of the workforce was Asian. There was a small white middle class, an all-powerful white elite, and a single political party ruled by that elite. Education, however, was always highly prized, and by the late 1800s all racial groups were encouraged to attend school. By 1900, almost 90 percent of Hawaiians were literate (far above the national norm), and schooling was mandatory for all children ages 6–15. Intermarriage was accepted, and there was a mixing of the races like nowhere else on earth. The military became increasingly important to Hawaii. It brought in money and jobs, dominating the islands' economy. The Japanese attack on Pearl Harbor, which began U.S. involvement in World War II, bound Hawaii to America forever. Once the islands had been baptized by blood, the average Mainlander felt that Hawaii was American soil. A movement among Hawaiians to become part of the United States began to grow. They wanted a real voice in Washington, not merely a voteless delegate as provided under their territory status. Hawaii became the 50th state in 1959, and the jumbo-jet revolution of the 1960s made it easily accessible to growing numbers of tourists from all over the world.

Military History

A few military strategists realized the importance of Hawaii early in the 19th century, but most didn't recognize the advantages until the Spanish-American War. It was clearly an unsinkable ship in the middle of the Pacific from which the United States could launch military operations. Troops were stationed at Camp McKinley, at the foot of Diamond Head, the main military compound until it became obsolete in 1907. Pearl Harbor was first surveyed in 1872 by General Schofield. Later a military base named in his honor, Schofield Barracks, was a main military post in central O'ahu. It first housed the U.S. 5th Cavalry in 1909 and was heavily bombed by the Japanese at the outset of World War II. Pearl Harbor,

first dredged in 1908, was officially opened on December 11, 1911. The first warship to enter was the cruiser *California*. Ever since, the military has been a mainstay of island economy. Unfortunately, there has been long-standing bad blood between locals and military personnel. Each group has tended to look down on the other.

Pearl Harbor Attack

On the morning of December 7, 1941, the Japanese carrier *Akagi*, flying the battle flag of the famed Admiral Togo of the Russo-Japanese War, received and broadcast over its public address system island music from Honolulu station KGMB. Deep in the bowels of the ship a radio man listened for a much different message, coming thousands of miles from the Japanese mainland. When the ironically poetic message "east wind rain" was received, the attack was launched. At the end of the day, 2,325 U.S. servicemen and 57 civilians were dead; 188 planes were destroyed; 18 major warships were sunk or heavily damaged; and the United States was in the war. Japanese casualties were ludicrously light. The ignited conflict would rage for four years until Japan, through the atomic bombing of Nagasaki and Hiroshima, was vaporized into total submission. At the end of hostilities, Hawaii would never again be considered separate from America.

Statehood

Several economic and political reasons explain why the ruling elite of Hawaii desired statehood, but simply, most people who lived there, especially after World War II, considered themselves Americans. The first serious mention of making the Sandwich Islands a state was in the 1850s under President Franklin Pierce, but the idea wasn't taken seriously until the monarchy was overthrown in the 1890s. For the next 50 years statehood proposals were made repeatedly to Congress, but there was stiff opposition, especially from the southern states. With Hawaii a territory, an import quota system beneficial to Mainland producers could be enacted on produce, especially sugar.

Also, there was prejudice against creating a state in a place where the majority of the populace was not white.

During World War II, Hawaii was placed under martial law, but no serious attempt to intern the Japanese population was made, as in California. There were simply too many Japanese, who went on to gain the respect of the American people through their outstanding fighting record during the war. Hawaii's own 100th Battalion became the famous 442nd Regimental Combat Team, which gained notoriety by saving the Lost Texas Battalion during the Battle of the Bulge and went on to be *the* most decorated battalion in all of World War II. When these GIs returned home, *no one* was going to tell them that they were not loyal Americans. Many of these Americans of Japanese Ancestry (AJAs) took advantage of the GI Bill and received higher education. They were from the common people, not the elite, and they rallied grassroots support for statehood. When the vote finally occurred, approximately 132,900 voted in favor of statehood with only 7,800 votes against. Congress passed the Hawaii State Bill on March 12, 1959, and on August 21, 1959, President Eisenhower announced that Hawaii was officially the 50th state.

Government

The only difference between the government of the state of Hawaii and those of other states is that it's "streamlined," and in theory more efficient. There are only two levels of government: the state and the county. With no town or city governments to deal with, considerable bureaucracy is eliminated. Hawaii, in anticipation of becoming a state, drafted a constitution in 1950 and was ready to go when statehood came. Politics and government are taken seriously in the Aloha State, which at one time consistently turned in the best national voting record per capita. For example, in the first state elections, 173,000 of 180,000 registered voters voted—a whopping 94 percent of the electorate. These days, Hawaiians give greater importance to and show greater turnout for state elections. Because of Hawaii's location in the far west, when presidential elections are held, the results are often known before many in the state have time to cast their ballots. In the election to ratify statehood, hardly a ballot went uncast, with 95 percent of the voters opting for statehood. The bill carried every island of Hawaii except Ni'ihau, where, coincidentally, most of the people (total population 250 or so) are of relatively pure Hawaiian blood. The U.S. Congress passed the Hawaii State Bill on March 12, 1959, and on August 21, 1959, President Eisenhower pro-

United States and Hawaii state flags

claimed Hawaii the 50th state. Honolulu became the state capital.

Breaking a 40-year Democratic hold on power in the state and becoming the first female to hold the position, former Maui mayor and Republican Linda Lingle was elected as governor in 2002.

Maui County

Maui County encompasses Maui island, as well as Lana'i, Moloka'i, and the uninhabited island of Kaho'olawe. Of the 25 State Senatorial Districts, Maui County is represented by three, all Democrats. The county also has six House districts of the 51 total, represented by three Democrats and three Republicans. Not surprisingly, the districts with the Republican representatives are the heavily touristed areas of West Maui, South Maui, and Upcountry. West Maui, with Ka'anapali and Lahaina, is one of the most developed and financially sound areas in all of Hawaii. It's a favorite area with tourists and is one of the darlings of developers. South Maui, with the tourist areas of Kihei, Wailea, and Makena, has a similar orientation. With both the Senate and House districts, the islands of Lana'i, Moloka'i, and Kaho'olawe are pared with the sparsely populated but heavily local area of East Maui. Lana'i has a tiny pop-

ulation, a growing tourist industry, and, in comparison, a minuscule economy. Moloka'i has the largest per capita concentration of native Hawaiians, a "busted economy" with a tremendous share of its population on welfare, and a grassroots movement determined to preserve the historical integrity of the island and the dignity of the people.

Following four years of Democratic control of the mayor's office, Republicans once again control the mayor seat. In 2002, Alan Arakawa won over then incumbent James "Kimo" Apana, who, at age 36, became the youngest mayor in Maui's history in 1998. Although Maui, like the rest of the state, is overwhelmingly Democratic, the Republicans had had their candidate in the mayor's office for most of the 30 years prior to 1998. The mayor is assisted by an elected county council consisting of one member from each council district around the county.

Economy

Hawaii's mid-Pacific location makes it perfect for two prime sources of income: tourism and the military. Tourists come in anticipation of endless golden days on soothing beaches, while the military is provided with the strategic position of an unsinkable battleship. Each economic sector nets Hawaii about $4 billion annually, money that should keep flowing smoothly and even increase in the foreseeable future. These revenues remain mostly aloof from the normal ups and downs of the Mainland U.S. economy. Also contributing to the state revenue are, in descending proportions, manufacturing, construction, and agriculture (mainly sugar and pineapples). As long as the sun shines and the balance of global power requires a military presence, the economic stability of Hawaii is guaranteed.

Tourism

Maui's economy is a mirror image of the state's economy: It's based on tourism, agriculture, and government expenditures. The primary growth is in tourism, with Maui being the second most

ECOTOURISM IN HAWAII

Ecotourism is economically, culturally, socially, and environmentally sensitive and sustainable tourism that helps promote local communities and organizations and works in harmony with nature. Although small potatoes yet in the Hawaiian (and worldwide) tourism economy, ecotourism and its goals are growing in importance and will become a major factor in the economic vitality of tourism in the state. For more information on ecotourism in Hawaii, contact the Hawaii Ecotourism Association, P.O. Box 61435, Honolulu, HI 96822, 808/956-2866, hea@aloha.net, www.planet-hawaii.com/hea. The following organization can also provide related information and contacts: The International Ecotourism Society, P.O. Box 668, Burlington, VT 05420, 802/651-9818, www.ecotourism.org.

frequently chosen Hawaiian destination after O'ahu. On average, Maui attracts about two million tourists per year, and on any given day about 40,000 visitors are enjoying the island. Maui's most popular attractions, in terms of visitor numbers, are Haleakala National Park, Lahaina Town, 'Iao Valley, and Hana district. More than 17,000 rooms are available on Maui in all categories, and they're filled 75 percent of the time. Most rooms are in the Kihei to Wailea and Ka'anapali to Kapalua strips. With tourists finding Maui more and more desirable every year, and with agriculture firmly entrenched, Maui's economic future is bright.

Agriculture

Maui generates agricultural revenue through cattle, sugar, pineapples, and flowers, along with a substantial subculture economy in *pakalolo*. **Cattle grazing** occurs on the western and southern slopes of Haleakala, where 35,000 acres are owned by the Haleakala Ranch, and more than 23,000 acres by the Ulupalakua Ranch. The upper slopes of Haleakala around Kula are a gardener's dream. Delicious onions, potatoes, and all sorts of garden vegetables are grown, but they are secondary to large plots of gorgeous flowers, mainly carnations and the amazing protea.

Sugar, actually in the grass family, is still very important to Maui's economy, but without federal subsidies it wouldn't be a viable cash crop. The largest acreage is in the central isthmus area, which is virtually all owned by the Alexander and Baldwin Company. Maui's one remaining operational mill is located at Pu'unene; the mill in Pa'ia is not being used but has not been dismantled. The Lahaina mill closed in 1996, and the cane fields on the Ka'anapali side have all been abandoned, the land given to pineapple production, developed into residential subdivisions, or simply left fallow. Reflecting a gradual shift, in 1997 the value of the sugarcane crop fell slightly below the value of the pineapple crop on Maui. In 2000, there were still about 37,000 acres of sugarcane fields in cultivation, producing some 200,000 tons of raw sugar. Those lodging in Ma'alaea and north Kihei will become vividly aware of the cane fields when

they're burned off just before harvesting, putting tons of black smoke and ash into the air, otherwise known as black snow. Making these unsightly burnings even worse is the fact that the plastic pipe used in the drip irrigation of the fields is left in place. Not cost-efficient to recover, it is burned along with the cane, adding its noxious fumes to the air. Luckily, the wind blows strong and constantly across the isthmus of Maui, so the smoke doesn't hang around long, but the ash and smell stay longer.

Maui Land and Pineapple Company grows **pineapples** in central east Maui between Pa'ia and Makawao and on substantial acreage in Kapalua in the far northwest. Some of the pineapples are shipped throughout the state and to the Mainland as whole fruits, while much is canned. Maui's first cannery (1914–20) was located in Honokohau, north of Kapalua. From 1920–62, canning was done at the cannery in Lahaina. Today, Maui's only cannery is located in Kahului, behind the Ka'ahumanu Shopping Center. With slightly fewer acres in production than sugarcane, pineapple now garners a larger value in total sales.

Renegade entrepreneurs grow patches of *pakalolo* wherever they can find a spot that has the right vibes and is away from the prying eyes of authorities. Deep in the West Maui Mountains and along the Hana coast are favorite areas.

Military

The small military presence on Maui amounts to a tiny Army installation near Kahului and the U.S. Coast Guard facility at Ma'alaea.

Land Ownership

Maui County is about 750,000 acres in size, and of that 465,000 belongs to Maui, 165,000 to Moloka'i, 90,000 to Lana'i, and 28,800 to the uninhabited island of Kaho'olawe. Almost 30,000 acres is owned by the federal government— Haleakala National Park. The state controls about four times that acreage in its various forest and protected land holdings. Large chunks of Hawaiian Home Lands are located on the south slope of Haleakala near Kaupo, above Kihei on the western slope of the mountain, and three separate sizable sections on Moloka'i between Kaunakakai

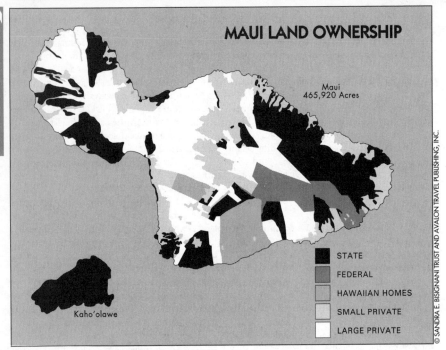

MAUI LAND OWNERSHIP

Maui
465,920 Acres

Kaho'olawe

STATE
FEDERAL
HAWAIIAN HOMES
SMALL PRIVATE
LARGE PRIVATE

© SANDRA E. BISIGNANI TRUST AND AVALON TRAVEL PUBLISHING, INC.

and Mo'omomi Beach. Land held by large landowners is greater than that held by small landowners. On Maui these players are Alexander and Baldwin, C. Brewer, Amfac, Maui Land and Pineapple Company, Haleakala Ranch, and the Ulupalakua Ranch. The two largest landowners on Moloka'i are the Moloka'i Ranch, which owns about one-third of the island, and Pu'u O Hoku Ranch. Lana'i is owned 98 percent by Castle and Cooke.

The People

Nowhere else on earth can you find such a kaleidoscopic mixture of people as in Hawaii. Every major race is accounted for, and more than 50 ethnic groups are represented throughout the islands, making Hawaii the most racially integrated state in the country. Its population of 1.2 million includes 90,000 permanently stationed military personnel and their dependents. Until the year 2000, when California's white population fell below 50 percent, Hawaii was the only state where whites are not the majority. About 56 percent of Hawaiian residents were born there, 24 percent were born on the Mainland United States, and 20 percent are foreign-born.

The population of Hawaii has grown steadily in recent times, but it fluctuated wildly in times past. Most European sources gave estimates of between 300,000 and 400,000 for the population of the Hawaiian islands before the arrival of Captain Cook. Some now estimate that number as low as 200,000 or as high as 800,000. In any case, following the arrival of Europeans, the native Hawaiian population declined steadily for a century. In 1876 it ebbed to its lowest, with only 55,000 permanent residents in the islands. This was the era of large sugar plantations; their constant demand for labor was the primary cause of the importation of various peoples from around the world and led to Hawaii's racial mix. World War II saw Hawaii's population swell from 400,000 just before the war to 900,000 during the war. Naturally, 500,000 were military personnel who left at war's end, but many returned to settle after getting a taste of island living.

Maui County Population Figures

With 128,000, Maui has the third-largest island population in Hawaii, about 10.5 percent of the state's total; about 7,200 people live on Moloka'i, and just over 3,200 live on Lana'i. Maui's population density is 176 people per square mile, with Moloka'i and Lana'i at 27 and 23 per square mile, respectively. The Kahului/Wailuku area has the island's greatest density of population, with about 41,000 people. The Upcountry population is just over 22,500, some 18,000 live along the west coast, 20,000 make South Maui their home, while some 10,000 live along the Hana Highway, less than 2,000 of which live in Hana itself. For Maui County, 78 percent are urban while 22 percent live rurally. The ethnic breakdown of Maui's 128,000 people is as follows: 34 percent Caucasian, 31 percent Asian, 22 percent Mixed, 11 percent Hawaiian, and 2 percent Other.

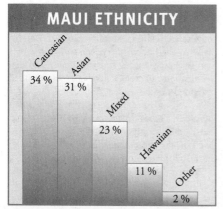

MAUI ETHNICITY

Caucasian 34 %
Asian 31 %
Mixed 23 %
Hawaiian 11 %
Other 2 %

THE HAWAIIANS

The study of the native Hawaiians is ultimately a study in tragedy because it nearly ends in their demise as a viable people. When Captain Cook first sighted Hawaii in 1778, there were an estimated 300,000 natives living in relative harmony with their ecological surroundings; within 100 years a scant 50,000 demoralized and dejected Hawaiians existed almost as wards of the state. Today, although more than 240,000 people claim varying degrees of Hawaiian blood, experts say that fewer than 1,000 are pure Hawaiian, and this is stretching it.

It's easy to see why people of Hawaiian lineage can be bitter over what they have lost, being strangers in their own land now, much like Native Americans. The overwhelming majority of Hawaiians are of mixed heritage, and the wisest take the best from all worlds. From the Hawaiian side comes simplicity, love of the land, and acceptance of people. It is the Hawaiian legacy of *aloha* that remains immortal and adds that special elusive quality that *is* Hawaii.

Polynesian Roots

The Polynesians' original stock is muddled and remains an anthropological mystery, but it's believed that they were nomadic wanderers who migrated from both the Indian subcontinent and Southeast Asia through Indonesia, where they learned to sail and navigate on protected waterways. As they migrated they honed their sailing skills until they could take on the Pacific, and as they moved, they absorbed people from other cultures and races until they had coalesced into what we now know as Polynesians.

Abraham Fornander, still considered a major authority on the subject, wrote in his 1885 *An Account of the Polynesian Race* that he believed the Polynesians started as a white (Aryan) race that was heavily influenced by contact with the Cushite, Chaldeo-Arabian civilization. He estimated their arrival in Hawaii at A.D. 600, based on Hawaiian genealogical chants. Modern science seems to bear this date out, although it remains skeptical about his other surmises. According to others, the intrepid Polynesians who actually settled Hawaii are believed to have come from the Marquesas Islands, 1,000 miles southeast of Hawaii. The Marquesans were cannibals known for their tenacity and strength, attributes that would serve them well.

The Caste System

Hawaiian society was divided into rankings by a strict caste system determined by birth, and from which there was no chance of escaping. The highest rank was the *ali'i*, the chiefs and royalty. The impeccable genealogies of the *ali'i* were traced back to the gods themselves, and the chants *(mo'o ali'i)* were memorized and sung by professionals (called *ku'auhau*), who were themselves *ali'i*. Ranking passed from both father and mother and custom dictated that the first mating of an *ali'i* be with a person of equal status.

A *kahuna* was a highly skilled person whose advice was sought before any major project was undertaken, such as building a house, hollowing a canoe log, or even offering a prayer. The *mo'o kahuna* were the priests of Ku and Lono, and they were in charge of praying and following rituals. They were very powerful *ali'i* and kept strict secrets and laws concerning their various functions.

Besides this priesthood of *kahuna*, there were other *kahuna* who were not *ali'i* but commoners. The two most important were the healers *(kahuna lapa'au)* and the black magicians *(kahuna 'ana'ana)*, who could pray a person to death. The *kahuna lapa'au* had a marvelous pharmacopoeia of herbs and spices that could cure more than 230 diseases common to the Hawaiians. The *kahuna 'ana'ana* could be hired to cast a love spell over a person or cause his or her untimely death. They seldom had to send out a reminder of payment!

The common people were called the *maka'ainana*, "the people of land"—the farmers, craftsmen, and fishermen. The land that they lived on was owned by the *ali'i*, but they were not bound to it. If the local *ali'i* was cruel or unfair, the *maka'ainana* had the right to leave and reside on another's lands. The *maka'ainana* mostly loved their local *ali'i* much like a child loves a parent, and the feeling was reciprocal. *Maka'ainana* who lived close to the *ali'i* and could be counted on as

The *ali'i* wore magnificent feathered capes that signified their rank. The noblest colors were red and yellow, provided by specialized hunters who snared and plucked just the right birds.

BOB RACE

warriors in times of trouble were called *kanaka no lua kaua*, "a man for the heat of battle." They were treated with greater favor than those who lived in the backcountry, *kanaka no hi'i kua*, whose lesser standing opened them up to discrimination and cruelty. All *maka'ainana* formed extended families called *'ohana*, and they usually lived on the same section of land, called *ahupua'a*. Those farmers who lived inland would barter their produce with the fishermen who lived on the shore, and thus all shared equally in the bounty of land and sea.

A special group called *kauwa* was a landless, untouchable caste confined to living on reservations. Their origins were obviously Polynesian, but they appeared to be descendants of castaways who had survived and become perhaps the aboriginals of Hawaii before the main migrations. It was *kapu* for anyone to go onto *kauwa* lands, and doing so meant instant death. If a human sacrifice was needed, the *kahuna* would simply summon a *kauwa*, who had no recourse but to mutely comply. To this day, to call someone *kauwa*, which now supposedly only means servant, is still considered a fight-provoking insult.

Kapu and Day-to-Day Life

Occasionally there were horrible wars, but mostly the people lived quiet and ordered lives based on a strict caste society and the *kapu* system. Famine was known but only on a regional level, and the population was kept in check by birth control, crude abortions, and the distasteful practice of infanticide, especially of baby girls. The Hawaiians were absolutely loving and nurturing parents under most circumstances and would even take in *hanai* (an adopted child or oldster), a lovely practice that lingers to this day.

A strict division of labor existed among men and women. Men were the only ones permitted to have anything to do with taro: This foodstuff was so sacred that there were more *kapu* concerning taro than concerning man himself. Men pounded poi and served it to the women. Men were also the fishermen and the builders of houses, canoes, irrigation ditches, and walls. Women tended to other gardens and shoreline fishing and were responsible for making tapa cloth. The entire family lived in the common house called the *hale noa*.

Certain things were *kapu* between the sexes. Primarily, women could not enter the *mua* (man's eating house), nor could they eat with men. Certain foods, such as pork, coconut, red fish, and bananas were forbidden to women, and it was *kapu* for a man to have intercourse before going fishing, engaging in battle, or attending a religious ceremony. Young boys lived with the women until they underwent a circumcision rite called *pule ipu*. After this ritual was performed, they were required to keep the *kapu* of men. A true Hawaiian settlement required a minimum of five huts:

the men's eating hut, women's menstruation hut, women's eating hut, communal sleeping hut, and prayer hut. Without these five separate structures, Hawaiian society could not happen because the *i'a kapu* (forbidden eating between men and women) could not be observed.

Ali'i could also declare a *kapu* and often did so. Certain lands or fishing areas were temporarily made *kapu* so that they could revitalize. Even today, it is *kapu* for anyone to remove all the *'opihi* (a type of limpet) from a rock. The great King Kamehameha I even placed a *kapu* on the body of his notoriously unfaithful child bride, Ka'ahumanu. It didn't work! The greatest *kapu* *(kapu moe)* was afforded to the highest-ranking *ali'i:* Anyone coming into their presence had to prostrate themselves. Lesser-ranking *ali'i* were afforded the *kapu noho:* Lessers had to sit or kneel in their presence. Commoners could not let their shadows fall on an *ali'i* or enter an *ali'i's* house except through a special door. Breaking a *kapu* meant immediate death.

The Causes of Decline

Less than 100 years after Captain Cook's arrival, King Kalakaua found himself with roughly 48,000 Hawaiian subjects. Wherever the king went, he would beseech his people, *"Ho'oulu lahui,"* "Increase the race," but it was already too late. It was as if nature had turned her back on these once proud people. Many of their marriages were barren; in 1874, when only 1,400 children were born, a full 75 percent died in infancy. The Hawaiians could do little as their race nearly faded from existence.

The ecological system of Hawaii has always been exceptionally fragile, and this included its people. When the first whites arrived, they found a great people who were large, strong, and virile. But when it came to fighting off the most minor diseases, the Hawaiians proved as delicate as hothouse flowers. To exacerbate the situation, the Hawaiians were totally uninhibited toward sexual intercourse between willing partners, and they engaged in it openly and with abandon. Unfortunately, the sailors who arrived were full of syphilis and gonorrhea. The Hawaiian women brought these diseases home and, given the nature of Hawaiian society at the time, the diseases spread like wildfire. By the time the missionaries came in 1820 and helped halt the unbridled fornication, they estimated the native population at only 140,000, less than half of what it had been only 40 years since initial contact! In the next 50 years measles, mumps, influenza, and tuberculosis further ravaged the people. Furthermore, Hawaiian men were excellent sailors, and it's estimated that during the whaling years at least 25 percent of all able-bodied Hawaiian men sailed away, never to return.

But the coup de grâce that really ended the Hawaiian race, as such, was that all racial newcomers to the islands were attracted to the Hawaiians and the Hawaiians were in turn attracted to them. With so many interracial marriages, the Hawaiians nearly bred themselves out of existence. By 1910, there were still twice as many full-blooded Hawaiians as mixed-bloods, but by 1940 mixed-blood Hawaiians were the fastest growing group, and full-blooded the fastest declining.

Hawaiians Today

Many of the Hawaiians who moved to the cities became more and more disenfranchised. Their folk society stressed openness and a giving nature but downplayed the individual and ownership of private property. These cultural traits made them easy targets for the users and schemers until they finally became either apathetic or angry. Most surveys reveal that although Hawaiians number only 13 percent of the population, they account for almost 50 percent of the financially destitute families and about half of all arrests and illegitimate births. Ni'ihau, a privately owned island, is home to about 160 pure-blooded Hawaiians, representing the largest concentration of them, per capita, in the islands. The Robinson family, which owns the island, restricts visitors to invited guests only.

The second largest concentration is on Moloka'i, where 2,700 Hawaiians, living mostly on 40-acre *kuleana* of Hawaiian Home Lands, make up 40 percent of that island's population. Most mixed-blood Hawaiians, 240,000 or so, live on O'ahu, where they are particularly strong in the hotel and entertainment fields. People of

Hawaiian extraction are still a delight to meet, and anyone so lucky as to be befriended by one long regards this friendship as the highlight of his or her travels. The Hawaiians have always given their *aloha* freely to all the people of the world, and we must acknowledge this precious gift.

THE CHINESE

Next to Yankees from New England, the Chinese are the oldest migrant group in Hawaii, and their influence has far outshone their meager numbers. They brought to Hawaii, along with their individuality, Confucianism, Taoism, and Buddhism, although many have long since become Christians. The Chinese population at 56,000 makes up only 5 percent of the state's total, and most reside on O'ahu. As an ethnic group they account for the least amount of crime, the highest per capita income, and a disproportionate number of professionals.

The First Chinese

No one knows his name, but an unknown Chinese immigrant is credited with being the first person in Hawaii to refine sugar. This Asian wanderer tried his hand at crude refining on Lana'i in 1802. Fifty years later the sugar plantations desperately needed workers, and the first Chinese brought to Hawaii under the newly passed Masters and Servants Act were 195 coolies from Amoy who arrived in 1852. These conscripts were contracted for three to five years and given $3 per month plus room and board. This was for 12 hours per day, six days per week, and even in 1852 these wages were the pits. The Chinese almost always left the plantations the minute their contracts expired. They went into business for themselves and promptly monopolized the restaurant and small shop trades.

The Chinese Niche

Although many people in Hawaii considered all Chinese ethnically the same, they were actually quite different. The majority came from Guangdong Province in southern China. They were two distinct ethnic groups: the Punti made up 75 percent of the immigrants, and the Hakka made up the remainder. In China, they remained separate from each other, never mixing; in Hawaii, they mixed out of necessity. For one thing, hardly any Chinese women came over at first, and the ones who followed were at a premium and gladly accepted as wives, regardless of ethnic background. The Chinese were also one of the first groups who willingly intermarried with the Hawaiians, from whom they gained a reputation for being exceptionally caring spouses.

The Chinese accepted the social order and kept a low profile. For example, during the turbulent labor movements of the 1930s and '40s in Hawaii, the Chinese community produced not one labor leader, radical intellectual, or left-wing politician. When Hawaii became a state, one of the two senators elected was Hiram Fong, a racially mixed Chinese. Since statehood, the Chinese community has carried on business as usual as they continue to rise both economically and socially.

THE JAPANESE

Most scholars believe that (inevitably) a few Japanese castaways floated to Hawaii long before Captain Cook arrived and might have introduced the iron with which the islanders seemed to be familiar before the white explorers arrived. The first official arrivals from Japan were ambassadors sent by the Japanese shogun to negotiate in Washington, D.C.; they stopped en route at Honolulu in March 1860. But it was as plantation workers that the Japanese were brought en masse to the islands. A small group arrived in 1868, and mass migration started in 1885.

In 1886, because of famine, the Japanese government allowed farmers, mainly from southern Honshu, Kyushu, and Okinawa, to emigrate. Among these were members of Japan's little-talked-about untouchable caste, called *eta* or *burakumin* in Japan and *chorinbo* in Hawaii. They gratefully seized this opportunity to better their lot, which was an impossibility in Japan. The first Japanese migrants were almost all men. Between 1897 and 1908 migration was steady, with about 70 percent of the immigrants being men. Afterward, migration slowed because of a "gentlemen's agreement," a euphemism for racism

against the "yellow peril." By 1900 there were more than 60,000 Japanese in the islands, constituting the largest ethnic group.

AJAs: Americans of Japanese Ancestry

Parents of most Japanese children born before World War II were *issei* (first generation), who considered themselves apart from other Americans and clung to the notion of "we Japanese." Their children, the *nisei* or second generation, were a different matter altogether. In one generation they had become Americans, and they put into practice the high Japanese virtues of obligation, duty, and loyalty to the homeland, but that homeland was now unquestionably America. After Pearl Harbor was bombed, the FBI kept close tabs on the Japanese community, and the menace of the "enemy within" prompted the decision to place Hawaii under martial law for the duration of the war. It has since been noted that not a single charge of espionage or sabotage was ever reported against the Japanese community in Hawaii during the war.

AJAs as GIs

Although Japanese had formed a battalion during World War I, they were insulted by being considered unacceptable as American soldiers in World War II. Some Japanese-Americans volunteered to serve in labor battalions, and because of their flawless work and loyalty, it was decided to put out a call for a few hundred volunteers to form a combat unit. More than 10,000 signed up! AJAs formed two distinguished units in World War II: the 100th Infantry Battalion and later the 442nd Regimental Combat Team. They landed in Italy at Salerno and even fought from Guadalcanal to Okinawa. They distinguished themselves by becoming *the* most decorated unit in American military history.

The AJAs Return

Many returning AJAs took advantage of the GI Bill and received college educations. The "Big Five" corporations for the first time accepted former AJA officers as executives, and the old order was changed. Many Japanese became involved with Hawaiian politics, and the first elected to Congress was Daniel Inouye, who had lost an arm fighting in World War II. Hawaii's past governor, George Ariyoshi, elected in 1974, was the country's first Japanese-American to reach such a high office. Most Japanese, even as they climb the economic ladder, tend to remain Democrats.

Today, one out of every two political offices in Hawaii is held by a Japanese-American. In one of those weird quirks of fate, the Hawaiian Japanese are now accused by other ethnic groups of engaging in unfair political practices—nepotism and reverse discrimination. Many of these accusations against AJAs are undoubtedly motivated by jealousy, but the AJAs' record in social fairness issues is not without blemish; true to their custom of family loyalty, they do stick together.

There are now 290,000 people in Hawaii of Japanese ancestry (another 100,000 of mixed Japanese blood), nearly one-quarter of the state's population. They are the least likely of any ethnic group in Hawaii to marry outside of their group—especially the men—and they enjoy a higher-than-average standard of living.

CAUCASIANS

White people have a distinction separating them from all other ethnic groups in Hawaii: They are lumped together as one. You can be anything from a Protestant Norwegian dockworker to a Greek Orthodox shipping tycoon, but if your skin is white, in Hawaii, you're a *haole*. What's more, you could have arrived at Waikiki from Missoula, Montana, in the last 24 hours, or your *kama'aina* family can go back five generations, but again, if you're white, you're a *haole*.

The word *haole* has a floating connotation that depends on the spirit in which it's used. It can mean everything from a derisive "honky" or "cracker" to nothing more than "white person." The exact Hawaiian meaning is clouded, but some say it meant "a man of no background" because white men couldn't chant a genealogical *kanaenae* telling the Hawaiians who they were. The word eventually evolved to mean "foreign white man" and today, simply "white person."

White History

Next to Hawaiians, white people have the oldest stake in Hawaii. They've been there as settlers in earnest since the missionaries of the 1820s and were established long before any other migrant group. From the 19th century until statehood, old *haole* families owned and controlled mostly everything, and although they were generally benevolent, philanthropic, and paternalistic, they were also racist. They were established *kama'aina* families, many of whom made up the boards of the "Big Five" corporations or owned huge plantations and formed an inner social circle that was closed to the outside. Many managed to find mates from among close family acquaintances.

Their paternalism, which they accepted with grave responsibility, at first extended only to the Hawaiians, who saw them as replacing their own *ali'i*. Asians were considered primarily instruments of production. These supremacist attitudes tended to drag on in Hawaii until recent times. They are today responsible for the sometimes sour relations between white and nonwhite people in the islands. Today, all individual white people are resented to a certain degree because of these past acts, even though they personally were in no way involved.

White Plantation Workers

In the 1880s the white landowners looked around and felt surrounded and outnumbered by Asians, so they tried to import white people for plantation work. None of their schemes seemed to work out. Europeans were accustomed to a much higher wage scale and better living conditions than were provided on the plantations. Although only workers and not considered the equals of the ruling elite, they still were expected to act like a special class. They were treated preferentially, which meant higher wages for the same jobs performed by Asians. Some of the imported workers included 600 Scandinavians in 1881; 1,400 Germans from 1881–85; 400 Poles from 1897–98; and 2,400 Russians from 1909–12. Many proved troublesome, like the Poles and Russians who staged strikes after only months on the job. Many quickly moved to the Mainland. A contingency of Scots, who first came as mule skinners, did become successful plantation managers and supervisors. The Germans and Scandinavians were well received and climbed the social ladder rapidly, becoming professionals and skilled workers.

The Depression years, which were not as economically bad in Hawaii as in the continental United States, brought many Mainland whites seeking opportunity, mostly from the South and the West. These new people were even more racist toward brown-skinned people and Asians than the *kama'aina haole*, and they made matters worse. They also competed more intensely for jobs. The racial tension generated during this period came to a head in 1932 with the infamous Massie Rape Case, in which five local men were accused on circumstantial evidence of raping the wife of a naval officer. The five were finally acquitted, but Thomas Massie and his mother-in-law, with the assistance of several others, killed one of the boys. Found guilty at their trial, these whites served just one hour for the murder.

The Portuguese

The last time anyone looked, Portugal was still attached to the European continent, but for some anomalous reason the Portuguese weren't considered *haole* in Hawaii for the longest time. About 12,000 arrived between 1878–87, and another 6,000 came between 1906–13. Accompanied during this period by 8,000 Spanish, they were considered one and the same. Most of the Portuguese were illiterate peasants from Madeira and the Azores, and the Spanish hailed from Andalusia. They were very well received, and because they were white but not *haole* they made a perfect buffer ethnic group. Committed to staying in Hawaii, they rose to be skilled workers—the *"luna* class" on the plantations. However, they deemphasized education and became racist toward Asians, regarding them as a threat to their job security.

By 1920, the 27,000 Portuguese made up 11 percent of the population. After that they tended to blend with the other ethnic groups and weren't counted separately. Portuguese men tended to marry within their ethnic group, but a good portion of Portuguese women married other white men and became closer to the *haole* group, whereas another large portion chose Hawaiian mates and grew further away. Although they didn't originate pidgin English (see Language section), the unique melodious quality of their native tongue did give pidgin that certain lilt it has today. Also, the ukulele was closely patterned after the *cavaquinho*, a Portuguese stringed folk instrument.

The White Population

Today Caucasians make up the largest racial group in the islands at about 25 percent of the population. With mixed white blood, that number jumps to nearly 40 percent. There are heavy white concentrations throughout O'ahu, especially in Waikiki, Kailua/Kane'ohe, and around Pearl City. In terms of pure numbers, the white population is the fastest growing in the islands because most people resettling in Hawaii are white Americans predominantly from the West Coast.

FILIPINOS AND OTHERS

The Filipinos who came to Hawaii brought high hopes of amassing personal fortunes and returning home as rich heroes, but for most it was a dream that never came true. Filipinos had been American nationals ever since the Spanish-American War of 1898, and as such weren't subject to immigration laws that curtailed the importation of other Asian workers at the turn of the 20th century. The first to arrive were 15 families in 1906, but a large number came in 1924 as strikebreakers. Most were illiterate peasants called Ilocanos from the northern Philippines, with about 10 percent Visayans from the central cities. The Visayans were not as hardworking or thrifty but were much more sophisticated. From the first, Filipinos were looked down on by all the other immigrant groups and were considered particularly uncouth by the Japanese. The value they placed on education was the least of any group, and even by 1930 only about half could speak rudimentary English, the majority remaining illiterate. They were billeted in the worst housing, performed the most menial jobs, and were the last hired and first fired.

One big difference between Filipinos and other groups was that the men brought no Filipino women to marry, so they clung to the idea of returning home. In 1930 there were 30,000 men and only 360 women. Many of these terribly lonely bachelors would feast and drink on weekends and engage in their gruesome but exciting pastime of cockfighting on Sundays. When some did manage to find wives, their mates were inevitably part Hawaiian. Today, there are still plenty of old Filipino bachelors who never managed to get home.

The Filipinos constitute 14 percent of Hawaii's population, some 170,000 individuals, with almost 75 percent living on O'ahu. Some 275,000 are of mixed Filipino blood. Many visitors to Hawaii mistake Filipinos for Hawaiians because of their dark skin, and this is a minor irritant to both groups. Some streetwise Filipinos even claim to be Hawaiians because being Hawaiian is "in" and goes over well with the tourists, especially the young women tourists. For the most part, these people are hardworking, dependable laborers who do tough work for little recognition. They remain low on the social totem pole and have not yet organized politically to stand up for their rights.

About 10 percent of Hawaii's population is a conglomerate of small ethnic groups. Of these, one of the largest and fastest growing is

Korean, with 25,000 people. About 8,000 Koreans came to Hawaii from 1903–05, when their own government halted emigration. During the same period about 6,000 Puerto Ricans arrived, and today about 30,000 consider themselves a Puerto Rican mix. Two attempts were also made in the 19th century to import other Polynesians to strengthen the dying Hawaiian race, but they were failures. In 1869 only 126 central Polynesian natives could be lured to Hawaii, and from 1878–85, 2,500 Gilbert Islanders arrived. Both groups became immediately disenchanted with Hawaii. They pined for their own islands and departed as soon as possible.

Today, however, 16,000 Samoans have settled in Hawaii, and with more on the way they are the fastest growing minority in the state. For inexplicable reasons, Samoans and native Hawaiians get along extremely poorly and have the worst racial tensions and animosity of any groups. The Samoans ostensibly should represent the archetypal Polynesians that the Hawaiians are seeking, but it doesn't work that way. Samoans are criticized by Hawaiians for their hot tempers, lingering feuds, and petty jealousies. They're clannish and often are the butt of "dumb" jokes. This racism seems especially ridiculous, but that's the way it is.

Just to add a bit more exotic spice to the stew, there are about 22,000 blacks, 3,500 Native American Indians, 4,000 Tongans, 7,000 other Pacific Islanders, and 8,000 Vietnamese living on the islands.

Language

Hawaii is part of the United States and people speak English there, but that's not the whole story. If you turn on the TV to catch the evening news, you'll hear "Walter Cronkite" English, unless of course you happen to tune in to a Japanese-language broadcast designed for tourists from that country. You can easily pick up a Chinese-language newspaper or groove to the music on a Filipino radio station, but let's not confuse the issue. All of your needs and requests at airports, car rental agencies, restaurants, hotels, or wherever you happen to travel will be completely understood, as well as answered, in English. However, when you happen to overhear islanders speaking, what they're saying will sound somewhat familiar, but you won't be able to pick up all the words, and the beat and melody of the language will be noticeably different.

Hawaii—like New England, the deep South, and the Midwest—has its own unmistakable linguistic regionalism. The many ethnic people who make up Hawaii have enriched the English spoken there with words, expressions, and subtle shades of meaning that are commonly used and understood throughout the islands. The greatest influence on English has come from the Hawaiian language, and words such as aloha, hula, lu'au, and mahalo are familiarly used and understood by most Americans.

Other migrant peoples, especially the Chinese, Japanese, and Portuguese, influenced the local dialect to such an extent that the simplified plantation lingo they spoke has become known as "pidgin." A fun and enriching part of the island experience is picking up a few words of Hawaiian and pidgin. English is the official language of the state, business, education, and perhaps even the mind, but pidgin is the language of the people, the emotions, and life, while Hawaiian remains the language of the heart and the soul.

Note: Many Hawaiian words are commonly used in English, appear in English dictionaries, and therefore would ordinarily be subject to the rules of English grammar. The Hawaiian language, however, does not pluralize nouns by adding an "s"; the singular and plural are differentiated in context. For purposes of this book, and to highlight the Hawaiian culture, the Hawaiian style of pluralization will be followed for common Hawaiian words. The following are some examples of plural Hawaiian nouns treated this way in this book: *haole* (not haoles), hula, *kahuna,* lei, lu'au, and *nene.*

PIDGIN

The dictionary definition of pidgin is "a simplified language with a rudimentary grammar used as a means of communication between people speaking different languages." Hawaiian pidgin is a little more complicated than that. It had its roots during the plantation days of the 19th century when white owners and *luna* (foremen) had to communicate with recently arrived Chinese, Japanese, and Portuguese laborers. It was designed as a simple language of the here and now, and was primarily concerned with the necessary functions of working, eating, and sleeping. It has an economical noun-verb-object structure (although not necessarily in that order).

Hawaiian words make up most of pidgin's non-English vocabulary, but it includes a good smattering of Chinese, Japanese, and Samoan as well. The distinctive rising inflection is provided by the melodious Mediterranean lilt of the Portuguese. Pidgin is not a stagnant language. It's kept alive by hip new words introduced by people who are "so radical," or especially by slang words introduced by teenagers. It's a colorful English, like "jive" or "ghettoese" spoken by American blacks, and is as regionally unique as the speech of Cajuns from Louisiana's bayous. *Maka'ainana* of all socioethnic backgrounds can at least understand pidgin. Most islanders are proud of it, but some consider it a low-class jargon. The Hawaiian House of Representatives has given pidgin an official sanction, and most people feel that it adds a real local style and should be preserved.

CAPSULE PIDGIN

The following are a few commonly used words and expressions that should give you an idea of pidgin. It really can't be written properly, merely approximated, but for now, *"Study da' kine an' bimbye it be mo' bettah, brah! OK? Lesgo."*

an' den—and then? big deal; so what's next?

auntie—respected elderly woman

bad ass—very good

bimbye—after a while; bye and bye. "Bimbye, you learn pidgin."

blalah—brother, but actually only refers to a large, heavy-set, good-natured Hawaiian man

brah—all the bros in Hawaii are brahs; brother; pal. Used to call someone's attention. One of the most common words even among people who are not acquainted. After a fill-up at a gas station, a person would say "Tanks, brah."

chicken skin—goose bumps

cockaroach—steal; rip off. If you really want to find out what *cockaroach* means, just leave your camera on your beach blanket when you take a little dip.

da' kine—a catchall word of many meanings that epitomizes the essence of pidgin. *Da' kine* is a euphemism for pidgin and is substituted whenever the speaker is at a loss for a word or just wants to generalize. It can mean you know? watchamacallit; of that type.

geev um—give it to them; give them hell; go for it. Can be used as an encouragement. If a surfer is riding a great wave, the people on the beach might yell, "Geev um, brah!"

grinds—food

hana ho—again. Especially after a concert the audience shouts "hana ho" (one more!).

hele on—let's get going

howzit?—as in "howzit, brah?" what's happening? how's it going? The most common greeting, used in place of the more formal "How do you do?"

huhu—angry! "You put the make on the wrong da' kine wahine, brah, and you in da' kine trouble if you get one big Hawaiian blalah plenty huhu."

lesgo—let's go! do it!

li'dis an' li'dat—like this or that; a catch-all grouping especially if you want to avoid details; like, ya' know?

lolo buggah—stupid or crazy guy (person). Words to a tropical island song go, "I want to find the lolo who stole my pakalolo."

mo' bettah—better, real good! great idea. An island sentiment used to be, "mo' bettah you *come* Hawaii." Now it has subtly changed to "mo' bettah you *visit* Hawaii."

ono—number one! delicious; great; groovy. "Hawaii is ono, brah!"

pakalolo—literally "crazy smoke"; marijuana; grass; reefer

pakiki head—stubborn; bull-headed

pau—a Hawaiian word meaning finished; done; over and done with. *Pau hana* means end of work or quitting time. Once used by plantation workers, now used by everyone.

seestah—sister, female

shaka—hand wave where only the thumb and baby finger stick out, meaning thank you, all right!

sleepah—slippers, flip-flops, zori

stink face—(or stink eye) basically frowning at someone; using facial expression to show displeasure. Hard looks. What you'll get if you give local people a hard time.

swell head—burned up; angry

talk story—spinning yarns; shooting the breeze; throwing the bull; a rap session. If you're lucky enough to be around to hear *kupuna* (elders) "talk story," you can hear some fantastic tales in the tradition of old Hawaii.

tanks, brah—thanks, thank you

to da max—all the way

waddascoops—what's the scoop? what's up? what's happening?

Pidgin Lives

Pidgin is first learned at school, where all students, regardless of background, are exposed to it. The pidgin spoken by young people today is "fo' real" different from that of their parents. It's no longer only plantation talk but has moved to the streets and picked up some sophistication. At one time there was an academic movement to exterminate it, but that idea died away with the same thinking that insisted on making left-handed people write with their right hands. It is strange, however, that pidgin has become the unofficial language of Hawaii's grassroots movement, when it actually began as a white owners' language that was used to supplant Hawaiian and all other languages brought to the islands.

Although hip young *haole* use pidgin all the time, it has gained the connotation of being the language of the nonwhite locals and is part of the "us against them" way of thinking. All local people, *haole* or not, do consider pidgin their own island language and don't really like it when it's used by *malihini* (newcomers). If you're in the islands long enough, you don't have to bother learning pidgin; it'll learn you. There's a book sold all over the islands called *Pidgin to da Max,* written by (you guessed it) a *haole* from Nebraska named Doug Simonson. You might not be able to understand what's being said by locals speaking pidgin (that's usually the idea), but you should be able to *feel* what's being meant.

HAWAIIAN

The Hawaiian language sways like a palm tree in a gentle wind. Its words are as melodious as a love song. Linguists say that you can learn a lot about people through their language: When you hear Hawaiian you think of gentleness and love, and it's hard to imagine the ferocious side so evident in Hawaii's past. With its many Polynesian root words easily traced to Indonesian and Malay, Hawaiian is obviously from this same stock. The Hawaiian spoken today is very different from old Hawaiian. Its greatest metamorphosis occurred when the missionaries began to write it down in the 1820s, but in the last couple of decades there has been a movement to reestab-

lish the Hawaiian language. Not only are courses in it offered at the University of Hawai'i, but there is also a successful elementary immersion school program in the state, some books are being printed in it, and more and more musicians are performing it. Many scholars have put forth translations of Hawaiian, but there are endless, volatile disagreements in the academic sector about the real meanings of Hawaiian words. Hawaiian is, by and large, no longer spoken as a language except on Ni'ihau and in Hawaiian-language immersion classes, and the closest tourists will come to it is in place names, street names, and in words that have become part of common usage, such as aloha and mahalo. A few old Hawaiians still speak it at home, and there are sermons in Hawaiian at some local churches. Kawaiaha'o Church in downtown Honolulu is the most famous of these.

Wiki Wiki Hawaiian

Thanks to the missionaries, the Hawaiian language is rendered phonetically using only 12 letters. They are the five vowels, a-e-i-o-u, sounded as they are in Italian, and seven consonants, h-k-l-m-n-p-w, sounded exactly as they are in English. Sometimes "w" is pronounced as "v," but this only occurs in the middle of a word and always follows a vowel. A consonant is always followed by a vowel, forming two-letter syllables, but vowels are often found in pairs or even triplets. A slight oddity about Hawaiian is the glottal stop called *'okina.* This is an abrupt break in the middle of a word, such as "oh-oh" in English, and is denoted with a reverse apostrophe ('). A good example is *ali'i* or, even better, the O'ahu town of Ha'iku, which actually means "abrupt break."

Note on Diacritics

In addition to the *'okina,* or glottal stop, there is the macron *kahako,* a short line written over a vowel indicating that the vowel is stressed. The *kahako* is not used in this book. The *'okina* is used in Hawaiian place names, names of historical persons, and ordinary Hawaiian words, where appropriate. It is not used in business names if the business itself does not use this symbol. The name Hawai'i, written with an 'okina refers to the island of Hawai'i, the Big Island; without the 'okina, it refers to the state. The word Hawaiian, written without the glottal stop, refers to both the Polynesian inhabitants of the islands before Western contact and to those people of all races who currently reside in the state.

Pronunciation Key

For those unfamiliar with the sounds of Italian or other Romance languages, the vowels are sounded as follows:

A—in stressed syllables, pronounced as in "ah" (that feels good!). For example, Haleakala is pronounced "hah-lay-AH-kah-lah." Unstressed syllables are pronounced "uh" as in "again" or "above." For example, Kamehameha would be "kuh-MAY-huh-MAY-huh."

E—short "e" is "eh," as in "pen" or "dent" (thus *hale* is "HAH-leh"). Long "e" sounds like "ay" as in "sway" or "day." For example, the Hawaiian goose *(nene)* is a "nay-nay," not a "nee-nee."

I—pronounced "ee" as in "see" or "we" (thus *pali* is pronounced "PAH-lee").

O—pronounced as in "no" or "oh," such as "KOH-uh" (koa) or "OH-noh" (ono).

U—pronounced "oo" as in "do" or "stew"; for example, "KAH-poo" *(kapu)* or "POO-nuh" (Puna).

Diphthongs

Eight vowel pairs are known as "diphthongs" (ae-ai-ao-au-ei-eu-oi-ou). These are the sounds made by gliding from one vowel to another within a syllable. The stress is placed on the first vowel. In English, examples would be s**oi**l and b**ai**l. Common examples in Hawaiian are lei and *heiau*.

Stress

The best way to learn which syllables are stressed in Hawaiian is by listening closely. It becomes obvious after a while. There are also some vowel sounds that are held longer than others; these can occur at the beginning of a word, such as the first "a" in *"aina,"* or in the middle of a word, like the first "a" in *lanai*. Again, it's a matter of tuning your ear and paying attention. When written, these stressed vowels, called *kahako,* occur with a macron, or short line, over them. Stressed vowels with marks are not written as such in this book.

No one is going to give you a hard time if you mispronounce a word. It's good, however, to pay close attention to the pronunciation of street and place names because many Hawaiian words sound alike and a misplaced vowel here or there could be the difference between getting to where you want to go and getting lost.

Religion

The Lord saw fit to keep His island paradise secret from humanity for a few million years, but once we finally arrived we were awfully thankful. Hawaii sometimes seems like a floating tabernacle; everywhere you look there's a church, temple, shrine, or *heiau*. The islands are either a very holy place or there's a powerful lot of sinning going on that would require so many houses of prayer. Actually, it's just America's "right to worship" concept fully employed in microcosm. All of the peoples who came to Hawaii brought their own forms of devotion. The Polynesian Hawaiians praised the primordial creators, Wakea and Papa, from whom their pantheon of animistically inspired gods sprang. Obviously, to a modern world, these old gods would never do. Unfortunately for the old gods, there were too many of them, and belief in them was looked on as superstition, the folly of semicivilized pagans. So the famous missionaries of the 1820s brought Congregational Christianity and the "true path" to heaven.

Inconveniently, the Catholics, Mormons, Reformed Mormons, Adventists, Episcopalians, Unitarians, Christian Scientists, Lutherans, Baptists, Jehovah's Witnesses, Salvation Army, and every other major and minor denomination of Christianity that followed in their wake brought their own brand of enlightenment and never quite agreed with each other. Chinese and Japanese immigrants established major sects of Buddhism, Confucianism, Taoism, and Shintoism. Allah is praised, the Torah is chanted in Jewish synagogues, and nirvana is available at a variety of Hindu temples. If the spirit moves you, a Hare Krishna devotee will be glad to point you in the right direction and give you a free flower for only a dollar or two. If the world is still too much with you, you might find peace at a Church of Scientology, or meditate at a Kundalini yoga institute, or perhaps find relief at a local assembly of Baha'i. Anyway, rejoice, because in Hawaii you'll find not only paradise but perhaps also salvation.

HAWAIIAN BELIEFS

The Polynesian Hawaiians worshipped nature. They saw its forces manifested in a multiplicity of forms to which they ascribed godlike powers, and they based daily life on this animistic philosophy. Handpicked and specially trained storytellers chanted the exploits of the gods. These ancient tales, kept alive in a special oral tradition called *mo'olelo*, were recited only by day. Entranced listeners encircled the chanter; in respect for the gods and in fear of their wrath, they were forbidden to move once the tale was begun. This was serious business during which a person's life could be at stake. It was not like the telling of *ka'ao*, which were simple fictions, tall tales, and yarns of ancient heroes related for amusement and to pass the long nights. Any object, animate or inanimate, could be a god. All could be infused with mana, especially a dead body or a respected ancestor.

'Ohana had personal family gods called *'aumakua* on whom they called in times of danger or strife. There were children of gods called *kupua* who were thought to live among humans and were distinguished either for their beauty and strength or for their ugliness and terror. It was told that processions of dead *ali'i*, called "Marchers of the Night," wandered through the land of the living, and unless you were properly protected it could mean death if they looked upon you. There were simple ghosts known as *akua lapu* who merely frightened people. Forests, waterfalls, trees, springs, and a thousand forms of nature were the manifestations of *akua li'i*, "little spirits" who

could be invoked at any time for help or protection. It made no difference who or what you were in old Hawaii; the gods were ever present, and they took a direct and active role in your life.

Behind all of these beliefs was an innate sense of natural balance and order. It could be interpreted as positive-negative, yin-yang, plus-minus, life-death, light-dark, whatever, but the main idea was that everything had its opposite. The time of darkness when only the gods lived was *po*. When the great gods descended to the earth and created light, this was *ao* and humanity was born. All of these *mo'olelo* are part of *The Kumulipo*, the great chant that records the Hawaiian version of creation. From the time the gods descended and touched the earth at Ku Moku on Lana'i, the genealogies were kept. Unlike the Bible, these included the noble families of female as well as male *ali'i*.

Heiau

A *heiau* is a Hawaiian temple. The basic *heiau* was a masterfully built and fitted rectangular stone wall that varied in size from about as big as a basketball court to as big as a football field. Once the restraining outer walls were built, the interior was backfilled with smaller stones and the top dressing was expertly laid and then rolled, perhaps with a log, to form a pavementlike surface. All that remains of Hawaii's many *heiau* are the stone platforms. The buildings on them, made from perishable wood, leaves, and grass, have long since disappeared.

Some *heiau* were dreaded temples where human sacrifices were made. Tradition says that this barbaric custom began at Waha'ula Heiau on the Big Island in the 12th century and was introduced by a ferocious Tahitian priest named Pa'ao. Other *heiau*, such as Pu'uhonua o Honaunau, also on the Big Island, were temples of refuge where the weak, widowed, orphaned, and vanquished could find safety and sanctuary.

Idols

The Hawaiian people worshipped gods who took the form of idols fashioned from wood, feathers, or stone. The eyes were made from shells, and until these were inlaid, the idol was dormant. The hair used was often human hair, and the arms and legs were usually flexed. The mouth was either gaping or formed a wide figure-eight lying on its side, and more likely than not was lined with glistening dog teeth. Small figures made of woven basketry were expertly covered with feathers. Red and yellow feathers were favorites taken from specific birds by men whose only work was to roam the forests in search of them.

Ghosts

The Hawaiians had countless superstitions and ghost legends, but two of the more interesting involve astral travel of the soul and the "Marchers of the Night." The soul, *'uhane,* was considered by Hawaiians to be totally free and independent of its body, *kino.* The soul could separate, leaving the body asleep or drowsy. This disincorporated soul *(hihi'o)* could visit people and was considered quite different from a *lapu,* an ordinary spirit of a dead person. A *kahuna* could immediately recognize if a person's *'uhane* had left the body, and a special wreath was placed on the head to protect him or her and to facilitate reentry.

If confronted by an apparition, one could test to see if it was indeed dead or still alive by placing leaves of an *'ape* plant on the ground. If the leaves tore when they were walked on, the spirit was merely human, but if they remained intact it was a ghost. Or you could sneak up and startle the vision, and if it disappeared it was a ghost. Also, if no reflection of the face appeared when it drank water from an offered calabash, it was a ghost. Unfortunately, there were no instructions to follow once you had determined that you had a ghost on your hands. Maybe it was better not to know! Some people would sprinkle salt and water around their houses, but this kept away evil spirits, not ghosts.

There are also many stories of *kahuna* restoring a soul to a dead body. First they had to catch it and keep it in a gourd. They then placed beautiful tapa and fragrant flowers and herbs around the body to make it more enticing. Slowly, they would coax the soul out of the gourd until it reentered the body through the big toe.

Death Marchers

One inexplicable phenomenon that many people attest to is Ka Huaka'i o Ka Po, "Marchers of the Night." This march of the dead is fatal if you gaze on it, unless one of the marchers happens to be a friendly ancestor who will protect you. The peak time for the march is 7:30 P.M.–2 A.M. The marchers can be dead *ali'i* and warriors, the gods, or the lesser *'aumakua.* When the *'aumakua* march there is usually chanting and music. *Ali'i* marches are more somber. The entire procession, lit by torches, often stops at the house of a relative and might even carry him or her away. When the gods march, there is often thunder, lightning, and heavy seas. The sky is lit with torches, and they walk six abreast, three gods and three goddesses. If you get in the way of a march, remove your clothing and prostrate yourself. If the marching gods or *'aumakua* happen to be ones to which you prayed, you might be spared. If it's a march of the *ali'i,* you might make it if you lie face upward and feign death. If you *do* see a death march, the last thing you'll worry about is lying naked on the ground and looking ridiculous.

THE STRIFES OF MAUI

Of all the heroes and mythological figures of Polynesia, Maui is the best known. His "strifes" are like the great Greek epics, and they make excellent tales of daring that elders loved to relate to youngsters around the evening fire. Maui was abandoned by his mother, Hina of Fire, when he was an infant. She wrapped him in her hair and cast him upon the sea, where she expected him to die, but he lived and returned home to become her favorite. She knew then that he was a born hero and had strength far beyond that of ordinary mortals. His first exploit was to lift the sky. In those days the sky hung so low that humans had to crawl around on all fours. A seductive young woman approached Maui and asked him to use his great strength to lift the sky. In fine heroic fashion, the big boy agreed, if the beautiful woman would euphemistically "give him a drink from her gourd." He then obliged her by lifting the sky, and he might even have made the earth move for her once or twice.

More Land

The territory of humankind was small at that time. Maui decided that more land was needed, so he conspired to "fish up islands." He descended into the land of the dead and petitioned an ancestress to fashion him a hook from her jawbone. She obliged and created the mythical hook, *Manai ikalani*. Maui then secured a sacred *'alae* bird that he intended to use for bait and bid his brothers to paddle him far out to sea. When he arrived at the deepest spot, he lowered *Manai ikalani* baited with the sacred bird, and his sister, Hina of the Sea, placed it into the mouth of "Old One Tooth," who held the land fast to the bottom of the waters. Maui then exhorted his brothers to row but warned them not to look back. They strained at the oars with all their might, and slowly a great landmass arose. One brother, overcome by curiosity, looked back, and when he did so, the land shattered into all of the islands of Polynesia.

Further Exploits

Maui still desired to serve humankind. People were without fire, the secret of which was held by the sacred *'alae* birds, who learned it from Maui's far-distant mother. Hina of Fire gave Maui her burning fingernails, but he oafishly kept dropping them into streams until all had fizzled out and he had totally irritated his generous progenitor. She pursued him, trying to burn him to a cinder; Maui chanted for rain to put out her scorching fires. When she saw that they were being quenched, she hid her fire in the barks of special trees and informed the mud hens where they could be found, but first made them promise never to tell humans. Maui knew of this and captured a mud hen, threatening to wring its scrawny, traitorous neck unless it gave up the secret. The bird tried trickery and told Maui first to rub together the stems of sugarcane, then banana, and even taro. None worked, and Maui's determined rubbing is why these plants have hollow roots today.

Finally, with Maui's hands tightening around

the mud hen's gizzard, the bird confessed that fire could be found in the *hau* tree and also the sandalwood, which Maui named *'ili aha* (fire bark) in its honor. He then rubbed all the feathers off the mud hen's head for being so deceitful, which is why their crowns are featherless today.

The Sun Is Snared

Maui's greatest deed, however, was in snaring the sun and exacting a promise that it would go slower across the heavens. The people complained that there were not enough daylight hours to fish or farm. Maui's mother could not dry her tapa cloth because the sun rose and set so quickly. She asked her son to help. Maui went to his blind grandmother, who lived on the slopes of Haleakala and was responsible for cooking the sun's bananas, which he ate every day in passing. She told him to personally weave 16 strong ropes with nooses from his sister's hair. Some say these came from her head, but other versions insist that it was no doubt Hina's pubic hair that had the power to hold the sun god. Maui positioned himself with the rope, and as each of the 16 rays of the sun came across Haleakala, he snared them until the sun was defenseless and had to bargain for his life. Maui agreed to free him if he promised to go more slowly. From that time forward the sun agreed to move slowly, and Haleakala (The House of the Sun) became his home.

MISSIONARIES ONE AND ALL

In Hawaii, when you say "missionaries," it's taken for granted that you're referring to the small and determined band of Congregationalists who arrived aboard the brig *Thaddeus* in 1820, and the follow-up groups called "companies" or "packets" that reinforced them. They were sent from Boston by the American Board of Commissioners for Foreign Missions (ABCFM), which learned of the supposed sad and godless plight of the Hawaiian people through returning sailors and especially through the few Hawaiians who had come to America to study.

The person most instrumental in bringing the missionaries to Hawaii was a young man named Henry Opukaha'ia. He was an orphan befriended by a ship's captain and taken to New England, where he studied theology. Obsessed with the desire to return home and save his people from certain damnation, Opukaha'ia wrote accounts of life in Hawaii that were published and widely read. These accounts were directly responsible for the formation of the Pioneer Company to the Sandwich Islands Missions in 1819. Unfortunately, Opukaha'ia died in New England from typhus the year before they left.

"Civilizing" Hawaii

The first missionaries had the straightforward task of bringing the Hawaiians out of paganism and into Christianity and civilization. They met with terrible hostility—not from the natives, but from the sea captains and traders who were very happy with the open debauchery and wanton whoremongering that was status quo in the Hawaii of 1820. Many direct confrontations between these two factions even included the cannonading of missionaries' homes by American sea captains, who were denied the customary visits of island women, thanks to meddlesome "do-gooders." The most memorable of these incidents involved "Mad Jack" Percival, the captain of the USS *Dolphin,* who bombed a church in Lahaina to show his rancor. In actuality, the truth of the situation was much closer to the sentiments of James Jarves, who wrote: "The missionary was a far more useful and agreeable man than his Catholicism would indicate; and the trader was not so bad a man as the missionary would make him out to be." The missionaries' primary aim might have been conversion, but the most fortuitous by-product was education, which raised the consciousness of every Hawaiian, regardless of religious affiliation. In 40 short years Hawaii was considered a civilized nation well on its way into the modern world, and the American Board of Missions officially ended its support in 1863.

Non-Christians

By the late 1800s, both Shintoism and Buddhism, brought by the Japanese and Chinese, were firmly established in Hawaii. The first official Buddhist temple was Hongpa Hongwanji, established on O'ahu in 1889. All the denominations of Buddhism account for 17 percent of the island's religious total, and there are about 50,000 Shintoists. The Hindu religion has perhaps 2,000 adherents, and roughly 10,000 Jewish people live throughout Hawaii. The largest number of people in Hawaii (300,000) remain unaffiliated, and about 10,000 people are in new religious movements and lesser-known faiths such as Baha'i and Unitarianism.

Arts and Music

Referring to Hawaii as paradise is about as hackneyed as you can get, but when you combine it into artists' paradise, it's the absolute truth. Something about the place evokes art (or at least personal expression) from most people. The islands are like a magnet: They not only draw artists to them, but they draw art *from* the artists.

The inspiration comes from the astounding natural surroundings. The land is so beautiful yet so raw; the ocean's power and rhythm are primal and ever present; the riotous colors of flowers and fruit leap from the deep-green jungle background. Crystal water beads and pale mists turn the mountains into mystic temples, while rainbows ride the crests of waves. The stunning variety of faces begging to be rendered appears as if all the world sent delegations to the islands— and in most cases it did! Inspiration is everywhere, as is art, good or bad.

Sometimes the artwork is overpowering in itself and in its sheer volume. Although geared to the tourist's market of cheap souvenirs, there is hardly a shop in Hawaii that doesn't sell some item that falls into the general category of art. You can find everything from carved monkey-face coconut shells to true masterpieces. The Polynesian Hawaiians were master craftspeople, and their legacy still lives in a wide variety of wood carvings, basketry, and weavings. The hula is art in swaying motion, and the true form is rigorously studied and taken seriously. There is hardly a resort area that doesn't offer the "bump and grind" tourist's hula, but even these revues are accompanied by proficient local musicians. Nightclubs offer "slack key" balladeers and island music performed on ukuleles, and Hawaii's own steel guitars spill from many lounges.

Vibrant fabrics, which catch the spirit of the islands, are rendered into mu'umu'u and aloha shirts at countless local factories. They're almost a mandatory purchase! Pottery, heavily influenced by the Japanese, is a well-developed craft at numerous kilns. Local artisans fashion delicate jewelry from coral and olivine, while some ply the whaler's legacy of etching on ivory, called scrimshaw. There is a fine tradition of quilting, flower art in lei, and street artists working in everything from airbrush to glass.

ARTS OF OLD HAWAII

Because everything in old Hawaii had to be fashioned by hand, almost every object was either a genuine work of art or the product of a highly refined craft. With the "civilizing" of the natives, most of the "old ways" disappeared, including the old arts and crafts. Most authentic Hawaiian art exists only in museums, but with the resurgence of Hawaiian roots, many old arts are being revitalized, and a few artists are becoming proficient in them.

Magnificent Canoes

The most respected artisans in old Hawaii were the canoe makers. With little more than a stone adze and a pump drill, they built canoes that could carry 200 people and last for generations—sleek, well proportioned, and infinitely seaworthy. The main hull was usually a gigantic koa log, and the gunwale planks were minutely drilled and sewn to the sides with sennit rope. Apprenticeships lasted for years, and a young man knew that he had graduated when one day he was nonchalantly asked to sit down and eat with the master builders. Small family-sized canoes with outriggers were used for fishing and perhaps carried a spear rack; large oceangoing double-hulled canoes were used for migration and warfare. On

these, the giant logs had been adzed to about two inches thick. A mainsail woven from pandanus was mounted on a central platform, and the boat was steered by two long paddles. The hull was dyed with plant juices and charcoal, and the entire village helped launch the canoe in a ceremony called "drinking the sea."

Carving and Weaving

Wood was a primary material used by Hawaiian craftsmen. They almost exclusively used koa because of its density, strength, and natural luster. It was turned into canoes, woodware, calabashes, and furniture used by the *ali'i*. Temple idols were another major product of wood carving. A variety of stone artifacts were also turned out, including poi pounders, mirrors, fish sinkers, and small idols.

Hawaiians became the best basket makers and mat weavers in all of Polynesia. *Ulana* (mats) were made from *lau hala* (pandanus) leaves. Once split, the spine was removed and the leaves stored in large rolls. When needed they were soaked, pounded, and then fashioned into various floor coverings and sleeping mats. Intricate geometrical patterns were woven in, and the edges were rolled and well fashioned. Coconut palms were not used to make mats in old Hawaii, but a wide variety of basketry was made from the aerial root *'ie'ie*. The shapes varied according to use. Some baskets were tall and narrow, some were cones, others were flat like trays, and many were woven around gourds and calabashes.

A strong tradition of weaving and carving has survived in Hawaii, and the time-tested material of *lau hala* is still the best, although much is now made from coconut fronds. You can purchase anything from beach mats to a woven hat, and all share the desired qualities of strength, lightness, and ventilation.

Featherwork

This highly refined art was found only on the islands of Tahiti, New Zealand, and Hawaii, while the fashioning of feather helmets and idols was unique to Hawaii. Favorite colors were red and yellow, which came only in a very limited supply from a small number of birds such as the *'o'o, 'i'iwi, mamo,* and *'apapane.*

MAUI MUSEUMS AND HISTORICAL SOCIETIES

Alexander and Baldwin Sugar Museum, at the corner of Pu'unene Ave. and Hansen Rd. in Pu'unene, 808/871-8058, is a small but highly informative museum on the history and culture of sugar and sugar production on Maui and the corresponding plantation life. See a functioning sugar mill across the street. Open Mon.–Sat. 9:30 A.M.–4:30 P.M.; $5 admission.

Baldwin Home, on Front St. across from the harbor in Lahaina, is the two-story home of medical missionary Rev. Dwight Baldwin. This showcase museum is the oldest stone structure on the island, and it portrays the early days of the missions on Maui. Open daily 10 A.M.–4 P.M.; $3 admission.

Hale Pa'i is a printing house located on the grounds of Lahainaluna School on the hillside above Lahaina. It has an operational replica printing press, original Lahainaluna Press publications, and exhibits about the early days of Western contact in Lahaina. Open Mon.–Fri. 10 A.M.–4 P.M.

Bailey House Museum, at 2375-A Main St., Wailuku, is a repository of Hawaiian historical precontact objects, artifacts from the early days of the missionaries on Maui, and the paintings of Edward Bailey. From the 1830s, this stone house itself is of interest. Once Bailey's home, it also served at one time as a dormitory for the Wailuku Female Seminary boarding school. Open Mon.–Sat. 10 a.m.–4 P.M.; $5 admission.

Maui Historical Society, 808/244-3326, is housed in the lower level of the Bailey House Museum. This organization promotes interest in and knowledge of the history of Maui County and maintains an invaluable historical archive. Sponsors free lectures, classes, and events during the year.

Hana Cultural Center, 808/248-8622, is located across from the entrance to Hana Bay. It preserves and restores historical artifacts, photos, and documents from the Hana area. On the grounds are a restored courthouse and jail. This cultural center also has four traditional-style buildings and maintains an ethnobotanical garden. Open daily 10 A.M.–4 P.M.; $2 admission.

The private and nonprofit **Paper Airplane Museum** in Kahului, 808/887-8916, is a collection of model paper airplanes, photographs and artifacts from Maui's aviation history, and a collection of planes and other objects made from tin cans. An eclectic display, this museum will not fail to please and educate. Open daily at a storefront in the Maui Mall; donation suggested.

The **Whale Museum,** 808/661-4567, at the Whalers Village shopping mall in Ka'anapali, displays whaling artifacts and portrays the history and culture of whaling in Hawaii, and the whaler's life. This excellent display includes a reconstructed fo'castle (ship's quarters) and many photographs. In the courtyard is a 40-foot sperm whale skeleton. Self-guided learning experience while you shop. Open daily 9:30 A.M.–10 P.M.; free.

Professional bird hunters in old Hawaii paid their taxes to *ali'i* in prized feathers. The feathers were fastened to a woven net of *olona* cord and made into helmets, idols, and beautiful flowing capes and cloaks. These resplendent garments were made and worn only by men, especially during battle when a fine cloak became a great trophy of war. Featherwork was also employed in the making of *kahili* and lei that were highly prized by the noble *ali'i* women.

Tapa Cloth

Tapa, cloth made from tree bark, was common throughout Polynesia and was a woman's art. A few trees such as the *wauke* and *mamaki* produced the best cloth, but other types could be utilized. First the raw bark was pounded into a feltlike pulp and beaten together to form strips (the beaters had distinctive patterns that also helped make the cloth supple). They were then decorated by stamping (using a form of block printing) and then were dyed with natural colors from plants and sea animals in shades of gray, purple, pink, and red. They were even painted with natural brushes made from pandanus fruit, with an overall gray color made from charcoal. The tapa cloth was sewn together to make bed coverings, and fragrant flowers and herbs were either sewn or pounded in to produce a permanent fragrance. Tapa cloth is still available today, but the Hawaiian methods have been lost, and most comes from other areas of Polynesia.

HULA AND LEI

Hula

The hula is more than an ethnic dance; it is the soul of Hawaii expressed in motion. It began as a form of worship during religious ceremonies and was danced only by highly trained men. It gradually evolved into a form of entertainment, but in no regard was it sexual. The hula was the opera, theater, and lecture hall of the islands all rolled into one. It was history portrayed in the performing arts. In the beginning an androgynous deity named Laka descended to earth and taught men how to dance the hula. In time the male aspect of

Laka departed for the heavens, but the female aspect remained. The female Laka set up her own special hula *heiau* at Ha'ena Point on the Na Pali coast of Kaua'i, where it still exists. As time went on women were allowed to learn the hula. Scholars surmise that men became too busy wresting a living from the land to maintain the art form.

Men did retain a type of hula called *lua*. This was a form of martial art employed in hand-to-hand combat that evolved into a ritualized warfare dance called *hula ku'i*. During the 19th century, the hula almost vanished because the missionaries considered it vile and heathen. King Kalakaua is generally regarded as saving it during the 1800s, when he formed his own troupe and encouraged the dancers to learn the old hula. Many of the original dances were forgotten, but some were retained and are performed to this day. Although professional dancers were highly trained, everyone took part in the hula. *Ali'i,* commoners, young, and old all danced.

Today, hula *halau* (schools) are active on every island, teaching hula and keeping the old ways and culture alive. (Ancient hula is called *hula kahiko,* and modern renditions are known as

MAUI ARTS AND CULTURE ORGANIZATIONS

Lahaina Arts Society, 808/661-0111, is a non-profit organization that has two galleries in the Old Lahaina Courthouse, open daily 9 A.M.–5 P.M. All artwork displayed there is juried artwork by the groups 175 members. Every other weekend, members also display their artwork under the banyan tree behind the courthouse. The Lahaina Arts Society also organized a year-round outreach program at a dozen sites throughout the island where classes are taught by society members.

The **Lahaina Town Action Committee,** 808/667-9175, www.visitlahaina.com, organizes cultural events and other activities in Lahaina, including the ever-popular Friday evening Art Night. This group also sponsors the **Lahaina Visitor Center,** which has its office on the first floor of the Old Lahaina Courthouse.

The **Maui Historical Society,** 808/244-3326,

www.mauimuseum.org, collects and preserves artifacts and disseminates information about the history and culture of Maui. It is located in the basement of the Bailey House Museum in Wailuku.

The Lahaina Restoration Foundation, 808/661-3262, is a community organization in Lahaina created to preserve the flavor and authenticity of old Lahaina without the context of continued growth and development. They own and maintain numerous historical buildings as museums and try to educate the visiting public about the history of the area.

Friends of Moku'ula, 808/661-3659, www.moku-ula.com, is a nonprofit organization with the goal of bringing to the attention of the public the importance of the old royal compound of Moku'ula in Lahaina and to its eventual re-creation.

ROBERT NILSEN

While some of the best hula is performed by local hula *halau* at community events, visitors will see the hula performed mostly at tourist lu'au and hotel venues.

hula auana.) Performers still spend years perfecting their techniques. They show off their accomplishments during the fierce competition of the Merrie Monarch Festival in Hilo every April. The winning *halau* is praised and recognized throughout the islands.

Hawaiian hula was never performed in grass skirts; tapa or *ti*-leaf skirts were worn. Grass skirts came to Hawaii from the Gilbert Islands, so if you see grass or cellophane skirts in a "hula revue," it's not traditional. Almost every major resort offering entertainment or a lu'au also offers a revue. Most times, young island beauties accompanied by local musicians put on a floor show for the tourists. It'll be fun, but it won't be traditional. Hula, like all art forms, has its own highly specialized techniques. A dancer has to learn how to control every part of his or her body, including the facial expressions, which help set the mood. The hands are extremely important and provide instant background scenery. For example, if the hands are thrust outward in an aggressive manner, this can be a battle; if they

sway gently overhead, they refer to the gods or to creation; they can easily symbolize rain, clouds, sun, sea, or moon. Watch the hands to get the gist of the story, but remember the words of one wise guy, "You watch the parts you like, and I'll watch the parts I like." The motion of swaying hips can denote a long walk, a canoe ride, or sexual intercourse. The foot motion can portray a battle, a walk, or any kind of movement or conveyance. The correct chanting of the *mele* is an integral part of the performance. These story chants, accompanied by musical instruments, make the hula very much like opera; it is especially similar in the way the tale unfolds.

Lei Making

Any flower or blossom can be strung into a lei, but the most common are carnations or the lovely smelling plumeria. Lei, like babies, are all beautiful, but special lei are highly prized by those who know what to look for. Of the different stringing styles, the most common is *kui*—stringing the flower through the middle or side. Most airport-quality lei are of this type. The *humuhumu* style, reserved for making flat lei, is made by sewing flowers and ferns to a *ti*, banana, or sometimes *hala* leaf. A *humuhumu* lei makes an excellent hatband. *Wili* is the winding together of greenery, ferns, and flowers into short, bouquet-type lengths. The most traditional form is *hili*, which requires no stringing at all but involves braiding fragrant ferns and leaves such as *maile*. If flowers are interwoven, the *hili* becomes the *haku* style, the most difficult and most beautiful type of lei.

The Lei of the Land

Every major island is symbolized by its own lei made from a distinctive flower, shell, or fern. Each island has its own official color as well, although it doesn't necessarily correspond to the color of the island's lei. Maui is the pink island, and its lei is the corresponding small pink rose called the *lokelani*. These flowers are not native, but were imported and widely cultivated at one time. In recent years they've fallen prey to a rose beetle, and sometimes when they're scarce, a *roselani* is substituted for Maui's lei.

THAT GOOD OLD ISLAND MUSIC

The missionaries usually take a beating when it's recounted how much Hawaiian culture they destroyed while "civilizing" the natives. However, they seem to have done one thing right. They introduced the Hawaiians to the diatonic musical scale and immediately opened a door to latent and superbly harmonious talent. Before the missionaries, the Hawaiians knew little about melody. Although sonorous, their *mele* were repetitive chants in which the emphasis was placed on historical accuracy and not on "making music." The Hawaiians, in short, didn't *sing*. But within a few years of the missionaries' arrival, they were belting out good old Christian hymns, and one of their favorite pastimes became group and individual singing.

Early in the 1800s, Spanish *vaqueros* from California were imported to teach the Hawaiians how to be cowboys. With them came guitars and moody ballads. The Hawaiian *paniolos* (cowboys) quickly learned how to punch cows and croon away the long, lonely nights on the range. Immigrants who came along a little later in the 19th century, especially from Portugal, helped create a Hawaiian-style music. Their biggest influence was a small, four-stringed instrument called a *braga* or *cavaquinho*. One owned by Augusto Dias was the prototype of a homegrown Hawaiian instrument that became known as the ukulele. "Jumping flea," the translation of ukulele, is an appropriate name devised by the Hawaiians when they saw how nimble the fingers were as they jumped over the strings.

King Kalakaua (The Merrie Monarch) and Queen Lili'uokalani were both patrons of the arts who furthered the Hawaiian musical identity at the turn of the 20th century. Kalakaua revived the hula and was also a gifted lyricist and balladeer. He wrote the words to "Hawaii Pono," which became the national anthem of Hawaii and later the state anthem. Lili'uokalani wrote the hauntingly beautiful "Aloha O'e," which is often pointed to as the "spirit of Hawaii" in music. Detractors say that its melody is extremely close to the old Christian hymn, "Rock Beside the Sea," but the lyrics are so beautiful and perfectly fitted that this doesn't matter.

Just before Kalakaua's reign, a Prussian bandmaster, Captain Henry Berger, was invited to head the fledgling Royal Hawaiian Band, which he turned into a respectable orchestra lauded by many visitors to the islands. Berger was open-minded and learned to love Hawaiian music. He collaborated with Kalakaua and other island musicians to incorporate their music into a Western format. He headed the band for 43 years until 1915 and was instrumental in making music a serious pursuit of talented Hawaiians.

Popular Hawaiian Music

Hawaiian music has a unique twang, a special feeling that says the same thing to everyone who hears it: "Relax, sit back in the moonlight; watch the swaying palms as the surf sings a lullaby." This special sound is epitomized by the bouncy ukulele, the falsettos of Hawaiian crooners, and by the smooth ring of the "steel" or

"Hawaiian" guitar. The steel guitar is a variation originated by Joseph Kekuku in the 1890s. Stories abound of how Joseph Kekuku devised this instrument; the most popular versions say that Joe dropped his comb or pocketknife on his guitar strings and liked what he heard. Driven by the faint rhythm of an inner sound, he went to the machine shop at the Kamehameha School and turned out a steel bar for sliding over the strings. To complete the sound he changed the cat-gut strings to steel and raised them so they wouldn't hit the frets. Voila! Hawaiian music as the world knows it today.

The first melodious strains of **slack-key guitar** (*ki ho'alu*) can be traced back to the time of Kamehameha III and the *vaqueros* from California. The Spanish had their way of tuning the guitar and played difficult and aggressive music that did not sit well with Hawaiians, who were much more gentle and casual in their manners.

Hawaiians soon became adept at making their own music. At first, one person played the melody, but it lacked fullness. There was no body to the sound. So, as one *paniolo* fooled with the melody, another soon learned to play bass, which added depth. But, a player was often alone, and by experimenting he or she learned to get the right hand going with the melody and at the same time play the bass note with the thumb to improve the sound. Singers also learned that they could "open tune" the guitar to match their rich voices.

Hawaiians believed knowledge was sacred, and what is sacred should be treated with utmost respect, which meant keeping it secret, except from sincere apprentices. Guitar playing became a personal art form whose secrets were closely guarded, handed down only to family members, and only to those who showed ability and determination. When old-time slack-key guitar players were done strumming, they loosened all the strings so no one could figure out how they had tuned them. If they were playing, and some folks came by who were interested and

> *Hawaiian music has a unique twang, a special feeling that says the same thing to everyone who hears it: "Relax, sit back in the moonlight; watch the swaying palms as the surf sings a lullaby."*

weren't part of the family, the Hawaiians stopped what they were doing, put their guitars down, and put their feet across the strings to wait for the folks to go away. As time went on, more and more Hawaiians began to play slack-key, and a common repertoire emerged.

Accomplished musicians could easily figure out the simple songs, once they had figured out how the family had tuned the guitar. One of the most popular tunings was the "open G." Old Hawaiian folks called it the "taro patch tune." Different songs came out, and if you were in the family and were interested in the guitar, your elders took the time to sit down and teach you. The way they taught was straightforward—and a test of your sincerity at the same time. The old master would start to play. He just wanted you to listen and get a feel for the music—nothing more than that. You brought your guitar and *listened.* When you felt it, you played it, and the knowledge was transferred. Today, only a handful of slack-key guitar players know how to play the classic tunes classically. The best-known and perhaps greatest slack-key player was Gabby Pahinui, with The Sons of Hawaii. When he passed away he left many recordings behind. A slack-key master still singing and playing is Raymond Kane. Not one of his students is from his own family, and most are *haole* musicians trying to preserve the classical method of playing.

Hawaiian music received its biggest boost from a remarkable radio program known as "Hawaii Calls." This program sent out its music from the Banyan Court of Waikiki's Moana Hotel from 1935–75. At its peak in the mid-1950s, it was syndicated on more than 700 radio stations throughout the world. Ironically, Japanese pilots heading for Pearl Harbor tuned in island music as a signal beam. Some internationally famous classic tunes came out of the '40s and '50s. Jack Pitman composed "Beyond the Reef" in 1948; more than 300 artists have recorded it, and it has sold more than 12 million records. Other million-sellers include "Sweet Leilani," "Lovely Hula Hands," "The Cross-eyed Mayor of Kaunakakai," and "The Hawaiian Wedding Song."

By the 1960s, Hawaiian music began to die. Just too corny and light for those turbulent years, it belonged to the older generation and the good times that followed World War II. One man was instrumental in keeping Hawaiian music alive during this period. Don Ho, with his "Tiny Bubbles," became the token Hawaiian musician of the 1960s and early '70s. He's persevered long enough to become a legend in his own time, and his Polynesian Extravaganza at the Hilton Hawaiian Village packed visitors in until the early 1990s. He now plays at the Waikiki Beachcomber Hotel five nights a week. Al Harrington, "The South Pacific Man," had another Honolulu "big revue" that drew large crowds until his recent retirement. Of this type of entertainment, perhaps the most Hawaiian was Danny Kaleikini, who entertained his audience with dances, Hawaiian anecdotes, and tunes on the traditional Hawaiian nose flute.

The Beat Goes On

Beginning in the mid-1970s, islanders began to assert their cultural identity. One of the unifying factors was the coming of age of Hawaiian music. It graduated from the "little grass shack" novelty tune and began to include sophisticated jazz, rock, and contemporary rhythms. Accomplished musicians whose roots were in traditional island music began to highlight their tunes with this distinctive sound. The best embellish their arrangements with ukuleles, steel guitars, and traditional percussion and melodic instruments. Some excellent modern recording artists have become island institutions. The local people say that you know the Hawaiian harmonies are good if they give you "chicken skin."

Each year special music awards, **Na Hoku Hanohano,** or Hoku for short, are given to distinguished island musicians. The following are some of the Hoku winners considered by their contemporaries to be among the best in Hawaii: Barney Isaacs and George Kuo, Na Leo Pilimihana, Robi Kahakalau, Keali'i Reichel, Darren Benitez, Sonny Kamahele, Ledward Kaapana, Hapa, Israel Kamakawiwio'ole, and Pure Heart. If they're playing on one of the islands while you're in Hawaii, don't miss them. Some, unfortunately, are no longer among the living, but their recorded music can still be appreciated.

Past Hoku winners who have become renowned performers include the Brothers Cazimero, who are blessed with beautiful harmonic voices; Krush, highly regarded for their contemporary sounds; The Peter Moon Band, fantastic performers with a strong traditional sound; Kapono and Cecilio; and The Beamer Brothers. Others include Loyal Garner, Del Beazley, Bryan Kessler and Me No Hoa Aloha, George Kahumoku, Jr., Olomana, Genoa Keawe, and Irmagard Aluli.

Those with access to the Internet can check out the Hawaiian music scene at one of the following: Hawaiian Music Island, www.mele.com; Nahenahenet, www.nahenahe.net; and Hawaiian Music Guide, www.hawaii-music.com. While not the only sites on the Net, they are a good place to start. For listening to Hawaiian music on the Net, try http://kkcr.org or www.hotspots.hawaii.com/IRH.

Festivals, Holidays, and Events

National holidays and Hawaiian state events are all celebrated and commemorated in Maui County. Events such as Aloha Festivals and Lei Day are celebrated on all of the islands, but several other unique happenings occur only on the Valley Isle, Moloka'i, and Lana'i. If you happen to be visiting when any of the following are in progress, be sure to attend! Most are either free or at nominal price. Many happenings are annual events, whereas others are one-time affairs. Check local newspapers and the free island magazines for dates. Island-specific information is also available on the web; check the calendar listing at www.visitmaui.com/calendar.html.

For additional events of all sorts throughout the state, visit the calendar of events listing on the Hawaii Visitors Bureau (HVB) website at http://calendar.gohawaii.com, the Hawaii vacation planner website at www.hshawaii.com/vacplanner/calendar, or the State Foundation of Culture and the Arts calendar, which features arts and cultural events, activities, and programs, at www.state.hi.us/sfca/culturecalendar.html.

January

Late January brings the televised college all-star **Hula Bowl** football game to the War Memorial Stadium in Kahului.

The **Mercedes Championship** PGA tour plays golf at Kapalua, while the Senior PGA tour hosts the **Senior Skins Game** at Wailea.

February

Lunar New Year celebrations are held in the evening along Front Street in Lahaina and include a lion's dance, martial arts demonstrations, live music, food, and, of course, firecrackers.

Marking the yearly return to Hawaiian waters of the humpback whale, February is whale month. The annual weeklong **Whalefest** happens in Lahaina with sailing and diving tours, demonstrations, and seminars; the **Great Whale Count** takes place islandwide; the **Annual Whale Day Celebration** is a Kihei event

with lots of music, dance, and food; and **Whale Week on Maui** is a Wailea event with all sorts of events, including a regatta, fun run, and parade.

March

The Valley Island Road Runners, 808/871-6441, sponsor the **Maui Marathon** in mid-March from the Queen Ka'ahumanu Center in Kahului to Whalers Village in Ka'anapali.

The **East-Maui Taro Festival,** 808/248-8972, www.tarofestival.org, is celebrated in Hana with traditional ceremonies, music, food markets, symposiums, demonstrations, and exhibitions to honor one of the island's most basic food sources and the resurgence of Hawaiian cultural traditions.

April

The **Da Kine Classic Windsurfing Event,** 808/877-2111, professional windsailing competition for men and women is held at Kanaha Beach. This is part of the Maui Race series.

The "Ulupalakua Thing," also called the **Maui Agricultural Trade Show and Sampling,** is the largest event for displaying and promoting Hawaii-grown and Hawaii-manufactured products. Held at the Tedeschi Winery at the Ulupalakua Ranch, 808/878-1266, www.mauiag.org; admission is charged.

May

The annual **Lei Festival** takes place at the Outrigger Wailea Beach Hotel with a flower lei competition, Hawaiian music, and numerous cultural demonstrations.

Lahaina's signature cultural event is **In Celebration of Canoes.** This cultural gathering honors the voyaging canoe, which brought the ancestors of modern Hawaiians from the South Pacific. Cultural arts demonstrations, lu'au, musical performances, and the carving of canoes from logs are some of the activities. Representatives from Pacific island nations participate.

June

The **Annual Upcountry Fair** at the Eddie Tam Center, Makawao, is an old-fashioned farm fair right in the heart of Maui's *paniolo* country. Crafts, food, and competitions are all part of the fair, as are the county 4-H championship and auctions.

June 11 is **King Kamehameha Day** in Lahaina. Festivities include a parade through town, crafts, and lots of food and entertainment.

The annual **Slack Key Guitar Festival** at the Maui Arts and Cultural Center in Kahului features some of Hawaii's best musicians.

The **Maui Film Festival,** 808/572-3456 or 808/579-9244, www.mauifilmfestival.com, shows a handful of art films in December and January at the Maui Arts and Culture Center in Kahului and then weekly throughout the rest of the year. Outdoor film events take place in Wailea in June.

July

Head for the coolness of Upcountry Makawao for the annual **Makawao Rodeo.** *Paniolo* are an old and very important tradition in Hawaiian life. Held at the Oskie Rice Arena, this old-time Upcountry rodeo can't be beat for fun and entertainment anywhere in the country. Always accompanied by the Paniolo Parade through town.

The **Fourth of July** brings the best fireworks display on Maui to the Lahaina Roads. Thousands congregate for the show.

July also brings the annual **Kapalua Wine and Food Symposium,** 808/669-0244, where foods prepared by local master chefs get paired with international wines.

Late July or early August brings the **Quicksilver Cup Windsurfing Championships** to Kanaha Beach in Kahului.

August

The Japanese **Bon Odori** takes place in late July–Aug. at Buddhist temples throughout the island, featuring dance, drumming, and lantern boats. Everyone is invited to participate.

Late July or early August also offers *the* most difficult marathon in the world. The annual **Maui Marathon** takes runners from Kahului

down to Ma'alaea and then along the ocean to Ka'anapali. For information, call 808/871-6441.

Maui Onion Festival, at Whalers Village in Ka'anapali, celebrates the island's most famous commercial herb. All sorts of music, chef's demonstrations, and cooking-related events take place.

September

Labor Day weekend brings the well-respected **Maui Writers Conference,** usually held at one of the fancy hotels on the island.

A culinary event featuring some of the best chefs in the islands, **A Taste of Lahaina** is not only a tasty treat of food, wine, and beer, but also offers cooking demonstrations and local music.

Head back up to Makawao for another excellent **Maui County Rodeo** as well as plenty of good happenings during the statewide **Aloha Festivals.**

October

The **Maui County Fair** at the Wailuku War Memorial Complex brings out the kid in everyone. An old-fashioned fair with Western and homespun flavor, this event offers rides, booths, and games. May be held in late September.

Wild costumes and outlandish behavior set the mood for **Halloween** in Lahaina, the largest celebration of Halloween in Hawaii, often called the "Mardi Gras of the Pacific." For information, call 808/667-9194.

The **Kaanapali Classic Senior PGA Golf Tournament** lures some of the game's living legends to the Ka'anapali links.

The **XTERRA World Championships** are held yearly in Wailea. This is an off-road triathlon that combines a 1.5-mile ocean swim, 30K mountain-bike ride, and an 11K trail run.

November

The **Hawaii International Film Festival,** 808/528-3456, www.hiff.org, showcases new and engaging films, mainly from Asian and Pacific Rim countries, at the Maui Arts and Cultural Center in Kahului.

The **Maui Invitational Basketball Tournament** holds a preseason college team playoff at the Civic Center in Lahaina.

Each year the Ka'anapali Beach Hotel hosts **Hula O Na Keiki,** the state's only children's solo and partner hula contest. Two days of competition make this an entertaining event for everyone.

December

This month remembers Maui of old with the **Na Mele O Maui** festival in Lahaina and Ka'anapali. Hawaiian music, dance, arts, and crafts are featured.

The **Festival of Art and Flowers** in Lahaina incorporates displays of flowers grown on the island, including the beautiful protea, flower displays, demonstrations, workshops, and music, plus the **Holiday Lighting of the Banyan Tree** and decorating the Old Courthouse for Christmas.

Exploring the Islands

Sports and Recreation

Maui won't let you down when you want to go outside and play. More than just a giant sandbox for big kids, its beaches and surf are warm and inviting, and there are all sorts of water sports from scuba diving to parasailing. You can fish, hunt, camp, or indulge yourself in golf or tennis to your heart's content. The hiking is marvelous, and the horseback riding on Haleakala is some of the most exciting in the world. The information offered in this chapter is merely an overview to let you know what's available. Have fun!

CAMPING

A major aspect of the "Maui experience" is found in the simple beauty of nature and the outdoors. Some visitors come to Maui to luxuriate at resorts and dine in fine restaurants, but everyone heads for the sand and surf, and most are captivated by the lush mountainous interior. What better way to savor this natural beauty than by hiking slowly through it or pitching a tent in the middle of it? Maui offers a full range of hiking but more limited camping, and most of it is easily accessible. Camping facilities are located both along the coast and amid the scenic forest areas of Haleakala. They range in amenities from

outrigger canoes off Ka'anapali beach

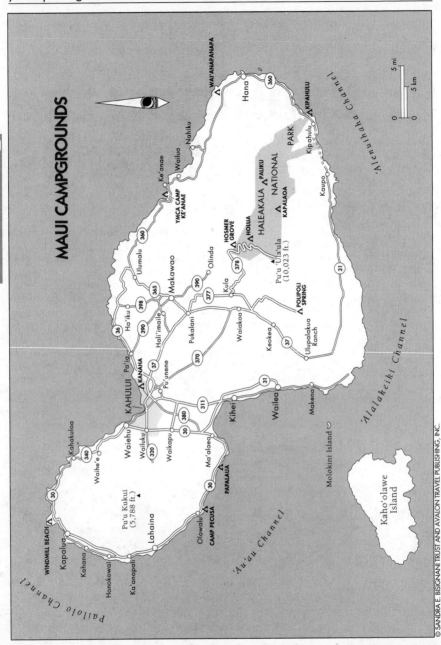

MAUI CAMPGROUNDS

© SANDRA E. BISIGNANI TRUST AND AVALON TRAVEL PUBLISHING, INC.

housekeeping cabins to primitive hike-in sites. Most require camping permits—inexpensive for the county and state parks, free for the national park. Camping permits can be obtained by walk-in application to the appropriate office or by writing. Although there is usually no problem obtaining sites, request reservations well in advance when writing, allowing a minimum of one month for letters to go back and forth.

General Information

Most campgrounds have pavilions, fireplaces, toilets (sometimes the pit variety), and running water, but usually no individual electrical hookups. Pavilions may have electric lights, but sometimes campers appropriate the bulbs, so it's wise to carry your own. Drinking water is available at all except for the national park's Kipahulu campground, the spots within Haleakala Crater, and Papalaua County Beach Park, but brackish water may be used for flushing toilets and for showers, so read all signs regarding water. Never hike without an adequate supply of your own drinking water. Cooking fires are allowed in established fire pits, but no wood is provided. Bringing your own charcoal is a good idea, but a camp stove is better. When camping in the mountains, be prepared for cold and rainy weather. Women especially should never hike or camp alone, and everyone should take precautions against theft.

Haleakala National Park

Camping at Haleakala National Park is free, but there is an automobile entrance fee of $10, $5 for hikers and bikers. Permits are not needed to camp at Hosmer Grove, just a short drive from park headquarters, or at Kipahulu Campground along the coastal road 10 miles south of Hana. Camping is on a first-come, first-served basis, and there's an official three-day stay limit, but it's a loose count, especially at Kipahulu, which is almost always empty. The case is much different at the campsites located inside Haleakala Crater proper. On the floor of the basin are two primitive tenting campsites, one at Paliku on the east side and the other at Holua on the northwest corner. For these you'll need a wilderness per-

mit from park headquarters, picked up on the first morning of your trip. Because of ecological considerations, only 25 campers per night can stay at each site, and a three-night, four-day per-month maximum stay is strictly enforced, with tenting allowed at any one site for only two consecutive nights. However, because of the strenuous hike involved, campsites are open most of the time. You must be totally self-sufficient and equipped for cold-weather camping to be comfortable at these two sites.

Also, Paliku, Holua, and another site at Kapalaoa on the south edge of the basin offer cabins. Fully self-contained with stoves, water, and nearby pit toilets, they can handle a maximum of 12 campers each. Bunks are provided, but you must have your own warm bedding. The same maximum-stay limits apply as in the campgrounds. Staying at these cabins is at a premium—they're popular with visitors and residents alike. Reservations for the cabins must be made at least two months in advance by mail using only a special cabin reservation request form. A lottery of the applicants chosen for sites keeps it fair for all. These cabins are geared toward groups, with rates at $40 for 1–6 people or $80 for up to the limit of 12. To have a chance at getting a cabin, write well in advance for complete information to Haleakala National Park, P.O. Box 369, Makawao, HI 96768, or call 808/572-4400.

State Parks

There are eight state parks on Maui, two with overnight camping. **Polipoli Spring State Recreation Area** and **Wai'anapanapa** offer free tenting, and housekeeping cabins are available; reservations highly necessary. Permits are required at each, and RVs technically are not allowed. Day use is free and open to everyone.

Tent camping **permits** are $5 per site and good for a maximum stay of five consecutive nights at any one park. A permit to the same person for the same park is again available only after 30 days have elapsed. Campgrounds are open every day. You can arrive after 2 P.M. and you should check out by 11 A.M. The minimum age for park permits is 18, and anyone under that age must be accompanied by an adult. Alcoholic beverages are prohibited, as is nude sunbathing. Plants and wildlife are protected, but reasonable amounts of fruits and seeds may be gathered for personal consumption. Fires are on cookstoves or in designated pits only. Dogs and other pets must be under control at all times and are not permitted to run around unleashed. Hunting and freshwater fishing are allowed in season and only with a license, but ocean fishing is permitted, unless prohibited by posting. Permits are required for certain trails, so check at the state parks office.

Housekeeping cabins are available. The dozen cabins at Wai'anapanapa have a maximum capacity of six and have all necessary amenities, while the one at Polipoli Spring (gas stove, no electricity) can handle up to 10 people. As with camping, permits are required with the same five-day maximum stay (the cabin at Polipoli Spring is closed on Tuesday nights). Reservations are absolutely necessary, especially at Wai'anapanapa, and a 50 percent deposit is required at time of confirmation. There's a three-day cancellation requirement for refunds, and payment is to be made in cash, by money order, certified check, or personal check, the latter only if it's received 30 days before arrival so that cashing procedures are possible. The balance is due on date of arrival. Cabins are $45 per night for up to four people, and $5 for each additional person up to the limit. These units are completely furnished down to the utensils, with heaters for cold weather and private baths.

Permits can be reserved up to one year in advance, but you must confirm at least seven days before arrival by writing a timely letter including your name, address, phone number, number of persons in your party, type of permit requested, and duration of your stay. They can be picked up on arrival with proof of identification. Office hours are Monday–Friday 8 A.M.–3:30 P.M. Tent camping permits are usually no problem to secure on the day you arrive, but reserving ensures you a space and alleviates anxiety. Permits are available from the Maui Division of State Parks, 54 S. High St., Rm. 101, Wailuku, HI 96793, 808/984-8109. This office also issues permits for camping at Pala'au State Park on Molokai.

County Parks

There are 16 county parks scattered primarily along Maui's coastline, and because of their locations, they're generally referred to as **beach parks.** Most are for day use only, where visitors fish, swim, snorkel, surf, picnic, and sunbathe, but only **Kanaha Beach County Park** in Kahului and **Papalaua Beach Park** near the Lahaina Tunnel have overnight camping. The rules governing use of these parks are just about the same as those for state parks. The differences between individual parks are too numerous to mention, but most have a central pavilion for cooking, restrooms, cold-water showers, individual fire pits, and picnic tables, with electricity usually only at the central pavilion. RVs are allowed to park in appropriate spaces. One safety point to consider is that beach parks are open to the general public, and most are used with regularity. This means that quite a few people pass through, and your chances of encountering a hassle or running into a rip-off are slightly higher in beach parks. Be aware when planning your trip that the Kanaha Beach Park camping area is closed Tuesdays and Wednesdays for maintenance. Camping **fees** are quite reasonable at $3 per night per adult, $.50 for children, with no more than three consecutive nights at the park. To get a permit and pay your fees, either write in advance and an application will be mailed to you or visit the Department of Parks and Recreation permit issuing office Monday–Friday 8 A.M.–4 P.M. at 1580-C Ka'ahumanu Ave. (at the front of the War Memorial Gym), Wailuku, HI 96793. Call 808/270-7389 for more information.

Private Campgrounds

YMCA Camp Keanae is perhaps the best-known private campground on the island, and it's a beauty. It lies on the rugged north shore, halfway along the Hana Highway. This camp offers bunkhouses (you must provide your own bedding), tenting space, bathrooms with showers, and a gymnasium. Tents can be pitched on the broad, grassy lawn. Bring your own cooking gear. The dining room and kitchen are open for large-group use only. Check-in is 3–7 P.M. A fee of $15 per person or $30 per family is charged, with a three-day maximum stay. Y members have reduced rates. All accommodations are by reservation only. For information and reservations, call the camp at 808/248-8355, YMCACamp-Keanae@aol.com.

Camp Pecusa in located about one-quarter mile east of Olowalu, along the coast east of Lahaina. Owned and operated by the Episcopal Church in Hawaii, this camp often fills with groups staying in the cabins during the summer. Tent space is open any time of the year for public use. A fee of $5 is charged per person per night. No reservations are taken, but it's best to call to ask if space is available. For information, call 808/661-4303 or write Camp Pucusa, 800 Olowalu, HI 96761.

Camping is also permitted at **Windmill Beach,** just north of Honolua Bay on the northwest coast, on land owned by Maui Land and Pineapple Company. This is primitive camping—there are *no* facilities. No reservations are necessary, but a permit is. Camping permits are issued by the company office at 4900 Honoapi'ilani Hwy. (across the highway from Napili Plaza), Monday–Friday 7 A.M.–3:30 P.M. Fees are $5 per party with three nights maximum. For information, call 808/669-6201.

HIKING

The hiking on Maui is excellent. Most times you have the trails to yourself, and the wide possibility of hikes ranges from a family saunter to a strenuous trek. Some restrictions to hiking apply because much of the land is privately owned, but plenty of public access trails along the coast and deep into the interior would fill the itineraries of even the most intrepid hikers. If you enjoy the great outdoors, you'll be thrilled by these "mini-continents," where in one day you can go from the frosty summits of alpine wonderlands down into baking arid scrubland and emerge through jungle foliage onto a sun-soaked subtropical shore.

Perhaps the most adventurous hiking on Maui is done along the 27 miles of trails within Haleakala National Park. This is all high-elevation hiking with virtually no shade cover or water

available, so you must be well prepared. Two trails start at different locations along Haleakala Highway and drop into the crater basin, traversing it to its far end. Several secondary trails connect these two main trails, while a third heads out and over the Kaupo Gap to descend the mountain to the south.

Not all hiking on the island requires such preparation or endurance. The Polipoli Spring area offers many miles of trails that are much lower in elevation and through sheltered forests, yet give you some great views over the countryside. There are also short hikes at 'Iao Needle near Wailuku, and longer hikes up the Waihe'e Stream and Waihe'e Ridge, both north of Wailuku. Longer, drier, and more exhausting is the Lahaina Pali Trail, which cuts across the mountain ridge from Ma'alaea to the coast road heading toward Lahaina.

Coastal trails are also an option, and the easiest to approach are sections of the old "King's Highway" at Wai'anapanapa State Park. Another section of this ancient paved trail can be accessed from the end of the road at La Pérouse Bay.

Refer to the appropriate travel chapter for specific information about each of these hikes.

Hiking Tips

Hike with someone—share the experience. If possible, don't hike or camp alone, especially if you're a woman. Don't leave your valuables in your tent, and always carry your money, papers, and camera with you. At the least, let someone know where you are going and when you plan to be back; supply an itinerary and your expected route, and then stick to it. Stay on designated trials: This not only preserves Maui's fragile environment, but it also keeps you out of dangerous areas. Occasionally, trails will be closed for maintenance, so stay off these routes. Many trails are well maintained, but trailhead markers are sometimes missing. The trails themselves can be muddy, which can make them treacherously slippery. Buy and use a trail map.

Wear comfortable clothing. Shorts and a T-shirt will suffice on many trails, but long pants and long-sleeve shirts are better where it's rainy and overgrown and at higher elevations. Bring a windbreaker or raingear because it can rain and blow at any time. Wear sturdy walking or hiking shoes that you don't mind getting wet and muddy, which is almost guaranteed on some trails. Sturdy shoes will be imperative on trails over lava. Some very wet spots and stream crossings may be better done in tabi or other watershoes. Your clothes may become permanently stained with mud—a wonderful memento of your trip. Officials and others often ask hikers to pick clinging seeds off their clothes when coming out at the trailhead and to wash off boots so as not to unintentionally transport seeds to non-native areas.

Always bring food because you cannot, in most cases, forage from the land. Carry plenty of drinking water, at least two quarts per day. Heat can cause your body to lose water and salt. If you become woozy or weak, rest, take salt, and drink water as you need it. Remember: It takes much more water to restore a dehydrated person than to stay hydrated as you go; take small, frequent sips. No matter how clean it looks, water in most streams is biologically polluted and will give you bad stomach problems if you drink it without purifying it first; either boil it or treat it with tablets. For your part, please don't use streams as a toilet.

Use sunscreen. The sun can be intense and UV rays go through clouds. Bring and use mosquito lotion. Even in paradise these pesky bugs abound. Do not litter. Carry a trash bag and take out all that you bring in.

Some trails are used by hunters of wild boar, deer, or game birds. It's best not to use these trails during hunting season, but if you do hike in hunting areas during hunting season, wear brightly colored or reflective clothing. Forest reserve trails often have check-in stations at trailheads. Hikers and hunters must sign a logbook, especially if they intend to camp. The comments by previous hikers are worth reading for up-to-the-minute information on trail conditions.

Twilight is short in the islands, and night sets in rapidly. In June, sunrise is around 6 A.M. and sunset 7 P.M.; in December, these occur at 7 A.M. and 6 P.M. If you become lost, find an open spot and stay put; at night, stay as dry as you can. If you must continue, walk on ridges and avoid the gulches, which have more obstacles and make it harder for rescuers to spot you. Do not light a fire. Some forest area can be very dry, and fire could spread easily. Fog is only encountered at the 1,500- to 5,000-foot level; be careful of disorientation.

Be careful of elevation sickness, especially on Haleakala. The best cure is to head down as soon and as quickly as possible.

Generally, stay within your limits, be careful, and enjoy yourself.

Camping and Hiking Equipment

Like everything else you take to Maui, your camping and hiking equipment should be lightweight and durable. Camping equipment size and weight should not cause a problem with baggage requirements on airlines: If it does, it's a tipoff that you're hauling too much. One odd luggage consideration you might make is to bring along a small styrofoam cooler packed with equipment. Exchange the gear for food items when you get to Hawaii; if you intend to car camp successfully and keep food prices down, you'll definitely need a cooler. You can also buy one on arrival for only a few dollars.

Consider an internal-frame **backpack** or a convertible pack that turns into a soft-side suitcase, and a day pack. You'll need a lightweight **tent,** preferably with a rainfly and a sewn-in waterproof floor. This will save you from getting wet and miserable and will keep out mosquitoes, cockroaches, ants, and the few stinging insects on Maui. In Haleakala Crater, where you can expect cold and wind, a tent is a must; in fact, you probably won't be allowed to camp without one. **Sleeping bags** are a good idea, although you can get along at sea level with only a blanket. Down-filled bags are necessary for Haleakala—you'll freeze without one.

Campstoves are needed because there's very little available wood; it's often wet in the deep forest, and open fires are often prohibited. If you'll be car camping, take along a multiburner stove; for hiking, a backpacker's stove will be necessary. Buy stove gas in Hawaii because these containers are not allowed on planes. The grills found only at some campgrounds are popular with many families, who go often to the beach parks for an open-air dinner. You can buy a very inexpensive charcoal grill at many variety stores throughout Maui. It's a great idea to take along a **lantern.** This will give car campers added safety. Definitely take a **flashlight,** replacement batteries, and a few small **candles.** A complete **first-aid kit** can mean the difference between life and death and is worth the extra bulk.

Hikers, especially those leaving the coastal areas, should take rain gear, a plastic ground cloth, utility knife, compass, safety whistle, mess kit, water purification tablets, biodegradable "Camp Suds" or similar soap, canteen, nylon twine, sewing kit (dental floss works as thread), and waterproof matches (buy matches in Hawaii because it is illegal to take flammables on an airplane). In a film container, pack a few nails, safety pins, fishhooks, line, and bendable wire. Nothing else does what these do, and they're all handy for a million and one uses. If you find a staff or hiking stick at the beginning of a trail, consider using it—others obviously found it useful—but leave it at the trailhead for others to use when you return.

Equipment Sales

You can find only a few stores that sell **camping and hiking equipment** on Maui, and it seems that no one currently rents equipment. For sales, try **Sports Authority, Costco,** and **Kmart** in Kahului.

Hiking Tours

Hike Maui, P.O. Box 330969, Kahului, Maui, HI 96733, 808/879-5270, fax 808/893-2515, hikemaui@hikemaui.com, www.hikemaui.com, as its name implies, offers walking tours to Maui's best scenic areas accompanied by Ken Schmitt, a professional nature guide, or one of his fine staff. Ken has dedicated years to hiking Maui and has accumulated an unbelievable amount of knowledge about this awesome island. He's proficient in Maui archaeology, botany, geology, anthropology, zoology, history, oceanography, and ancient Hawaiian cosmology, and the hikes are actually workshops in Maui's natural history. Ken has ex-

panded his operation to include a small hand-picked staff of assistants, each trained in the sciences, with the soul of an adventurer and the heart of an environmentalist. The hikes require a minimum of four people and a maximum of eight. All special equipment is provided, but you are requested to wear comfortable walking/hiking shoes. Gourmet lunches and fruits are provided. These hikes take in sights from Hana to West Maui, the coast, forest, and crater summit of Haleakala, and range from the moderate to the hardy ability level. Good physical conditioning is essential. Half-day hikes last about five hours, and all-day hikes go for eight hours or more. The rates vary from $61–140. A day with Ken Schmitt or one of his dedicated guides is a classic outdoor experience. You'll be in the hands of experts. Don't miss it!

Mango Mitch Ecotours is another well-established company that offers small groups customized half-day, full-day, and overnight hikes, kayak trips, 4WD excursions, as well as multiple-day expeditions to other islands. Half-day hikes and snorkel trips run $60–70; the full-day Hana-area hike and swim is $90. An overnight in Haleakala Crater runs $120. Call for information on other options and multiday trips. For Maui tours, refreshments and some gear are provided; all meals and equipment are provided on the overnight tours. Aside from the hiking experience itself, Mango Mitch imparts knowledge about Hawaii's natural history and culture to all his guests. For more information, contact P.O. Box 2511, Wailuku, HI 96793, 808/873-1848.

Maui Hiking Safaris, P.O. Box 11198, Lahaina, HI 96761, 808/573-0168 or 888/445-3963, fax 808/572-3037, mhs@maui.net, www.mauihikingsafaris.com, also offers organized group hikes led by Randy Weaver for $59–69 per half day or $89–99 for a full day, all gear, snacks, and beverages provided. Various hikes are offered through valleys and forests, to waterfalls and up along ridges, and each hike is narrated with special attention to history and botany. Hikes generally are 4–8 miles in length, and groups go with no more than six people.

Paths in Paradise offers a full range of hikes, easy to strenuous, from half day to full day, most on Haleakala and its slope, with an emphasis on natural history and birds. Fees run $95–150. All food and necessary gear are provided. Hikes are led by Renate Gassmann-Duvall, Ph.D.; tours in German are available. For information and reservations, contact P.O. Box 667, Makawao, HI 96768, 808/573-2022, fax 808/573-2021, renate@lava.net, www.maui.net/~corvusco.

Latitudes & Attitudes offers hikes on West Maui and Haleakala. Usually 4–6 hours in length, covering 2–6 miles, these hikes take you to a private arboretum tucked up the mountainside, into a valley used by ancient Hawaiians, through the thick jungle to a waterfall and the crater of Haleakala. Hikes are easy to moderate in endurance. Rates are $80–120 for adults, with a minimum of four needed for a hike. All hiking equipment and breakfast and/or lunch is provided, and there is hotel pickup in the Kapalua and Ka'anapali area. For information and reservations, contact the company at 808/661-7720 or 877/661-7720 or 877/661-7720, www.ecomaui.com.

Helpful Departments and Organizations

The **Department of Land and Natural Resources (DLNR),** Division of Forestry and Wildlife, 1151 Punchbowl St., Rm. 325, Honolulu, HI 96813, 808/587-0058, is helpful in providing trail maps, accessibility information, hunting and fishing regulations, and general forest rules. On Maui, contact the DLNR, Division of Forestry and Wildlife, 54 S. High St., Rm. 101, Wailuku, HI 96793, 808/984-8100. The department's *Maui Recreation Map* is useful and free. The following organizations can provide general information on wildlife, conservation, and organized hiking trips: **Sierra Club, Hawaii Chapter,** P.O. Box 2577, Honolulu, HI 96803; or the Sierra Club of Maui Group, 808/579-9802 or 808/573-4147 for the hike line, www.hi.sierraclub.org; and **Hawaiian Audubon Society,** 850 Richards St., Honolulu, HI 96813, 808/528-1432, for information about bird-watching hikes and other outings.

Hiking and Camping Books

Two helpful camping books are *Hawaii: A Camping Guide,* by George Cagala, and Richard McMahon's *Camping Hawaii.*

For well-written and detailed hiking guides complete with maps, check out *Maui Trails* by Kathy Morey and *Hiking Maui* by Robert Smith.

Topographical Maps and Nautical Charts

For detailed topographical maps, contact **U.S. Geological Survey, Information Services,** P.O. Box 25286, Denver, CO 80225, or call 888/ASK-USGS (888/275-8747), www.usgs.gov. Many types of maps are available at Borders Books at the Maui Marketplace mall in Kahului. Also useful, but not for hiking, are the University of Hawaii Press reference maps of each island. For nautical charts, write **National Ocean Service,** Greenbelt, MD 20770-1479, 301/436-8301 or 800/638-8972.

BEACHES

Because the island is blessed with 150 miles of coastline, more than 32 of which are wonderful beaches, your biggest problem is to choose which one you'll grace with your presence. All beaches are open to the public. Most are accessed through beach parks, but some access is over private property. All hotels and condominiums must by law offer pathway access to beaches they front, and each has some parking set aside for public use. The following should help you choose just where you'd like to romp about. But before you romp, pick up and read the brochures *Maui Beach Safety Tips,* by the American Red Cross, and *Beach and Ocean Safety Information,* both found at most free information stands around the island.

Generally speaking, beaches and shorelines on the north and west have high surf conditions and strong ocean currents during winter—use extreme caution—and those on the south and east experience some high surf during summer. A few county beaches have lifeguards. For lifeguard hours and locations in Maui County, call 808/270-6136. At some beaches, flags will warn you of ocean conditions. A yellow flag means use caution. A half-yellow, half-red sign signifies caution because of strong winds. A red flag indicates hazardous water conditions—beach closed, no swimming. In addition, yellow and black signs are sometimes posted at certain beaches to indicate other warnings: dangerous shore break, high surf spot, strong currents, presence of jellyfish, or beach closed.

Before you head to the beach, take a drive to the local shop for a cheap woven beach mat. Whalers General Store, ABC markets, other sundries shops, Longs Drug, Wal-Mart, Kmart, and the like have them for less than $2. Hotel sundries shops sometimes also carry the exact same thing for about a dollar more. On occasion, condos will have them to borrow, and often B&Bs and vacation rental homes will have them for guest use, but don't necessarily count on it.

West Maui Beaches

The most plentiful and best beaches for swimming and sunbathing are on West Maui, strung along 18 glorious miles from Kapalua to Olowalu. For all-purpose beaches, you can't beat **D.T. Fleming Beach, Kapalua Bay Beach,** or **Napili Beach** on Maui's western tip. They have everything: safe surf (except in winter), great swimming, snorkeling, and bodysurfing in a first-class, family-oriented area. Then comes **Ka'anapali Beach,** bordered by the hotels and condos, the most well-known beach on the island. Black Rock, at the Sheraton here, is the best for snorkeling. In Lahaina, **Lahaina Beach** is convenient but not private and just so-so. **Puamana Beach** and **Launiupoko Beach** have only fair swimming but great views and picnic areas. The beach at **Olowalu** has very good swimming and is one of the best and most accessible snorkeling spots on the island, while farther down, **Papalaua Wayside** offers camping and a nar-

Because the island is blessed with 150 miles of coastline, more than 32 of which are wonderful beaches, your biggest problem is to choose which one you'll grace with your presence. The most plentiful and best beaches for swimming are on West Maui.

row beach fringed by *kiawe* trees that surround tiny patches of white sand.

Kihei and Wailea Beaches

The 10 miles stretching from Ma'alaea to Wailea are dotted with beaches that range from poor to excellent. **Ma'alaea Beach** and **Kealia Beach** extend four miles from Ma'alaea to Kihei. These are excellent for walking, windsurfing, and enjoying the view, but little else. **Kama'ole Beach I, II,** and **III** are at the south end of Kihei. Top-notch beaches, they have it all—swimming, snorkeling, and safety. **Keawakapu Beach** is more of the same. Then come the great little crescent beaches of Wailea, which get more secluded as you head south: **Mokapu, Ulua, Wailea,** and **Polo.** All are surrounded by the picture-perfect hotels of Wailea and all have public access. **Makena Beach,** down the road from Wailea, is very special. It's one of the island's best. At one time, alternative-lifestyle people made Makena a haven, and it still attracts free-spirited souls. There's nude bathing in secluded coves, unofficial camping, and freedom. It gets the highest compliment when locals and those staying at hotels and condos around Maui come here to enjoy themselves.

Wailuku and Kahului Area

Poor ugly ducklings! The beaches in town are shallow and unattractive, and no one spends any time there. However, **Kanaha Beach** near the airport isn't bad at all, and it's a favorite of beginning windsurfers and kitesurfers. **H.P. Baldwin Beach** in Pa'ia has a reputation for hostile locals protecting their turf, but the beach is good and you won't be hassled if you "live and let live." **Ho'okipa Beach** just east of Pa'ia isn't good for the average swimmer, but it is the "Sailboarding Capital" of Hawaii, and you should visit here just to see the exciting, colorful spectacle of people skipping over the ocean with bright sails.

EXPLORING THE ISLANDS

Hana Beaches

Everything about Hana is heavenly, including its beaches. There's **Kaihalulu Beach,** almost too pretty to be real with its red cinder sand. Black-sand **Wai'anapanapa Beach,** surrounded by the state park and good for swimming and snorkeling, even provides a legendary cave whose waters turn blood red. **Hana Bay** is well protected and safe for swimming and kayaking. Just south of town is the white-sand **Hamoa Beach,** described by James Michener as looking like the South Pacific.

SCUBA

Maui is as beautiful from under the waves as it is above them. There is world-class snorkeling and diving at many coral reefs and beds surrounding the island. You'll find some of the best, coincidentally, just where the best beaches are: mainly from Kihei to Makena, up around Napili and Kapalua bays, and especially around Olowalu. For a total thrill, try diving Molokini, the submerged volcano off Makena, just peeking above the waves and designated a Marine Life Conservation District. There are underwater caves at Nahuna ("Five Graves") Point, just up from Makena landing; magnificent caves, arches, and lava tubes out at Lana'i. *Only* advanced divers should attempt the back side of West Maui, the coast at Kipahulu, and beyond Pu'uiki Island in Hana Bay. For these and other locations, with a brief description, check out the Maui Dive Shop's pamphlet, *Maui Dive Guide.*

With a name like Chuck Thorne, what else can you expect but a world-class athlete of some kind? Well, Chuck is a diver who lives on Maui and receives the highest accolades from his peers. He's written *The Divers' Guide to Maui,* the definitive book on all the best dive/snorkel spots on the island. He's a no-nonsense kind of guy who's out to show you some great spots, but he never forgets about safety first. Although he's no longer available as a guide, his book is still available at many scuba outlets, or you can write for it direct: Maui Dive Guide, P.O. Box 40, Hana, HI 96713. This book is an invaluable resource, well worth the money and the effort to check it out.

WATER SAFETY TIPS

Observe the water before you enter. Note where others are swimming or snorkeling and go there. Don't turn your back on the water. Dive under incoming waves before they reach you. Come in *before* you get tired.

When the wind comes up, get out. Stay out of the water during periods of high surf. High surf often creates riptides that can pull you out to sea. If you get caught in a riptide, don't panic. Swim parallel to the shore until you are out of the strong pull. Be aware of ocean currents, especially those within reefs that can cause riptides when the water washes out a channel.

If you are using water equipment, make sure it all works properly. Wear a T-shirt when snorkeling; it could save you from a major sunburn.

Stay off coral. Standing on coral damages it, as does breaking it with your hands.

Leave the fish and turtles alone. Green sea turtles are an endangered species, and a fine of up to $10,000 can be levied on those who knowingly disturb them. Have a great time looking, but give them space.

The number and variety of scuba options is astounding, with each company seemingly offering something slightly different. Generally, you're looking at $80–90 for an introductory dive, $70–90 for a beach dive, $70–80 for a night dive, $100 for a scooter dive, and $100–150 for boat dives. Several Maui companies take you from your first dive to PADI, NAUI, or NASDS certification. Prices range from inexpensive quickie refresher dive up to three- to five-day certification courses for $300–600. Shops also rent equipment and fill tanks. You might also consider buying an underwater camera for $15–20.

Scuba Shops and Tour Companies

Many boats will take you out diving. Some also do snorkel trips, deep-sea fishing, moonlight cruises, and other charters. A few rafting and kayak companies also offer dives as part of their package. All "activities centers" on the island can arrange these excursions for no extra charge. Although there is some crossover, boats leaving from Lahaina Harbor typically go to Lana'i or to spots along the west and north Maui coast to dive; those out of Ma'alaea or Makena go to Molokini or along the south coast of Maui. Companies that do shore dives pick their spot according to ocean conditions and the weather.

Mike Severns Diving, 808/879-6596, www.mikesevernsdiving.com, is one of the most experienced and respected diving companies on Maui. Mike is a marine scientist/explorer who's extremely knowledgeable about Maui both above and below the waves. He has his own boat and accepts both beginning and advanced divers, and he dives mostly along the south coast. Diving with Mike is an extraordinary educational experience. The two-tank dives run $120 and leave from the Kihei boat ramp; no snorkel tours. Special three-tank and night dives can be accommodated.

Ed Robinson's Diving Adventures, 808/879-3584 or 800/635-1273, www.mauiscuba.com, offers a great deal for those staying in South Maui. The company runs tours from two fully equipped boats to spots mostly in South Maui and to Molokini and Lana'i. Offered are introductory and refresher dives, certification, and two- and three-tank boat dives.

The **Maui Dive Shop,** 1455 S. Kihei Rd., 808/879-3388 or 800/542-3483, www.mauidiveshop.com, with its six other locations in Kihei and Lahaina, is Maui's largest scuba operation. The retail outlet is a full-service water sports store, and it and all locations offer a variety of shore and boat dives along with certification. Rates are moderate, and your experience will be memorable.

Scuba Shack, 2349 S. Kihei Rd., 808/879-3483, www.scubashack.com, has a shop with all the gear and offers numerous boat and shore dives plus classes at competitive rates. No hype, just personalized service with plenty of experience.

Lahaina Divers, 143 Dickenson St., Lahaina, next to Pacific Whale Foundation, 808/667-7496 or 800/998-3483, www.lahainadivers.com, offers a snorkeling experience, various scuba dives to Lana'i, Molokini, and the Maui coast, night dives, and certification courses. Lahaina Divers uses its own boats for all of the excursions and offers beverages and snacks on all trips. This company is well regarded and has an established reputation. Boats leave from Lahaina Harbor.

Pacific Dive, 150 Dickenson St., Lahaina, 808/667-5331 or 877/667-7331, www.pacificdive.com, offers open-water certification classes, beach dives, boat dives, night dives, and scooter dives. This full-service scuba/snorkel store offers daily rentals on scuba and snorkel equipment, boogie boards, and other water gear, and also has a complete repair facility and air fill station for those who are already certified. Nitrox is available.

Dive Maui, 900 Front St., Lahaina, 808/667-2080 or 866/281-7450, www.divemauiscuba.com, covers the whole range of shore and boat dives, night dives, certification, snorkel trips, and rentals. Boats leave from the most convenient boat ramp or pier.

Among the many other companies in South Maui, check out **Makena Coast Charters,** 808/874-1273 or 800/833-6483, or **Dive and Sea Maui,** 808/874-1952. In West Maui, try **Tropical Divers Maui,** 808/669-6284; **Extended Horizons,** 808/667-0611 or 888/348-3628; or **Maui Diving,** 808/667-0633 or 800/959-7319.

SNORKEL AND SNUBA

Use the same caution when scuba diving or snorkeling as when swimming. Be mindful of currents. It's generally safer to enter the water in the center of a bay than at the sides where ripcurrents are more likely to occur. The following sites are suitable for beginners to intermediates: on Maui's western tip Honolua Bay and nearby Mokule'ia Bay, both part of a Marine Life Conservation District; Kapalua and Napili bays for usually good and safe conditions; in Ka'anapali you'll enjoy Black Rock at the Sheraton Hotel; at Olowalu, the ocean is very gentle with plenty to see. Also try the rocky headlands between the Kama'ole beaches in Kihei and farther down between the beaches

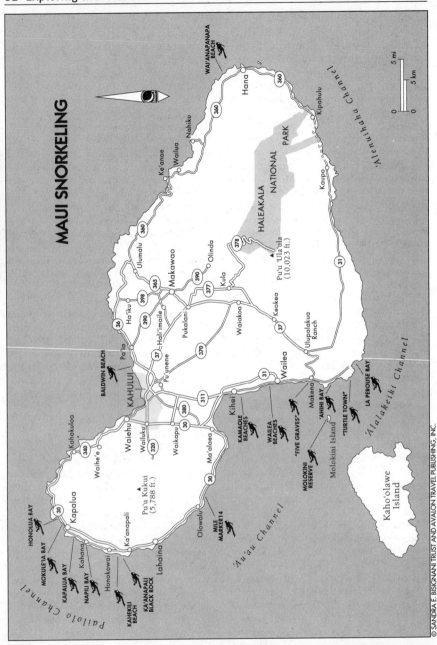

MAUI SNORKELING

WAI'ANAPANAPA BEACH

Nahiku

Hana

360

360

Wailua

Ke'anae

Kipahulu

HALEAKALA NATIONAL PARK

Ulumalu

Makawao

Olinda

378

Pu'u 'Ula'ula
(10,023 ft.)

365

398

Ha'iku

390

Pa'ia

390

Holi'imaile

377

Kula

Pukalani

31

BALDWIN BEACH

36

37

Pu'unene

370

Waiakoa

Keokea

37

Waiohuli

Ranch

KAHULUI

311

Kihei

31

Wailea

Ulupalakua
Ranch

Waiehu

Waikapu

30

380

320

Waikapu

Kahakuloa

340

Waihe'e

KAMAOLE BEACHES

WAILEA BEACHES

Makena

'AHIHI BAY

LA PEROUSE BAY

Kapalua

Pu'u Kukui
(5,788 ft.)

Ka'anapali

Ma'alaea

30

"FIVE GRAVES"

MOLOKINI
RESERVE

Molokini Island

"TURTLE TOWN"

HONOLUA BAY

30

MOKULE'IA BAY

KAPALUA BAY

NAPILI BAY

Kahana

Honokowai

Olowalu

MILE
MARKER 14

Kaho'olawe
Island

KAHEKILI
BEACH

KA'ANAPALI
BLACK ROCK

Lahaina

Pailolo Channel

'Au'au Channel

'Alalakeiki Channel

'Alenuihaha Channel

5 mi

5 km

in Wailea. 'Ahihi Bay and La Pérouse Bay in South Maui are great spots and fairly isolated. On the windward side, Waihe'e Beach north of Wailuku, Baldwin Beach in Pa'ia, and Wai'anapanapa State Park beach near Hana are generally good. Under no circumstances should you miss taking a boat out to Molokini. It's worth every penny, even though it's getting rather crowded! Some boats also stop at **Turtle Town** off of Maui's last lava flow. Manele and Hulopo'e bays on Lana'i are like aquariums, both also a Marine Life Conservation District. And there are plenty more.

Equipment

Sometimes condos and hotels have snorkeling equipment free for their guests, but if you have to rent it, don't do it from a hotel or condo; go to a snorkel or dive shop where it's much cheaper. Expect to spend $5–10 per day for mask, fins, and snorkel, or $25–30 per week.

One of the best snorkel deals is through **Snorkel Bob's,** 808/879-7449 in Kihei, 808/667-2553 in Lahaina, and 808/669-9603 in Napili, www.snorkelbob.com. Old Snorkel Bob will dispense information and full snorkel gear for only $9–29 per week. Add $7 per week if you add a dry snorkel tube. You can return it to any store on Maui or on a Neighbor Island if you'll be heading off Maui before the week is up. Daily rates are similarly reasonable. Slick-bottom boogie boards run $26 per week, and other water gear are also available for rent.

A & B Rentals and Sportswear, in Honokowai at the Da Rose Mall, 808/669-0027, open daily 9 A.M.–5 P.M., rents snorkel gear for $2.50 per day and $9 per week, as well as boogie boards.

Located in the Kahana Plaza, **Boss Frogs** 808/669-6700, has snorkel gear for $2.50–9 per day or $9–30 per week. This shop also rents surfboards, boogie boards, and bikes. Boss Frogs also has shops in Napili, Lahaina, and Kihei.

West Maui Sports, behind Lahaina Cannery mall, 808/661-6252, rents ordinary snorkel gear for $2.50 per day or $10 per week. Also rent bodyboards, kayaks, beach gear, and golf clubs.

In Lahaina, try **Duke's Rental Shop,** along Front Street at the south end of downtown, for snorkel gear at $3 per day, as well as surfboards, bikes, golf clubs, and an assortment of other items.

Numerous other shops on the island also rent snorkel gear at comparable but variable rates depending on the quality of the equipment. Some also sell snorkel gear, as do the Sports Authority, Wal-Mart, and other large shops in Kahului, where you can find a set from about $20 and up depending on the quality.

Snorkel Excursions

For a pure snorkeling adventure, unlike those offered by the tour boats, try **Snorkel Maui,** 808/572-8437, www.maui.net/~annf, with Ann Fielding, the naturalist author of *Hawaiian Reefs and Tide Pools* and *An Underwater Guide to Hawai'i,* which details many of the invertebrates and reef fish you will encounter on one of her fantastic dives. Ms. Fielding will instruct you in snorkeling and in the natural history and biology of what you'll be seeing below the waves. She tailors the dive to fit the participants. A basic half-day morning snorkel dive costs $85 adults, $75 kids.

Literally dozens of snorkel boat excursions take place in Maui's waters every week. Most boats leave either from Lahaina or Ma'alaea harbors, while others leave from the beaches that front the large hotels of Ka'anapali, Wailea, and Makena. Catamarans, monohulls, sailing ships, power boats, or rafts: They come in all shapes and sizes. Prices range from $50–80 for half-day adventures; full-day tours with lunch and sail are around $150.

For a magnificent day of sailing, exploring, and snorkeling, you can't beat **Trilogy Excursions,** 808/661-4743 or 888/628-4800, whose sleek catamarans leave Lahaina Harbor for a day trip to Lanai, Ma'alaea Harbor for Molokini, or Ka'anapali Beach for trips up the coast.

Others to check out are *Pride of Maui,* 808/242-0955; **Classic Charters'** *Four Winds II,* 808/879-8188; **Island Marine Activities'** *Lahaina Princess,* 808/661-8397; *Prince Kuhio,* 808/242-8777; *Blue Dolphin,* 808/661-3333; or **Boss Frog's** *Frogman,* 808/874-6325.

EXPLORING THE ISLANDS

REEF FISH

Achilles tang

red-lipped parrotfish

moorish idol

Hawaiian lionfish

lagoon *humu*

manini

blue-spotted cowfish

bluestripe butterflyfish

Potter's angelfish

threadfin butterflyfish

trumpetfish

saddleback wrasse

mottled moray

manta ray

uhu

Snuba

No, that's not a typo. Snuba is half snorkeling and half scuba diving. You wear a regulator, weight belt, mask, and flippers, and you're tethered to scuba tanks that float 20 feet above you on a sea-sled. The idea is that many people become anxious diving under the waves encumbered by tanks and all the scuba apparatus. Snuba frees you. You would think that being tethered to the sled would slow you down, but actually you're sleeker and can make better time than a normal scuba diver. If you would like to start diving, this is a wonderful and easy way to begin. Try **The Four Winds,** 808/879-8188, a snorkel-dive boat that goes to Molokini Crater; **Island Scuba,** 808/667-4608; or the kayak company **Maui Eco-tours,** 808/891-2223. A few other outfits are now starting to offer snuba on Maui. A snuba experience will run $45–70, depending on whether it's part of a boat tour or an activity by itself.

MORE WATER SPORTS

Bodysurfing

All you need are the right wave conditions and a sandy beach to have a ball bodysurfing and boogie boarding. Always check conditions first because bodysurfing has led to some very serious neck and back injuries for the ill-prepared. The following are some decent beaches: Ulua, Wailea, Polo, or Makena, the north end of Kama'ole Beach Park I in Kihei, Napili Bay, D. T. Fleming, and Baldwin Park. Typical boogie board rental prices are $5 per day to $25 per week—similar to the rate for snorkel gear. If you want to buy a board, head for Sports Authority, Wal-Mart, and smaller water sports shops where body boards are available for about $50 and up.

Surfing

While the north coast of O'ahu is known as the best surfing area in Hawaii—and arguably the best in the world—Maui has a few decent spots for the enthusiast. For good surfing on Maui, try Honolua Bay, Napili Bay, Lahaina Harbor, Ma'alaea Harbor, and Ho'okipa Beach, but surfers find acceptable waves all around the island. Beginners should stay at the more gentle beaches

between Lahaina and Olowalu, Launiupoko Park, and the beaches in Kihei.

Maui does have one spot, however, that has gained worldwide notoriety over the last several years. This is "Jaws." Jaws is a place where, on a good day, waves rise 30–50 feet high! The conventional method of catching a wave—paddling belly down on your board until you gain enough speed and momentum to slip down the front of the wave—doesn't work here because of the height and speed of these waves. Ingenious (and maybe a bit crazy) surfers have come up with a solution: Use a jet ski to gain speed and tow the surfer to the right spot before dashing out of harm's way. Some surfers use the tow rope as a big slingshot to propel themselves even faster from behind the jet ski. Some surfboards used at Jaws have straps for the feet similar to a sailboard. So far, no one has died in this highly risky endeavor, but it seems likely that over time someone will bite it big. Jaws is located about 10 minutes past Ho'okipa Beach on the road to Hana and then down a road toward the ocean. People are reluctant to give the exact location, although locals know the spot well. Some fear, and rightly so, that inexperienced surfers will give this monster a try, but homeowners in the area just don't like the traffic and congestion. On a high surf day, there may be as many as 350 cars parked on the approach road.

Surfing Instruction

There are more than two dozen shops on Maui that rent surfboards and perhaps a dozen or more companies and additional individuals that teach the basics of surfing. Some are listed as follows. You can get surfing lessons in groups or individually. Lessons generally run in the vicinity of $60–80 for a group lesson that lasts about two hours or about $100–160 for a private lesson. Many lessons are taught directly south of Lahaina Harbor, while some instruction is done at the beach parks between Lahaina and Olowalu or in Kihei. The surfing schools offer several quality multiday packages.

A "learn in one day" guarantee is offered by the well-respected **Nancy Emerson School of Surfing,** 808/244-7873 or 808/662-4445, www.surfclinics.com. Nancy and her instructors offer lessons just to the side of Lahaina harbor. The **Surf School on Kaanapali Beach,** 808/244-6858, www.mauisurfschool.com, offers lessons in Ka'anapali Beach. Also in Lahaina are **Goofy Foot,** 808/244-9283; **Surf Dog Maui,** 808/250-7873, www.surfdogmaui.com; and **Outragious Adventures,** 808/669-1400, www.you-cansurf.com. In Kihei, call **Maui Waveriders,** 808/875-4761, www.mauiwaveriders.com; or **Big Kahuna,** 808/875-6395, www.bigkahunaadventures.com.

Sailboarding

Ho'okipa Beach, just east of Pa'ia, is the "Sailboarding Capital of the World," and the big-money championship used to be held here every year in March and April. Today, the **Aloha Classic,** held in late October or early November, with prize money at $5,000–10,000, is as big as it gets. Smaller local and national competitions are held in spring and winter, usually at Kooks Beach, Kanaha Beach Park, in Kahului, but for details ask at any of the big windsurfing shops on the island.

Kanaha Beach Park has perfect gentle winds and waves for learning the sport, and the beach at Spreckelsville has virtually the same characteristics. Summer is best for windsurfing because of the characteristics of the winds, which blow steadily from the east. Mornings are good for the novice and for instruction because winds are lighter. As winds and chop pick up in the afternoon, the more advanced board riders hit the water. Any sailboard shop will point you in the right direction for location and gear according to your skill level. When the winds come from the south, most windsurfers head to the north end of Kihei and set in at Mai Poina 'Oe La'u Beach park to sail on Ma'alaea Bay. Sometimes in the winter, you'll see boarders out on the water with the whales. Wherever you decide to try the water, pick up a copy of *Guidelines For Windsurfing on Maui* before you put together your gear—if you can find one.

Rental equipment with a board and one mast runs roughly $30 per day or $50 with two sails, up to $350–550 for two weeks, depending on the quality of gear. Group lessons for three or more usually run 2–3 hours, and private lessons that

Strong and consistent trade winds make the beaches of central Maui some of the best in the world for the sport of sailboarding.

ROBERT NILSEN

run 1–2 hours will be about $70–80. Remember: Start with a big board and a small sail! Take lessons to save time and energy. To rent equipment or take instructions, try **Maui Windsurf Company,** 808/877-4816 or 800/872-0999. Several others to try, with comparable rates for lessons and rentals, are **Hi-Tech Surf Sports,** 808/877-2111, www.htmaui.com; **Second Wind,** 808/877-7467 or 800/936-7787, www.maui.net/~secwind; **Neilpryde Maui,** 808/877-7443 or 800/321-7443, www.neilprydemaui.com; **Extreme Sports Maui,** 808/871-7954 or 877/376-6284, www.extremesportsmaui.com; **Hawaiian Island Surf and Sports,** 808/871-4981 or 800/231-6958, www.hawaiianisland.com; **Sailboards Maui,** 808/579-8432; and **Simmer Hawaii,** 808/879-8484. For lessons only, inquire at one of the shops or directly with **Alan Cadiz's HST,** 808/871-5423 or 800/968-5423, www.hstwindsurfing.com; or **Action Sports Maui,** 808/871-1590, www.actionsportsmaui.com. **Al West's,** 808/877-0090 or 800/870-4084, www.mauivans.com, also does lessons and rents vans to transport your gear.

Kiteboarding

A cross between wakeboarding and flying a kite, kiteboarding (also known as kitesurfing) is one of the newest water sports to hit the island. If you want to see it, head for "Kite Beach," just west of Kanaha Beach park in Kahului.

Lessons are offered by several shops in Kahului that run from a three-hour introductory lesson to a five-day advanced course. For most, the three-hour course works best and will run about $240. Rental gear is also available at local shops. If you decide to really get into the sport, you can get set up for about $1,000. Perhaps the premier organization offering lessons and equipment is the **Kiteboarding School of Maui,** 22 Hana Hwy., www.ksmaui.com. Others are **Second Wind,** 808/877-7467 or 800/936-7787, www.secondwindmaui.com; and **Hawaiian Islands Surf and Sport,** 808/871-4981 or 800/231-6958, www.kitesails.com. If you are new on the island, be sure to familiarize yourself with kitesurfing regulations. Pick up a copy of the *Safe Kiteboarding Guidelines* printed by the Maui Kiteboarding Association and available at shops that rent or sell kiteboarding equipment, or check the association's website at www.maui.net/~hotwind/mka.html.

THRILL CRAFT

Usually the term "thrill craft" refers to jet skis, water-ski boats, speedboats, parasailing, and other such motorized watercraft. In years past, a controversy raged about their use. The feeling among conservationists was that these craft disturb humans, and during whale season they disturb the whales that come to winter over in the rather small Lahaina Roads and Ma'alaea Bay. This is definitely a case of "one man's pleasure is another man's poison." On March 31, 1991, a law was passed that bans these type of crafts from operating in west and south Maui waters during whale season, December 15 through May 15. Although you might assume that this is due to the sound of the motors roaring through the waters—some research has also been done to determine if this too is a problem—the restriction was set in place because of the speed and unpredictable nature of these watercraft.

Jet Skis

To try this exciting sport in season, contact **Pacific Jet Sports,** 808/667-2001, for use of jet skis and waverunners. From 9 A.M.–4 P.M. daily, you can meet their shuttle boat on the beach in front of the Hyatt Hotel in Ka'anapali, and it will take you out to their pontoon and riding area, where you'll get instruction on how to operate these machines. Rates are $50 per half hour or $78 per hour, and $13 extra for each additional person up to three for the waverunners. You must be 15 years old to operate.

Parasailing

If you've ever wanted to soar like an eagle, here's your chance with no prior experience necessary. Basically a parasail is a parachute tethered to a speedboat. And away we go! The most dangerous part seems to be getting in and out of the boat when you leave the harbor. On the powerboat is a special harness attached to a parachute. You're put in a life vest and strapped to the harness that forms a cradle on which you sit while aloft. Make sure, once you're up, to pull the cradle as far under your thighs as you can. It's much more comfortable. Don't be afraid to loosen your steel grip on the guide ropes because that's not what's holding you anyway. In the air, you are as free as a bird and the unique view is phenomenal. You don't have time to fret about going up. The boat revs and you're airborne almost immediately. Once up, the feeling is very secure. The technology is simple, straightforward, and safe. Relax and have a ball. Cost is about $60–70 for a 10-minute joyride that lets out about 800 feet of line or $40–50 for a seven-minute ride where you are at the end of a 400-foot line. Some pull singles only; others take doubles. **UFO Parasail,** 808/661-7UFO or 800/359-4UFO, operates on Ka'anapali Beach; **Parasail Kaanapali,** 808/669-6555, leaves from Mala Wharf; and **Parasail in Paradise,** 808/661-4060, uses a slip in the Lahaina Harbor.

EXPLORING THE ISLANDS

OCEAN TOURS

You haven't really seen Maui unless you've seen it from the sea. Tour boats take you fishing, sailing, whale-watching, dining, diving, and snorkeling. You can find powerboats, sailboats, catamarans, and Zodiac rafts that offer a combination of some or all of these options or just sail you around for pure pleasure. Maui presents one of the premier sailing venues in the Pacific. Many take day trips to Lana'i. Others visit Molokini, a submerged volcano with only half the crater rim above water, which has been designated a Marine Life Conservation District. Most of Maui's pleasure boats are berthed in Lahaina Harbor, and most have a booth right there on the wharf where you can sign up. Many other boats come out of Ma'alaea Harbor, and a few companies are based in Kihei. The following are basically limited to sailing/dining/touring activities, with snorkeling often part of the experience. To add to the mix, there are even a few submarine tour possibilities, where you can see underwater sights without getting wet.

A cruise or snorkel trip is a popular activity on Maui.

Excursions/Dinner Sails

Trilogy, 808/661-4743 or 888/628-4800, www.sailtrilogy.com, founded and operated by the Coon Family, is a success in every way, and its cruises are the best on Maui. Although the hand-picked crews have made the journey countless times, they never forget that it's your first time. They run catamarans that carry up to 50 passengers, and once aboard, you're served refreshments and Mama Coon's famous cinnamon rolls. The Discover Lana'i tour leaves Lahaina Harbor weekdays. Once at Lana'i, you can frolic at Hulopo'e Bay, which is great for swimming and renowned as an excellent snorkeling area. Scuba and kayaking are also options. All gear is provided. While you play, the crew is busy at work preparing a delicious barbecue at the picnic facilities at Manele Harbor. You couldn't have a more memorable or enjoyable experience than sailing with Trilogy. But don't spoil your day; be sure to bring along (and use!) a wide-brim hat, sunglasses, sunscreen, a long-sleeve shirt, and a towel. For this full day's experience, adults

pay $169, children (3–15) half price. Leaving later in the day is the Discover Lana'i Sunset Sail for the same price. Trilogy Excursions also runs a popular half-day trip to Molokini Crater, sailing daily from Ma'alaea Harbor, adults $95, children half price, which includes breakfast, lunch, and all snorkeling gear; a five-hour midday picnic sail from Ka'anapali Beach for $95; two-hour whale-watching sails during whale season, also from Ka'anapali Beach for $39; and a Saturday all-day Zodiac tour to Lana'i with Jeep tour of the island for $199. Trilogy periodically adds new adventures to its lineup, so explore the options.

If you've had enough of Front Street Lahaina, **Club Lanai,** 808/667-9595 or 800/531-5262, is a Maui-based company with two boats that run day excursions and do whale-watching, sunset cocktail, and sunset dinner cruises, too. You board your catamaran at Lahaina Harbor, leaving at 7 A.M. and returning at around 3:30 P.M. after a full day. En route you're served a breakfast. The club provides you with snorkel gear, and scuba diving can also be arranged at an extra charge. Family oriented with plenty of activities for children of all ages, Club Lanai lets you set your own pace—do it all, or do nothing at all. Departing in the late afternoon, the sunset cocktail and dinner cruises bring an easy end to a busy day.

Pacific Whale Foundation, 808/249-8811, www.pacificwhale.org, runs four powered catamarans out of the Lahaina and Ma'alaea harbors. All trips to Lana'i and Molokini involve snorkeling and dolphin encounters, with whale-watching in season. Trips to Lana'i run $37–75, a snorkel trip to Molokini is $64, and whale-watch trips in season from Lahaina and Ma'alaea harbors go for $20. In addition, the *Manute'a*, a 50-foot catamaran, runs from Lahaina Harbor for a sunset dinner sail for $49.95. Kids 4–12 go free with a paying adult, and it's half price for additional children the same age. This eco-friendly company has great credibility. Three of their boats are powered by biofuel—reprocessed vegetable oil.

The *Prince Kuhio,* 800/242-8777 or 800/468-1287, offers a different kind of trip altogether. Comfort, luxury, and stability come with this 92-foot monohull ship. Departing from Ma'alaea Harbor daily, the *Prince Kuhio* does a four-hour snorkel cruise to Molokini and turtle town ($84 adults, $48 children 5–15), including a continental breakfast, buffet lunch, open bar, and champagne on the return voyage. In season, the *Prince Kuhio* also does whale-watch cruises for $21. A similar large ship that also does the Molokini trip is *Lahaina Princess,* 808/667-6165.

The 44-foot catamaran *Frogman,* 808/662-0075, and its partner *Blue Dolphin* depart from Ma'alaea Harbor for trips to Molokini. The glass-bottom *Four Winds* does similar morning and afternoon cruises for $40–78, as do *The Pride of Maui,* 808/242-0955, and Friendly Charter's *Lani Kai,* 808/244-1979. The quickest way to Molokini, which means more time in the water, is aboard the catamaran *Kai Kanani,* 808/879-7218, which departs from in front of the Maui Prince Hotel in Makena. Equipment and food are provided. Other resort catamarans leave from westside beaches, all doing a combination of snorkel sails, sunset cruises, and private charters. These sunset tours generally run about $60, and half-day snorkel tours are around $80. *Teralani* and *Teralani II* leave from Ka'anapali Beach in front of Whalers Village, *Gemini* from the Westin Maui, and *Kiele V* from the Hyatt Regency. Up

EXPLORING THE ISLANDS

SEASICKNESS

Many people are affected by motion sickness, particularly on sailing vessels. If you tend to get queasy, try one of the following to prevent symptoms.

Oral medications widely available through pharmacies are **Dramamine, Bonine,** and **Triptone.** Running about $4 a pop, Dramamine and Bonine may cause drowsiness in some people, but Triptone seems not to. Although these medications are usually taken just before boarding a ship, they might work better if one half-dose is taken the night before and the second half-dose is taken the morning of your ride. In all cases, however, take medication as prescribed by the manufacturer.

For those who don't want to take medication, try **Seabands,** an elastic band worn around the wrist that puts gentle pressure on the inside of the wrist by way of a small plastic button. Seabands are also available at pharmacies and at most scuba shops for about $8.50 and can be reused until the elastic wears out. Follow directions for best results.

Without medication or pressure bands, you can still work to counter the effects of motion sickness. The night before, try not to eat too much, particularly greasy food, and don't drink an excess of alcohol. If your stomach begins to feel upset, try eating a few soda crackers. If you begin to feel dizzy, focus on the horizon or a mountain top—something stationary—and try to direct your thoughts to something other than your dizziness or queasiness. With children (and perhaps adults as well), talking about what animal figures they can see in the clouds or how many houses they can spot along the shoreline may be enough to distract them for a time to begin feeling better.

the coast, the *Kapalua Kai* sails from the Ka-palua Bay Hotel.

Scotch Mist Sailing Charters, 808/661-0386, has one racing yacht, *The Scotch Mist II*. It is the oldest sailing charter on Maui (since 1970) and claims to have the fastest monohull sailboat in Lahaina Harbor, boasting the lightest boat, the biggest sail, and the best crew. A sail/snorkel in the morning costs $60 per person; the afternoon sail-ing trip is best to catch the trade winds; or take the sunset sail (up to 25 passengers) for $35 per per-son. A champagne and chocolate sunset cruise also runs for $40. When the season is right, whale-watching sails are also offered for $25–40.

Other sailing ships that do a variety of snorkel, sunset, or sailing tours include the following: The sloops *Flexible Flyer,* 808/244-6655, and *Cinderella,* 808/244-0009, also leave from Ma'alaea Harbor. The *Flexible Flyer* charges $142 per person with a six-guest capacity to $660 for the boat on a five-hour run. Also with six pas-sengers maximum, the *Cinderella* charges $135 per person for short tours. The entire ship can be chartered at the rate of $400 for four hours, $800 for a full day, or $360 for a two-hour sunset run. America's Cup contender *America II,* 808/667-2195, sailing out of Lahaina Harbor, can carry up to 28 passengers, leaves twice daily at $33 per person, and runs $32.95 for a sunset sail. **Paragon Sailing Charters,** 808/244-2087, runs their two catamarans on a twice-daily snorkel and sail schedule with evening sunset sails for $51–149 per person. Running private charters only, the rate for *Island Star,* 808/669-7827, runs $500–3,000.

Sunset cruises are very romantic and very pop-ular. They last for about two hours and cost $40–70 for the basic cruise, but for a dinner sail expect to spend $70–90. Remember, too, that the larger established companies are usually on Maui to stay, but that smaller companies come and go with the tide! The big 149-passenger *Maui Princess,* 808/667-6165, offers dinner cruises aboard its sleek 118-foot motor yacht for $79 ($59 children), which includes open bar, dinner, entertainment, and dancing. **Windjam-mer,** 808/661-8600, also does a salmon and prime rib dinner cruise for $75 on its 93-pas-senger three-masted schooner, with sailings daily at 5:30 P.M. and 7:30 P.M. Others to check out are the sunset cocktail cruise on the *Pride of Maui,* Is-land Marine's barefoot buffet sunset cruise, and sunset cruise, dinner sail, and dance party hosted by Club Lanai.

Some companies offer a variety of cocktail sails and whale-watches for much cheaper prices, but many tend to pack people in so tightly that they're known derisively as "cattle boats." Don't expect the personal attention you'd receive on smaller boats, and always check the number of passengers when booking.

Whale-Watching

Anyone on Maui from Nov.–Apr. gets the added treat of watching humpback whales as they frolic just off Lahaina, one of the world's major win-tering areas for the humpback. Almost every boat in the harbor runs a special whale-watch during this time of year. If you're susceptible to seasick-ness, take a ride in the morning because the water usually gets a little choppier in the afternoon.

Highly educational whale-watch trips are spon-sored by the **Pacific Whale Foundation,** Ma'alaea Harbor Village, 300 Maalaea Rd., Ste. 211, 96793, 808/249-8811, www.paci-ficwhale.org; open daily 6 A.M.–10 P.M. A non-profit organization founded in 1980, it is dedicated to research, education, and conserva-tion and is one of the only research organiza-tions that has been able to survive by generating its own funds through membership, donations, and excellent whale-watch cruises. The founda-tion has one of the best whale-watches on the island aboard its own ships, berthed for your convenience at Ma'alaea and Lahaina Harbors and going out several times daily. The scientists and researchers who make up the crew rotate shifts and come out on the whale-watch when they're not in the Lahaina Roads getting up close to identify, and make scientific observations of, the whales. Most of the information that the other whale-watches dispense to the tourists is generated by the Pacific Whale Foundation. The foundation also offers an "Adopt-a-Whale Pro-gram" and various reef and snorkel cruises that run throughout the year.

Rafting

For a totally different experience, try a rafting trip. Numerous rafting companies have sprung up in the last decade or more, so there's plenty of competition. These rafts are small rigid-bottom crafts with a sun shade that mostly seat 6–24 people. The vessels are highly maneuverable, totally seaworthy, high-tech motorized rafts whose main features are their speed and ability to get intimate with the sea as the supple form bends with the undulations of the water. You're right on the water, so you'll get wet, and you often ride right on the inflatable rubber tubes. Like boat tours, these rafts do one or a combination of tours that involve whale-watching, snorkeling, scuba, sea caves, coastal cruises, or the circumnavigation of Lana'i. For half-day rides, you can expect a charge of about $70–80; $110–135 for full-day adventures. Some shorter whale-watch runs last about two hours and run around $40–50.

The first company in Maui waters was **Blue Water Rafting,** 808/879-7238, www.bluewaterrafting.com, which departs from the Kihei Boat Ramp for trips along the rugged Makena coast or out to Molokini. Other options include **Ocean Rafting,** 808/661-7238 or 888/677-7238, www.hawaiioceanrafting.com, which heads to Lana'i; **Hawaiian Rafting Adventures,** 808/661-7333, www.hawaiianrafting.com, which leaves from Mala Wharf for Lana'i; **Ultimate Rafting,** 808/667-5678, www.ultimatewhalewatch.com, which leaves from the Lahaina Harbor and goes to Lana'i; and **Ocean Riders,** 808/661-3586, which leaves Mala Wharf for Lana'i or Moloka'i depending on the weather.

Submarine

Undersea adventures have also come to Maui. With *Atlantis Submarine,* 808/667-2224 or 800/548-6262, www.atlantisadventures.com, you can dive to more than 130 feet to view the undersea world through glass windows. The basic tour in this 48-passenger true submarine starts at $85 adults, $43 kids; you must be at least three feet tall to board. These trips leave from the Lahaina Harbor pier every hour from 9 A.M. and travel to the sub loading area about two miles

east of town. The trip underwater lasts about 50 minutes. Atlantis offers several combo packages with other island activity vendors.

The 34-passenger *Reefdancer,* 808/667-2133, www.galaxymall.com/stores/reefdancer, is a submersible that lets you view the underwater world from the depth of no more than 10 feet, but it's a great view nonetheless and you might see more fish. The *Reefdancer* leaves from Lahaina Harbor and fares run $33–45 for 60- and 90-minute tours.

Kayaking

Kayaking has also become quite popular over the last decade and more. Much of the kayaking is done in the Makena area, but some companies take trips to the north coast and other locations. **South Pacific Kayaks,** in the Rainbow Mall, 2439 S. Kihei Rd., 808/875-4848 or 800/776-2326, www.southpacifickayaks.com, offers a half-day introductory trip (with drinks and snacks) for $59, an advanced explorer trip along the remote coastline of South Maui (including drinks and full lunch) for $89, a shorter sunset trip for $55, and several location options. Tours include plenty of snorkeling opportunities as you glide in and out of tiny bays fashioned from jutting lava rock fingers. South Pacific Kayaks offers rentals and sales of single

OUTRIGGER CANOES

Historically, outrigger canoes have been made from the trunks of koa trees. Koa trees large enough to build a canoe out of are scarce these days, however, and most are legally protected. To have one made today from available logs would run $40,000–100,000. By far the majority of outrigger canoes in the islands these days are made from fiberglass. Much cheaper, they still must meet rigorous specifications. On Maui there are eight or nine canoe clubs, and most have 100-plus members. In all of Hawaii, outrigger canoeing is the team sport that has the greatest participation, with more than 10,000 active canoe club members in about 60 canoe clubs throughout the state.

and double kayaks, snorkel sets, and also offers hiking adventures.

Kelii's Kayak Tours, 808/874-7652, www.keliiskayak.com, has several tours to various sites around the island ranging $49–99. **Makena Kayak,** 808/879-8426, has two- to four-hour trips at Makena or the westside cliffs for $55–85. **Big Kahuna Kayak,** 808/875-6395, www.maui.net/~paddle, has two kayak tours in South Maui for $60–85, but also does surfing lessons, hiking tours, and outrigger canoe rides. **Maui Eco-tours,** 808/891-2223, www.mauiecotours.com, departs from La Pérouse Bay. **Pacific Coast Kayak,** 808/879-2391, also tours various Makena sites. Out in Hana, you can explore Hana Bay and the nearby coastline with **Hana-Maui Sea Sports,** 808/248-7711. If renting a kayak to go on your own, expect single kayaks to go for about $25 per day while tandem kayaks will be about $40 per day.

HORSEBACK RIDING

Those who love sightseeing from the back of a horse are in for a big treat on Maui. Stables dot the island, so all you have to do is choose the terrain for your trail ride: a breathtaking ride through Haleakala Crater, across rangeland, or a backwoods ride into the rainforest. There is no riding on the beach. Choose the stable by area or type of ride offered. Unfortunately, none of this comes cheap, but you won't be disappointed by either the quality of the trail guide or the scenery. It's advisable to wear jeans (jogging suit bottoms will do) and a pair of closed-toe shoes. Sunscreen and a hat are also recommended on most rides. All stables have age and weight restrictions, so be sure to check with them directly for all details.

You'll have your choice of rides at **Ironwood Ranch:** sunset, mountain, pineapple field, or extended trips for experienced riders. The West Maui Journey, for all skill levels, costs $80 for 90 minutes and runs through the foothills of the mountains. Also for all riders are the two-hour sunset ride for $110 and a two-hour Hawaiian Excursion for $110. No one weighing more than 220 pounds, please. Horses are matched to the rider's experience level and all rides are escorted.

Ironwood Ranch, 808/669-4991 or 887/699-4529, www.ironwoodranch.com, is located at mile marker 29 along Route 30 above Napili. Because all rides are conducted on private ranch land, meet at the pickup point across the highway from Napili Plaza.

Makena Stables, 808/879-0244, www.makenastables.com, is located at the end of the road at the edge of La Pérouse Bay. Owners Helaine and Pat Borge will take you on a two-hour introductory ride through low-elevation rangeland, lava flows, and along the mountain trails of Ulupalakua Ranch; on three-hour morning or sunset rides; or on a five- to six-hour bay and lunch ride. Rides range from $120–165, and only one ride goes a day. Must be at least 13 years old and no more than 205 pounds.

Pony Express Tours, 808/667-2200, www.maui.net/~ponex, offers trail rides into Haleakala Crater—full day $190, partial day $155, lunch provided. One- and two-hour rides ($60–105) are also offered across Haleakala Ranch land at the 4,000-foot elevation. Riders must be at least 10 years old and not more than 235 pounds.

Thompson Ranch Riding Stables, 808/878-1910, a family-operated stable that will even mount up children under 10, guides you over the lower slopes of Haleakala on one of Maui's oldest cattle ranches. Located at 3,700 feet, just outside of Keokea, rides go downhill from here. A 1.5-hour ride runs $60, while the two-hour ride is $70 and the sunset ride is $80.

Adventures On Horseback, 808/242-7445, www.mauihorses.com, offers waterfall rides along the north coast over lands of a private estate in Ha'iku for $185. Rides go with a maximum of six riders, who must be at least 12 years old and five feet tall, and not more than 225 pounds. Bring your own swimming suit and towel. A full-day "horse whisperer" program is also offered for $300.

Hotel guests are given priority for use of the horses at the **Hana Ranch Stables,** 808/248-8811, but you can call ahead to arrange a trail ride on this truly magnificent end of the island. The one-hour easy guided rides ($50) and two-hour rides ($90) go either along the coast or into the upper pastureland; riders must be seven years old. Private rides can be arranged.

In Kipahulu you'll find **Oheo Stables,** 808/667-2222, www.maui.net/~ray. Two rides (10:30 A.M. and 11 A.M.) are given every day, both three hours on the trail, and the destination is the highland above Makahiku and Waimoku Falls in Haleakala National Park. Only six riders maximum per ride; must be 12 years old and not more than 225 pounds. Both rides include snacks and drinks, and both run $129.

Mendes Ranch, 808/871-5222, www.mendes ranch.com, offers two different rides daily over their 3,000-acre working cattle ranch on the rugged north coast of Maui; $85 and $130 per person. Riders must be at least 11 years old and no more than 250 pounds. On both of these rides, you'll have a look at the shoreline, pastureland, lush valleys, and waterfalls, and a real *paniolo* barbecue picnic is provided on the longer ride. This is a local experience led by real cowboys. Mendes Ranch is located just past mile marker 6 on Route 330 north of Wailuku. Check-in is at 8:15 A.M. and 12:15 P.M.

Fun for the whole family, rides at the **Piiholo Ranch,** 808/357-5544, www.piiholo.com, in Makawao take you over a small working cattle ranch. Groups are limited to six riders. A morning picnic ride runs $140, while the afternoon ride with refreshments is $120; private rides can be arranged as well. Daily except Sunday.

BICYCLING

Bicycle enthusiasts should be thrilled with Maui, but the few flaws might flatten your spirits as well as your tires. The countryside is great, the weather is perfect, but the roads are heavily trafficked and the most interesting ones are narrow and have bad shoulders. Pedaling to Hana will give you an up-close and personal experience, but for bicycle safety this road is one of the worst. Haleakala is stupendous, but with a rise of more than 10,000 feet in less than 40 miles it is considered one of the most grueling rides in the world going up but superb coming down. You may be better off bringing your own bike rather than renting. If you do rent, instead of a delicate road bike, get a mountain bike that can handle the sometimes-poor road conditions as well as open up the possibilities of off-road biking (mostly along the access road to and several trails near Polipoli Spring State Recreation Area). Cruiser bikes are best for those who plan to ride on level ground to and from the store or near the beach. In short, cycling on Maui as your primary means of transportation is not for the neophyte; because of safety factors and the tough rides, only experienced riders should consider it.

Wear a helmet, bring sunglasses, use bike gloves, and wear appropriate bike shoes. If possible, have a bike pump, extra tube, and repair kit with you. Bring plenty of water and some snacks. Take a map, but get information from a bike shop for the kind of riding you want to do before you head out.

Getting your bike to Maui from one of the Neighbor Islands is no problem. All of the interisland and commuter carriers will fly it for you for about $20 one-way on the same flight as you take—just check it as baggage. Bikes must be packed in a box or hard case, supplied by the owner. Handlebars must be turned sideways and the pedals removed or turned in. Bikes go on a space-available basis only, which is usually not a problem, except perhaps during bicycle competitions. In addition, a release of liability for damage must be signed before the airline will accept the bike. If you plan ahead, you can send your bike the previous day by air freight. The freight terminal at Kahului is just a few minutes' walk from the passenger terminal and opens at 7 A.M. You can also take your bike on the interisland ferries between Maui and both Lana'i and Moloka'i. It will cost you $20 each way to Lana'i, but you don't need to pack it, and $15 each way to Moloka'i.

Getting your bike to Hawaii from the Mainland will depend on which airline you take. Some will accept bicycles as baggage traveling with you (approximate additional charge of $50) if the bikes are properly broken down and boxed in a bicycle box, but others will only take them as air freight, in which case the rates are exorbitant. Check with the airlines well before you plan to go or explore the possibility of shipping it by sea through a freight company.

For general information on biking in Hawaii, contact **Hawaii Bicycling League,** P.O. Box

4403, Honolulu, HI 96812-4403. This non-profit organization promotes biking as recreation, sport, and transportation, encourages safe biking practices, conducts biking education, and advocates for biking issues. It publishes a monthly newsletter, *Spoke-n-Words*, filled with news of the organization's business, its bicycle safety program for kids, and rides that are open to the public, as well as current bicycle issues and sponsored bicycle competitions throughout the state. If you are a bicycle rider living in the islands or simply want a subscription to the newsletter, write for membership information.

For mountain biking and trail information on all the major islands, pick up a copy of *Mountain Biking the Hawaiian Islands* by John Alford.

Bicycle Rentals

Some bicycle rental shops will tell you that the Park Service does not allow you to take your bike up to Haleakala National Park—horse pucky! You *cannot* ride the bike on the hiking paths, but going up the road (40 miles uphill) is okay if you have the steam. You are given this misinformation because the bike rental shops don't want the wear and tear on their bikes, but for the prices they charge, they shouldn't squawk. For off-road riding, try the trails in Kula Forest Reserve near Polipoli Spring State Recreation Area. Helmets should come with the rental cost; car racks will be an extra $5–10.

South Maui Bicycles, 1993 S. Kihei Rd. across from Kalama Park, 808/874-0068, open Mon.–Sat. 10 A.M.–6 P.M., Sunday until 2 P.M., is a rental and bike repair shop that boasts the largest fleet on Maui from which to choose. Rates are street bikes $22 per day, $99 per week; road bikes $29 per day, $129 per week; and simple mountain bikes $19 per day, $89 per week. Frank Hackett, the shop owner, will take the time to give you tips including routes and the best times to travel.

West Maui Cycles, 840 Waine'e St. in Lahaina, 808/661-9005, is a full-service bike sale and rental store that also carries other sporting equipment. The store has mostly Cannondale, GT, and Schwinn bikes. Standard road bike rates run from $30 per day to $120 per week, tandems run $55–65 per day or $220–260 per week, and cruisers are $15 per day or $60 per week. Moun-

tain bikes vary from $30 per day to $160 per week, depending on suspension.

Cruisers can also be rented in Lahaina from **Duke's Rental Shop,** across from Kamehameha School along Front Street, for $10 per day.

In Kahului, **The Island Biker,** 415 Dairy Rd., 808/877-7744, rents mostly mountain bikes along with its sales and repair services. They go for $29 per day, $95 per week, or $250 per month. Open Monday–Saturday 9 A.M.–6 P.M. Also try **Extreme Sports Maui,** 808/871-7954, which has mountain bikes for $29–39 per day or $162–218 per week.

For other bike rentals, try **A & B Rental and Sales,** in Honokowai at 3481 Lower Honoapi'ilani Rd., 808/669-0027, open daily 9 A.M.–5 P.M., which rents basic mountain bikes at $15 for 24 hours or $60 per week. Aside from running bike tours, **Haleakala Bike Company,** 808/572-2200, in Ha'iku also rents Gary Fisher mountain bikes, all equipment, and a rack if you need one for $45 per day or $120 per week.

Haleakala Bicycle Tours

An adventure on Maui that's become famous is riding a specially equipped bike from the summit of Mt. Haleakala for 40 miles to the bottom at Pa'ia. These bikes are mountain bikes or modified cruisers with padded seats, wide tires, and heavy-duty drum brakes, front and back. Typically, these tours take about eight hours with about three hours on the bike. Most offer a shuttle pickup and drop-off at your hotel. For tours that go to the top of the mountain for sunrise, expect to get picked up about 3 A.M.—get to bed early! Every bike rider on tours that ride through the national park must wear a full motorcycle helmet. Other tours that start outside the park will provide you with a regular bicycle helmet. Warm, layered clothing is a must, and long pants and closed-toe shoes are recommended. All bike companies have some guidelines—like no pregnant women, minimum age of 12, must be at least five feet tall—but each company's requirements may be slightly different, so check. These safety requirements are not without reason. Although comparatively safe, a few deaths have occurred on these bike trips over the years. No one wants to take a chance of your safety.

A pioneer in this field is **Maui Downhill,** 199 Dairy Rd., Kahului, 808/871-2155 or 800/535-BIKE, www.mauidownhill.net. Included in the bike ride for $150 you get two meals (continental breakfast, brunch or a gourmet picnic lunch), and a windbreaker, gloves, and helmet to use. To drench yourself in the beauty of a Haleakala sunrise, you have to pay your dues. You arrive at the base yard in Kahului at about 3:30 A.M. after being picked up at your condo by the courtesy van. Here, you'll muster with other bleary-eyed but hopeful adventurers and munch donuts and coffee, which at this time of the morning is more like a transfusion. Up the mountain, in the van, through the chilly night air takes about 90 minutes, with singing and storytelling along the way. Once atop, find your spot for the *best* natural light show in the world: The sun goes wild with colors as it paints the sky and drips into Haleakala Crater. This is your first reward. Next comes your bicycle environmental cruise down the mountain with vistas and thrills every

Early-morning bicycle tours start from Haleakala Visitor Center on the crater rim — it's downhill all the way.

ROBERT NILSEN

inch of the way, with stops for sightseeing, food, and to let cars pass. For the not-so-early risers, other mountain descent tours are available for $150 and $104.

Maui Mountain Cruisers of Kahului, 808/871-6014 or 800/232-6284, www.mauimountaincruisers.com; **Mountain Riders,** 808/242-9739 or 800/706-7700, www.mountainriders.com; **Cruiser Phil's,** 808/893-2332 or 877/764-2453, www.cruiserphil.com; **Emerald Island Bicycle Rides,** 808/573-1278 or 800/565-6615, www.mauibiking.com; and **Hawaii Downhill,** 808/893-2332, are other major bike touring companies that offer pretty much the same guided bike services at competitive rates.

A twist to this convoy guided bike tour is offered by **Haleakala Bike Company,** 808/575-9575, www.bikemaui.com, in Ha'iku. With this outfit, you meet at the bike store and get fitted with your bike and are given all necessary equipment. For the sunrise tours, the van leaves at about 4:15 A.M. and brings you to the top of the mountain in the park for your sunrise experience. When the riders start down the mountain, the company van stays with them until they are comfortable with the bikes and route and then lets them go the rest of the way by themselves, taking their time or zipping down the hill as they like, stopping when they want and eating where they desire. All that is required is that they return by about 4 P.M. It's bike freedom. Later in the morning, another drop-off goes to the crater rim. These rides are $84 and $74. Later drop-offs at the park entrance go for $65, but you can do the "takeaway option" for $45.

Another company that encourages a go-at-your-own-pace unguided tour is **Upcountry Cycles,** 808/573-2888 or 800/373-1678, www.bikemauihawaii.com.

Aloha Bicycle Tours, 808/249-0911, www.maui.net/~bikemaui, does trips through upcountry.

For going off road with a guided tour, see **Maui Eco-adventures,** 808/661-7720, www.ecomaui.com, who have access to private ranch land on the side of Haleakala.

MAUI GOLF COURSES

Course	Par	Yards	Fees	Cart	Clubs
The Dunes at Maui Lani Kuihelani Highway Kahului, 808/873-0422	72	6,413	$95	Incl.	$30
Elleair Maui Golf Club 1345 Pi'ilani Highway Kihei, 808/874-0777	70	5,979	$85	Incl.	$30
Kaanapali Golf Courses 2290 Kaanapali Pkwy. Kaanapali, 808/661-3691					
North Course	71	6,136	$150	Incl.	$35
South Course	71	6,067	$142	Incl.	$35
Kapalua Golf Club 300 Kapalua Drive (Bay) Kapalua, 808/669-8044					
Bay Course	72	6,051	$180	Incl.	$40
Village Course	71	5,753	$180	Incl.	$40
Plantation Course	73	6,547	$220	Incl.	$40
Makena Golf Courses 5415 Makena Alanui Makena, 808/879-3344					

Bicycle Touring

For those interested in long-distance bicycle touring on Maui, contact **Go Cycling Maui,** 808/572-0259. This company provides all the gear and the know-how for small group tours of 1–5 days in length for $135–575 per person. You just need to show up and enjoy; routes can be negotiated. Fit and experienced bicyclists only. Call for rates.

For those who like to strike out on their own, two routes are recommended. One takes you for a 50-mile loop from Wailuku (or Lahaina) up the Ka'anapali coast and around the head of Maui back to Wailuku. The road starts out in good repair, but the traffic will be heavy until you pass Kapalua. Here the road begins to wind along the north coast. Since this road has been paved, traffic around the north end has picked up, so the road will not be just yours anymore.

Around the north end there is no place to get service. Go prepared, and be on the lookout for cars. The second route is from Kahului up to Kula or Pukalani via Pulehu Road and back down the mountainside via Pa'ia, Ha'iku, or Ulumalu, taking you through irrigated cane fields, the cool Upcountry region, and the lush and sculpted north slope of Haleakala.

GOLF

Maui has 10 golf courses with 16 links; all but one have 18 holes. These range from modest municipal courses to world-class private clubs. Some are set along the coast, while others back against the mountain with sweeping views of the lowlands. The high-class resort areas of Ka'anapali, Kapalua, and Wailea are built around golf courses.

Course	Par	Yards	Fees	Cart	Clubs
North Course	72	6,914	$155	Incl.	$35
South Course	72	7,014	$175	Incl.	$35
Maui Country Club	72	6,339	$75	Incl.	$20
Sprecklesville, 808/877-7270			$38 (9 holes)		
Pukalani Country Club	72	6,882	$50	Incl.	$20
360 Pukalani Street					
Pukalani, 808/572-1314					
Sandalwood Golf Course	72	6,469	$80	Incl.	$35
2500 Honoapiʻilani Highway					
Wailuku, 808/242-4653					
Waiehu Municipal Golf Course	72	6,330	$26 (weekdays)	$8	$15 (18)
Wailuku, 808/270-7400			$30 (weekends)		$10 (9)
Wailea Golf Club					
120 Kuakahi Street (Blue)					
Wailea, HI 96753					
Blue Course 808/875-5155	72	6,797	$140	Incl.	$35
Gold Course 808/875-7450	72	6,653	$160	Incl.	$35
Emerald Course	72	6,407	$150	Incl.	$35

EXPLORING THE ISLANDS

The three Kapalua golf courses have all been certified as Audubon Cooperative Sanctuaries, which means they take measures to protect native birds, reduce the use of chemicals, reduce water consumption, and replant some native vegetation.

Municipal and public courses are open to everyone. Resort courses cater to the public as well as to resort guests. Most golf courses offer lessons and have driving ranges, some that are lighted. All have pro shops and clubhouses with a restaurant or snack shop; some have cocktail lounges. Greens fees listed in the chart are for non-Hawaii residents. Many courses offer reduced *kamaʻaina* rates and discount rates for play that starts later in the day. Be sure to ask about these rates because they often afford substantial savings. Guests of resorts affiliated with a golf course also have reduced greens fees. Deciding at the last minute to golf? Want a discount rate? Willing to golf where it may not necessarily be your first choice? Try **Stand-by Golf,** 888/645-2665, where you can arrange tee times for great savings. Call one day in advance or the morning you want to play. **Maui Golf Shop,** 808/875-4653, also offers some reduced-rate greens fees on short notice. If you want to rent clubs other than at the golf course, try **Maui Golf Shop** 808/875-4653, at the Kihei Gateway Center in Kihei; **Maui Golf Repair,** 808/661-0889; or **West Maui Sports,** 808/661-6252, in Lahaina.

For printed information on golf in Hawaii, pick up a copy of *Maui Golf Review* magazine or the newspaper-format *Hawaiʻi Golf.*

Some tipping is the norm. A $1 tip to the bag drop attendant is customary, $2 if a bag boy takes your bags from the car, and a couple bucks extra if he cleans your clubs for you.

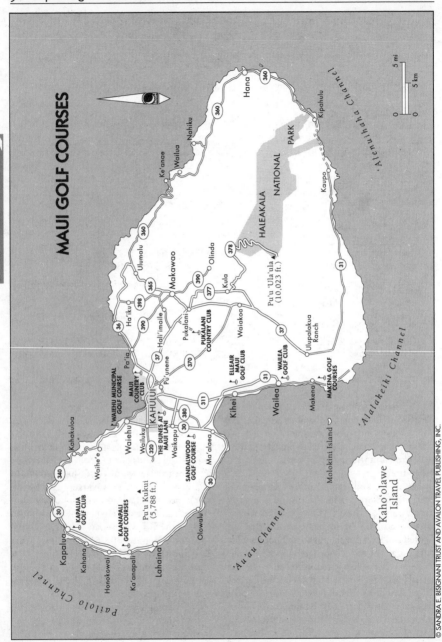

MAUI GOLF COURSES

TENNIS

There are many tennis courts on Maui, and plenty of them are free. County courts are under the control of the Department of Parks and Recreation, which maintains a combination of lighted and unlit courts around the island. No fees are charged for these public courts, but play is on a first-come, first-served basis and limited to 45 minutes if people are waiting. Weekends are often fairly busy, but it's relatively easy to get a court on weekdays. Court rules apply and only soft-sole shoes are allowed. Some resort and private courts are open to the public for a fee, while others restrict play to members and guests only. Most private courts have a plexi-pave or similar surface. Although each facility differs, private clubs usually have pro shops, offer equipment rental, and arrange clinics and lessons. Court play is regulated according to accepted rules, and proper attire is required, including proper shoes. The accompanying chart is a partial listing of what's available.

LAND TOURS

Bus and Van Tours

It's easy to book tours to Maui's famous areas such as Lahaina, Hana, 'Iao Valley, and Haleakala. Normally they're run on either half- or full-day schedules (Hana is always a full day) and range anywhere from $40–85 with hotel pickup included, kids at reduced prices. Some even do special cultural tours to such places as Kahakuloa Valley on the north shore. Big bus tours are run by **Roberts Hawaii,** 808/871-6226 or 800/831-5541, www.roberts-hawaii.com, and they're quite antiseptic—you sit behind tinted glass in an air-conditioned bus. Other companies with smaller tour buses and vans also hit the high points but have specialty tours. Try **Ekahi Tours,** 808/877-9775 or 888/292-2422, www.ekahi.com; **Polynesian Adventure Tours,** 808/877-4242 or 800/622-3011, www.polyad.com; **Akina Aloha Tours,** 808/879-2828 or 800/800-3989, www.akinatours.com; and **Valley Isle Excursions,** 808/661-8687 or 877/871-5224, www.tourmaui.com.

Temptation Tours, 808/887-8888 or 800/817-1234, www.temptationtours.com, operates the ultimate in luxury van tours for the discriminating traveler. The deluxe vans, more like limousines, seat each of the eight passengers in a comfortable captain's chair for trips to Hana and Haleakala. This outfit runs over a half-dozen tours, all out to Hana or up to Haleakala, many combined with other activities. One Hana tour combines with a great cave tour, while a second lets you fly by helicopter one way. The Haleakala trips take you up for sunrise or let you experience a day on the mountain. Rates run $134–239.

Off-Road Tours

Maui ATV Tours, 808/878-2889, www.mauiatvtours.com, has opened tours across the uplands of the Ulupalakua Ranch. These *mauka* tours take you up on the hillsides of this working cattle ranch, through pastures, and past lava caves to panoramic scenes of the island, with a good chance of seeing wildlife. Tours are conducted on single-passenger, four-wheel automatic ATVs. Instruction is given on the operation of these machines, so no experience is necessary. Each trip runs in a circular route so there are new sights through the entire trip. A morning four-hour ride starts at 7:30 A.M. and runs $125 while the two-hour afternoon ride is $90 and begins at 1:30 P.M. Refreshments are provided. Must be 16 years old to ride on your own, but youngsters can be taken on a three-passenger ATV. All protective gear is provided, but you should wear long pants and close-toe shoes. No one over 300 pounds, pregnant women, or those with back problems are allowed to ride. Private tours can be accommodated. For those who do not care to drive an ATV, a 4WD Pinzgauer truck tour is offered that also takes you to places you cannot ordinarily go. These three-hour tours go morning and afternoon and run $125 per person. For all activities, meet at the office across from the Ulupalakua Store near the winery.

Haleakala Ranch, 808/661-0288, www.atv-maui.com, also offers ATV tours across the vast acreage of its ranch. Meet at the office on the highway up to the summit and from there head

MAUI TENNIS COURTS

County Courts

Under jurisdiction of the Department of Parks and Recreation, 808/270-7230. Courts listed are in or near visitor areas and open to the public.

Town	Location	No. of Courts	Lighted
Hali'imaile	Hali'imaile Park	1	Yes
Hana	Hana Ball Park	2	Yes
Kahului	Kahului Community Center	2	Yes
Kihei	Kalami Park	4	Yes
	Waipu'ilani Park	6	Yes
Lahaina	Lahaina Civic Center	5	Yes
	Malu'ulu O Lele Park	4	Yes
Makawao	Eddie Tam Center	2	Yes
Pukalani	Pukalani Park	2	Yes
Wailuku	Wailuku War Memorial Complex	4	Yes
	Wells Park	7	Yes

Hotel and Private Courts Open to the Public

Town	Location	No. of Courts	Lighted
Ka'anapali	Hyatt Tennis Center 808/661-1234	6	Yes
	Maui Marriott Tennis Club 808/661-6200	5	No
	Royal Lahaina Tennis Ranch 808/667-5200	10	6
	Sheraton Maui Tennis Club 808/667-9200	3	Yes
Kapalua	Kapalua Tennis Center 808/665-0112	10	5
	Kapalua Tennis Garden 808/669-5677	10	4
Makena	Makena Tennis Club 808/879-8777	6	2
Napili Bay	Napili Kai Beach Resort 808/669-6271	2	No
Wailea	Wailea Tennis Club 808/879-1958	11	3

into the ranch property. These tours start at about 4,000 feet and go up from there, so the views can be wonderful. Morning and afternoon tours are offered. Two-hour tours run $90 while the 3.5-hour tours go for $130.

Personal Guided Tours

For a personalized tour where a guide drives your rental car and takes you to "local" places, try the following: **Guides of Maui,** 808/877-4060 or 800/231-8022, www.guidesofmaui.com, offers a Hana tour, circle-island tour, Hana and Haleakala combination tour, a honeymooner's tour, and others. Trips start at 8 A.M. and return late afternoon; the rate is $235 per car with your rental car.

A similar service is provided by **Hapa Papa's Tours,** 808/242-8500, where a trip to Hana, 'Iao Valley, or Haleakala runs $75–95 per person depending on the tour, and they supply the van.

Tape Tours

For those who desire a go-at-your-own-pace alternative to van tours, yet want the convenience of an escort, **Best of Maui Cassette Tours,** 333 Dairy Rd., Kahului, 808/871-1555, may be for you. Buy a quality tape for $13 or a CD for $17 describing the Hana Highway and what to see and do along the way. This rental comes with a small pamphlet of sights, history, and legends, a route map, a video, and coupons. Pick up your cassettes from 5 A.M.–1 P.M.; reservations are appreciated. You can also get one of these tapes at **Woo-wee Maui's Cafe** next door, where they will also provide you with a boxed lunch for the road for $8.95.

Offering roughly the same service at a similar price is **Hana Cassette, CD Guide,** 808/572-0550. Pick up your tape and all the extras from 5 A.M. at their booth at the Shell gas station along Dairy Road in Kahului, or inside the station after the booth closes.

You will also find that several condos and other accommodations, as well as some other activities, have these tapes for use by their guests for free.

AIR TOURS

Maui is a spectacular sight from the air. A few small charter airlines, a handful of helicopter companies, and a hang gliding outfit swoop you around the island. These joyrides are literally the highlight of many people's experiences on Maui, but they are expensive.

Helicopter Tours

Everyone has an opinion as to which company offers the best ride, the best narration, or the best service. All of the helicopter companies on Hawai'i are safe and reputable—although there have been a few accidents—and nearly all pilots have been trained by the military. Most companies fly air-conditioned six-seat A-Stars or Eco-Stars, with a few four-passenger Bell Jet Rangers, Hughes 500s, and Robinson Ravens in use. For all, tours are narrated over specially designed earphones, and most have two-way microphones so you can communicate with the pilot. Some offer a video of your helicopter tour of Maui (or a generic tape of highlights) as a souvenir at the end of the flight for an extra $20 or so. Each gives a preflight briefing to go over safety regulations and other details. Remember, however, that the seating arrangement in a helicopter is critical to safety. The preflight crew is expertly trained to arrange the passengers so that the chopper is balanced, and with different people in various sizes flying every day, their job is very much like a chess game. This means that the seating goes strictly according to weight. If you are not assigned the seat of your choice, for safety's sake, please do not complain. Think instead that you are part of a team whose goal is not only enjoyment but also to come back safe and sound. It's very difficult not to have a fascinating flight—no matter where you sit.

Nearly everyone wants to take photographs of the sights from their helicopter tour. Who wouldn't? Here are a few things to consider. Most of the newer helicopters are air-conditioned, which means that the windows don't open, so you might experience glare or some distortion. If you need absolutely clear shots, choose a chopper where the windows open or go with the one that

ROBERT NILSEN

While the islands can be appreciated from their many beautiful locations, the best way to see much of the land, particularly the heavily forested mountain slopes and deep penetrating valleys, is from the seat of a helicopter.

flies with its doors off. Also, if you are the only one taking pictures on a tour and you're seated in the middle of the rear seat, you won't be happy. Again, ask for a ride in a smaller rig where everyone gets a window seat.

On certain flights the craft will touch down for a short interlude, and on some flights a complimentary lunch will be served. Several companies combine a flight with a van tour either to or from Hana. Most companies can make special arrangements to design a package especially for you. Helicopter rides are particularly attractive because you can sightsee from a perspective not possible from the ground and you can get close to areas not accessible by foot. There may be a tradeoff, however. Steep turns, quick descents, and unstable pockets of air can cause some riders to get airsick.

Chopper companies are competitively priced, with tours of West or East Maui at around $125, with a Hana/Haleakala flight at about $180. Circle-island tours are approximately $225, but the best option might be to include a trip to Moloka'i at approximately $225 in order to experience the world's tallest sea cliffs along the

isolated windward coast. While the most spectacular ones take you over Haleakala Crater, or perhaps to the remote West Maui Mountains, where inaccessible gorges lie at your feet, the 45-minute east Maui tour is the most popular. Know, however, that many hikers have a beef with the air tours: After they've spent hours hiking into remote valleys in search of peace and quiet, out of the sky comes the mechanical whir of a chopper to spoil the solitude.

All flights leave from the heliport at the back side of Kahului Airport—access off Haleakala Highway extension road. Each company has an office at the Kahului Airport, where you check in and receive your preflight instructions. There is a parking lot here, free the first 15 minutes, $1 for 15–30 minutes, $1 each additional hour, maximum of $7 per day.

Air Maui, 808/877-7005 or 877/238-4942, www.airmaui.com, is one of the "little guys," but it works hard to please by offering many options at competitive prices with a great safety record. Family owned and operated, Air Maui offers all the standards and can customize a tour for you.

Alex Air, 808/871-0792 or 888/418-8455, www.helitour.com, is a small, personable company that runs a tight ship. It offers a wide variety of flights on two types of helicopters, the A-Star and a smaller Hughes 500. Two of its flights make landings at a black-sand beach.

Sunshine Helicopter, 808/871-0722 or 800/469-3000, www.sunshinehelicopters.com, is another local, family-run outfit that flies "Black Beauties." The seating is two-by-two, and each pilot goes out of his way to give you a great ride. Aside from the usual tours, this company does charters and combinations with Atlantis Submarine tours. Sunshine Helicopters also operates on the Big Island.

Blue Hawaiian Helicopters, 808/871-8844 or 800/745-2583, www.bluehawaiian.com, operates on Maui and the Big Island. It's a company that does lots of advertising, gets a lot of passengers, and has done work for film companies. Standard flights are offered plus one that touches down and a combination fly/drive to/from Hana tour with Temptation van tours.

If you want a private flight, try **Mauiscape Helicopters,** 877-7272 or 888/440-7272, www .mauiscape.net. This company uses a four-seat Robinson Raven and usually takes two passengers, although three passengers can fit, so everyone has a window seat. Other options are a four-seat EC110 or a six-seat A-Star. With East Maui, West Maui, Haleakala, and circle-island flights, tours run $180–250. The Mauiscape office is near the corner of Dairy Road and Hana Highway in Kahului.

Fixed-Wing Tours

For a Maui joyride out of Kahului Airport, contact **Paragon Air,** 808/244-3356 or 800/ 248-1231, www.paragon-air.com. Paragon offers several different options, like a flight to Moloka'i with a tour of Kalaupapa for $210 or a flight to Moloka'i coupled with the mule ride down to Kalaupapa for $279. Others include a four-hour Big Island volcano tour for $495 and a five-island tour for $165. Paragon Air can also be hired for point-to-point charter travel for those who don't want to wait in lines at the airport.

An alternate for a Big Island volcano tour, a sunset tour, or private charter is **Maui Air,** 808/ 877-5500, www.volcanoairtours.com. Maui Air runs the two-hour volcano tour from either Kahului or Kapalua airports at $279 per person. Taking a slightly different route to the Big Island, the sunset tour leaves from Kahului Airport only and is $255 per passenger. Flights are conducted in nine-passenger air-conditioned, twin-engine planes, and everyone gets a comfortable window seat with stereo headset for the tour narration.

Paragliding

For motorized hang gliding, contact **Hang Gliding Maui,** 808/572-6557, www.hanggliding-maui.com. These powered flight runs $115 for 30 minutes and $190 for 60 minutes. Longer tours and instruction can be arranged. Flights leave from the Hana Airport only.

Want to try paragliding off the side of Haleakala? Contact **Proflyght Hawaii Paragliding,** 808/874-5433 or 877/463-5944, www .paraglidehawaii.com. They'll set you up on a tandem flight with a certified instructor. Depending on launch site, flights can be 5–10 minutes or up to 40 minutes; rates are $75–275. All necessary equipment is provided, but you should wear warm, comfortable clothing and sturdy shoes.

FISHING

Surrounding Maui are some of the most exciting and productive "blue waters" in all the world. Here you can find a sportfishing fleet made up of skippers and crews who are experienced professional anglers. You can also fish from jetties, piers, rocks, and from shore. If rod and reel don't strike your fancy, try the old-fashioned throw-net or take along a spear when you go snorkeling or scuba diving. There's nighttime torch fishing that requires special skills and equipment. Streams and irrigation ditches yield introduced trout, bass, and catfish, but there are no state-maintained, public freshwater fishing areas in Maui County. While you're at it, you might want to try crabbing for Kona and Samoan crabs or working low-tide areas after sundown hunting octopus, an island delicacy.

EXPLORING THE ISLANDS

Deep-Sea Fishing

Most game-fishing boats work the waters on the calmer leeward sides of the islands. Some skippers, carrying anglers who are accustomed to the sea, will also work the much rougher windward coasts and island channels where the fish bite just as well. Trolling is the preferred method of deep-sea fishing; this is done usually in waters of 1,000–2,000 fathoms (a fathom is six feet). The skipper will either "area fish," which means running in a crisscross pattern over a known productive area, or "ledge fish," which involves trolling over submerged ledges where the game fish are known to feed. The most advanced marine technology, available on many boats, sends sonar bleeps searching for fish. On deck, the crew and anglers scan the horizon in the age-old Hawaiian tradition—searching for clusters of seabirds feeding on baitfish pursued to the surface by the huge and aggressive game fish. "Still fishing" or "bottom fishing" with hand lines yields some tremendous fish.

The Game Fish

The most thrilling game fish in Hawaiian waters is marlin, generically known as "billfish" or *a'u* to the locals. The king of them is the blue marlin, with record catches of well more than 1,000 pounds. Although the Big Island is best known for big game sports fishing and its big catches, Maui has had some great catches too. The biggest seems to have been a 1,201-pound marlin (more than 14 feet in length) that was weighed in at the Lahaina pier. You can see it mounted over the bar at the private Maui Yacht Club. Also check out the 1,100 pounder hanging at Coolers restaurant in Lahaina and the grander at the Blue Marlin restaurant at Ma'alaea Harbor. There are also striped marlin and sailfish, which often weigh more than 200 pounds.

The best times for marlin are during spring, summer, and fall. The fishing tapers off in January and picks up again by late February. "Blues" can be caught year-round, but, oddly enough, when they stop biting it seems as though the striped marlin pick up. Second to the marlin are tuna.

GAME FISH

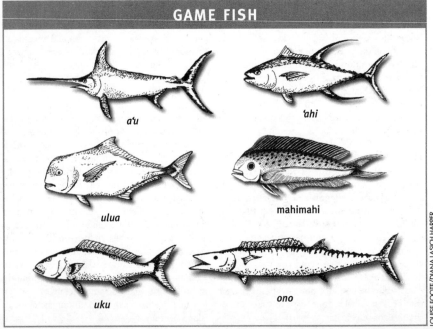

a'u

'ahi

ulua

mahimahi

uku

ono

LOUISE FOOTE/DIANA LASICH HARPER

'Ahi (yellowfin tuna) are caught in Hawaiian waters at depths of 100–1,000 fathoms. They can weigh 300 pounds, but 25–100 pounds is common. There are also *aku* (skipjack tuna) and the delicious *ono,* which average 20 and 40 pounds, respectively. Mahimahi is another strong-fighting, deep-water game fish abundant in Hawaii. These delicious fish can weigh up to 70 pounds.

Shorefishing and bait casting yield *papio,* a jack tuna. *Akule,* a scad (locally called *halalu*), is a smallish schooling fish that comes close to shore and is great to catch on light tackle. *Ulua* are shore fish and can be found in tide pools. They're excellent eating, average 2–3 pounds, and are taken at night or with spears. *'O'io* are bonefish that come close to shore to spawn. They're caught by bait casting and bottom fishing with cut bait. They're bony, but they're a favorite for fish cakes and *poke. Awa* is a schooling fish that loves brackish water. It can get up to three feet long and is a good fighter; a favorite for throw-netters, it's even raised commercially in fish ponds. Besides these, there are plenty of goatfish, mullet, mackerel, snapper, sharks, and even salmon.

Fishing Charters

The fishing around Maui ranges from very good to excellent. A sizable fleet of charter boats with skilled captains and tested crews is ready, willing, and competent to take you out. Most are berthed at Lahaina Harbor, while others are at Ma'alaea Harbor. The best times of year for marlin are July–Sept. and Jan.–Mar. (when the generally larger females arrive). August is the optimum month. Rough seas can keep boats in for a few days during December and early January, but by February all are generally out.

You can hire a boat for a private or share charter, staying out for four, six, or eight hours. Some captains like to go for longer runs because there is a better chance of a catch and they can get farther into the water; some now do only private charters. Boat size varies, but four anglers per midsize boat is about average. No matter the size, most boats will take no more than six anglers. Although some provide it, be sure to bring

food and drink for the day; no bananas, please—they're bad luck.

Deep-sea fishing on a share basis costs approximately $120 per half day (four hours) or $160 full day, per person. On a private basis, expect $500 per half day or $800 or more for a full day. If you're thinking of having a go at catching that "big one," go down to the harbor first and check out the boats, preferably in the afternoon when they're returning from sea. Be sure to talk with the captains and ask what success they've had lately, how they fish, where they try, and what happens to the fish.

Some of the best boats at Ma'alaea Harbor include *Carol Ann,* 808/877-2181; *No Ka Oi III* and *Maka Kai,* 808/879-4485, run by Ocean Activities Center; and *Makoa Kai,* 808/875-2251, captained by Dave Ventura, who does only private fishing charters. In Lahaina you can't go wrong with the *Judy Ann,* 808/667-6672; *Aerial III* or *No Problem,* 808/667-9089; *The Finest Kind* and *Reel Hooker,* 808/661-0338; or *Lucky Strike II,* 808/661-4606.

Coastal Fish

You don't have to hire a boat to catch fish! The coastline is productive too. Catch limits for 21 species of marine fish and eight crustaceans and shellfish are regulated, so check state guidelines. Also check state guidelines for Maui's County's limited or prohibited areas of shore fishing: Kaho'olawe Island Reserve, Molokini Shoal Marine Life Conservation District, Honolua-Mokule'ia Marine Life Conservation District, Kahului Harbor, Kaunakakai Harbor, Manele Small Boat Harbor, and Manele-Hulopo'e Marine Life Conservation District. If you need instruction or gear, contact **Off-Road Shorefishing Expeditions,** 808/572-3470.

Freshwater Fish

Freshwater fishing on Maui is poor from an angler's point of view, but small populations of freshwater fish can be found in island streams and ponds. Hawaii has only one native freshwater game fish, the *'o'opu.* This goby is an oddball with fused ventral fins. It grows to 12 inches and is found on all islands, especially Kaua'i.

EXPLORING THE ISLANDS

Introduced species include largemouth and smallmouth bass, bluegills, catfish, *tucunare,* oscar, carp, and tilapia. The *tucunare* is a tough-fighting, good-tasting game fish introduced from South America, similar to the oscar from the same region. Both have been compared to bass but are of a different family.

The tilapia is from Africa and has become common in Hawaii's irrigation ditches. It is a mouth breeder—the young will take refuge in their parents' protective jaws even a few weeks after hatching. The snakehead are eel-like fish that inhabit the reservoirs and are great fighters. The channel catfish can grow to more than 20 pounds; it bites best after sundown. Or go for carp—with its broad tails and tremendous strength, it's the poor man's game fish. All of these species are best caught with light spinning tackle or with a bamboo pole and a trusty old worm. The catch limit of eight species of fresh-water fish is regulated.

Fishing Licenses

All game fish may be taken year-round, except trout, *'ama'ama, moi,* and certain crustaceans (check specific regulations). A **Freshwater Game Fishing License** is good July 1–June 30. Licenses cost $25 for nonresidents, $10 for seven-day tourist use, $20 for 30-day tourist use, $5 for residents over age 15 and active-duty military personnel, their spouses, and dependents under age 15, $3 for children ages 9–15; free to senior citizens and children under age nine when accompanied by an adult with a license. You can pick up a license at sporting goods stores or at the Division of Aquatic Resources, 130 Mahalani St., Wailuku, 808/243-5294. Be sure to ask for the *Hawaii Fishing Regulations* and *Freshwater Fishing in Hawaii* booklets. Fishing is usually allowed in most State Forest Reserve Areas. Owner permission must be obtained to fish on private property. Shoreline and recreational fishing is permitted without a license.

HUNTING

Most people don't think of Hawaii as a place for hunting, but actually it's quite good. Seven species of introduced game mammals and 15 species of game birds are regularly hunted. Some species of game animals are restricted on all islands, but every island offers hunting. Public game lands are located throughout Maui County; a license is required to take birds and game.

Information

Hunting rules and regulations are always subject to change. Also, environmental considerations often change bag limits and seasons. Make sure to check with the State Division of Forestry and Wildlife for the most current information. Request *Rules Regulating Game Bird Hunting, Rules Regulating Game Mammal Hunting,* and *Hunting in Hawaii.* Direct inquiries to the Department of Land and Natural Resources, Division of Forestry and Wildlife Office, 54 S. High St., Rm. 101, Wailuku, HI 96793, 808/984-8100. Office hours are 8 A.M.–3:30 P.M. Monday–Friday.

General Hunting Rules

Hunting licenses are mandatory in order to hunt on public, private, or military land anywhere in Hawaii. They're good for one year beginning July 1 and cost $20 residents and service personnel, $105 nonresidents, free to senior citizens. Licenses are available from sporting goods stores and from the various offices of the Division of Forestry and Wildlife. This government organization also sets and enforces the rules, so contact it with any questions. Generally, hunting hours are from one-half hour before sunrise to one-half hour after sunset. Checking stations are maintained, where the hunter must check in before and after hunting.

Rifles must have a muzzle velocity greater than 1,200 foot-pounds. Shotguns larger than .20 gauge are allowed, and muzzle-loaders must have a .45-caliber bore or larger. Bows must have a minimum draw of 40 pounds for straight bows, 35 pounds for a recursive bow, and 30 pounds for compounds. Arrows must be broadheads. The use of hunting dogs is permitted only for certain species of birds and game, and when dogs are permitted, only smaller-caliber rifles and shotguns, and spears and knives, may be used—no big-bore guns/shotguns. Hunters must wear orange safety cloth on front and back no smaller than a 12-inch square. Certain big-game species are hunted only by lottery selection; contact the Division of Forestry and Wildlife two months in advance. Guide service is not mandatory but is advised if you're unfamiliar with hunting in Hawaii. You can hunt on private land only with permission, and you must possess a valid hunting license. Guns and ammunition brought into Hawaii must be registered with the chief of police of the corresponding county within 48 hours of arrival. Also, firearms must be unloaded and stored in an appropriately locked case as checked luggage to be transported by plane to the state.

Game Animals

All game animals in Hawaii have been introduced. Some have adapted admirably and are becoming well entrenched, while the survival of others is still precarious. **Axis deer** originated in India and were brought to Lana'i and Moloka'i, where they're doing well. The small herd on Maui is holding its own. Their unique flavor makes them one of the best wild meats; they're hunted on Lana'i from mid-February to mid-May by public lottery. **Mouflon sheep** are native to Corsica and Sardinia. They do well on the windswept slopes of Mauna Loa and Mauna Kea on the Big Island and on Lana'i, where they're hunted Aug.–Oct., also by public lottery.

Feral pigs are escaped domestic pigs and are found on all islands except Lana'i. The stock is a mixture of original Polynesian pigs and subsequently introduced species. Involving dogs and killing with a spear or long knife, pig hunting is not recommended for the timid or tenderhearted. These beasts' four-inch tusks and fighting spirits make them tough and dangerous. **Feral goats** come in a variety of colors. Found on all islands except Lana'i, they have been known to cause erosion and are considered a pest in some areas, especially on Haleakala. Openly hunted on all islands, their meat is considered delicious when properly cooked.

Game Birds

Several game birds are found on most of the islands. Bag limits and hunting seasons vary, so check with the Division of Forestry and Wildlife for details. **Ring-necked pheasants** are one of the best game birds and found on all the islands. **Green pheasants** are found on Maui. **Francolins,** gray and black, from India and the Sudan, are similar to partridges. They are hunted with dogs and taste great roasted. There are also **chukar** from Tibet, found on the slopes of all islands; **quail,** including the Japanese and California varieties; **doves;** and the wild Rio Grande **turkey,** to name a few.

SPORTING CLAYS

An outgrowth of hunting, sporting clays is a sport that helps develop and maintain your hand-eye coordination. Shooting is done from different stations around a course, and the object is to hit a small, round clay disk. Different from trap or skeet shooting, sporting clays relies on moving targets that mimic different animals and birds, hopping along the ground as if a rabbit, springing off the ground like a teal, or flying high like a pheasant. Maui County has two sporting clay grounds, one on Maui and one on Lana'i. Each is designed differently but both provide the same basic service. Although a variety of options are available for the beginner to the advanced shooter, a typical round of 100 shots with a 20-gauge shotgun would take about an hour and cost around $125. Open daily 8:30 A.M.–dusk, **Papaka Sporting Clays,** 808/879-5649, is located in Makena. Call for reservations and directions.

BOOKING AGENCIES

Ocean Activities Center, 808/879-4484, is one of the biggest agencies for booking any and all kinds of activities on Maui. For much of the fun events like snorkeling, scuba diving, whale-watching, sunset cruises, and deep-sea fishing, the center has its own facilities and equipment, which means it not only provides you with an excellent outing, but it also offers very competitive prices. Ocean Activities can also book you on helicopters and land tours, and rent boogie boards, snorkel equipment, sailboards, surfboards, and kayaks. It has booking agencies in the Kihei area at the Mana Kai Maui Resort, Maui Hill Resort, and the Kamaole Shopping Center, at the Ma'alaea Harbor Village Shops, and at the Maui Marriott in Ka'anapali. Prices on all of their activities are very reasonable, and the service is excellent. If you had to choose one agency for all your fun needs, this would be a good bet.

Another very reputable outfit with one booking office in Lahaina is **Barefoot's Cashback Tours,** 834 Front St., 808/661-8889 or 888/222-3601, www.tombarefoot.com. Barefoot's gives you up to a 10 percent discount on all your activities if you pay by cash or traveler's checks or 7 percent discount with credit cards. It too can set you up with virtually any activity around the island or throughout the state. Shop here; you'll be glad you did.

Activity Warehouse can provide the same service, often with last-minute reservations, and it also rents some ocean equipment. You can find Activity Warehouse in Lahaina, at 900 and 602 Front St., 808/667-4000, at the Embassy Vacation Resorts in Honokowai, 808/667-6062, and in Kihei, at 247 Pi'ikea Ave., Ste. 103, 808/875-4000. **Activity World,** 808/667-7777, has more than a dozen booths throughout the is-

land, many at condos and resorts. They're convenient and offer good reductions in prices for all sorts of activities on the island. These are legitimate vendors with solid reputations. You will, however, find a horde of other activities desks up and down Front Street and in other locations; you don't have to search for them—they'll find you, especially to make an exhausting high-pressured pitch for time shares! Avoid them, unless you want to listen to the rap in exchange for your reduced ticket price.

One of the easiest ways to book a fishing activity and sightseeing trip at the same time is to walk along the Lahaina Wharf. There's an information booth here operated by many of the companies who rent slips at the harbor. Check it out first, and then plan to be there when the tour boats return. Asking the passengers, right on the spot, if they've had a good time is about the best you can do. You can also check out the boats and do some comparative pricing of your own.

For boats out of quiet Ma'alaea Harbor and a full range of activities around the island, contact the **Ma'alaea Activity Center,** 808/242-6982, www.activityshack.com. The center does it all, from helicopters to horseback, but specializes in the boats berthed at Ma'alaea.

Shopping

This chapter provides general information about shopping on Maui; you'll find greater detail in the individual travel chapters. Here, you should get an overview of what's available and where, with enough information to get your pockets twitching and your credit cards smoldering! Happy bargain hunting!

SHOPPING CENTERS

Those who enjoy one-stop shopping will be happy with the choices in Maui's various malls. You'll find regularly known department stores as well as small shops featuring island-made goods. The following are Maui's main shopping malls.

Kahului/Wailuku

Along Ka'ahumanu Avenue, you'll find **Queen Ka'ahumanu Center,** the largest shopping mall on the island. Here's everything from Sears and Macy's to Sew Special, a tiny store featuring island fabrics. The mall is full-service with apparel and shoe stores, book and music shops, jewelry stores, and health, beauty, and specialty shops. This is where local residents shop. You can eat at numerous restaurants or enjoy a movie at Kaahumanu Theater.

Down the road is **Maui Mall,** featuring Longs Drug for everything from aspirin to film, numerous restaurants and food outlets, and another multiplex theater. Sandwiched between these two modern facilities is **Kahului Shopping Center,** definitely down-home with old-timers sitting around outside. The shops here aren't fancy, but they are authentic, and you can make some off-beat purchases while strolling through.

The newest and the second largest mall in town is **Maui Marketplace.** This mall is located on the south side of Dairy Road, where you can find Sports Authority, OfficeMax, several clothing shops, jewelry stores, and a Borders Books and Music outlet.

The past few years have seen a rapid expansion of mercantile outlets in Kahului. In the triangle by Kahana Pond is **Triangle Square** center, and many of its shops are dedicated to sports. Several small malls are strung along Dairy Road between Hana Highway and Hulilike Street, and here too you'll find the big-box stores of Wal-Mart, Kmart, Costco, and Home Depot.

Lahaina

You can't beat Lahaina's Front Street for the best, worst, most artistic, and tackiest shopping on Maui. This is where the tourists are, so this is where the shops are . . . shoulder to shoulder. The list is endless, but you'll find art studios and galleries, T-shirts galore, scrimshaw, jewelry, silks, boutiques, leathers, souvenir junk, eelskins, and even a permanent tattoo memory of Maui. No wimps allowed! Lahaina also has the best special-interest shopping on Maui in various little shops strung out along Front Street.

The following are the local malls: **The Wharf Cinema Center** on Front Street has a multitude of eating establishments, as well as stores and boutiques, and a movie theater in its multilevel shopping facility. Nearly across the street are the **Pioneer Inn Shops,** again with a multitude of clothing and gift shops, but all on street level. **Lahaina Market Place,** tucked down an alley off Front Street near Lahainaluna Road, features established art shops along with open-air stalls. **Lahaina Square Shopping Center, Lahaina Shopping Center,** and **Anchor Square,** all set between Route 30 and Front Street, have various stores and are the most *local* of the Lahaina malls. The **505 Front Street Mall** is at the south end of Front Street and offers distinctive and quiet shopping away from the frenetic activity.

The **Lahaina Cannery Mall,** on Lahaina's north end, features restaurants, boutiques, specialty shops, fast food, and plenty of bargains. It's the largest mall on West Maui and has some of the best shopping under one roof on the island. The newest mall in town is the open-air **Lahaina Center,** located along Front Street at Papalaua Street. Stores include Hilo Hattie, Banana Republic, Wet Seal, Maui Dive Shop, Hard Rock Cafe, and the Front Street Theaters. There are plenty of fine eateries here.

Ka'anapali to Kapalua

Whalers Village, the only mall in Ka'anapali, is set right on the ocean and features a wonderful self-guided whaling museum. There are various eateries, upscale boutiques, art galleries, a film processing center, and a sundries store. It's a great place to stroll, buy, and learn a few things about Maui's past. All of the big resorts have shopping arcades. You'll need a suitcase stuffed with money to buy anything there, but it's a blast just walking around the grounds and checking out the big-ticket items.

Along Lower Honoapi'ilani Road, the villages of Honokowai, Kahana, and Napili all have small local shopping malls, mostly for everyday items. Three new and larger malls have opened on Honoapi'ilani Highway, however, with a smattering of shops from clothing and sporting goods to fine restaurants. At the junction where the old road splits from the newer highway is **Honokowai Marketplace.** Up the way is **Kahana Gateway Mall,** while farther up is **Napili Plaza.**

Aside from the swanky arcade at the Ritz-Carlton and **Honolua Store,** which has a mix of clothing, gifts, and deli foods, the only place to shop in Kapalua is at the **Kapalua Shops** attached to the Kapalua Bay Hotel. Here are high-end clothing retailers, an import store, art gallery, gift shop, and one great restaurant.

Kihei and Wailea

Azeka Place, Azeka Place II, and **Longs Shopping Center** are all located along South Kihei Road in what could be considered the center of Kihei. Here there's food shopping, a multitude of clothing, gift, and specialty shops, with a few sporting goods stores, dive shops, and activities centers thrown in. Strung south along Kihei Road, one after another, are **Kukui Mall, Kihei Town Center, Kalama Village Marketplace, Dolphin Shopping Center, Kamaole Beach Center, Rainbow Mall, Kamaole Shopping Center,** and **Kai Nani Kai Village Plaza,** where restaurants, food outlets, boutiques, and all manner of gift shops can be found. Aside from these larger malls, there are numerous small arcades and individual shops throughout the area.

Newly rebuilt and the only shopping plaza within the fashionable resort area of Wailea, **The Shops at Wailea** is an exclusive assortment of both chic and affordable boutiques and eateries. It gives Whaler's Village in Ka'anapali a run for its money as the most exclusive mall on the island. In addition, all the hotels within Wailea have ritzy shopping arcades of their own, but you may need a wad of cash even to look.

SPECIALTY SHOPS

Some truly nifty and distinctive stores are wedged in among Maui's run-of-the-mill shopping centers; however, for real treasures you'll find the solitary little shop the best. Lahaina's Front Street has the greatest concentration of top-notch boutiques, but others are dotted here and there around the island. The following is only a sampling of the best; many more are listed in the individual chapters.

Tattered sails on a rotted mast, tattooed sea dogs in wide-striped jerseys, grim-faced Yankee captains squinting at the horizon, exotic (probably extinct) birds on the wing, flowers and weather-bent trees, and the beautiful, simple faces of Polynesians staring out from ancient days are faithfully preserved at **Lahaina Printsellers Ltd.,** one of the most unusual purveyors of art on Maui. This shop, like a mini-museum, is hung with original engravings, drawings, maps, charts, and naturalist sketches ranging in age from 150–400 years. Marked with an authenticity label, each piece can come from anywhere in the world, but the Hawaiiana collection is amazing in its depth. Many

works feature a nautical theme, reminiscent of the daring explorers who opened the Pacific. Lahaina Printsellers has been collecting for years and has the largest collection of material relating to Captain Cook in the entire Pacific Basin. The store also keeps Maui's art alive by representing modern artists as well. Find it at the Whalers Village in Ka'anapali.

For a unique memento of Maui, have your photo taken along Front Street in front of the Pioneer Inn Shops. Here, you'll become the human perch for macaws and cockatoos. The birds are very tame, natural hams, and the only thing on Maui guaranteed to be more colorful than your Hawaiian shirt. For about $25, vendors take your picture and deliver your developed photos the next day.

Pa'ia is quickly becoming an unofficial art center of Maui, along with being the windsurfing capital of Hawaii. Lahaina has slicker galleries, but you come much closer to the source in Pa'ia. The **Maui Crafts Guild** is an exemplary crafts shop that displays the best in local island art. All artists must be selected by active members before their works can be displayed. All materials used must be natural, with an emphasis on those found only in Hawaii.

Upcountry's Makawao is a wonderful and crazy combination of old-time *paniolo,* matured hippies who now worry about drugs and their kids, those into alternative health practices, and up-and-coming artists. This hodgepodge makes for a town with general merchandise shops, exclusive boutiques, numerous art galleries, a health food store, and Asian health clinics, all strung along two Dodge City–like streets.

The **Maui Swap Meet** on Pu'unene Avenue in Kahului is open every Saturday and Wednesday 8 A.M.–1 P.M. Great junk!

Wailuku is Maui's **antique attic** turned out on the street. About half a dozen odd little shops on Market Street display every kind of knick-knack, curio, art treasure, white elephant, grotesque and sublime piece of furniture, jewelry, stuffed toy, game, or oddity that ever floated, sailed, flew, or washed up on Maui's beaches.

Whalers General Store and **ABC Discount Stores** are good places to look for sundries, but they can hardly be beat for prices on such things as snacks, bottles of liquor, beach towels, straw mats and hats, zoris, gift items, Hawaiian-made products, and postcards.

Bookstores

The bookshop with the largest selection of books on the island is **Borders Books and Music,** at the Maui Marketplace in Kahului, 808/877-6160. Open daily 9 A.M.–10 P.M., until 11 P.M. Friday and Saturday. Borders also has a huge selection of magazines and newspapers and a thorough selection of books and maps relating to Hawaii and Hawaiiana. Their Cafe Espresso coffee shop is open the same hours, and there is a full schedule of music, presentations, and discussions throughout the month. Also with a full selection of books in Kahului is **Waldenbooks,** at the Queen Ka'ahumanu Center in Kahului, 808/871-6112. For the esoteric and the spiritual, stop at **Miracles Bookery,** 3682 Baldwin Ave. in Makawao, 808/572-2317.

There are several good used book shops on the island, and these also usually carry a fine selection of new Hawaiiana. In Wailuku, try **Paperbacks Plus,** 1977 Main St., 808/242-7135. The best place to look while in Lahaina is the **Old Lahaina Book Emporium,** 834 Front St., 808/661-1399. Open daily, most books in stock are used, but you can find some new books and new and used CDs as well.

Camera and Film

Ritz Camera Centers, with four shops, is the largest film sales and developing chain on the island and offers one-hour color print developing. The **Longs Drugs** around the island and some of the big-box stores also offer this service. Individual shops include **Paradise Photo** at the Kukui Mall in Kihei, **Flashback Photo Systems** in Piilani Village Shopping Center in Kihei, and **Wiki Wiki Photo** in Kahana. Camera service

centers on the island are limited. Ritz Camera on Lahainaluna Street in Lahaina can repair certain makes of cameras if the repair is not too technical; otherwise, they can refer you to an independent service technician.

ARTS TO BUY

Wild Hawaiian shirts or bright mu'umu'u, especially when worn on the Mainland, have the magical effect of making wearers feel as if they're in Hawaii, while eliciting spontaneous smiles from passersby. Maybe it's the colors, or perhaps it's just the vibe that signifies party time or hang loose, but nothing says Hawaii like alohawear. More than a dozen fabric houses in Hawaii turn out distinctive patterns, and many dozens of factories create their own personalized designs. These factories often have attached retail outlets, but in any case you can find hundreds of shops selling alohawear. Aloha shirts were the brilliant idea of a Chinese merchant in Honolulu, who used to hand-tailor them and sell them to the tourists who arrived by ship in the glory days before World War II. They were an instant success. Mu'umu'u or "Mother Hubbards" were the idea of missionaries, who were appalled by Hawaiian women running about *au naturel* and insisted on covering their new Christian converts from head to foot. Now the roles are reversed, and it's Mainlanders who come to Hawaii and immediately strip down to as little clothing as possible.

> *Wild Hawaiian shirts or bright mu'umu'u, especially when worn on the Mainland, have the magical effect of making the wearer feel as if they're in Hawaii, while eliciting spontaneous smiles from passersby.*

Alohawear

At one time alohawear was exclusively made of cotton or from man-made, natural fiber–based rayon, and these materials are still the best for any tropical clothing. Beware, however: Polyester has slowly crept into the market! No material could possibly be worse for the island climate, so when buying your alohawear make sure to check the label for material content. On the bright side, silk also is used and makes a good material, but is a bit heavy for some. Mu'umu'u now come in various styles and can be worn for the entire spectrum of social occasions in Hawaii. Aloha shirts are basically cut the same as always, but the patterns have undergone changes, and apart from the original flowers and ferns, modern shirts might depict an island scene in the manner of a silk-screen painting. A basic good-quality mu'umu'u or aloha shirt is guaranteed to be worth its price in good times and happy smiles. The connoisseur might want to purchase *The Hawaiian Shirt, Its Art and History* by R. Thomas Steele. It's illustrated with more than 150 shirts that are now considered works of art by collectors the world over.

Scrimshaw

This art of etching and carving on bone and ivory has become an island tradition handed down from the times of the old whaling ships. Although scrimshaw can be found throughout

a scrimshaw whaling scene

BOB RACE

Hawaii, the center remains in the old whaling capital of Lahaina. There along Front Street are a few shops specializing in scrimshaw. Today, pieces are carved on fossilized walrus ivory that is gathered by Inuit and shipped to Hawaii. It comes in a variety of shades from pure white to mocha, depending on the mineral content of the earth in which it was buried. Elephant ivory or whale bone is no longer used because of ecological considerations, but there is a "gray market" in Pacific walrus tusks. Inuit can legally hunt the walrus. They then make a few minimal scratches on the tusks, which technically qualifies them to be Native American art and free of most governmental restrictions. The tusks are then sent to Hawaii as art objects, but the superficial scratches are immediately removed and the ivory is reworked by artisans. Scrimshaw is made into everything from belt buckles to delicate earrings and even into coffee-table centerpieces. The prices can go from a few dollars up to the thousands.

Wood Carvings

One surviving Hawaiian art is wood carving. Old Hawaiians used koa almost exclusively because of its density, strength, and natural luster, but koa is becoming increasingly scarce. Many items are still available, but they are costly. Milo and monkeypod are also excellent woods for carving and have largely replaced koa. You can buy tikis, bowls, and furniture at numerous shops. Countless inexpensive carved items are sold at variety stores, such as hula dancers or salad servers, but most of these are imported from Asia or the Philippines.

Weaving

The minute you arrive in Hawaii, you should shell out $2 for a woven beach mat. This is a necessity, not a frivolous purchase, but it definitely won't have been made in Hawaii. What is made in Hawaii is *lau hala*. This is traditional Hawaiian weaving from the leaves (*lau*) of the pandanus (*hala*) tree. These leaves vary greatly in length, with the largest over six feet, and they have a thorny spine that must be removed before they can be worked. The color ranges from light tan to dark brown. The leaves are cut into strips one-eighth to one-inch wide and are then employed in weaving. Any variety of items can be made or at least covered in *lau hala*. It makes great purses, mats, baskets, and table mats.

Woven into a hat, it's absolutely superb but should not be confused with a palm-frond hat. A *lau hala* hat is amazingly supple and will pop back into shape even when squashed. A good one is expensive and will last for years with proper care. All *lau hala* should be given a light application of mineral oil on a monthly basis, especially if it's exposed to the sun. For flat items, iron over a damp cloth and keep purses and baskets stuffed with paper when not in use. Palm fronds also are widely used in weaving. They, too, are a great natural raw material, but not as good as *lau hala*. Almost any woven item, such as a beach bag woven from palm, makes a good authentic yet inexpensive gift or souvenir.

Quilts

Along with the gospel and the will to educate, the early missionaries brought skills and machines to sew. Aside from wanting to cover the naked bodies of their new converts, many taught the Hawaiians how to quilt together small pieces of material into designs for the bed. Quilting styles and patterns varied over the years and generally shifted from designs familiar to New Englanders to those more pleasing to Hawaiian eyes, and standard patterns include leaves, fruits, and flowers of the islands. Most Hawaiian-design quilts seen for sale in the islands today are now made in the Philippines under the direction of Hawaiian designers. Because of labor costs, they are far less expensive than any quilt that is actually made in Hawaii. Generally speaking, quilts 24 inches square run about $75, those 48 inches square about $180–250, and those for queen- and king-size beds from $1,200–1,500. When available, quilts made in Hawaii can be several times as expensive.

Gift Items

Jewelry is always an appreciated gift, especially if it's distinctive, and Hawaii has some of the most original. The sea provides the basic raw materials of pink, gold, and black corals that are as beautiful and fascinating as gemstones. Har-

vesting coral is dangerous work. The Lahaina beds off Maui have one of the best black coral lodes in the islands, but unlike reef coral, these trees grow at depths bordering the outer limits of a scuba diver's capabilities. Only the best can dive 180 feet after the black coral, and about one diver per year dies in pursuit of it. Conservationists have placed great pressure on the harvesters of these deep corals, and the state of Hawaii has placed strict limits and guidelines on the firms and divers involved.

Pink coral has long been treasured by humans. The Greeks considered it a talisman for good health, and there's even evidence that it has been coveted since the Stone Age. Coral jewelry is on sale at many shops throughout Hawaii. The value comes from the color of the coral and the workmanship.

Puka shells (with small, naturally occurring holes) and *'opihi* shells are also made into jewelry. These items are often inexpensive, yet they are authentic and are great purchases for the price. Hanging macramé planters festooned with seashells are usually quite affordable and are sold at roadside stands along with shells.

Hawaii also produces some unique food items appreciated by most people. Various-sized jars of macadamia nuts and butters are great gifts, as are tins of rich, gourmet-quality Kona coffee. Guava, pineapple, passion fruit, and mango are often gift-boxed into assortments of jams, jellies, and spicy chutneys. And for that special person in your life, you can bring home island fragrances in bottles of perfumes and colognes in the exotic odors of gardenia, plumeria, and even ginger. All of these items are reasonably priced, lightweight, and easy to carry.

Accommodations

With about 18,000 rooms available, in some 225 properties, Maui is second only to Oʻahu in the number of visitors it can accommodate. There's a tremendous concentration of condos on Maui, approximately 9,000 units, predominating in the Kihei, Maʻalaea, Honokowai, Kahana, and Napili areas; plenty of hotels, the majority in Kaʻanapali and Wailea; and a growing number of bed-and-breakfasts. Camping is limited to a handful of parks, but what it lacks in number it easily makes up for in quality.

More than 90 hotels and condos have sprouted on West Maui, from Lahaina to Kapalua. The most expensive are strung along some of Maui's best beaches in **Kaʻanapali** and **Kapalua** and include the Hyatt Regency, Westin Maui, Sheraton, Kapalua Bay, and Ritz-Carlton. The older condos in Honokowai are cheaper, with a mixture of expensive and moderate as you head north. **Lahaina** offers only a handful of places to stay: condos at both ends of town, three old-style inns, and a handful of bed-and-breakfasts. Most people find the pace a little too hectic, but you couldn't get more in the middle of it if you tried. **Maʻalaea Bay,** between Lahaina and Kihei, has 11 quiet condos. Prices are reasonable, the beach is fair, and you're within striking distance of the action in either direction.

Kihei is condo row, with close to 100 of them along the six miles of Kihei Road, plus a few hotels. This is where you'll find top-notch beaches and the best deals on Maui. **Wailea** just down the road is expensive, but the hotels here are world-class and the secluded beaches are gorgeous. **Kahului** often takes the rap for being an unattractive place to stay on Maui, but it isn't all that bad. You're smack in the middle of striking out to the best of Maui's sights, and the airport is minutes away for people staying only a short time. Prices are cheaper and Kanaha Beach is a sleeper, with great sand, surf, and few visitors. **Hana** is an experience in itself. You can camp, rent a cabin, or stay at an exclusive hotel. Always reserve in advance and consider splitting your stay on Maui, spending your last few nights in Hana. You can really soak up this wonderful area, and you won't have to worry about rushing back along the Hana Highway.

HOTELS

Even with the variety of other accommodations available, most visitors, at least first-timers, tend to stay in hotels. At one time, hotels were the only places to stay. Lahaina's Pioneer Inn dates from the turn of the 20th century, and if you were Maui-bound, it and a handful that haven't survived were about all that were offered on Maui. Hotels come in all shapes and sizes, from 10-room, family-run affairs to high-rise giants. The Neighbor Islands have learned an aesthetic lesson from Waikiki, however, and build low-rise resorts that don't obstruct the view and blend more readily with the surroundings. Whatever kind of accommodations you desire, you should be able to find it somewhere on Maui.

Types of Hotel Rooms

Most readily available and least expensive is a bedroom with bath. Some hotels can also offer you a studio (a large sitting room that converts to a bedroom), a suite (a bedroom with sitting room), or an apartment with full kitchen plus at least one bedroom. Kitchenettes are often available and contain a refrigerator, sink, and stove usually in a small corner nook or fitted together as one space-saving unit. Kitchenettes cost a bit more but save you a bundle by allowing you to prepare some of your own meals. To get that vacation feeling while keeping costs down, eat breakfast in, pack a lunch for the day, and go out to dinner. If you rent a kitchenette, make sure all the appliances work as soon as you arrive. If they don't, notify the front desk immediately, and if the hotel will not rectify the situation, ask to be moved or ask for a reduced rate. Hawaii has cockroaches, so put all food away.

Check-in is usually 3 P.M. or 4 P.M., although if your room is ready, they can get you in early. Call first. Checkout is most often 11 A.M. or noon. Some of the more expensive hotels and resorts have express checkout, and a TV/video checkout system is offered by others.

Amenities

All hotels have some of them, and some hotels have all of them. Air-conditioning is available in most, but under normal circumstances you won't need it. Balmy trade winds provide plenty of breezes, which flow through louvered windows and doors in many hotels. Ceiling fans are better. TVs are most often included, but not always, as are entertainment centers with stereos and CD players; pay-per-view movies are almost always an option. In-room phones are usually provided, but a service charge of up to one dollar per call is often tacked on, even for local calls. A few hotels have purposefully created an environment without phone, TV, or entertainment centers so that you can get plugged into your surroundings and stay disconnected from other distractions. Swimming pools are common, even though the hotel may sit right on the beach. There is always a restaurant of some sort—usually several—a coffee shop or two, a bar, a cocktail lounge, and sometimes a sundries shop, clothing store, or art gallery. While most stock complimentary coffee and tea, goodies from the honor bar will be charged to your bill.

Some hotels also offer tennis courts or golf courses either on the premises or affiliated with the hotel; usually an activities or concierge desk can book you into a variety of daily outings. Plenty of hotels offer laundromats on the premises, and the better places also have pickup and delivery laundry services. Hotel towels can be used at the pool and beach. Many hotels have installed clotheslines that pull out over the bathtub and are to be used for drying wet clothes. Dry your swimsuits there because hotels don't want you to drape your wet suit over the balcony outside. Bellhops generally get about $1 tip per bag or $5 per load on a rolling cart, and while maid service is complimentary, maids are customarily tipped $1–2 per time—a bit more if kitchenettes are involved or if you've been a piggy. Self-parking is (usually) free, and valet parking is often provided at a nominal fee or by tip. Most have in-room safes for securing your valuables but may charge between $1.50–3.75 for the privilege. Most hotels offer a children's program with supervised activities, excursion, and food during weekday daytime hours—sometimes seasonally—for children 5–12, which ranges from free to $50 per kid. Hotels can often arrange special services like baby-sitters (in house or with a local licensed caregiver), all kinds of lessons, and special entertainment activities. A few even have bicycles and snorkeling equipment to lend. They'll receive and send mail for you, cash your traveler's checks, and take messages. For your convenience, each room should be equipped with a directory of hotel services and information, and some hotels also include information about area sights, restaurants, and activities.

Hotel Rates

Every year Hawaiian hotels welcome in the New Year by hiking their rates by about 10 percent. Because of its gigantic tourist flow and tough competition, Hawaii offers hotel rooms at universally lower rates than most developed resort areas around the world; even with the 11.4 percent tax (7.25 percent accommodations tax, plus 4.16 percent state excise tax), there are still many reasonable rates to be had. The basic **daily rate** is geared toward double occupancy; singles are hit in the pocketbook. Single rates, when offered, are cheaper than doubles, but not usually by much. Many hotels will charge for a double and then add an additional charge ($10–100) for extra persons up to a certain number. Plenty of hotels offer the **family plan,** which allows children, usually 17 or 18 and under, to stay in their parents' room free if they use the existing bedding. If another bed or crib is required, there is an additional charge. Some hotels—not always the budget ones—let you cram in as many people as can sleep on the floor with no additional charge. Only a limited number of hotels offer the **American plan,** where breakfast and dinner are included with the night's lodging. **Discounts** of various sorts are offered, but these vary by hotel. Some of the typical discounts are AAA, AARP, car and room, room and breakfast, fifth night free, and *kama'aina* (state resident) rates, but

EXPLORING THE ISLANDS

many now offer special lower Internet rates when booking online because it's cheaper for hotels to sell rooms that way. **Business/corporate rates** are usually offered to anyone who can at least produce a business card. **Weekly and monthly** rates will save you approximately 10 percent off the daily rate. In all cases, make sure to ask about other-than-published rates because this information won't usually be volunteered. In addition to regular hotel charges and taxes, some luxury hotels and resorts now charge a "resort fee," generally $10–15, which is used to offset a variety of activity, service, and parking costs that would otherwise be charged for individually.

Some hotels have a single basic rate throughout the year, but most have a tiered pricing policy based on times of the year. This often translates as regular- and value-season rates (which may be referred to differently at different hotels), while some also include holiday rates. Some hotels have a policy of **minimum stay,** usually 3–7 days, during Christmas and New Year. While the difference between "high season" and "low season" is less distinct than it used to be, Hawaii's **peak season** still runs from just before Christmas until after Easter, and then again throughout the summer, when rooms are at a premium. Value-season rates, when rooms are easier to come by, are often about 10 percent below the regular rate.

In Hawaiian hotels you always pay more for a good view. Terms vary slightly, but usually "oceanfront" means your room faces the ocean and your view is mostly unimpeded. "Oceanview" is slightly more vague. It could be a decent view or it could require standing on the dresser and craning your neck to catch a tiny slice of the sea sandwiched between two skyscrapers. "Garden view" means just that, and "mountain view" may mean that you have a view of a mountain or simply that you have a view away from the ocean. Rooms are designated and priced upward, with garden view or mountain view being the least expensive, then oceanview and oceanfront rooms. Suites are invariably larger and more expensive, and these usually get the best locations and views.

Note: Prices listed are based on a standard published rate, double occupancy, without taxes or other charges added, unless otherwise noted.

Payments, Deposits, and Reservations

Most Hawaiian hotels accept foreign and domestic traveler's checks, personal checks preapproved by the management, foreign cash, and most major credit cards. Reservations are always the best policy, and they're easily made through travel agents or by contacting the hotel directly. In all cases, bring documentation of your confirmed reservations with you in case of a mix-up.

Deposits are not always required to make reservations, but they do secure them. Some hotels require the first (or several) night's payment in advance. Reservations without a deposit can be legally released if the room is not claimed by 6 P.M. Whether by phone call, email, fax, or letter, include your dates of stay and type of room in your request for a reservation, and make sure that the hotel sends you a copy of the confirmation. All hotels and resorts have **cancellation requirements** for refunding deposits. The time limit on these can be as little as 24 hours before arrival or as much as a full 30 days. Some hotels require full **advance payment** for your entire stay, especially during peak season or during times of crowded special events. Be aware of the time required for a cancellation notice *before* making your reservation deposit, especially when dealing with advance payment. If you have confirmed reservations, especially with a deposit, and there is no room for you, or one that doesn't meet prearranged requirements, you should be given the option of accepting alternate accommodations. You are owed the difference in room rates if there is any. If there is no room whatsoever, the hotel is required to find you one at a comparable hotel and to refund your deposit in full.

CONDOMINIUMS

The main qualitative difference between a condo and a hotel is in amenities. At a condo, you're more on your own. You're temporarily renting an apartment, so there won't be any bellhops and rarely a bar, restaurant, or lounge on the premises, although many times you'll find a sundries store. The main lobby, instead of having that grand-entrance feel of many hotels, is more like an apartment house entrance, although there might be a front desk. Condos can be studios (one big room), but mostly they are one- or multiple-bedroom affairs with a complete kitchen. Reasonable housekeeping items should be provided: linens, all furniture, and a fully equipped kitchen. Most have TVs and phones, but remember that the furnishings provided are all up to the owner. You can find brand-new furnishings that are top of the line, right down to garage-sale bargains. Inquire about the furnishings when you make your reservations. Maid service might be included on a limited basis (for example, once weekly) or you might have to pay extra for it.

Condos usually require a minimum stay, although some will rent on a daily basis, like hotels. Minimum stays when applicable are often three days, but seven is also commonplace, and during peak season two weeks isn't unheard of. Swimming pools are common, and depending on the theme of the condo, you can find saunas, weight rooms, hot tubs, and tennis courts. A nominal extra fee, often $10–15, is usually charged for more than two people. Generally speaking, studios can sleep two, a one-bedroom place will sleep four, two-bedroom units will sleep six, and three-bedroom units will sleep eight. Most have a sleeper couch in the sitting room that folds out into a bed. You can find clean, decent condos for as little as $450 per week, all the way up to exclusive apartments for well more than $2,000. Most fall into the $700–1,000 range per week. The method of paying for and reserving a condo is just about the same as for a hotel. However, requirements for deposit, final payments, and cancellation charges are much stiffer than in hotels. Make absolutely sure you fully understand all of these requirements when you make your reservations.

The real advantage of condos is for families, friends who want to share accommodations, and especially travelers on long-term stays, for which you will always get a special rate. The kitchen facilities save a great deal on dining costs, and it's common to find units with their own mini-washers and dryers. To sweeten the deal, many condo companies offer coupons that can save you money on food, gifts, and activities at local establishments. Parking space is ample for guests, and like hotels, plenty of stay/drive deals are of-

fered. Like hotels, condos usually charge for local calls and credit card or collect calls. Some have in-room safes, but there will be a daily charge of $1.50–1.75 for their use. Pay-per-view, in-room movie service is usually available from $8.95–16.95 per movie. Many now also have a lost key fee, which may be as steep as $75, so don't lose it! If you can't produce it, you pay for it.

Hotel/Condominium Information

The best source of hotel/condo information for the vacationer is the **Hawaii Visitors Bureau (HVB).** While planning your trip, either visit one nearby or write to the bureau in Hawaii. (Addresses are given in the Information and Services section later in this chapter.) Request a free copy of the current Accommodation/Dining/Entertainment Guide. This handy booklet lists all of the hotel/condo members of the HVB, with addresses, phone numbers, facilities, and rates. General tips are also given.

For those who are thinking of living in a condominium long-term or perhaps of buying a condo unit, invest in a copy of the *Maui County Condominium Directory.* This 600-plus-page tome is a complete listing of all condominium properties on Maui, Moloka'i, and Lana'i. It details specific information and features about the properties and their units, provides photographs, contact numbers, recent sales information, and added general information about living in the county. At $39.95 plus shipping and handling charges, it's not for everyone, but it might come in handy for those who are seriously shopping around. Contact Paradise Publishing, P.O. Box 1647, Wailuku, HI 96793; 808/242-4970 or 800/354-1450, info@maui-book.com, www.mauibook.com.

Condo Booking and Reservations

The following is a partial listing of booking agents handling properties on Maui. Some of these rental agencies also offer services for arranging other types of vacation rentals.

Aston Hotels and Resorts, 2250 Kuhio Ave., Honolulu, HI 96815, 800/321-2558 in Hawaii, 808/931-1400 or 800/922-7886 Mainland, or 800/445-6633 Canada, www.aston-hotels.com

Outrigger Hotels and Resorts, 2375 Kuhio Ave., Honolulu, HI 96815, 800/688-7444, www.outrigger.com

Marc Resorts Hawaii, 2155 Kalakaua Ave., Honolulu, HI 96815, 808/926-5900 or 800/535-0085, www.marcresorts.com

Destination Resorts Hawaii, 3750 Wailea Alanui, Wailea, HI 96753, 808/879-1595 or 800/367-5246, fax 808/874-3554, rents condos in six separate luxury villages in Wailea, www.destinationresortshi.com.

Go Condo Hawaii, 800/452-3463, www.gocondohawaii.com

Maui Condominium and Home Realty, 2511 S. Kihei Rd., P.O. Box 1840 Kihei, Maui, HI 96753, 808/879-5445 or 800/451-5008, fax 808/874-6144, www.mauicondo.com, has more than 300 listings in all price categories with most in the Kihei area.

Condominium Rentals Hawaii, 362 Huku Li'i Place, #204, Kihei, HI 96753, 808/879-2778 or 800/367-5242 Mainland, 800/663-2101 Canada, fax 808/879-7825, www.crhmaui.com, can arrange your stay in 10 condos in Kihei.

Maui Beachfront Rentals, 256 Papalaua St., Lahaina, HI 96761, 808/661-3500 or 888/661-7200, fax 808/661-5200, www.mauibeachfront.com, has high-end homes and condo units on West Maui.

AA Oceanfront Condo Rentals, 1279 S. Kihei Rd., Suite 107, Kihei, HI 96753, 808/879-7288 or 800/488-6004, fax 808/879-7500, www.aaoceanfront.com, manages properties from north Kihei to Makena, economy to deluxe.

Kumulani Vacations and Realty, P.O. Box 1190, Kihei, HI 96753, 808/879-9272 or 800/367-2954, fax 808/874-0094, www.kumulani.com, handles rentals in 10 condos in Kihei and Wailea.

Kihei Maui Vacations, P.O. Box 1055, Kihei, HI 96753, 808/879-7581 or 888/568-6284, fax 808/879-2000, www.kmvmaui.com, has several dozen units mostly in Kihei.

Maui Resort Vacation Rentals, P.O. Box 1755, Kihei, HI 96753, 808/879-5973 or 800/441-3187, fax 808/879-1357, www.mauiresort4u.com, handles units in more than two dozen condos along the Kihei coast and also has a few rental homes.

Klahani Resorts, P.O. Box 11108, Lahaina, HI 96761, 808/667-2712 or 800/669-6284, fax 808/661-5875, www.klahani.com, offers units in half a dozen properties from Lahaina to Kahana.

Maalaea Bay Rentals, 280 Hauoli St., Maalaea, HI 96793, 808/244-7012 or 800/367-6084, fax 808/242-7476, www.maalaeabay.com, handles more than 100 units in a majority of the condos in Ma'alaea.

Chase'n Rainbows, 118 Kupuohi St., Lahaina, HI 96761, 808/667-7088 or 800/367-6092, www.chasenrainbows.com

Sullivan Properties, P.O. Box 55, Lahaina, HI 96767; 808/669-0423 or 800/332-1137, fax 808/669-8409, www.kapalua.com, has rental units is a handful of condo properties along this stretch and in Kapalua up the coast.

For condos mostly in west Maui, see **Accommodations Hawaii,** 808/661-6655 or 877/661-6655, fax 808/669-9199, infor@accommodations-hawaii.com, www.accommodations-hawaii.com.

VACATION RENTALS

Vacation rentals are homes or cottages that are rented to visitors, usually for a week or longer, sometimes shorter. These rentals come with all the amenities of condo units, but they are usually freestanding homes. Meals are not part of the option, so that is your responsibility. There are numerous vacation rentals throughout the island, and many of these advertise by word of mouth, ads in magazines, and with websites. Perhaps the best way to locate a vacation rental, at least for the first time that you visit the island, is through a rental/real-estate agent: see the previous listing for a starter. This can be handled either on Hawai'i, or by phone, fax, email, or through the mail. Everything from simple beach homes to luxurious hideaways are put into the hands of rental agents. The agents have descriptions of the properties and terms of the rental contracts, and many will furnish photographs. Be aware that some places, although not all, have outgoing cleaning fees that are in addition to the rental rate. When contacting an agency, be as specific as possible about your needs, length of stay, desired location, and how much you're willing to spend. If handled through the mail, the process may take some time; write several months in advance. Be aware that during high season, rentals are at a premium; if you're slow to inquire there may be slim pickins.

BED-AND-BREAKFASTS

Bed-and-breakfast (B&B) inns are hardly a new idea. The Bible talks of the hospitable hosts who opened the gates of their homes and invited the wayfarer in to spend the night. B&Bs have a long tradition in Europe and were common-place in Revolutionary America. Nowadays, lodging in private homes called bed-and-break-fasts is becoming increasingly fashionable throughout America, and Hawaii is no excep-tion, with about 100,000 B&B guests yearly. Maui County has perhaps 300 B&Bs, of which about 30 are legally licensed and registered with the county office.

Points to Consider

The primary feature of bed-and-breakfasts is that every one is privately owned and there-fore uniquely different from every other. The range of B&Bs is as wide as the living stan-dards in America. You'll find everything from a semi-mansion in the most fashionable resi-dential area to a little grass shack offered by a down-home fisherman and his family. This means that it's particularly important for the guest to choose a host family with whom his or her lifestyle is compatible.

Unlike at a hotel or a condo, you'll be staying *with* a host (usually a family), although your room will be private, with private baths and separate entrances quite common. You can make arrangements directly or you might want to go through an agency (listed as follows), which acts as a go-between, matching host and guest. It is best to call these agencies, but you can also write. Agencies have a description of each B&B they rent for, its general location, the fees

charged, and a good idea of the lifestyle of the host family. The agency will want to know where you want to stay, what type of place you're looking for, the price range you're willing to pay, arrival and departure dates, and other items that will help them match you with a place (for example: Are you single? Do you have children? Do you smoke?) You can do all the legwork yourself, but these people know their territory and guarantee their work. If you find that a sit-uation is incompatible, they will find another that works. They also inspect each B&B and make sure that each has a license and insurance to operate. Most can also arrange discount rental car and interisland airfares for you.

Because B&Bs are run by individual families, the times they will accept guests can vary ac-cording to what's happening in their lives. This makes it imperative to write well in advance: three months is good; earlier is too long and too many things can change. Four weeks is about the minimum time required to make all necessary arrangements. Expect a minimum stay require-ment (three days is common). B&Bs are not long-term housing, although it's hoped that guest and host will develop a friendship and that future stays can be as long as both desire.

As with condos, B&Bs have different re-quirements for making and holding reservations and for payment. Most will hold a room with a credit card deposit or check covering a certain percentage of the total bill. Be aware, however, that some B&Bs do not accept credit cards or personal checks, so you must pay in cash, trav-eler's checks, or money orders. Always inquire about the method of payment when making your initial inquiries.

B&B Agencies

Maui Bed and Breakfast Association, www.bed-breakfastmaui.com, is an entity established to represent bed-and-breakfast inns of Maui on the Internet. All listed accommodations are fully li-censed by the county, and all current members are located on West Maui.

A top-notch B&B agency with more than 200 homes is **Bed-and-Breakfast Hawaii,** P.O. Box 449, Kapa'a, HI 96746, 808/822-7771 or

800/733-1632, reservations@bandb-hawaii.com, www.bandb-hawaii.com, operated by Evelyn Warner and Al Davis. They've been running this service since 1978, and their reputation is excellent.

One of the most experienced agencies, **Bed-and-Breakfast Honolulu (Statewide)**, 3242 Kaohinanai Dr., Honolulu, HI 96817, 808/595-7533, fax 808/595-2030, or 800/288-4666, rainbow@hawaiibnb.com, www.hawaiibnb.com, owned and operated by Mary Lee and Gene Bridges, began in 1982. Since then, they've become masters at finding visitors the perfect accommodations to match their desires, needs, and pocketbooks. Their repertoire of guest homes offers more than 400 rooms, with half on O'ahu and the other half scattered around the state.

All Island Bed-and-Breakfast, 823 Kainui Dr., Kailua, HI 96734, 808/263-2342, fax 808/263-0308, or 800/542-0344, cac@aloha.net, can match your needs up with about 700 homes throughout the state.

Hawaii's Best Bed-and-Breakfast, P.O. Box 520, Kamuela, HI 96743, 808/885-4550 or 800/262-9912, fax 808/885-0559, bestbnb @aloha.net, www.bestbnb.com, has listings all over the state and is known for excellent service.

Since 1982, **Go Native Hawaii**, 808/935-4178 or 800/662-8483, reservations@gonativehi.com, www.gonativehi.com, has helped people find the right place to stay on the five major islands.

HOSTELS

Maui has several reasonably priced hostels in Wailuku and Lahaina. **Banana Bungalow**, 310 N. Market St., Wailuku, HI 96793, 808/244-5090 or 800/846-7835, fax 808/244-3678, info@mauihostel.com, www.mauihostel.com, has office hours 8 A.M.–11 P.M. This laid-back hostel has bunks for $17.50 per night and rooms for $32 single, $40 double, and $50 triple. Extras include shuttle service, tours, on-site kitchen, and a hot tub in the garden.

Just up the street and around the corner is the **North Wind Hostel**, 2080 Vineyard St., tel/fax 808/242-1448 or 866/946-7835, maui@northwind-hostel.com, www.northwind-hostel.com. Look for the row of international flags on the streetfront balcony. The North Wind offers most of the same amenities as Banana Bungalow. Bunks are $18, rooms $32 single and $38 double.

With only 16 places, the smaller **Aloha Windsurfers' Hostel**, 167 N. Market St., 808/249-0206 or 800/249-1421, fax 808/249-0705, email alohawindsurf@yahoo.com, www.accommodations-maui.com, offers dorm beds for $17.50, with privates $42–56. Amenities include a free simple breakfast, Internet access, and local calls, as well as airport and beach pickup and drop-off.

Patey's Place Maui Hostel, 761 Waine'e St. in Lahaina, 808/667-0999, maui@hawaiian-hostels.com, www.hawaiian-hostels.com, is a smaller, spartan, home-turned-hostel set two blocks back from the water that has a kitchen, TV room, and some storage. A bunk runs $20, a small single room $45, a private room with shared bath $50–55, and the private room with private bath $60.

HOME EXCHANGES

One other method of staying in Hawaii, open to homeowners, is to offer the use of your home in exchange for use of a home in Hawaii. This is done by listing your home with an agency that facilitates the exchange and publishes a descriptive directory. To list your home and to find out what is available, contact one of the following agencies:

Homelink USA, P.O. Box 47747, Tampa, FL 33647, 813/975-9825 or 800/638-3841, fax 813/910-8144, usa@homelink.org, www.homelink.org

Intervac U.S., 30 Corte San Fernando, Tiburon, CA 94920, 808/756-4663, fax 415/435-7440, info@intervacus.com, www.intervacus.com

Vacation Homes Unlimted, 16654 Soledad Canyon Rd., Ste. 214, Santa Clarita, CA 91387, 808/298-0376, fax 808/298-0576 or 800/848-7927, www.exchangehomes.com

Food and Drink

Hawaii is a gastronome's Shangri-la, a sumptuous smorgasbord in every sense of the word. The varied ethnic groups that have come to Hawaii in the last 200 years have each brought their own special enthusiasm and culture. And lucky for all, they didn't forget their cookpots, hearty appetites, and exotic taste buds.

The Polynesians who first arrived found a fertile but barren land. Immediately they set about growing taro, coconuts, and bananas and raising chickens, pigs, fish, and dogs, although the latter were reserved for the nobility. Harvests were bountiful and the islanders thanked the gods with the traditional feast called the lu'au. Most foods were baked in the underground oven, the *imu*. Participants were encouraged to feast while relaxing on straw mats and enjoying the hula and various entertainments. The lu'au is as popular as ever and a treat guaranteed to delight anyone with a sense of eating adventure.

The missionaries and sailors came next, and their ships' holds carried barrels of ingredients for puddings, pies, dumplings, gravies, and roasts—the sustaining "American foods" of New England farms. The mid-1800s saw the arrival of boatloads of Chinese and Japanese peasants, who wasted no time making rice instead of bread the staple of the islands. The Chinese added their exotic spices, cooking complex Sichuan dishes as well as workers' basics like chop suey. The Japanese introduced shoyu (soy sauce), sashimi, boxed lunches (bento), delicate tempura, and rich, filling noodle soups. The Portuguese brought their luscious Mediterranean dishes of tomatoes, peppers, and plump, spicy sausages; nutritious bean soups; and mouthwatering sweet treats like *malasadas* (holeless donuts) and *pao dolce* (sweet bread). Koreans carried crocks of zesty kimchi and quickly fired up grills for pulgogi, a marinated beef cooked over a fire. Filipinos served up their delicious adobo stews—fish, meat, or chicken in a rich sauce of vinegar and garlic.

Recently, Thai and Vietnamese restaurants have been offering their irresistible dishes next door to restaurants serving fiery burritos from Mexico or elegant marsala cream sauces from France. The ocean breezes of Hawaii not only cool the skin but waft with them some of the most delectable aromas on earth, to make the taste buds tingle and the spirit soar.

HAWAIIAN CUISINE

Hawaiian cuisine, the oldest in the islands, consists of wholesome, well-prepared, and delicious foods. All you have to do on arrival is notice the size of some of the local men (and women) to know immediately that food to them is indeed a happy and serious business. An oft-heard island joke is that "local men don't eat until they're full; they eat until they're tired." Many Hawaiian dishes have become standard fare at a variety of restaurants, eaten at one time or another by anyone who spends time in the islands. Hawaiian food in general is called *kaukau*, cooked food is *kapahaki*, and something broiled is called *ka'ola*. Any of these prefixes on a menu will let you know that Hawaiian food is served. Usually inexpensive, it will definitely fill you and keep you going.

Traditional Favorites

In old Hawaii, although the sea meant life, many more people were involved in cultivating beautifully tended garden plots of taro, sugarcane, breadfruit, and various sweet potatoes *('uala)* than with fishing. They husbanded pigs and barkless dogs *('ilio)*, and prized *moa* (chicken) for their feathers and meat, but found eating the eggs repulsive. Their only farming implement was the *'o'o*, a sharpened hardwood digging stick. The Hawaiians were the best farmers of Polynesia, and the first thing they planted was taro, a tuberous root that was created by the gods at the same time as humans. This main staple of the old Hawaiians was made into poi. Every lu'au will have poi, a glutinous purple paste. It comes in liquid consistencies referred to as one-, two-, or three-finger poi. The fewer fingers you need to eat it, the thicker it is. Poi is one of the most nutritious carbohydrates known, but people unaccustomed to it find it bland and tasteless. Some of the best, fermented for a day or so, has an acidic bite. Poi is made to be eaten *with* something, but locals who love it pop it in their mouths and smack their lips. Those unaccustomed to it will suffer constipation if they eat too much.

Although poi grew out of favor during the middle of the 20th century, it is once again becoming more popular, and several sizable factories are now producing poi for sale. You can find plastic containers of this food refrigerated in many supermarkets and local food stores. In addition, deep-fried slices of taro root, plain or spiced, are now packaged and sold like potato chips.

A favorite dessert is *haupia,* a custard made from coconut. *Limu* is a generic term for edible seaweed, which many people still gather from the shoreline and eat as a salad or mix with ground *kukui* nuts and salt as a relish. A favorite Hawaiian snack is *'opihi,* small shellfish (limpets) that cling to rocks. Those who gather them always leave some on the rocks for the future. Cut from the shell and eaten raw by all peoples of Hawaii, *'opihi* sell for $150 per gallon in Honolulu—a testament to their popularity. A general term that has come to mean "hors d'oeuvres" in Hawaii is *pu pu.* Originally the name of a small shellfish, it is now used for any finger food. A traditional liquor made from *ti* root is *'okolehao.* It literally means "iron bottom," reminiscent of the iron blubber pots used to ferment it.

Pacific Rim (a.k.a. "Hawaiian Regional") Cuisine

At one time the tourist food in Hawaii was woeful. Of course, there have always been a handful of fine restaurants, but for the most part the food lacked soul, with even the fine hotels opting to offer second-rate renditions of food more appropriate to large Mainland cities. Surrounded by some of the most fertile and pristine waters in the Pacific, you could hardly find a restaurant offering fresh fish, and it was an ill-conceived boast that even the fruits and vegetables lying limply on your table were imported. Beginning with a handful of extremely creative and visionary chefs

in the early 1980s, who took the chance of perhaps offending the perceived simple palates of visitors, a delightfully delicious new cuisine was born. Based on the finest traditions of continental cuisine—including, to a high degree, its sauces, pastas, and presentations—the culinary magic of Pacific Rim boldly adds the pungent spices of Asia, the fantastic fresh vegetables, fruits, and fish of Hawaii, and, at times, the earthy cooking methods of the American Southwest. The result is a cuisine of fantastic tastes, subtle yet robust, and satiating but health-conscious—the perfect marriage of fresh foods prepared in a fresh way. Now restaurants on every island proudly display menus labeled "Hawaiian Regional" or some version of this. As always, some are better than others, but the general result is that the tourist food has been vastly improved and everyone benefits. Many of these exemplary chefs left lucrative and prestigious positions at Hawaii's five-diamond hotels and opened signature restaurants of their own, making this fine food much more available and affordable.

In 1998, a new and younger group called Hawaiian Island Chefs came together to further enhance the variety and offering of innovative foods made with island-grown produce and the bounty of the sea. In addition, this group strives to influence culinary programs in the state to help carry on this fine tradition. With the incredible mix of peoples and cultures in Hawaii, the possibilities are endless, and this new group of chefs intends to shepherd the experience along.

Lu'au

The lu'au is an island institution. For a fixed price, you get to gorge yourself on a tremendous variety of island foods, sample a few free island drinks, and have an evening of entertainment as well. Generally, lu'au run from about 5 or 5:30 P.M. to 8:30 or 9 P.M. On your lu'au day, eat a light breakfast, skip lunch, and do belly-stretching exercises! Food is usually served buffet-style, and while all have pretty much the same format, the type of food and entertainment differ somewhat.

To have fun at a lu'au you have to get into the swing of things. Entertainment is provided by local performers in what is often called a Polynesian Revue. This includes the tourist's hula—the fast version with swaying hips and dramatic lighting—a few wandering troubadours singing Hawaiian standards, and someone swinging flaming torches. Some also offer an *imu* ceremony where the pig is taken from the covered oven. All the Hawaiian standards like *poi, haupia, lomi* salmon, *laulau*, a package of meat, fish, and veggies wrapped in *ti* leaves, and *kalua* (*imu*-baked) pig are usually served. If these don't suit your appetite, various Asian dishes, plus chicken, fish, and roast beef, are most often also on the table. If you leave a lu'au hungry, it's your own fault!

The lu'au master starts the *imu* on the morning of the gathering; stop by and watch. He lays the hot stones and banana stalks so well that the underground oven maintains a perfect 400°F. In one glance, the lu'au master can gauge the weight and fat content of a succulent porker and decide just how long it should be cooked. The water in the leaves covering the pig steams and roasts the meat so that it falls off the fork. Local wisdom has it that "All you can't eat in the *imu* are the hot stones."

Lu'au range in price from about $67–80 for adults and about half that for children and include entertainment. This is the tourist variety—a lot of fun, but definitely a show. The least expensive, most authentic, and best lu'au are often put on by local churches or community groups. If you ask locals "Which is the best?" you won't get two to agree. It's literally a matter of taste. Following is a list of the lu'au presently available on Maui.

Old Lahaina Lu'au, on the beach at its location near the Lahaina Cannery Mall, 808/667-1998, www.oldlahainaluau.com, has an excellent reputation because it is as close to authentic as you can get. Doors open at 6 P.M. daily, 5:30 P.M. during winter, but reserve at least 3–6 days in advance to avoid disappointment, perhaps two weeks in advance during peak season. The lu'au, featuring a "locals' favorite," all-you-can-eat buffet and all-you-can-drink bar, costs $79 adults, $49 children 2–12. The traditional hula dancers use *ti*-leaf skirts, and the music is *fo' real*. The Old Lahaina Lu'au is one of the oldest, and it

gets the nod from nearly everyone as being the best lu'au on the island.

Renaissance Wailea Beach Resort, 808/891-7811, recounts tales of old Hawaii with its professional hula show and lu'au every Tuesday, Thursday, and Saturday at 5:30 P.M. Hawaiian music, hula, drumming, and a fire dancer entertain as you dine through the evening on a wonderful assortment of foods expertly prepared by the chefs. Price includes open bar at $70 adults, $33 children 3–12. Reservations are required.

The Royal Lahaina Resort has been offering the nightly **Royal Lahaina Lu'au** for years in their Lu'au Gardens starting at 5 P.M. Although definitely designed for the tourist, the show is entertaining and the food offered is authentic and tasty. Prices are $67 adults, free for children 12 and under with a paying adult; reservations at 808/661-3611.

Wailea's Finest Lu'au, at the Wailea Marriott Resort, 808/879-1922, has garnered awards for its lu'au fare and Polynesian show, and its fire/knife dancer is an international award winner for his skill. Held Mondays, Tuesdays, Thursdays, and Fridays 5–8 P.M., $68 adults, $30 children 6–12.

Hyatt Regency Maui's **Drums of the Pacific,** 808/667-4420, is held every evening 5–8 P.M., for $78 adults, $37 kids 6–12. This meal and show always gets high marks from those who know on the island.

The **Maui Marriott** also presents its version of the lu'au and Polynesian show, starting the night with Polynesian games and activities. The Marriott's niche is its funny and entertaining twists. The evening starts at 5 P.M. and runs until 8 P.M. Cost is $78 adults, $38 children 3–8. Call 808/661-5828 for reservations.

Although not the typical lu'au per se, **The Feast at Lele,** at the beachfront 505 Front Street Mall venue in Lahaina, 808/667-5353, www.feastatlele.com, does a wonderful job of combining food with entertainment. Each of the five courses of this sit-down, served meal is accompanied by a Hawaiian, Tongan, Tahitian, or Samoan music and dance performance. Prepared under the direction of chef James McDonald, who also owns and operates the i'o and pacific'O restaurants, the food is top-notch, and the show, designed by those who bring you the Old La-haina Lu'au, is well coordinated with the meal. This evening runs $95 adults, $65 children, daily from 6–9 P.M. (5:30–8:30 P.M. during winter). Reservations are a must.

MONEY-SAVERS

Only one thing is better than a great meal: a great meal at a reasonable price. The following are island institutions and favorites that will help you eat well and keep prices down.

Kaukau Wagons

These are lunch wagons, but instead of slick, stainless-steel jobs, most are old delivery trucks converted into portable kitchens. Some say they're a remnant of World War II, when workers had to be fed on the job; others say that the meals they serve were inspired by the Japanese bento, a boxed lunch. You'll see the wagons parked along beaches, in city parking lots, or on busy streets. Usually a line of local people will be placing their orders, especially at lunchtime—a tip-off that the wagon serves delicious, nutritious island dishes at reasonable prices. They might have a few tables, but basically they serve food to go. Most of their filling meals are about $3.50, and they specialize in the "plate lunch."

Plate Lunch

One of the best island standards, these lunches give you a sampling of authentic island food that can include teriyaki chicken, mahimahi, *lau lau*, and *lomi* salmon, among others. They're on paper or Styrofoam plates, are packed to go, and usually cost less than $3.50. Standard with a plate lunch is "two-scoop rice" and a generous dollop of macaroni or other salad. Full meals, they're great for keeping down food costs and for instant picnics. Available everywhere, from *kaukau* wagons to restaurants.

Bento

Bento are the Japanese rendition of the box lunch. Aesthetically arranged, they are full meals. They are often sold in supermarkets and in some local eateries with takeout counters.

Saimin

Special "saimin shops," as well as restaurants, serve this hearty, Japanese-inspired noodle soup. Saimin is a word unique to Hawaii. In Japan, these soups would be called "ramen" or "soba," and it's as if the two were combined into "saimin." A large bowl of noodles in broth, stirred with meat, chicken, fish, shrimp, or vegetables, costs only a few dollars and is big enough for an evening meal. The best place to eat saimin is at a local hole-in-the-wall shop run by a family.

Okazu-ya

A Hawaiian adaptation of the Japanese restaurant that sells side dishes and inexpensive food, "okazu-ya" usually have a full menu of savory entrées as well as side dishes that take their inspiration, like much in the islands, from all the peoples who have made Hawaii their home. Sometimes they specialize in one type of dish or another. Usually small family-run shops that cater to the local community, they have loyal clients who demand top quality and cheap prices. While not usually on the list of dieters' delights, the food you find at these fine places is filling and will sustain you through the day, yet some places are adapting to a leaner menu selection. Some but not all have okazu-ya as part of the restaurant name.

Early-Bird Specials

Even some of the island's best restaurants in the fanciest hotels offer early-bird specials—the regular-menu dinners offered to diners who come in before the usual dinner hour, which is approximately 6 P.M. You pay as little as half the normal price and can dine in luxury on some of the best foods. The specials are often advertised in the "free" tourist books, which might also include coupons for two-for-one meals or limited dinners at much lower prices. Just clip them out.

Buffets

Buffets are also quite common in Hawaii, and like lu'au are all-you-can-eat affairs. Offered at a variety of restaurants and hotels, they usually cost $12 and up, but will run $25–35 in the better hotels. The food, however, ranges considerably from passable to quite good. At lunchtime, they're priced lower than dinner, and breakfast buffets are cheaper yet. Buffets are often advertised in free tourist literature, which always include discount coupons.

FOOD MARKETS

If you're shopping for general food supplies and are not interested in gourmet, specialty items, or organic foods, you'll save money by shopping at the big-name supermarkets, located in Lahaina, Kahului, and Kihei, often in malls. Smaller towns have general food stores, which are adequate but a bit more expensive. You can also find convenience items at sundries shops in many condos and hotels, but these should be used only for snack foods or when absolutely necessary because the prices are just too high.

Kahului and Wailuku

The greatest number of supermarkets is found in Kahului. Three are conveniently located along Ka'ahumanu Avenue or adjacent to the three malls. **Foodland,** open daily until 10 P.M., is at the Queen Ka'ahumanu Center. Just down the road in the Kahului Shopping Center is the ethnic **Ah Fooks Super Market,** open Mon.–Fri. until 8 P.M., closing early Saturday and Sunday, specializing in Japanese, Chinese, and Hawaiian foods. Farther along in the Maui Mall is **Star Market,** open every day until 10 P.M. Just behind the Maui Mall on East Kamehameha Avenue is a **Safeway.** The biggest and most well-stocked in Wailuku is **Ooka Super Market.** Along with the usual selection of items, it has a great ethnic food section. Open daily into the evening.

Kihei

In Kihei you've got your choice of **Foodland** in the Kihei Town Center and **Star Market** up the way on South Kihei Road, open 5 A.M.–2 A.M.

West Maui

In Lahaina you can shop at **Foodland** and **Nagasako General Store** at the Old Lahaina Center. Nagasako's has all you need, plus a huge selection of Hawaiian and Asian items, and is

open daily 7 A.M.–10 P.M., Sunday until 7 P.M. If you're staying at a condo and doing your own cooking, the largest and generally least expensive supermarket on West Maui is the **Safeway,** open 24 hours daily, in the Lahaina Cannery Mall. North of Lahaina are the smaller but full-service **Star Market** in Honokowai and the **Napili Market** in Napili Plaza. All others are smaller convenience stores with more limited selection and higher prices.

Around and About

At **Pukalani Superette** in Pukalani, open seven days a week, you can pick up supplies and food to go, including sushi. Larger yet, with a greater selection, is **Foodland** in the Pukalani Terrace Center. In Hana, the **Hana Store** carries all of the necessities and even has a selection of health foods and imported beers; open daily 7 A.M.–7:30 P.M.

Health Food

Those who are into organic foods, fresh vegetables, natural vitamins, and takeout snack bars have it made on Maui. At the island's fine health food stores you can have most of your needs met. In Kahului, **Down to Earth Natural Foods,** 305 Dairy Rd., 808/877-2661, is an excellent full-service health food store complete with vitamins, minerals, and supplements, bulk foods, canned and boxed goods, and fresh vegetables and fruit. This store also has a deli counter, salad bar, and bakery (open Mon.–Sat. 7 A.M.–7 P.M., Sunday 7 A.M.–8 P.M.). A **Down To Earth Natural Foods** sister store, 1169 Makawao Ave. in Makawao, 808/572-1488, is smaller but with the same basic items and the same philosophy; open daily 8 A.M.–8 P.M. **Down To Earth Natural Foods** also has a store in Lahaina at the corner of Lahainaluna and Waine'e streets. Open Monday–Saturday 7 A.M.–9 P.M., Sunday 8:30 A.M.–8 P.M.), it's a full-service health food store, featuring bulk items, and a full selection of vitamins, minerals, and supplements. You can even get food to go from the salad bar and hot item counter. In Pa'ia is **Mana Natural Foods,** 49 Baldwin Ave., 808/579-8078, open daily 8:30 A.M.–8:30 P.M. You can pick up whatever you need for your trip to Hana at this old establishment. It has a full range of bulk and packaged items, supplements, drinks, a deli and hot-food counter, and picnic foods.

Farmers Markets

For the best and freshest fruits, veggies, baked goods, flowers, and sometimes crafts and clothing, search out the farmers markets. Most of what is sold is local, some is organic. Gardeners bring their goods to the parking lot across from Honokowai Beach Park in Honokowai Mondays, Wednesdays, and Fridays 7–11 A.M. and then move to the parking lot of Suda's Store in Kihei for the afternoon of the same days, 1:30–5:30 P.M. Be early for the best selection. The Longs Shopping Center in Kihei also hosts a farmers market every Saturday 8 A.M.–noon, and another market is held at the Da Rose Mall in Honokowai every day but Saturday 7:30 A.M.–3:30 P.M. Kahului holds an organic farmers market at the Kahului Shopping Center on Wednesday mornings from 8 A.M.–noon. If you're in Ha'iku on a Saturday morning, stop by the Ha'iku Farmers Market in front of the Ha'iku Town Center 8 A.M.–noon for produce and crafts. All along the road to Hana are family fruit and flower stands. Many times no one is in attendance and the very reasonable prices are paid on the honor system.

FISH AND SEAFOOD

Anyone who loves fresh fish and seafood has come to the right place. Island restaurants specialize in seafood, and it's available everywhere. Pound for pound, seafood is one of the best dining bargains on Maui. You'll find it served in every kind of restaurant, and often the fresh catch of the day is proudly displayed on ice in a glass case. The following is a sampling of the best.

Mahimahi

This excellent eating fish is one of the most common, most popular, and least expensive in Hawaii. It's referred to as "dolphin" but is definitely a fish, not a mammal. Mahimahi can weigh 10–65 pounds; the flesh is light and moist. This fish is broadest at the head. When caught it's a dark olive color, but after a while the skin turns iridescent shades of blue, green, and yellow. It can be served as a main course or as a patty in a fish sandwich.

A'u

This true island delicacy is a broadbill swordfish or marlin. It's expensive even in Hawaii because the damn thing's so hard to catch. The meat is moist and white and truly superb. If it's offered on the menu, order it. It'll cost a bit more, but you won't be disappointed.

Ono

Ono means "delicious" in Hawaiian, so that should tip you off to the taste of this wahoo, or king mackerel. *Ono* is regarded as one of the finest eating fishes in the ocean, and its flaky, white meat lives up to its name.

Manini

These five-inch fish are some of the most abundant in Hawaii and live in about 10 feet of water. They school and won't bite a hook but are easily taken with spear or net. Not often on menus, they're favorites with local people who know best.

Ulua

This member of the crevalle jack family ranges 15–100 pounds. Its flesh is white and has a steak-like texture. Delicious and often found on the menu.

Uku

This gray snapper is a favorite with local people. The meat is light and firm and grills well.

'Ahi

A yellowfin tuna with distinctive pinkish meat, *'ahi* is a great favorite cooked or served raw in sushi bars.

Moi

This is the Hawaiian word for "king." The fish has large eyes and a sharklike head. Considered one of the finest eating fishes in Hawaii, it's best during the autumn months.

Seafood Potpourri

Other island seafood include *'opihi,* a small shell-fish (limpet) that clings to rocks and is considered one of the best island delicacies, eaten raw; *'alo'alo,* similar to tiny lobsters; crawfish, plentiful in taro fields and irrigation ditches; *'ahipalaka,* albacore tuna; various octopuses and squid (calamari); and sharks of various types.

'A'ama are the ubiquitous little black crabs that you'll spot on rocks and around pier areas. They're everywhere. For fun, local fishers will try to catch them with poles, but the more efficient way is to throw a fish head into a plastic bucket and wait for the crabs to crawl in and trap themselves. The *'a'ama* are about as big as two fingers and make delicious eating.

Limu is edible seaweed that has been gathered as a garnish since precontact times and is frequently found on traditional island menus. There's no other seaweed except *limu* in Hawaii. Because of this, the heavy, fishy-ocean smell that people associate with the sea but that is actually seaweed is absent in Hawaii.

Poke is raw, cubed fish, usually made into a seafood salad with salt, vinegar, seaweed, onions, or other such ingredients, that is often found in deli sections of supermarkets.

Sushi

A finger-size block of sticky rice, topped with a pickled vegetable and a slice of raw fish. A delicacy in Japan and appreciated in Hawaii as a fine food. In addition to the traditional offerings, cutting-edge chefs now create a mind-boggling variety of innovative sushi morsels.

MUNCHIES AND ISLAND TREATS

Certain finger foods, fast foods, and island treats are unique to Hawaii. Some are meals in themselves, whereas others are snacks. Here are some of the best and most popular.

Pu Pu

Pronounced as in "Winnie the Pooh Pooh," these are little finger foods and hors d'oeuvres. They can be anything from crackers to cracked crab.

Often, they're given free at lounges and bars and can even include chicken drumettes, fish kebabs, and tempura. At a good display, you can have a free meal.

Crackseed

A sweet of Chinese origin, crackseed is preserved and seasoned fruits and seeds. Favorites include coconut, watermelon, pumpkin seeds, mango, plum, and papaya. Distinctive in taste, they take some getting used to but make great trail snacks. They are available in all island markets. Also look for dried fish (cuttlefish) on racks, usually near the crackseed. Nutritious and delicious, it makes a great snack.

Shave Ice

This real island institution makes the Mainland "snow cone" melt into insignificance. Special machines literally shave ice to a fluffy consistency. It's mounded into a paper cone, and your choice from dozens of exotic island syrups is generously poured over it. Given a straw and spoon, you just slurp away.

Taro Chips

Like potato chips, but made from the taro root. If you can find them fresh, buy a bunch because they are mostly available packaged.

Malasadas and Pao Dolce

Two sweets from the Portuguese, *malasadas* are holeless donuts and *pao dolce* is sweet bread. Sold in island bakeries, they're great for breakfast or as treats.

Lomi Lomi Salmon

This salad of salmon, tomatoes, and onions with garnish and seasonings often accompanies plate lunches and is featured at buffets and lu'au.

TROPICAL FRUITS AND VEGETABLES

Some of the most memorable taste treats from the islands require no cooking at all: the luscious tropical and exotic fruits and vegetables sold in markets and roadside stands or just found hanging on trees, waiting to be picked. Experience as many as possible. The general rule in Hawaii is that you are allowed to pick fruit on public lands, but the amount should be limited to personal consumption. The following is a sampling of some of Hawaii's best produce.

Bananas

No tropical island is complete without them. There are more than 70 species in Hawaii, with hundreds of variations. Some are for peeling and eating while others are cooked. A "hand" of bananas is great for munching, backpacking, or picnicking. Available everywhere—and cheap.

Avocados

Brought from South America, avocados were originally cultivated by the Aztecs. They have a buttery consistency and nutty flavor. Hundreds of varieties in all shapes and colors are available fresh year-round. They have the highest fat content of any fruit besides the olive.

Coconuts

What tropical paradise would be complete without coconuts? Indeed, these were some of the first plants brought by the Polynesians. When a child was born, a coconut tree was planted to provide fruit for the child throughout his or her lifetime. Truly tropical fruits, coconuts know no season. Drinking nuts are large and green, and when shaken you can hear the milk inside. You get about a quart of fluid from each. It takes skill to open one, but a machete can handle anything. Cut the stem end flat so that it will stand, then bore a hole into the pointed end and put in a straw or hollow bamboo. Coconut water is slightly acidic and helps balance alkaline foods. Spoon meat is a custardlike gel on the inside of drinking nuts. Sprouted coconut meat is also an excellent food. Split open a sprouted nut, and inside is the yellow fruit, like a moist sponge cake. "Millionaire's salad" is made from the heart of a coconut palm. At one time an entire tree was cut down to get to the heart, which is just inside the trunk below the fronds and is like an artichoke heart except that it's about the size of a

ROBERT NILSEN

What would a trip to the islands be without a tasty tropical fruit like these hearty bananas?

watermelon. In a downed tree, the heart stays good for about two weeks.

Breadfruit

This island staple provides a great deal of carbohydrates, but many people find the baked, boiled, or fried fruit bland. It grows all over the islands and is really thousands of little fruits growing together to form a ball that can be as big as a watermelon.

Mangos

These are some of the most delicious fruits known to humans. They grow wild all over the islands; the ones on the leeward sides of the islands ripen Apr.–June, while the ones on the windward sides can last until October. They're found in the wild on trees up to 60 feet tall. The problem is to stop eating them once you start!

Papayas

This truly tropical fruit has no real season but is mostly available in the summer. Papayas grow on branchless trees and are ready to pick as soon as any yellow appears. Of the many varieties, the "solo papaya," meant to be eaten by one person, is the best. Split them in half, scrape out the seeds, and have at them with a spoon.

Passion Fruit

Known by their island name of *liliko'i,* passion fruit make excellent juice and pies. The small yellow fruit (similar to lemons but smooth-skinned) is mostly available in summer and fall. Many grow wild on vines, waiting to be picked. Slice off the stem end, scoop the seedy pulp out with your tongue, and you'll know why they're called "passion fruit."

Guavas

These small, round, yellow fruits are abundant in the wild, where they ripen from early summer to late fall. They're often considered a pest, so pick all you want. A good source of vitamin C, they're great for juice, jellies, and desserts.

Macadamia Nuts

The king of nuts was brought from Australia in 1882. Now it's the state's fourth-largest agricultural product. Until the year 2000, Hawaii produced more of these nuts than anywhere else in the world. Now it follows Australia in total production. These nuts are cream-colored, crispy, about the size of a marble, slightly sweet, and available plain, roasted, candied, or buttered.

Litchis

Called nuts but really small fruit with thin red shells, litchis have sweet, juicy white flesh that tastes somewhat like a green grape that surrounds a hard inner seed. **Rambutan** are similar in flesh but have a soft spikey and somewhat thicker red covering.

Potpourri

Along with the above, you'll find pineapples (including the white, sweet, and less acidic Sugarloaf variety), oranges, limes, kumquats, thimbleberries, and blackberries in Hawaii, as well as carambolas, wild cherry tomatoes, and tamarinds.

ISLAND DRINKS

To complement the fine dining in the islands, bartenders have been busy creating their own tasty concoctions. The full range of beers, wines, and standard drinks is served in Hawaii, but for a real treat you should try mixed drinks inspired by the islands. Most look very innocent because they come in pineapples, coconut shells, or tall frosted glasses, but they can still pack a wallop. They're often garnished with little umbrellas or sparklers, and most have enough fruit in them to give you your vitamins for the day. Rum is the basis of many of them; it's been an island favorite since it was introduced by the whalers of the 19th century. At fancy hotels expect to pay $6–7 for a drink, at other locations, about $5–6. Here are some of the most famous: Mai Tai, a mixture of light and dark rum, orange curaçao, orange and almond flavoring, and lemon juice; Chi Chi, a simple concoction of vodka, pineapple juice, and coconut syrup—a real sleeper because it tastes like a milk shake; Blue Hawaii, made with vodka and blue curaçao; Planter's Punch, composed of light rum, grenadine, bitters, and lemon juice—a great thirst quencher; and Singapore sling, a sparkling mixture of gin and cherry brandy with lemon juice and/or pineapple, lime, and orange juices.

Drinking Laws

There are no state-run liquor stores; all kinds of spirits, wines, and beers are available in markets and shops, generally open during normal business hours, seven days a week. The drinking age is 21, and no towns are "dry." Legal hours for serving drinks depend on the type of establishment. Hours generally are: hotels, 6 A.M.–4 A.M.; discos and nightclubs where there is dancing, 10 A.M.–4 A.M.; bars and lounges where there is no dancing, 6 A.M.–2 A.M. Most restaurants serve alcohol, and in many that don't, you can bring your own.

Local Brews

Several local brew houses and brewpubs on

Maui have come and gone over the past decade. Currently, there is only one establishment on Maui that brews its own beer on property. Since 1998, **Fish and Game Brewing Company and Rotisserie** has been handcrafting beer on Maui's west side at the Kahana Gateway Mall. Of the half-dozen varieties that are always on tap, you could try the Plantation Pale Ale, Wild Hog Stout, or the lighter Honolua Lager. The brewing apparatus is behind glass in the restaurant.

Coffee

Kona coffee at one time held the distinction of being the only coffee grown in the United States. It's been grown for about 150 years in the upland district of Kona on the Big Island and is a rich, aromatic, truly fine coffee. If it's offered on the menu, have a cup. More recently, coffee from Maui, Moloka'i, O'ahu, and Kaua'i has entered the market. While the acreage on Maui is still fairly small, there are some 500 acres on Moloka'i planted in coffee trees.

Getting There

With the number of visitors each year approaching seven million—and another several hundred thousand just passing through—the state of Hawaii is one of the easiest places in the world to get to by plane. More than half a dozen large North American airlines (plus additional charter airlines) fly to and from the islands. About the same number of foreign carriers, mostly from Asia and Oceania, also touch down there on a daily basis. Hawaii is a hotly contested air market. The competition among carriers is fierce, and this sometimes makes for sweet deals and a wide choice of fares for the money-wise traveler. It also makes for pricing chaos. It's impossible to quote airline prices that will hold true for more than a month, if that long. Familiarize yourself with the alternatives at your disposal so you can make an informed travel selection. Now more than ever, you should work with a sharp travel agent who's on your side or do some research on the web.

Almost all travelers to Maui arrive by air. A few lucky ones come by private yacht, the interisland ferries from Lana'i and Moloka'i, and others make a stop on a cruise ship. Maui, the Hawaiian destination second only to O'ahu, attracts about two million visitors per year. A limited number of direct air flights from the Mainland United States, Canada, and Japan are offered, but most airlines servicing Hawaii, both domestic and foreign, land at Honolulu International Airport and then carry on to Maui or offer connecting flights on interisland carriers. In most cases they're part of the original ticket

price with no extra charge. Different airlines have interline agreements with different Hawaiian carriers, so check with your travel agent. All major and most smaller interisland carriers service Maui from throughout Hawaii, with more than 100 flights per day in and out of Kahului Airport and less than a dozen a day to Kapalua–West Maui airport.

Airlines usually adjust their flight schedules about every three months to account for seasonal differences in travel and route changes. Before planning a trip to and around the islands, be sure to contact the airlines directly, view the airline's Internet site, or go through your travel agent for the most current information on routes and flying times.

When to Go

The prime tourist season starts two weeks before Christmas and lasts until Easter. It picks up again with summer vacation in early June and ends once more in late August. Everything is usually much more heavily booked and prices are inflated. Hotel, airline, and car reservations are a must at this time of year. You can generally save considerably and deal with a lot less hassle if you go in the off-season—September to early December, and mid-April (after Easter) until early June. Recently, the drop in number of tourists during the off-season has not been nearly as substantial as in years past, indicating the increasing popularity of the island at all times of the year, but you'll still find the prices better and the beaches, trails, campgrounds, and even restaurants less crowded. The local people will be happier to see you, too.

BY AIR

There are two categories of airlines that you can take to Hawaii: **domestic,** meaning American-owned, and **foreign**-owned. An American law, penned at the turn of the 20th century to protect American shipping, says that only an American carrier can transport you to and from two American cities. In the airline industry, this law is still very much in effect. It means, for example, that if you want a round-trip between San Francisco and Honolulu, you *must* fly on a domestic carrier. If, however, you are flying San Francisco to Tokyo, you are at liberty to fly a foreign airline, and you may even have a stopover in Hawaii, but you must continue to Tokyo or some other foreign city and cannot fly back to San Francisco on the foreign airline. Canadians have no problem flying round-trip from Toronto to Honolulu because this route does not connect two U.S. cities, and so it is with all foreign travel to and from Hawaii. Travel agents know this, but if you're planning your own trip, be aware of this fact.

Kinds of Flights

Depending on where you are coming from, you may have to fly from your home to a gateway city, from where flights go to Hawaii, either direct or nonstop. On direct flights you fly from point A to point B without changing planes; it doesn't mean that you don't land in between. Direct flights do land, usually once to board and deplane passengers, but you sit cozily on the plane along with your luggage and off you go again. Nonstop is just that; you board and when the doors open again you're at your destination. All flights from the West Coast gateway cities are nonstop "God willing"—because there is only the Pacific in between!

Flights to Maui

Until not too long ago, United Airlines was the only carrier that offered nonstop flights from the Mainland to Maui. Now, Delta Air Lines, American Airlines, Hawaiian Airlines, and Aloha Airlines offer daily flights from various Mainland cities to Maui. All other major domestic and foreign carriers fly you to Honolulu and have arrangements with either Hawaiian Airlines or Aloha Airlines for getting you to Maui. This involves a plane change, but your baggage can be booked straight through. If you fly from the Mainland with Hawaiian or Aloha, you have the added convenience of dealing with just one airline. Several charter airlines also fly to Maui nonstop from the Mainland.

Travel Agents

At one time people went to a travel agent the same way they went to a barber or beautician, loyally sticking with one, but now increased competition and the Internet have made many of these relationships a thing of the past. Most agents are reputable professionals who know what they're doing. They should be members of the American Society of Travel Agents (ASTA) and licensed by the Air Traffic Conference (ATC). Most have the inside track on the best deals, and they'll save you countless hours calling 800 numbers and listening to elevator music while on hold or checking with umpteen Internet ticket sellers. Unless you require them to make very special arrangements, their services are free or nearly so. They are paid a commission by the airlines and hotels they book for you. In recent years these commissions have been greatly reduced, in some cases abandoned altogether, causing some agents to start charging a small fee for their services.

If you've done business with a travel agent in the past and were satisfied with the services and prices, by all means stick with him or her. If no such positive rapport exists, then shop around. Ask friends or relatives for recommendations; if you can't get any endorsements, go to the *Yellow Pages.* Call two or three travel agents to compare prices. Make sure to give all of them the same information and to be as precise as possible. Tell them where and when you want to go, how long you want to stay, which class you want to travel, and any special requirements. Write down their

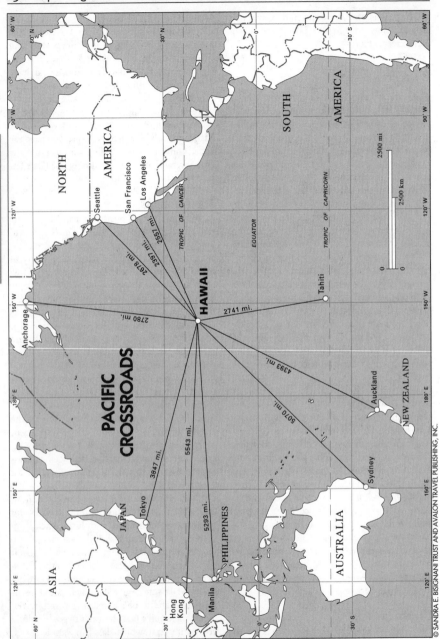

information. It's amazing how confusing travel plans can be when you have to keep track of flight numbers, times, prices, and all the preparation information. When you compare, don't look only for the cheapest price. Check for convenience in flights, amenities of hotels, and any other fringe benefits that might be included. Then make your choice of agent and, if he or she is willing to give you individualized service, stick with that agent from then on.

Agents become accustomed to offering the same deals to many clients because they're familiar with the arrangements and because the deals have worked well in the past. Sometimes these are indeed the best, but if they don't suit you, don't be railroaded into accepting them. Any good agent will work with you. After all, it's your trip and your money.

Consolidators are companies that buy blocks of seats on certain flights and then turn around and sell them. Their buying price must be very cheap because their prices are some of the best you can find. They often list their toll-free phone numbers in local phone directories and just as often run ads in large city newspapers—often in a Sunday Travel section. With the proliferation of the Internet, the number of online travel companies has also mushroomed, and these companies offer great deals. As with consolidators, online travel companies come and go, so use a company that has previously worked with you or someone you know. Again, the range in prices in substantial, so check around with many before you send your money.

Package Tours

For the independent traveler, practical package deals that include only flight, car, and lodging are okay. Agents put these together all the time and they just might be the best, but if they don't suit you, make arrangements separately. A package *tour* is totally different. On these you get your hand held by an escort, eat where they want you to eat, go where they want you to go, and watch Hawaii slide by your bus window. For some people, especially groups, this might be the way to do it, but everyone else should avoid the package tour. You'll see Hawaii best on your own, and if

you want a tour you can arrange one there, often cheaper. Once arrangements have been made with your travel agent, make sure to take all receipts and letters of confirmation (hotel, car) with you to Hawaii. They probably won't be needed, but if they are, nothing will work better in getting results.

Mainland and International Fares

There are many categories of airline fares, but only three apply to the average traveler: first class, coach, and excursion. Traveling **first class** seats you in the front of the plane, gives you free drinks, a wider choice of meals, more leg room, and access to VIP lounges, if they exist. There are no restrictions, no penalties for cancellations or rebooking of return flights, and no advance-booking or minimum-stay requirements.

Coach, the way that most people fly, is totally adequate. You sit in the plane's main compartment behind first class. Your seats are comfortable, but they're narrower and you don't have as much legroom or as wide a choice of meals. Movie headsets and drinks cost you a few dollars, but that's about it. Coach offers many of the same benefits as first class and costs about 30 percent less. You can buy tickets up until takeoff; you have no restrictions on minimum or maximum stays; you receive liberal stopover privileges, and you can cash in your return ticket or change your return date with no penalties.

Excursion or advance payment excursion (APEX) fares are the cheapest. You are accommodated on the plane exactly the same as if you were flying coach; however, there are some restrictions. You must book and pay for your ticket in advance (usually 7–14 days; sometimes up to 30 days). At the same time, you must book your return flight, and under most circumstances you can't change either without paying a stiff penalty. Also, your stopovers are severely limited and you will have a minimum/maximum stay period. Only a limited number of seats on any one plane are set aside for APEX fares, so book as early as you can. Also, if you must change travel plans, you can go to the airport and get on as a standby passenger using a discounted ticket, even if the airline doesn't have an official standby policy.

There's always the risk that you won't get on, but you do have a chance, as well as priority over an actual standby customer.

Standby is exactly what its name implies: You go to the airport and wait around to see if any flights going to Hawaii have an empty seat. You can save some money, but you cannot have a firm itinerary or limited time. Since Hawaii is such a popular destination, standbys can wait days before catching a plane.

Charters

Charter flights were at one time only for groups or organizations that had memberships in travel clubs. Now they're open to the general public. A charter flight is an entire plane or a block of seats purchased at a quantity discount by a charter company and then sold to customers. Because they are bought at wholesale prices, charter fares can be the cheapest available. As in package deals, only take a charter flight if it is a "fly only," or perhaps includes a car and/or a room. You don't need one that includes a guide and a bus. Most important, make sure that the charter company is reputable. It should belong to the same organizations (ASTA and ATC) as most travel agents. If not, check into the company at the local chamber of commerce.

More restrictions apply to charters than to any other flights. You must pay in advance. If you cancel after a designated time, you can be penalized severely or lose your money entirely. You cannot change departure or return dates and times; however, up to 10 days before departure the charter company is legally able to cancel, raise the price by 10 percent, or change time and dates. It must return your money if cancellation occurs or if changed arrangements are unacceptable to you. Mostly, charter companies are on the up-and-up and flights go smoothly, but there are horror stories. Be careful. Be wise. Investigate!

Tips

Flights from California take about five hours, a bit longer from the Northwest or Pacific Canada; you gain two hours over Pacific Standard Time when you land in Hawaii (three hours during daylight savings time). From the East Coast it takes about 11 hours and you gain five hours over Eastern Standard Time. Flights from Japan take about seven hours and there is a five-hour difference between the time zones. Travel time between Sydney, Australia, or Auckland, New Zealand, and Hawaii is about nine hours. They are ahead of Hawaii time by 20 and 22 hours, respectively. Try to fly Monday–Thursday, when flights are cheaper and easier to book. Pay for your ticket as soon as your plans are firm. If prices go up, there will be no charge added, but merely booking doesn't guarantee the lowest price. Make sure that airlines, hotels, and car agencies get your phone number too—not only your travel agent's—in case any problems with availability arise (travel agents are sometimes closed on weekends). It's not necessary, but it's a good idea to call and reconfirm flights 24–72 hours in advance.

First-row (bulkhead) seats are good for people who need more legroom, but bad for watching the movie. Airlines will give you special meals (vegetarian, kosher, low cal, low salt) often at no extra charge, but you must notify them in advance. If you're bumped from an overbooked flight, you're entitled to a comparable flight to your destination within one hour. If more than an hour elapses, you get denied-boarding compensation, which goes up proportionately with the amount of time you're held up. Sometimes this is cash or a voucher for another flight to be used in the future. You don't have to accept what an airline offers on the spot, if you feel they aren't being fair.

Traveling with Children

Fares for children ages 2–12 are often 30–50 percent less than adult fares, although the exact amount will depend on the season and flight; children under two not occupying a seat travel free. If you're traveling with an infant or active toddler, book your flight well in advance and request the bulkhead seat or first row in any section and a bassinet if available. Many carriers have fold-down cribs with restraints for baby's safety and comfort. Toddlers appreciate the extra space provided by the front-row seats. Be sure to reconfirm, and arrive early to ensure this special seating. On long flights you'll be glad that you took these extra pains.

Although most airlines have coloring books, puppets, and so forth to keep your child busy, it's always a good idea to bring your own. These items can make the difference between a pleasant flight and a harried ordeal. Also, remember to bring baby food, diapers, and other necessities because many airlines may not be equipped with exactly what you need. Make all inquiries ahead of time so you're not caught unprepared.

Baggage

You are allowed two free pieces of luggage—one large, the other smaller—and a carry-on bag. The two checked pieces can weigh up to 70 pounds each; an extra charge is levied for extra weight. The larger bag can have an overall added dimension (height plus width plus length) of 62 inches; the smaller, 55 inches. Your carry-on must fit under your seat or in the overhead storage compartment. Purses and camera bags are not counted as carry-ons and may be taken aboard. Surfboards and bicycles may run $50 extra from the Mainland, but this may vary by airline; enclosed golf bags can be sent as checked luggage at no extra charge. Although they make great mementos, remove all previous baggage tags from your luggage; they can confuse handlers. Attach a sturdy holder with your name and address on the handle, or use a stick-on label on the bag itself. Put your name and address inside the bag, and the address where you'll be staying in Hawaii if possible. Carry your cosmetics, identification, money, prescriptions, tickets, reservations, change of underwear, camera equipment, and perhaps a change of shirt or blouse in your carry-on.

Visas

Entering Hawaii is like entering anywhere else in the United States. Foreign nationals must have a current passport and most must have a proper visa, an ongoing or return air ticket, and sufficient funds for the proposed stay in Hawaii. A visa application can be made at any U.S. embassy or consular office outside the United States and must include a properly filled-out application form, two photos 1.5 inches square, and a nonrefundable fee of $65. Canadians do not need a visa or passport but must have proper identification such as passport, driver's license, or birth certificate. Visitors from 28 countries do not need a visa to enter the United States for 90 days or less. This list is amended periodically, so be sure to check in your country of origin to determine if you do not need a visa for U.S. entry.

Agricultural Inspection

Everyone visiting Hawaii must fill out a "Plant and Animals Declaration Form" and present it to the appropriate official upon arrival in the state (or to the airline personnel). Anyone carrying any of the listed items must have those items inspected by an agricultural inspection agent at the airport. For information on just what is prohibited, contact any U.S. Customs Office or check with an embassy or consulate in foreign countries.

Remember that before you leave Hawaii for the Mainland, all of your bags are again subject to an agricultural inspection, a usually painless procedure taking only a minute or two. To facilitate your departure, leave all bags unlocked until after inspection. There are no restrictions on beach sand from below the high-water line, coconuts, prepackaged sugarcane, dried flower arrangements, fresh flower lei, pineapples, certified pest-free plants and cuttings, seashells, seed lei, and wood roses. However, avocado, litchi, and papaya must be treated before departure. Some other restricted items are berries, fresh gardenias, roses, jade plants, live insects, snails, cotton, plants in soil, soil itself, and raw sugarcane. Raw sugarcane is okay, however, if it is cut between the nodes, has the outer covering peeled off, and is split into fourths. For any questions pertaining to plants that you want to take to the Mainland, call the Agricultural Quarantine Inspection office, 808/873-3556 in Kahului.

Foreign countries may have different agricultural inspection requirements for flights from Hawaii (or other points in the United States) to those countries. Be sure to check with the proper foreign authorities for specifics.

Pets and Quarantine

Hawaii has a rigid pet quarantine policy designed to keep rabies and other Mainland diseases from reaching the state. All domestic pets are subject to **120 days' quarantine** (a 30-day quarantine is allowed by meeting certain prearrival and postarrival requirements—inquire). Unless you are contemplating a move to Hawaii, it is not feasible to take pets. For complete information, contact the Department of Agriculture, Animal Quarantine Division, 99-951 Halawa Valley Street., 'Aiea, HI 96701, 808/483-7151.

Maui's Airports

There are three commercial airports on Maui, but most travelers will be concerned only with **Kahului Airport,** which accommodates 95 percent of the flights in and out of Maui. Kahului Airport is only minutes from Kahului city center,

on the north-central coast of Maui. A full-service facility with all amenities, it has a few gift and snack shops, a restaurant, two tourist information booths, a newsstand, display cases of Hawaiian arts and crafts, a lost and found office, bathrooms, public telephones, car rental agencies, and limited private transportation. Of the tourist information booths, one of which is in the arrival lounge and the other in the upstairs courtyard, at least one will be open from 6:30 A.M.–10 P.M. daily. As you face the terminal building, the departure lounge is on your right, the arrival lounge is on your left, and splitting the two is an upper-level courtyard with shops, a restaurant, and lounge. For your entertainment, a hula and music show is performed here for two hours at midday. Between the baggage claim and car rental booths is a 10 by 20 foot, 1,200-gallon state-of-the-art aquarium with accompanying signboards,

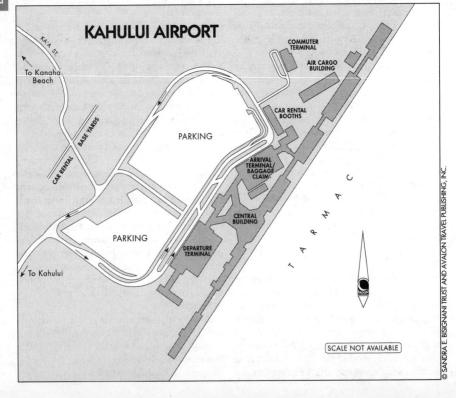

constructed and maintained by the Maui Ocean Center, that presents to visitors a sample of the lively and colorful world that surrounds the island. A few steps beyond the rental car booths at the front of the arrival building is the commuter terminal, and on the far side of the runway is the heliport. Public parking at the airport costs $1 for the first half hour, $1 for each additional hour, or $7 maximum per day. There is metered parking at the commuter terminal. In 1990, the Kahului Airport underwent a major expansion that allows it to land large commercial planes and handle a great increase in traffic, including direct international flights. An additional runway expansion was then considered, but this plan has been permanently shelved because of sustained and overwhelming popular disapproval. Major roads lead from Kahului Airport to all primary destinations on Maui.

Hawaiian Airlines opened the one-strip **Kapulua-West Maui Airport** in early 1987. You fly in over pineapple fields. This facility is conveniently located between the Ka'anapali and Kapalua resort areas, on the *mauka* side of the Honoapi'ilani Highway at Akahele Street, just a few minutes from the major Ka'anapali hotels and condos of Honokowai and Kahana. As convenient as it is to this area of West Maui, it is not heavily used. Hawaiian Airlines no longer operates connecting flights to West Maui with the rest of Hawaii. There is on-again, off-again scheduled service with both Island Air and Pacific Wings, but you can't always count on it, and some charter companies use this strip for their flights. The small terminal is user-friendly with a snack bar, sundries shop, tourist brochures, and courtesy phones for car rental pickup in the baggage claim area. Parking is in the metered lot: $1 for the first half hour, $1 for each additional hour, or $7 maximum for the day.

The third airstrip is **Hana Airport,** an isolated runway with a tiny terminal on the northeast coast just west of Hana, serviced only by Pacific Wings. It has no amenities aside from a bathroom and telephone, and transportation is available only to the Hotel Hana-Maui via the hotel shuttle. People flying into Hana Airport generally plan to vacation in Hana for an extended period and have made prior arrangements for being picked up. The only car rental available in Hana is by Dollar Rent A Car, 808/248-8237—call before you arrive!

DOMESTIC CARRIERS

The following are the major domestic carriers to and from Hawaii. The planes used are primarily wide-body D10s, L10s, and 747s, with a smaller 737, 767, and the like flown now and again. A list of the gateway cities from which they fly direct and nonstop flights is given, but connecting cities are not. Most flights, by all carriers, land at Honolulu International Airport, with the remainder going directly to Maui, Kaua'i, and Hawai'i. Only the established companies are listed. Entrepreneurial small airlines such as the now-defunct Mahalo Air pop up now and again and specialize in dirt-cheap fares. There is a hectic frenzy to buy their tickets and business is great for a while, but then the established companies lower their fares and the gamblers fold.

Hawaiian Airlines

Hawaiian Airlines, 800/882-8811 in Hawaii, 800/367-5320 Mainland and Canada, www.hawaiianair.com, operates daily flights from Los Angeles, San Francisco, San Diego, Ontario (California), Las Vegas (via Los Angeles), Phoenix, Seattle, and Portland to Honolulu, with flights several times a week from Los Angeles, San Francisco, and Portland nonstop to Kahului, Maui. Scheduled flights to the South Pacific run twice a week between Honolulu and Pago Pago, Samoa, and once weekly to Papeete, Tahiti. Since about 2000, Hawaiian Airlines has expanded its service to the West Coast, so there may very well be additional destinations and service in the future. Hawaiian Airlines offers special discount deals with Dollar rental cars and select major-island hotels, and has a partnership agreement with American, Continental, Alaska, and Northwest airlines.

Aloha Airlines

Aloha Airlines, 808/244-9071 on Maui, 800/367-5250 Mainland and Canada, www.alohaairlines.org, flies between Honolulu and Kahului, Maui in the islands and Vancouver, Canada,

Oakland, Las Vegas (via Oakland), Burbank, Sacramento (via Burbank), Orange County, California, and Phoenix (via Orange County) on the Mainland. It also has a direct connection between Kaua'i and Oakland, and Kona on the Big Island with Vancouver and Oakland. In addition, Aloha Airlines now operates a weekly flight on Saturdays to Midway Island and twice-weekly flights to Johnston Atoll in the South Pacific that carry on to Majuro Atoll and Kwajalein. Periodically, charter flights also go to Christmas Island and Rorotonga in the South Pacific. If you are interested in visiting these remote islands, check with the airlines to see if those flights are currently in operation. Like Hawaiian, Aloha Airlines has been expanding its West Coast operation, so greater variety will undoubtedly be in store in the future.

United Airlines

Since their first island flight in 1947, United Airlines, 800/241-6522, www.ual.com, has become top dog in flights to Hawaii. United's Mainland routes connect more than 100 cities to Honolulu. The main gateway cities of San Francisco and Los Angeles have direct flights to Honolulu, with additional flights from Denver on some weekends; flights from all other cities connect through these cities. United also offers direct flights to Maui, Kona, and Kaua'i from San Francisco and Los Angeles. Continuing through Honolulu, United flights go to Tokyo (Narita), where connections can be made for other Asian cities. United offers several packages, including flight and hotel on O'ahu, and flight, hotel, and car on the Neighbor Islands. United interlines with Aloha Airlines and deals with Hertz Rent A Car. United is the "big guy" and intends to stay that way. Its packages are hard to beat.

American Airlines

American Airlines, 800/433-7300, www.aa.com, offers direct flights to Honolulu from Los Angeles, San Francisco, Dallas/Fort Worth, and Chicago. It also flies daily from Los Angeles and Chicago direct to Maui, and from Los Angeles to Lihue. American does not fly to points in Asia or other Pacific destinations from Hawaii. American interlines with Hawaiian Airlines.

Continental Airlines

Continental Airlines, 800/523-3273, www.continental.com, flights from all Mainland cities to Honolulu connect via Los Angeles, Newark, and Houston. Also available are direct flights from Honolulu to Guam, from where flights run to numerous other Asian and Pacific cities and islands. Continental interlines with Hawaiian Airlines.

Northwest Airlines

Northwest Airlines, 800/225-2525, www.nwa.com, flies into Honolulu from Los Angeles and Seattle. There are onward nonstop flights to Narita and Osaka in Japan, from where all other Asian destinations are connected.

Delta Air Lines

In 1985, Delta Air Lines, 800/221-1212, www.delta.com, entered the Hawaiian market; when it bought out Western Airlines its share became even bigger. It has nonstop flights to Honolulu from Dallas/Fort Worth, Los Angeles, San Francisco, Salt Lake City, and Atlanta, and a flight to Maui from Los Angeles.

FOREIGN CARRIERS

The following carriers operate throughout Asia and Oceania but have no U.S. flying rights. This means that for you to vacation in Hawaii using one of these carriers, your flight must originate or terminate in a foreign city. You can have a stopover in Honolulu with a connecting flight to a Neighbor Island. For example, if you've purchased a flight on Japan Air Lines from San Francisco to Tokyo, you can stop in Hawaii, but you must then carry on to Tokyo. Failure to do so will result in a stiff fine, and the balance of your ticket will not be refunded.

Air Canada

Air Canada, 888/247-2262, www.aircanada.ca, nonstop flights from Canada to Honolulu originate in Vancouver and Toronto, and to Maui from Vancouver.

Air New Zealand

Air New Zealand, 800/262-1234 in the United States and 800/663-5494 in Canada, www.airnz.com, flights link New Zealand, Australia, and numerous South Pacific islands to Honolulu, with continuing flights to Mainland cities. All flights run via Auckland, New Zealand.

Japan Air Lines

The Japanese are the second-largest group, next to Americans, to visit Hawaii. JAL, 800/525-3663, www.jal.co.jp/en, flights to Honolulu originate in Tokyo (Narita), Nagoya, and Osaka (Kansai). In addition, there are flights between Tokyo (Narita) and Kona on the Big Island. JAL flights continue beyond Hawaii to San Francisco and Los Angeles.

Qantas

Daily flights on Qantas, 800/227-4500, www.qantas.com.au, connect Sydney and Melbourne, Australia with Honolulu; all other flights feed through these hub.

China Airlines

Routes to Honolulu with China Airlines, 800/227-5118, www.china-airlines.com, are only from Taipei, and all go through Tokyo. Connections are available in Taipei to most Asian capitals.

Korean Air

Korean Air, 800/438-5000, www.koreanair.com, offers some of the least expensive flights to Asia. All flights are direct between Honolulu and Seoul, with connections there to many Asian cities.

Air Pacific

Air Pacific, 808/227-4446, www.airpacific.com, offers once-weekly nonstop flights between Nadi, Fiji and Honolulu.

Polynesian Airlines

If flying to Samoa, use Polynesian Airlines, 808/842-7659, www.polynesianairlines.co.nz, for weekly flights directly from Honolulu to Apia.

Philippine Airlines

Three times weekly, direct nonstop flights between Honolulu and Manila are handled through Philippine Airlines, 808/435-7725, www.philippineair.com.

Other Airlines

Aside from the listed airlines, large-volume charter operators book flights to the various islands with such carriers as **Canada 3000, American Trans Air, Ryan International,** and **Skyservice USA.**

TOUR AND TRAVEL COMPANIES

Many tour companies advertise packages to Hawaii in large-city newspapers every week. They offer very reasonable airfares, car rentals, and accommodations. The following companies offer great deals and most have excellent reputations. This list is by no means exhaustive.

Pleasant Hawaiian Holidays

A California-based company specializing in Hawaii, Pleasant Hawaiian Holidays, 2404 Townsgate Rd., Westlake Village, CA 91361, 800/742-9244, www.pleasantholidays.com, makes arrangements for flights, accommodations, and transportation only. For flights, it primarily uses American Trans Air but also uses select commercial airlines and regularly scheduled flights. Aside from the air connection, Pleasant Hawaiian offers a choice of accommodation levels from budget to luxury, a fly/drive option if you have your own accommodation, and numerous perks, like a flower greeting lei, first morning orientation, service desks at hotels, and coupons and gift certificates. Pleasant Hawaiian is easy to work with and stands behind its services. A deposit is required after booking and there is a time frame for full payment that depends on when you make your reservation. Fees are accessed for changing particulars after booking, so be sure to apprise yourself of all financial particulars. Most major travel agents work with Pleasant Hawaiian.

SunTrips

Another California-based tour company, Sun-Trips, 2350 Paragon Dr., San Jose, CA 95131, 800/786-8747, www.suntrips.com, runs flights to Hawaii from Los Angeles and San Francisco. It offers flight, accommodation, and/or car rental packages that match any for affordability. Your price will depend on your choice of accommodations and type of car. Using both charter and commercial air carriers, SunTrips does not offer assigned seating until you get to the airport. They recommend you get there two hours in advance, and they ain't kidding! This is the price you pay for getting such inexpensive air travel. Remember that everyone on your incoming flight makes a beeline for the rental car's shuttle van after landing and securing their baggage. If you have a traveling companion, work together to beat the rush by leaving your companion to fetch the baggage while you head directly for the van as soon as you arrive. Pick your car up, then return for your partner and the bags. Even if you're alone, you could zip over to the car rental center and then return for your bags without having them sit very long on the carousel. SunTrips' financial regulations are similar to those at Pleasant Hawaiian; be sure to inquire.

Other Similar Companies

Several other companies offer similar package options from the Mainland to Hawaii. Try the following: **Happy Vacations,** 4604 Scotts Valley Dr., Scotts Valley, CA 95066, 831/461-0113 or 800/877-4277, fax 831/461-1604, www.happy-vacations.com; an older and reputable company that gives good service and stands by its policies. **Creative Leisure International,** 951 Transport Way, Petaluma, CA 94954, 707/778-1800 or 800/413/1000, fax 707/778-1223, www.creativeleisure.com; utilizes United Airlines. **United Vacations,** 8907 Port Washington Rd., Milwaukee, WI 53217, 800/328-6877, 414/228-7472 or 414/351-5826; a United Airlines affiliate.

Council Travel Services

These full-service, budget-travel specialists are a subsidiary of the nonprofit Council on International Educational Exchange and the official U.S. representative to the International Student Travel Conference. They'll custom-design trips and programs for everyone from senior citizens to college students. Bona fide students have extra advantages, however, including eligibility for the International Student Identification Card (ISIC), which often gets you discount fares and waived entrance fees to tourist attractions. Groups and business travelers are also welcome. For full information, call 800/226-8624, or write to Council Travel Services at one of these offices: 530 Bush St., San Francisco, CA 94108, 415/421-3473; or 205 E. 42nd St., New York, NY 10017, 212/822-2700. For additional retail locations and information, see www.counciltravel.com.

STA Travel

STA Travel, 800/781-4040, www.statravel.com, is a full-service travel agency specializing in student travel, regardless of age. Those under 26 do not have to be full-time students to get special fares. Older independent travelers can avail themselves of services, although they are ineligible for student fares. STA works hard to get you discounted or budget rates. Many tickets issued by STA are flexible, allowing changes with no penalty, and are open-ended for travel up to one year. STA has some 300 offices around the world. STA also maintains Travel Help, a service available at all offices designed to solve all types of problems that may arise while traveling. STA is a well-established travel agency with an excellent and well-deserved reputation.

Ocean Voyages

This unique company offers multiday itineraries aboard two yachts in the Hawaiian Islands. The ships, one a six-passenger catamaran and the other a six-passenger sloop, ensure individualized sail training and service. These vessels sail throughout the islands, exploring hidden bays and coves, and berth at different ports as they go. This opportunity is for anyone who wishes to see the islands in a timeless fashion, thrilling to sights experienced by the first Polynesian settlers and Western explorers. For rates and information, contact Ocean Voyages, 1709 Bridgeway, Sausalito, CA 94965, 415/332-4681 or 800/299-4444 Mainland, fax 415/332-7460.

Ecotours to Hawaii

Sierra Club Trips offers Hawaii trips for nature

lovers who are interested in an outdoor experience. Various trips include birding on the Big Island and kayak and camping trips on Kaua'i. All trips are led by experienced guides and are open to Sierra Club members only ($35 per year to join). For information, contact the Sierra Club Outing Department, 85 2nd St., 2nd Fl., San Francisco, CA 94105, 415/977-5522, www.sierraclub.org/outings.

Backroads, 801 Cedar St., Berkeley, CA 94710, 510/527-1555 or 800/462-2848, fax 510/1444, backtalk@backroads.com, www.backroads.com, arranges an easy-on-the-environment six-day cycling, hiking, and kayaking trip on the Big Island for $2,398. This price includes hotel/inn accommodations, most meals, and professional guide service. Airfare is not included, and bicycles and sleeping bags can be rented (BYO okay) for reasonable rates.

Educational Trips

Not a tour per se, but an educational opportunity, **Elderhostel Hawaii** offers short-term programs on five of the Hawaiian islands. Different programs focus on history, culture, cuisine, and the environment in association with one of the colleges or universities on the islands. Most programs use hotels for accommodations. For information, write Elderhostel, 11 Avenue de Lafayette, Boston, MA 02111-1746, or call 877/426-8056; www.enderhostel.org.

BY SHIP
Cruise Ships

Cruise lines offering ships that stop in Hawaii for day trips only on their varied routes include the following. Most travel agents can provide information on these cruise lines.

Norwegian Cruise Lines, 800/327-7030, www.ncl.com

Holland America Lines, 800/426-0327, www.hollandamerica.com

Cunard, 800/528-6273, www.cunardline.com

Carnival Cruise Line, 800/327-9501, www.carnival.com

Princess Cruises, 800/421-0522, www.princesscruises.com

Royal Caribbean International, 800/327-6700, www.royalcaribbean.com

Crystal Cruises, 800/446-6620, www.cruisecrystal.com

Freighter Travel

Travel by freighter is on a working cargo ship. Although their routes are usually longer than cruise ship itineraries and the ships do not contain all the luxuries and amenities of the cruise liners, fares are often 30–40 percent less per day than travel on a cruise ship. If you're especially interested in traveling by freighter, contact **Freighter World Cruises,** 180 South Lake Ave., Ste. 335, Pasadena, CA 91101-2655, 626/449-3106 or 800/531-7774, freighter@freighterworld.com, www.freighterworld.com. This company is an agent that arranges passage for travelers on more than 100 ships around the world. They publish the *Freighter Space Advisory* newsletter.

Also arranging travel is **Maris Freighter Cruises, USA,** 215 Main St., Westport, CT 06880, 203/222-1500 or 800/996-2747, fax 203/222-9191, maris@freightercruises.com, www.cruisemaris.com/frieghters.html. Maris publishes the monthly *Freighter Travel Newsletter*. For additional information, check *Ford's Freighter Travel Guide & Waterways of the World* quarterly, which can be contacted at 19448 Londelius St., Northridge, CA 91324, 818/701-7414.

EXPLORING THE ISLANDS

Getting Around

If it's your intention to *see* Maui when you visit, and not just to lie on the beach in front of your hotel, the only efficient way is to rent a car. Limited public transportation, a few free shuttles, taxis, and the good old thumb are available, but all of these methods are flawed in one way or another. Other unique and fun-filled ways to tour the island include renting a motorcycle, bicycle, or moped, but these conveyances are highly specialized and are more in the realm of sports than touring.

INTERISLAND AIR CARRIERS

Getting to and from Maui via the other islands is easy and convenient. The only effective way for most visitors to travel between the Hawaiian Islands is by air. Luckily, Hawaii has excellent air transportation that boasts one of the industry's safest flight records. All interisland flights have a no-smoking regulation. There are no assigned seats on interisland flights, so if you have a seating preference, get to the boarding gate early and grab your place in line. Items restricted on flights from the Mainland and from overseas are also restricted on flights within the state. Baggage allowances are the same as anywhere, except that due to space constraints, carry-on luggage on the smaller prop planes may be limited in number and size.

Hawaiian and Aloha have competitive prices, with interisland flights at about $80 each way, with substantial savings for state residents. With both airlines, you can save per ticket by purchasing a booklet of six **flight coupons** that run $408. These are only available in-state at any ticket office or airport counter and they are *transferable*. Just book a flight as normal and present the filled-in voucher to board the plane. Perfect for families or groups of friends. Hawaiian Airlines coupons are good for six months, Aloha Airlines coupons for one year. Hawaiian also offers a 10-coupon booklet that can be mailed to Mainland visitors for $732—allow two weeks.

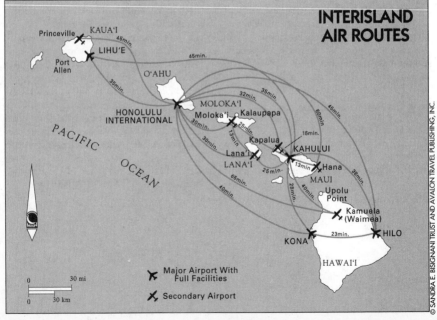

ROBERT NILSEN

While most interisland flights are via large jet planes, routes to some of the less frequented island airports are covered by smaller prop planes.

Additionally, each airline offers passes that are good for unlimited travel anywhere that the airlines flies, but they are nontransferable and may only be used on consecutive days. You may purchase these passes in-state or before you arrive in Hawaii. Hawaiian Airlines has the "Hawaiian Island Pass": five days at $310, seven days at $320, 10 days at $419, and 14 days at $479. Fares for children ages 2–11 are about 10 percent less. Aloha Airlines offers one "7-day Island Pass" with up to four flights per day for $336 with the same conditions.

Note: Although every effort has been made for up-to-date accuracy, remember that schedules change constantly. The following should be used only as a point of reference. Please call the airlines listed for their latest schedules.

Hawaiian Airlines

Hawaiian Airlines, 800/367-5320 Mainland and Canada, 800/882-8811 statewide, www .hawaiianair.com, runs flights to and from Honolulu (average flight time 35 minutes) about two dozen times per day in each direction.

Hawaiian Airlines flights to Kahului, Maui, from Honolulu begin at 5:15 A.M., with flights thereafter about every 30 minutes until 7:15 P.M. Flights from Kahului to Honolulu begin at 6:15 A.M. and go all day until 8:15 P.M. There are two flights to/from Hilo daily, one at midmorning and one in the late afternoon. Kona, also on the Big Island, is serviced with one afternoon flight from Kahului. For flights to Kaua'i, Lana'i, and Moloka'i, you must go through Honolulu. Although there are many flights to Kaua'i, Moloka'i and Lana'i are connected to Maui by one daily direct flight.

Aloha Airlines

Aloha Airlines, 808/244-9071 Maui, 800/367-5250 Mainland and Canada, www.alohaairlines.com, with its all-jet fleet of 737s, flies between Honolulu and Maui about 20 times per day beginning at 5:30 A.M. with the last flight at 7:30 P.M.; return flights to Honolulu start at 6:24 A.M., with the last at 8:30 P.M. Kahului is also connected by numerous daily flights to Lihue, Kaua'i and to both Kona and Hilo on the Big Island, but only a few times a day.

Island Air

A subsidiary of Aloha Airlines, **Island Air,** 800/652-6541 in Hawaii, 800/323-3345 Mainland, connects Honolulu, Kahului, and Kona with the state's smaller airports, including Kapalua–West Maui, Lana'i, and Ho'olehua on Moloka'i. About half the flights are on jet aircraft and half on Dash-8 turboprop airplanes. Four flights a day connect Honolulu to Kahului, making a stop on Moloka'i or Lana'i. Direct flights to and from Honolulu and Kapalua–West Maui Airport run five times daily from 7:25 A.M.–4:40 P.M. There are also numerous direct flights spread throughout the day connecting Honolulu with both Lana'i and Moloka'i. Island Air uses the commuter terminal at the Kahului Airport.

Pacific Wings

A local company operating eight-seat, twin-engine Cessna 402C planes, Pacific Wings, 888/575-4546 or 808/873-0877, www.pacificwings.com, does the pickup routes. They connect Kahului nonstop with Hana, Lana'i, Moloka'i, and Kamuela on the Big Island. To Honolulu, flights are either nonstop or through one of these other airports. Pacific Wings also flies from Hana, Moloka'i, and Kalaupapa to Honolulu. Pacific Wings uses the commuter terminal at the Kahului Airport.

Charter Airlines

If you've got the bucks or just need to go when there's no regularly scheduled flight, try one of the following for islandwide service: **Paragon Air,** 808/244-3356 or 800/428-1231 Mainland, www.paragon-air.com; **Pacific Wings,** 808/873-0877 or 888/575-4546 Mainland, www.pacificwings.com; or **Maui Air,** 808/877-5500, www.volcanoairtours.com. These airlines use the commuter terminal at the Kahului Airport.

BY SHIP
Cruise Ships

In 2001, American Hawaii Cruises stopped all service within the Hawaiian Islands. For years, this company had operated seven-day cruises to four of the islands, and hopefully it will resume operation at some time in the future.

Seen at port here in Kahului, the *Norwegian Star* makes a one-week circuit through the Hawaiian Islands with a one-day stop at Fanning Island.

ROBERT NILSEN

From December 2001, Norwegian Cruise Lines (a subsidiary of Star Cruises PLC of Malaysia), 7665 Corporate Center Dr., Miami FL, 33126, 800/327-7030, www.ncl.com, has run a weekly seven-day round-trip cruise with their luxury liner *Norwegian Star*. This ship leaves Honolulu harbor Sunday evenings and cruises to Hilo for its first stop. Leaving there, it spends a day at sea before arriving at Fanning Island in the Republic of Kiribati. One day of sailing back returns the ship to Kahului, from where it goes to Nawiliwili Harbor on Kaua'i and then back to port in Honolulu. This trip can also be started on Maui.

Lahaina–Lana'i Interisland Ferry

Expeditions runs a passenger ferry between Lahaina Harbor and Manele Bay on Lana'i. This shuttle service is not luxury travel but offers a speedy, efficient, and convenient transportation alternative to the plane when going to the Secluded Island. You are allowed to take luggage free of charge, but there's an extra $20 fee for a bicycle. The one-hour crossing leaves Lahaina's public pier daily at 6:45 A.M., 9:15 A.M., 12:45 P.M., 3:15 P.M., and 5:45 P.M.; from Manele Bay at 8 A.M., 10:30 A.M., 2 P.M., 4:30 P.M., and 6:45 P.M.; $25 adults one-way, $20 children 2–11, *kama'aina* rates available. It is best to reserve your place. Because only two bikes are permitted on each ferry, be sure to let the company know well ahead of time so your bike can go with you.

Ground transportation on Lana'i from the pier at Manele Bay is provided by Lana'i City Service, which will take you up to Lana'i City for $20 round-trip or $10 round-trip to the Manele Bay Hotel. An added perk of this trip is that you will see dolphins from the boat most of the year, and there's good whale-watching during winter. For information and reservations, call 808/661-3756 on Maui or 800/695-2624 on Lana'i and elsewhere, or write 658 Front St., Ste. 127, Lahaina, HI 96761; www.go-lanai.com.

Maui–Moloka'i Interisland Ferry

The *Maui Princess* used to sail daily between Kaunakakai and Lahaina, but for economic reasons the service was stopped in 1997, affecting many businesses on Moloka'i. Island Marine,

the company that operates this ship, started ferry operation again in 2001 with the refurbished and faster *Molokai Princess*, which is able to make the crossing in about one hour and 15 minutes. Although the schedule is open to change, the yacht currently runs daily, leaving Kaunakakai at 5:45 A.M. and 3:30 P.M., and returning from Lahaina at 7:30 A.M. and 5:15 P.M. The fares are $40 one-way for adults and $20 for kids. Bikes are an extra $15 each way but don't need to be packed. For information and reservations, contact Island Marine at 808/667-6165 or 800/275-6969; www.molokaiferry.com.

CAR RENTAL

Rental car options in Maui are as numerous as anywhere in the state, from a subcompact to a full-size luxury land yacht. Even so, if you visit the islands during a peak tourist frenzy without reserving your wheels in advance, you could be marooned at the airport.

There's a tremendous field of cars and agencies from which to choose. Special deals come and go like tropical rain showers; swashbuckling price-slashings and come-ons are common all over the rental car market. A little knowledge combined with some shrewd shopping around can save you a bundle. And renting a car is the best way to see the islands if you're going to be there for a limited time.

The most common rentals seem to be compact and midsize sedans, but convertibles, 4WD jeeps, and SUVs are becoming very popular, and some vans are also available. Automatics far outnumber standard-shift cars, and some companies don't even carry vehicles with manual transmissions anymore. What's best for you must meet your needs—and your pocketbook. If your vacation will mostly be spent at the hotel, seeing a few sights, and going out to dinner, get yourself a comfortable midsize or luxury car. If you get a big fatso luxury car, it'll be great for puttin' on the ritz at the resort areas, but you'll feel like a hippopotamus in the backcountry. Are you young and/or adventurous, on a honeymoon perhaps? Try a sporty model. There's nothing like cruising along the coast with the top down.

M
EXPLORING THE ISLANDS

Got kids? Be sure to rent a car with four doors or get a van. Want to get off the main highway? A compact with standard shift or a jeep might be best for you.

The main roads on Maui are broad and well paved, but the back roads, where much of the fun is, can be narrow, twisty affairs. You'll appreciate the downshifting ability of standard transmissions on curves and steep inclines, if you can get it. Most cars now come with cloth seats. If yours doesn't, sitting on your towel will help. Air-conditioning is standard on all but the cheapest, but it hardly seems necessary in this environment. Automatic window and door locks are common but will not come on all rentals. Although you'll want to be paying attention to the scenes around you, a radio is great for getting in touch with local Hawaiian tunes and for weather and surf reports. Most companies have child seats available for rent on a daily basis, $6 per day or $40–50 maximum. They can also install right- or left-hand controls for handicapped drivers; most agencies require 48–72 hours advance notice to install hand controls.

Maui has about two dozen car rental agencies that can put you behind the wheel of anything from an exotic convertible to a used station wagon with chipped paint and torn upholstery. There are national companies, interisland firms, good local companies, and a few fly-by-nights that'll rent you a clunker. The national chains have booths at the Kahului Airport. No rental agency has a booth at the Kapalua–West Maui Airport (there are courtesy phones), but one company has a booth at the Hana Airport. The rest are scattered around the island, with a heavy concentration in Kahului, on Halawai Drive in Ka'anapali, and along South Kihei Road. Those without an airport booth either have a courtesy phone or a number to call; some will pick you up and shuttle you to their lots. Stiff competition tends to keep the prices more or less reasonable. Good deals are offered off season, with price wars flaring at any time and making for real savings. Even with all of these companies, it's best to book ahead. You might not save money, but you can save yourself headaches.

Requirements

A variety of requirements are imposed on the renter by car agencies, but the most important clauses are common. Before renting, check that you fulfill the requirements. Generally, you must be 21 years old—a few agencies will rent to 18-year-olds and others require you to be 25 for certain types of vehicles. You must possess a valid driver's license—licenses from most countries are accepted, but if you are not American, get an International Driver's License to be safe. You should also have a major credit card in your name. This is the easiest way to rent a car. Some companies will take a deposit, but it will be very stiff. It could easily be $50 per day on top of your rental fees and sometimes much more. In addition, they may require a credit check on the spot, complete with phone calls to your employer and bank. If you damage the car, charges will be deducted from your deposit, and the car company determines the extent of the damages. Some companies *will not* rent you a car without a major credit card in your name, no matter how much of a deposit you are willing to leave, and this is often true for Hawaiian residents who want to rent a car on an island where they are not a resident.

When to Rent

You'll have to make up your own mind on this one, because it's a bet that you can either win or lose. But it's always good to know the odds before you plop down your money. You can reserve your car in advance when you book your air ticket or play the field when you get there. If you book in advance, you'll obviously have a car waiting for you, but the deal that you made is the deal you'll get; it may or may not be the best around, but it may be quite good. On the other hand, if you wait, you can often take advantage of on-the-spot deals; however, you're betting that cars are available. You might be totally disappointed and not be able to rent a car at all, or you might make a honey of a deal.

If you're arriving during the peak seasons of Christmas, Easter, or late summer vacation, absolutely *book your car in advance*. Rental companies have their numbers down pretty well and seem to have plenty of cars, but all may be accounted for during this period. Even if you can find a junker from a fly-by-night, they'll price-gouge you mercilessly. If you're going off peak, you stand a good chance of getting the car you want at a price you like. It's generally best to book ahead; most car companies have toll-free numbers. At least call them for an opinion of your chances of getting a car upon your intended arrival.

Rates

The super-cheap rates on eye-catcher brochures refer to subcompacts. The price goes up with the size of the car. As with options on a new car, the more luxury you get, the more you pay. All major car rental companies in Hawaii use a flat-rate option. The flat rate is best, providing a fixed daily rate and unlimited mileage. Some of the smaller local companies may have a mileage-rate option. Mileage rate costs less per day, but you are charged for every mile driven. Mileage rates are best if you drive less than 30 miles per day, but even on an island that isn't much! With either rate, you buy the gas.

Rental rates vary by company, as do the names they refer to their types of vehicles. The following rates are fairly representative for most categories: subcompact, $45 per day, $225 per week; compact, $55/260; midsize, $65/300; full size, $75/350; luxury, $110/575; convertible and jeep, $100/500; van, $110/$575. Substantial discounts, often 10–15 percent, are offered for weekday, weekly, and monthly rentals. It's sometimes cheaper to rent a car for the week even if you're only going to use it for five days. If you'll be on more than one island, check to see if weekly and monthly rates can be split between Neighbor Islands. Most of the car companies, local and national, offer special rates and deals, like AAA discounts. These deals fluctuate too rapidly to give any hard-and-fast information. They are common, however, so make sure to inquire. Don't expect that rental companies will let you know about any deal they have. Also, peak periods have blackouts, during which normally good deals no longer apply.

These rates aren't your only charges, however. On top of the actual rental fee, you must pay an airport access fee, airport concession fee, state tax, and a road tax surcharge—in total, an additional 25–30 percent. For cars not rented at the airports, you'll realize savings of about 7.5 percent because some of the taxes cannot be charged.

You may be asked about refueling options. Ordinarily, you fill the tank when you return the car or the company will fill the tank at an inflated rate. Some now offer you the option of prepaying for a half or full tank of gas at a reduced rate, and they fill the car when it comes back. In order to get your money's worth this way, bring the car back exactly half empty or all the way empty; otherwise, you may lose a little bit over pumping the gas yourself. Gas prices are generally higher in Hawaii than anywhere on the Mainland, and may be higher yet in distant locations like Hana, Moloka'i, and Lana'i.

Warning: If you keep your car beyond your contract, you'll be charged the highest daily rate unless you notify the rental agency beforehand. *Don't keep your car longer than the contract without notifying the company.* Companies are quick to send out their repossession specialists. You might find yourself in a situation with your car gone, a warrant for your arrest, and an extra charge on your bill. A simple courtesy call notifying them of your intentions saves a lot of headaches and hassle.

Insurance

Before signing your car rental agreement, you'll be offered various "insurance" coverage. Although these too vary somewhat by company, they fall into general categories: loss/damage option runs about $15 per day; uninsured motorist protection, $7 per day; and liability protection, $13 per day. In addition, some also offer personal effects protection for $5 per day in case your property gets stolen. Because insurance is already built into the contract (don't expect the rental agency to point this out), what you're really buying is a waiver on the deductible ($500–1,000), in case you crack up the car. If you have insurance at home, you will almost always have coverage on a rental car—including your normal deductible—although not all policies are the same, so check with your agent. Also, if you haven't bought the waiver and you do have a mishap, the rental agencies may put a claim against your credit card on the spot for the amount of the deductible, even if you can prove that your insurance will cover the charge. They'll tell *you* to collect from your insurance company because they don't want to be left holding the bag on an across-the-waters claim. If you have a good policy with a small deductible, it's hardly worth paying the extra money for the waiver, but if your own policy is inadequate, buy the insurance. Also, most major credit cards offer complimentary car rental insurance as an incentive for using their cards to rent the car. Simply call your credit card company to see if this service is included.

Driving Tips

Wear your seat belt—it's the law! Police keep an eye out for miscreants and often ticket those who do not use their restraints. Protect your small children as you would at home with car seats. Either bring one from home or rent one from a car rental company. Rental prices and availability vary, but all of the agencies can make arrangements if you give them enough notice.

Mile markers on roads are great for pinpointing sights and beaches. The lower number on these signs is the highway number, so you can always make sure you're on the right road.

In most cases, you'll get only one key for your rental car. Don't lose it or lock it inside. If you do lock it inside the vehicle, call AAA (or other auto emergency service that you have) and ask for assistance. Failing that, a local locksmith can open your car for a fee or the rental car agency can send out a second key by taxi, but both of these options can get quite pricey.

There are few differences between driving in Hawaii and on the Mainland. Just remember that many people on the roads are tourists and can be confused about where they're going. Because many drivers are from somewhere else, there's hardly a "regular style" of driving in the islands. A farmer from Iowa accustomed to poking along on back roads can be sandwiched between a frenetic New Yorker who's trying to drive over his roof and a super-polite but horribly confused Japanese tourist who normally drives on the left.

In Hawaii, drivers don't generally honk their horns except to say hello or in an emergency. It's considered rude, and honking to hurry someone might earn you a knuckle sandwich. Hawaiian drivers reflect the climate: they're relaxed and polite. Often on small roads, they'll brake to let you turn left when they're coming at you. They may assume you'll do the same, so be ready, after a perfunctory turn signal from another driver, for him or her to turn across your lane. The more rural the area, the more apt this is to happen. Don't expect it in the large cities.

It may seem like common sense, but remember to slow down when you enter the little towns strung along the circle-island route. It's easy to bomb along on the highway and flash through these towns, missing some of Hawaii's best scenery. Also, rural children expect *you* to be watchful and will assume that you are going to stop for them when they dart out into the roadway.

Traffic can get heavy at times on Maui. Rush-hour morning and evening traffic slows down the flow considerably. Areas to avoid, if possible, at these times are along Pi'ilani Highway in Kihei, the highway through Lahaina, the intersection of Highways 30 and 31 near Ma'alaea, Honoapi'ilani Highway between Ka'anapali and Kapalua, and Haleakala Highway just outside of Kahului.

Respect "Do not enter" and "Private property" signs—"Kapu" means the same thing.

Most insurance companies warn you that their cars are not supposed to be driven off paved roads—read your policy. This seems absolutely ridiculous for 4WD vehicles but may be true nonetheless. When a road is signed for 4WD only, assume that that's the case for a good reason. Also, most rental companies prohibit you from taking their rental vehicles around the south side of the island—that section between 'Oheo Gulch and Ulupalakua.

Speed limits change periodically along the highways of Hawai'i, particularly when they pass through small towns. Police routinely check the speed of traffic by use of radar equipment. Be aware of this so you don't go home with more than a suntan.

The State Department of Transportation has installed solar-powered emergency call boxes on Maui highways that are linked directly to an emergency response network. These boxes are located along major roadways, on the Hana Highway, the Haleakala Highway, and on the road around the north end of the island in Kahakuloa. They can be located by a yellow box on a tall pole topped by a small solar panel and blue light.

B.Y.O. Car

If you want to bring your own car, write for information to the Director of Finance, Division of Licenses, 1455 S. Beretania St., Honolulu, HI 96814. However, unless you'll be in Hawaii for a bare minimum of six months and will spend all of your time on one island, don't even think about it. It's an expensive proposition and takes time and plenty of arrangements. To ship a car from the U.S. West Coast to Hawaii, the cost is at least $825 to Honolulu and an additional $50 to any other island. To save on rental costs, it would be better to buy and sell a car there or to lease for an extended period. For information about licensing and insurance on Maui, contact the County Department of Finance, Motor Vehicle and Licensing Division, 808/270-7363.

RENTAL AGENCIES

The following are major firms that have booths at Kahului Airport—exit the arrival terminal and go to your right. Many prebooked cars are waiting at these booths, but if not, and if you want to rent a car upon arrival, you must take a company shuttle to the base yard behind the airport parking lot or in town to arrange for your car.

Dollar Rent A Car, 808/877-2731 in Kahului, 808/667-2651 in Ka'anapali, 808/248-8237 in Hana, 800/342-7398 statewide, or 800/800-4000 worldwide, www.dollarcar.com, has an excellent reputation and very competitive prices. Dollar rents mostly Chrysler vehicles: sedans, jeeps, convertibles, and 4WDs. Great weekly rates, and all major credit cards accepted.

Alamo, 808/871-6235 in Kahului and 808/661-7181 in Ka'anapali, or 800/327-9633, www.goalamo.com, has good weekly rates. Mostly GM cars.

National Car Rental, 808/871-8851 in Kahu-

lui, 808/667-9737 in Ka'anapali, or 800/227-7368 nationwide, www.nationalcar.com, features GM cars and accepts all major credit cards.

Avis, 808/871-7575 in Kahului, 808/661-4588 Ka'anapali, 800/321-3712 nationwide, www.avis.com, features late-model GM cars as well as most imports and convertibles.

Budget, 800/527-7000 on Maui, or nationwide 800/527-0700, www.budget.com, offers competitive rates on a variety of late-model Ford and Lincoln-Mercury cars, trucks, and specialty vehicles.

Hertz, 808/877-5167 Kahului, 808/661-7735 in Ka'anapali, 800/654-3011 nationwide, www.hertz.com, is competitively priced with many fly/drive deals. They feature Ford vehicles.

Enterprise, 808/871-1511 Kahului, 808/661-8804 in Ka'anapali, or 800/736-8222 nationwide, www.enterprise.com, rents all types of vehicles at decent rates.

Thrifty, 808/871-2860 or 800/367-5238 statewide, or 808/367-2277 worldwide, www.thrifty.com, offers mostly Chrysler-made vehicles.

The following local companies are based in Maui. None have a booth at the airport, but a few have pickup service through courtesy phones. **Word of Mouth Rent-A-Used Car,** 150 Hana Hwy., 808/877-2436 or 800/533-5929, www.mauirentacar.com, offers some fantastic deals on their used, but not abused, cars; pickup van provided. They're a reputable agency, having been around for more than 25 years. Office hours are 8 A.M.–5 P.M., but they will leave a car at the airport at earlier or later hours with prior arrangement. Others include **Kihei Rent A Car,** 96 Kio Loop behind the Maui Dive shop in Kihei, 808/879-7257 or 800/251-5288, www.kiheirentacar.com; and **Maui Cruisers,** 808/249-2319 or 877/749-7889 Mainland, 800/488-9083 Canada, www.mauicruisers.net, who will put you in a car that will make you "look local."

Four-Wheel Drive

Although much more expensive than cars, some people might feel safer in 4WDs for completely circling Maui or driving some roads in Upcountry. Also, unlike for cars, the rental companies offering 4WDs put no restrictions on driving past ʻOheʻo Gulch. Four-wheel drives can be obtained from **Dollar** and a few of the other "big boys," as well as the following: **Maui Rent A Jeep,** 808/877-6626 or 800/701-JEEP, www.mauijeep.com; **Kihei Rent A Car;** 808/879-7257 or 800/251-5288, www.kiheirentacar.com; or one of the vanity vehicle dealers listed as follows. Rates vary from company to company but are mostly around $75–100 per day, depending on availability, model, and length of rental.

Vanity Vehicles

If you feel like stepping out in style, consider renting a flashy sports car. **Island Riders,** 808/661-9966 in Lahaina or 808/874-0311 in Kihei, www.islandriders.com, rents a Dodge Viper, Ferrari 348TS, Prowler, Porsche Cabriolet, and Corvette convertible, as well as a few jeeps, vans, and Mazda Miatas. The vanity cars are classy but they're not cheap, and you may have to be 25 years old to rent. However, for that one night of luxury, it may be worth it to you. Rates run from around $200 per day to $850 per day depending on the type of car. Rental by the hour is also possible. The **Aloha Toy Store,** with locations at 640 Front St., 808/662-0888, The Shops at Wailea, 808/891-0888, or The Fairway Shops in Kaʻanaplai, 808/661-9000, www.alohatoystore.com, also has a variety of these fancy cars at comparable rates, as does **Hawaiian Riders,** 196 Lahainaluna St. in Lahaina, 808/662-4386, and in Kihei, 808/891-0889, www.hawaiianriders.com.

Travelers with Disabilities

Accessible Vans of Hawaii, 296 Alamaha St., Ste. C, Kahului, HI 96732, 808/871-7785, 800/303-3750 in Hawaii, 888/282-8267 nationwide, fax 808/871-7536, info@accessalohatravel.com, www.accessiblevanshawaii.com, is a private company, owned and operated by Dave McKown, who has traveled the world with his paraplegic brother. Dave knows firsthand the obstacles faced by people with disabilities, and his disabled associate does as well. Accessible Vans of Hawaii provides a full-service travel agency, booking rooms, flights, and activities for the physically disabled. Wheelchair-lift-equipped vans are

rented on Maui and Oʻahu for $115 per day, $599 per week, or $2,250 per month, plus tax and pickup and delivery charge. This company also sells new and used vans set up for disabled owners and mobility equipment and travel accessories. Dave and his associate are good sources of information for any traveler with disabilities.

Motorcycles

A few companies also rent motorcycles for the intrepid traveler. Virtually all rental bikes are Harley-Davidson big hogs or sportsters. Rates vary but run around $100 for half a day and $140–190 for 24 hours; longer rentals can be arranged. All drivers must be at least 21 years old, have a valid motorcycle endorsement on your license, and own a major credit card. Insurance is available. Companies want you to stay on good paved roads and don't usually allow trips to Hana. Although it is not required by state law to wear them, helmets are available, but you must wear eye protection. To ride one of these big steeds, contact **Mavriks',** at Halawai Drive in Kaʻanapali, 808/661-3099; **Island Riders,** 808/661-9966 in Lahaina or 808/874-0311 in Kihei; the **Aloha Toy Store,** 808/662-0888 or 808/661-1212 in Lahaina, The Shops at Wailea, 808/891-0888, or The Fairway Shops in Kaʻanaplai, 808/661-9000; **Hawaiian Riders,** 808/662-4386 in Lahaina or 808/891-0889 in Kihei; or **Hula Hogs,** 808/875-7433 in Kihei.

Mopeds

Just for running around town or to the beach, mopeds are great. Expect to pay about $25 for two hours, $35 for four hours, and $45 for eight hours; some offer weekly rates. Most will ask for a cash deposit; some companies will not let you keep mopeds overnight. You must be at least 18 years old. Check with **Hawaiian Island Cruzers,** 2395 S. Kihei Rd., 808/879-0956; **Mavriks',** Halawai Drive in Kaʻanapali, 808/661-3099; **Aloha Toy Store,** 640 Front St., Lahaina, 808/662-0888, the Shops at Wailea in Wailea, 808/891-0888, or The Fariway Shops in Kaʻanapali, 808/661-9000; or **Hawaiian Riders,** 196 Lahainaluna Rd. in Lahaina, 808/662-4386, or in Kihei, 808/891-0889.

ALTERNATIVE TRANSPORTATION

Maui Bus System

There is limited public bus service on Maui that operates between Wailuku and Kahului, within the South Maui and West Maui areas, between these two regions, with a connection up to Wailuku and Kahului through Maʻalaea. Unfortunately, there is still no public bus service to Upcountry or along the Hana Highway. This public transportation system is operated by MEO (Maui Economic Opportunity, Inc.) and Akina Aloha Tours: the MEO Public Shuttle and the Akina Holo Kaʻa Transit.

The MEO Public Shuttle runs two circular routes between Kahului and Wailuku 6–8 times per day Monday through Saturday, allowing for easy access between these two towns. Overlapping seven of these stops is the Akina Holo Kaʻa Transit Route 5, which runs down to Maʻalaea and on to Lahaina Harbor, Whaler's Village in Kaʻanapali, and the Ritz-Carlton in Kapalua or from Maʻalaea down to the Shops at Wailea in Wailea. Four of these overlapping stops are the state office building in Wailuku and the Queen Kaʻahumanu Center, the Maui Mall, and K-Mart in Kahului. There is no fare for the MEO Public Shuttle, although donations are accepted.

The Holo Kaʻa Transit buses operate within the South Maui and West Maui areas and between these two areas. The point-to-point one-way fare for rides within the Lahaina–Kaʻanapali section is $1, $2 for the routes between Kapalua and Kaʻanapali as well as the Kihei–Makena route, $5 one-way to or from Maʻalaea, and an all-day systemwide pass is $10, which includes the connection from Wailuku or Kahului.

West Maui Route 1 runs approximately one dozen times a day between Kapalua and Kaʻanapali from 9 A.M. Route 2 starts at 8:45 A.M. and goes more than a dozen times a day between Kaʻanapali and Lahaina. The Route 3 Express runs six times a day from Kaʻanapali Whaler's Village to Lahaina, then on to Maʻalaea, and finally through Kihei to The Shops at Wailea. An Early Bird Route also runs twice a morning between Kihei at Kapalua, via Maʻalaea, Lahaina, and Kaʻanapali. Route 4 runs seven times a day within South Maui, stopping at more than a dozen stops on the way. The Suda's Store is at the north end and the Maui Prince in Makena is at the south end.

For information on routes, schedules, and fares for this public transit system, contact MEO at 808/877-7651, www.meoinc.com; or Akina Aloha Tours, 808/879-2828, www.akinatours.com. Systemwide schedules and timetables are also printed in some of the free tourist literature available across the island.

Shuttle Services

Speedi Shuttle, 808/875-8070, connects the Kahului Airport to virtually anywhere on the island and operates daily during the hours that the planes fly. Pickup can be either from the airport or from any hotel or condo if going to the airport. Use the telephone next to the information booth in the baggage claim area when at the airport. Rates vary according to distance and how many are in your party, but as an example, a party of two from the airport to Wailea would run about $32, to Kaʻanapali $46, to Kapalua $60, and between Wailea and Lahaina $45. **Executive Airport Shuttle,** 808/669-2300, offers virtually the same service to and from the airport and to points around the island for nearly the same rates, like $30 from the airport in Kahului to the harbor in Lahaina. Although these companies will service their calls as soon as they can, they prefer several hours or even 24 hours advance notice if possible in order to best facilitate use of their vehicles.

The free **Kaanapali Trolley** runs along the Kaʻanapali strip about every half hour 10 A.M.–10 P.M., stopping at all major resorts, the golf course, and the Whalers Village shopping complex. Look for the green jitneys. Pick up free printed tourist literature or ask at any hotel desk for a schedule.

The **Wailea Shuttle** is a complimentary van that stops at several of the major hotels in Wailea, The Shops at Wailea, and the golf course clubhouses in Wailea every 30 minutes. It operates 6:30 A.M.–8 P.M. Be sure to check with the driver about the last pickup times if you are out in the evening.

Taxis

About two dozen taxi companies on Maui operate pretty much an islandwide service. Some operate by area. Most, besides providing normal taxi service, also run tours all over the island. While sedans predominate, some minivans are being used as well. Taxis are expensive and metered by the distance traveled. For example, a ride from Kahului Airport to Lahaina is $49, Ka'anapali is $55, to Kapalua $75, and to Wailea about $40. Expect $5–10 in and around Kahului, and about $12 to the hostels in Wailuku. Any taxi may drop off at the airport, but only those with permits may pick up there. In the Kihei/Wailea area, try **Wailea Taxi,** 808/874-5000, or **Kihei Taxi,** 808/879-3000. **Kahului Taxi Service,** 808/877-5681, operates in central Maui. In West Maui, options include **Alii Cab,** 808/661-3688; **AB Taxi,** 808/667-7575; and Island Taxi, 808/667-5656. **Classy Taxi,** 808/665-0003, uses renovated old cars from the '20s and '30s. A ride from Lahaina to Ka'anapali will run about $11 and from there to Kapalua about $18.

For those who desire private limo service, several companies on the island can fit the bill. These are expensive rides, however, and will run, for example, more than $120 one-way from the Kahului Airport to Ka'anapali. Private tours might run $60 for two persons for two hours or $90 for a full load for the same time frame. Ask your hotel concierge for assistance in arranging for this service, or contact one of the following: **Wailea Limousine,** 808/875-4114; **Executive Service, 808/669-2300; or Bob and Sons Limousine Service,** 808/877-7800.

Hitchhiking

After three decades of being a "criminal act," hitchhiking is once again legal in Maui County. Use the old tried-and-true method of thumb out, facing traffic, with a smile on your face. You can get around quite well by hitchhiking if you're not on a schedule. The success rate of getting a ride to the number of cars that go by isn't that great, but you will get picked up eventually. Locals and the average tourist with family will generally pass you by. Recent residents and single tourists will most often pick you up, and 90 percent of the time these will be white males. Hitching short hops along the resort beaches is easy. People can tell by the way you're dressed that you're not going far and will give you a lift. Catching longer rides to Hana or up to Haleakala can be done, but it'll be tougher because the driver will know that you'll be with him or her for the duration of the ride. Women under no circumstances should hitch alone.

Health and Conduct

In a survey published some years ago by *Science Digest,* Hawaii was cited as the healthiest state in the United States in which to live. Indeed, Hawaiian citizens live longer than anywhere else in America: men to 76 years and women to 82. Lifestyle, heredity, and diet help with these figures, but Hawaii is still an oasis in the middle of the ocean, and germs just have a tougher time getting there. There are no cases of malaria, cholera, or yellow fever. Because of a strict quarantine law, rabies is also nonexistent. On the other hand, tooth decay, perhaps because of the wide use of sugar and the enzymes present in certain tropical fruits, is 30 percent above the national average. With the perfect weather, a multitude of fresh-air activities, soothing negative ionization from the sea, and a generally relaxed and carefree lifestyle, everyone seems to feel better in the islands. Hawaii is just what the doctor ordered: a beautiful, natural health spa. That's one of its main drawing cards. The food and water are perfectly safe, and the air quality is the best in the country.

Handling the Sun

Don't become a victim of your own exuberance. People can't wait to strip down and lie on the sand like beached whales, but the tropical sun will burn you to a cinder if you're silly. The burning rays come through more easily in

Hawaii because of the sun's angle, and you don't feel them as much because there's always a cool breeze. The worst part of the day is 11 A.M.–3 P.M. Maui lies about 19 degrees north latitude, not even close to the equator, but it's still over 1,000 miles south of sunny southern California beaches. You'll just have to force yourself to go slowly. Don't worry; you'll be able to flaunt your best souvenir—your golden Hawaiian tan—to your green-with-envy friends when you get home. It's better than showing them a boiled lobster body with peeling skin! If your skin is snowflake white, 15 minutes per side on the first day is plenty. Increase by 15-minute intervals every day, which will allow you a full hour per side by the fourth day. Have faith; this is enough to give you a start on a deep golden, uniform tan. If you lie out on the beach or are simply out in the sun during the day, use sunblock lotion that has greater strength than you use at home—most people recommend SPF 25 or higher—and reapply every couple of hours. If you do burn, try taking aspirin as quickly as you can. No one knows exactly what it does, but it seems to provide some relief. Alternately, apply a cold compress or aloe juice, but be careful with aloe because it may stain clothing.

Whether out on the beach, hiking in the mountains, or just strolling around town, be very aware of dehydration. The sun (and wind) tend to sap your energy and your store of liquid. Bottled water in various sizes is readily available in all parts of Hawaii. Be sure to carry some with you or stop at a store or restaurant for a filler-up.

Don't forget about your head and eyes. Use your sunglasses and wear a brimmed hat. Some people lay a towel over their neck and shoulders when hiking and others will stick a scarf under their hat and let it drape down over their shoulders to provide some protection.

Haole Rot

A peculiar condition caused by the sun is referred to locally as *haole* rot. It's called this because it supposedly affects only white people, but you'll notice some dark-skinned people with the same condition. Basically, the skin becomes mottled with white spots that refuse to tan. You get a blotchy effect, mostly on the shoulders and back. Dermatologists have a fancy name for it, and they'll give you a fancy prescription with a not-so-fancy price tag to cure it. It's common knowledge throughout the islands that Selsun Blue shampoo has some ingredient that stops the white mottling effect. Just wash your hair with it and then make sure to rub the lather over the affected areas, and it should clear up.

Bugs

Everyone, in varying degrees, has an aversion to vermin and creepy crawlers. Hawaii isn't infested with a wide variety, but it does have its share. Mosquitoes were unknown in the islands until their larvae stowed away in the water barrels of the *Wellington* in 1826 and were introduced at Lahaina. They bred in the tropical climate and rapidly spread to all of the islands. They are a particular nuisance in the rainforests. Be prepared, and bring a natural repellent like citronella oil, available in most health stores on the islands, or a commercial product available in grocery and drugstores. Campers will be happy to have mosquito coils to burn at night as well.

Cockroaches are very democratic insects. They hassle all strata of society equally. They breed well in Hawaii and most hotels are at war with them, trying desperately to keep them from being spotted by guests. One comforting thought is that in Hawaii they aren't a sign of filth or dirty housekeeping. They love the climate like everyone else, and it's a real problem keeping them under control. Of a number of different roaches in Hawaii, the ones that give most people the jitters are big bombers over two inches long. Roaches are after food crumbs and the like and very infrequently bother with a human. Be aware of this if you rent a room with a kitchenette or condo. If you are in a modest hotel and see a roach, it might make you feel better to know that the millionaire in the $1,000-a-night suite probably has them too. Bring your own spray if you wish, call the desk if you see them, or just let them be.

WATER SAFETY

Hawaii has one very sad claim to fame: More people drown here than anywhere else in the world. Moreover, there are dozens of yearly swimming victims with broken necks and backs or with injuries from scuba and snorkeling accidents. These statistics shouldn't keep you out of the sea because it is indeed beautiful—benevolent in most cases—and a major reason to go to Hawaii. But if you're foolish, the sea will bounce you like a basketball and suck you away for good. The best remedy is to avoid situations you can't handle. Don't let anyone dare you into a situation that makes you uncomfortable. "Macho men" who know nothing about the power of the sea will be tumbled into Cabbage Patch dolls in short order. Ask lifeguards or beach attendants about conditions, and follow their advice. If local people refuse to go in, there's a good reason. Even experts get in trouble in Hawaiian waters. Some beaches are as gentle as a lamb, whereas others, especially on the north coasts during the winter, are frothing giants.

While beachcombing, or especially when walking out on rocks, never turn your back to the sea. Be aware of undertows (the waves drawing back into the sea). They can knock you off your feet. Before entering the water, study it for rocks, breakers, reefs, and riptides. Riptides are powerful currents, like rivers in the sea, that can drag you out. Mostly they peter out not too far from shore, and you can often see their choppy waters on the surface. If caught in a "rip," don't fight to swim directly against it; you'll lose and only exhaust yourself. Swim diagonally across it, while going along with it, and try to stay parallel to the shore. Don't waste all your lung power yelling, and rest by floating.

When bodysurfing, never ride straight in; come to shore at a 45-degree angle. Remember, waves come in sets. Little ones can be followed by giants, so watch the action awhile instead of plunging right in. Standard procedure is to duck under a breaking wave. You can survive even thunderous oceans using this technique. Don't try to swim through a heavy froth and never turn your back and let it smash you. Don't swim

alone if possible, and obey all warning signs. Hawaiians want to entertain you and they don't put up signs just to waste money. The last rule is, "If in doubt, stay out."

Yikes!

Sharks live in all the oceans of the world. Most mind their own business and stay away from shore. Hawaiian sharks are well fed—on fish—and don't usually bother with unsavory humans. If you encounter a shark, don't panic! Never thrash around because this will trigger their attack instinct. If they come close, scream loudly.

Portuguese man-of-wars put out long, floating tentacles that sting if they touch you. It seems that many floating jellyfish are blown into shore by winds on the eighth, ninth, and tenth days after the full moon. Don't wash the sting off with freshwater because this will only aggravate it. Hot saltwater will take away the sting, as will alcohol (the drinking or the rubbing kind), after-shave lotion, or meat tenderizer (MSG), which can be found in any supermarket or some Chinese restaurants.

Coral can give you a nasty cut, and it's known for causing infections because it's a living organism. Wash the cut immediately and apply an antiseptic. Keep it clean and covered, and watch for infection.

Poisonous sea urchins, such as the lacquer-black *wana*, can be beautiful creatures. They are found in shallow tide pools and will hurt you if you step on them. Their spines will break off, enter your foot, and burn like blazes. There are cures. Vinegar and wine poured on the wound will stop the burning. If those are not available, the Hawaiian solution is urine. It might seem ignominious to have someone pee on your foot, but it'll put the fire out. The spines will disintegrate in a few days, and there are generally no long-term effects.

Hawaiian reefs also have their share of moray eels. These creatures are ferocious in appearance but will never initiate an attack. You'll have to poke around in their holes while snorkeling or scuba diving to get them to attack. Sometimes this is inadvertent on the diver's part, so be careful where you stick your hand while underwater. Present in streams, ponds, and muddy soil, *lep-*

tospirosis is a freshwater-borne bacteria, deposited by the urine of infected animals. From 2–20 days after the bacteria enter the body, there is a *sudden* onset of fever accompanied by chills, sweats, headache, and sometimes vomiting and diarrhea. Preventive measures include staying out of freshwater sources and mud where cattle and other animals wade and drink, not swimming in freshwater if you have an open cut, and not drinking stream water. Although it may not always be the case, *leptospirosis* may be fatal if left untreated.

HAWAIIAN FOLK MEDICINE AND CURES

Hawaiian folk medicine is well developed, and its cures for common ailments have been used effectively for centuries. Hawaiian *kahuna* were highly regarded for their medicinal skills, and Hawaiians were by far some of the healthiest people in the world until the coming of the Europeans. Many folk remedies and cures are used to this day and, what's more, they work. Many of the common plants and fruits you'll encounter provide some of the best remedies. When roots and seeds and special exotic plants are used, the preparation of the medicine is as painstaking as in a modern pharmacy. These prescriptions are exact and take an expert to prepare. They should never be prepared or administered by an amateur.

Common Curative Plants

Arrowroot, for diarrhea, is a powerful narcotic used in rituals and medicines. Kava *(Piper methisticum),* also called *'awa,* is chewed and the juice is spat into a container for fermenting. Used as a medicine for urinary tract infections, rheumatism, and asthma, it also induces sleep and cures headaches. A poultice for wounds is made from the skins of ripe bananas. Peelings have a powerful antibiotic quality and contain vitamins A, B, and C, phosphorous, calcium, and iron. The nectar from the plant was fed to babies as a vitamin juice. Breadfruit sap is used for healing cuts and as a moisturizing lotion. Coconut is used to make moisturizing oil, and the juice was chewed, spat into the hand, and used as a shampoo. Guava is a source of vitamins A, B, and C. Hibiscus has

ALL-PURPOSE KUKUI

Reaching heights of 80 feet, the *kukui* (candlenut) was a veritable department store to the Hawaiians, who made use of almost every part of this utilitarian giant. Used as cure-alls, its nuts, bark, or flowers were ground into potions and salves and taken as a general tonic, applied to ulcers and cuts as an effective antibiotic, or administered internally as a cure for constipation or asthma attacks. The bark was mixed with water, and the resulting juice was used as a dye in tattooing, tapa-cloth making, and canoe painting, and as a preservative for fishnets. The oily nuts were burned as a light source in stone holders, and ground and eaten as a condiment (mixed with salt) called *'inamona.* Polished nuts took on a beautiful sheen and were strung as lei. Lastly, the wood itself was hollowed into canoes and seeds as fishnet floats.

been used as a laxative. *Kukui* nut oil makes a gargle for sore throats and a laxative, plus the flowers are used to cure diarrhea. *Noni,* an unappetizing hand-grenade-shaped fruit that you wouldn't want to eat unless you had to, reduces tumors, diabetes, and high blood pressure, and the juice is good for diarrhea. Sugarcane sweetens many concoctions, and the juice of toasted cane was a tonic for sick babies. Sweet potato is used as a tonic during pregnancy and juiced as a gargle for phlegm. Tamarind is a natural laxative and contains the most acid and sugar of any fruit on earth. Taro has been used for lung infections and thrush and as suppositories. Yams are good for coughs, vomiting, constipation, and appendicitis.

MEDICAL SERVICES

Maui Memorial Medical Center, 221 Mahalani St., Wailuku, 808/244-9056, is the only full-service hospital on the island.

There are several clinics around the island, including the following: **Urgent Care Maui/Kihei Physicians,** 1325 S. Kihei Rd., Ste. 103, 808/879-7781, where doctors, a clinical lab, and X-rays are available from 6 A.M.–midnight daily. **Kihei-Wailea Medical Center,** in the Pi'ilani Village Shopping Center, 808/874-8100, has physicians, a pharmacy, physical therapy, and a clinical laboratory and is open Monday–Friday 8 A.M.–8 P.M., Saturday and Sunday until 5 P.M. **Kaiser Permanente** has a clinic in Lahaina at 910 Waine'e, 808/662-6900, in Wailuku at 80 Mahalani St., 808/243-6000, and in Kihei at 1279 S. Kihei Rd., 808/891-6800; open Monday–Friday 8 A.M.–5 P.M., closed noon –1 P.M., weekends, and holidays. At Dickenson Square in Lahaina, **Aloha Family Practice Clinic,** 808/662-5642, has hours weekdays 8:30 A.M.–4:30 P.M. for preventive and urgent care needs. In the center of Wailuku, try **Maui Medical Group,** 2180 Main St., 808/249-8080; they also have clinics in Lahaina and Pukalani. The **West Maui Healthcare Center** maintains an office at the Whalers Village shopping mall, 808/667-9721; open 8 A.M.–8 P.M. daily.

Of the numerous drugstores throughout the island, the following should meet your needs: **Longs Drug** in Kihei, Lahaina, and Kahului; **Kihei Pharmacy,** 41 E. Lipoa, 808/879-8499; and **Lahaina Pharmacy,** in the Lahaina Shopping Center, 808/661-3119.

SERVICES FOR TRAVELERS WITH DISABILITIES

A person with a disability can have a wonderful time in Hawaii; all that's needed is a little pre-planning. The following is general advice that should help your planning.

Commission on Persons with Disabilities

This state commission was designed with the express purpose of aiding handicapped people. It is a source of invaluable information and distributes self-help booklets, which are published jointly by the Disability and Communication Access Board and the Hawaii Centers for Independent Living. Any person with disabilities heading to Hawaii should write first or visit their offices on arrival. For the *Aloha Guide To Accessibility* (Part I is free; $3–5 charge for Parts II and III), write or visit: Hawaii Centers for Independent Living, 414 Kuwili St., #102, Honolulu, HI 96817, 808/522-5400; or the Commission on Persons with Disabilities, 919 Ala Moana Blvd., Rm. 101, Honolulu, HI 96814, 808/586-8121. On Maui, contact either the Commission on Persons with Disabilities, 54 High St., Wailuku, HI 96793, 808/984-8219; or Maui Center for Independent Living, 220 Imi Kala St., Ste. 103, Wailuku, HI 96793, 808/242-4966.

General Information

The key for a smooth trip is to make as many arrangements ahead of time as possible. Tell the transportation companies and hotels you'll be dealing with the nature of your handicap in advance so they can make arrangements to accommodate you. Bring your medical records and notify medical establishments of your arrival if you'll be needing their services. Travel with a friend or make arrangements for an aide on arrival. Bring your own wheelchair if possible and let airlines know if it is battery-powered. Boarding interisland carriers requires steps. They'll board wheelchairs early on special lifts, but they must know that you're coming. Most hotels and restaurants accommodate persons with disabilities, but always call ahead just to make sure.

Maui Services

On arrival at Kahului Airport, parking spaces are directly in front of the main terminal. Elevators are available for those going between levels. There are no special emergency medical services, but visitor information is available at

808/872-3893. There is no centralized medical service, but Maui Memorial Medical Center in Wailuku, 808/244-9056, will refer. Getting around can be tough because there is little public transportation on Maui, and most tour operators do not accommodate nonambulatory persons; however, rental cars can be fitted with hand controls (both right and left), but some restrict these controls to certain size or type vehicles. They generally require prior arrangements, one or two days at least, preferably when making your advance reservation. Rates are comparable with or the same as for standard rental cars. A private special shuttle company with handivans operating on Maui is **Executive Shuttle, 808/669-2300 or 800/833-2303; it takes wheelchair-bound persons. Accessible Vans of Hawaii,** 808/871-7785 or 800/303-3750, fax 808/871-7536, info@accessalohatravel.com, www.accessible-vanshawaii.com, rents wheelchair-lift-equipped vans on Maui and O'ahu for $115 per day, $599 per week, or $2,250 per month. This is a full-service travel agency and a good source of information on traveling with disabilities. Valid, out-of-state, **handicapped parking placards** may be used throughout the state of Hawaii. A Hawaiian **handicapped parking permit** can be obtained from the county drivers' licensing section, 808/243-7363.

For medical support services, contact **Maui Center for Independent Living,** 808/242-4966; **Action Medical Personnel,** 808/875-8300; or **CareResource Hawaii,** 808/871-2115. Medical equipment is available through **Gammie Homecare,** 808/877-4032.

ILLEGAL DRUGS

The use and availability of illegal, controlled, and recreational drugs are about the same in Hawaii as throughout the rest of America. Cocaine is available on the streets of the main cities, especially Honolulu. Although most dealers are small-time, the drug is brought in by organized crime. Cocaine trafficking fans out from Honolulu.

Another drug menace on the streets is "ice." Ice is smokable methamphetamine that will wire a user for up to 24 hours. The high lasts longer and is cheaper than cocaine or its derivative, "crack." Users become quickly dependent, despondent, and violent because ice robs them of their sleep as well as their dignity. Its use is particularly prevalent among late-night workers. Many of the violent deaths in Honolulu have been linked to the growing use of ice.

The main drug available and commonly used in Hawaii is marijuana, which is locally called *pakalolo.* Also, three varieties of psychoactive mushrooms contain the hallucinogen psilocybin; they grow wild but are considered illegal controlled substances.

Pakalolo Growing

In the 1960s and '70s, mostly *haole* hippies from the Mainland began growing pot in the more remote sections of the islands, such as Puna on Hawaii and around Hana on Maui. They discovered what legitimate planters had known for centuries: Plant a broomstick in Hawaii, treat it right, and it'll grow. *Pakalolo,* after all, is a weed, and it grows in Hawaii like wildfire. The locals quickly got into the act when they realized that they, too, could grow a "money tree." As a matter of fact, they began resenting the *haole* usurpers, and a quiet and sometimes dangerous feud has been going on ever since. Much is made of the viciousness of the backcountry growers of Hawaii. There are tales of booby traps and armed patrols guarding their plants in the hills, but mostly it's a cat-and-mouse game between the authorities and the growers. If you, as a tourist, are tramping about in the forest and happen upon someone's "patch," don't touch anything. Just back off and you'll be okay. Pot has the largest monetary turnover of any crop in the islands and, as such, is now considered a major source of agricultural revenue, albeit illicit and underground. There are all kinds of local names and varieties of pot in Hawaii. Dealers will sometimes approach you. Their normal technique is to stroll by and in a barely audible whisper say, "Buds?" All passengers leaving Hawaii are subject to a thorough agricultural inspection, and you can bet they're not looking only for illegal papayas.

THEFT AND HASSLES

Theft and minor assaults can be a problem, but they're usually not violent or vicious as in some Mainland cities. Mostly, it's a local with a chip on his shoulder and few prospects, who will ransack your car or make off with your camera. A big Hawaiian or local guy will be obliged to flatten your nose if you look for trouble, but mostly it will be sneak thieves out to make a fast buck.

From the minute you sit behind the wheel of your rental car, you'll be warned not to leave valuables unattended and to lock up your car tighter than a drum. Signs warning about theft at most major tourist attractions help fuel your paranoia. Many hotel and condo rooms offer safes so you can lock your valuables away and relax while getting sunburned. Stories abound about purse snatchings and surly locals just itching to give you a hard time. Well, they're all true to a degree, but Hawaii's reputation is much worse than the reality. In Hawaii you'll have to observe two golden laws: (1) If you look for trouble, you'll find it; and, (2) a fool and his camera are soon parted.

Theft

Most theft in Hawaii is of the sneak thief variety. If you leave your hotel door unlocked, a camera sitting on the seat of your rental car, or valuables on your beach towel, you'll be inviting an obliging thief to pad away with your stuff. You have to learn to take precautions, but they won't be anything like those employed in rougher areas of the world—just normal everyday precautions.

If you must walk alone at night, stay on the main streets in well-lit areas. Always lock your hotel door and windows and place valuable jewelry in the hotel safe. When you leave your hotel for the beach, there is absolutely no reason to carry all of your traveler's checks and credit cards or a big wad of money. Just take what you'll need for drinks and lunch. If you're uptight about leaving money in your beach bag, stick it in your bathing suit. American money is just as negotiable when damp. Don't leave your camera on the beach unattended. Ask a person nearby to watch your things for you while you go for a dip. Most people won't mind at all, and you can repay the favor.

While sightseeing in your shiny new rental car—which immediately brands you as a tourist—again, don't take more than what you'll need for the day. Many people lock valuables away in the trunk, but remember that most good car thieves can "jimmy" it as quickly as you can open it with your key. If you must, for some reason, leave your camera or valuables in your car, lock them in the trunk, stash them under a seat back that's been reclined, or consider putting them under the hood. Thieves usually don't look there, and on most modern cars you can only pop the hood with a lever inside the car. It's not fail-safe, but it's worth a try.

Campers face special problems because their entire scene is open to thievery. Most campgrounds don't have any real security, but who, after all, wants to fence an old tent or a used sleeping bag? Many tents have zippers that can be secured with a small padlock. If you want to go hiking and are afraid to leave your gear in the campground, take a large green garbage bag with you. Transport your gear down the trail and then walk off through some thick brush. Put your gear in the garbage bag and bury it under leaves and other light camouflage. That's about as safe as you can be. You can also use a variation on this technique instead of leaving your valuables in your rental car.

Hassles

Another self-perpetuating myth about Hawaii is that "the natives are restless." An undeniable animosity exists between locals (especially those with some Hawaiian blood) and *haole*. Fortunately, this prejudice is directed mostly at the group and not at the individual. The locals are resentful of those *haole* who came, took their land, and relegated them to second-class citizenship. They realize that this is not the average tourist and they can tell what you are at a glance. Tourists usually are treated with understanding and are given a type of immunity. Besides, Hawaiians are still among the most friendly, giving, and understanding people on earth.

Haole who live in Hawaii might tell you stories of their children having trouble at school. They could even mention an unhappy situation at some schools called "beat-up-a-*haole*" day, and you might hear that if you're a *haole* it's not a matter of if you'll be beaten up, but when. Truthfully, most of this depends on your attitude and your sensitivity. The locals feel infringed upon, so don't fuel these feelings. If you're at a beach park and there is a group of local people in one area, don't crowd them. If you go into a local bar and you're the only one of your ethnic group in sight, you shouldn't have to be told to leave. Much of the hassle involves drinking. Booze brings out the worst prejudice on all sides. If you're invited to a beach party, and the local guys start getting drunk, make this your exit call. Don't wait until it's too late.

Most trouble seems to be directed toward white men. White women are mostly immune from being beaten up, but they have to beware of the violence of sexual abuse and rape. Although plenty of local women marry white men, it's not a good idea to try to pick up a local woman. If you're known in the area and have been properly introduced, that's another story. Women out for the night in bars or discos can be approached if they're not in the company of local guys. Maintain your own dignity and self-respect by treating others with dignity and respect. Most times you'll reap what you sow.

What to Take

It's a snap to pack for a visit to Maui. Everything is on your side. The weather is moderate and uniform on the whole, and the style of dress is delightfully casual. The rule of thumb is to pack lightly: few items and light clothing both in color and weight. What you'll need will depend largely on your itinerary and your desires. Are you drawn to the nightlife, the outdoors, or both? If you forget something at home, it won't be a disaster. You can buy everything you'll need in Hawaii. As a matter of fact, Hawaiian clothing, such as mu'umu'u and aloha shirts, is one of the best purchases you can make, both in comfort and style. It's quite feasible to bring only one or two changes of clothing with the express purpose of outfitting yourself while there. Prices on bathing suits and summer wear in general are quite reasonable.

Matters of Taste

A grand conspiracy in Maui adhered to by everyone—tourist, traveler, and resident—is to "hang loose" and dress casually. Best of all, alohawear is just about all you'll need for comfort and virtually every occasion. The classic mu'umu'u is large and billowy, and aloha shirts are made to be worn outside the pants. The best of both are made of cool cotton. Rayon is a natural fiber that isn't too bad, but polyester is hot, sticky, and not authentic. Not all mu'umu'u are of the tent persuasion. Some are very fashionable and form-fitted with peek-a-boo slits up the side, down the front, or around the back. *Holomu* are mu'umu'u fitted at the waist with a flowing skirt to the ankles. They are not only elegant, but perfect for stepping out.

Basic Necessities

As previously mentioned, you really have to consider only two modes of dressing in Hawaii: beachwear and casual clothing. The following list is designed for the midrange traveler carrying one suitcase or a backpack. Remember that there are laundromats and that you'll be spending a considerable amount of time in your bathing suit. Consider the following: one or two pairs of light cotton slacks for going out and about and one pair of jeans for hiking and riding horses; two or three casual sundresses; three or four pairs of shorts for beachwear and sightseeing; four to five short-sleeve shirts or blouses and one long-sleeve; three or four colored and printed T-shirts that can be worn anytime from hiking to strolling; a beach cover-up; a brimmed hat for rain and sun—the crushable floppy type is great for purse or daypack, or pick up a straw or woven hat on the island for about $10; two or three pairs of socks are sufficient, nylons you won't generally need; two bathing suits; plastic bags to hold wet bathing suits and laundry; five to six pairs of underwear; towels (optional, because hotels provide them, even for the beach); a first-aid kit, pocket-size is sufficient; suntan lotion and insect repellent; and a daypack or large beach purse. And don't forget your windbreaker, perhaps a light sweater for the evening, and an all-purpose jogging suit. A few classy restaurants in the finest hotels require men to wear a sport coat for dinner. If you don't have one, most hotels can supply you with one for the evening.

In the Cold and Rain

Two occasions for which you'll have to consider dressing warmly are visits to mountaintops and boat rides where wind and ocean sprays are a factor. You can conquer both with a jogging suit or sweat suit and a featherweight, water-resistant windbreaker. If you intend to visit Haleakala, it'll be downright chilly. Your jogging suit with a hooded windbreaker/raincoat will do the trick for all occasions. If you're going to camp or hike, you should add another layer, a woolen sweater being one of the best. Wool is the only natural fiber that retains most of its warmth-giving properties even if it gets wet. Several varieties of "fleece" synthetics currently on the market also have this ability. If your hands get cold, put a pair of socks over them. Tropical rain showers can happen at any time, so you might consider a fold-up umbrella, but the sun quickly breaks through and the warming winds blow. Nighttime winter temps may drop into the lower 60s or upper 50s, so be sure to have a sweater and long pants along.

Shoes

Dressing your feet is hardly a problem. You'll most often wear zoris (rubber thongs) for going to and from the beach, leather sandals for strolling and dining, and jogging shoes for hiking and sightseeing. Teva and other types of outdoor strap sandals are good for general sightseeing and beach and water wear. A few discos require dress shoes, but it's hardly worth bringing them just for that. If you plan on heavy-duty hiking, you'll definitely want your hiking boots. Lava, especially 'a'a, is murderous on shoes. Most backcountry trails are rugged and muddy, and you'll need those good old lug soles for traction. If you plan moderate hikes, jogging shoes should do.

Specialty Items

The following is a list of specialty items that you might consider bringing along. They're not necessities, but most will definitely come in handy. A pair of binoculars really enhances sightseeing—great for viewing birds and sweeping panoramas, and almost a necessity if you're going whale-watching. A folding, Teflon-bottomed travel iron makes up for cotton's one major shortcoming, wrinkles. Most accommodations have them, but you can't always count on it. Nylon twine and miniature clothespins are handy for drying garments, especially bathing suits. Commercial and hotel laundromats are around, but many times you'll get by with hand-washing a few items in the sink. A radio/tape recorder provides news, weather, and entertainment, and can be used to record impressions, island music, and a running commentary for your slide show. Although the wind can be relied on to dry wet hair, it leaves a bit to be desired in the styling department, so you may want a hair dryer. As with the iron, most accommodations have these, but not all. Flippers, mask, and snorkel can easily be bought in Hawaii but don't weigh much or take up much space in your luggage.

Information and Services

HAWAII VISITORS BUREAU OFFICES

The HVB is a top-notch organization providing help and information to all of Hawaii's visitors. Anyone contemplating a trip to Hawaii should visit or write the HVB and inquire about any specific information that might be required, or visit its website, www.gohawaii.com. The HVB's advice and excellent brochures on virtually every facet of living, visiting, or simply enjoying Hawaii are free. The material offered is too voluminous to list, but for basics, request individual island brochures, maps, vacation planners (also on the web at www.hshawaii.com), and an all-island members directory of accommodations, restaurants, entertainment, and transportation. Allow 2–3 weeks for requests to be answered.

HVB Offices Statewide

The best information on Maui is dispensed by the **Maui Visitors Bureau,** 1727 Wili Pa Loop, Wailuku, HI 96793, 808/244-3530 or 800/525-6284, www.visitmaui.com.

Statewide offices include **HVB Administrative Office,** Waikiki Business Plaza, 2270 Kalakaua Ave., Ste. 801, Honolulu, HI 96815, 808/923-1811; **Visitor Information Office,** 808/924-0266, Waikiki Shopping Plaza, 2250 Kalakaua Ave., Ste. 502, Honolulu, HI 96815; **O'ahu Visitors Bureau,** 733 Bishop St., Ste. 1872, Honolulu, HI 96813, 808/524-0722 or 877/525-3530, www.visit-oahu.com; **Big Island HVB, Hilo Branch,** 250 Keawe St., Hilo, HI 96720, 808/961-5797 or 800/648-2441, www.bigisland.org; **Big Island HVB, Kona Branch,** 250 Waikoloa Beach Dr., Ste. B15, Waikoloa, HI 96738, 808/886-1655; **Kaua'i HVB,** 4334 Rice St., Ste. 101, Lihu'e, HI 96766, 808/245-3971 or 800/262-1400, www.kauaivisitorsbureau.org.

Two other helpful organizations are the **Moloka'i Visitors Association,** P.O. Box 960, Kaunakakai, HI 96748, 808/553-3876 or 800/800-6367 Mainland and Canada, or 800/553-0404 interisland, www.molokai-hawaii.com; and **Destination Lana'i,** P.O. Box 700 Lana'i City, HI 96763, 808/565-7600 or 800/947-4774, fax 808/565-9316, www.visitlanai.net.

Additional online information pertaining to Maui County can be found at the official County of Maui website: www.co.maui.hi.us.

North American Offices

West Coast: 4150 Mission Blvd., Ste. 200A, San Diego, CA 92109, 858/270-2390; 1172 South Main St., #369, Salinas, CA 93901, 831/455-1839

Midwest: 625 N. Michigan Ave., Ste. 1737, Chicago, IL 60611, 312/654-4542

East Coast: 1100 N. Glebe Rd., #760, Arlington, VA 22201, 703/525-7770

Canada: c/o Comprehensive Travel, 1260 Hornby St., #104, Vancouver, BC, Canada V6Z 1W2, Canada, 604/669-6691

European Offices

United Kingdom: P.O. Box 208, Sunbury on Thames, Middlesex, England, TW16 5RJ, 208/941-4009

Germany: Noble Kommunikation GmbH, Luisenstrasse 7, 63262 Neu-Isenburg, Germany, 180/223-040

South American Office

Uruguay: c/o Yamandu Rodriguez 1390, 11500 Montevideo, Uruguay, 2/606-0277

Asian/Pacific Offices

Tokyo: Kokusai Bldg., 2F, 3-1-1, Marunouchi, Chiyoda-ku, Tokyo 100, Japan, 3/3201-0430

Osaka: Sumitomo Nakanoshima Bldg., 2F, 3-2-18, Nakanoshima, Kita-gu, Osaka 530, Japan, 6/6443-8015

Korea: c/o Travel Press, Seoul Center Bldg., 12th Fl., 91-1, Sokong-dong, Chung-gu, Seoul 100-070, Korea, 2/777-0033

Beijing: A606, COFCO Bldg., 8 Jianguomen Nei Dajie, Beijing, China 100005, 10/6527-7530

EXPLORING THE ISLANDS

Shanghai: Shanghai Centre, 1376 Nanjing Rd. West, Rm. 527, Shanghai, China 200040, 21/6279-8099

Taiwan: Wish (Wei Yuan) Company, 9F-1, #21, Lane 22, Hsein Yen Road, Wen Shan Area, Taipei 117, Taiwan, 2/2934-8323

Hong Kong: Pacific Leisure Group, c/o Pacam Limited, 10F, Tung Ming Bldg., Rm. 1003, 40 Des Voeux Rd. Central, Hong Kong SAR, China, 2524-1361

New Zealand: c/o Walshes World, 14 Shortland St., Level 6, Auckland, New Zealand, 9/379-3708

Australia: c/o The Sales Team, Ste. 602A, Level 6, 97-103 Pacific Highway, North Sydney, NSW 2060, Australia, 2/9955-2619

Other Tourism-related Information Sources

The state operates two **visitors information booths** at Kahului Airport, one in the center building upper level and the other in the baggage claim area of the arrival terminal. One or the other should be open daily 6:30 A.M.–10 P.M., offering plenty of practical brochures and helpful information. Call 808/872-3892. Also, scattered around the arrival terminal lower level are numerous racks of free brochures, magazines, and other tourist literature.

LOCAL RESOURCES

Emergencies

To summon **police, fire, or ambulance** anywhere on Maui, dial **911.**

For **nonemergency police** assistance and information, call 808/244-6400.

Civil Defense: In case of natural disaster such as hurricanes or tsunamis on Maui, call 808/270-7285.

Coast Guard: 800/552-6458

Sexual Assault Crisis Line: 808/873-8624

Weather, Marine Report, and Time of Day

For recorded information on **local island weather,** call 808/877-5111; for the **marine report,** call 808/877-3477; and for conditions on

Haleakala, call 808/871-5054. For **time of day** on Maui, dial 808/242-0212; on Moloka'i it's 808/553-9211, and on Lana'i call 808/565-9211.

Consumer Protection

If you encounter problems with accommodations, bad service, or downright rip-offs, try the following: **Maui Chamber of Commerce,** 250 Ala Maha, Kahului, 808/871-7711; the **Office of Consumer Protection,** 808/984-8244; or the **Better Business Bureau** (O'ahu), 877/222-6551.

Post Offices

There are 12 branch post offices on Maui, five on Moloka'i, and one on Lana'i. Window service is offered Monday–Friday 8:30 A.M.–5 P.M.; some offices are open Saturday 9 A.M.–1 P.M. For information, dial 800/275-8777.

Laundromats

Laundromats are located in sizable towns on Maui, in Lana'i City, and in Kaunakakai on Moloka'i. Hours are generally early morning to midevening. Some are a bit run-down, but several new laundromats have been built recently with the best machines. You'll find prices here about the same as on the Mainland, with a load of wash running $1.75. Dryers take $.25 for a 10-minute spin, and usually require 40–50 minutes to dry a full load. Little boxes of laundry soap go for $.75, and there is often a change machine and maybe a folding table in the establishment. Machines take quarters only. Some offer drop-off service and dry cleaning for a fee. On Maui, try **W & F Washerette,** 125 S. Wakea in Kahului, 808/877-0353; **Lipoa Laundry Center,** 41 E. Lipoa in Kihei, 808/875-9266; and **Kahana Koin-Op Laundromat,** in the Kahana Gateway Center, 808/669-1587.

Luxury hotels usually do not have self-service laundry facilities on premises but provide cleaning service for a fee. Condos most often do have washers and dryers, sometimes in their units, but more often on each floor of a building or in a detached structure, and rental homes almost always provide washers and dryers. Some B&Bs also provide this service, while others do not. Ask when you make your reservation, if it's important. Some sort of laundry facility can be found at hostels.

Reading Material

The main branch of the **library** is at 251 High Street, Wailuku, 808/243-5766; other branches are in Kahului, Lahaina, Makawao, Kihei, and Hana. The libraries are open a hodgepodge of hours throughout the week. Library cards are available free for Hawaii state residents and military personnel stationed in Hawaii, $25 for nonresidents (valid for five years), and $10 for three months for visitors.

Free tourist literature is well done and loaded with tips, discounts, maps, happenings, and so forth. Found in hotels, restaurants, and street stands, they include *This Week Maui, Maui Gold, Maui Magazine, Maui Beach and Activity Guide, Maui Activities and Attractions,* and *The Best Guidebook.* Published three times per year, the *Drive Guide,* with excellent maps and tips, is given out free by all car rental agencies; similar is the *Driving Magazine of Maui. Maui Menus* and *Menu* are all about food, *101 Things to do in Maui* is a great resource for activities and also has money-saving coupons, and the *Maui Visitor* is worth a look.

Both the *Honolulu Advertiser* and *Honolulu Star Bulletin,* are available on Maui for $.75 apiece or $2 on Sunday. Aside from these two big Honolulu newspapers, local papers available on Maui include the *Maui News,* published Monday–Friday, $.50 daily and $1.50 on Sunday, which has a good listing of local events; www.mauinews.com. *Lahaina News,* www.west-maui.com, is a daily community paper of news, feature stories, and entertainment listings, $.25. Free local papers include the *Maui Time, Haleakala Times, Gold Coast,* and *Maui Weekly.* Of the Mainland papers, the *USA Today,* $.75 daily, seems the most prominent.

Island Radio

More than a dozen radio stations broadcast on Maui. Popular ones are KHPR 88.1 FM (also 90.7 FM), which broadcasts from Honolulu and is the island's public radio station; KPOA 93.5 FM out of Lahaina does a mix of contemporary Hawaiian and standard rock; KAOI 95.1 FM

in Wailuku is mostly adult rock with a request line; KAPA 99.1 FM is good for island sounds; KNUI 900 AM does traditional Hawaiian; and KAOI 1110 AM offers news, talk, and sports.

OTHER INFORMATION

Telephone

The telephone system on the main islands is modern and comparable to any system on the Mainland. All of Hawaii uses the area code 808. Any phone call to a number on that island is a local call; it's long distance when dialing to another island or beyond the state. As they do everywhere else in the United States, long-distance rates go down at 5 P.M. and again at 11 P.M. until 8 A.M. the next morning. Rates are cheapest from Friday at 5 P.M. until Monday at 8 A.M. Local calls from public telephones cost $.50. Emergency calls are always free. Public telephones are found at hotels, street booths, restaurants, most public buildings, and some beach parks. It is common to have a phone in most hotel rooms and condominiums, although a service charge is usually collected, even on local calls. You can "direct dial" from Hawaii to the Mainland and more than 160 foreign countries. Undersea cables and satellite communications ensure top-quality phone service. Toll-free calls are preceded by 800, 888, 877, or 866; there is no charge to the calling party. Many are listed in the text. For directory assistance: local, 1-411; interisland, 1-555-1212; Mainland, 1-(area code)-555-1212; toll free, 800/555-1212. The area code for all the islands of Hawaii is 808.

Time Zones

There is no daylight saving time in Hawaii. When daylight saving time is not observed on the Mainland, Hawaii is two hours behind the West Coast, four hours behind the Midwest, five hours behind the East Coast, and 11 hours behind Germany. Hawaii, being just east of the international date line, is almost a full day behind most Asian and Oceanic cities. Hours behind these countries and cities are Japan, 19 hours; Singapore, 18 hours; Sydney, 20 hours; New Zealand, 22 hours; Fiji, 22 hours.

Electricity

The same electrical current is in use in Hawaii as on the U.S. Mainland and is uniform throughout the islands. The system functions on 110 volts, 60 cycles of alternating current (AC). Appliances from Japan will work, but there is some danger of burnout, while those requiring the normal European voltage of 220 will not work.

Distance, Weights, and Measures

Hawaii, like all of the United States, employs the English method of measuring weights and distances. Basically, dry weights are in ounces and pounds; liquid measures are in ounces, quarts, and gallons; and distances are measured in inches, feet, yards, and miles. The metric system is known but is not in general use.

MONEY AND FINANCES

Currency

U.S. currency is among the drabbest in the world. It's all the same size and color; those unfamiliar with it should spend some time getting acquainted so they don't make costly mistakes. U.S. coinage in use is one cent (penny), five cents (nickel), 10 cents (dine), 25 cents (quarter), 50 cents (half dollar), and $1 (uncommon); paper currency is $1, $2 (uncommon), $5, $10, $20, $50, $100. Bills larger than $100 are not in common usage. Since 1996, new designs have been issued for the $100, $50, $20, $10, and $5 bills. Both the old and new bills are accepted as valid currency.

Banks

Full-service bank hours are generally 8:30 A.M.–4 P.M. Monday–Thursday and Friday until 6 P.M. There are no weekend hours, and weekday hours will be a bit longer at counters in grocery stores and other outlets. All main towns on Maui have one or more banks. Virtually all branch banks have automated teller machines

(ATMs) for 24-hour service, and these can be found at some shopping centers and other venues around the island. ATMs work only when the Hawaiian bank you choose to use is on an affiliate network with your home bank. Of most value to travelers, banks sell and cash traveler's checks, give cash advances on credit cards, and exchange and sell foreign currency (sometimes with a fee). Major banks on Maui are American Savings Bank, Bank of Hawaii, and First Hawaiian Bank. All have branches in Kahului, Wailuku, Kihei, Lahaina, and Pukalani. First Hawaiian has a branch in Napili, and Bank of Hawaii also has offices in Kahana, Pa'ia, and Hana.

Traveler's Checks

Traveler's checks are accepted throughout Hawaii at hotels, restaurants, and car rental agencies and in most stores and shops; however, to be readily acceptable, they should be in U.S. currency. Some larger hotels that frequently have Japanese and Canadian guests will accept their currency. Banks accept foreign-currency traveler's checks, but it'll mean an extra trip and inconvenience. It's best to get most of your traveler's checks in $20–50 denominations; anything larger will be hard to cash in shops and boutiques, although not in hotels.

Credit Cards

More and more business is transacted in Hawaii using credit cards. Almost every form of accommodation, shop, restaurant, and amusement accepts them. For renting a car they're almost a must. With credit card insurance readily available, they're as safe as traveler's checks and sometimes even more convenient. Write down the numbers of your cards in case they're stolen and keep them separate from the checks. Don't rely on them completely because some establishments won't accept them, or perhaps won't accept the kind that you carry.

Central Maui: The Isthmus

Kahului

It is generally believed that Kahului means "The Winning," but perhaps it should be "The Survivor." Kahului suffered attack by Kamehameha I in 1790, when he landed his war canoes here in preparation for battle at 'Iao Valley. In 1900 it was purposely burned to thwart the plague, and then rebuilt. Combined with Wailuku, the county seat just up the road, this area is home to 38,800 Mauians, more than one-quarter of the island population. Here's where the people live. It's a practical, homey, commercial town, the only deep-water port from which Maui's sugar and pineapples are shipped out and other commodities shipped in, and it now has the island's only pineapple cannery. Although Kahului was an established sugar town by 1880, it's really only grown up in the last 40 years. In the 1960s,

'Iao Needle

ROBERT NILSEN

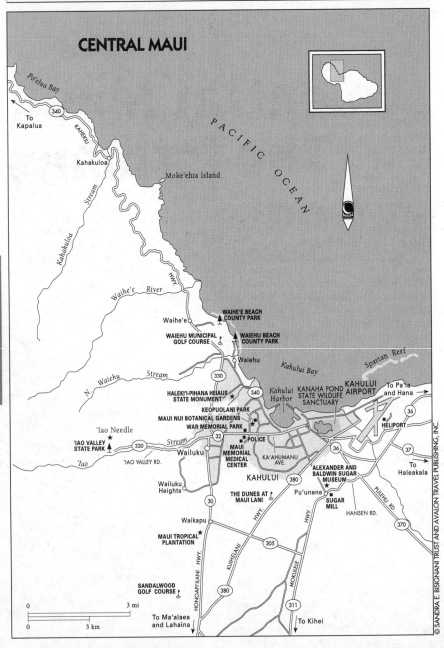

Hawaiian Commercial and Sugar Co. began building low-cost housing for its workers, which became a model development for the whole of the United States. Most people land at the airport, blast through for Lahaina or Kihei, and never give Kahului a second look. It's in no way a resort community, but it has the best general-purpose shopping on the island, a few noteworthy sites, one of the island's best windsurfing beaches, and a convenient location to the airport.

SIGHTS

Kanaha Pond State Wildlife Sanctuary

This one-time royal fish pond is located between downtown and the airport on the ocean side of the airport approach road. It's on the migratory route of various ducks and Canada geese, temporary home to dozens of vagrant bird species, but most important it's home to the endangered Hawaiian stilt *(ae'o)* and the Hawaiian coot *('alae ke'oke'o).* The stilt is a slender, 16-inch bird with a black back, white belly, and sticklike pink legs. The coot is a gray-black ducklike bird that builds large floating nests. An observation pavilion is maintained on the south edge of the pond, accessed by a short walkway from a small parking area. This pavilion is always open and free of charge. Bring your binoculars. Entry to the walking trails within the sanctuary is free to individuals or groups but by permit only on weekdays from the first day of September to the last day of March. Apply Monday–Friday 8 A.M.–3:30 P.M. at the Department of Natural Resources, Division of Forestry and Wildlife office, 54 S. High St., Rm. 101, Wailuku, HI 96793. For more information, call 808/984-8100. You must supply exact dates and times of your intended visit.

Kanaha Beach County Park

This is the only beach worth visiting in the area. Good for a swim (roped-off area) and a picnic, the broad beach here is flanked by plenty of trees so you can get out of the sun. In this strip of tall ironwood trees are broad lawns, picnic tables, barbecue pits, bathrooms, and a public phone. Permit camping is allowed at the western end of

the park. This beach is used by one of the outrigger canoe clubs on the island, and you'll see their canoes drawn up on shore near their pavilion when they're not out on the water practicing their strokes. Kanaha is a favorite of windsurfers, and it's also *the* best place to learn windsurfing. Many windsurf instructors bring their students here at midmorning. The wind is steady but not too strong, and the wave action is gentle. Others don't generally come until late morning or early afternoon when the wind picks up. Most use the section of beach farthest to the east, locally known as Kooks Beach. From Ka'ahumanu Avenue or the Hana Highway, turn onto Hobron Avenue, and then immediately right onto Amala Street, and follow the signs to the park. Alternately, follow Keolani Place to the airport, swing back around and turn right on Ka'a Street. Pass the rental car agencies and carry on to Amala Street. There are two entrances to the park and plenty of parking. The only drawback might be the frequent and noisy arrivals and departures of aircraft at the airport, which is only a few hundred yards away.

A short way in toward the harbor from Kanaha Beach Park and across the road from the wildlife sanctuary is a stretch of beach known as "Kite Beach." Kitesurfers congregate here, as the kitesurfing and windsurfing areas have been segregated in order to reduce the risk of accidents. Having become popular in Hawaii over the last several years, this beach area is perhaps the best place in the state to see this rather new extreme water sport. There is no developed parking here; just pull off the road onto the edge of the sand dune.

Kahului Harbor

This is the island's principal commercial harbor, the conduit through which most goods flow in and out of the island, including pineapples and raw sugar. Several piers along the water's edge are a hive of shipping activity. Although no fishing boats or other tourist ventures operate at Kahului Harbor, the *Norwegian Star,* which makes a one-week tour of the islands, docks here once a week, disembarking passengers for a day's sightseeing on the island, before floating away to its next stop. Local fishermen try their luck along both the breakwaters, and a canoe club launches its out-

CENTRAL MAUI

Kahului Bay

KANAHA BEACH COUNTY PARK

To Kanaha Beach

To Kahului Airport

To Hana

KEOLANI PL.

AMALA ST.

Kite Beach

KANAHA POND STATE WILDLIFE SANCTUARY

HALEAKALA HWY

PULEHU RD.

HANA HWY

380

0.25 mi

0.25 km

COSTCO

GAS STATION

WINDSURF SHOP

KMART

DAIRY CENTER

GAS STATION

MAUI MARKETPLACE

MAUI DOWNHILL

WAL-MART

OBSERVATION PAVILION

MARCO'S GRILL

TRIANGLE SQUARE

DOWN TO EARTH NATURAL FOODS

DAIRY

PAPA PL.

LALO ST.

FIRE STATION

HOME DEPOT

ALANAHA

HUIILIKE ST.

KAHULUI

HOBRON AVE.

32A

328

WINDSURF SHOPS

MAUI MALL

SAFEWAY

POST OFFICE

SWAP MEET

CATHOLIC CHURCH

HONGWANJI

PU'UNENE AVE.

350

To Kihei

To Lahaina

OLD KAHULUI SHOPPING CENTER

HIDEAWAY RESTAURANT

TWO FROGS HUGGING

BANK OF HAWAII

MAUI MEDICAL CENTER

AMERICAN SAVINGS BANK

FIRST HAWAIIAN BANK

KAHULUI SHOPPING CENTER

KAULAWAHINE ST.

ST.

AVE.

LANAI AVE.

ONO ST.

HOALOHA PARK

Kahului Harbor

MAUI SEASIDE HOTEL

MANANA GARAGE

GAS STATION

LIBRARY

KANE ST.

WAKEA AVE.

HINA AVE.

MAUI BEACH HOTEL

FOODLAND

MAUI PINEAPPLE PLANT

KAMEHAMEHA

To Waihe'e

340

MAUI ARTS AND CULTURAL CENTER

KAHULUI BEACH RD.

KA'AHUMANU AVE.

MAUI COMMUNITY COLLEGE

MAUI MOUNTAIN CRUISERS

QUEEN KA'AHUMANU CENTER

W&F WASHERETTE

32

KEA ST.

ONEHE'E AVE.

© SANDRA E. BISIGNANI TRUST AND AVALON TRAVEL PUBLISHING, INC.

riggers from Hoaloha Park for early morning practice on the smooth harbor waters.

Maui Community College

Just across the street from the Queen Ka'ahumanu Center on Route 32, the college is a good place to check out bulletin boards for various activities, items for sale, and cheaper long-term housing. The Student Center is conspicuous as you drive in and is a good place to get most information about the school. Maui Community College, www.mauicc.hawaii.edu, is a branch of the University of Hawaii and the only college-level school in the county, although it maintains learning centers in Hana and on Moloka'i and Lana'i. Concentrating mostly on two-year-degree courses, the school's focus is on vocational and technical fields with some liberal arts added. Its culinary arts program is reasonably well known around the state.

Maui Arts and Cultural Center

This complex is surrounded by Maui Community College and Keopuolani Park. Opened in 1994, the Maui Arts and Cultural Center, 808/242-7469, www.mauiarts.org, is a big draw for the island, attracting well-known local and national musicians, international dancers, visual arts exhibitions, and films. The Maui Film Festival uses this venue, as does the Hawaii International Film Festival. Educational programs are offered, and free art shows are held at the Shaffer Gallery Tuesday–Sunday 11 A.M.–5 P.M. and before shows. Performance tickets can be picked up at the box office Monday–Saturday 10 A.M.–6 P.M.

Keopuolani Park

Lying between the Maui Arts and Cultural Center and Kanaloa Avenue is the 110-acre Keopuolani Park, the largest county park on the island. Open 7 A.M.–10 P.M., this greenway has broad expanses of grass and sidewalks, jogging trails and exercise stations, as well as baseball and soccer fields, a sand volleyball court, children's play areas, horseshoe pits, picnic pavilions, and in the corner near Ka'ahumanu Avenue, a skateboard park. Landscaped

and open to the public in 1999, this is a welcome addition to the developed parklands of the island.

War Memorial Park and Center

Across Kanaloa Avenue is Wailuku War Memorial Park and Center, basically a large-arena athletic venue. Here you'll find a football stadium, baseball field, gymnasium, Olympic-size swimming pool, tennis courts, and track. After years of being played at the Aloha Stadium in Honolulu, the college all-star Hula Bowl now takes place at the War Memorial Stadium. You can pick up county camping permits from the recreation director's office at the front of the building.

Paper Airplane Museum

For the curious, the unusual Paper Airplane Museum at the Maui Mall, 808/877-8916, www.flex.com/~edynray/pam, is an eclectic place displaying all sizes of model paper airplanes (not the folded-paper type) from those small enough to fit on the palm of a man's hand to those as large as a local boy, with plenty of photos, commentary, and artifacts on the island's aviation history. More than 2,500 model paper airplane kits and other memorabilia are for sale in the gift shop. Known as "The Tin Can Man," the owner also displays airplanes and numerous other objects that he's constructed by using old soda cans. Open Monday–Thursday and Saturday 10 A.M.–6 P.M., Friday until 8 P.M., and Sunday until 4 P.M. Admission is free to this nonprofit museum, yet donations are gladly accepted and will be used to support their children's outreach programs.

Alexander and Baldwin Sugar Museum

The museum, 808/871-8058, www.sugarmuseum.com, is located at the intersection of Pu'unene Avenue (Route 311) and Hansen Road, about one-half mile from Dairy Road. Hours are Monday–Saturday 9:30 A.M.–4:30 P.M.; admission $5 adults, $2 children 6–17, ages five and under free. (Avoid the area around 3 P.M. when the still-working mill across the street changes shifts.) This small but highly informative museum could easily be your first stop after arriving at Kahului Airport only 15 minutes away, especially if you're heading to Kihei. Once you get off the plane, you'll realize that you're in the midst of sugarcane fields. If you want to know the history of this crop and the people who worked and developed it, visit the museum. The vintage museum building (circa 1890) was the home of the sugar plantation superintendent, who literally lived surrounded by his work. Outside on the lawn are several old pieces of machinery from decades past, once used at the plantation. Inside is a small but well-stocked bookstore and gift shop featuring Hawaiiana and handmade clothing and artifacts, with goodies like guava and coconut syrups and raw sugar.

As you begin your tour, notice the ancient refrigerator in the hallway that the staff still uses. In the first room, you are given a brief description of the natural history of Maui, along with a rendition of the legends of the demigod Maui. Display cases explain Maui's rainfall and use of irrigation for a productive sugarcane yield. There is an old-fashioned copper rain gauge along with pragmatic artifacts from the building of the Haiku Ditch. A collection of vintage photos features the Baldwin and Alexander families, while a historical plaque recalls when workers lived in ethnic camps, each with its own euphemistic name (Chinese at Ah Fong, Japanese at Nashiwa, Portuguese at Cod Fish). This setup was designed to discourage competition (or cooperation) among the ethnic groups during labor disputes and to ease the transition to the new land. These people are represented by everything from stuffed fighting cocks to baseball mitts from the '30s. Included is an educational video on sugarcane production. The museum is in the shadow of the state's largest and the island's only active sugar mill, and you can hear the wheels turning and the mill grinding. It's not an antiseptic remembrance, but a vital one where the history still continues. No tours are given at the mill across the street, but you can view a scale model of the crushers to get an idea of what goes on inside its hulking exterior.

ACCOMMODATIONS

Kahului features two economical hotels, just right for the traveler looking for a good deal away from the island's tourist hubs, yet in a convenient location to many island sites, the airport, and business and government offices. These accommodations are west of Hoaloha Park on the harbor side of Ka'ahumanu Avenue (Rte. 32).

The **Maui Beach Hotel**, 808/877-0051, 888/649-3222, or fax 808/871-5797, is a low-rise affair with a Polynesian-style peaked roof over its lobby. On the lobby level are the front desk, small gift shop, and a banquet hall. Upstairs, daily buffets at the Rainbow Dining Room are a good value, and cocktails and *pu pu* are served at the Lokelani Lounge near the dining room from 5:30 P.M., with entertainment on the weekends. Open 9 A.M.–5:30 P.M., the small swimming pool is located on the second floor next to the pool. Lying between two arms of rooms, the central lawn leads down to the narrow beach fronting Kahului Harbor. Rates are $98–185 for standard to oceanfront rooms and $450 for an oceanfront suite. Each room has a small refrigerator, color television, safe for valuables, a lanai, and air-conditioning. For the convenience of its guests, a complimentary shuttle runs to the airport every hour 6:30 A.M.–9 P.M.; reservations necessary. The Maui Beach Hotel has offered the same friendly hospitality to *kama'aina* and visitors alike since the 1960s.

About 100 yards to the east is the **Maui Seaside Hotel**, 808/877-3311 or 800/560-5552, fax 808/877-4618, www.mauiseasidehotel.com, part of the Sand and Seaside Hotels, a small island-owned chain. Friendly and economical, this too is a two-story facility with a swimming pool in the central courtyard, access to the beach, and Vi's Restaurant for breakfast and dinner. All rooms hold two double beds or a king-size bed, have a color TV, small refrigerator, ceiling fan, and air-conditioning. Some kitchenettes are available, and there is a self-service laundry on premises. More motel-like than the Maui Beach, the Maui Seaside is clean, neat, and well cared for, and the owners show obvious pride in the way they keep up the property. AAA approved, rates are $98–135, or

$105–125 with rental car; numerous discounts, including through the Internet, are offered.

FOOD

The Kahului area has an assortment of inexpensive to moderate eating establishments and one that is a notch above the rest. Many are found in the shopping malls.

Inexpensive

Several basic restaurants and other food purveyors are located along Dairy Road. If you're looking for a wholesome, natural deli item, fresh salad, hot entrée, or freshly baked pastry, there's not a better place to look than the deli counter at **Down to Earth Natural Foods,** 305 Dairy Rd. Prices for items from the hot bar and salad bar run just over $6 per pound; prices for other items are marked and moderate. Open daily, it's also a full-service grocery store.

At the Dairy Center just up the road, you'll find the inexpensive eateries **Koko Ichiban Ya** for Japanese food and **Piñata's** Mexican restaurant. In the second half of this complex, around the corner and fronting Hana Highway, is **Maui Coffee Roasters,** 808/877-2877, for those who want a hot brew or take-home beans, available from all the islands. Tea, cold drinks, smoothies, sandwiches, wraps, soups, salads, veggie burgers, and baked goods are also available in this good-time, upscale, yuppie-ish coffeehouse-type place. Open weekdays at 7 A.M. and weekends at 8 P.M.

With an unlikely location in an industrial area among car repair shops is **Ajiyoshi Okazuya,** 385 Hoohana St., Unit 5C, 808/877-9080. Once here, try grilled fish, oxtail soup, or any of the other inexpensive Japanese dishes.

Follow your nose in the Queen Ka'ahumanu Center to **The Coffee Store,** 808/871-6860, open Mon.–Fri. 7:30 A.M.–9 P.M., Saturday 8 A.M.–7 P.M., and Sunday 8 A.M.–5 P.M. Light lunches include savories like a hot croissant or a spinach roll pastry puff, mostly in the $6–7 range. Coffee by the cup is $1.25 and up. The coffees, roasted on the premises, are from more than 20 gourmet varieties hand-picked in Hawaii and from around the world. Gifts and giftwear are

sold too. In addition, the Queen Ka'ahumanu Center also has a food court with half a dozen international fast-food outlets. You'll be sure to find something you can eat here.

The Maui Mall has a selection of inexpensive fast-food-type shopping center restaurants that include **Siu's Chinese Kitchen,** where most of their typical Chinese dishes are under $5, **Maui Mixed Plate** for local hot entrées, **Island Breeze Cafe,** and **IHOP.** All are good choices for a quick lunch during the day. Other fast-food eateries can be found in the food courts at Maui Marketplace.

Finally, for those who need their weekly fix of something fried and wrapped in Styrofoam, Kamehameha Avenue and adjacent streets behind the Maui Mall are dotted with a slew of fast-food chain restaurants.

Moderate

The Maui Beach Hotel serves food in its second-floor, open-air **Rainbow Dining Room** restaurant. You can fill up here at the breakfast buffet from 7–9:30 A.M. Monday–Saturday for $5.99, or try the Sunday buffet for $7.99. A lunch buffet is served 11 A.M.–2 P.M. daily for $10.95. Nearly every evening there's a different theme buffet from 5:30–8 P.M. for $21.99, except for the special Thursday king crab, prime rib, seafood, and lobster buffet for $28.99. At the Rainbow Dining Room, you'll have no complaint about value for price.

Vi's Restaurant, at the Maui Seaside Hotel, 808/871-6494, serves a standard American fare breakfast 7–9 A.M. for $6 or less and dinner 6–8 P.M. for under $13.50. Vi's offers more than 20 dinners such as fresh fish and steak, and breakfasts include their well-known omelets and hotcakes, and other island favorites.

In the Kahului Shopping Center you'll find **Ichiban Restaurant,** 808/871-6977, an authentic and inexpensive Japanese eatery, open daily except Sunday 7 A.M.–2 P.M. (Saturday from 10:30 A.M.), dinner 5–9 P.M., featuring full and continental breakfast, along with Japanese, American, and local specialties. Much of the breakfast menu is typically American, like eggs and bacon, omelets, and pancakes, most around $5. The lunch menu includes teriyaki chicken or shrimp tempura, chicken cutlet, don buri dishes, a variety of udon, and basic noodles, most $5–8. Dinner features combination plates, with your choice of any two items like shrimp and vegetable tempura, sashimi, or teriyaki chicken for around $14, along with more expensive special combinations like steak and lobster, the most expensive item on the menu, for $20–27. In addition, the sushi bar is open for lunch and dinner, with individual pieces ranging $3.75–6.75.

Koho Grill and Bar, 808/877-5588, at the Queen Ka'ahumanu Center, is an easygoing, good-time family dining place. The breakfast menu items are fairly standard, but Koho combines appetizers and salads with burgers, plate lunches, a few Mexican and Italian dishes, plus fish and standard American meat entrées for lunch and dinner. The food is not special, but you won't be disappointed either.

At the corner of Dairy Road and the Hana Highway is **Marco's Grill and Deli,** 808/877-4446, a casual place with black and white leather booths and cane chairs set around tiled tables. It's very Italian, and you might hear Tony Bennett being played as background music. For breakfast try chocolate cinnamon French toast for $6.95, pancakes, omelets, or pastries. A quick lunch might be one of the many deli sandwiches or a hot sandwich from the grill, most for under $13. Among the usual Italian fare items are Italian sausage and linguini for $16.95, pasta and basil for $14.95, and veal parmigiano for $22.95. Other specialties are vodka rigatoni for $16.95 and grilled salmon for $20.95. Take-out is available for anything on the menu, or choose something from the deli case. Open daily 7:30 A.M.–10 P.M.

The only on-the-water dining in Kahului is the **Hideaway** restaurant, 808/873-6555, next to Hoaloha Park. Hideaway does breakfast, lunch, and dinner buffets along with their à la carte menu, which has a combination of American standard and local dishes. The dinner menu is heavy on the meats and seafood, with pork ribs a signature item. Entrées run $13–23, and the *keiki* menu makes this a more affordable place for families. The Sunday breakfast buffet and the Monday–Saturday lunch buffets runs $10.99, while the nightly dinner buffet is $18.99. With dark wood overtones and low lighting, the Hideaway might also be a romantic spot for those who don't want to spend a bundle.

Perhaps the best of the bunch, and with the most outstanding menu, is **Mañana Garage,** 808/873-0220, located at the corner of Lono and Ka'ahumanu avenues. This trendy "nuevo latino" eatery serves lunch and dinner inside and out on the patio, and mixed drinks and Mexican beer at the bar. Fitting with its name, the Mañana Garage has a semi-industrial look mixed with bright Latin colors. While the lunch and dinner menus differ somewhat, a few items you will find are fried calamari and quesadilla con queso appetizers and entrées like fresh fish chimichanga, roasted habanero chicken, Cuban fried steak, chili adobo pulled pork, and pumpkin seed crusted shrimp. Lunch items run $8–13, while dinner entrées are $14–25. Weekdays, lunch is served 11 A.M.–2:30 P.M. with an abbreviated midday menu available 2:30–5 P.M. Dinner is served nightly from 5–9 P.M., but evening revelers can get food off the late-night menu until 10:30 P.M. Wednesday–Saturday, when the place is filled with the sounds of sultry live jazz or Latin instrumental music. While not the most romantic spot—the restaurant sits across from a gas station on a busy street—it does, however, have tasty food with a south-of-the-border zing in a vibrant and visually pleasing atmosphere. Call for reservations.

Groceries

For basic grocery items, try any of the following full-service stores in Kahului: **Star Market** at the Maui Mall, **Ah Fooks** at the Kahului Shopping Center, **Foodland** at the Queen Ka'ahumanu Center, and **Safeway** at 170 E. Kamehameha Avenue behind the Maui Mall. **Down to Earth Natural Foods,** 305 Dairy Rd., across from Maui Marketplace, is open Monday–Saturday 7 A.M.–9 P.M. and Sunday 7 A.M.–8 P.M. A full-service natural foods grocery with bulk items, canned and boxed goods, fresh vegetables and fruit, vitamins, minerals, and supplements, and health and beauty items, the store also has a deli counter, salad bar, hot entrée bar, and a bakery.

For a quick stop at a basic bottle shop, try Ah Fooks at the Kahului Shopping Center, Star Market at the Maui Mall, or the **Hawaii Liquor Superstore** at the Maui Marketplace.

ENTERTAINMENT

The six-plex **Kaahumanu Theater,** on the second floor of the Queen Ka'ahumanu Center, 808/875-4910, screens shows for $7.75 adults, $4.50 teens, and $2 children. At the Maui Mall, the **Maui Mall Megaplex Cinemas,** 808/249-2222, has eight screens and tickets run $7.50 adults, $4.50 ages 3–11.

You can hear free musical entertainment at both the Maui Mall and Queen Ka'ahumanu Center, usually over the lunch hour or early evening. These schedules vary throughout the month, but definitely stop and listen if the music is going when you are there shopping.

The **Maui Arts and Cultural Center,** 808/242-7469, has a varied program of music, dance, film, and visual arts showings at their complex near the harbor. This is one of the finest arts venues in the state. The box office is open 10 A.M.–6 P.M. Monday–Saturday.

RECREATION

Kahului is by no means a recreational center on the island, but it does offer a variety of options for sports and recreation. Nearby beaches are known throughout the world for excellent windsurfing and kitesurfing. Although the mountain is a distance away, you can start your journey for a bike ride down the mountain here.

Located southwest of downtown Kahului in the rolling sand hills of the isthmus is the "Irish

KITESURFING

The newest watersport to make a splash in the islands is kitesurfing, which may be described as a cross between flying a kite and wakeboarding. A foil-sail kite, perhaps six meters or more in length, is attached by long ropes to a grab bar that is clipped to a harness worn around the waist. Steering is done by pulling one end of the bar or the other to raise or lower the kite, catching more or less wind. A wide ski is used, similar to a wakeboard ski, except with a short rudder. Booties, a neoprene version of snowboard boots, keep you attached to the board. Some beginners content themselves with being dragged through the water as they learn to control the kite, while the proficient skim the water as fast and as freely as windsufers. Those who really know how to use the wind to their advantage can get 20–30 feet of loft. Sound intriguing? Approach with caution and take lessons. Those who know the sport say that it's not for the timid, nor as easy as it might appear.

Linksland Design" **The Dunes at Maui Lani,** the island's newest golf course. Undulating over the sand dunes, with plenty of elevation change, this course is a welcome addition to the range of courses offered on the island. Designed by Nelson and Haworth, the facility opened in 1999 with rudimentary facilities, but a full-service pro shop, restaurant, and driving range were added in 2000. Located north and south of Wailuku, respectively, are the shoreline **Waiehu Municipal Golf Course,** a family-friendly course used mostly by locals. This course is beautiful to play yet open to the bay, so it can get strong winds. The more challenging **Sandalwood Golf Course** lies on the lower slope of the West Maui Mountains.

SHOPPING

Because of its malls, Kahului has the best all-around shopping on the island. Combine this with the smaller shopping plazas, Kmart, Wal-Mart, Costco, and individual shops around town, and you can find absolutely everything you might need. For something different, don't miss the **Maui Swap Meet,** 808/877-3100, on Pu'unene Avenue next to the post office, every Saturday 7 A.M.–noon.

You can also shop almost the minute you arrive or just before you leave at two touristy but good shops along Keolani Place. Less than one-half mile from the airport are the **T-shirt Factory,** with original Maui designs and custom inexpensive T-shirts, as well as aloha shirts, sarongs, and pareu; and **Coral Factory,** for pink and black coral and jewelry sets with semiprecious stones. The Coral Factory seems to be set up largely to cater to Japanese tour groups.

On Dairy Road between Haleakala and Hana highways are the two huge stores housing **Kmart** and **Costco.** Farther down Dairy Road are the equally as large **Wal-Mart** and **Home Depot** stores. Mainland American mercantilism has invaded!

The two-story **Queen Ka'ahumanu Center** along Ka'ahumanu Avenue is Kahului's largest mall, with the widest selection of stores on the island with goods priced for the local

market and plenty of free parking. The mall's central courtyard is covered with a big skylight and a huge sail-like expanse of canvas—a good way to let the light and breezes through. You'll find the big stores like **Macy's** and **Sears** anchoring this mall, with the smaller **Shirokiya** here as well. Numerous apparel, shoe, jewelry, and specialty stores and three restaurants fill this center, and a half dozen inexpensive international fast-food eateries are located in the food court. In addition, the center hosts a farmers market on Fridays 8 A.M.–3 P.M. Several of the specialty shops are a large **Waldenbooks** for one of the best selections of books on Maui; **Serendipity** for oriental furniture, home accessories, and inspired clothing; **Ho'opomaika'i,** which carries Hawaiian gifts and crafts; **Maui Hands** for arts and crafts; a **Whaler's General Store** for sundries; and **GNC** for nutritional supplements. On the upper level, you can relax in the cool, dark comfort of the **Kaahumanu Theater** and catch a movie. For something free, entertainment is often offered at the center stage over the lunch hour and at about 7 P.M. on Fridays.

The low-rise, open-air, and renovated **Maui Mall** is more pedestrian, yet it has a pleasant ambiance as its buildings are set around courtyards. At the intersection of Hana Highway and Ka'ahumanu Avenue, Maui Mall has **Longs Drugs** for everything from aspirin to film, a **Star Market,** the unusual **Paper Airplane Museum** (see the Sights section), a megaplex theater, a handful of clothing and specialty shops, and a couple places for quick foods. On Fridays, there is free live entertainment at the mall's center stage.

While **Kahului Shopping Center,** 47 Ka'ahumanu Ave., has lost much of its vitality, you'll still find **Ah Fooks** supermarket, open daily from 6:30 A.M. and specializing in Asian foods, the smaller **Ji-Mi Asian Food Mart,** the moderate and pleasant **Ichiban Restaurant,** a **Salvation Army Thrift Store,** and **Central Pacific Bank.** Maui Organic Farmers Market holds court here on Wednesdays 8 A.M.–noon. This mall is less distinctive than the other two along Ka'ahumanu Avenue and seems to have suffered most because of the newer and larger malls in town.

The Old Kahului Shopping Center, 55 Ka'ahumanu Ave., just across from the Maui Mall, is just that, an old building from 1916 that held a bank and a series of shops that was modernized and brought back to life in the late '80s. Once full of boutiques and specialty shops, it now has only two ordinary shops and a chiropractic office. **Lightning Bolt** specializes in surfboards and surf attire, modern fashions, women's apparel, hats, and sunglasses, while **Fabric Mart** has miles of cloth and craft and sewing supplies.

The newest mall in Kahului, with a style from Anywhere U.S.A., occupies a huge area along Dairy Road. This is **Maui Marketplace,** and here you'll find such stores as **Borders Books and Music** for the best selection of books on the island; **The Sports Authority** for a large selection of athletic clothing and equipment, bicycles, and camping and fishing supplies; the clothing stores **Hawaiian Island Creations** and **Old Navy;** a **Sunglass Hut** outlet; the huge **Lowe's** home improvement warehouse for anything you might need for your house or yard; **OfficeMax** for your business needs; **Pier 1 Imports** for home furnishings; several jewelry stores; other smaller shops; and a food court.

Kahului has the greatest concentration of windsurfing and watersport shops on the island, many of them at or near the corner of Hana Highway and Dairy Road. Shop here and comparison shop before going anywhere else. **Hawaiian Island Surf and Sport** carries a multitude of water sports equipment, new and used, for sale and rental. Next door is **Island Biker,** which sells and services road bikes and mountain bikes and rents mountain bikes. A boardsail away at the **Triangle Square** mall across from Kahana Pond, you'll find **High Tech Surf Sport** for all water sports equipment and information, and across Hana Highway is **Neilpryde Maui.** Several other water sport shops are located within a stone's throw of the Kanaha Pond near Kamehameha Avenue.

At the **Dairy Center,** at the intersection of Dairy Road and Hana Highway, you'll find **Extreme Sports Maui** and **Kinko's** along with several eateries, **Marco's Grill** and **Maui Coffee Roasters.** Extreme Sports rents the usual water equipment, plus skateboards and bikes, and has a small climbing wall.

Of the freestanding shops in town, **Two Frogs Hugging,** 808/873-7860, at the corner of Ka'ahumanu and Pu'unene Avenues, is one of the most unusual with its collection of wooden furniture and wood and stone carvings imported mostly from Indonesia. Look for the two hugging frogs stone sculpture out front.

SERVICES

Medical Services

For medical emergencies, try **Maui Memorial Medical Center,** 808/244-9056, at 221 Mahalani. Clinics include **Kaiser Permanente,** 808/243-6000, at 20 Mahalani. Both of these facilities are located between downtown Kahului and downtown Wailuku, the medical center up behind the county police station, the clinic across the road from the police station.

Banks

Kahului has numerous **banks,** most with ATMs, and the majority are near the intersection of Ka'ahumanu and Pu'unene Avenues. There is a Bank of Hawaii, 808/871-8250, at 27 S. Pu'unene Avenue and at the Maui Marketplace; First Hawaiian Bank, 808/877-2311, at 20 W. Ka'ahumanu Avenue; American Savings Bank branches at 73 Pu'unene Avenue, 808/871-8411, and at the Queen Ka'ahumanu Center; and Central Pacific Bank, 808/877-3387, at 85 W. Ka'ahumanu Avenue.

Post Office

The Kahului **post office,** 138 S. Pu'unene Ave. (Rte. 350), is open Monday–Friday 8:30 A.M.–5 P.M. and Saturday 9 A.M.–noon. For information, call 800/275-8777.

If you need to check your email while on Maui, stop at **Kinko's,** 395 Dairy Rd. 808/871-2000, and use a computer for $.20 per minute, or avail yourself of any of the facility's other numerous copy and office services. Open daily 7 A.M.–11 P.M. For other copy, postal, and business services, try **Mail Boxes Etc.,** 415 Dairy Rd., 808/877-0333, across from Kmart.

Library

The **library,** 808/873-3097, tucked quietly under the trees at 90 School Street, is open Mondays, Thursdays, Fridays, and Saturdays 10 A.M.–5 P.M., and Tuesdays and Wednesdays 10 A.M.–10 P.M.; closed Sundays.

Laundry

The **W & F Washerette,** 125 S. Wakea, 808/877-0353, features video games to while away the time as well as a little snack bar. Soap and change machines, drop-off service, and dry cleaning are available. Open daily 6 A.M.–9 P.M.

Wailuku

Historical towns often maintain a certain aura long after their time of importance has passed. Wailuku is one of these. Maui's county seat since 1905, the town has the feel of one that has been important for a long time. Wailuku earned its name, "Water of Destruction," from a ferocious battle fought by Kamehameha I against Maui warriors just up the road in 'Iao Valley. The slaughter was so intense that more than four miles of the local stream literally ran red with blood. In the 1800s, the missionaries settled in Wailuku, and their architectural influences, such as a white-steeple church and the courthouse at the top of the main street, give an impression of a New England town. Later in the 19th century, sugar came to town, and this vast industry grew with muscle and pumped great vitality into the community. After the turn of the 20th century, Wailuku strengthened its stance as the island's center of government, business, and industry, and the wealthy and influential built homes here. Wailuku maintained this strong position until the 1960s when the sugar industry declined and the growth of tourism began to create other centers of population and industry on the island. Although still a vibrant government and population center, much of Wailuku's importance to the island's economy has been eclipsed.

Some of Wailuku is pretty, but it's a mixed bag in others areas, including much of the downtown area. The town center, while once dignified, has lost its blush, yet there has been and continues to be a concerted effort to revitalize it. Comely rows of plantation-era bungalows are scattered here and there around town, yet fading sections past their prime also exist, not always too far from the new and modern developments. Built on the rolling foothills of the West Maui Mountains, this adds some character—unlike the often-flat layout of many other Hawaiian towns. You can tour Wailuku in only an hour, although most people don't even give it that much time. They just pass through on their way to 'Iao Needle, where everyone goes, or simply skirt the edge of town and head on to Kahakuloa, around the back side, and West Maui.

> *Historical towns often maintain a certain aura long after their time of importance has passed. Wailuku is one of these. Maui's county seat since 1905, the town has the feel of one that has been important for a long time.*

You can see Wailuku's sights from the window of your car, but don't shortchange yourself this way. Definitely visit the Bailey House Museum (1833), and while you're out, walk the grounds of Ka'ahumanu Church (1876). Clustered near these two are other historical buildings, several of which are listed on the Hawaii and National Registers of Historic Places. These include the small Alexander House (1836), which is set just above the cemetery near the corner of Main and High streets, the Circuit Courthouse (1907), Old County Building (1925), Territorial Building (1930), Wailuku Public Library (1928), Wailuku Union Church (1911), and the Wailuku Public School (1904). One block away is the Church of the Good Shepherd (1911), and beyond that the 'Iao Theater (1928), the last remaining of the 19 theaters that dotted the island in the era between the world wars. Built somewhat later

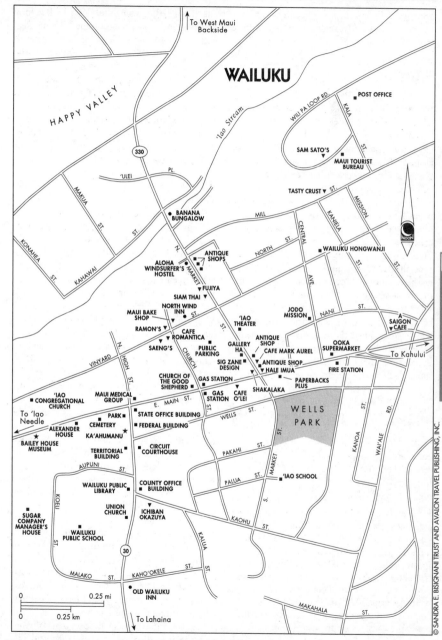

WAILUKU

HAPPY VALLEY

To West Maui Backside

POST OFFICE

WILI PA LOOP RD.

KALA ST.

SAM SATO'S

MAUI TOURIST BUREAU

TASTY CRUST ST.

'Iao Stream

330

'ULEI PL.

MILL

NORTH ST.

CENTRAL AVE.

KANIELA ST.

MISSION ST.

WAILUKU HONGWANJI

BANANA BUNGALOW

ANTIQUE SHOPS

ALOHA WINDSURFER'S HOSTEL

FUJIYA

SIAM THAI

NORTH WIND INN

MAUI BAKE SHOP

RAMON'S

CAFE ROMANTICA

SAENG'S

'IAO THEATER

JODO MISSION

NANI ST.

SAIGON CAFE

GALLERY HA

ANTIQUE SHOP

CAFE MARK AUREL

OOKA SUPERMARKET

To Kahului

PUBLIC PARKING

SIG ZANE DESIGN

ANTIQUE SHOP

HALE IMUA

FIRE STATION

CHURCH OF THE GOOD SHEPHERD

GAS STATION

SHAKALAKA

PAPERBACKS PLUS

'IAO CONGREGATIONAL CHURCH

MAUI MEDICAL GROUP

E. MAIN ST.

GAS STATION

CAFE O'LEI

WELLS PARK

To 'Iao Needle

PARK

CEMETERY

KA'AHUMANU

STATE OFFICE BUILDING

FEDERAL BUILDING

WELLS ST.

KANOA ST.

WAI'ALE RD.

ALEXANDER HOUSE

BAILEY HOUSE MUSEUM

TERRITORIAL BUILDING

CIRCUIT COURTHOUSE

PAKAHI ST.

AUPUNI ST.

WAILUKU PUBLIC LIBRARY

COUNTY OFFICE BUILDING

PALUA ST.

'IAO SCHOOL

KOELI

UNION CHURCH

ICHIBAN OKAZUYA

KAOHU ST.

SUGAR COMPANY MANAGER'S HOUSE

WAILUKU PUBLIC SCHOOL

30

KAIUA ST.

MALAKO ST.

KAHO'OKELE ST.

0   0.25 mi

0   0.25 km

OLD WAILUKU INN

To Lahaina

MAKAHALA

MOON

CENTRAL MAUI

© SANDRA E. BISIGNANI TRUST AND AVALON TRAVEL PUBLISHING, INC.

are the Wailuku Sugar Company manager's house (1936) and the 'Iao Congregational Church (1936).

SIGHTS

Ka'ahumanu Church

It's fitting that Maui's oldest existing stone church is named after the resolute but loving Queen Ka'ahumanu. This rock-willed woman is the "Saint Peter" of Hawaii, upon whom Christianity in the islands was built. She was *the* most important early convert, often attending services in Kahului's humble grass-hut chapel. It is also worth noting that the church was erected on Maui king Kahekili's *heiau*—the squashing of one religion with the growing presence of another. In 1832, when the congregation was founded, an adobe church was built on the same spot and named in her honor. Rain and time washed it away, to be replaced by the island's first stone structure in 1837. In 1876 the church went through its fourth metamorphosis, the church tower and clock being delayed until 1884, and what remains is the white and green structure we know today. Its construction was supervised by the missionary Edward Bailey, whose home stands to the rear. A three-year renovation project

ended in 1976, bringing the church back to form and allowing it placement on the National Register of Historic Places. Oddly enough, the steeple was repaired in 1984 by Skyline Engineers, who hail from Massachusetts, the same place from which the missionaries came 150 years earlier! You can see the church sitting there on High Street (Rte. 30), but it's sometimes closed during the week. Sunday services are at 9 A.M., when the Hawaiian congregation sings the Lord's praise in their native language. An excellent cultural and religious event to attend!

Bailey House Museum

This is the old Bailey House, 2375-A Main St., built 1833–1850, with various rooms added throughout the years. From 1837 it housed the Wailuku Female Seminary, of which Edward Bailey was principal until the school closed in 1849. After that, the Baileys bought the property, began to raise sugar cane, and lived here until the 1890s. During this time, Edward Bailey became the manager of the Wailuku Sugar Company. More important for posterity, he became a prolific landscape painter of various areas around the island. Most of his paintings, 26 in the museum's holdings, record the period 1866–1896 and are now displayed in the Bailey Gallery, once the sitting room of the house. The onetime seminary dining room, now housing the museum gift shop, was his studio. In July 1957 this old missionary homestead formally became the Maui Historical Society Museum, at which time it acquired the additional name of Hale Hoikeike, "House of Display." It closed in 1973 when it was placed on the National Register of Historic Places, then was refurbished and reopened in July 1975.

You'll be amazed at the two-foot-thick walls the missionaries taught the Hawaiians to build, using goat hair as the binding agent. Years of whitewashing make them resemble new-fallen snow. The rooms inside are given over to various themes. The Hawaiian Room houses excellent examples of the often practical artifacts of precontact Hawaii like stone tools, bone fishhooks, and wooden weapons; especially notice the fine displays of tapa cloth and cal-

MAUI SAND DUNES

The isthmus of Maui connects the island's two great mountains. This low, broad plain was formed by lava that spewed over thousands of years, connecting the two mountains (and at one time also connecting Maui to Lana'i and Kaho'olawe) before the fire ceased and Maui drifted to the northwest. Over the eons, coral and sand formed along the periphery of the island, and strong winds from the northeast lifted this mixture off the beaches along the isthmus's north shore and deposited it inland forming sand dunes. The isthmus is windswept and fairly flat, but dunes have formed as mostly low, rounded hills, principally on the western side of the isthmus, that rise to about 200 feet in height where they push against the mountainside at Wailuku.

ROBERT NILSEN

the Bailey House, a museum of Hawaii's missionary era

abashes. Hawaiian tapa, now nearly a lost art, was considered Polynesia's finest and most advanced. Upstairs is the bedroom. It's quite large and dominated by a four-poster bed. In this and an adjoining room, there's a dresser with a jewelry box, other pieces of furniture, toys for children, and clothes including hats and fine lace gloves. Downstairs you'll discover the sitting room and kitchen, the heart of the house: the "feelings" are strongest here, and perhaps more so because original paintings by Edward Bailey adorn the walls. The solid ʻohiʻa lintel over the doorway is as stout as the spirits of the people who once lived here. The stonework on the floor is well laid but now covered for preservation, and the fireplace is totally homey.

Now look outside: The lanai runs across the entire front and down the side. Around back is the canoe shed, housing a refurbished sennit-sewn outrigger canoe from the late 1800s, as well as Duke Kahanamoku's redwood surfboard from about 1910. On the grounds you'll also see exhibits of sugarcane, sugar pots, konane boards, and various Hawaiian artifacts around the lush and landscaped lawn. Open Monday–Saturday 10 A.M.–4 P.M. Admission is well worth the $5

adults, $4 seniors, and $1 children 7–12. Upon arrival, a docent will introduce you to the house and then let you make a self-guided tour at your leisure. Adjacent in the gift shop is a terrific selection of high-quality souvenirs, books, music, and Hawaiiana at better-than-average prices. All are done by Hawaiian artists and craftspeople, and many are created specifically for this shop.

The office of the **Maui Historical Society,** 808/244-3326, office@mauimuseum.org, www.mauimuseum.org, is in the basement of the Bailey House. It seems appropriate that this society, which collects and preserves artifacts and disseminates information about the history and culture of Maui, should be located on the grounds where Kahekili, Maui's last king, had his compound.

Kepaniwai Park

As you head up Route 320 to ʻIao Valley, you're in for a real treat. Two miles after leaving Wailuku, you come across Kepaniwai Park and Heritage Gardens. Here the architect, Richard C. Tongg, envisioned and created a park dedicated to all of Hawaii's people. See the Portuguese villa and

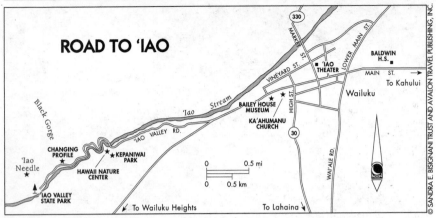

garden complete with an outdoor oven, a thatch-roofed Hawaiian grass shack, a New England "salt box," a Chinese pagoda, a Japanese teahouse with authentic garden, a Korean pavilion, and a bamboo house—the little "sugar shack" that songs and dreams are made of. Admission is free and there are pavilions with picnic tables often used by families for a Sunday picnic. This now-tranquil spot is where the Maui warriors fell to the invincible Kamehameha and his merciless patron war god, Ku. Kepaniwai means "Damming of the Waters"—literally with corpses. Kepaniwai is now a monument to man's higher nature: harmony and beauty.

Hawaii Nature Center, 'Iao Valley

Located at the upper end of Kepaniwai Park is the Hawaii Nature Center, 'Iao Valley, 808/244-6500, www.hawaiinaturecenter.org, a private, nonprofit educational and interactive science center—good for kids and grown-ups alike and highly recommended. Open daily 10 A.M.–4 P.M., $6 adults, $4 children, this center boasts 30 exhibits that will beg you to participate, challenge your mind, and teach you about all aspects of Hawaiian nature at the same time. This seems an appropriate spot for a nature center because the West Maui Mountains harbor 12 distinct plant communities, about 300 species of plants, of which 10 are endemic to this locale, and literally thousands of varieties of animals and insects. One-mile, 1.5-hour nature walks are guided

through the valley daily to bring you face to face with some of the wonders this valley has to offer. These hikes generally start at 1:30 P.M. and cost $25 adults, $23 children, which includes entrance to the exhibits. Reservations are required.

The Changing Profile

Up the road toward 'Iao Valley you come to a scenic area long known as Pali 'Ele'ele, or Black Gorge. This stream-eroded narrow slit canyon has attracted attention for centuries. It was one of the places in 'Iao Valley where *ali'i* were buried, so that no one would discover their final resting place. Amazingly, after President Kennedy was assassinated, people noticed his likeness portrayed there by a series of large boulders on one side of the valley wall; mention of a profile had never been noted or recorded there before. Bring your binoculars, as the pipe that once served as a rudimentary sighting instrument is gone. The likeness—with eyes closed in deep repose—is uncanny and easily seen, unlike most of these formations, where you have to stretch your imagination to the breaking point. Recently, however, the powers that be (a committee of the State Department of Land and Natural Resources) have pronounced that this image is really that of the late-15th-century *kahuna* Kauaka'iwai. Legend has it that he was turned to stone to protect the *ali'i* buried in this valley. Go figure. You obviously see what you want to in these stones anyway.

'Iao Valley State Park

This valley has been a sacred spot and a place of pilgrimage since ancient times. Before Westerners arrived, the people of Maui, who came here to pay homage to the "Eternal Creator," named this valley 'Iao, "Cloud Supreme" or "Supreme Light." Facing almost directly east, the valley catches the warming morning sunlight. According to legend, the gods Maui and Hina raised their daughter 'Iao in this valley. As 'Iao grew, she became entranced with a half-man, half-fish god, and they became lovers. This arrangement did not please her father, who, in revenge, turned 'Iao's lover into a stone pinnacle, the peak we know as 'Iao Needle.

Historically, 'Iao Valley was a place set aside and did not belong to the traditional *ahupua'a* land-division system. No commoners were allowed into the valley except on special occasions, and royalty were buried here in secret graves. During the Battle of Kepaniwai in 1790, when King Kamehameha defeated Maui's King Kahekili, this valley was valiantly defended but overrun. Countless commoners perished while the *ali'i* escaped over the mountains to Olowalu.

In the center of this velvety green amphitheater-like valley is a pillar of stone rising more than 1,200 feet (actual height above sea level is 2,250 feet), its grassy top at one time a natural altar and lookout for defense. Kuka'emoku, now commonly called "The Needle," is a tough basaltic ridge that remained after water swirled away the weaker stone surrounding it, leaving only a saddle that connects it to the valley wall, unseen from below. 'Iao Valley is actually the remnant of the volcanic caldera of the West Maui Mountains, whose grooved walls have been smoothed and enlarged by the restlessness of mountain streams. Robert Louis Stevenson had to stretch poetic license to create a word for 'Iao when he called it "viridescent."

The road ends in a parking lot. Signs point you to paved paths, tame and well maintained, with plenty of vantage points for photographers. If you take the lower path to the river below, you'll find a good-size, popular swimming hole; but remember, these are the West Maui Mountains, and it can rain at any time, causing water to rise rapidly. Pu'u

ROBERT NILSEN

'Iao Needle, one of the most unusual natural features on the island, draws a great number of visitors every year.

Kukui, West Maui Mountains' tallest peak, lies on the western edge of this crater rim and gets about 400 inches of rain per year! On the east side of the stream below the bridge, a loop path leads though a garden of native plants. Beyond the bridge, steps lead up to an observation pavilion. You can escape the crowds, however, even in this heavily touristed area. As you head back, take the paved path that bears to the right skirting the river and the tourists magically disappear. Here are several pint-size pools where you can take a refreshing dip. A rudimentary path continues up this valley. About one mile up is a fork in the stream, beyond which it is not recommended to go.

'Iao is for day use only; hours are 7 A.M.–7 P.M. On your way back to Wailuku you might take a five-minute side excursion up to Wailuku Heights. Look for the road on your right. There's little here besides a mid- to upper-end residential area, but the view below over the isthmus is tops!

Maui Tropical Plantation and Country Store

This attraction is somewhat out of the ordinary. The 60-acre Maui Tropical Plantation, 808/244-7643, presents a model of a working plantation that you can tour by small tram. Most interesting is the up-close look at Maui's agricultural abundance. Displays of each of these products are situated around the taro patches at the plantation village. A 40-minute tram ride takes you through fields of cane, banana, guava, mango, papaya, pineapple, coffee, and macadamia nuts; flowers here and there add exotic color. Leaving every 45 minutes 10 A.M.–3:15 P.M., the tram ride is $9.90 adults, $3.65 children 3–12. The plantation, with its restaurant, gift shop, and tropical flower nursery, is near Waikapu, a small village along Route 30 between Wailuku and Ma'alaea. If you visit over the noon hour, stop by the Plantation Cafe for lunch, open 11 A.M.–2 P.M. daily. The Country Store here sells Maui-produced goods and can mail gift packages of fruits, nuts, and coffee, while the nursery will ship flowers to anywhere in the country. Look for the windmill! Open daily 9 A.M.–5 P.M.

ACCOMMODATIONS

Visitors to Wailuku mostly stay elsewhere on Maui because there are only a few specialized and humble hostels and one historic bed-and-breakfast inn.

Bed-and-Breakfast

The only fine place to stay in Wailuku is at the attentively renovated **Old Wailuku Inn at Ulupono,** 2199 Kaho'okele St., 800/305-4899 or 808/244-5897, fax 808/242-9600, Mauibandb@aol.com, www.mauiinn.com, now on the Hawaii Register of Historic Places. Built in 1924 for the son and daughter-in-law of Maui's first bank president, this was the queen of homes in one of Maui's most posh neighborhoods. Refurbished in 1997, this house was brought back to its early charm, lovingly detailed, filled with period furniture that evokes the feeling of grandma's house, and decorated with Hawaiian and Asian an-

tiques and artwork. It's a gem. Yet no modern amenity or comfort is left out. Each room has a TV, VCR, telephone, private bath, ceiling fan, and gorgeous Hawaiian quilt on its spacious bed. A fax machine, photocopier, and computer are also available for use. The house has central air-conditioning, but the cooling trade winds are generally enough to moderate the temperature. Catching the morning sun, the screened breakfast room looks out over the rear garden. The open-air front porch is a perfect spot for afternoon tea or reading a book from the extensive house library, and the living room is a fine place to relax in the evening. Each of the seven guest rooms is named for a Hawaiian flower, and their color and design motifs follow. The four upstairs rooms are spacious and grand, with native hardwood floors and 10-foot ceilings. The downstairs rooms are cozier, and two have their own courtyards. In the back garden, the Vagabond House was built on the site of an old garage and opened for guests in 2002. It contains three rooms that, like the rest of the house, are in keeping with the period of the 1920s and '30s. A gourmet breakfast accompanies each night's stay and, no matter what the offering, is tasty, filling, nutritious, and well presented. You'll be pampered. Born and raised on the island, the gracious and personable hosts, Janice and Tom Fairbanks, have intimate knowledge of what to do, what to see, and where to eat throughout the island and will gladly share their knowledge and recommendations with you. Rooms in the main house run $120–180 double occupancy, $140–160 for the Vagabond House; two nights minimum. Parking is on property.

Hostels

The **Banana Bungalow,** 310 N. Market St., 808/244-5090, 800/846-7835, fax 808/244-3678, info@mauihostel.com, www.mauihostel.com, is located on the edge of Happy Valley. It's a clean and spartan hostel, with a coat of (yellow) paint, some artistic decorations, refurbished bathrooms up and down, and a renovated common room. Typically, you're liable to hear languages from a half dozen countries, and if you're into windsurfing or just after a cross-cultural experience, this is the spot. The Banana Bungalow offers basic accommodations, and if you care more about your experience than your sleeping arrangements, it's the place for you. Rates are $32 single, $40 double, $50 triple, or $17.50 for a bunk in a four- to six-person dorm (co-ed and female-only), which includes the bed linens but not towels. All rooms and dorms share bathrooms. Monthly rates can be arranged for dorm use. A departure air ticket and/or a foreign passport are required to stay. Extra services include a free and convenient morning airport/beach shuttle; laundry and storage facilities; a common room for conversation, TV, or music; free Internet access; a hot tub, barbecue grill, hammocks in the garden under tropical fruit trees; discount rates on water equipment and lessons; and discount car rental deals. Because the Banana Bungalow is in a residential neighborhood, the 10 P.M.–8 A.M. quiet hours are enforced. Also, no smoking and no drugs are allowed. The hostel's no-cost adventure van tours, different every day, are sign-up tours open to anyone, guests or not, on a first-come, first-served basis. Tours change periodically due to interest, but typical outings include a hike over swinging bridges into a lush nearby valley, a road trip to Hana, a snorkel and sunset tour to a marine sanctuary, an 'Iao Valley walk, and a drive to Haleakala for sunset. There is no cost for these tours, but you should tip the driver. Reception hours are 8 A.M.–11 P.M.; there is no curfew. The Banana Bungalow is the premier hostel accommodation on Maui.

The **North Wind Hostel,** 2080 Vineyard St., tel/fax 808/242-1448 or 866/946-7835, maui@northwind-hostel.com, www.northwind-hostel.com, is easily spotted with its row of international flags fluttering from the second-floor balcony. Enter via the alley sidewalk; 24-hour access. With a capacity of about 45, this single-floor hostel caters mostly to young, independent travelers and surfers. Bunk rooms go for $18 a bed, single rooms $32, and double rooms $38, exclusive of tax but including bed linens; all rooms share four bathrooms with showers. You'll need an air ticket off Maui or a foreign

passport to check in. Good for socializing, the lounge has a television and a computer for Internet access. There are laundry facilities; a safe for valuables; storage facilities for sailboards, backpacks, and large items, and much more. No smoking is permitted inside the hostel. In a previous incarnation, this hostel won the respect of the community for transforming the former fleabag Wailuku Grand Hotel into a viable business and dealing equitably with the locals; however, the hostel has gone through several changes of ownership in the last few years, so only time will tell if it manages to maintain its integrity.

The newest inexpensive accommodation in town is the **Aloha Windsurfers' Hostel,** 167 N. Market St., 808/249-0206 or 800/249-1421, fax 808/249-0705, alohawindsurf@yahoo.com, www.accommodations-maui.com. With only 16 places, this remodeled old structure is small and quiet, with a common room, kitchen, and several bathrooms. The rate for a dorm bed is $17.50, $42–49 for a single private room, and $46–56 for a private double room. Weekly, monthly, and room and car rates are also available. Amenities include a free simple breakfast, Internet access, and local calls, as well as airport and beach pickup and drop-off.

FOOD
Downtown

Wailuku has some of the best and most inexpensive restaurants on Maui. The establishments listed as follows are all in the bargain or reasonable range. The decor in most is basic and homey, with the emphasis placed on the food. Even here in this nontouristy town, however, some of the restaurants are sprucing up and becoming a bit gentrified.

Saeng's, 2119 Vineyard, 808/244-1567, serves excellent Thai food at great prices. Dishes include appetizers like Thai crisp noodles for $4.95 and green papaya salad for $6.50. The savory soups, enough for two, include spicy coconut shrimp soup for $9.50 and po teak, a zesty seafood combination soup for $10.95. Thai specialties such as pad thai vegetables, chicken Thai curry, and eggplant shrimp are all under $10, while vegetarian selections like stir-fry vegetables and Evil Prince tofu are under $7.50. Only some seafood plates are more expensive at $12.95. Although the interior is quite tasteful with linen tablecloths and paisley booths, the best seating is outside in the covered garden patio, where a small waterfall gurgles pleasantly. Open Monday–Friday for lunch 11 A.M.–2:30 P.M. and dinner nightly 5–9:30 P.M., except for Sunday when it closes at 8:30 P.M.

Siam Thai, 123 N. Market, 808/244-3817, is a small restaurant (open Mon.–Sat. 11:30 A.M.–2:30 P.M., daily 5–9:30 P.M.). It serves excellent Thai food with an emphasis on vegetarian cuisine, at prices that are comparable with Saeng's. Extensive menu; a perennial favorite.

Ramon's Restaurant, 2102 Vineyard, 808/244-7243, is open from 8 A.M. and serves food throughout the day. It also has the only bar in town and provides live music on some weekends. Ramon's has a good mix of Mexican and Hawaiian dishes, with plenty of plate dishes, specials, combinations, and burritos. Some items off the menu are teriyaki chicken plate for $6.95, fiesta combination plates for $9.95, a bean burrito for $7.95, and enchilada del mar for $14.95.

Maui Bake Shop and Deli, 2092 Vineyard St., 808/242-0064 (open weekdays 7 A.M.–3 P.M., Saturday 7 A.M.–1 P.M., closed Sunday) has a full selection of home-baked goods, and sandwiches for about $3.95, with soup du jour $6.75. Daily specials can be pizza, quiche, filled croissants, or even lox and bagels for under $5. Tantalizing baked goods include apple strudel, coconut macaroons, apricot twists, fruit tarts, and homemade pies. Enjoy your selection with an espresso, cappuccino, or hot tea. Maui Bake Shop is a common stop for morning nourishment.

Kitty-corner across the intersection and open Tuesday–Friday 11 A.M.–3 P.M. for vegetarian cuisine is **Cafe Romantica,** 808/249-0697. Short on hours, but heavy on quality, they offer a variety of soups and salads, pastries, samosa, crepes, lasagna, and quiche.

The tiny **Ichiban Okazuya** take-out restaurant is located just around the corner from the county office building on Kaohu Street. They're open 10 A.M.–2 P.M. and 4–7 P.M. for katsu, teriyaki,

and other quick eats. They have a good reputation that's growing.

An unassuming little storefront shop that serves wonderful food and that's been a hit with local patrons is **Cafe O'lei On Main Street,** 808/244-6816. Stop by Monday–Friday 10:30 A.M.–3:30 P.M. for coffee, sandwiches, and other entrées. Most everything is under $7.

Just down the street on the corner of Main and Market streets, **Shakalaka Fish and Chips,** 808/986-0855, serves up quick and inexpensive eats Monday–Friday 10:30 A.M.–8 P.M.

For a spot of coffee, tea, pastries, bagels, or light lunches, head to the sophisticated **Cafe Mark Aurel,** 28 N. Market St., 808/244-0852 (open Mon.–Fri. 7 A.M.–6 P.M., Saturday and holidays 7 A.M.–1 P.M.).

One block down on the corner of Maluhia Street is **Hale Imua Internet Cafe,** 808/242-1896, which not only offers Internet access but also serves all manner of coffee and other drinks, sandwiches, and salads. Open Monday–Friday 9 A.M.–5:30 P.M., Saturday until 4 P.M.

A little out of the way but well worth the effort to find is **A Saigon Cafe,** 1792 Main St., 808/243-9560. A great family place, clean but not fancy, this may be the best Vietnamese cuisine on the island. It gets a thumbs up from everyone. Although there's no large sign yet advertising its location, it's a favorite local stop, and you'll know why once you try. Start with spring rolls at $5.75 or shrimp pops for $7.25 and move on to one of the tasty soups like hot and sour fish soup for $9.20 or a green papaya salad for $5.50. Entrées, all under $10 except the Saigon fondue, which is cooked at your table, include a wide range of noodle, meat, fish, and vegetarian dishes, all with good portions. The menu is extensive. Open daily 10 A.M.–10 P.M., Sunday until 8:30 P.M., this restaurant is behind Ooka Super Market, below the bridge.

On the edge of town toward Kahului near the underpass is **Stillwell's Bakery and Cafe,** 1740 Ka'ahumanu Ave., 808/243-2243. Having established a fine reputation with locals, it's now becoming known to visitors. The surroundings are nothing special, but the food is worthy of the reputation, and the breads, baked goods, and cakes are delicious—and served at some fine restaurants on the island. Stop in for a pastry and coffee, cookies, a lunch sandwich and soup, or other hot entrée. Open Monday–Saturday 6 A.M.–4 P.M.

Off the Main Drag

If you get out of downtown, you'll be rewarded with some of the *most* local and *least* expensive restaurants on West Maui, many of them along Mill Street and Lower Main. They are totally unpretentious and serve hefty portions of tasty, homemade local foods. If your aim is to *eat* like a local, search out one of these.

The **Tasty Crust Restaurant,** 1770 Mill St., 808/244-0845, opens daily 5:30 A.M.–11 P.M., Friday and Saturday until midnight. Similar to a diner, with bar stools at the counter, booths, and a few tables, the welcome sign says "This is where old friends meet." If you have to carbo-load for a full day of sailing, snorkeling, or windsurfing, order the famous giant homemade hotcakes.

Sam Sato's, 1750 Wili Pa Loop Rd. in the Mill Yard, 808/244-7124, is famous for *manju,* a pufflike pastry from Japan usually filled with lima or adzuki beans. This is one of those places that, if you are a local resident, you *must* bring Sato's manju when visiting friends or relatives off-island. Aside from the manju there are noodles, saimin, sandwiches, and plate lunches for lunch, and omelets and banana hotcakes for breakfast. Many think that Sam serves the best dry mein noodles on the island. Most everything is under $5.50. Open Monday–Saturday 7 A.M.–4 P.M., pickup until 2 P.M. A highly specialized place, but worth the effort.

Another well-established local place is **Nazo's Restaurant,** 1063 Lower Main St., 808/244-0529, on the second floor of the Puuone Plaza, an older yellowish two-story building. Park underneath and walk upstairs. Daily specials cost under $9, but Nazo's is renowned for its oxtail soup, a clear-consommé broth with peanuts and water chestnuts floating around, a delicious combination of East and West. Open Monday–Saturday 10 A.M.–2 P.M. and again 5–9 P.M.

Tokyo Tei, 808/242-9630, in the same complex but downstairs, is another institution that has been around since 1937 serving Japanese dishes to a devoted clientele. Eating here is as consistent as eating at grandma's kitchen, with traditional Japanese dishes like tempura, various don buri, and seafood platters. If you want to sample real Japanese food at affordable prices, come here! Open daily 11 A.M.–1:30 P.M. for lunch, 5–8:30 P.M. dinner, open Sunday for dinner only.

Romeo's Café, 740 Lower Main St., 808/242-5957, is in a no-nonsense part of town, in a place of local atmosphere, where the inside is pink, white, and yellow, with booths and a few tables. Breakfast starts at 6 A.M. and includes items like pancakes, omelets, and loco moco. Lunch is also served (but not dinner), and nothing on the menu is more than $7.

For a different taste treat, try the traditional-style manju and mochi made fresh daily at Wailuku's **Shishido Manju Shop,** 758 Lower Main St., 808/244-5222. If you're in the mood for a more contemporary manju with new flavors or hot malasadas, traditional or fancy, try **Home Maid Bakery,** 1005 Lower Main St.,808/244-7015.

Groceries

For general grocery shopping, go to **Ooka Super Market,** 1870 Main St., where you'll find not only the usual groceries but also a deli section and many ethnic foods. For decades, this has been Wailuku's major food supplier. A new addition, **Sack 'N Save,** is located in the Wailuku Town Center on the north edge of town along Waiehu Beach Road. In Happy Valley, you can get a few basic necessities, including sashimi and plate lunches to go, at the tiny **Takamiya Market** along Market Street from 6 A.M.–5 P.M.

You can pick up fresh produce at the tiny **Wailuku Town Open Market,** held along Market Street near Sig Zane Design and open Monday–Friday 7 A.M.–7 P.M.

ENTERTAINMENT

Wailuku is not a hotbed for entertainment by any stretch of the imagination, yet there are a few items worthy of note. Live theater is offered by **Maui Onstage,** 68 N. Market St., 808/242-6969, in the remodeled 'Iao Theater building. Major productions occur several times a year, while traveling stage performances and other events take the stage periodically. Plays are generally performed in the evening, with some matinee shows on the weekends. Tickets run $15 adult, $13 seniors and students.

The only bar in town and about the only place for live entertainment is **Ramon's** restaurant on Vineyard Street.

SHOPPING

Most shopping in this area is done in Kahului at the big malls, but for an interesting diversion, some people shop closer to home. Wailuku's attic closets used to overflow with numerous discovery shops all in a row hung like promnight tuxedos, limp with old memories, and each with its own style. Today, most of these specialty shops are gone, but the few that hang on are all along Market Street. Here you'll find **Brown-Kobayashi,** 808/242-0804, for Asian art and furniture; **Bird of Paradise,** 808/242-7699, which handles blue willow china, vintage bottles, Depression and carnival glass, license plates from around the world, and even a smattering of antique furniture; and **Gottling, Ltd.,** 808/244-7779, specializing in Oriental art and furnishings. If you're still on a roll, other shops are **Ali'i Antiques,** 808/243-9497; **Old Daze Antiques and Collectibles,** 808/249-0014; and **Sheila's Junktique,** 808/244-9610.

Lucky for those who live or visit here, **Sig Zane Designs,** 808/249-8997, a well-known women's apparel and fabric design store from Hilo, has opened a shop here, and a few steps up Market Street, **Gallery Ha,** 808/244-3993, has opened it doors. **Paperbacks Plus,** 1977 Main St., 808/242-7135, is the only book purveyor in town, dealing mostly in used titles and some new Hawaiiana.

The best place in Wailuku to pick up a high-quality gift to take home is at the **Bailey House Museum gift shop.** Here you'll find books, CDs, and a wide assortment of crafts made by island artists with native materials at a decent price.

SERVICES

For **banking,** there's a Bank of Hawaii branch office at 2105 Main, 808/871-8200, and an American Savings Bank, 808/244-9148, at 69 N. Market Street. The state office building, county office building, federal building, old courthouse, and library are all situated along High Street in the center of town, and the **post office** is out in the Mill Yard near the **Maui Visitors Bureau** office, 808/244-3530, both on Wili Pa Loop Road.

Camping permits for county parks are available at the War Memorial Gym, 808/270-7389, Monday–Friday 8 A.M.–4 P.M. They cost $3 adults, $.50 children, per person per night. State park permits can be obtained from the State Building, 54 S. High St., Rm. 101, Wailuku, HI 96793, 808/984-8109, weekdays 8 A.M.–4:15 P.M. only.

Kahakuloa: West Maui's Back Side

To get around to the back side of West Maui you can head north from Ka'anapali or north from Wailuku. A few short years ago, this road was in rugged shape, closed to all but local traffic, and forbidden to rental cars by their companies. It's still narrow and very windy in part—there are still a few short one-lane sections near the Wailuku end—but now it's paved all the way. What once took three hours might now take only an hour. Because many people drive it these days, there is more traffic, so it still has hazards.

Additionally, loose rock tumbles onto the roadway from embankments (particularly after rainfalls), so be mindful and aware of debris. Drive slowly, carefully, and defensively. In large part, the road is the journey.

Sights

Route 340, or Kahekili Highway, runs north from Kahului to Kahakuloa Bay and beyond, where it changes number to Route 30 not too much before reaching Kapalua. Before you start this 18-mile stretch, make sure you have adequate gas and water. From Wailuku, head north on Market Street through the area called Happy Valley. This road continues out of town as Route 330. Before it meets Route 340, you'll see an overgrown macadamia nut farm on the upland side of the road, a failed attempt at diversifying the agricultural base of this region.

Just north of the bridge over 'Iao Stream along Route 340 will be Kuhio Place on your left. Turn here and then again onto Hea Place to **Haleki'i and Pihana Heiau State Monument,** which sits on a bluff overlooking lower 'Iao Stream. This was a place of great prominence during the centuries that Maui kings called Wailuku home and when a large population filled the surrounding land cultivating it in taro. Although uninspiring, this 10-acre site is historical and totally unvisited. Originally constructed around 1240 for other reasons, Haleki'i became a house of images. Pihana was made a temple of war and rededicated to the war god Ku by Kahekili, Maui's last king. Legend says that the last human sacrifice on Maui was performed here for Kamehameha I as a demonstration of his control over the island. These *heiau* are on the National Register of Historic Places.

A short way north and down Lower Waiehu Road toward the water—a Shoreline Access sign will point the way—you'll reach **Waiehu Beach County Park.** This strip of sand meets the southern end of the Waiehu Golf Course and is a decent place for sunbathing, as well as swimming when the water is calm. Surfers sometimes come for

WEST MAUI'S BACK SIDE

CENTRAL MAUI

© SANDRA E. BISIGNANI TRUST AND AVALON TRAVEL PUBLISHING, INC.

the waves, but people mostly come to use the athletic fields.

Back on Route 340 you come shortly to the small town of **Waiheʻe** (Slippery Water), where you'll find the reconstructed **Waiheʻe Protestant Church,** established in 1828 as one of the first churches on the island, standing next to the Waiheʻe School. Turn at the town Park (softball on Saturday) and follow the sign pointing you to **Waiehu Municipal Golf Course;** call 808/243-7400 for tee times. Mostly local people golf here; it's full of kids and families on the weekend. The fairways, strung along the sea, are beautiful to play. Waiehu Inn Restaurant is an adequate little eatery at the golf course.

Like its sister on the south edge of the golf course, **Waiheʻe Beach County Park** is tucked into its northern corner. It too is secluded and frequented mostly by local people. Some come here to picnic or snorkel and spear fish inside the reef. The reef is quite a ways out and the bottom is rocky, but the shore is sandy. Although both parks are for day use only, they'd probably be okay for an unofficial overnight stay. To reach this park, go left and follow the fence just before the golf course parking lot.

At mile marker 5, the pavement narrows and begins to climb the hillside. The road hugs the coastline and gains elevation quickly; the undisturbed valleys are resplendent. Here are several one-lane sections. Slow down and use the pulloffs if you want to take pictures of the wild coastline below or Haleakala in the distance. Soon you pass Maluhia Road, the access road to a Boy Scout camp and the Waiheʻe Ridge trail, which leads up into the West Maui Mountains. Across from the entrance to Maluhia Road is Mendes Ranch, and beyond that—oddly enough—is the new upper-end residential subdivision of Maluhia Country Ranches. With the paving of this coastal road, several commercial establishments have been opened along this back route. One of these is **Aina Anuhea Tropical Gardens,** a private garden between mile markers 8 and 9. While not spectacular, this garden is fine for a short stop. Walkways take you through the diminutive gardens, from where you're able to see not only the bay below but also Haleakala off in the

distance. Smitty will greet you as you come up the driveway, collect your $5 entrance fee, and set you on the right path.

In a few miles you skirt a tall headland—easily seen from Paʻia and points along the north shore—and pass the **Kaukini Gallery,** 808/244-3371, probably the most remote gallery on the island. A place of arts, crafts, and gifts, the gallery displays the work of more than four dozen island artists. From here the road rounds the shoulder and drops down to the fishing village of **Kahakuloa** (Tall Lord), with its dozen weatherworn houses and two tiny churches. St. Francis Xavier Mission, above the village on the east side of the stream, was founded in 1846. Being on the north coast, the turbulent waters constantly wash the beach of round black stones. Although a tiny community (you are greeted with Aloha, Welcome, and Farewell all on one sign), each house is well kept with pride, and a new house or two have popped up in the last decade or so. To cater to the increased through traffic, several roadside stands have popped up selling fruit, shave ice, banana bread, and other delicacies. Overlooking Kahakuloa on the western side is a pullout and promontory where you have good views over the rugged coast and back at the village. Here the road is at its absolute narrowest. The valley is very steep-sided and beautiful. Supposedly, great Maui himself loved this area.

A mile or so past Kahakuloa and near mile marker 15, you come to **Pohaku Kani,** the bell stone. It's about six feet tall and the same in diameter, and it sits directly on the inland edge of the road. The seascapes along this stretch are tremendous. The surf pounds along the coast below and sends spumes skyward, roaring through a natural blowhole. **Nakalele blowhole** sits near the Nakalele Lighthouse coast guard beacon site. Park at the entrance road to the lighthouse at mile marker 38 or about one-half mile to the east of there. From the road, it's a short walk down to the water-a good spot for the family. Enjoy the spume close-up, but be aware that it's a rough coastline with occasional heavy surf, churning seas, and lots of wind and spray. After the bell stone, the road becomes wider again but still curvy, the mileage markers start over and reduce in number, and you're soon at D. T. Fleming Beach Park. Civilization comes again too quickly.

Hiking Trails

The **Waiheʻe Valley Trail** runs into this picturesque narrow valley. North of the town of Waiheʻe, turn left onto Waiheʻe Valley Road, just before mile marker 5 and the Waiheʻe Stream bridge. Proceed to the village and park in the pulloff near the middle of this community. Leave a couple of bucks in the collection box! Walk right at the T-intersection and go to a gate. Inside the gate, the trail first follows the maintenance road that skirts the stream, with the flume on the opposite bank. This level track then takes you over two suspension footbridges, through a bamboo forest, and under huge banyan trees until you reach the head dam, where you can leap off a rope swing into the pool. Count on at least two hours, more if you intend to swim in the pool.

Waiheʻe Ridge Trail is a 2.5-mile trek leading up Kanoa Ridge on the windward slope of the West Maui Mountains. Follow Route 340 around the back side to Maluhia Road at the Mendes Ranch. Turn inland here and follow the road up about one mile—almost to the Boy Scout camp—where there's a parking area, trail sign, and vehicular gate. Walk through the adjacent trail gate, go *steeply* up the hill on the cement track, cross the pasture, and head for the trees and another gate where the trail actually begins. This trail starts innocently enough but does become a switchback farther up and crosses some areas that are boggy during the rains. The trail rises swiftly to over 2,560 feet. Along the way, views into Waiheʻe and Makamakaʻole valleys are spectacular, and you even

on the swinging bridge trail

get distance views of Wailuku, the isthmus, and Haleakala. Maintained and marked by mileage markers, the trail continues on to Lanilili summit, where on clear days you can see the northern slope of the mountain. This trail takes energy; count on three hours for the more than five miles there and back. If you think you'll be on the trail after 5:30 P.M. or so, park your car down near the highway at the entrance to Maluhia Road because the gate across this road closes at 6 P.M.; for those wanting an early start, it opens at 7 A.M.

ROBERT NILSEN

M

CENTRAL MAUI

West Maui

Lahaina

Lahaina (Merciless Sun) is and always has been the premier town on Maui. It's the most energized town on the island as well, and you can feel it from the first moment you walk down Front Street. Maui's famed warrior-king Kahekili lived here and ruled until Kamehameha, with the help of newfound cannon power, subdued Kahekili's son in 'Iao Valley at the turn of the 19th century. When Kamehameha I consolidated the island kingdom, he chose Lahaina as his seat of power. It served as such until Kamehameha III moved to Honolulu in the mid-1840s. Lahaina is where the modern world of the West and the old world of Hawaii collided, for better or worse. The *ali'i* of Hawaii loved to be entertained here; the royal surf spot, mentioned numerous times as an area of revelry in old missionary diaries, is just south of the Small Boat Harbor. Kamehameha I built in Lahaina the islands' first Western structure in 1801, known as the Brick Palace; the site, near the harbor entrance, still remains. Queens Ke'opuolani and Ka'ahumanu, the two most powerful wives of the great Kamehameha's harem of more than 20, were local Maui women who remained after their husband's death and helped to usher in the new order.

Lahaina Harbor

ROBERT NILSEN

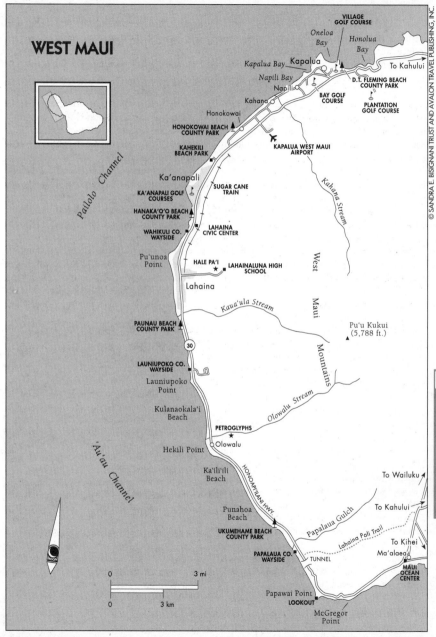

WEST MAUI

Pailolo Channel

'Au'au Channel

VILLAGE GOLF COURSE

Oneloa Bay

Honolua Bay

To Kahului

Kapalua Bay · Kapalua

Napili Bay

D.T. FLEMING BEACH COUNTY PARK

Napili

BAY GOLF COURSE

Kahana

PLANTATION GOLF COURSE

Honokowai

HONOKOWAI BEACH COUNTY PARK

KAHEKILI BEACH PARK

KAPALUA WEST MAUI AIRPORT

Ka'anapali

KA'ANAPALI GOLF COURSES

SUGAR CANE TRAIN

HANAKA'O'O BEACH COUNTY PARK

WAHIKULI CO. WAYSIDE

LAHAINA CIVIC CENTER

Kahana Stream

Pu'unoa Point

HALE PA'I

LAHAINALUNA HIGH SCHOOL

West Maui Mountains

Lahaina

Kaua'ula Stream

PAUNAU BEACH COUNTY PARK

30

Pu'u Kukui (5,788 ft.)

LAUNIUPOKO CO. WAYSIDE

Launiupoko Point

Olowalu Stream

Kulanaokala'i Beach

PETROGLYPHS

Olowalu

Hekili Point

To Wailuku

Ka'ili'ili Beach

Honoapiilani Hwy

To Kahului

Punahoa Beach

UKUMEHAME BEACH COUNTY PARK

Papalaua Gulch

Lahaina Pali Trail

To Kihei

PAPALAUA CO. WAYSIDE

Ma'alaea

TUNNEL

MAUI OCEAN CENTER

0   3 mi

0   3 km

Papawai Point
LOOKOUT

McGregor Point

© SANDRA E. BISIGNANI TRUST AND AVALON TRAVEL PUBLISHING, INC.

WEST MAUI

The whalers came preying for "sperms and humpbacks" in 1819 and set old Lahaina Town a-reelin'. Island girls, naked and willing, swam out to meet the ships, trading their favors for baubles from the modern world. Grog shops flourished, and drunken sailors owned the debauched town. The missionaries, invited by Queen Ke'opuolani, came praying for souls in 1823. Led by the Reverends Stuart and Richards, they tried to harpoon moral chaos. In short order, there was a curfew, a *kapu* placed on the ships by wise but ineffectual old Governor Hoapili, and a jail and a fort to discourage the strong-arm tactics of captains and unruly seamen. The pagan Hawaiians transformed like willing children to the new order, but the Christian sailors damned the meddling missionaries. They even whistled a few cannonballs into the Lahaina homestead yard of the Reverend Richards, hoping to send him speedily to his eternal reward. Time, a new breed of sailor, and the slow death of the whaling industry eased the tension.

Meanwhile, the missionaries built the first school and printing press west of the Rockies at Lahainaluna in the mountains just above the town, along with downtown's Waine'e Church, the first stone church on the island. Lahaina's glory days slipped by and it became a sleepy "sugar town" dominated by the Pioneer Sugar Mill, which operated from 1860–1996. In 1901, the Pioneer Inn was built to accommodate interisland ferry passengers, but few *came* to Lahaina. In the 1960s, Amfac Inc. had a brilliant idea. It turned Ka'anapali, a magnificent stretch of beach just west, into one of the most beautifully planned and executed resorts in the world. The Pioneer Sugar Mill had long used the area as a refuse heap, but now the ugly duckling became a swan, and Lahaina flushed with new life. With superb farsightedness, the Lahaina Restoration Foundation was begun in those years and almost the entire town was made a national historical landmark. Lahaina, subdued but never tamed, throbs with its special energy once again.

Parking

Traffic congestion is a problem that needs to be addressed. It's best to be parked and settled 4:30–5:30 P.M., when traffic is heaviest. There are still no traffic lights on Front Street, but a spree of construction in the last several years has increased the number of lights on the highway from two to more than half a dozen. The other thing to know to make your visit carefree is where to stash your car. The two lots along Dickenson Street, the one at Dickenson Square, and the lot directly to its south are centrally located and charge a reasonable daily rate, as do the two lots along Lahainaluna Road and the small lots behind the Baldwin Home and the Lahaina Inn. A little more expensive but very central are the two lots behind Burger King near the Banyan Tree. These private lots charge $5–10 per day; exact fee is usually required because few lots have attendants on duty. Often, you'll find a reduced overnight fee or an all-day special. Also close is a smallish free public parking lot along Luakini Street, but it usually fills early in the day. A bit more distant is the larger free public parking lot at the corner of Front and Prison streets, but it has a three-hour limit. The lots at Malu'ulu O Lele and Kamehameha Iki parks are

DAVID MALO: LAHAINALUNA SCHOLAR

Every year, in April, the Lahainaluna High School celebrates the anniversary of the death of one of its most famous students, David Malo. Educated here as an adult in the 1830s, he stayed on to become a teacher. His house was down in town across the street from the Hale Pa'i Prison. Considered Hawaii's first native scholar, he authored the definitive *Hawaiian Antiquities,* an early history of the Hawaiian islands. His final wish was to be buried "high above the tide of foreign invasion," and his grave is close to the giant "L" atop Mount Ball, behind Lahainaluna. At graduation, students from the school follow a decades-old tradition of surrounding the "L" with lighted tiki torches, making quite a sight from town. On the way back down to town, you have an impressive panorama of former cane fields, the port, Lahaina Roads, and Lana'i, and you realize that Lahaina is not a big place, as you can see it all easily from end to end.

THE LAHAINA RESTORATION FOUNDATION

Begun in 1961 by Jim Luckey, a historian who knows a great deal about Lahaina and the whaling era, the **Lahaina Restoration Foundation,** 808/661-3262, is now headed by Keoki Freeland, an old Maui resident and grandson of the builder of the Pioneer Inn. Its office is the upstairs of the Baldwin Home. The main purpose of the foundation is to preserve the flavor and authenticity of Lahaina without stifling progress—especially tourism. The foundation is privately funded and has managed to purchase or lease many of the important historical sites in Lahaina for their continued maintenance. It owns the Baldwin Home, Masters' Reading Room, and the Seaman's Hospital, leases the Wo Hing Temple and the old Courthouse, and maintains Hale Pa'i, Hale Aloha, and the old prison. The people on the board of directors come from all socioeconomic backgrounds. You don't get on the board by how much money you give but by how much effort and time you are willing to invest in the foundation; the members are extremely dedicated. Merchants approach the foundation with new ideas for business and ask how they can best comply with the building codes. The townspeople know that their future is best served if they preserve the feeling of old Lahaina rather than rush headlong into frenzied growth. The historic village of Williamsburg, Virginia, is sometimes cited as Lahaina's model, except that Lahaina wishes to remain a "real" living, working town.

also free and for use by park users only, but people do park and walk into town from there. An underground lot below the 505 Front Street Mall is safe but the most expensive with fees up to $20 per day. Aside from these public parking lots, all shopping centers in town have parking: Some are free with time limits, some charge beyond a certain time, and some offer validated parking. All are reasonably priced. Street parking has a three-hour limit. Watch your time as the "meter patrol" is very efficient, and your car may wind up in the pound if you're not careful! Parking fines are $35, and it will cost more than $100 if your car is towed. Those staying in Ka'anapali should leave cars behind and take the Holo Ka'a shuttle for the day or hop on the Sugar Cane Train.

SIGHTS

In short, strolling around Lahaina offers the best of both worlds. It's busy, but it's bite-size. It's engrossing enough, but you can see it in half a day. The main attractions are mainly downtown within a few blocks of each other. Lahaina technically stretches, long and narrow, along the coast for about four miles, but you may only be interested in the central core, a mere mile or so. All along Front Street, the main drag, and the side streets running off it are innumerable shops, restaurants, and hideaways where you can browse, recoup your energy, or just wistfully watch the sun set. Go slowly and savor, and you'll feel the dynamism of Lahaina past and present all around you. Enjoy!

The Banyan Tree

The best place to start your tour of Lahaina is at this magnificent tree at the corner of Hotel and Front streets. You can't miss it because it spreads its shading boughs over almost an entire acre. It is the largest banyan in the state. Use the benches to sit and reconnoiter while the sun, for which Lahaina is infamous, is kept at bay. Children love it, and it seems to bring out the Tarzan in everyone. Old-timers sit here chatting, and on Saturdays and Sundays, various artists gather here to display and sell their artwork under the tree's broad branches. Every Christmas, the tree is covered in lights, and numerous other festivities are held in its shade. This banyan was planted in April 1873 by Sheriff Bill Smith in commemoration of the Congregationalist Missions' golden anniversary. One hundred years later, a ceremony was held here and more than 500 people were accommodated under this natural canopy. Symbolic as it is, this banyan is truly the heart of Lahaina.

Courthouse

Behind the banyan tree on Wharf Street is the old county Courthouse. Built in 1859 from coral blocks recycled from Kamehameha III's ill-fated

WEST MAUI

DOWNTOWN LAHAINA

To Lahainaluna

LAHAINALUNA RD.

KUHUA ST.

To Ka'anapali

THE BAKERY

TRAIN DEPOT

HONOAPI'ILANI HWY.

30

PIZZA HUT

FIRST HAWAIIAN BANK

ST.

GAS

ANCHOR SQUARE

PIONEER SUGAR MILL

GAS

DOWN TO EARTH NATURAL FOODS

ERIK'S SEAFOOD AND SUSHI

LAHAINA SQUARE

GAS

TRILOGY

SEAMEN'S CEMETERY

MARIA LANAKILA CHURCH

DICKENSON ST.

DICKENSON SQUARE

P

P

WAINE'E ST.

PATEY'S PLACE

PLANTATION INN

BJ'S CHICAGO PIZZERIA

PACIFIC WHALE FOUNDATION

KAISER PERMANENTE CLINIC

HILO HATTIE

AM. SAVINGS BANK

PAPALAUA

BANK OF HAWAII

MAUI THEATRE

WO HING TEMPLE

FOX CAMERA

P

LAHAINA INN

LAHAINA MARKETPLACE

P

POST OFFICE

LONGHI'S

LAHAINA CENTER

OLD LAHAINA CENTER

KIMO'S

MOOSE McGILLYCUDDY'S

CHEESEBURGER IN PARADISE

THE LAHAINA FISH COMPANY

SEAWALL

BAKER ST.

KENUI ST.

SEAMEN'S HOSPITAL

FRONT ST.

To Ka'anapali

LAHAINA JODO MISSION

MOON

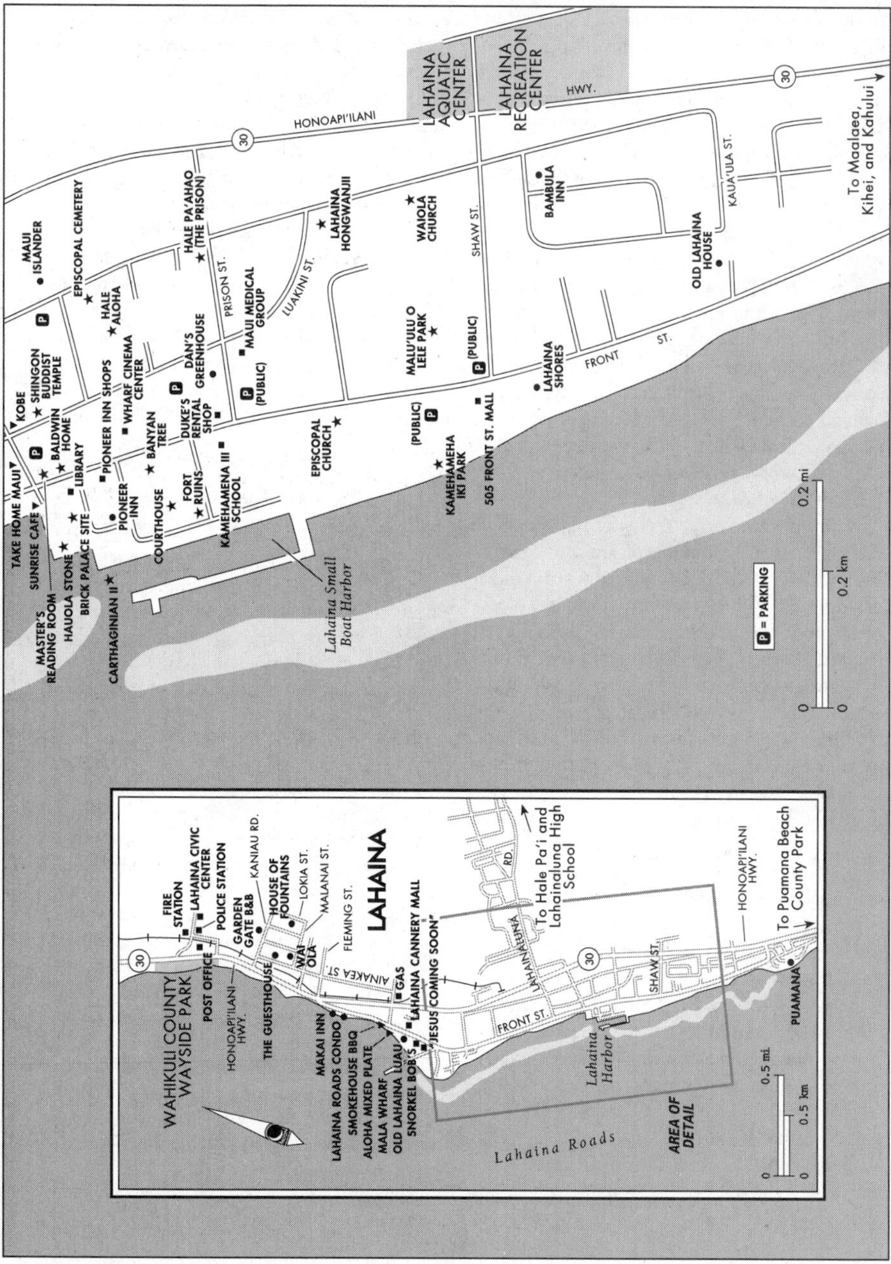

LAHAINA

Map labels (top detail map):

- HONOAPI'ILANI
- 30
- LAHAINA AQUATIC CENTER
- LAHAINA RECREATION CENTER
- HWY.
- 30
- To Maalaea, Kihei, and Kahului
- MAUI ISLANDER
- EPISCOPAL CEMETERY
- HALE PA'AHAO (THE PRISON)
- LAHAINA HONGWANJI
- WAIOLA CHURCH
- SHAW ST.
- BAMBULA INN
- KAUA'ULA ST.
- OLD LAHAINA HOUSE
- KOBE
- SHINGON BUDDHIST TEMPLE
- BALDWIN HOME
- TAKE HOME MAUI
- HALE ALOHA
- PRISON ST.
- DAN'S GREENHOUSE
- LUAKINI ST.
- MAUI MEDICAL GROUP
- P (PUBLIC)
- MALU'ULU O LELE PARK
- LAHAINA SHORES
- FRONT ST.
- P
- LIBRARY
- PIONEER INN SHOPS
- WHARF CINEMA CENTER
- P
- SUNRISE CAFE
- BRICK PALACE SITE
- HAUOLA STONE
- PIONEER INN
- BANYAN TREE
- DUKE'S RENTAL SHOP
- COURTHOUSE
- FORT RUINS
- KAMEHAMEHA III SCHOOL
- MASTER'S READING ROOM
- CARTHAGINIAN II
- EPISCOPAL CHURCH
- (PUBLIC) P
- KAMEHAMEHA IKI PARK
- 505 FRONT ST. MALL
- Lahaina Small Boat Harbor
- P = PARKING
- 0.2 mi
- 0.2 km

Map labels (inset map):

- WAHIKULI COUNTY WAYSIDE PARK
- 30
- FIRE STATION
- LAHAINA CIVIC CENTER
- POLICE STATION
- POST OFFICE
- HONOAPI'ILANI HWY.
- GARDEN GATE B&B
- KANIAU RD.
- THE GUESTHOUSE
- HOUSE OF FOUNTAINS
- LOKIA ST.
- MALANAI ST.
- FLEMING ST.
- WAI OLA
- LAHAINA
- MAKAI INN
- LAHAINA ROADS CONDO
- SMOKEHOUSE BBQ
- ALOHA MIXED PLATE
- MALA WHARF
- OLD LAHAINA LUAU
- SNORKEL BOB'S
- GAS
- LAHAINA CANNERY MALL
- "JESUS COMING SOON"
- AINAKEA ST.
- LAHAINALUNA
- FRONT ST.
- To Hale Pa'i and Lahainaluna High School
- RD.
- HONOAPI'ILANI HWY.
- SHAW ST.
- To Puamana Beach County Park
- Lahaina Harbor
- PUAMANA
- AREA OF DETAIL
- Lahaina Roads
- 0.5 mi
- 0.5 km

WEST MAUI

palace, Hale Piula, it also served as governor's office, post office, customs office, and the police station, complete with a jail in the basement. The jail is now home to the Lahaina Arts Society's **Old Jail Gallery,** where paintings and artifacts are kept behind bars, waiting for patrons to liberate them. The society has its main **Banyan Tree Gallery** on the first floor. Since its renovation in 1998, another project of the Lahaina Restoration Foundation, the **Lahaina Visitor Center,** 808/667-9193, has also occupied a room on the main floor, and here anyone can come for all sorts of tourist information and brochures about the town. Located in the old courtroom on the second floor, a small museum displays historical and cultural objects pertaining to the area; open daily from 9 A.M.–5 P.M. with free entrance. Public bathrooms are located upstairs; use either the stairway or the elevator.

Adjacent is the **Fort,** built in the 1830s to show the sailors that they couldn't run amok in Lahaina. Even with its 20-foot-high walls, it was not much of a deterrent. When it was torn down, the blocks were hauled over to Prison Street to build the real jail, Hale Pa'ahao. A corner battlement of the fort was restored, but that's it, because restoring the entire structure would mean mutilating the banyan. The cannons, from a military vessel sunk in Honolulu harbor a few years prior and now set along the wharf in front of the courthouse, are in approximately the location that they had been when they were fixtures on the fort wall.

Just south of the fort was one of the several canals that ran through Lahaina. At one point, this canal was widened to land small boats coming in from the ships anchored offshore. Just beyond it, in what is now part of the school yard, was the Government Market. A notorious place, all kinds of commodities, manufactured and human, were sold here during the whaling days, and it was given the apt name of "Rotten Row."

Small Boat Harbor

Walking along the harbor stimulates the imagination and the senses. The boats waiting at anchor sway in confused syncopation. Hawser ropes groan and there's a feeling of anticipation and adventure in the air. Here you can board for all kinds

of seagoing excursions. In the days of whaling there was no harbor; the boats tied up one to the other offshore in the "roads," at times forming an impromptu floating bridge. The whalers came ashore in their chase boats; with the winds always up, departure could be made at a moment's notice. The activity here is still dominated by the sea.

Although whaling has long since ceased to be, and commercial fishing is not really a player either, the Lahaina Roads still plays host to some big ships. More than four dozen modern cruise ships make a stop annually at Lahaina so their fun-seeking voyagers can taste a bit of what West Maui has to offer. Without a large pier, all ships park out in the deep water and, as in the days of old, passengers are tendered from ship to shore in

THE CARTHAGINIAN II

The masts and square rigging of this ship were a replica of the enterprising freighters that braved the Pacific some two hundred years ago. Everyone was drawn to it. Until its demise in 2003, it was the only truly square-rigged ship left afloat on the seas. It replaced the *Carthaginian I* after that ship went aground in 1972 while being hauled to Honolulu for repairs. The Lahaina Restoration Foundation found the steel-hulled ship that became the *Carthaginian II* in Denmark; built in Germany in 1920 as a two-masted schooner, it tramped around the Baltic under converted diesel power. The foundation had it sailed 12,000 miles to Lahaina, where it underwent extensive conversion until it became the beautiful replica of those older vessels. The *Carthaginian II* was a floating museum dedicated to whaling and to whales. On deck, it was easy to check out the rigging, masts, and steering platform, and try to imagine sailing on a ship of this size for months around Cape Horn and then up and across the broad Pacific to Hawaii. Below decks was a museum containing artifacts and implements from the whaling days. After years of good use, this trusty old ship began to give way and in its later years began to sink at its moorings. In 2003, the ship was towed out to sea and sunk as a diving site, so its usefulness lives on in another capacity.

The Pioneer Inn overlooks Lahaina Harbor as it has done for a century.

smaller boats. These cruise ships tend to come in the winter, when the weather is warm and the waters of Alaska are just too cold.

Just as today, the old commercial and whaling boats used a light to guide their way to port. At the harbor's mouth is the site of Lahaina's first lighthouse. In 1840, before any were built along what would later be the West Coast of the United States, King Kamehameha III ordered a lighthouse to be constructed here. The original wooden nine-foot structure was rebuilt to 26 feet in 1869, and the present concrete structure was installed in 1916. As might be expected, a whale oil lamp was first used for light, later to be supplanted by electricity.

The Brick Palace Site

A rude structure was commissioned by Kamehameha I in 1801 and slapped together by two forgotten Australian ex-convicts. It was the first Western structure in Hawaii, but unfortunately the substandard materials have all disintegrated or been moved and only the site remains, marked by a slab in front of the library. Kamehameha never lived in it, but it was occupied and used as a

storehouse until the 1850s. Inland from this site was a taro patch (now occupied by the library), said to have been tended by King Kamehameha I and/or Kamehameha III as an inspiration of labor to his subjects. Just to the right of the Brick Palace site, as you face the harbor, is **Hauola Stone.** Formed like a chair, it was believed by the Hawaiians to have curative powers if you sat on it and let the ocean bathe you. One legend says it was a woman who was turned to stone and saved by the gods as she tried to escape those who were pursuing her. Best view is at low tide.

Pioneer Inn

This vintage inn, situated at the corner of Hotel and Wharf streets, is just exactly where it belongs. Stand on its veranda and gaze out at the banyan tree and harbor. Presto . . . it's magic time! You'll see. It was even a favorite spot for actors like Errol Flynn and later Spencer Tracy when he was in Lahaina filming *Devil at Four O'-clock.* The green and white inn was built in 1901 to accommodate interisland ferry passengers, but its style seems much older. If ironwork had been used on the veranda, you'd think you were in

ROBERT NILSEN

New Orleans. A new and larger wing of rooms and shops was built behind it in 1965 and the two form a courtyard. Make sure to read the hilarious rules governing behavior that are posted in the main lobby, and give your regards to the old salt who's greeted guests at the front door for years. Although the second-floor rooms of the old section are no longer used, the inn still retains character and atmosphere despite its recent major renovation.

Baldwin Home

One of the best attractions in Lahaina is the Baldwin Home, on the corner of Front and Dickenson streets. It was occupied by Doctor/Reverend Dwight Baldwin, his wife Charlotte, and their eight children, two of whom died in infancy. He was a trained teacher, as well as the first doctor/dentist in Hawaii. The building also served from the 1830s to 1868 as a dispensary, meeting room, and boarding home for anyone in need. The two-foot-thick walls are of cut lava, and the mortar was made of crushed coral over which plaster was applied. Originally, the downstairs had four rooms; only later were the side rooms and upstairs added. The men slept downstairs in the boys room; upstairs were rooms for the girls. When needed, the upstairs was used by guests, boarders, or the sick and could be occupied by several dozen at one time. As you enter, notice how low the doorway is and that the doors inside are "Christian doors"—with a cross forming the upper panels and an open Bible at the bottom. The Steinway piano that dominates the entrance was built in 1859. In the bedroom to the right, along with all of the period furniture, is a wooden commode. Also notice the lack of closets; all items were kept in chests. Most of the period furniture and other items were not owned or used by the Baldwins but are representative of the era.

The doctor's fees are posted and are hilarious. Payment was by "size" of sickness: very big $50, diagnosis $3, refusal to pay $10! The Reverend Baldwin was 32 when he arrived in Hawaii from New England, and his wife was 25. She was supposedly sickly, and he had heart trouble, so they moved to Honolulu in 1868 to receive better health care. The home

Wo Hing Temple

ROBERT NILSEN

became a community center, housing the library and meeting rooms. Today, the Baldwin Home is a showcase museum of the Lahaina Restoration Foundation. It's open daily 10 A.M.–4 P.M., admission $3 adults, $2 seniors, $5 couples or families.

The oldest coral-block house in Hawaii was built in 1827 for Rev. William Richards and his family who had come to serve in Lahaina three years earlier. Now gone, the house occupied the site of Campbell Park next door to the Baldwin Home.

Masters' Reading Room

Originally a missionaries' storeroom, the uniquely constructed coral-stone Masters' Reading Room was converted to an officers' club in 1834. It was restored to original condition in 1970, becoming the office of the Lahaina Restoration Foundation. For a short while in the 1990s, it was used as a native Hawaiian craft shop, but it is not used presently. Located next door to the Baldwin Home, these two venerable buildings constitute the oldest standing Western structures on Maui.

Wo Hing Temple

This structure on Front Street is a Lahaina Restoration Foundation reconstruction. Built in 1912 as a social and religious hall for Chinese workers and residents in the area, it's perhaps the best example of such a structure in the state and has been placed on the National Register of Historic Places. Leased from the Chee Kung Tong Chinese fraternal society, it was opened to the public in 1984 and shows the Chinese influence in Lahaina. Downstairs are displays, upstairs is the altar. In the cookhouse next door, you can see film clips of Hawaii taken by the Edison Company in 1899 and 1906. It's open daily 10 A.M.–4 P.M.; admission is by donation ($1).

Hale Pa'ahao

This is Lahaina's old prison, located midblock on Prison Street, and its name literally means "Stuck-in-Irons House." It was constructed by prisoners in 1852 from blocks of stone salvaged from the old defunct Fort. It had a catwalk for an armed guard and cells complete with shackles for hardened criminals, but most were drunks who yahooed around town on the Sabbath, wildly spurring their horses. The cells were rebuilt in 1959, the gatehouse in 1988, and the structure is maintained by the Lahaina Restoration Foundation. The cells, curiously, are made of wood, which shows that the inmates weren't that interested in busting out. Have a look at the prison rules posted on the gatehouse wall on your way in. It's open daily; admission is free but donations are accepted.

Kamehameha Iki Park

Across the street from Malu'ulu O Lele Park was the site of Hale Piula (Iron-roof House), a two-story royal stone palace built in the late 1830s for King Kamehameha III. Never finished, its stones were later used to construct the old courthouse

MALU'ULU O LELE

This park, a nondescript area at the corner of Shaw and Front, holding tennis and basketball courts, a baseball field, and a parking lot, was at one time the most important spot in Lahaina— "The Breadfruit Shelter of Lele." ("Lele" was the former name of Lahaina.) Here was a small pond with a diminutive island in the center. The 17-acre pond, Mokuhinia, was inhabited by a *mo'o*, a lizard spirit, said to be the deceased daughter of a proud Maui king, and protector of the tiny one-acre island, Moku'ula, home of Maui royalty and the Kamehamehas when they were in residence. King Kamehameha III and his sister Princess Nahi'ena'ena were raised together in Lahaina. They fell in love, but the new ways caused turmoil and tragedy. Instead of marrying and producing royal children, a favored practice only 20 years earlier, they were wrenched apart by the new religion. He, for a time, numbed himself with alcohol, while she died woefully from a broken heart. She was buried here, and for many years Kamehameha III could frequently be found at her grave, quietly sitting and meditating. Shortly afterward, the government of Hawaii moved to Honolulu, and although part of this island remained a royal mausoleum, it slowly fell into disrepair. By the early years of the 20th century, water that fed this pond had been largely diverted for use in irrigating the surrounding sugarcane fields. By 1918, all of the remains of the island were taken away, the pond was filled, and the ground was leveled for use as a park.

Friends of Moku'ula, www.mokuula.com, is a nonprofit organization based in Lahaina, which is trying to bring the historical and cultural significance of Malu'ulu O Lele to the public eye, and eventually to re-create the pond and island to its former physical shape. In association with this organization, the group Maui Nei offers an historical walking tour of Lahaina daily except Sunday for $37 per person. These tours are led by a *kupuna* and stop at more than a dozen sites around town, but there is a focus on Moku'ula and its significance. Tours last about 2 hours and start at 9:30 A.M. from the steps of the old Courthouse. Reservations are required, preferably 24 hours in advance.

that now stands between the banyan tree and harbor. This mostly barren spot is now known as Kamehameha Iki Park. On this site the 62-foot double-hulled sailing canoe, Mo'o Kiha (Sacred Lizard), has been built by the cultural group Hui O Wa'a Kaulua and is considered by them to be "Maui's flagship of Hawaiian culture and goodwill." Future plans for the park include additional canoes, canoe sheds, traditional-style buildings, landscaping, and educational and cultural training programs. Access to one of the two in-town beaches is here.

Waiola Church and Cemetery

The church is not impressive, but its history is. This is the spot where the first Christian services were held in Hawaii, in 1823. A Waine'e stone church was built here in 1832 that could hold 3,000 people, but it was razed by a freak hurricane in 1858. Rebuilt, it survived until 1894, when it was deliberately burned by an angry mob, upset with the abolition of the monarchy in Hawaii and the islands' annexation by the United States. Another church was built, but it too was hit not only by a hurricane but by fire as well. The present structure was built in 1951 and renamed Waiola. In the cemetery is a large part of Maui's history: Buried here are Hawaiian royalty. Lying near each other are Queen Ke'opuolani, her star-crossed daughter, Princess Nahi'ena'ena, and old Governor Hoapili, their royal tomb marked by two large headstones surrounded by a wrought-iron fence. Other graves hold missionaries such as William Richards and many infants and children.

Churches and Temples

You may wish to stop for a moment at Lahaina's other churches and temples dotted around town. They are reminders of the mixture of faiths and peoples that populated this village and added their particular cultural styles. **Holy Innocents Episcopal Church,** built in 1927, is on Front Street, near Kamehameha III school. Known for its "Hawaiian Madonna," its altar and pulpit are resplendent with paintings of fruits, plants, and birds of the islands. Stop by on Sundays when the church is full and hear the sermon preached and hymns sung in Hawaiian. **The Episcopal Cemetery** (from 1863) on Waine'e Street shows the English influence in the islands. Many of the royal family, including King Kalakaua, became Anglicans. This cemetery holds the remains of many early Maui families, and of Walter Murray Gibson, the notorious settler, politician, and firebrand of the 1880s. Just behind is **Hale Aloha,** "House of Love," a small structure built by Maui residents in thanksgiving for being saved from a terrible smallpox epidemic that ravaged O'ahu but largely bypassed Maui in 1853–54. The structure was restored in 1974. Also on Waine'e is **Maria Lanakila Church,** the site of the first Roman Catholic Mass in Lahaina, celebrated in 1841. The present structure dates from 1928. Next to the church's cemetery is the **Seamen's Cemetery,** where many infirm from the ships that came to Lahaina were buried after failing to recover. Most stones have been obliterated by time, and only a few remain. Herman Melville came here to pay his last respects to a cousin buried in this yard. **Hongwanjii Temple** is also on Waine'e, between Prison and Shaw. It's a Buddhist temple with the largest congregation in Lahaina and dates from 1910, although the present structure was raised in 1927. Down Luakini Street is the tall clapboard plantation-era structure **Hokuji Mission Shingon Buddhist Temple.**

The **Lahaina Jodo Mission** is near Mala Wharf on Ala Moana Street. When heading west, you'll leave the main section of town and keep going until you see a sign over a building that reads "Jesus Coming Soon." Turn left toward the beach and you'll immediately spot the three-tiered wooden pagoda. The temple bell welcomes you at the entrance gate, and a giant bronze Buddha sits exposed to the elements on a raised stone platform nearby. The largest outside of Asia, this seated Amita Buddha image was dedicated in 1968 in commemoration of the centennial of the arrival of Japanese workers in Hawaii. The grounds are impeccable and serenely quiet. You may stroll around, and while the buildings are closed to the public, you can climb the steps of the main building to peek into the temple. The entire area is a perfect spot for solitary meditation if you've had enough of frenetic Lahaina. Buddha's birthday is celebrated here every April. The

WEST MAUI

Pu'upiha Cemetery is across the street along the beach. It seems incongruous to see tombstones set in sand.

Mala Wharf

Built in 1922 and once an integral part of Lahaina commerce, the old Mala Wharf now stands decaying at the northern end of town. Next to it is a new boat launch ramp, which is used by local fishermen and some ocean activities companies. There are restrooms here but no other amenities or services.

U.S. Seamen's Hospital

This notorious hospital from 1833 was reconstructed by the Lahaina Restoration Foundation in 1982. Here is where sick seamen were cared for under the auspices of the U.S. State Department. Allegations during the late 1850s claimed that the care here extended past the grave! Unscrupulous medicos supposedly charged the U.S. government for care of seamen who had long since died. The hospital is located at Front and Baker, heading toward Ka'anapali, near the Jodo Mission. The stony exterior of this building has been maintained, but the building now houses a company that produces the visitor channel for television. In the front yard is a 10,000-pound, swivel-end Porter anchor, found off Black Rock in Ka'anapali. This building was supposedly constructed for King Kamehameha III as a place where he could gamble, carouse, and meet his sister Nahi'ena'ena for love trysts away from the puritanical eyes of the missionaries.

Lahainaluna

Head up the mountain behind Lahaina on Lahainaluna Road for approximately two miles. On your left you'll pass the **Pioneer Sugar Mill,** in operation until 1996. Once at Lahainaluna (Above Lahaina) you'll find the oldest school west of the Rockies, opened by the Congregationalist missionaries in 1831. Children from all over the islands, and many from California, came here if their parents could afford to send them away to boarding school. Today, the school is West Maui's public high school, but many children still come here to board. The first students

were given not only a top-notch academic education but a practical one as well. They built the school buildings, and many were also apprentices in the famous Hale Pa'i (Printing House), which turned out Hawaii's first newspaper (1834) and made Lahaina famous as a printing center.

One look at **Hale Pa'i** and you think of New England. It's a white stucco building with blue trim and a wood-shake roof. It houses a replica printing press and copies of documents once printed there. Placed on the National Register of Historic Places in 1976 and restored in 1982, it's open Monday–Friday 10 A.M.–4 P.M. Owned by the state, Hale Pa'i is maintained by the Lahaina Restoration Foundation. If you visit the campus when school is in session, you may go to Hale Pa'i, but if you want to walk around, please sign in at the vice principal's office. Lahainaluna High School is still dedicated to the preservation of Hawaiian culture.

Heading East

Five miles east of Lahaina along the coastal road (Route 30) is the little village of **Olowalu.** Today, little more than the Olowalu General Store and Chez Paul French Restaurant are here. This was the place of the Olowalu Massacre perpetrated by Captain Metcalfe, whose far-reaching results greatly influenced Hawaiian history. Two American seamen, Young and Davis, were connected with this incident, and with their help Kamehameha I subdued all of Hawaii. Only the remains of a pier and a few storage buildings mark the site of a once busy cane harbor and port facilities.

Behind the general store a dirt track leads about one-half mile to **petroglyphs;** make sure you pass a water tower at the start because there are three similar roads here. After about 20 minutes, you'll come to the dilapidated remains of a wooden stairway going up to a rock face on an outcrop. Etched into the flat face of this deep red rock are a small group of human figures and one crab claw sailing canoe, which are believed to be about 300 years old. Some modern graffiti defaces this rock, so it's a little difficult to determine just what's what, but these petroglyphs are still perhaps the most easily accessible of all such rock art on the island.

Near mile marker 14 is good snorkeling, some of the best on the island. Other good snorkeling is done near the highway tunnel, where boats come to anchor just off shore. You will see them from the road as you pass by. Just east of mile marker 11, the old **Lahaina Pali Trail** heads up the rugged dry hillside to cross the ridge and drop down to the isthmus north of Maʻalaea.

If you continue east on Route 30, you'll pass **Papawai** and **McGregor Point,** both noted for their vistas (here you can see South Maui, Molokini, Kahoʻolawe, and Lanaʻi) and as excellent locations to spot whales in season. The road sign merely indicates a scenic lookout.

BEACHES

The best beaches around Lahaina are just west of town in Kaʻanapali, or just east toward Olowalu. A couple of adequate places to spread your towel are right in Lahaina, but they're not quite on a par with the beaches just a few miles away.

In-Town Beaches

One beach stretches east of the harbor starting at Kamehameha Iki Park. It's crowded at times, on occasion used for beach volleyball, and there may be "wash up" at certain times of the year. It's cleaner and quieter at the east end down by Lahaina Shores Hotel. Close to the old royal compound, it was a favorite with the *aliʻi.* There are restrooms, the swimming is fair, it's gentle for kids, and the snorkeling is acceptable past the reef. **Lahaina Beach** is at the west end of town near Mala Wharf. Follow Front to Puʻunoa Place and turn down to the beach. This is a good place for families with tots because the water is clear, safe, and shallow. There is beach access also at the turnaround on Kai Pali Place, the next two streets in toward town.

Puamana Beach County Park

About two miles before you enter Lahaina from the southeast along Route 30, you'll see signs for this beach park, a narrow strip between the road and the sea. The swimming and snorkeling are only fair. The setting, however, is quite nice with picnic tables shaded by ironwood trees. The views

are terrific, and this is a great spot to eat your plate lunch only minutes from town.

Launiupoko Wayside Park

One mile farther southeast, this park has restrooms and showers, but only a small enclosed kiddie beach that's best at high tide when it fills with water. This is more of a picnic area than anything else, although many come to sunbathe on the grass below the coconut trees. Beginning surfers like this spot, and some beginning surf lessons are taught here because the waves are gentle.

South of here you'll see lots of shore fishermen and others out for a quiet afternoon. Although not a designated park, the water is adequate for swimming. Find parking where you can under the trees.

East of Olowalu

Between Olowalu and the highway tunnel are **Ukumehame Beach County Park** and **Papalaua Wayside.** The first is a small park with picnic tables, barbecue pits, toilets, and a tiny lawn for sunbathing; swimming is okay. At mile marker 11, Papalaua Wayside is a mostly unimproved area with lots of ironwood trees for shade, but there are toilets. This long, narrow beach is a favorite of shore fishermen, and camping is allowed with a county permit.

Wahikuli Wayside Park

Along Route 30 between Lahaina and Kaʻanapali, this county park is a favorite with local people and excellent for a picnic. It has a rocky shore and a short, narrow sand beach, but is known as a good swimming spot. The drawback is that it's right on the busy highway. With three parking areas, it's as if the park was split into three units. Tennis courts are located up across the street behind the main Lahaina post office.

Just up the highway, as if connected to this wayside park, is **Hanakaʻoʻo Beach County Park.** This beach, which is actually the south end of Kaʻanapali Beach, runs north past some of the most exclusive hotels on the island. Local canoe clubs put their canoes in the water here, and at certain times of the year paddling events will be held at this beach.

ACCOMMODATIONS

Lodging in Lahaina is not of the usual tourist resort variety that people head to Ka'anapali for. Lahaina tends to be hot and hot to trot, especially at night. You can find good bargains here, and if you want to be in the thick of the action, you're in the right spot.

The hotels in Lahaina are small, more along the lines of inns, as there names suggest. The only true hotel in town is the Pioneer Inn. Both the Lahaina Inn and Plantation Inn are much smaller, more intimate, and each serves a complimentary breakfast to all guests.

$100–150

The **Pioneer Inn,** 658 Wharf St., Lahaina, HI 96761, 808/661-3636 or 800/457-5457, fax 808/667-5708, info@pioneerinnmaui.com, www.pioneerinnmaui.com, is the oldest hotel on Maui still accommodating guests, and it was the only hotel on West Maui until 1963. The inn has undergone more than a facelift since its early days. The semiseedy, old-timey essence has now been spiffed and polished. Now a Best Western hotel, the Pioneer Inn had $500,000 poured into it in 1997–98, but all renovation was done in early-1900s taste. For decades, the Pioneer Inn had absolutely no luxury whatsoever, only a double scoop of atmosphere. It was the place to come if you wanted to save money and be the star of your own movie with the Inn as the stage set. Creaky stairways, threadbare carpets, low-light hallways, shared baths, and questionable merrymakers and occupants—the place had it all. Now the stairway doesn't creak anymore, new carpet has been laid, TVs installed, baths have shiny new tiles and some period fixtures, bedrooms have new furniture, trim and wall coverings renewed, and all rooms have air-conditioning. What does remain the same are the lanai, which, depending on the room, look out over the banyan tree or the hotel courtyard and pool, the posted house rules, and the old salt who still

> *Lahaina tends to be hot and hot to trot, especially at night. You can find good bargains here, and if you want to be in the thick of the action, you're in the right spot.*

stands at the front door. Rooms run $115–180; AAA and Best Western Gold Club discounts are available. Downstairs, food and drink are served daily at the grill and bar, and local live music in always on the menu. Shops occupy the perimeter of the ground floor fronting the banyan tree and Front Street.

Another reborn classic is the **Lahaina Inn,** 127 Lahainaluna Rd., Lahaina, HI 96761, 808/661-0577 or 800/669-3444, fax 808/667-9480, inntown@lahainainn.com, www.lahainainn.com. Completely renovated and remodeled, this one-time dowdy orphan, the old, down-at-the-heels traveler's classic, Lahainaluna Hotel, emerged in 1989 as a lovely lady. Gone from this cockroach paradise are the weather-beaten linoleum floors, bare-bulb musty rooms, and rusted dripping faucets. In their place are antique-stuffed, neo-Victorian, tastefully appointed rooms that transport you back to the late 1800s. Each room is individually decorated, and period pieces include everything from wardrobes to nightstands, rugs, ceramic bowls, mirrors, pictures, lamps, and books. The only deference to modernity are the bathrooms with their new-but-old-style fixtures, the air-conditioning, telephones, and safes—no TV. You can still peer from the balcony of this vintage hotel—each room has a lanai with two hardwood rocking chairs and a table—or observe the masses below from behind heavy drapes and lace curtains. The 12 units include three spacious suites. Rates are $119–129 for the rooms and $169 for parlor suites ($10 less during regular season) and include a complimentary continental breakfast, served every morning from about 7:30 A.M. at the sideboard at the end of the hall. There is a two-night minimum stay only on Fridays and Saturdays; children older than age 15 are welcome. For dinner, you might try downstairs at the renowned David Paul's Lahaina Grill, which offers Inn guests a discount. Free to guests, parking is in the public parking lot directly behind the inn.

WEST MAUI

$150–200

If Agatha Christie were seeking inspiration for *the* perfect setting for one of her mysteries, **The Plantation Inn,** 174 Lahainaluna Rd., Lahaina, HI 96761, 808/667-9225 or 800/433-6815, fax 808/667-9293, info@theplantationinn.com, www.theplantationinn.com, is where she would come. The neo-Victorian building is appointed with posted verandas, hardwood floors, natural wood wainscoting and trim counterpointed by floral wall coverings, bedspreads, and deep-cushioned furniture. Rays of sunlight stray through stained-glass windows and wide double doors. Each uniquely decorated room is comfortable, with four-poster beds and private tiled baths with bold porcelain and brass fixtures; most have sofas. The complete illusion is turn of the 20th century, but the modern amenities of air-conditioning, remote TV and VCR, a fridge, daily maid service, and a soothing spa and pool are included. The back addition brings the total room count to 19. Most of the back 12 units have lanai overlooking the garden courtyard with its pool, spa, and guest pavilion. Prices are a reasonable $157 standard, $177 superior, $197 deluxe, $220–240 suites (some with kitchenette and hot tub), and all include a filling continental breakfast at poolside. Rates are slightly higher during the peak Christmas season, when there is a seven-night minimum, and special packages are available. The Plantation Inn also offers a money-saving option for dinner at Gerard's, the fine French restaurant on the first floor. While now associated with the Ka'anapali Beach Hotel in Ka'anapali, it still maintains great autonomy. Set off the main drag and away from the bustle, it's simply one of the best accommodations that Maui has to offer, and although a relatively new building, it fits well into the 19th-century whaling port ambiance that Lahaina fosters.

Condominiums

Lahaina's few condos are listed from least expensive to most expensive. One is modern, new, and pricey. One is a more affordable renovated older place. The rest fall in between.

Out beyond the Lahaina Roads is **The Makai Inn,** 1415 Front St., 808/662-3200, fax 808/661-9027, info@makaiinn.net, www.makaiinn.net, a former concrete block two-story apartment building turned into rental units. Compact and landscaped in a pleasing manner, this neat and tidy complex is set right on the water where there's nothing blocking you from the sunset. Each of the more than one dozen units is small, yet all have full kitchens and bathrooms, queen or double beds, and a sitting room. While furnished in tropical style, there are no TVs or phones in the units nor daily maid service, but there is a laundry room on premises, a pay phone, and off-street parking. Units run $70–105 per night, $10 extra for each person more than two, and a discount is offered after seven nights. The Makai Inn offers an affordable option for staying in this exciting town.

The **Lahaina Roads,** 1403 Front St., is a condo/apartment at the far north end of town where all units have fully equipped kitchens, TV, and maid service on request. One-bedroom units (for two) run $125; two-bedroom units (for four) are $200. There is a three-night minimum stay and a deposit required to hold your reservation. There is no beach here because it sits right along the seawall, but there is a freshwater pool, and you couldn't have a better view, with every unit facing the ocean. Parking is on ground level below the rooms. Rentals are handled through Klahani Resorts, P.O. Box 11108, Lahaina, HI 96761, 808/667-2712 or 800/669-6284, fax 808/661-5875.

Located a few blocks away from the hubbub, the **Ohana Maui Islander,** 660 Waine'e St., Lahaina, HI 96761, 808/667-9766 or 800/462-6262, fax 808/661-3733, is an adequate hotel offering rooms with kitchenettes, studios, and one- and two-bedroom suites. Originally intended as a residential condo complex, these units are more spacious than most visitor accommodations. All have daily maid service, air-conditioning and TV, plus there's a swimming pool, lighted tennis court (hotel guests only), coin laundry facility, and a barbecue and picnic area on premises. The low-rise design in a garden setting lends a homey atmosphere; an activity desk at the front can help arrange your outings. Basic hotel rooms start at $149, family studios

$179, and suites $199–279. Studios and suites all have kitchens. Suites will take three guests, one-bedroom, one-bath suites will hold four guests, and the two-bedroom, two-bath suites up to six individuals. Take a botanical walk through the garden, where there are many varieties of exotic plants and flowers. This fine little hideaway is an Ohana Hotels property.

A six-story condo, the **Lahaina Shores,** at the south end of town, 475 Front St., Lahaina, HI 96761, 808/661-4835 or 800/642-6284, was constructed before the Lahaina building code limited the height of new structures. The condo has become a landmark for incoming craft. The Shores offers a swimming pool and spa and is the only accommodation in Lahaina located on a beach. From a distance, the Southern-mansion facade is striking; up close, though, it becomes painted cement blocks and false colonnades. The fully air-conditioned rooms, however, are good value for the money. The basic room contains a full bathroom, large color TV, and modern kitchen. They're all light and airy, and the views of the harbor and mountains are the best in town. Studios run $180 mountain-view and $215 oceanfront; one-bedroom suites are $250 mountain-view and $280 oceanfront. The penthouse suites run $290 and $315 for mountain and ocean views, respectively. Other amenities include a front desk, daily maid service, laundry facilities, and an activities desk. This facility is associated with the Classic Resorts group, info@classicresorts.com, www.classicresorts.com.

A 28-acre private community of condos located on the south edge of town along the ocean, **Puamana** is a quiet hideaway away from the hustle and bustle of town, definitely a high-end property. The clubhouse here was the Pioneer Sugar Company's former plantation manager's residence (built 1923), and it's a beauty. Surrounding it are broad lawns and the townhouses. One-bedroom condo units run $140–200, two-bedroom units $175–275, and three-bedroom townhouses $350–500; three- to five-night minimum stay. Discounts are given for long stays, and all rates are somewhat lower during the low season. All units have fully equipped kitchens, all linens, TVs and VCRs, air-conditioning, and outdoor barbecue grills. Puamana also features an oceanside swimming pool plus two others on property; a sauna, reading parlor, and lending library in the clubhouse; a guests-only tennis court; badminton and volleyball courts; and children's play areas. The only drawback is that it's wedged against the highway, but a thick hedge blocks out much of the noise. For rentals, contact Klahani Resorts, P.O. Box 11108, Lahaina, HI 96761, 808/667-2712 or 800/669-6284, fax 808/661-5875; or Whaler's Realty Management, 808/661-3484 or 800/676-4112, fax 808/661-8338.

B&Bs and Guesthouses

By and large, the B&Bs in Lahaina are clumped together in two areas of town: south of downtown near the water, and halfway to Ka'anapali and up above the highway in the area known as Kapunakea.

Barbier's **Old Lahaina House,** P.O. Box 10355, Lahaina, HI 96761, 808/667-4663 or 800/847-0761, fax 808/669-9199, info@oldlahaina.com, www.oldlahaina.com, is a big salmon-colored house, surrounded by a wall of the same color, has four rooms, all with private baths, that range $69–115 but $10–20 higher in the busy season. No breakfast is served. All rooms include air-conditioning, telephone, TV, small refrigerator and microwave, and everyone has access to the garden and the refreshing swimming pool and deck, which occupy the front yard. Reduced rental car rates can be arranged. Old Lahaina House is a relaxing, homey place, lived in by the family (so there may be kids around).

In a street behind, you'll find the **Bambula Inn** bed and breakfast, 518 'Ilikahi St., Lahaina, HI 96761, 808/667-6753 or 800/544-5524, fax 808/667-0979, bambula@maui.net, www.bambula.com. Here, a cottage and studio are separated at the back of the house so you're independent from the family, while a smaller studio is set to the side. Each unit has a full kitchen, queen-size beds, private bath, TV, phone, and lanai. The detached cottage for $110 has air-conditioning, while both studios have fans. The rear studio runs $100 and the side studio is $79; $20 for each additional person more than two, three nights minimum. Breakfast is brought to your room, and a complimentary sunset sail aboard the family sailboat *Bambula* is offered every evening, weather permitting. Contact Pierre for information and reservations. If these rooms are full, ask about his other accommodation options.

The peach color of the **Garden Gate Bed And Breakfast,** 67 Kaniau Rd., Lahaina, HI 96761, 808/661-8800 or 800/939-3217, fax 808/661-0209, jaime@gardengatebb.com, www.gardengatebb.com, beyond its private courtyard garden lets you know that this is an easygoing, restful, and welcoming place. There are three bedrooms in the main house, one larger unit off an upstairs lanai to the side, an efficiency unit under that, and a newer room at the front. All have private baths, and although each is different from the other, all are comfy and decorated in island style. Only the efficiency has a kitchen. The others have microwaves and refrigerators, but a breakfast of pastries, fruit, and drinks is served daily except Sunday on the patio unless the weather doesn't permit. All guests may use the barbecue and laundry facilities, and you can borrow bikes and beach gear. Rates run $79–139; three-night minimum stay. Knowledgeable and ready to share information about their island and what to see, the owners make you feel like part of the family.

The GuestHouse, 1620 Ainakea Rd., Lahaina, HI 96761, 808/661-8085 or 800/621-8942, fax 808/661-1896, relax@mauiguesthouse.com, www.mauiguesthouse.com, is a well-appointed contemporary B&B where the host will provide free snorkel gear and even scuba lessons for a fee. The GuestHouse caters largely to honeymooners and scuba enthusiasts. All rooms have queen beds, air-conditioning, ceiling fans, TVs, refrigerators, phones, and private lanai, and all have private baths with a hot tub or whirlpool tub. Full breakfast is provided. Everyone shares the living room, kitchen, barbecue, and laundry facility. Each of the four rooms runs $129 per couple or $115 single.

Wai Ola Vacation Paradise, 1565 Ku'uipo, 808/662-0812 or 800/572-5642, fax 808/661-8045, waiola@maui-vacations.com, www.waiola.com, is a private home with three units, all with private entrances; however, the entire house may

also be rented. Located just off the pool, the large one-bedroom Makai Apartment is more than 1,000 square feet, with full kitchen and amenities. It runs $150 per couple and $15 each extra person up to four. The Malanai Suite is about half as big but also has a full kitchen and all amenities. Located in the garden, it runs $135 per couple. With its own private lanai and large king bed, the Honeymoon Ohana room goes for $175 per night. If the two-bedroom, two-bath upper portion of the house is rented, the rate is $400 per night. Depending on the number of bedrooms, the entire house goes for $550–850 per night. The minimum stay is five nights. All units are well-appointed and have air-conditioning, TV, VCR, and phones, and everyone has use of the free laundry facilities and the swimming pool. As a vacation rental, no food is served, but all kitchens are stocked with basics. Very private; booked mostly by honeymooners.

The **House of Fountains,** 1579 Lokia St., Lahaina, HI 96761, 808/667-2121 or 800/789-6865, fax 808/667-2120, private@alohahouse.com, www.alohahouse.com, is farther up in this neighborhood. A large modern house, with tile floor throughout, native wood furniture, and overall Hawaiian-style decor, this B&B is a restful and relaxing spot that also has a pool and hot tub on the back patio. Room rates for the six suites are $95–145 per night, with $20 for extra individuals, which includes a filling breakfast of fruits and other goodies.

Hostel

If you're looking for the least expensive place in town, try **Patey's Place Maui Hostel,** 761 Waine'e St., 808/667-0999, maui@hawaiian-hostels.com, www.hawaiian-hostels.com, the only hostel-type accommodation in town. This single-story house, with additional rooms added to the side for space, is spartan and reasonably clean. There's no luxury at this easygoing hostel, but it's serviceable. Guests can hang out on the cushions in the common TV room, a kitchen is available for simple food preparation and storage, there's coin laundry available, and there are shared bathrooms with showers. Drugs and smoking are forbidden in the rooms, and quiet time is after

10 P.M. A bunk in the dorm room runs $20 per night, the small single room $45, a private room with shared bath $50–55, and the private room with private bath $60. Used by those visiting the island on the cheap and by those who've come to find work, this could be a good place to garner information about what to see and do on Maui.

FOOD

Lahaina's menu of restaurants is gigantic. All palates and pocketbooks can easily be satisfied: There's fast food, sandwiches, sushi, happy hours, vegetarian, and elegant cosmopolitan restaurants. Because Lahaina is a dynamic tourist spot, restaurants and eateries come and go with regularity. The following is not an exhaustive list of Lahaina's food spots—it couldn't be—but there is plenty listed here to feed everyone at breakfast, lunch, and dinner. *Bon appétit!*

Quick Food and Snacks

Hawaii's own **Lappert's Ice Cream,** next to the library, not only has rich ice cream, shave ice, and cookies, but also serves fat- and sugar-free ice cream—about the only thing on Maui that is fat-free! **Häagen-Dazs** can also serve up your favorite flavor at both the Pioneer Inn shops and near Lahaina Market Place.

A good spot for a quick snack is **Mr. Sub Sandwiches,** 129 Lahainaluna Rd., which features double-fisted sandwiches and packed picnic lunches. Your sweet tooth will begin to sing the moment you walk into **The Bakery,** 911 Limahana, 808/667-9062, near the Sugar Cane Train. You can't beat the stuffed croissants for under $3 or the sandwiches for under $5. The pastries, breads, and bagels are gooood! Open daily at 5:30 A.M. and closes at 2 P.M. weekdays, 1 P.M. on Saturday, and noon Sunday.

Take Home Maui, 121 Dickenson St., 808/661-8067 or 800/545-MAUI from the Mainland for mail order, is a food store and delicatessen that specializes in packaging agriculturally inspected Maui produce such as pineapples, papayas, Maui onions, protea, potato chips, macadamia nut products, and even Kona coffee, which they will deliver to you at the airport before your departing flight. For an on-the-spot treat, they prepare deli sandwiches for under $6, a variety of quiches, and sides of macaroni and potato salad. Take Home Maui is famous for its fresh-fruit smoothies, homemade soups, and picnic lunches. Choose a shaded spot on the veranda and enjoy your lunch while taking a break from the jostle of Front Street. Open 7:30 A.M.–6:30 P.M.

Inexpensive

Across from the Banyan Tree is **Swiss Cafe,** 808/661-6776, a simple European-style eatery with seating outside under the trellis, where you can order hot and cold sandwiches, pizzas, coffee, and juice for reasonable prices—nothing is over $8. Perhaps a bagel with cheese and tomato or fresh croissant will satisfy you for breakfast. All sorts of sandwiches and personal-size pizzas can be made for lunch, but the "melts" are the focus. Some stop by just for an espresso or iced mocha, while others come to cool off with a smoothie or ice cream. Open 9 A.M.–6 P.M., and while you're here, check your email—from $.10 per minute depending on the length of use.

Tacos, burritos, and other south-of-the-border foods are served up with a Hawaiian attitude at **Maui Taco,** 808/661-8883, at Lahaina Square Shopping Center. This is excellent Mexi-waiian food with a punch, and everything on the menu is less than $7.

Smokehouse BBQ, 1307 Front St., 808/667-7005, serves baby back ribs, chicken, and fish smoked over a kiawe grill and smothered in special barbecue sauce. Also available for lunch are a variety of burgers and sandwiches, and always sides like rice, barbecued beans, and cole slaw. This is where local people and those in the know come for a very good but no-frills meal. If eating hearty without caring about the ambiance (actually the sunset view couldn't be better) is your aim, come here. Open daily 11 A.M.– 9 P.M. Takeout available.

The **Thai Chef,** 808/667-2814, will please any Thai food lover who wants a savory meal at a good price. Search for this restaurant stuck in a corner at the Old Lahaina Center (open Mon.–Fri. 11 A.M.–3 P.M. for lunch, dinner

WEST MAUI

nightly 5–10 P.M.). As in most Thai restaurants vegetarians are well taken care of with plenty of spicy tofu and vegetable dishes. The extensive menu offers everything from scrumptious Thai soups with ginger and coconut for $8.95 (enough for two) to curries and seafood. Most entrées are under $14 with a good selection under $10. It's not fancy, but food-wise you won't be disappointed. Takeout is available. When in Kihei, visit the second Thai Chef restaurant in the Rainbow Mall.

Zushi's is a reasonably priced Japanese restaurant selling sushi and various other Japanese dishes in Lahaina Square Shopping Center on Waine'e Street. Zushi's serves lunch (take-out too) 11 A.M.–2 P.M., dinner 5–9:30 P.M. Authentic with most items under $6. Also in this shopping center is **Denny's,** which serves up inexpensive standard American fare.

Sunrise Cafe, 808/661-8558, open 6 A.M.–6 P.M. at 693 Front Street to the side of the library, is the kind of place locals keep secret. It's a tiny restaurant where you can have excellent coffee and a sandwich or more substantial gourmet food at down-home prices. The nutritious and wholesome food includes breakfast specials like freshly baked quiche for $6.95, and lunch salads from Chinese chicken to fresh island fruit all priced under $9. Those with heartier appetites can choose various hot or cold sandwiches for under $8, soups for $3.95, *kalua* pork, tofu dish, roasted beef, or other main entrée for under $12. The kitchen closes at 4 P.M. A deli case holds scrumptious award-winning pastries that are complemented by fine coffee selections always freshly brewed and a good selection of herbal teas. Eat inside or out on the back patio.

At the 505 Front Street Mall is **Bamboo Bar and Grill,** 808/667-4051, which serves inexpensive Thai and Vietnamese dishes for lunch and dinner until 11 P.M., with only a few items on the menu over $13. Many of the well-known seafood, meat, and vegetarian dishes are available plus a few that might not be familiar, like fish or shrimp simmered in a clay pot.

Next door to the new Old Lahaina Lu'au venue near Mala Wharf is **Aloha Mixed Plate,** 808/661-3322, a great spot for a simple, authentic, and award-winning meal and a cold drink. While noodle dishes, burgers, and sandwiches are on the menu, the specialties are the plate lunches. Available in three sizes, most run $2.95–8.95. Open 10:30 A.M.–10 P.M.; happy hour 3–6 P.M. You can't beat it.

Among the several eateries at the Wharf Cinema Center is the unpretentious **Yakiniku Lahaina,** which serves a fine rendition of Korean food.

Aside from the full range of produce, vitamins, health foods, and bulk foods, the **Down To Earth Natural Foods,** on Lahainaluna Rd., 808/667-2855, has some reasonably priced and healthily prepared hot and cold foods, fruit drinks, and smoothies. Items at the salad bar and hot-food counter are priced $6.50 per pound. Open Monday–Saturday 7 A.M.–9 P.M., Sunday 8:30 A.M.–8 P.M.

Penne Pasta Cafe, 808/661-6633, at the Dickenson Square, is an inexpensive Italian restaurant that serves quality food quickly at reasonable prices. Order at the counter and your meal will be brought to your table. Pastas include linguine pesto, baked penne, and chicken piccata. Pizza and flatbreads are also available, as are salads, and a few sandwiches, like prosciutto, pepper, onion, and provolone, and open-face roasted eggplant parmesan. Nothing on the menu is over $10. Run by Mark Ellman, a perennial favorite island chef who has started and run numerous restaurants over the years, Penne Pasta is a winner.

The trendiest of the inexpensive eateries in town, the open-air **Cheeseburger in Paradise,** 811 Front St., 808/661-4855, open 10:30 A.M.–11 P.M., with live music nightly, is a joint down by the sea overlooking the harbor out back. Served are a whole slew of burgers priced $6.75–8.50, Portuguese turkey burger for $8.50, the jumbo cheese dog covered with cheese and sautéed onions for $6.50, or the Maui classic BLT for $6.75. Other selections include the aloha fish and seasoned fries at $10.25, a huge Upcountry salad for $7.50, and calamari scallop gumbo for $6.95. Cheeseburger also has a full bar that sells a range of both imported and domestic beer, along with tropical concoctions. If you were going to pick one spot to have a beer, soak in the sights, and capture the flavor of old Lahaina, "the Burg" has all the trimmings.

Also a trendy place and up at the top end of the inexpensive spots is the **Hard Rock Cafe,** 808/667-7400, at the Lahaina Center on the corner of Front and Papalaua streets. Open daily from 11:30 A.M., this is a large breezy, screened restaurant keeping the rock-and-roll faith. Over the bar is a '59 Cadillac convertible woody, and on the walls are prints of rock stars and electric guitars, including a Gibson autographed by the Grateful Dead. The floors have a shiny patina, and the raised stools and round-top tables give you a view of the street and the sea beyond. Menu prices are moderate, with homemade onion rings at $4.29, Caesar salad for $7.79, Cajun chicken sandwich at $9.19, barbecued ribs for $15.99, and grilled burger for $7.59. Sit inside at the bar or dining section or outside under the umbrellas. Food is served until 10 P.M. Sunday–Thursday, until 10:30 Friday and Saturday; the bar is open two hours longer every night, and there's live music on Saturday.

Also reasonably cheap and an institution is **Moose McGillycuddy's,** 808/667-7758. A wild and zany place, there is music nightly (live on Fridays and Saturdays), the sports channel on the many TVs hanging here and there, daily specials, early-bird specials (both breakfast and dinner), and a happy hour 3–6 P.M. The large portions are filling, and the menu reads like a book, with burgers, sandwiches, fajitas, *pu pu,* and much else, most under $10. Take a moment (or an hour) and have a look at all the stuff hanging on the walls.

Moderate

Kobe Japanese Steak House, 136 Dickenson at the corner of Luakini, 808/667-5555, is open daily for dinner from 5:30 P.M. Service is teppanyaki-style, which means that the chef comes to you. His sharp blade flashes through the air and thumps the table, keeping the culinary beat as it slices, dices, and minces faster than any Veg-o-matic you've ever seen. The delectables of marinated meat, chicken, and vegetables are then expertly flash-fried at your own grill, often with aplomb in a ball of sake-induced flame. The ex-

perience is fun, the food very good, and the interior authentic Japanese. Teppan meals come complete with rice, soup, and tea. Expect to spend at least $18 for an entrée (less for the early-bird specials), $11 for an appetizer, and from $15 for four pieces of sushi. Other style fish and meat entrées are also available for up to $37. Complement your meal with a glass of sake or Japanese beer. Aside from the food, karaoke entertainment on the weekend draws a lively crowd.

Set right at the harbor, the **Pioneer Inn Bar and Grill,** 808/661-3636, at the historic Pioneer Inn, has a marine theme. It serves breakfast 6:30–11:30 A.M., offering two buttermilk pancakes for $6.25, eggs Benedict for $7.25, and a three-egg omelet for $8.25. Lunch and dinner, served noon–11 P.M., start with such items as a hearty bowl of Portuguese soup for $5.50 or Caesar salad for $8, and moves on to a full selection of sandwiches for under $9, pepper-grilled steak for $20.25, oven-roasted chicken for $13.95, sesame-seared ahi for $22.50, or primavera Alfredo for $12.50. In addition, the saloon is open for drinks from noon–midnight, with happy hour 3–7 P.M., and there's live music most evenings. Because the Pioneer Inn is the oldest hotel in town, and a true landmark with a great lanai from which you can view the harbor, the experience is really one of history and atmosphere.

The **Whale's Tail Bar and Grill,** 808/667-4044, is a casual, easygoing, open-air restaurant that overlooks the banyan tree from above the ABC Discount Store at the Wharf Cinema Center. Open 11 A.M.–11 P.M. daily for lunch and dinner, there is a full bar with happy hour from 2:30–5 P.M. and live entertainment nightly 4–7 P.M. At the Whale's Tale you'll find mostly salads, burgers, and sandwiches in the $6–9 range, with seafood dishes up to $11.

At the back of the Wharf Cinema Center is the fun-loving **Poncho and Lefty's Cantina and Restaurante,** 808/661-4666. Amble back and sit awhile for a margarita or cerveza, or stop by at lunch or dinner for tasty Mexican *comidas.* Food runs the gamut from nacho appetizers to two-fisted burritos to sizzling fajita plates. Most dishes run $8–15, but the more complex fajitas are priced around $25.

Kimo's, 845 Front St., 808/661-4811, is friendly and has great harbor and sunset views on the lower level. If you're in Lahaina around 6 P.M. and need a break, head here to relax with some "Kimo therapy." Popular, but no reservations taken. Kimo's offers seafood from $16.95, with most entrées $15–19 and is known for the catch of the day, usually the best offering on the menu; limited menu for children. Lunch prices are half the dinner prices, and you can get an assortment of *pu pu*, burgers, and sandwiches. Dine upstairs or down. The downstairs bar has top-notch well drinks featuring brand-name liquors. Kimo's is one of the well-established restaurants in town with a great reputation.

The Lahaina Fish Company, 831 Front St., 808/661-3472, open daily from 11 A.M. for lunch and 5–10 P.M. for dinner, buys from local fishermen so the fish is guaranteed fresh. Belly up to the Hammerhead Bar, fashioned from glass and brass, or choose a table that looks directly out onto Lahaina Harbor. Notice the vintage Coca-Cola vending machine and a display of knots that were tied by the old salts who visited Lahaina. The limited lunch/grill menu has sandwiches and other light foods, mostly for under $10. The evening dinner menu starts with dinner salads at $3.99, a fried calamari appetizer at $9.99, or a bowl of fresh seafood chowder for $3.95. Entrées can be island fish and chips at $9.99, fisherman's pasta with fish and vegetables for $12.99, or sautéed sea scallops for $16.99. Meat and poultry dishes include Hawaiian teriyaki chicken for $12.99, luau-style pork ribs for $15.99, or top sirloin steak for $12.99. The fresh fish, of which there might be half a dozen varieties to select from depending on what's caught that day, is grilled and basted, oven broiled, or blackened Cajun style and offered at market price. Every day brings a chef's special.

At 505 Front Street is **Hecock's,** 808/661-8810, open daily 8 A.M.–10 P.M. for food service, bar open until 2 A.M., owned and operated by Tom and Nancy, a husband and wife team who bring you good food at reasonable prices. Hecock's breakfast could be ranch eggs with a broiled mahimahi for $8.75 or a three-egg omelet for $6.95, along with the classics like French toast or buttermilk pancakes with the trimmings for under $7. The lunch menu offers a chef salad for $8.95, assorted burgers and sandwiches priced under $9.95. The dinner bill of fare includes fettuccine Alfredo for $16.95, scampi for $24.95, and rack of lamb for $24.95. A children's menu, happy hour, daily specials, and an early-bird special offered 5–6 P.M. help keep prices down.

Lahaina Coolers, 808/661-7082, at Dickenson Square, presents quick, easy meals throughout the day in an open-air setting. Try pancakes, omelets, or eggs Benedict for breakfast; salads, sandwiches, and burgers for lunch; and pasta, pizzas, fresh fish, steaks, and burgers for dinner. Few items on the evening menu are over $15.95. Coolers is a casual place, great for late-night revelers who can get food until midnight and drinks until 2 A.M.

BJ's Chicago Pizzeria, 808/661-0700, on the second floor overlooking the seawall at 730 Front St., is known throughout the island for its deep-dish pizzas. Various choices, ranging from the ordinary cheese and tomato to shrimp thermador and "the works," run about $10–24. All made to order, they take some time, but everyone agrees they're worth the wait. Along with the pizza are various calzone and pasta dishes, and fine salads. Eat in or take out. BJ's has one of the largest beer selections on the island and live contemporary music every evening.

Compadres Mexican Bar and Grill, 808/661-7189, at the Lahaina Cannery Mall, has a full menu ranging from nacho appetizers through soups, salads, and sandwiches to a complete list of entrées, most in the $10–18 range. Sit down, relax, and enjoy your meal and the surroundings, or have a beer or margarita at the spacious long bar.

Café Sauvage, 808/661-7600, has an intimate spot in the courtyard at 844 Front Street below Moose McGillycuddy's. Food prepared here has a definite Pacific Rim twist, with such offerings as shrimp cocktail in lemon juice, yellow ginger, toasted coconut, and fresh chilis, Thai chicken roulade, and braised veal shank with saffron risotto. Main entrées run $17–26. Call for reservations.

Fine Dining

When you feel like putting a major dent in your budget and satisfying your desire for gourmet food, you should be pleased with one of the following.

You won't be a pawn when you walk onto the black-and-white-checkered floor at **Longhi's**, 888 Front St., 808/667-2288, open daily 7:30 A.M.–10 P.M. Longhi owns the joint and he's a character. He feels that his place has healing vibes and that man's basic food is air. Longhi's has been around since 1976, and it's many people's favorite. Prices at Longhi's may seem expensive, but the portions are enormous and can easily fill two. If you don't want to stuff yourself, ask for a half-order. Mornings you can order frittatas, like spinach, ham, and bacon, eggs Benedict, or lox and bagels. A good lunch choice is pasta Siciliana with calamari, spicy with marinara sauce, a corned beef sandwich, or Greek salad; for dinner, the prawns amaretto and shrimp Longhi are signature dishes, but numerous pasta, meat, and other seafood dishes are on the menu. Dinner entrées generally run $19–30 with pastas somewhat less. Save room for the fabulous desserts or a cooling cocktail. Longhi's is a winner. It's hard not to have a fine meal here, and the wine list is outstanding. There's always a line, reservations accepted, never a dress code, and always complimentary valet parking! Live music is provided only on Friday and Saturday evenings.

After two decades of operating in Kahana, **Erik's Seafood and Sushi** moved into Lahaina and opened anew at the back end of the Old Lahaina Center. The entire staff came with the move, and the superb menu has stayed the same, but there is now the addition of a sushi bar. The new restaurant has kept the decoration in an appropriately nautical theme, with fish tanks, divers' helmets, and mounted trophy fish. Erik's is open weekdays for lunch 11 A.M.–2 P.M. and dinner nightly 5–10 P.M., and a light bar menu is available throughout the afternoon; call 808/662-8780 for reservations. Lunch is a variety of reasonably priced dishes. The early-bird specials, which run at the bargain price of $12.95 and $13.95, are offered 5–6 P.M. Bouillabaisse, cioppino, and seafood curry are among the chef's specialties, but you shouldn't forget to try one of the many appetizers first. Shellfish, lobster, steak, and poultry are on the menu, but the real focus is on the wide variety of fish that can be prepared in numerous ways. Most dinners run $21–30, with all fish quoted at the daily market price. Erik's is known to have the *best* selection of fresh fish on Maui—always more than half a dozen selections nightly. Sushi is created in its own section, but it can also be ordered from the main dining room. This is a quality restaurant with delicious food and excellent service.

Ruth's Chris Steak House, 808/661-8815, has captured the attention of those Midwestern corn-fed-beef lovers. If you're wanting a meal of meat and potatoes, this is your place. Entrées run $24–37 and include filet, rib eye, T-bone, and strip steaks, and pork, veal, and lamb chops. A few seafood items also appear on the menu at market price. A semi-formal affair with crystal on the linen-clad tables and a full bar, Ruth's is open for dinner only 5–10 P.M. in the Lahaina Center; reservations are a necessity.

The pacific'O Cafe, 808/667-4341, at 505 Front Street, has garnered a solid reputation. Foods and flavors from the West, the East, and the Pacific are blended together, using only the freshest ingredients from the islands, to create a delectable contemporary Pacific cuisine. Start with a fine Thai coconut seafood chowder for $6.50 or roasted Maui onion and Puna goat cheese salad for $9.50. Lunch entrées, like the seared fish or sautéed prawn pasta, are all reasonable at less than $15. Dinner entrées run $22–29 and might be fish tempura wrapped in wakame, pan-roasted scallops and pork, coconut macadamia nut–crusted fish, or sesame-crusted lamb. Comfortable seating, attentive servers, and the views out over the ocean might tempt you to linger over your meal and savor an excellent bottle of wine. Open daily for lunch 11 A.M.–4 P.M. and dinner 5:30–10 P.M. Dinner runs until 10:30 on Friday and Saturday, when there's live jazz 9 P.M.–midnight.

The **i'o** restaurant next door, 808/661-8422, is open 5:30–10 P.M. for dinner only; reservations are a must. Like pacific'O, i'o is owned by Chef James McDonald, but unlike its neighbor, i'o is more experimental with its food and the ambiance is more modern. Start your evening with tomato bread, served each night with a different dipping sauce. Appetizers include the "silken purse" steamed wonton, scallops on the half shell, and the signature i'o crab cakes, $8–12. The main entrée might be a luscious crispy ahi, another signature dish, the foie gras–crusted and pan-fried fresh fish, or the wok stir-fried lobster Thai-hitian with mango curry sauce, $23–34. No matter what your choice, each dish is artfully inspired and the symphony of flavors, particularly the sauces, compliment one another. If you think you've tried all manner of desserts, order the goat cheese ice cream for a new experience, or have your meal with one of the many tropical-flavored martinis that the restaurant is known for. Sleek, open, and airy inside, there is also seating outside on the patio where, if you time it right, you can watch the sunset paint the sky in bands of pink and red or the crescent moon rise into the inky night sky.

David Paul's Lahaina Grill, 127 Lahainaluna Rd. under the Lahaina Inn, 808/667-5117, open for dinner nightly 6–10 P.M., is one of Lahaina's finest gourmet restaurants. Here owner David Paul Johnson, famous for his sauces, presents "artwork on a plate." The dining room is quite lovely, with coved and pressed-metal ceilings from which hang punchbowl chandeliers illuminating the starched-white table settings that surround the central bar. With low lighting and soft music, this well-appointed room is meant for a long romantic evening of salubrious relaxation. The professional and friendly servers definitely give you attentive service. The menu is diverse and can be served at the bar as well. Start with a bowl of Maui onion soup for $9, a Kona lobster-crab cake appetizer for $15, or baby romaine Caesar salad for $11. Entrées include David Paul's signature dishes, tequila shrimp and firecracker rice, made from tiger prawns marinated in chili oil, lemons, cilantro, cumin, and brown sugar in a blend of vanilla bean and chili rice for $29, and Kona coffee–roasted rack of lamb for $39, plus others like Maui onion-crusted seared ahi for $38 and kalua duck with a plum sauce reduction for $29. Vegetarians will

find at least one meatless entrée on each menu, and other dietary restrictions can be accommodated by the masterful chefs. No matter what is on the changing menu, you can be assured that the ingredients are the freshest available. The very wicked dessert tray, with everything priced $10–12, combined with a cup of rich roasted coffee, ends a wonderful meal.

Gerard's elegant restaurant is in the Plantation Inn, 174 Lahainaluna Rd., 808/661-8939, open daily for dinner only 6–9 P.M., with validated free parking nearby. The epitome of neo-Victorian charm, the room is comfortable with puff-pillow wicker chairs and always set with fine crystal atop starched linen. Fronting the building is a small dining garden, and inside the interior is rich with hardwood floors and oak bar. Chef Gerard Reversade, trained in the finest French culinary tradition since age 14, creates masterpieces. He feels that eating is *the* experience of life, around which everything else that is enjoyable revolves. Gerard insists that the restaurant's servers share his philosophy, so along with the excellent food comes excellent service. The menu changes, but it's always gourmet. Gerard's is not cheap, but it's worth every penny because nothing on the menu is less than excellent. Appetizers range $10.50–24.50, entrées $32.50–42.50, and desserts are $8.50. Some superb salad choices are the island greens with heart of palm, or spinach salad with grilled scallops, shaved reggiano cheese, and balsamic vinaigrette. Appetizers feature mouth-watering choices like shiitake and oyster mushrooms in a puff pastry and duck foie gras. Full entrées like Confit of duck with fingerling potato cakes, venison cutlets with Jamaica pepper and an akala berry port sauce, or roast Hawaiian snapper with star anise and savory titillate the palate. The grilled rack of lamb with mint crust is one of Gerard's superb signature dishes. Even if you possess great self-control, you have less than an even chance of restraining yourself from choosing a luscious dessert like crème brûlée, chocolate mousse in cream puffs with raspberry sabayon, or even fresh strawberries glazed with suzette butter and macadamia nut cream. *C'est bon!*

Chez Paul, 808/661-3843, five miles east of

Lahaina in Olowalu, is secluded, romantic, very popular, and French—what else! Owner Patrick Callarec emphasizes Provençale regional cuisine with flavors of traditional French cooking. Chez Paul is open nightly 6–9 P.M.; reservations are a must. Local folks who are into elegant dining give it two thumbs up. The wine list is tops, the desserts fantastic, and the food *magnifique!* Start with luscious hors d'oeuvres like chilled leek and potato soup with chives or oven-roasted eggplant and tomatoes, or a warm appetizer such as Borgogne escargot in their shells or wild mushroom and brie cheese baked in a puff pasty, all priced $10–26. Salads lead to delightful entrées, which might be fresh island fish poached in champagne, bouillabaisse, filet mignon in caviar sauce, boneless crispy duck with tropical fruits and pineapple sauce bigarade, or herbed veal loin, all priced $30–45. If you have room after such a feast, try one of the fine desserts. Hot and runny chocolate cake is a favorite, but pineapple and vanilla crème brûlée in a pineapple shell or ice cream soufflé with mandarin liquor flavor will do as well. This is fine dining at its best. Chez Paul is definitely worth the trip from Lahaina, with a short stroll along the beach recommended as a perfect aperitif.

ENTERTAINMENT

Lahaina is one of those places where the real entertainment is the town itself. The best thing to do here is to stroll along Front Street and people-watch. As you walk along, it feels like a block party with the action going on all around you—as it does on Halloween. Some people duck into one of the many establishments along Front Street for a breather, a drink, or just to watch the sunset. It's all free, enjoyable, and safe.

Art Night

Friday night is Art Night in Lahaina. In keeping with its status as the cultural center of Maui, Lahaina opens the doors of its galleries 7–10 P.M., throws out the welcome mat, sets out food and drink, provides entertainment, and usually hosts a well-known artist or two for this weekly party. It's a fine social get-together where the emphasis

is on gathering people together to appreciate the arts and not necessarily on making sales. Take your time and stroll Front Street from one gallery to the next. Stop and chat with shopkeepers, munch the goodies, sip the wine, look at the pieces on display, corner the featured artist for comment on his or her work, soak in the music of the strolling musicians, and strike up a conversation with the person next to you who is eyeing that same piece of art with the same respect and admiration. It's a party. People dress up, but don't be afraid to come casually. Take your time and immerse yourself in the immense variety and high quality of art on display in Lahaina.

Halloween

This is one of the big events of the year. As many as 30,000 people head to town for the night. It seems that everyone dresses in costume, strolls Front Street, parties around town, and gets into the spirit of the evening. It's a party in the street with throngs of people, dancing, live music, swirling color, a costume contest at the banyan tree, an arts festival, and other activities that include a haunted house, a clown show, and *keiki* parade for the little ones. For the adults, the parade goes on all evening. Halloween in Lahaina has become so popular with some revelers that they fly in from Honolulu just for the night. To accommodate the fun, Front Street is closed to traffic from the Banyan Tree all the way past the Lahaina Center from midafternoon until past midnight.

Fourth of July

There is some musical entertainment and other special activities to celebrate this occasion, but the biggest excitement is created by the fireworks celebration out over the Lahaina Roads, with its multicolor puffballs, showers of streaming light, and blazing rocket trails. This is the best show on the island and can be seen for miles. Plenty of people crowd into town, sit along the seawall, or stop along the roadways to have an up-close look at the color show. On this day, it may be difficult to get to Lahaina if you're not staying there or haven't arrived by midafternoon, and parking can be a struggle or simply unattainable.

Nightspots and Dancing

All of the evening musical entertainment in Lahaina is in restaurants and lounges, except for the acclaimed Old Lahaina Lu'au and The Feast at Lele.

You, too, can be a disco king or queen on **Longhi's** black-and-white chessboard dance floor every weekend. Longhi's has live music on Friday and Saturday nights featuring island groups.

Moose McGillycuddy's (just listen for the loud music on Front Street) is still a happening place with occasional music, although it's becoming more of a cruise joint for post-adolescents. Those who have been around Lahaina for a while usually give it a miss, but if you want to get your groove on with a younger crowd, this place is for you.

The open-air **Cheeseburger in Paradise** rocks with live music nightly until 11 P.M. There's no cover charge, and you can sit upstairs or down listening to the tunes.

Similarly, you can hear live soft rock during dinner at the **Whale's Tail Bar and Grill** at the Wharf Cinema Center across from the banyan tree, at **BJ's Chicago Pizzeria** overlooking the water, and at the **Pioneer Inn Grill and Bar** at the Pioneer Inn. Live jazz happens every Thursday–Saturday evening at **pacific'O** restaurant at 505 Front Street Mall.

Maui Brews not only has a long bar—up to 16 beers on tap, half from Hawaii—a restaurant serving breakfast, lunch, and dinner, and a game room, but the back room becomes a nightclub with loud music, colored lights, and plenty of people. There's music and dancing nightly until 2 A.M., and this seems to be the most happening place in town. Music ranges from rock to techno to reggae, and while a DJ sets the stage most evenings, there are live acts on Fridays and occasionally on other nights.

Theater Shows

Lahaina is lucky to have two theater shows: one large, the other more intimate. Performed at the 700-seat Maui Theatre with its thrust stage and amphitheater seating is **'Ulalena,** a 1.5-hour historical review, cultural journey, and tale of legend and myth that is in essence the story of the

Hawaiian people. While the content is thoroughly Hawaiian, it's told in a manner that's modern and Western—and that's part of its magic. Colorful, captivating, and imaginative, it is full of fun visuals, dramatic dance, and superbly moving music. This is a show not to be missed. Tickets run $48 standard, $58 for preferred seating in the middle, and $68 for premium seats, a cocktail, and backstage pass; $28, $38, and $48, respectively for kids. Showtimes are 6 P.M. and 8:30 P.M. Tuesdays and 6 P.M. Wednesday–Saturday. The Maui Theatre is located at 878 Front Street, in the Old Lahaina Center; call 808/661-9913 for information and reservations or see the website: www.mauitheatre.com.

Warren and Annabelle's is a slight-of-hand, up-close magic show that's performed in a 78-seat theater at 900 Front Street, upstairs at the Lahaina Center. Before the show, guests gather in the theater's cocktail lounge for gourmet appetizers and drinks to be serenaded on piano by Annabelle, a 19th-century resident "ghost." Anyone who loves magic will be thrilled by this show, and it's particularly captivating because it all happens just a few feet from where you're sitting. You'll leave wondering, "How did he do that?" This show is open to those 21 years of age and older. Tickets for the show run $40 per person, and shows are performed every evening Monday–Saturday. Packages with various drinks and appetizers included are also available. Call 808/667-6244 for information and reservations.

Lu'au

Lahaina has two of the best dinner shows anywhere on the island. The **Old Lahaina Lu'au** is the most authentic lu'au on the island, and the all-you-can-eat buffet and all-you-can-drink bar has a well-deserved reputation. Located on the beach near the Lahaina Cannery Mall, it is the only lu'au on the island not associated with a hotel. Seating is daily at 6 P.M. (from 5:30 P.M. in winter), but because it's so popular, be sure to reserve tickets several days in advance, perhaps two weeks in advance during peak season; 808/667-1998. Tickets are $79 adults, $49 children 2–12.

The **Feast at Lele** combines food and entertainment. While not a lu'au per se, the five-course meal is masterfully coordinated with music and dance from the islands of Hawaii, Tonga, Tahiti, and Samoa. Reservations are a must; 808/667-5353. The dinner and show runs $95 adults, $65 children, daily 6–9 P.M. (from 5:30 in winter) on the beach at the 505 Front Street Mall.

Cinemas

Lahaina Cinemas, once the only multiplex theater on West Maui, is located on the third floor of the Wharf Cinema Center. Showing only first-run features, movies start at about noon and run throughout the day. Adults $7.25, kids 2–11 $4.25, seniors $4.75; all seats $4 until 5 P.M. Lahaina's second cinema is **Front Street Theaters.** Located at the Lahaina Center, this four-screen theater charges $7.25 adults, $4.25 kids, and $4.75 matinee. Call 808/249-2222 for what's showing at either theater.

The Hawaii Experience Domed Theater, 824 Front St., 808/661-8314, has continuous showings on the hour daily 10 A.M.–9 P.M. (40-minute duration); $6.95 adults, $3.95 children 4–12. The idea is to give you a total sensory experience by means of the giant, specially designed concave screen. You sit surrounded by it. You will tour the islands as if you were sitting in a helicopter or diving below the waves. And you'll be amazed at how well the illusion works. If you can't afford to fly through Kaua'i's Waimea Canyon, dive with the humpback whales, watch the sunrise over Haleakala, or view the power of an oozing volcano, this is about as close as you can get. A second film on a different subject is sometimes offered during the day. For both shows, tickets run $11.90 and $5.90, respectively. The lobby of the theater doubles as a gift shop where you can pick up souvenirs such as carved whales, T-shirts, and a variety of inexpensive mementos.

Hula and Polynesian Shows

For a different type of entertainment, stop to see the free *keiki* hula shows, Wednesdays at 2:30 P.M. and Fridays at 6 P.M., at Hale Kahiko in the parking lot of the Lahaina Center. Various singers also perform on Tuesdays and Thursdays around sunset. Hale Kahiko is a reproduction Hawaiian village displaying implements and items of everyday use; open daily 9 A.M.–6 P.M.

Various weekly shows are also offered at center stage at the Lahaina Cannery Mall. Tuesdays and Thursdays at 7 P.M. there's a free Polynesian show, and a *keiki* hula show is presented Saturdays and Sundays 1–2 P.M.

RECREATION

Lahaina is a center particularly for ocean-based activities on Maui. For further details on activity providers, see the Sports and Recreation section in the On the Road chapter.

Snorkel Bob's, at 1217 Front St. near the Mala Wharf, 808/661-4421, rents snorkel gear for $15 per week (daily rental also), which you can take to a neighboring island and return there for a small extra fee. Boogie boards are available at $13 per day or $26 per week, and Snorkel Bob's advice, whether you need it or not, is plentiful and free. Open 8 A.M.–5 P.M. daily, Snorkel Bob's can also fix you up with virtually any activity on the island through their activity desk.

Across from the banyan tree is **Duke's Rental Shop,** where snorkel gear runs $3 per day. Ordinary surfboards and longboards go for anywhere from $7 for two hours to $20. Water equipment are not the only items you can rent here; look also for cruiser bikes from $10 per day, golf clubs from $15, and a whole assortment of other items.

West Maui Cycles, at the Lahaina Square Shopping Center below Denny's Restaurant, 808/661-9005, rents snorkel gear, surfboards, and boogie boards, but its big thing is the sale, service, and rental of road and mountain bicycles. Mountain bikes run $30–40 per day, depending on the quality. Also available are cruisers at $15, road bikes at $30, and tandems at $55–65, car racks extra. Weekly rates are available. All bike rentals come with a helmet, pump, tool kit, and lock. Stop here for all of your cycling needs on West Maui.

West Maui Sports, 808/661-6252, rents snorkel gear for $2.50–10 per day or $10–35 per week. Boogieboards are $20 per day or $75 per week, single kayaks $35 per day and $120 per

ROBERT NILSEN

While the cane is now gone, a ride on the Sugar Cane Train still evokes images of the muscled farming economy that once dominated this coast.

week, tandem kayaks $50 per day or $150 per week. If you haven't brought them from home, beach chairs, coolers, umbrellas, other beach gear, fishing poles, and golf clubs can also be rented. Look for them behind Lahaina Cannery Mall next to Aloha Mixed Plate.

Activity Companies

Companies that can set you up with almost any activity offered on the island include the following: **Tom Barefoot's Cashback Tours,** 834 Front St., 808/661-8889 or 888/222-3601, www.tom barefoot.com, is a one-shop business that has a great handle on all types of tourist activities on Maui and throughout the state. They reduce the fee for activities by 10 percent for those who pay in cash or traveler's checks and a 7 percent discount is given for payment by credit card. You can also explore information and book activities before you come to town. This company has been around for more than 25 years and is a leader in the business.

The purveyor with the largest number of activity booths around the island (over a dozen—mostly at condo resorts and shopping centers)

is **Activity World,** 808/667-7777 or 800/624-7771, www.hawaiiactivityworld.com. In Lahaina, look for them at 910 Honoapi'ilani Highway, the Wharf Cinema Center, Lahaina Shores, and Maui Islander. **Activity Mart,** 808/667-6278 or 800/450-7736, www.activitymart.com, has an office at 624 Front Street and another at the Lahaina Cannery Mall. **Activity Warehouse,** 808/667-4000 or 800/343-2087, www.travel-hawaii.com, across from Kamehameha III School along Front St., can also set up your activity schedule. The **Lahaina Ticket Company,** 764 Front St. at the Pioneer Inn shops, 808/662-3430, can also arrange activities for you. For purely ocean activities, try the **Pier 1** booth at Lahaina Harbor, 808/667-0680.

A few of these companies and others not mentioned greatly discount their activities, but there is a trade-off. Usually, in order to get this vastly reduced fare for an activity, you must attend a time-share presentation and sit through the hard sell that follows. If you are interested in buying into a time-share property anyway, getting cheap tickets in the process may not be a bad idea. However, most people just give it a miss because they have better things to do on their vacations than be bombarded by high-pressure salespeople.

The Sugar Cane Train

The old steam engine puffs along from Lahaina to Pu'ukoli'i Depot in Ka'anapali pulling old-style open-air passenger cars through cane fields and the Ka'anapali golf course. The six miles of narrow-gauge track are covered in 25 minutes (each way), and the cost round-trip is $15.95 adults, $9.95 children 3–12. The train runs throughout the day 10:15 A.M.–4 P.M. It's very popular, so book in advance—more than 400,000 people ride the train every year. All rides are narrated and the conductor even sings. It's not just great fun for children; everybody has a good time. On Tuesdays and Thursdays, the dinner train leaves Pu'ukoli'i Depot at 5 P.M. for a sunset ride, followed by a paniolo barbecue dinner at the Ka'anapali Depot; $65 adults, $39 kids. All kinds of combination tours with other activity vendors are offered as well; they're tame, touristy, and fun. Contact the Lahaina Kaanapali and Pacific Railroad at 808/667-6851 or 800/499-2307; www.sugarcanetrain.com.

Hiking Trail

The **Lahaina Pali Trail** is a Na Ala Hele (Hawaii Trail and Access System) trail. Five miles in length, it starts near mile marker 11, about one-half mile west of the Lahaina Tunnel. Following an old established trail, it crosses the Kealaloloa Ridge at 1,600 feet and then descends to an access road that meets the highway near the junction of Highways 30 and 380. Starting at nearly sea level, you have a steady but not steep climb, yet overall you might consider this a rigorous climb. The trail passes in and out of several small and one deeper gulch, the largest of which is Malalowai'ole Gulch. This trail is hot and dry, with no shade, so bring plenty of water and wear a hat and sturdy hiking shoes because it's fairly rocky. If you're lucky, there will be some breeze blowing up the hill. On the way you might see cattle in the upland pastures or *nene* hiding in the grass near the trail. Near the halfway point, the trail flattens out as it rounds the bend of the hill, and for a short way it follows a Department of

Land and Natural Resources (DLNR) road before it zigzags down the east slope to the Ma'alaea side trailhead. If starting from the east side, park about 100 yards south of the turnoff to Kahului and walk about one-half mile in from the highway to the trailhead. Expect a hike of at least three hours one way. Several markers along the way indicate cultural and historical sites. If you're interested in more than just a hike, pick up a copy of the *Tales From the Trail: Maui History and Lore From the Lahaina Pali Trail: A Trail Guide* brochure put out by the DLNR, Division of Forestry and Wildlife, and available at their office in the state office building in Wailuku.

SHOPPING

Once learned, everybody loves to do the "Lahaina Stroll." It's easy. Just act cool, nonchalant, and give it your best strut as you walk the gauntlet of Front Street's exclusive shops and boutiques. The fun is just in being there. If you begin in the evening, go to the south end of town and park down by Prison Street; it's much easier to find a spot and you walk uptown, catching the sunset.

The Lahaina Stroll

On Prison Street, check out **Dan's Green House,** 808/661-8412, open daily 9 A.M.–5 P.M., specializing in *fuku-bonsai,* miniature plants originated by David Fukumoto. They're mailable (except to Australia and Japan), and when you get them home, just plop them in water and presto . . . a great little plant; from $26. Dan's also specializes in exotic birds like African gray parrots, macaws from Australia, common cockatoos, and various cheeky parrots, and has a few other miniature animals. Dan's is a great place to browse, especially for families.

Near the corner is **Mermaid's Dowry,** 113 Prison St., 808/662-3697, a small antique shop that has an amazingly diverse collection for the space—all collected by the owner (open Wed.–Sun. 9 A.M.–5 P.M.).

As you head up Front Street, the first group of shops includes **Activity Warehouse** and **Duke's Rental Shop,** where you can rent everything from snorkel gear and surfboards to cruiser bikes

Lahaina's Front Street is lined with shops.

and golf clubs. Visit the "pin and ink" artist upstairs at **Skin Deep Tattooing,** 626 Front St., 808/661-8531, open daily 10 A.M.–10 P.M., until 6 P.M. Sunday, where you can get a permanent memento of your trip to Maui. Skin Deep features "new-age primal, tribal tattoos," Japanese-style intricate beauties, with women artists available for shy female clientele. The walls are hung with sample tattoos you can choose from. A sobriety test is necessary to get tattooed. No wimps allowed! This is a legitimate place where the artists know what they're doing; they've been in business now for more than 20 years.

Up a ways are **Camellia** with a treasure chest laden with gifts and jewelry made from gold, silver, and ivory, and **Original Maui Divers,** which has some fancy jewelry including its specialty, black tree coral. Around the side are the **Aloha Toy Store,** with its motorcycle rentals, and **Swiss Cafe,** which offers early morning coffee and breakfast and other goodies during the day.

Moving down the Line

The following shops are all located along Front Street. By no means exhaustive, this list just gives you an idea of some of the unique shops here.

Between the Pioneer Inn and the seawall, walk onto the sandy floor of the Polynesian-style **Gecko Store,** where all of the items, including shorts, T-shirts, bathing suits, and sweatshirts, bear the bug-eyed sucker-footed logo of Hawaii's famous clicking geckos. Next door is the **Lahaina Hat Co.,** where you can find the perfect chapeau to shield your head from the "merciless" Lahaina sun; and at **Maui Mercantile** you can find all sorts of clothing fit for the sun.

Golden Reef, 695 Front St., is open daily 10 A.M.–10 P.M. Inside is all manner of jewelry from heirloom quality to costume baubles made from black, gold, red, and pink coral, malachite, lapis, and mother of pearl. All designs are created on the premises. Everyone will be happy shopping here because prices range from $1–1,000 and more. Contrast these gems with **Bijoux Pour Vous** heirloom Hawaiian jewelry only a few steps away.

Noah himself would have been impressed with the **Endangered Species Store,** open daily 9 A.M.–10:30 P.M., where a lifesize mountain gorilla, coiled python, flitting butterflies, and fluttering birds bid you welcome to this lovely jam-packed menagerie. The shelves hold world globes, maps, cuddly panda bears, posters of trumpeting elephants, sculptures of soaring eagles, parlor games, postcards, and memento flora- and fauna-inspired T-shirts of 100 percent cotton designed by local artists. A percentage of the profits from every purchase is set aside to advance environmental issues. Moreover, the store tries to deal with vendors who also contribute to the well-being of endangered species and the environment.

Back on the mountain side of the street, **Tropical Blues,** 754 Front, presents fine aloha shirts and women's alohawear. Next door at 752 Front, one of the four **Serendipity** shops on the island offers a unique collection of casual islandwear, furniture, wood carvings, and accouterments of an Asian and Hawaiian nature. In this stretch you will also find **Island Woodcarving** gallery, a prefect spot to choose a hand-carved art piece done in an island wood in a Hawaiian style, and both an **ABC Discount Store** and **E-Z Discount** for sundries, gifts, snacks, and liquor.

The **Whaler's Locker,** 780 Front St., 808/661-3775, open 9 A.M.–10 P.M., is a sea chest filled with hand-engraved scrimshaw on fossilized walrus and mammoth ivory. Lahaina, historically a premier whaling port, has long been known for this sailor's art etched on everything from pocket knives to whale-tooth pendants. Display cases also hold gold and amber jewelry, Ni'ihau shellwork, Japanese *netsuke,* shark's teeth, and even some coral necklaces. If you are looking for a distinctive folk-art gift that truly says Maui, the Whaler's Locker is an excellent store from which to make your choice. The 780 Front Street building is the second oldest shop in modern Lahaina, dating back to 1871.

Sharing the same address is **The South Seas Trading Post,** open daily 8:30 A.M.–10 P.M. It has artifacts from the South Pacific, like tapa cloth from Tonga, but also colorful rugs from India, primitive carvings from Papua New Guinea, and Burmese *kalaga* wall hangings with their beautiful and intricate stitching, jade from China, and bronze from Tibet. You can pick up a one-of-a-kind bead necklace for only a few dollars or a real treasure that would adorn any home, for a decent price. Both antiques and reproductions are sold; the bona fide antiques have authenticating dates on the back or bottom sides.

In the courtyard just off Front Street and Lahainaluna Road is **The Lahaina Market Place,** a collection of semi-open-air stalls and a handful of storefronts, open daily 9 A.M.–9 P.M. Some vendors have roll-up stands and sell trinkets and baubles. Some is junk, but it's neat junk, and they all compete for your business. A mainstay of this alleyway market, **Maui Crystal** has fine examples of handmade glass sculpture and some crystals that are not made on premises. Pyrex and softer colored glass is used to form these creations, an activity you can watch through the glass windows of the small workshop. Two art galleries, facing Lahainaluna Road, back up against this courtyard.

The Far End

On both sides of Front Street beyond Lahainaluna Road, the shops continue. In the Old Poi Factory, 819 Front St., is **David's of Hawaii.** The "sexually incorrect" will love David's, where you can find all kinds of lewd postcards, T-shirts, and souvenirs. If T-shirts bearing sexually implicit puns offend you, keep strolling—it's nasty in there. Funky and audacious. Open daily 9 A.M.–10:30 P.M. This little nook also has jewelry and gift shops.

The **Old Lahaina Book Emporium,** 808/661-1399, the best used bookstore on this side of the island, is crammed full of hardcover and paperback books, just right for a poolside read or serious study. Down the valley at 834 Front Street, this shop also has some new books and new and used CDs, with trades welcome; open Mon.–Sat. 10 A.M.–9 P.M. and Sunday until 6 P.M.

Scrimshaw is the art of carving and/or coloring ivory. Whaling and nautical scenes are perhaps the most common, but other designs are also found. **Lahaina Scrimshaw,** 845 Front St. (across from Wo Hing temple), 808/661-8820, open daily 9 A.M.–10 P.M., boasts its own master scrimshander who works in the window every day from about 7:30 A.M.–noon, and who is willing to answer questions about this seaman's art. Most of the scrimshaw is done on antique whale's teeth from the whaling era or on fossilized walrus and mastodon tusks. The scrimshaw offered is authentic and made by about 40 artists, most of whom are from Hawaii.

Elephant Walk is a gift and clothing store that's fairly representative of others you'll find along Front Street, and the prices are good. **Crazy Shirts** also has a great assortment of distinctive T-shirts and other clothes. Also in this store at 865 Front Street is the tiny but intriguing display of antiques, nautical instruments, scrimshaw, and whaling-related pictures.

Across the street is **The Whaler** for mostly new marine and nautical objects and some art glass. At the **Sunglass Hut** shop, you can pick up shades for the strong tropical sun. Depending on the type, these sunglasses run $40–350. Also available are a wide range of watches—waterproof and not—some economical and others that will bust your budget.

Off the Main Drag

Fox Camera, 139 Lahainaluna Rd., 808/667-6255, open daily, is a full-service, one-hour-developing camera store. It's good in West Maui for any specialized photo needs. A second one-hour lab is down the street and around the corner at 820 Front Street. Technicians here can do some camera repair or arrange to have it done.

Even if you haven't been out on a whale-watching tour, stop in at the Pacific Whale Foundation's **Ocean Store,** 143 Dickenson St., 808/667-7447, for a look at all the clothing, posters, jewelry, and gift items relating to the whale and other sea creatures. It's almost an education having a look here, and the proceeds help support this worthy organization.

The **Salvation Army Thrift Shop,** on Shaw St. just up from Front St., has the usual collection of inexpensive used goods but occasionally some great buys on older aloha shirts. Open Monday–Saturday, regular business hours.

505 Front Street

With most shops open daily 9 A.M.–9 P.M., this mall offers a barrel full of shops and restaurants at the south end of Front Street, away from the heavy foot traffic. The complex looks like a New England harbor village, and the shopping is good

and unhurried with validated underground parking for customers. Some shops include a **Whalers General Store** for sundries; **Foreign Intrigue Imports; Maui to Go** for arts and crafts; **Colors of Maui Clothing;** and the wonderful **Elizabeth Doyle Gallery,** which has a superb collection of art glass, ceramics, and paintings—some island artists.

Check your email at **Ali'i Espresso Cafe** as you linger over a snack and coffee. Rates are $.20 cents per minute, $6 per half-hour, or $12 per hour; printouts are extra. Several other shops inhabit this mall, as do half a dozen restaurants.

The Wharf Cinema Center

The Wharf Cinema Center at 658 Front offers three floors of fast-food eateries, clothing and jewelry stores, souvenir shops, and a movie theater. Most shops are open 9 A.M.–9 P.M. Playing first-run movies, the triplex **Lahaina Cinemas** occupies much of the third floor. Browse **Crazy Shirts** with its excellent selection of quality T-shirts or the **Red Dirt Shirt** shop for distinct T's from Kaua'i. **Hawaiian Styles and Creations** offers tropical sportswear, and **Island Swimwear** carries bathing suits for men and women. For a ready-made bed covering or cloth to sew your own tropical dress, head for **Quilts 'N Fabric Land,** and if a take-home souvenir is what you're after, look at **A Piece of Maui Gallery and Gifts.**

Island Coins and Stamps on the third floor is a shop as frayed as an old photo album. It specializes in philatelic supplies. Also on the third floor is the **Atlantis submarine** office, where you can arrange a memorable underwater Maui adventure. If all of this shopping gets you down, sit and relax at **Maui Island Coffee** or have a bite to eat at **The Blue Lagoon** in the central courtyard. For postal needs and gifts, stop by the **Lahaina Mail Depot** on the lower level at the rear; open weekdays 10 A.M.–4:30 P.M., Saturday until 1 P.M. Across the walk is **Island Sandals,** 808/661-5110, a small shop run in the honest old-style way that produces fully adjustable leather tie sandals, styled from the days of Solomon. As the gregarious sandal maker says, he creates the right sandal for $155 ($135 women's) and gives you the left as a gift. Stop in and have him trace your feet for an order. As he works, he'll readily talk about political, social, or local island issues, and definitely tell you why it's much better to have leather on the bottom of your feet than any man-made material. See his work at www.islandsandals.com. Out front is an **ABC Discount Store.** For those coming from Ka'anapali, the West Maui Shopping Express stops at the rear of this complex.

Pioneer Inn Shops

Below Pioneer Inn is a clutch of shops that includes **Products of Hawaii Too** for gift and craft items; a **Lifestyle** alohawear clothing shop; and a **Whalers General Store.** Several other clothing stores are here, as are **Trouvaille Gallery** for jewelry, gifts, and artwork, **Maui Divers** for unique jewelry made from the harvest of the sea, and **Häagen-Dazs** for ice cream treats. Most shops are open 9 A.M.–9 P.M.

On the sidewalk in front of these shops is a stand where you can get your picture taken with a multicolored macaw on your shoulder (or with one on each shoulder and one sitting on your head!). Taken one day, the photos are ready the next day. The fee ranges upward from $20, depending on the number and size of your photographs.

Old Lahaina Center

The Old Lahaina Center, in front of the midtown post office and between Front and Waine'e streets, has an **Ace Hardware,** a new **Foodland,** the **Lahaina Ticket Company,** and a **Starbuck's Coffee** shop. In the midst of this complex is the **Maui Theatre,** where the 'Ulalena theater show is performed, while along Papalaua Avenue are **Bank of Hawaii** and **American Savings Bank** branches. In the portion closest to Waine'e Street, you'll find **Nagasako General Store, Lahaina Pharmacy, Lahaina Fishing Supplies** for fishing gear and marine hardware, and **Ji Mi's Asian Food Mart.**

Across Waine'e Street is the **Lahaina Square Shopping Center,** with its several inexpensive eateries, **West Maui Cycles,** and **Gold's Gym.** You'll find an Activity Warehouse center and additional eateries next door at the small **Anchor Square** center.

The Lahaina Center

Lahaina's newest shopping center is at the corner of Front and Papalaua streets at the north edge of downtown. The signature establishments of this mall are the **Hard Rock Cafe,** filled with memorabilia of rock-and-roll greats and serving American standards and cold beer; a **Banana Republic** for livable fashions; and **Hilo Hattie** for Hawaiian clothing and gifts. In the center you will also find **Local Motion,** a hip clothing store selling tank tops, swimwear, and locally designed T-shirts; **Wet Seal** for young women's clothing; several other fashion shops; an **ABC Discount Store** for sundries and inexpensive beach gear; a **Dive Maui** outlet for water activities and equipment; **Diamond Head Gallery** and **Pictures Plus** for art; and several activity companies. You can also cool down at the long bar at **Maui Brews,** have a meal at the restaurant, spend some extra change in the game room, or come in the evening for music and dancing at their nightclub. For finer food, try **Ruth's Chris Steak House** and follow that with an evening of magic at **Warren and Annabelle's.** Lahaina's second cinema complex, the **Front Street Theaters,** occupies one of the center buildings. There is a pay parking lot here that's free with validation. The Holo Ka'a shuttle stops at the Hilo Hattie store more than 10 times per day on its route between Lahaina and Ka'anapali; $1 per person each way.

After shopping, stop by **Hale Kahiko** and have a look at the traditional-style Hawaiian buildings and items of everyday use displayed as a cultural showcase in a landscaped enclosure to the side of the parking lot. Open daily 9 A.M.–6 P.M. While here enjoy the *keiki* hula shows at 2:30 P.M. on Wednesdays and 6 P.M. on Fridays.

Lahaina Cannery Mall

As practical looking as its name on the outside—it is a converted pineapple cannery, after all—the center's bright, well-appointed, and air-conditioned interior features some of the best and most convenient shopping on West Maui; open daily 9:30 A.M.–9 P.M. The mall is located at 1221 Honoapi'ilani Highway, near Mala Wharf. If you'll be staying at a condo and doing your own cooking, the largest and generally least expensive supermarket on West Maui is **Safeway,** open daily 24 hours. To book any activities, from a whale-watch to a dinner cruise, you'll find **Activity Mart** offering the right price. Sundries can be picked up at the **ABC Discount Store,** and you can beat the sun's glare by stopping into **Shades of Hawaii.** Some of the clothing shops you'll find here are **Crazy Shirts, Maui WaterWear, Escape to Maui, Panama Jacks,** and **Blue Ginger Designs.** Food is available at **Compadres Mexican Bar and Grill,** as well as half a dozen smaller stalls for international food in the food court.

Waldenbooks has one of its excellent, well-stocked stores in the mall. One of the most unusual shops is **The Kite Fantasy,** featuring kites, windsocks, and toys for kids of all ages. You can buy kites like a six-foot flexifoil for more than $100 or a simple triangular plastic kite for only a few bucks. Cloth kites are made from nylon with nice designs for a reasonable $15.95. Another unique shop, well worth the effort to explore, is **Na Mea Hawai'i Store.** This unique shop carries only native Hawaiian arts and crafts, block prints, clothing, printed fabric, tapa fabric, feather and shell lei, and food items, as well as a good selection of local music and books on Hawaiian subjects. This is the real thing. You won't find tourist junk or imported goods here. Open daily 10 A.M.–7 P.M., stop in for an authentic gift from the island. Along the same lines, **Totally Hawaiian Gift Gallery** carries quilts, carved bowls, shellwork, woodwork, and other fine gift items.

If you're into designer coffees and cigars, come to **Sir Wilfred's.** It's one of the few places on this side of the island for such delicacies. If you're hungry, try the deli case for pastries and the like, or order a cup of soup, quiche, lasagna, or a sandwich. A good assortment of gift items round out what's sold here. **Longs Drugs** is one of the cheapest places to buy and develop film. You can also find a selection of everything from aspirin to boogie boards. There's plenty of free parking at this mall, but the Holo Ka'a shopping shuttle stops here a dozen times a day shuttling between Lahaina and Ka'anapali; $1 per person each way or $2 for a trip all the way from Kapalua.

Booths are set up in the mall Monday–Friday 10 A.M.–4 P.M., displaying and selling Hawaiian art and crafts. Also, a free **Polynesian Show** is presented every Tuesday and Thursday evening 7–8 P.M., and there's a **Keiki Hula Show** every Saturday and Sunday 1–2 P.M.

Arts

Dubbed the "Art Capital of the Pacific," it's said that Lahaina is the world's third-largest art market. Who determined that to be so is a question unanswered, yet it is certain that you can view countless works of art here and spend a fortune acquiring it. Many artists on display at the galleries in Lahaina are local island artists and others from the state, although other Americans and numerous foreigners are also represented. Although not all, many of the galleries in town are open until 10 P.M.

The Lahaina Arts Society has its **Old Jail Gallery** in the basement of the Old Lahaina Courthouse and its **Banyan Tree Gallery** on the first floor. Both are open daily 9 A.M.–5 P.M. The Lahaina Arts Society is a nonprofit venture, and all artworks hung in its galleries are juried pieces of its 175 members, all island residents. You can get some good bargains here. Contact the Lahaina Arts Society at 808/661-0111 for information. Every other Saturday and Sunday 8 A.M.–5 P.M., society members display and sell their art at **Banyan Tree Craft Fair,** under the big banyan behind the courthouse. On alternate weekends, other artists and craftspeople display their wares at the same location at the **Na Kupuna O Maui He U'i Cultural Arts Festival.** Sometimes you'll get demonstrations and music to boot. Many of the artists here are up and coming, and the prices for sometimes remarkable works are reasonable. They're trying to make a living by their skills, and most are not displayed at the well-known galleries in town.

The Village Galleries, with two locations open daily 9 A.M.–9 P.M. at 120 Dickenson St., 808/661-4402, and at 180 Dickenson St., 808/661-5559, were founded by Lynn Shue in 1970 and are among the oldest continuous galleries featuring original works of Maui artists. At the original gallery at 120 Dickenson, enter to find everything from raku pottery to hand-blown glass and sculptures done in both wood and metal. Some of the accomplished painters on display are George Allan, who works in oils; Joyce Clark, another oil painter noted for her seascapes; Betty Hay-Freeland, a landscape artist; Fred KenKnight, who uses watercolors to depict island scenes; and Lowell Mapes, who also uses oil to render familiar landmarks and island scenes. The galleries also have inexpensive items like postcards, posters, and limited-edition prints, all perfect as mementos and souvenirs. The gallery at 180 Dickenson features more contemporary and abstract works.

With several shops around the islands, **Dolphin Galleries,** 697 Front St., 808/661-5000, has a wide collection of internationally known artists, many from Hawaii. One of the most unusual is the teenage sensation Alexandra Nechita, who produces abstract impressionist pieces not unlike Picasso.

The Wyland Gallery, 711 Front St., 808/667-2285, showcases the works of Wyland, renowned worldwide for his "whaling wall" murals of cavorting whales. Wyland's visionary oil and watercolor paintings of marvelous aquatic scenes adorn the walls, while his compassionate bronze renderings of whales and dolphins sing their soul songs from white pedestals. Other featured paintings are done by Al Hogue, William DeShazo, Neolito, Steven Power, and John Pitre. Also displayed are the organic sculptures of Dale Joseph Evers, a pioneer in functional furnishings, who has turned bronze and acrylic into dolphin-shaped tables. A second Wyland Gallery, 136 Dickenson St., 808/661-0590, vibrates with fantastic colors and images. Galleries are open 9 A.M.–9 P.M. daily.

The two **Galerie Lassen,** 700 and 844 Front St., 808/661-1101 and 808/667-7707, showcase original and limited-edition prints by Christian Riese Lassen, who boldly applies striking colors to bring to life his landscapes and two-worlds perspective of sea and earth. Complementing the exaggerated hues of Lassen's mystical works is the subtle patina of Richard Steirs' cast-iron sculptures of supple whales and dolphins. Mr. Steirs, an Upcountry resident, is among the most admired sculptors on Maui with his limited-edition castings.

After many successful years in Kula, Curtis Cost has opened a second gallery, the **Curtis Wilson Cost Gallery,** 808/661-4140, at 710 Front Street. All works on display are by Cost, and his style is one of realism, portraying bucolic country scenes in rich colors with strong greens.

Displaying only contemporary oil paintings is the **Elizabeth Edwards Fine Art** gallery, 808/667-6711, at 716 Front Street. **The Lahaina Galleries,** 728 Front St., 808/667-2152, is one of the oldest galleries on the island. The gallery, with a central room and two in the rear, is hung with the works of Dario Campanile, Lau Chun, Guy Buffet, Aldo Luongo, and other widely acclaimed painters, and the mesmerizing acrylic sculptures of Frederick Hart. Branch galleries are located at the Kapalua Shops in Kapalua and at The Shops at Wailea.

At **Celebrities** gallery, 764 Front St., 808/667-0727, you can find paintings, drawings, photographs, and other artworks by well-known personalities who are generally not known for their artwork. Some of those whose works are shown include Bob Dylan, John Lennon, Tony Bennett, Anthony Quinn, and David Bowie. Surprisingly, much of it is reasonably good. Stop in for a look.

Robert Lynn Nelson Studio, 802 Front St. near the corner of Lahainaluna Road, 808/667-2100, shows originals and prints only of Robert Lynn Nelson, the father of the modern marine art movement, which splits the canvas between land and undersea scenes. Although most well-known for his marine scenes, Nelson pursues other styles and themes that he is not known for, like landscapes and abstracts, that you may only find displayed in this gallery. A second gallery is found at the West Maui Center on the mountain side of Honoapi'ilani Highway.

Showing modern art with bright colors is **Sargents Fine Art** gallery right on the corner of Front Street and Lahainaluna Road. Some of what hangs on these walls are abstract sailing ships by Rick Lawrence, impressionist landscapes by Anne Good, surreal scenes by Vladimir Kush, portraits by Bill Mack, fairies by St. Clair, impressionist pieces by Andrea Smith, and immense brightly painted fruit by Carmelo Sortino.

Nearly across Lahainaluna Road is the **Martin Lawrence Gallery,** 808/661-1788, which shows an eclectic and pleasing collection of pop and contemporary art by such artists as Warhol, Chagall, Picasso, Miro, Etré, and Kordakova. Around the corner at 126 Lahainaluna Road, in a one-man shop, is **Island Art Collection,** 808/667-6782, showing island scenes by owner Jim Kingwell.

The **One World Gallery,** 816 Front St., 808/661-3984, is a zany collection of modern art, jewelry, glass, ceramics, and multimedia art pieces, full of fun and with a sense of humor. Clown faces by Red Skelton, African wildlife scenes by Craig Bone, and portraits of Hawaiians by Lori Higgins are some of what you will find at **Addi Galleries,** 844 Front St., 808/661-4900.

Displaying idyllic home scenes, waterfalls, snowscapes, and the like by Thomas Kinkade are the **Thomas Kinkade Galleries,** 808/667-7175, at 780 Front Street. Closed on Sunday.

Food/Liquor Stores

The following markets/supermarkets are in and around Lahaina. The larger ones also stock beer, wine, and liquor. **Safeway,** at the Lahaina Cannery Mall, open 24 hours, is a large supermarket complete with deli, fish market, floral shop, and bakery. **Foodland,** at the Old Lahaina Center, is a new and well-stocked supermarket. **Nagasako General Store,** also at the Old Lahaina Center, open daily 7 A.M.–10 P.M., Sunday until 7 P.M., has a smaller selection of ethnic Hawaiian, Japanese, Chinese, and Korean foods, along with liquor selections, fresh fish, and produce.

For bulk foods, health food items, vitamins, minerals, and supplements, and hot and cold prepared foods, try the full-service **Down To Earth Natural Foods,** 808/667-2855, at the corner of Lahainaluna Road and Waine'e Street. Open Monday–Saturday 7 A.M.–9 P.M. and Sunday 8:30 A.M.–8 P.M.

The Olowalu General Store, 808/661-3774, located five miles east of Lahaina along Rte. 30, open Mon.–Fri. 6 A.M.–6:30 P.M., Sat. 7 A.M.–6:30 P.M., Sun. 7 A.M.–5 P.M., is fairly well stocked and the only place to pick up supplies in this area. It also has light snacks, including sandwiches and hot dogs, making it a perfect stop if you are snorkeling or swimming on the nearby beaches.

Mr. Wine, on the corner of Lahainaluna Road and Waine'e Street, 808/661-5551, not only has a huge selection of wines, and some beer, liquors, and liqueurs, but also keeps the better wines and champagnes under cellar conditions in a climatically controlled room at 55°F and 70 percent humidity. While classic wines are stocked, the shop also has many economical wines just right for any wallet. Beat the hot Lahaina sun and stop in for a perfect bottle for the evening. Open Monday–Saturday 11 A.M.–7 P.M.

INFORMATION AND SERVICES
Information

The following groups and organizations should prove helpful: Lahaina Restoration Foundation, P.O. Box 338, Lahaina, HI 96761, 808/661-3262. The foundation is a storehouse of information about historical Lahaina; be sure to pick up its handy brochure, *Lahaina, A Walking Tour of Historic and Cultural Sites,* for an introduction to historically significant sites around town.

The Lahaina Town Action Committee, 648 Wharf St., Lahaina, HI 96761, 808/667-9175, sponsors cultural events and other activities throughout the year, including Art Night and Halloween, and can provide information about what's happening in the area. It operates the **Lahaina Visitor Center** on the first floor of the Old Lahaina Courthouse. For popular events and activities happening in Lahaina, contact the events hotline at 808/667-9194 or 888/310-1117, or visit the center's website at www.visitlahaina.com. Pick up its *Maui Historical Walking Guide* brochure. It has information mostly on Lahaina and Ka'anapali.

The nonprofit Lahaina Arts Society, 808/661-0111, las@mauigateway.com, has information about the art scene and art events in town. They maintain two galleries at the old Courthouse and run an art program for children.

The Lahaina **public library,** 680 Wharf St., 808/662-3950, is open Tuesday noon–8 P.M., Wednesday and Thursday 9 A.M.–5 P.M., and Friday and Saturday 10:30–4:30 P.M.

Medical Services

A concentration of all types of specialists is found at the Maui Medical Group, 130 Prison St., 808/661-0051 (open Mon.–Fri. 8 A.M.–5 P.M. and Saturday 8 A.M.–noon); call for emergency hours. Professional medical care can also be found at the Kaiser Permanente clinic, 910 Waine'e St., 808/662-6900, during the same hours. Alternatively, the Aloha Family Practice Clinic, 180 Dickenson St. at Dickenson Square, Ste. 205, 808/662-5642, offers scheduled and urgent care services.

Pharmacies in Lahaina include the Lahaina Pharmacy at the Old Lahaina Center, 808/661-3119; Longs Drugs at the Lahaina Cannery Mall, 808/667-4390; and Valley Isle Pharmacy, 130 Prison St., 808/661-4747.

Banks

In Lahaina during normal banking hours, try the Bank of Hawaii, 808/661-8781, or the American Savings Bank, 808/667-9561, in the Old Lahaina Center; or First Hawaiian Bank, just a few steps away at 215 Papalaua St., 808/661-3655.

Post Office

The main post office is on the very northwest edge of town where Ka'anapali begins; the midtown postal branch is located at the Old Lahaina Center. Both are open Monday–Friday 8:30 A.M.–5 P.M. and Saturday 9 A.M.–1 P.M.

Lahaina Mail Depot is a post office contract station located at The Wharf Cinema Center, 808/667-2000. It's open weekdays 10 A.M.–4:30 P.M. and Saturday until 1 P.M., and along with the normal stamps and such, it specializes in sending packages home. Mailing boxes, tape, and packaging materials are all available, as are souvenir packs of coffee, nuts, candies, and teas, which might serve as a last-minute purchase, but are expensive.

Ka'anapali

Five lush valleys, nourished by streams from the West Maui Mountains, stretch luxuriously for 10 miles from Ka'anapali north to Kapalua. All along the connecting **Honoapi'ilani Highway** (Rte. 30), the dazzle and glimmer of beaches is offset by black volcanic rock. This is West Maui's resort coast. Two sensitively planned and beautifully executed resorts are at each end of this drive. Ka'anapali Resort is 500 acres of fun and relaxation at the south end. It houses six luxury hotels, a handful of beautifully appointed condos, a shopping mall and museum, 36 holes of world-class golf, tennis courts galore, and epicurean dining in a chef's salad of cuisines. Two of the hotels, the Hyatt Regency and Sheraton, are inspired architectural showcases that blend harmoniously with Maui's most beautiful seashore surroundings. At the northern end is another gem, the Kapalua Resort, 1,650 of Maui's most beautifully sculpted acres with its own showcases, prime golf, fine beaches, exclusive shopping, and endless activity.

Ka'anapali, with its four miles of glorious beach, is Maui's westernmost point. It begins where Lahaina ends and continues north along Route 30 until it runs into the village of Honokowai. Along this shore, Maui flashes its most captivating pearly white smile. The sights here are either natural or man-made, but not historical. This is where you come to gaze from mountain to sea and bathe yourself in natural beauty. Then, after a day of surf and sunshine, you repair to one of the gorgeous hotels or restaurants for a drink or dining, or just to promenade around the grounds.

History

Western Maui was a mixture of scrub and precious *lo'i*, irrigated terrace land reserved for taro, the highest life-sustaining plant given by the gods. The farms stretched to Kapalua, skirting the numerous bays all along the way. The area was important enough for a "royal highway" to be built by Chief Pi'ilani, and it still bears his name.

Westerners used the lands surrounding Ka'anapali to grow sugarcane, and **The Lahaina, Kaanapali, and Pacific Railroad,** known today as the "Sugar Cane Train," chugged to Ka'anapali Beach

WEST MAUI

to unburden itself onto barges that carried the cane to waiting ships. Ka'anapali, until the 1960s, was a blemished beauty where the Pioneer Sugar Mill dumped its rubbish. Then Amfac, who owned the mill and this land, decided to put the land to better use. In creating Hawaii's first planned resort community, it outdid itself. Robert Trent Jones, Sr. was hired to mold the golf course along this spectacular coast, while the Hyatt Regency and its grounds became an architectural counterpoint. The Sheraton Maui was built atop, and integrated with, Pu'u Keka'a, "Black Rock," a wave-eroded cinder cone, and the architects used its sea cliffs as part of the walls of the resort. Here, on a deep underwater shelf, daring divers used to descend to harvest Maui's famous black coral trees. The Hawaiians believed that Pu'u Keka'a was a very holy place where the spirits of the dead left this earth and migrated into the spirit world. Kahekili, Maui's most famous 18th-century chief, often came here to leap into the sea below. This old-time daredevil was fond of the heart-stopping activity and made famous "Kahekili's Leap," an even more treacherous sea cliff on nearby Lana'i. Today, the Sheraton puts on a daily sunset show where this "leap" is reenacted.

Pu'u Keka'a

One of the most easily accessible and visually engaging snorkeling spots on Maui is located at the Sheraton's Black Rock. Approach this either from the beach in front of the hotel, where you can snorkel west around the rock, or from around back. The entire area offshore is like an underwater marine park. There are schools of reef fish, rays, and even lonely turtles. Follow the main road past the Sheraton until it begins to climb the hill. Walk along the pathway that leads to the North Ka'anapali Beach and head for the remnants of an old pier. This pier was built as the end of a spur line of the sugarcane railroad and used to ship bags of sugar. After the Mala Wharf was constructed closer to Lahaina in the 1920s, the rail lines were taken up and cattle were shipped off island from here. There is limited free public parking in Ka'anapali, so you may have to park in one of the few pay lots. Alternately, park at Kahekili Beach Park at the far north end of Ka'ana-

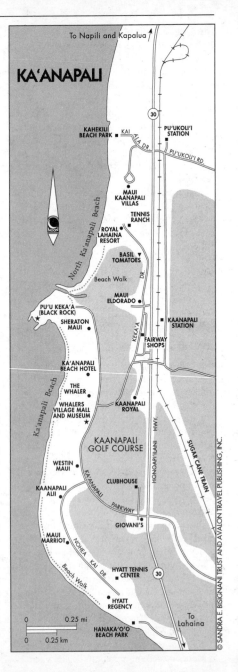

ROBERT NILSEN

rainbow over Ka'anapali

pali near the Maui Kaanapali Villas, from where it's only a 15-minute walk.

Whale Museum

The free Whale Museum, at Whaler's Village shopping mall, 808/661-5992, has a few outside displays, but most items are inside on the upper level of the mall. The most dramatic outside display is the skeleton of a 40-foot sperm whale. This big boy greets you at the entrance to the mall as you come up the steps. There is also a whaling boat in a side courtyard. The compact display area upstairs on the mezzanine level is full of whaling history, photographs, drawings, artifacts from whaling ships, a reconstructed forecastle, a video on whaling, and many informative descriptions and stories about the whaling industry, whaling life, and the whalers themselves. After a walk through the museum, pick up a memento at the museum gift shop. Open 9 A.M.–10 P.M. daily. This is a must-see stop for anyone who wishes to have a better understanding of whales, sailors, life on board, and this integral aspect of Hawaiian history.

Transportation

Ka'anapali is serviced by the free **Kaanapali Trol-**ley within the resort area. It runs throughout the day from 10 A.M.–10 P.M. on a prescribed schedule and stops at each resort and at the Whalers Village.

Holo Ka'a public transit shuttle runs south between Ka'anapali and Lahaina Harbor in Lahaina and north to Kapalua. Shuttles operate about a dozen times a day between 9 A.M.–10 P.M., stopping at hotels, condos, and shopping centers on the way. Rides between Ka'anapali and Lahaina are $1 each way and between Ka'anapali and Kapalua are $2 each way. Several times a day, shuttles connect the West Maui and South Maui regions through Ma'alaea. Fares are $5 either way to/from Ma'alaea and $10 per day for the entire system.

Fun for the entire family, the **Sugar Cane Train** takes the scenic route between Ka'anapali and Lahaina.

The Kapalua–West Maui Airport is the most convenient for air travel to this end of the island, but there are only a limited number of daily flights in and out of this airstrip. Most air traffic to Maui still goes via Kahului. For access to the airport in Kahului from Ka'anapali and Lahaina, try **Speedy Shuttle** or **Executive Shuttle.** From Lahaina, the fare will be about $35 one way, a bit more from Ka'anapali.

WEST MAUI

ROBERT NILSEN

Its fine sand, gentle water, plethora of activities, and nearby accommodations and restaurants make Ka'anapali Beach Maui's best-known vacation spot.

BEACHES

Ka'anapali Beach

The two-mile stretch of pristine sand at Ka'anapali is what people come to experience in Maui, and they are never disappointed. Just as you leave Lahaina and enter Ka'anapali you'll find **Hanaka'o'o Beach Park.** It's a good swimming and sailboarding spot, with lifeguards, showers, and parking; and while so close, it's away from the hotel crowds. Napili, Lahaina, and Kahana canoe clubs are based here, and you can often see rowers out on the water practicing their strokes. This beach, called Makaiwa, is also referred to as Canoe Beach. Between the beach and the road is an old cemetery with mostly Chinese characters written on the headstones. A path runs between here and Wahikuli Wayside Park just down the road.

Just north around the corner opens the expanse of **Ka'anapali Beach,** an uninterrupted stretch of sand running from the park to Black Rock. Ka'anapali Beach is sometimes referred to as Little Waikiki for all the resorts along its shore and the crowds of people who frequent it, and it has earned the moniker "Dig Me Beach" because

it's known for people-watching and those who come to be watched. Ka'anapali Beach is a center for water activities in West Maui. Aside from swimming and snorkeling, you can take surfing and windsurfing lessons, rent an ocean kayak, ride on a catamaran or outrigger canoe, or be lifted into the air by parasail. Options abound. Although the hotels that line this beach are some of the most exclusive on the island, public access to the beach is guaranteed. There are numerous right-of-way walkways to the beach that run between the various properties, but parking your car here is definitely a hassle. Several of the hotels have set aside a few parking spaces in their area—usually less than a dozen spots—to accommodate the general public who come to enjoy the beach, but these spaces are usually taken early in the day and remain full. A good idea is to park at either Hanaka'o'o or Wahikuli parks and walk northward along the beach. You can park in the Hyatt's lower lot and enter along a right-of-way. There's access between the Hyatt and the Marriott's pay parking ramp, between the Marriott and the Kaanapali Alii, which also has limited parking, and between the Kaanapali Alii

WEST MAUI

and the Westin Maui. There is also some parking near the Sheraton and at the Whalers Village parking ramp, but you must pass through the gauntlet of shops.

North Ka'anapali Beach

Continue past Black Rock and the beach continues north. Quieter than the main Ka'anapali Beach, it's much less frequented, has no lifeguards, and only the Royal Lahaina Resort has frontage here. In the early 20th century, pigs and cattle were raised where the Royal Hawaiian Hotel now stands, and before that some of the area back from the beach was a village site. This North Ka'anapali Beach is also known as Keka'a Beach, and the section fronting and just north of Kahekili Beach Park is locally called Airport Beach because the small Ka'anapali airstrip and terminal were located here during the 1960s and '70s.

Located just north of the Royal Lahaina Resort, **Kahekili Beach Park** is dedicated to Maui's last major king, Kahekili. Open 6 A.M. to 30 minutes past sunset, this small park is a commodious place with a broad lawn, palm trees, a pavilion for cooking, and tables for a picnic. The large shaded parking area can accommodate many cars, and you can count on always finding someone here. The beach, sometimes used for scuba lessons and not bad for snorkelers, runs uninterrupted to Black Rock.

Beach Walk

As in Wailea, a beach walkway has been created in Ka'anapali that parallels the edge of the sand from the Hyatt Regency in the south to the Sheraton in the north. This walkway is a convenient way to pass from one property to another: Peruse your neighbor hotel, try one of the restaurants down the line, or walk to shop. During the cool hours of the day and at sunset, this walkway is also used by joggers out for exercise and those who want the perfect location to watch the sun go down. If you cut through the Sheraton property and duck out the other side, you can connect with a similar pathway that skirts the golf course and runs along the North Ka'anapali Beach into the Royal Lahaina Resort.

LUXURY HOTELS

The Ka'anapali Resort offers hotels that are all in the luxury category—no budget or midrange accommodations here. The following should give you an idea of what's available.

Ka'anapali Beach Hotel

Not as large or as luxurious as its chain-hotel neighbors, but an excellent hotel nonetheless, the Ka'anapali Beach Hotel, 2525 Ka'anapali Pkwy., 808/661-0011 or 800/262-8450, fax 808/667-5978, www.kbhmaui.com, is a bargain and the least expensive hotel property on the beach. This is undoubtedly the most Hawaiian of the hotels in Ka'anapali and perhaps in the state. As you arrive, you'll be greeted with *ho'okipa* (hospitality), and throughout your stay experience the *po'okela* (excellence) of the staff. There is no glitz here, just warm and friendly service, reasonably priced restaurants, a wonderful beachfront location, and nearly as many amenities as the big boys down the line. Guest service provides many free activities and demonstrations, including lei-making, hula lessons, *lau hala* weaving, and a free torchlighting ceremony and sunset hula show nightly. The tour desk can always hook you up with any activity on the island, and the gift and sundries shop has items that you forgot to bring with you or you want to take back as souvenirs.

A delight is the 11 A.M. music and dance performance put on by the hotel staff on Mondays, Wednesdays, and Fridays—they even have their own CD! On these days, and also on Sundays, a craft fair is held in the lobby 9–11 A.M. If you're staying here, don't miss it; if you're not, drop on by anyway—everyone is welcome. Have a swim in the hotel's distinctive whale-shaped pool or check with the Trilogy Ocean Sports activity booth for water equipment to rent and water tours. Over the past few years, most of the rooms have been totally renovated with new wicker furniture, island-inspired wall coverings, a unique sliding-glass door arrangement for the lanai, and larger and updated bathrooms, and the rest of the property repainted and spiffed up. The two restaurants and one snack shop provide a wide variety of food for everyone's taste, and the courtyard bar offers libations into the evening. The Aloha Passport for Kids program will keep the little ones busy as they go from spot to spot around the property collecting mementos from each "destination." Standard rooms range $195–265 for an ocean view, oceanfront rooms are $290, and suites are priced $255–600. Numerous special packages are available.

Sheraton Maui

The 510 rooms and suites of the Sheraton Maui, 2605 Ka'anapali Pkwy., Lahaina, HI 96761, 808/661-0031 or 800/782-9488, fax 808/661-0458, www.sheraton-maui.com, are built around Ka'anapali's most conspicuous natural phenomenon, Pu'u Keka'a, "Black Rock." Originally opened in 1963, the Sheraton reopened in 1997 after a two-year complete and extensive renovation. Open, bright, and breezy, the lobby looks out over the finely landscaped gardens and an enticing meandering pool with a water slide and spa. Two classy restaurants grace the hotel, as does one indoor lounge, where you can shoot billiards in the evening, and one bar situated at poolside, which features evening entertainment. The guest activities desk can arrange almost any activity that the island offers, and you can rent water equipment and have lessons from the beach activity booth. The snorkeling around Black Rock is the best in the area, and every evening there is a torchlighting ceremony and cliff dive from the rock.

As a guest, you can avail yourself of several daily catamaran rides aboard the *Teralani* or head for some sporting competition at the resort's tennis club. The fitness center, day spa, business center, and clothing and sundries shops are all for guest use. Kids ages 5–12 can be taken care of as well through the daily Keiki Aloha program, which operates half-day, full-day, and evening services that combine arts and crafts with history and culture. The north end of the Ka'anapali beach walk ends at the Sheraton, so you can stroll all the way to the Hyatt at the south end without leaving the oceanside. Most rooms at the Sheraton face the ocean; all are air-conditioned and have full

amenities. Rates are $350–420 for garden and mountain-view rooms, $510–610 for oceanview and oceanfront rooms, $750 for an Ohana family suite, and other suites from $825. The extra adult charge is $50, but children 17 years old and under stay free in the same room as an adult if existing bedding is used. The Sheraton Maui has a superb location and is a superb property. You'll be entranced by the beauty, welcomed by the friendly and helpful staff, and thoroughly enjoy your well-deserved vacation.

Hyatt Regency Maui

The moment you enter the main lobby of this luxury hotel, the magic begins. A multithread architectural extravaganza opens to the sky, birds fly freely, and magnificent potted plants and full-size courtyard palm trees create the atmosphere of a modern Polynesian palace located at Ka'anapali's southern extremity, at 200 Nohea Kai Dr., Lahaina, HI 96761, 808/661-1234 or 800/554-9288, fax 808/667-4498, www.maui.hyatt.com. Nooks and crannies abound and wildlife inhabits the impeccable landscaped gardens and ponds. The swimming pools are inspired by the islands: grottoes, caves, waterfalls, and a 150-foot slide are all built in. A swinging wooden bridge connects sections of the pool deck. There are four fine restaurants on property, half a dozen lounges (one is a swim-up bar at the pool), and the Drums of the Pacific lu'au. The covey of specialty shops and boutiques will please parents, and the little kids will love it here too. Camp Hyatt for children ages 5–12 runs daily 9 A.M.–3 P.M. and includes activities and excursions that change daily. An evening camp 6–10 P.M. is also available, so put those little kiddies in the care of professionals and have a romantic night out.

All beach activities, equipment rentals, and lessons, including a sail/snorkel ride on the *Kiele V* catamaran, can be arranged through the beach activities center at oceanside. Expend some energy at the health club and tennis center, or try the oceanfront Spa Moana for the relaxing royal treatment. For those with less physical activity in mind, check out the daily Hawaiian demonstrations in the lobby, the hotel wildlife tour, the art and garden tour ($2 million worth of art—most from Asia and the Pacific), or the nightly astronomy show ($25 per person) on the hotel roof. The lobby activity desk or Aloha Services will help you make reservations for activities throughout the island, and if you're here on business, the business center can help take care of your office needs. Rates for the 806 rooms and suites are $345 for terrace rooms, $385 for golf/mountain rooms, $445 for oceanview rooms, and $565 for oceanfront rooms. Rates are higher for the special Regency floors, and suites run $900–4,500. If you visit, valet parking is in front of the hotel. Or you can self-park out front or around in the back. From here, both the north end of Lahaina, pretty at night with its colored lights reflecting on the water, and Lana'i, floating across the Lahaina Roads, are easily visible.

Westin Maui

The Westin Maui, 2365 Ka'anapali Pkwy., Lahaina, HI 96761, 808/667-2525 or 866/500-8313, fax 808/661-5764, www.westinmaui.com, is actually a phoenix, risen from the old Maui Surf Hotel. True to the second life of that mythical bird, it is a beauty. Westin is known for its fabulous entranceways, lobbies, and quiet nooks, and you won't be disappointed here. A series of strolling paths takes you through resplendent manicured grounds that surround an extensive multipool area, one of the largest on Maui. Waterfalls, water slides, and natural rock formations all blend to create civilized paradise. To the left of the main lobby is a collection of exclusive boutique shops and a business center. You'll find just what you want to eat or drink at any time of the day at one of the hotel's three restaurants and three lounges. The ocean activity center can set you up with all sorts of rentals on the beach or a ride on *Gemini*, the hotel's sailing catamaran. The kids are taken care of at the supervised daily Keiki Kamp. The daily kids' program runs 9 A.M.–3 P.M., with an evening program from 6:30–9:30.

For the experience of all, each Friday 8 A.M.–4 P.M. brings Ho'olauna, a Hawaiian culture and arts program, and throughout the week are other activities set up especially for the guests. Perhaps a soothing massage or healing facial is

what you're looking for. The Health Spa and Beauty Salon is open daily 6 A.M.–8 P.M. for your needs. If you just want to soak in some beauty, have a tour of the hotel's art collection. The Westin Maui has more than 750 guest rooms. Standard terrace rooms run $350, a garden-view room $380, golf/mountain-view $420, ocean-view $445–510, oceanfront $580, and suites go upward from $850.

Royal Lahaina Resort

Twenty-seven idyllic acres surround 542 rooms at the Royal Lahaina Resort, 2780 Keka'a Dr., Lahaina, HI 96761, 808/661-3611 or 800/222-5642, fax 808/661-6150, www.2maui.com, the largest complex in Ka'anapali. Here the tropical landscaping leads directly to the sun-soaked beach. One of the first properties to be developed, the Royal Lahaina is divided into cottages and a tower. Rates range from a standard room at $320 to an oceanfront room at $460. Cottages rent for $390 and $500, suites $550–750; condo/car and other deals and packages are available. The renovated rooms are decorated in a comfortable Hawaiian style with all amenities and private lanai; some of the cottages have kitchens. The adjacent and newly remodeled Royal Hale building also has rooms for $240–270. There are two restaurants at the resort, a poolside grill, a nightly lu'au, music in the lounge, and two swimming pools on the well-maintained grounds. A handful of sundries shops are located at the hotel entrance for your convenience. The beach activities booth rents snorkel equipment, windsurfing boards, and kayaks, and arranges scuba lessons. The resort is also home to the **Royal Lahaina Tennis Ranch**, boasting 11 courts and a 3,500-seat stadium along with special tennis packages for those inclined.

Maui Marriott

The Maui Marriott, 100 Nohea Kai Dr., Lahaina, 96761, 808/667-1200 or 800/763-1333, fax 808/667-8300, www.marriott.com, recently finished a year-long reconstruction process, which included, among other things, renovating the lobby, building a new courtyard and pool area, and turning some rooms into time-share units. With nearly 400 rooms, a Trilogy Ocean Sports beach activity booth for water recreation activities and tours, on-site tennis courts, two dozen shops, three restaurants, one bar, an evening lu'au, and indoor and outdoor parking, the Marriott is one of the largest properties on West Maui. Open to the beach and facing the setting sun, the hotel is graced with cooling breezes that waft across its manicured gardens and through the open atriums of its buildings. Indoors, the many flowers and potted plants bring the outdoors inside; outdoors, the grounds are more finely landscaped and tended than ever. The centerpiece of the reconstruction is the courtyard and swimming pool area, which incorporates a huge pool with lagoons, waterfalls, a water slide, and a children's beach area. It is now one of the premier courtyard garden areas in Ka'anapali. The hospitable staff orchestrates the numerous daily handicraft and recreational activities, and there's plenty to keep every family busy. Snorkel sets, boogie boards, and kayaks can be rented at the beach activities center, and scuba lessons are given. Room rates are $329 for a standard room, $369 oceanfront, and $414 deluxe oceanfront; suites run $579–1,499. Special honeymoon, tennis, golf, and family plans are available.

CONDOMINIUMS

Generally less expensive than the hotels, but still in the luxury category, most of these condos offer full kitchens, TVs, some maid service, swimming pools, tennis courts, and often a convenience store and laundry facilities. Combinations of the above are too numerous to mention, so it's best to ask all pertinent questions when booking. Off-season rates and discounts for longer stays are usually offered.

Located right on the water amid the hotels are the fancy high-rise Kaanapali Alii and The Whaler condos. Set along the golf links and following the lay of the land are the low-rise Kaanapali Royal and Outrigger Maui Eldorado Resort. A short way north up the beach and off on a road by itself is Maui Kaanapali Villas.

Kaanapali Alii

The Kaanapali Alii, 50 Nohea Kai Dr., Lahaina, HI 96761, 808/667-1400 or 800/642-6284, fax 808/661-5686, www.kaanapalialii.com, managed by Classic Resorts, lies in a finely landscaped yard right on the ocean. The four high-rise towers are aesthetically pleasing and are set off by flowers and greenery hanging from many of the balconies. If you need space, try staying here because each of the 200 or so large one- and two-bedroom units runs 1,500–1,900 square feet. All have full kitchens, dining and living rooms, two bathrooms, air-conditioning, and washers and dryers. Services include free parking on premises, a beach activity center, complimentary tennis, daily maid service, room service, and many area activities, and restaurant bills can be put on your room charge as a service. On the property are an exercise room, a swimming pool that overlooks the beach, a whirlpool spa, and barbecue grills. Room rates are $350–740 per night, three-night minimum.

The Whaler on Kaanapali Beach

The Whaler, 2481 Ka'anapali Pkwy., Lahaina, HI 96761, 808/661-4861 or 800/922-7866, fax 808/661-8315, www.the-whaler.com, comprises two high-rise buildings set right on the beach next to Whalers Village shopping mall. Outwardly, it has less character than the Kaanapali Alii but offers numerous amenities. On property are a pool and spa, exercise room, tennis courts for guests, sundries shop, and concierge desk. These units run from a 640-square-foot studio to a 1,950-square-foot two-bedroom, two-bath suite. Rates are $235–700, with substantially lower rates during the low season. There is a two-night minimum stay, and several car/condo, honeymoon, and senior packages are available. Covered parking is offered and signing privileges are granted at some nearby restaurants. The Whaler is managed by Aston, but some units are available through **Whalers Realty Management,** 808/661-3484 or 800/676-4112.

Maui Eldorado Resort

An Outrigger Hotels and Resorts property, the Maui Eldorado Resort, 2661 Keka'a Dr., 808/661-0021, fax 808/667-7039, www.outrigger.com, drapes the hillside along the fourth and fifth fairways of the golf course and has a beachfront cabana on the water. Guests can avail themselves of three small swimming pools and a sundries store on property, and an activity desk will help you plan your day. These privately owned studios and one- and two-bedroom suites run $195–395 year-round. All have full kitchens, air-conditioning, TV, in-unit safes, washers and dryers, and daily maid service. For toll-free reservations and information, call Outrigger direct at 800/688-7444. Some units here are also offered for rent directly by their owners or through independent agents, such as Whalers Realty Management, 808/661-3484 or 800/367-4112.

Kaanapali Royal

A golfer's dream right on the course, the Kaanapali Royal, 2560 Keka'a Dr., 808/667-7200, has only two-bedroom, two-bath, privately owned units that run about $280 per night during peak season but less during the regular season. Each suite has a full kitchen and a lanai that faces the fairway, a sunken living room, an entertainment center, and washer and dryer. Take advantage of the guest-only swimming pool, lighted tennis courts, and barbecue pit. Units are rented through agents only. Contact Whalers Realty Management, 808/661-3484 or 800/676-4112; Maui Beachfront Rentals, 808/661-2684 or 888/661-7201; Chase'n Rainbows, 808/667-7088 or 800/367-6093; or Maui Resort Rentals, 808/879-5973 or 800/441-3188.

Aston Maui Kaanapali Villas

Enjoy the surroundings of 11 sculpted acres at this affordable condo at 45 Kai Ala Dr., 808/667-7791 or 800/922-7866, fax 808/667-0366. The extensive grounds of cool, swaying palms harbor three pools, a beach service booth, the Castaway Restaurant, an activity desk, and a sundries shop. Rates begin at $220 for a hotel room with refrigerator. Studios with kitchens run $285–375, and it's $385–600 for one- and two-bedroom suites with air-conditioning, cable TV, full kitchens, plus maid service daily. This property, located at the far north end of the Ka'anapali development, has an added bonus of peace and quiet, although you remain just minutes from the action and a short stroll from Black Rock.

These units are very large with spacious bedrooms; even the studios are capable of handling four people. A good choice.

FOOD

Every hotel in Ka'anapali has at least one restaurant, with several others scattered throughout the area. Some of the most expensive and exquisite restaurants on Maui are found in these hotels, but surprisingly, at others you can dine very reasonably. The only cheap eats in the area are the few fast-food restaurants at Whalers Village shopping mall.

Nonresort Restaurants

Reilley's Steak and Seafood, an Irish restaurant and bar, is located in the clubhouse at Ka'anapali Golf Courses, 808/667-7477. Open for lunch and dinner, Reilley's is known for its twice-weekly prime rib dinner. Other meat and seafood entrées are generally in the $19–28 range. Nightly dinner specials are offered, as is lobster on Sundays. During the day, a simple pub menu is offered at the bar. Reilley's has a full bar—their single-malt Scotch selection is remarkable—so come and have a drink after a round of golf or just to watch the sun set over the fairway. Live jazz is on tap every Monday and Tuesday.

Giovani's Tomato Pie, 808/661-3160, a moderately priced "Italian American Ristarante," is located at the entrance to Ka'anapali Resort. Here you'll find everything you'd expect at such a restaurant and much more. Start your meal with a fine antipasto, salada, or zupa, most in the $4–9 range. Pizza and pasta selections of all kinds are numerous, but full-course meals like veal parmigiana, seafood pescatore, calamari and peas with bacon, and shrimp scampi are also great choices. Basic pizzas run $9–15, pasta dishes are in the same range, and full meals run up to $20. This is a pleasant, family-oriented restaurant, and the kid's menu makes the bill easier on mom and dad. Open for dinner 5:30–9:30 P.M.

Downstairs is **Jonny's Burger Joint,** open 11:30 A.M.–2 A.M. for cold drinks from the bar, fist-size burgers until midnight, and games. Jonny's serves meat, veggie, fish, and chicken burgers with all the trimmings and a variety of deep-fried side items. This is a good-time place to relax after a day in the sun.

At Whalers Village

This shopping mall has three restaurants and a clutch of fast-food joints. You can find everything from pizza and frozen yogurt to lobster tails. Prices range from bargain to pricey.

The well-established **Leilani's On The Beach,** 808/661-4495, has a downstairs Beachside Grill open 11 A.M.–11 P.M., while the upstairs fine-dining section is open for dinner only 5–10 P.M. A daily dinner special is featured 5–6:30 P.M. The Beachside Grill offers plate lunches of barbecued ribs, *paniolo* steak, or stir-fry chicken all priced around $10, along with appetizers like sashimi at a daily quote, and creamy seafood chowder for $4. The burgers range $7–9.50. A more formal dinner from the upstairs broiler can be fresh fish of the day, filet mignon for $23 from the lava rock broiler, baby back pork ribs at $17 from the kiawe-wood smoker, or fried coconut prawns for $16. A children's menu helps keep prices down. Cocktails are served until midnight at the bar, and there's entertainment daily 2:30–5:30 P.M.

Another favorite here is the partially indoors but mostly outdoors **Hula Grill and Barefoot Bar,** 808/667-6636. Open 11 A.M.–11 P.M., with dinner served 5–9:30 P.M. You can eat either in the casual Barefoot Bar under a thatch cabana or in the more formal dining area. Reservations are taken for inside but not for the barefoot bar outside. No matter where you sit, however, the sunsets are always great. At the Barefoot Bar, try burgers, sandwiches, salads, and pizza. The dining room features seafood and steak. Expect entrées in the $20–25 range, with such choices as firecracker mahimahi, shrimp scampi, and black angus New York steak. Music runs 3–5 P.M. at the Barefoot Bar and 6:30–9 P.M. in the dining room.

The **Rusty Harpoon,** 808/661-3123, offers a pleasing atmosphere, a dozen satellite TVs showing sports events, and plenty of seafood items. It also has a bar that claims to serve the best daiquiris on Maui, along with a happy hour 2–6 P.M. and again from 10 P.M.–2 A.M. Breakfast served 8–11 A.M. gets you started for the day with create-your-own three-egg omelets for $8.95, a homestyle breakfast with potatoes, eggs, and sausage links for $7.95, continental breakfast for $7.95, and a Belgian waffle bar with your choice of various fruit toppings and garnishes for $7.95. Lunch, served 11 A.M.–5 P.M., is an extensive menu starting with appetizers like a house salad for $4.95 or crab-stuffed mushrooms for $9.95. Sandwiches are priced $8.95–9.95, burgers around the same. Dinner, served 5–10 P.M., offers entrées mostly in the $22–28 range, including linguine Mediterranean, pineapple teriyaki chicken, and rack of lamb, and lighter bistro fare is served from the bar until midnight. Don't forget about the sushi and seafood bar or the luscious desserts. To save money, the Rusty Harpoon has a $14.95 early-bird special from 5–6 P.M. and a children's menu.

Ka'anapali Beach Hotel

The restaurants here are down-to-earth, reasonably priced, and provide some food from the native Hawaiian diet that's unlike anything else in the area. The **Tiki Terrace** is the main food venue of the Ka'anapali Beach Hotel and offers casual dining in an open-air setting. Breakfast can be à la carte or buffet style ($9–12) and consists mostly of American standards, but a local-style breakfast is on the menu. It runs 7–11 A.M. daily, except for Sunday when it gives way to a champagne Sunday brunch that runs 9 A.M.–1 P.M. More Hawaiian-inspired dishes are on the table for this brunch, $28.95, and the whole affair is accompanied by Hawaiian music. Dinner in the Tiki Terrace runs 5:30–9 P.M. and reservations are recommended, 808/667-0124. Most entrées run $17–33. Aside from more usual items on the menu, there is a Hawaiian combo selection that consists of poi, taro, steamed fish or chicken, sweet potatoes, and Pahole fern salad, that is totally Hawaiian in essence. On Fridays the Tiki Terrace does a *huli huli* barbecue of whole pig. Aside from the eats, a free hula show is given nightly at 6:30 P.M.

Open daily 6 A.M.–2 P.M., and again 4–9 P.M., the **Ka'anapali Mixed Plate** restaurant serves all-you-can-eat breakfast and lunch buffets for $9.75 and a dinner buffet for $12.95. An early-bird prime rib plate runs $10.95. In the courtyard next to the whale-shaped pool, have a salad, sandwich, or burger from the **Tiki Grill,** 11 A.M.–6 P.M., or just stop for a drink at the **Tiki Bar** when the *pu pu* are put out 3–6 P.M. The bar stays open until 10 P.M.

Royal Lahaina Resort

The **Royal Ocean Terrace,** the resort's only dining room, is open daily for breakfast and dinner. The breakfast buffet runs $11.50 and is a very good deal—à la carte also. Most evening entrées are in the $13–20 range and include fresh catch, top sirloin, and island-style chicken that can be prepared in half a dozen ways. Sunday brunch 9 A.M.–2 P.M. is a winner. The attached lounge serves *pu pu* in the afternoon and provides entertainment every evening. It overlooks the ocean. When the resort is very busy, a second restaurant and pool grill may also be open for business. You can get ice cream, sandwiches, and pastries from the **Royal Scoop Ice Cream Parlor.**

Located at the entrance to the Royal Lahaina Resort, but an independent establishment, is **Basil Tomatoes,** 808/662-3210, an Italian grill that's open for dinner only 5:30–9 P.M.; reservations suggested. Basil's has garnered a fine reputation for its wonderful Northern Italian food. Start with an antipasto of fried green tomatoes at $8 or cheese-stuffed artichokes at $12 and move on to the house salad for $9 or another fine bowl of greens. The entrées cover the whole range of meats, poultry, and fish, and are generally in the $22–30 range, with pastas $17–22. To complement any dinner selection, choose from a variety of beers, wine, or aperitifs, and round out your meal with a cup of coffee and a sweet dessert.

Westin Maui

Located on the pool level, the **'Ono Surf Bar and Grille** is open all day for bistro dining. While the à la carte menu is an option, the 'Ono is known especially for its breakfast buffet at $19.95. For lunch, sandwiches rule, but dinner entrées are more substantial with fish, meats, and poultry in the $18–25 range. Just as well attended as the breakfast buffet is the Saturday evening prime rib and seafood buffet that runs $29.95. The 'Ono bar runs a happy hour daily 5–7 P.M., during which time there is musical entertainment with the addition of a hula show on Fridays and afternoon music on Fridays and Saturdays. Perhaps the most well-known dining at the Westin is the champagne Sunday brunch, $29.95, served 9:30 A.M.–1 P.M. at the oceanfront **tropica** restaurant. The Sunday brunch at this open-air venue is a tradition at the Westin, and it too is always accompanied by live music. For those with smaller eyes (and stomachs), the **Colonnade Cafe** along the lobby-level open-air hallway to the pool serves pastries, fruits, and coffee from 6–11:30 A.M. More formal evening dinners are also served at the tropica, and entrées might be filet mignon, roasted lobster, guava-crusted rack of lamb, or any of several fish selections done in one of five different preparations. The early-bird special runs $24.95. Reservations are a must; 808/667-2525.

Maui Marriott

Serving casual food all day at poolside is the **Beachwalk Market and Pantry.** With mostly light fare on the menu, it's perfect for a midday snack. Open, airy, and very pleasant, **Va Bene** serves a bit more elegant breakfast, but in the evening turns into the hotel's fine-dining Italian restaurant. The à la carte menu has items in the $19–28 range as well as two prix fixe menus for $22 and $28. Special to this restaurant is the Friday night prime rib buffet dinner for $28 and the Saturday night Alaskan king crab buffet dinner at $35. Expanding the bar and its scope of appetizers, **Nalu Sunset Bar** (formerly the Makai Bar) is still a great place for excellent *pu pu,* sushi, and entertainment some evening as you watch the sun set into the distant horizon. *Pu pu* run $6–12, sushi mostly $4–8 with specials up to $10, and there are specials some evenings. The Nalu Sunset Bar is open daily 5–10:30 P.M.

Hyatt Regency Maui

The **Swan Court** is the Hyatt's signature restaurant. Save this one for a very special evening. You don't come here to eat, you come here to dine! Anyone who has been enraptured by those old movies where couples regally glide down a central staircase to make their grand entrance will have his or her fantasies come true. Although expensive, with entrées up to $38, you get your money's worth not only with the many wonderful tastes but also with the attention to detail. Dinner, served 6–10 P.M., is grand and the style is continental; reservations are recommended, and resort attire is required. The Swan Court offers a sumptuous breakfast buffet daily and much-talked-about Sunday brunch. For reservations, call 808/667-4727.

Spats Trattoria, open for dinner only, is downstairs near the entrance and decorated in heavy dark wood and carpets, premodern artwork, and intimate low light. Spats specializes in "country homestyle" Northern Italian food, with the average entrée around $20 for pasta dishes and $25 for fish and meat. Casual attire, reservations recommended. Set in the more casual setting of the garden, yet overlooking the grotto pool, is the open-air **Cascades Grille and Sushi Bar,** with a full complement of selections for lunch and dinner from about $22–34, yet some come especially for the sushi. Stop by **Pavilions** at the garden level during the day for light food and quick dining. After a full and pleasing meal, you might want to try **Cascade Lounge** or **Swan Court Lounge** for an aperitif, or the **Weeping Banyan Lounge** off the main lobby for a nightcap and soft music before heading off for a stroll along the beach.

Sheraton Maui

A blend of Asia and America, in theme, decor, and cuisine, **Teppan Yaki Dan** is the hotel's signature restaurant. Appetizers like blackened ahi or Oriental duck salad get you ready for the main meal of meat or fish, all cooked at your table teppanyaki style. It's a delight for the eyes and taste buds, but not cheap, as most entrées run $22–32. Teppan Yaki Dan serves Tuesday–Saturday 6–9 P.M., reservations recommended. Less formal is the **Keka'a Terrace** restaurant, where you can order all day long while surveying the gardens, pool, and Black Rock. Aside from the à la carte menu, regular and continental breakfast buffets can be selected. Lunch is mostly salads, sandwiches, and

wraps in the under $13 range. More extensive and heartier, evening entrées run $20–32, and include fresh catch of the day on one of four preparations, coconut shrimp, barbecued baby back ribs, and roast boneless pork loin. To reserve at either restaurant, call 808/661-0031. In addition, the poolside Lagoon Bar offers light barbecued eats throughout the day, music until 7 P.M., and the perfect seating for the evening torchlight and cliff dive performance at Black Rock.

Maui Kaanapali Villas

This is the only Ka'anapali condo that has a restaurant. The casual and moderately priced **Castaway Cafe,** 808/661-9091, is located only steps from the beach and is open for breakfast, lunch, and dinner. Breakfast items include omelets, items from the griddle, and fruit, most for under $8.50. Burgers, sandwiches, and salads are served for lunch, and for dinner, a variety of seafood, pasta, chicken, and steaks go for $15–24. Every day there are specials, and the full bar can set you up with a drink any time until 9:30 P.M.

ENTERTAINMENT

Lu'au

The dinner show accompanying the lu'au at the Hyatt Regency features pure island entertainment. **Drums of the Pacific** is a musical extravaganza that you would expect from the Hyatt. There are torch-lit processions and excitingly choreographed production numbers, with all the hula-skirted *wahines* and *malo*-clad *kanes* you could imagine. Flames add drama to the setting and the grand finale is a fire dance. The Hyatt lu'au, 808/667-4720, is held every evening 5–8 P.M.; $78 adults, $37 kids 6–12.

Similarly, the lu'au at the Royal Lahaina Resort and Maui Marriott entertain you with music and dance while you stuff yourself on fine island cuisine. These two are fairly tourist-oriented but great fun nonetheless. Follow your nose nightly at 5 P.M. to the Luau Gardens for the **Royal Lahaina Lu'au** banquet and show, where the biggest problem after the Polynesian Revue is standing up after eating mountains of traditional food. Reservations needed, 808/661-3611; adults $67, children 12 and under free with a paying adult. The **Maui Marriott Lu'au** presents its version nightly except Monday, starting with an *imu* ceremony and Polynesian games. The Marriott's niche is its funny and entertaining twists. The evening starts at 5 P.M. and runs until 8 P.M.; $78 adults, $38 children 3–8; 808/661-5828.

Musical Entertainment

The Ka'anapali Beach Hotel presents a free hula and music show in its courtyard at 6 P.M. for everyone's pleasure. In addition, Monday, Wednesday, and Friday around 11 A.M., the staff of this hotel put on a music and hula show for guests. It's good fun in a family atmosphere.

Hawaiian music is also presented outdoors at 7 P.M. Monday, Wednesday, and Saturday on the center stage at Whalers Village. If you are into lively music, try the **Hula Grill** at the shopping center. Across the way, **Leilani's on the Beach** has softer music in the afternoon. The **'Ono Grille** at the Westin has music nightly 5–7 P.M. and during the afternoons on Friday and Saturday. Several of the bars and lounges, like the Weeping Banyan Lounge and Swan Court Lounge at the Hyatt and the Lagoon Bar at the Sheraton, also have live late afternoon and/or evening music.

Away from the hotels, live jazz on Monday and Tuesday evenings at **Reilley's** at the Kaanapali Golf Clubhouse is about the only option.

Illusion Show

Sunday through Thursday, the Ka'anapali Beach Hotel hosts the **Black Rock Illusions** dinner show at its Kanahele Room. This show is not only one of slight of hand, but also presents larger magic tricks and special effects. Hula and Hawaiian legends are woven into the fabric of the show making, this a nonillusory Hawaiian experience. Seating starts at 5:30 P.M. for the full buffet dinner, and the main show is preceded by tricks done at your table by a wandering magician. Dinner and show are by reservation only; call 808/661-3424; adults $69–79, children $29–49. Entrance at 6 P.M. for cocktails and the show runs $35 adults, $25 kids.

RECREATION

Golf

Ka'anapali Resort, www.kaanapali-golf.com, is dominated by two gold courses. Designed by Robert Trent Jones, Sr., the North Course is a challenge and requires masterful putting. While a bit shorter, the South Course by Arthur Synder calls for more overall accuracy. The clubhouse for both sits right at the resort entrance, and the pro shop rents clubs, arranges lessons, and can set you up on a putting green or the driving range. The Kaanapali Classic Senior PGA Tournament is played here. For nonresidents, greens fees run $150 for the North Course and $142 for the South Course, with twilight rates at half the regular fee. Call 808/661-3691 for tee times.

Tennis

The Royal Lahaina Tennis Ranch, Sheraton Maui Tennis Club, and the Maui Marriott Tennis Club are all operated by the same company. Rates are the same for all, and it rents racquets, balls, machines, and can arrange round robins, lessons, and clinics. The court fee runs $10 per person daily, racquets go for $2.50, and ball machines are $20 per hour. The Tennis Ranch at the Royal Lahaina has a 3,500-seat stadium that's rated for non-pro tournaments (it's occasionally used for concerts) and 10 other courts. Open 8 A.M.–noon and again 2–7 P.M. Call 808/667-5200 for court time. The Sheraton has three lighted courts open 8 A.M.–noon and 2–8 P.M.; 808/667-9200. Five courts are open at the Marriott 7 A.M.–8 P.M.; 808/661-6200 to arrange time on a court.

The Hyatt runs its own tennis center of five courts that's open from 7 A.M. until dusk. All equipment is available, and lessons and clinics can be arranged. Court time runs $12 per hour for guests or $20 for nonguests. To set a time for play, call 808/661-1234.

Water Activities

A whole variety of water activities and gear are available at Ka'anapali, some from established activity booths, some from the hotels, and some from private vendors that operate right on the beach. Not all provide all services. The following is a sampling of what you might expect to find somewhere along the beach: Hobie Cats $45 per hour or $69 for a one-hour lesson; single kayak $15 per hour, tandem kayak $25 per hour; sea cycle (pedal boat) $25 per hour; windsurf board $20 per hour or a 90-minute lesson for $69; boogie board $5 per hour; and snorkel gear $10 per day. Jet Ski rental and parasailing are other options. Scuba lessons and a variety of rentals can be arranged at the beach activity booths at each hotel. The *Gemini* at the Westin Maui, the *Kiele V* from the Hyatt, the *Teralani* at the Sheraton, and others leaving from the beach in front of Whalers Village make sailings every day that weather permits. For a full listing, contact any of the activity desks at the hotels on this strip, or the Maui Ocean Activities booth on the beach at Whalers Village, 808/667-2001. You can arrange water activities and all other activities islandwide at reduced rates at Activity World, located on Halawai Drive just off the highway north of the main Ka'anapali strip.

SHOPPING

Ka'anapali provides a varied shopping scene: the **Whalers Village** shopping complex, which has a mix of the affordable and exorbitant; the **Royal Lahaina Resort** for some distinctive purchases; and the **Hyatt Regency, Westin Maui,** and **Maui Marriott,** where most people get financial jitters even window-shopping.

Whalers Village

Open daily 9:30 A.M.–10 P.M., you can easily find anything at this shopping complex that you might need. Some of the shops are **Reyn's,** for upscale tropical clothing; **Giorgiou** and others for expensive women's fashions; the exclusive **Louis Vuitton** for designer luggage; **Blue Ginger Designs,** for women's and children's resortwear and alohawear; **Dolphin Gallery,** with beautiful creations in glass, sculptures, paintings, and jewelry; **Lahaina Scrimshaw,** for fine scrimshaw pieces and other art objects ranging from affordable to expensive; **Endangered Species Store,** where you are greeted by a stuffed python and proceeds go to help endangered species; **Eye-**

catcher Sunglasses, where you can take care of your eyes with shades from $150 Revos to $5 cheapies; **Jessica's Gems,** featuring the work of designer David Welty, along with coral jewelry and black Tahitian pearl rings; **Ritz Camera** for film developing; **Waldenbooks,** a full-service book shop; and an **ABC Discount Store** for sundries. There are many other shops tucked away here and there.

A fascinating shop is **Lahaina Printsellers,** www.printsellers.com, featuring original and reproduction engravings, drawings, maps, charts, and naturalist sketches. The collection comes from all over the world, but the Hawaiiana collection is amazing in its depth, with many works featuring a nautical theme reminiscent of the amazing explorers who opened the Pacific or naturalist theme showing the flora and fauna of the islands.

The Whalers Village also has plenty of fast-food shops, three fine restaurants, the West Maui Healthcare Center, the Whale Museum, and ATMs. The Kaanapali Trolley and the westside public shuttle make stops at the mall.

Be sure to catch the free entertainment performed at 7 P.M. at the center stage some evenings of the week, and the weekly creation of sand sculpture in front of the stage on the lower level during the day. Every year in late July or early August, the Maui Onion Festival is held here at the mall, celebrating the most well known of Maui's agricultural crops with chef's demonstrations, food products, and music. Everyone is welcome.

There is free parking for three hours at the parking structure with validation from one of the mall shops. For others, the Whaler's Village parking lot charges $2.50 per hour or $20 maximum for the day, making parking an expensive proposition in Ka'anapali unless you have free parking as a guest of one of the hotels or condos here.

Fairway Shops

A new group of shops located along the highway across from the Ka'anapali train depot is called the Fairway Shops. Access is from both Honoapi'ilani Highway and Keka'a Drive. Two of the shops that might be of interest to visitors are the **Toy Store** for car and motorcycle rentals and **Maui Dive Shop,** which rents gear and offers tours.

INFORMATION AND SERVICES

Information

All hotels have concierge desks and/or activity desks that offer guests free information about their hotels and the Ka'anapali area.

For a source of general information on all aspects of the Ka'anapali area as well as several brochures, contact Kaanapali Beach Resort Association, 2530 Keka'a Dr., Ste. 1-B, Lahaina, HI 96761, 808/661-3271 or 800/245-9229, kbra@kaanapaliresort.com, www.kaanapaliresort.com.

Car Rentals

Between Ka'anapali and Honokowai, along the edge of the highway on Halawai Drive, are several rental companies that service all of West Maui. Dollar, Budget, Avis, Alamo, Hertz, and National car rental companies have offices and small lots here, as does Mavrik Motorcycles.

While the availability is somewhat limited, the car rental companies do carry sedans and jeeps. Renting here eliminates one fee that is charged at the airport lots in Kahului. Mavrik only rents motorcycles and scooters.

Medical Services

The West Maui Healthcare Center maintains an office on the upper level at the Whalers Village shopping mall, 808/667-9721; open 8 A.M.–8 P.M. daily. Doctors On Call, 808/667-7676, operates daily 8 A.M.–9 P.M. out of the Hyatt Regency, Westin Maui, and at the Kapalua Resort but makes house calls.

Banks

There are no banks in Ka'anapali; the closest are in Lahaina. Most larger hotels can help with some banking needs, especially with cashing traveler's checks. An ATM is located on the lower level of the Whalers Village mall.

Honokowai, Kahana, and Napili

Between Ka'anapali and Kapalua are the villages of Honokowai, Kahana, and Napili, which service the string of condos tucked away here and there along the coast. After Ka'anapali started to be built, developers picked up on Amfac's great idea and built condos here. Unfortunately, they seemed to be interested more in profit than beauty, earning this strip the dubious title of "condo ghetto." While somewhat softened over time by a great deal of thoughtful landscaping, some redevelopment, and the addition of private homes, beaches, and markets, this stretch remains overwhelmingly a string of condominium accommodations and vacation rentals. Each of these villages is a practical stop where you can buy food, gas, and all necessary supplies to keep your vacation rolling. You head for this area if you want to enjoy Maui's west coast and not spend a bundle of money. These towns are not quite as pretty as Ka'anapali or Kapalua, but proportionate to the money you'll save, you come out ahead. These areas are not clearly distinct from one another, so you may

have some trouble determining where one ends and the next begins, but generally they are separated by some stretch of residential neighborhood. With the development of the new Ka'anapali Ocean Resort at the far northern end of Ka'anapali, the boundary between Ka'anapali and Honokowai will become less distinct. Napili, at the far north end of this strip, adjoins and in some ways is connected to Kapalua. To get to this area, travel north along Honoapi'ilani Highway past Ka'anapali and then take Lower Honoapi'ilani Road through Honokowai, and continue on it to Kahana and Napili. Three short connector roads link the new highway with the old road. For those who need to use it, the Kapalua–West Maui Airport sits above the highway in Kahana surrounded by acres of pineapple fields.

Beaches

The whole strip here is rather rocky and full of coral, so not particularly good for swimming except in a few isolated spots.

WEST MAUI

Honokowai Beach Park is right in Honokowai just across from a small shopping plaza and the well-cared-for and still used Lahuiokalani Ka'anapali Congregational Church (1850). The park has a large lawn with palm trees and picnic tables, but a small beach with a reef in close. The water is shallow and tame—good for tots. While the swimming is not as nice as at Ka'anapali, snorkeling is fair and you can get through a break in the reef at the north end.

Kahana Beach is near the Kahana Beach Resort; park across the street. Nothing spectacular, but the protected small beach is good for catching some rays and it's decent swimming between the bands of rock when the waves are not too strong. There's a great view of Moloka'i, and the beach is never crowded. Just south of there is **Pohaku Park.** It's a narrow strip with only a few parking stalls but is often used for picnics or by surfers—no restroom.

By far the best beach in this area, and one of the best on the island, is that at **Napili Bay.** This gentle crescent slopes easily into the water, and its sandy bottom gives way to coral, so snorkeling is good here as well. There are rights-of-way to this perfect, but condo-lined, beach. Look for beach access signs along Napili Place and on Hui Drive. They're difficult to spot, but once on the beach there's better-than-average swimming, snorkeling, and a good place for beginning surfers and boogie boarders.

ACCOMMODATIONS

At last count there were more than three dozen condos and apartment complexes in the four miles encompassing Honokowai, Kahana, and Napili. There are plenty of private homes out there as well, which gives you a good cross-section of Hawaiian society. A multimillion-dollar spread may occupy a beach, while out in the bay is a local fisherman with his beat-up old boat trying to make a few bucks for the day—and his house may be up the street. Many of the condos built out here were controversial. Locals refused to work on some because they were on holy ground, and a few actually experienced bad-luck jinxes as they were being built. The smarter owners called

in *kahuna* to bless the ground and the disturbances ceased.

As usual, condos are more of a bargain the longer you stay, especially if you can share costs with a few people by renting a larger unit. As always, you'll save money on food costs. Most of these are in the $200 per night and up category. Only a handful fall into the $100 per night or less group, with a remainder falling somewhere in between. Because of the mixture of studio, one-, two-, and three-bedroom units, some properties have a wide price range. The following should give you an idea of what's available in this area, starting from the south end moving north.

Mahana at Kaanapali

Aston's Mahana at Kaanapali, 110 Ka'anapali Shores Place, 808/661-8751 or 800/922-7866, is billed as an "all oceanfront resort," and in fact all units have an ocean view at no extra cost because the two long and tall buildings parallel the shoreline. The second you walk into the entry of this condo and look through a large floor-to-ceiling window framing a swimming pool and the wide blue sea, your cares immediately begin to slip away. A AAA three-diamond property, this condo sits on a point of beach and is one in the first group of condos north of Ka'anapali. Enjoy a complete kitchen plus heated pool, sauna, two tennis courts, maid service, activities desk, and a money-saving family plan. Restaurant signing privileges and the kids Camp Kaanapali are available at and in coordination with the Aston Kaanapali Shores just up the way. Rates begin with studios at $295, one-bedroom suites at $385, and huge two-bedroom suites (up to six people) for $625, but greatly reduced rates are offered during the spring and autumn "value seasons."

Maui Kai

Smaller and older, yet offering great value, is the Maui Kai condominium resort, 106 Ka'anapali Shores Place, 808/667-3500 or 800/367-5635, fax 808/667-3660, reservation@mauikai.com, www.mauikai.com. These well-kept and privately owned units each have a full kitchen, an entertainment center, air-conditioning, a lanai that overlooks the water, daily maid service, and tile throughout. Relax at the swimming pool or inquire at the activity desk to arrange off-property tours. Studios run $155, one-bedrooms $188–198, and two-bedrooms $294, with rates reduced by about 10 percent during the value season. Two nights' minimum stay except for the last two weeks of December, when there is a seven-night minimum. The Maui Kai is an intimate place that gives you a good location and great value for the money.

Embassy Vacation Resort

Open, airy, and with an atrium courtyard, this huge pink pyramid occupies a sliver of beach. Each of the more than 400 air-conditioned suites has a kitchen, separate living area, large-screen TV, and lanai. Daily maid service is offered, as are a children's program, two restaurants, an activity desk, a Maui Ocean Activities ocean sports booth, and laundry facilities. Kids will love the water slide at the pool, while the adults may gravitate to the spa and fitness center. The resort's Ohana Grill is a casual restaurant that serves quick food such as burgers, salads, and pizza for under $10. It's open for lunch and dinner and features live entertainment from 6–9 P.M. The North Beach Grille, a dinner-only restaurant, is the resort's better eatery, where you'll find a greater variety of entrées in the under $25 range and a nightly all-you-can-eat buffet. In a way, the Embassy is like a smaller version of the more exclusive resorts down the beach in Ka'anapali. Rates run $349–489 for a one-bedroom suite and $629 for a two-bedroom suite that sleeps six. The Embassy is located at 104 Ka'anapali Shores Place, 808/661-2000 or 800/669-3155, fax 808/667-1353, www.mauiembassy.com. There is shoreline access next to this resort.

Aston Kaanapali Shores

The green tranquility of this created oasis at 3445 Lower Honoapi'ilani Road, 808/667-2211 or 800/922-7866, offers an unsurpassed view of sun-baked Lana'i and Moloka'i just across the channel. You enter a spacious and airy open lobby, framing a living sculpture of palms and ferns that's protected by the two arms of guest rooms that reach nearly to water's edge. The grounds are a trimmed garden in large proportions dappled with sunlight and flowers. Soak away your cares in two whirlpools, one tucked away in a quiet corner of the central garden area for midnight romance, the other near the pool. Visit the gift shop, sundries store, fitness center, lighted tennis courts, and activities desk, or enroll the little ones in Camp Kaanapali, a program for children. Enjoy a romantic dinner at the Beach Club Restaurant, which serves meals all day and offers entertainment in the evening. All studios and suites have been refurbished and include full kitchens, sweeping lanai, TVs, air-conditioning, and daily maid service. Prices range from a studio at $300 to a two-bedroom oceanfront suite for $730. Several hotel rooms with refrigerators are also available at a more affordable $200, as are suites for $900–1,000. The Aston Kaanapali Shores is a AAA three-diamond accommodation.

Paki Maui Resort

At 3615 Lower Honoapi'ilani Road, 808/669-8235 or 800/922-7866, this Aston-managed, excellent-value condo presents airy and bright rooms with sweeping panoramas of the Lahaina Roads. Well-appointed studios for two begin at $210, up to $345 for a two-bedroom oceanfront apartment for up to six people; additional guests are $20. Amenities include maid service, air-conditioning, cable TV, complete kitchens, pool with spa, and coin laundry facilities. Every unit in this gracefully curved building has a private lanai overlooking a gem of a courtyard or the ocean. You can save money by getting a garden-view unit without sacrificing that delightful feeling that you are in the tropics. A complimentary mai tai party is held weekly for all guests. Although the Paki Maui is in town, it feels secluded the moment you walk onto this property, which forms a little oasis of tranquility. There is no sand beach fronting the condo, but the snorkeling along the reef is excellent.

Honokowai Palms

At 3666 Lower Honoapi'ilani Road, this condo is an old standby for budget travelers. A basic two-story cinder block affair, originally used as housing for workers constructing the Sheraton down the road, it's basically a long-term place now with a few rental units. The Palms is older, but not run-down; no tinsel and glitter, but neat, clean, and adequate. There is no view. Fully furnished with kitchens, TVs, full baths, and queen- or king-size beds. A swimming pool and coin laundry are on the premises. The least expensive condos along the coast, a one-bedroom unit runs $80; three nights minimum. Contact the Klahani Resorts Corp. for details and reservations, 808/667-2712 or 800/669-6284, fax 808/661-5875.

Hale Maui

This very reasonably priced mustard-yellow apartment hotel, owned and operated by Hans Zimmerman, offers one-bedroom apartments that can accommodate up to five people. All have a full kitchen, private lanai, color TV, and limited maid service, with coin washers and dryers, barbecue grills, and beach access available to guests. All units are bright, tasteful, clean, and neat as a pin. One of the most reasonable condos along the coast, rates are $85–105, extra person $15, weekly and monthly discount rates available; three nights minimum. The Hale Maui is an excellent choice for budget travelers who would rather spend money on having fun than on a luxurious hotel room. Contact Hale Maui at P.O. Box 516 Lahaina, HI, 96767, 808/669-6312, fax 808/669-1302, halemaui@maui.net,www.maui.net/~halemaui.

Hale Ono Loa

Four floors high with a pool in the garden, this place will give you a basic condo experience. Amenities include complete kitchens, separate living and dining areas, TVs, lanai, partial maid service, and laundry facility. Hale Ono Loa, 3823 Lower Honoapi'ilani Rd., has peak- and low-season rates with about a $20 difference. High-season one-bedroom, ocean-view is $116, a two-bedroom oceanview runs $173; three nights minimum, discounts for stays more than 28 days. For information and reservations, contact Maui Lodging, 808/669-0089 or 800/487-6002, fax 808/669-3937.

Noelani

This AAA-approved condo located at 4095 Lower Honoapi'ilani Road, 808/669-8374 or 800/367-6030, fax 808/669-7904, www.noelani-condo-resort.com, is last in the line before Kahana. All units are oceanfront, with fully equipped kitchens, ceiling fans, color TVs, VCRs (video rental available), washer/dryers in the non-studio units, and midweek maid service. On the grounds are two heated pools, a hot tub, and a barbecue area. You're welcomed on the first morning with a complimentary continental breakfast served poolside, where you are given an island orientation by the concierge. You'll find peace and quiet here; you can't go wrong. Studios rent from $122–135, one bedrooms are $165, two and three bedrooms for $217 and $267; 10 percent discount offered after 28 days. Car/condo, senior, AAA, and honeymoon discounts are given.

Sands of Kahana

You know you're in Kahana when you pass Pohaku Park and spot the distinctive blue roofs of this gracious complex, which forms a central courtyard area at 4299 Lower Honoapi'ilani Road. The condo boasts the poolside Kahana Terrace Restaurant, which serves breakfast, lunch, and dinner daily. The narrow sandy-bottomed beach fronting the property is very safe and perfect for swimming and sunbathing. The Sands of Kahana gives you extraordinarily large units for the money, with lots of glass for great views, and to sweeten the pot, they're beautiful and well appointed, mostly in earth tones and colors of the islands. Some studios in this complex are timeshare units. Of the rental units, one bedrooms are $150–225, two-bedroom units at $205–285, and three-bedroom units at $305–350 are massive with two lanai, two baths with a tub built for two, walk-in closets, and great ocean views. Each unit offers a gourmet kitchen, cable TV, daily maid service, and washer/dryer units. The property, with pool, three tennis courts, putting green, barbecue area, fitness center, and spa, exudes a sense of peace and quiet, and although there are plenty of guests, you never feel crowded. This is where you come when you want to get away from it all but still be within reach of the action.

All arrangements are made through Sullivan Properties, P.O. Box 55, Lahaina, HI 96767; 808/669-0423 or 800/332-1137, fax 808/669-8409; www.sands-of-kahana.com.

Royal Kahana Resort

A tall, imposing structure in a flying V-wing shape gives all rooms a perfect view of the ocean and the islands across the channel. Light in color and accented by floral patterns, all units have full kitchens, living areas, and washers and dryers, plus there are two tennis courts on the property for guest use only, a swimming pool by the beach, an activities desk, and a fitness center. Regular-season rates are $210–230 for a studio, $265–400 for a one bedroom, and $320–460 for a two-bedroom unit; value season has rates reduced 10–15 percent with more drastic discounts at certain times of the year. The Royal Kahana is located at 4365 Honoapi'ilani Road. Call 808/669-5911, fax 808/669-5950, or Outrigger Hotels and Resorts direct at 800/668-7444.

Kahana Village

Up the road at 4531 Lower Honoapi'ilani Road, 808/669-5111 or 800/824-3065, fax 808/669-0974, www.kahanavillage.com, this graceful vacation condominium is a group of low beach houses surrounded by well-manicured lawns on three acres. Each of the pleasantly comfortable units is individually owned, so all have a slightly different character. All are light and breezy, appointed in earth tones, and each has a complete kitchen, color TV, VCR, and large lanai. Ground-level apartments are large at 1,700 square feet and feature three bedrooms and two baths. The upper-level units are a bit smaller but still spacious at 1,200 square feet and have two bedrooms (one as a loft), two baths, and high open-beam ceilings. There is a narrow pebble beach out front, and the property has a swimming pool, hot tub, and barbecue grills. Rates are $240–280 for second-floor units, $330–395 for ground-level units, and $20 per night for each extra person; five nights minimum. Low-season rates are about 20 percent less; 10 percent discount for stays longer than 14 days.

WEST MAUI

Kahana Sunset

This property has a superb spot on a wonderful little beach. Set alone on the small and protected Keoninue Bay, the finely sculpted gardens and trellised lanai set off the attractive and privately owned condo units that step down to the water. All units have full kitchens, private lanai, color TVs, washers and dryers, and daily maid service. Ceiling fans are used in each unit, and louvered windows catch the cooling sea breezes. Rates are $130–240 for one-bedroom, garden- and oceanview units, two bedroom oceanview units run $195–275, while two-bedroom oceanfront units run $280–370. Substantial off-season and monthly discounts are offered and some packages are available. There is a two-night minimum, except during the year-end holidays. Some credit cards accepted. Kahana Sunset, 4909 Lower Honoapi'ilani Rd., 808/669-8700 or 800/669-1488, fax 808/669-4466, www.kahanasunset.com, is managed by Premier Resort.

Napili Point Resort

Napili Point, 5295 Honoapi'ilani Rd., 808/669-9222 or 800/669-6252, fax 808/669-7984, www.napili.com, is one of the most beautifully situated complexes on Maui. This low-rise property sits on its own promontory of black lava separating Kahana and Napili. The reef fronting the condo is home to a colorful display of reef fish and coral, providing some of the best snorkeling on the west end. Not graced with a sand beach (it's only 100 yards north along a path), nature, however, was generous in another way. Each room commands an unimpeded panorama with a breathtaking sunset view of Lana'i and Moloka'i. You get a deluxe room for a standard price. Because of the unique setting, the condo is secluded although convenient to shops and stores. The two-story buildings offer fully furnished one- and two-bedroom units from an affordable $229–399, less during regular season, with full kitchens, washers and dryers, walk-in closets, and large dressing and bath areas. Amenities include maid service, two pools, and barbecue grills. Two-bedroom units on the second floor include a loft with its own sitting area. Floor-to-ceiling windows frame the living still life of sea and surf so you can enjoy the view from every part of the apartment.

Napili Shores

Next door to Napili Point and overlooking Napili Bay from the lava-rock shoreline is the two-story Napili Shores condominium, 5315 Lower Honoapi'ilani Rd., 808/669-8061 or 800/688-7444, fax 808/669-5407, an Outrigger property. All units surround a tropical garden, fish pond, manicured lawn, hot tub, and two swimming pools. Although not large or ostentatious, each unit is comfortable and contains a full kitchen, color TV, and large lanai. Rates run $182–238 for studios, $216–244 for one-bedroom units, with many packages available. There are two restaurants on the premises: the Orient Express Thai Restaurant and the Gazebo; an activity desk; and a guest laundry.

Napili Surf Beach Resort

Located at 50 Napili Place, these are reasonably priced full condo units at the south end of Napili Beach that attract mostly an older crowd with some younger families, particularly during the summer. Both the buildings and grounds have been upgraded recently. The grounds are not luxurious but nicely manicured and have two pools and three shuffleboard lanes. Very clean rooms with full kitchens have ceiling fans, TVs, and their own lanai. Daily maid service is provided, and there's a laundry facility on premises. Garden-view studio units run $130, oceanview and oceanfront studios are $175–190, while the one-bedroom units range $205–280. Minimum stay is five nights, 10 during the Christmas holiday season; 10 percent discount for 30 days or longer. Car/condo packages and other special deals are offered. Contact Napili Surf at 808/669-8002 or 800/541-0638, fax 808/669-8004, relax@napilisurf.com, www.napilisurf.com.

Napili Sunset

At 46 Hui Drive, this AAA-approved condo has two buildings on the beach and one away from the water. All units have fully equipped kitchens, ceiling fans, color TVs, and daily maid service and share the pool, the beachfront barbecue grill,

ROBERT NILSEN

Napili Bay, one of the best on the island for swimming and snorkeling

and a laundry area. Studio apartments in the building away from the beach go for $120, one bedrooms $225, and two bedrooms $315; all have reduced rates during the low season. For additional information and reservations, contact Napili Sunset at 808/669-8083 or 800/447-9229, fax 808/669-2730, www.napilisunset.com.

The Mauian

Opened in 1959, this property is the oldest on the bay, and it couldn't have a better location. Don't let the age fool you, however, because all 44 units have been attentively renovated with new kitchens and bathrooms, pleasing period-style reproduction bamboo and hardwood furniture, and Hawaiian artwork that helps conjure up the feeling of a slower, more hospitable Hawaii. And you'll find hospitality here—lots of it. This is a gem. The '50s-era buildings blend well with the garden, in which you'll find not only tropical flowers and bushes, but also taro and medicinal plants. The open central lawn holds a pool and shuffleboard courts (join a tournament), and every unit has a lanai with a view of the beach and ocean. It's the kind of place where you might expect to hear slack-key guitar wafting across the

garden, and you'll certainly hear the water lapping at the shore, lulling you to sleep at night. Ceiling fans and louvered windows create air flow; there is no air-conditioning. There also are no TVs or phones in the studios, but there is a TV and a phone as well as video and book libraries in the community Ohana Room, where a complimentary continental breakfast is served daily 7:30–9 A.M. and the sunset Thursday Aloha Party is a tradition. Because of the hospitality and sense of *ohana* (family), many guests return year after year. Based on double occupancy, rates for low and high seasons are $180/$195 for a beachfront unit, $165/$185 for beach-view units, and $145/$165 for garden units; $10 each extra person. The Mauian is located at 5441 Lower Honoapi'ilani Road, 808/669-6205 or 800/367-5034, fax 808/669-0129, info@mauian.com, www.mauian.com.

Napili Kai Beach Resort

At 5900 Honoapi'ilani Road, 808/669-6271 or 800/367-5030, fax 808/669-0086, www.napilikai.com, this accommodation is the last in Napili before you enter the landscaped expanse of Kapalua. The Napili Kai Beach Resort, the dream-come-true of now-deceased Jack Millar, was built before regulations forced properties back from the water. Jack Millar's ashes are buried near the restaurant under a flagpole bearing the United States, Canadian, and Hawaiian flags. The setting is idyllic, with the beach a crescent moon with gentle wave action. The bay is a swim-only area with no pleasure craft allowed. Rates run $190 for a garden-view hotel room up to $700 for an oceanfront luxury two-bedroom suite, but amenities include a kitchenette (refrigerators in the hotel rooms), private lanai, air-conditioning in most units, complimentary snorkel gear, daily tea party, activities desk, and all the comforts of home. Several special packages are available. There are four pools, "Hawaii's largest whirlpool," an exercise room, a croquet lawn, putting greens, and tennis courts on property, and the Kapalua Bay Golf Course is just a nine-iron away. All rooms have Japanese touches complete with shoji screens. There's fine dining, dancing, and entertainment at the on-site Sea House Restaurant overlooking the beach.

Bed-and-Breakfasts

True to its name, the **Blue Horizons B&B,** 3894 Mahinahina St., P.O. Box 10578, Lahaina, HI 96761, 808/669-1965 or 800/669-1948, fax 808/665-1615, innkeeper@blue horizensmaui.com, www.bluehorizensmaui .com, has good views of the blue Pacific looking to the west over Honokowai and Kahana. Set in a residential neighborhood below the Kapalua–West Maui Airport, this modern-style bed-and-breakfast offers three rooms. All have private bathrooms, one has a kitchenette, and all have refrigerators. The living room, kitchen, screened lanai, lap pool, barbecue grill, and washer/dryer are for everyone's use. Breakfast is included Monday–Saturday. Room rates run $99–129 for two, $15 per additional person; two nights minimum. The Blue Horizon is perhaps the only B&B north of Lahaina on the west coast.

Agencies

Aside from booking a room direct, you can work through a condo booking agenc,y which will do all the arranging for you. For condos and homes throughout West Maui, try the following:

Whalers Realty Management, 808/661-3484 or 800/676-4112, fax 808/661-8338, www.va-cation-maui.com, has more units in Ka'anapali properties than Honokowai, but does have a presence here.

With condos stretching from Lahaina to Napili is **Maui Beachfront Rentals,** 808/661-3500 or 888/661-7200, www.mauibeachfront.com.

With units in seven properties, **Klahani Resorts,** 808/667-2712 or 800/669-6284, fax 808/661-5875, www.klahani.com, deals mostly in the low to midrange places.

Sullivan Properties, P.O. Box 55, Lahaina, HI 96767, 808/669-0423 or 800/332-1137, fax 808/669-8409, www.kapalua.com, has rental units in a handful of condo properties along this stretch and in Kapalua up the coast.

Maui Lodging, 808/669-0089 or 800/487-6002, fax 808/669-3937, www.mauilodging .com, concentrates on a dozen oceanfront condo properties in the Honokowai area of West Maui.

FOOD AND ENTERTAINMENT

Inexpensive

At Da Rose Mall, just as you enter Honokowai proper, **Lourdes Kitchenette,** 808/669-5725, offers take-out or delivery service along with a few picnic tables out front where you can eat. Open daily 10 A.M.–4 P.M., they prepare plate lunches and simple Filipino food such as adobo, with everything under $7. Lourdes is small, simple, clean, and adequate. Across the parking lot is **Cha Cha's Place,** a basic eatery for local-style grinds and priced, like Lourdes, with nothing over $7.

For a quick bite, **Honokowai Okazuya and Deli,** 808/665-0512, is available for an amazing selection of Chinese, Japanese, Italian, Mexican, and vegetarian foods at very affordable prices. Located in 5-A Rent a Space mall, 3600 Lower Honoapi'ilani Rd., Honokowai Okazuya has well-deserved popularity. Eat in or take out. Open Monday–Saturday only 10 A.M.–2:30 P.M. and again 4:30–9 P.M.

The following three restaurants are all located at Napili Plaza. **Maui Tacos** has reasonably priced, health-conscious fast food and a variety of drinks. Try a chimichanga for $5.99, a tostada for $5.25, tacos for about $3.50, or a two-fisted burrito that will keep you full all day for $6.95 or less. The salsa and guacamole are made fresh daily. No MSG or lard is used. Food is served form 9 A.M. For those who need a little pick-me-up during the day, stop at **The Coffee Shop,** open 6:30 A.M.–6 P.M. Down at the end of the line is **Mama's Ribs 'N Rotisserie,** a small take-out place that does all their cooking on the spot from fresh ingredients. Try a plate meal of ribs or chicken, done teriyaki- or traditional-style, with rice and barbecue beans, or choose a full rack of ribs or whole chicken. Side dishes are barbecue beans, macaroni salad, or rice. Aside from the full rack of ribs at $18.99, virtually everything else is under $11.75. This is a local eatery of good repute. Open Monday–Saturday 11 A.M.–6 P.M. Mama knows best.

The **Gazebo,** 808/669-5621, open daily 7:30 A.M.–2 P.M., one of the best-kept secrets in the area, is a little brown gazebo with louvered windows next to the pool at the Napili Shores Resort. Be prepared for a line. Locals in the know come here for a breakfast of the Gazebo's famous banana, pineapple, and especially the macadamia nut pancakes for $6.50. There are also eggs and omelets of all sorts under $8.95. The lunch menu features a range of sandwiches from $6.25–8.25, along with burgers and lunch plates under $8.25. You can enjoy a world-class view sitting inside or outside the Gazebo for down-home prices.

Moderate

Whether you're a guest or not, a quiet and lovely restaurant in which to dine is **The Beach Club** at the Aston Kaanapali Shores. One of Honokowai's best-kept secrets, the restaurant is centered in the condo's garden area and opens directly onto the sea. The restaurant changes throughout the day from a casual café in the morning to a more formal candlelit room in the evening, but the service is always friendly. Breakfast, served 7–11:30 A.M., with early-bird specials until 9 A.M., is mostly standard American fare. Lunch, served 11:30 A.M.–3 P.M., offers sandwiches and lighter fare. The evening dinner menu, served

5:30–9:30 P.M., whets your appetite with scrumptious appetizers. Soup of the day and salad lead to main entrées such as chicken Marsala, grilled scallops, or clams pesto with linguine, with most in the $15–20 range. A children's menu is also offered, and entertainment is provided several nights a week.

Under the blue roof by the pool at the Sands of Kahana Resort, the open-air and moderately priced **Kahana Terrace Restaurant,** 808/669-5399, is just right for sunsets. Breakfast offerings feature omelets and items from the griddle; lunch is mostly sandwiches and burgers that go for less than $10. Appetizers like coconut shrimp and hot buffalo wings and various salads precede dinner entrées that can be fresh catch of the day for $19.95, New York strip steak for $19.95, or chicken-fried steak for $13.95. Every night brings early-bird specials where you get even more for your money, and on Sunday an all-you-can-eat poolside barbecue packs them in. While not haute cuisine, food here is nutritious and satisfying. Live music nightly 5–7 P.M.

Located at the Kahana Manor Shops, **Dollie's Pub and Café,** 808/669-0266, is open daily 11 A.M.–midnight, with happy hour 3–6 P.M. Dollie's features several TVs with satellite hookup for sporting events, cappuccino, and weekend entertainment. The good food and fair prices on Dollie's menu feature more than a dozen sandwiches from which to choose, all priced $5.25–8.95; *pu pu* like nachos and potato skins; plates of various fettuccine from $9.95–11.95; and pizza by the tray for $15–21 or by the slice for $1.50 from 3–6 P.M. and 10 P.M. to closing. The sandwiches and other entrées are good, but the pizza is the best. The bar has a wide selection of domestic and imported beers, wines, and a daily exotic drink special. One of the few eateries in the area, Dollie's is usually a laid-back pub/pizzeria but can get hopping on the weekends and is perhaps the most happening place for late-night get-togethers in Kahana.

The **China Boat** restaurant, 4474 Lower Honoapi'ilani Hwy. in Kahana, 808/669-5089, is open Monday–Saturday for lunch 11:30 A.M.–2 P.M. and daily for dinner 5–9 P.M. It's almost elegant with its highly polished,

WEST MAUI

black-lacquer furniture, pink tablecloths, scroll paintings, and island-inspired prints, but the food quality is variable. A typically large MSG-free Chinese menu offers seafood, beef, chicken, vegetables, pork, and noodle dishes at a reasonable price. Most entées run $10–15, with some vegetarian and rice dishes less.

At the Kahana Gateway Shopping Center, the **Outback Steakhouse,** 808/665-1822, is an Australian meat house serving down under grilled and flame-broiled favorites. The Outback is open 4–10 P.M. for dinner, until midnight for drinks. Get your meal going with a Kookaburra wings appetizer or bonzer Brisbane Caesar salad. Sirloin, porterhouse, and tenderloins are favorites, as are smoked and grilled baby back ribs and seasoned and grilled chicken and shrimp. Most entrées run $16–22.

The **Orient Express,** at the Napili Shores Resort, 808/669-8077, is open daily for dinner only 5:30–10 P.M. The restaurant serves Thai and Chinese food with a flair for spices; duck salad and stuffed chicken wings are a specialty. The early-bird special, served before 6:30 P.M., is a five-course dinner for $11.95. The full menu of finely spiced foods includes Orient Express's well-known curry dishes; take-out is available. Most entrées are in the $12–15 range. Overlooking the koi pond at the resort, this restaurant is a good choice. Sharing the same space is Harry's sushi and *pu pu* bar, where everything is prepared before you at the counter. Nigiri sushi orders run $4.50–7, sashimi $9.50–15, with a few other items on the menu.

Expensive

Finally McDonald's has a culinary purpose: to landmark **Roy's Kahana Bar and Grill,** 808/669-6999, located at the Kahana Gateway Shopping Center and open daily for dinner 5:30–10 P.M. At Roy's, the executive chef works kitchen magic preparing the best in Pacific Rim cuisine. Roy Yamaguchi, the inspirational founder, has a penchant for locating his Hawaii restaurants in pragmatic shopping malls. At Roy's Kahana, the surroundings are strictly casual, like a very upscale cafeteria. The enormous room, reverberating with the clatter of plates and the low hum of dinner conversations, has 40-foot vaulted ceilings, a huge copper-clad preparation area, heavy koa tables and booths, track lighting, and windows all around. Roy's philosophy is to serve truly superb dishes post haste, but impeccably, focusing on the *food* as the dining experience, not the surroundings. Although part of the menu changes every night, you could start your culinary extravaganza with island-style pot stickers with a spicy almond satay peanut sauce, grilled Sichuan-spiced baby back pork ribs, crispy Upcountry green salad with a creamy spinach and tarragon dressing, or an individual *imu* pizza, all for less than $12. Move on to main dishes like lemongrass chicken, grilled filet mignon, or blackened yellowfin ahi. Expect entrées to be $22–30. Desserts feature the chocolate macadamia tart or the signature fluffy dark-chocolate soufflé (allow 20 minutes to prepare). The full bar serves beer, mixed drinks, and personally selected wine by the bottle or glass. Eating at Roy's is no place to linger over a romantic cocktail. It's more like sipping the world's finest champagne from a beer mug, but the best by any other name is still the best!

Nicole Yamaguchi has a restaurant named in her honor, just next door to her dad's place at the Kahana Gateway Shopping Center, open daily from 5:30 P.M., 808/669-5000. **Roy's Nicolina Restaurant** features Euro-Asian cuisine heavily spiced with California and Southwestern dishes. For example, try a gourmet pizzalike flatbread covered in red onions, tomatoes, and pesto, or Cajun shrimp and handmade sausage. Appetizers can be pan-fried calamari with anchovy mayonnaise, or seared goat cheese and eggplant with cilantro pesto and red pepper vinaigrette. Entrées are delicious and fascinating, with offerings like roasted orange-ginger plum duck, or Yankee pot roast with mashed potatoes and garlic spinach. While much of the menu at Nicolina's is the same as across the hall at Roy's, about half is created only for this restaurant, and it too changes nightly. If dad's place is filled up, you'll love the quieter Nicolina's, a "Sichuan-spiced taco chip off the old block."

Since 1998 you've been able to get hand-crafted beer on Maui's west side at the **Fish and Game Brewing Company and Rotisserie,**

808/669-3474, at the Kahana Gateway Shopping Center. Of the half-dozen, brewed-on-property varieties that are always on tap, you could try the Plantation Pale Ale, Wild Hog Stout, or the lighter Honolua Lager. Beers run $3.75 a glass, or $5 for a sampler of five. The sports bar is in the back, and to its front is the deli counter and a sit-down space for lunch. Order your sandwiches and drink at the counter and have a look at the gourmet cheeses, seafood, and specialty meats that line the deli case. In the evening, the dark paneled dinner room is opened for full meals, and set behind glass in that room is the brewing apparatus. Start your dinner with spiced tomato steamed mussels, grilled brewers sausage, or oyster chowder. For the heart of the meal, try fresh fish in one of four preparations, which includes steamed Oriental and habanero cornmeal–crusted dungeness crab, or cioppino pasta. From the rotisserie and grill come such items as hoisin-glazed duckling, marinated pork loin, and rack of lamb, and most entrées are in the under $27 range. The rich surroundings, fine food flavors, and quality beer will make for a satisfying evening.

At the Napili Kai Beach Resort, the **Sea House Restaurant,** 808/669-1500, is open daily for breakfast 8–10:30 A.M., lunch 11:30–2 P.M., and dinner 6–9 P.M. (5:30 P.M. in winter); reservations suggested. Inside the semi-open-air restaurant, breakfast is standard American fare and lunch is sandwiches, salads, soups, and a few entrées. The restaurant shines more at night and has a list of appetizers that's nearly as long as the list of entrées. Dinner choices, served with vegetables and rice pilaf or potato, include fresh catch for $27, Sea House scampi for $26, seasoned and broiled rack of lamb for $27, and ancho chili chicken breast for $24. Besides the normal menu, every night brings a special dinner menu, but the best is the lobster tail dinner on Thursdays. A full wine list includes selections from California and France. There are the sweet sounds of Hawaiian music nightly and a wonderful Friday night Napili Kai Foundation children's Polynesian show put on by local children who have studied their heritage under the guidance of the foundation. Dinner seating is at 6 P.M., the show at 7:30 P.M.; $50 adults, $25

children. If you just want to soak up the rays and gorgeous view of Napili Bay, you can wear your swimwear and have a cool drink or light fare at the Whale Watcher's Bar, where you can also get lunch and *pu pu.*

SHOPPING

Honokowai Marketplace

This shopping plaza, located at the intersection where Lower Honoapi'ilani Road splits off from Honoapi'ilani Highway, is a new mall in the spirit of the Kahana Gateway Shopping Center and the Napili Village Shopping Center farther up the highway. Modern in design and convenient in location, it provides services for tourists and residents alike. Here you'll find a large **Star Market** for all basic food needs and deli items, a **Maui Dive shop, Java Jazz** coffee shop, a video rental shop, and a dry cleaners. **Maui Arts and Gifts** provides souvenirs and take-home art, **Aloha Shirt Shack** can set you up with something to wear, you can buy and develop film at **Imagine Photo,** and **Pizza Paradiso, Soup Nutz,** and **Hula Scoops** will give you something quick to eat and drink.

Da Rose Mall

Look for this tiny mall located oceanside at the south end of town at 3481 Lower Honoapi'ilani Road, where you'll find **A & B Rental and Sales,** 808/669-0027, open daily 9 A.M.–5 P.M., specializing in bicycles, snorkel gear, boogie boards, and surfboards. Prices are mountain bikes $15 for 24 hours, $60 per week; snorkeling gear $2.50 per day and $9 per week. Boogie boards, surfboards, and even fishing poles are rented by the day or week. The sportswear includes board shorts, sundresses, sarongs, aloha shorts, T-shirts, and sunglasses. In front is **Lourdes Kitchenette,** around the side are **Treasures From the Sea** gift shop and **Blooming Rose Boutique** studio for women's fashions, and across the parking lot is **Cha Cha's Place** restaurant. Maui No Ka Oi farmers sell their produce at a **farmers market** in the parking lot of Da Rose Mall Sunday–Friday 7:30 A.M.–3:30 P.M. This is a good chance to pick up locally grown foods. Next door is an

ABC Store, open daily 6:30–11 P.M., a mini-market selling everything from resort wear to wine.

5-A Rent a Space Mall

At 3600 Lower Honoapiʻilani Highway, this mall is usually located by reference to the Pizza Hut here. **Honokowai Okazuya and Deli** is the other eatery in this strip of shops, while **The Fish Market Maui** sells fresh fish, seafood, and prepared, ready-to-eat, or ready-to-cook items. Here you'll also find **Snorkels N' More,** 808/665-0804, open daily 8 A.M.–5 P.M., which has reasonable rates for sales and rental of snorkel gear, boogie boards, surfboards, other water equipment, and some golf clubs. There are usually a few bikes for rent as well, and same-day film processing is available.

Monday, Wednesday, and Friday 7–11 A.M. you'll find the West Maui **farmers market** in the parking lot across from Honokowai Beach Park. Pick up fresh fruit, produce, flowers, and other food products for a day on the beach or dinner ingredients for those staying at the condos nearby. Also in this small complex are **Gina's Food Mart** and **Boss Frog's,** where you can rent snorkel gear or sign up for a boat ride.

Kahana Manor Shops

Aside from **Dollie's,** in the Kahana Manor Shops, there is the **Kahana Manor Groceries,** a one-stop sundries and liquor store open Monday–Saturday 8 A.M.–10 P.M.; the **Women Who Run With Wolves** boutique for beach and athletic wear and accessories for active women; the **Wiki Wiki One-Hour Photo** for all your camera needs; and **Boss Frogs** water activity shop that rents snorkel gear and kayaks, and does activity reservations.

Kahana Gateway Shopping Center

At this newest shopping addition to the Kahana area, easily spotted along Route 30 by McDonald's golden arches, you'll find a **gas station,** a **Whalers General Store, Bank of Hawaii,** and the **Koin-Op Laundromat.** However, the premier stop is **Roy's Kahana Bar and Grill,** one of the finest gourmet restaurants on Maui, and

Roy's Nicolina Restaurant next door. But these aren't the only eateries here. Also try the **Fish and Game Brewing Company and Rotisserie,** one of only two on the island, and its accompanying restaurant where you can get gourmet foods and specialty meats, and the more casual **Outback Steakhouse.** Also at the center is the **Maui Dive Shop,** 808/669-3800, a full-service water activities store where you can rent snorkel equipment, scuba gear, and beach accessories; **Gallerie Hawaii** for contemporary international artwork; **Hutton's Jewelry; Leslie's Family Funwear** for contemporary fashions; and **Ashley's Internet Cafe** for ice cream, yogurt, hot and cold drinks, and sandwiches while you check your email ($.25 per minute, minimum $3).

Napili Plaza

Napili's shopping center offers the full-service **First Hawaiian Bank; Napili Supermarket,** open daily 6:30 A.M.–11 P.M., featuring fresh fish; and **Mail Services Plus,** open Monday–Saturday 8 A.M.–6 P.M., Saturday until 1 P.M., closed Sunday, for all your postal and shipping needs. You may want to pick up a video for the night at **Cinemagic Video** or snorkel gear at **Boss Frog's.** For food, the center has **Maui Tacos,** the **Coffee Store,** and **Mama's Ribs 'N Rotisserie.** If you stop by on Wednesday or Saturday from 9 A.M.–4 P.M., have a look at the craft fair for arts, crafts, gifts, and collectibles.

Napili Village Shopping Center

At 5425 Lower Honoapiʻilani Road, this tiny cluster of shops is hardly big enough to warrant the moniker "shopping center." The **Napili Village General Store,** 808/669-6773, is a well-stocked little store and known landmark, good for last-minute items, with fairly good prices for where it is. You can pick up picnic items and sandwiches, groceries, sundries, and liquor. Open daily 7 A.M.–9 P.M. Next door is **Snorkel Bob's,** 808/669-9603, open daily 8 A.M.–5 P.M., where you can rent snorkel equipment (prescription masks available) for as little as $9 per week and boogie boards for only $26 per week. Bob lets you return your gear at any of his shops for free. Snorkel Bob also arranges island tours.

Kapalua

Kapalua sits like a crown atop Maui's head. One of the newest areas on Maui to be developed, the 1,650-acre Kapalua Resort, www.kapalua-maui.com, was begun in 1975 as a vision of Colin Cameron, one of the heirs to the Maui Land and Pineapple Company. It's been nicely done. Within the resort are the Kapalua Bay and Ritz-Carlton luxury hotels, a half-dozen upscale condominium communities, exclusive shops, three championship golf courses, a golf academy, two tennis centers with multiple courts, sweeping vistas, and terrific beaches. Nearby are horseback-riding stables and plenty of water activity options. All of this has been carved out of the former Honolua Ranch, an outgrowth of land granted to Rev. Baldwin (of Lahaina) in 1836, that eventually grew to be 24,500 acres by 1902. From the beginning, the Honolua Ranch grazed cattle and farmed fruits and coffee. This is pineapple country now, and these golden fruits have been raised here since 1912. Following the introduction of this crop, a cannery was built; camps, a store, and a church were set up for plantation workers; and a railroad was established for transporting the goods. Currently, Maui Land and Pineapple Company has about 9,000 acre of pineapple under cultivation, here and near Makawao, and is the largest producer of these sweet fruits in the United States.

Of the annual special events that take place at Kapalua, a few have broad interest. Held in late June, the Kapalua Wine and Food Festival showcases culinary works of island chefs and couples these with select wines from around the world. The yearly Earth Maui Nature Summit conference is presented by the Kapalua Nature Society, which also sponsors an Earth Maui 5K Fun Run and Kapalua Fun Swim Challenge. These bring out plenty of enthusiastic local athletes, and part of the proceeds go to environmental organizations around the island. Both the Kapalua Open Tennis Tournament in September and the Senior Tennis Championship earlier in the year draw admiring crowds, but perhaps the most well-known event that takes place in Ka-

palua is the nationally broadcast Mercedes Championship golf tournament.

In 1993, the Bay Course was the first golf course in the nation to be certified by the Audubon Society as a cooperative sanctuary; by the next year, the Village and Plantation courses also had that designation. This certification means that, among other things, measures are taken to protect and promote wildlife habitat, plant native species of vegetation, reduce water consumption, and restrict the use of chemicals for fertilizers and pest control. For another example of the lengths that the landowners are willing to go in their stewardship of the natural environment, one need only look to a secluded and rather unusual sanctuary high above the West Maui Airport. There, land has been set aside and infrastructure begun on a gorilla preserve that will be the future home to Koko, the well-known great ape who talks in sign language.

Transportation

The complimentary **Kapalua Shuttle** runs throughout the resort for use by resort guests on an on-demand basis from 6 A.M.–11 P.M. While there is no regular schedule, it will make stops at the hotels and villas, tennis courts, golf courses, and the Kapalua–West Maui Airport. For information or pickup, call 808/669-3177. A dozen times a day, the Holo Ka'a public transit shuttle runs between the two hotels in Kapalua and the Ka'anapali Resort, stopping at nine points along the way in Napili, Kahana, and Honokowai. The fare is $2 one way.

BEACHES AND BAYS

Kapalua Beach

Just past Napili Bay is the equally as nice Kapalua Bay with its fine crescent beach that's popular although usually not overcrowded. Look for access just past the Napili Kai Beach Resort. Park in the public lot and follow the path through the tunnel below the Bay Club restaurant to the beach. The well-formed reef has plenty of fish

PU'U KUKUI PRESERVE

High in the hills above Kapalua is the **Pu'u Kukui Preserve**. Donated by the Maui Land and Pineapple company and managed by the Nature Conservancy, this 8,661-acre tract of rainforest real estate was dedicated in 1992 and is said to be the largest privately owned preserve in the state. It borders the remainder of the 13,000 acres that make up the whole of the West Maui Mountains rainforest, one of the most environmentally diverse areas in the state. Within its boundaries are several endangered species of birds, five endangered and brightly colored tree snails, and 15 distinct plant communities. Thickly wooded hillsides and deep ravines, a mist-shrouded mountaintop, boggy upland plateaus, and a swampy crater characterize this area. It is pristine wilderness that gets nearly as much rain (more than 400 inches per year) as Mt. Wai'ale'ale on Kaua'i (said to have the highest rainfall in the world), and has, in miniature, characteristics similar to the Alaka'i Swamp on Kaua'i. There is no public access to this preserve, except for a once-a-year guided group hike arranged by lottery and sponsored by the Kapalua Nature Society. In response to this rich environment and the deep cultural and historical past of the region, the Kapalua Nature Society was formed to promote an awareness and appreciation for the diversity of the land and a respect for holding it in trust for future generations.

for snorkeling, but swimming is good here too. Also here are restrooms, showers, and a hotel beach concession.

Oneloa Beach

Located around the point from Kapalua Beach, Oneloa is a small sandy beach down a steep path between condos, where swimming is good and locals come to surf. Seldom visited and private; parking available at the entrance to The Ironwoods.

D. T. Fleming Beach Park

One of Maui's best—a long, wide beach backed by wonderful shade trees. This beach park is on Honoapi'ilani Highway just past the Ritz-Carlton, where the road dips back down to the coast. Here you'll find parking, showers, barbecue grills, and excellent swimming except in winter, when there's a pounding surf. There's fair snorkeling here and good surfing, but many younger kids come for body boarding. This is the beach for the Ritz-Carlton, so the south end closest to the hotel has become a bit exclusive, while the rest maintains its very local flavor.

Mokule'ia Bay

Mokule'ia Bay is about 200–300 yards after mile marker 32. There is limited parking along the road, where cement stairs lead down to the water through a stand of trees. This beach has great bodysurfing but terribly dangerous currents in the winter when the surf is rough. Be careful. The surf here is known as "Slaughterhouse." This entire area, plus all of adjacent Honolua Bay, is a **Marine Life Conservation District** and the underwater life is fabulous—some of the best snorkeling in the area. Fish, crabs, eels, rays, octopus, and numerous other sea creatures use the bottom sand, multihued coral, and volcanic rock to play out their rhythm of life.

Honolua Bay

Just past Mokule'ia Bay heading north, look for a dirt road, then park, or park just after crossing the bridge. It's about a 10-minute walk to the beach from either spot. The bay is good for swimming, snorkeling, and especially surfing. Some people stay the night without much problem. For good views of the surfers, drive a little farther along the road and park along the cliff just as the road reaches the top, or drive down the dirt road at the edge of the pineapple field for a spot—there will be lots of cars on a good wave day.

Honokohau Bay

This rather sizable bay faces north and is the last bay before the "wilds" of the backside become predominant. Into the bay drains the water of the narrow but deep Honokohau Valley, from which water is taken by flume to irrigate the extensive fields of West Maui. A few houses constitute the community of Honokohau near mile

Situated within a marinelife conservation district, Mokule'ia Bay is a great spot to snorkel.

marker 36. A rocky beach and thin strip of gray sand are located where the stream enters the bay, which generally has a sandy bottom close to shore. In the uplands above this valley are extensive pineapple fields, and from 1914–20 the island's first pineapple cannery canned fruit here to be distributed to the world. Canning operations moved to Lahaina and continued there until 1962, when the business moved again to a new cannery in Kahului, which is still in operation.

LUXURY HOTELS

As in Ka'anapali, all accommodations in Kapalua fall into the luxury classification.

Kapalua Bay Hotel and Ocean Villas

This, like other grand hotels, is more than a place to stay; it's an experience. The hotel steps down the hillside from its sixth-level entrance. The main lobby is partially open, letting through the gentle breezes and opening up the ocean vista. Plants accent the lobby, and the walls are hung with paintings by Peggy Hopper. All colors are soothing and subdued. To one side is the Lehua Lounge, which is open for cocktails and light snacks. A tiny brook splits the Gardenia Court restaurant on the lower level, and the view over the garden lawns and out to sea is spectacular. The clean lines of the hotel, its sparse decoration, and contemporary elegance let the view speak for itself without distraction. The ocean view vies for your attention here, while the pool pulls you down to the garden, and the beach lures you to the water. Not overly ornamented, guest rooms are done in muted colors—off-whites, tans, and tropical greens. Each spacious room is neatly laid out with an entertainment center, three telephones, electronic safe, a soft couch and easy chairs, and louvered doors to the lanai. The well-lit bathrooms have his and hers sinks at each end of the room, separate dressing closets, and individual areas for the tub, shower, and commode. Marble, tile, and chrome are used throughout. Concierge service and twice-daily maid service are additional amenities.

There are three restaurants and a lobby lounge in the complex, a business center, fitness room, swimming pool and spa, beach activity center, arcade of shops, and a multitude of daily activities and cultural programs including Kamp Kapalua for kids. Every day from 9 A.M.–3 P.M. in the lobby, craftspeople and artisans share their work with hotel guests. The least expensive rooms in the hotel are ones with a garden view at $360–390. Oceanview rooms run $450–620, and suites from $1,200; $75 each additional person 18 and older. In addition, a dozen one- and two-bedroom oceanfront villa suites go for $530–800 per night. For reasonable sums, numerous packages are available. The Kapalua Bay Hotel is part of the Luxury Collection of Starwood Hotels and Resorts. Contact the Kapalua Bay Hotel at One Bay Drive, Kapalua, HI 96761, 808/669-5656 or 800/367-8000, www.kapaluabayhotel.com.

Ritz-Carlton Kapalua

The green sweep of tended lawns fading into the distant sea foaming azure heralds your entrance into an enchanted realm as you wind your way down the

WEST MAUI

roadway leading to the Ritz-Carlton Kapalua, a AAA five-diamond property at One Ritz-Carlton Drive, Kapalua, HI 96761, 808/669-6200 or 800/262-8440, fax 808/665-0026, www.ritzcarlton.com. At the porte cochere, a waiting bellman will park your car. Enter the main hall and relax in the formal parlor of overstuffed chairs, marble-topped tables, and enormous flower arrangements. Evenings in the hall bring mellow entertainment under soft illumination. Through a huge set of double doors is a terrace of Chinese slate. Below, in the floral heart of the hotel grounds, are the trilevel seashell-shaped swimming pools and fluttering palms. Reminiscent of the Orient, the roof line of this great hotel covers the two wings that descend the hill toward the sea, creating an enormous central area between them. All this, coupled with the dark and rich woodwork, thick patterned carpets, floral drapery, pineapple-pattern wallpaper, and halls hung with fine works by prominent island artists and 19th-century reproductions, define the Ritz as the epitome of elegance and luxury.

On the beach, a sweeping crescent of white sand is embraced by two sinewy arms of jet-black lava. It becomes immediately obvious why the diminutive promontory was called Kapalua, "Arms Embracing the Sea," by the ancient Hawaiians who lived here. Notice on the rise above the sea a rounded shoulder of banked earth separated from the main hotel grounds by a low hedge of beach naupaka: The spirits of ancient *ali'i* linger here. This 13.5-acre burial ground harbors perhaps 2,000 graves from around 850 to the 1800s, and it also contains a section of the old paved King's trail that at one time circled the island. With the discovery of this site, the original construction plans were altered, and the hotel was moved away from the area in an attempt to protect it. A *kahuna* was asked to perform the ancient *mele* to appease the spirits, and to reconsecrate the land, passing the *kahu* (caretaking) of it to the Ritz-Carlton. Although the small parcel was deeded to the state as the **Honokahua Preservation Site,** the hotel management and staff alike take their responsibility very seriously. Public access is restricted.

For those with physical fitness and pampering on their minds, the hotel has a fitness center complete with exercise machines, yoga classes, massage therapy, a beauty salon, sauna, and steam rooms. Other hotel offerings include the Ritz Kids children's program, the Aloha Fridays program of cultural activities, a croquet lawn, a putting green, a business center, and a clutch of exclusive shops. At the corner of the property, the Kumulani Chapel or adjacent gazebo can be arranged for weddings.

Located in two wings off the main reception hall, the nearly 550 luxury rooms and suites, all with their own private lanai and sensational view, are a mixture of kings and doubles. Done in muted neutral tones of coral or celadon, the rooms feature hand-crafted quilts, twice-daily room attendance, turndown service, color TVs, 24-hour room service, a fully stocked honor bar, and an in-room safe. The spacious marble bathrooms offer wide, deep tubs, separate shower stalls and commodes, and double sinks. Rates begin at $340 for a garden view to $535 for a deluxe ocean view. The Ritz-Carlton Club, an exclusive floor with its own concierge, and featuring continental breakfast, light lunch, cocktails, cordials, and a full spread of evening hors d'oeuvres, is $635. Suites from a one-bedroom garden view to the magnificent two-bedroom Ritz-Carlton Suite run $610–2,700. Many special packages are offered.

CONDOMINIUMS

Several groups of upscale condominiums dot this spacious resort, either fronting the water or overlooking the golf fairways. Condos in the Bay Villas, Ridge Villas, and Golf Villas range from one-bedroom fairway units to two-bedroom oceanfront hideaways—and a handful of luxury homes are thrown into the mix. Each is individually owned, so all are decorated differently, but all are equipped with full kitchens, air-conditioning and fans, washers and dryers, telephones, and TVs, and all amenities that you'll need for your vacation. Daily maid service can be arranged. All groups of villas also have swimming pools, barbecue grills, and maintained gardens. One-bedroom villas with a fairway view start at $199 and climb rapidly to the three-bedroom oceanfront villas for $499. Daily rates for the luxury homes run $1,650 for three bedrooms to $4,000–7,000 for five-bedroom ones. Some golf and tennis packages and car/condo deals are also offered. Check-in is at the Kapalua Villas Reception Center in a structure built in 1912 and used for decades as the plantation office. For information and reservations, contact Kapalua Villas, 550 Office Rd., Kapalua, HI 96761, 808/669-8088 or 800/545-0018, fax 808/669-5234, www.kapaluavillas.com. For rental options throughout the remainder of this luxury resort, contact Kapalua Vacation Rentals, 808/669-4144, and Sullivan Properties, 808/669-0423.

FOOD

Kapalua Bay Resort Restaurants

The resort has four dining spots. The elegant **Bay Club,** 808/669-8008, offers fine dining for dinner 6–9:30 P.M. on a promontory overlooking the beach and Moloka'i in the distance. Traditionally elegant, there is a dress code, and the soft evening entertainment creates a superb atmosphere. With selections like the signature crab and rock shrimp cake appetizer, Kona lobster, porcini mushroom–dusted opakapaka, seafood paella, and Basque-style rack of lamb, expect to spend at least $35 for a superbly prepared entrée with overtones of flavors from the Pacific and Asia. The menu changes seasonally.

The open-air and contemporary **Gardenia Court** on the lower lobby level of the main building is the principal dining room of the hotel. It serves breakfast daily 6–11 A.M., with a Sunday brunch overlapping from 9:30 A.M.–1:30 P.M. Sunday brunch runs $32 per person. Dinners run Tuesday–Saturday 6–9 P.M., while the Friday seafood buffet starts at 5:30 P.M. Most entrées are $24–32, and the seafood buffet is $38. Resortwear required.

For lunch, light favorites are served at **The Plumeria Terrace,** a relaxing poolside café open 11 A.M.–5 P.M. for food and until 5:30 P.M. for cocktails. In the entrance lobby, the **Lehua Lounge** serves *pu pu* and a light à la carte menu 4:30–9 P.M. and drinks until 10 P.M., with relaxing music in the evening to help let the cares of the day slip away.

Ritz-Carlton Restaurants

Dining at the Ritz-Carlton is a wonderful gastronomic experience, with two main restaurants from which to choose, plus a lobby lounge, sushi bar, and both beachside and poolside cafés. **The Terrace Restaurant,** set below the main lobby and open daily for breakfast 7–11 A.M., informal and relaxed, overlooks the central courtyard with the dramatic sea vista beyond and features fish and seafood with undertones of Asian flavors. Although there is an extensive à la carte breakfast menu, the house specialty is a breakfast buffet for $24.

The Banyan Tree, a semiformal outdoor restaurant oceanside of the swimming pool, is open for lunch 11:30 A.M.–3:30 P.M. and dinner 5:30–9 P.M., with live entertainment at dinnertime Friday–Tuesday. Food is a mix of Asian and Hawaiian. Fashioned like a Mediterranean court, the restaurant offers seating in highbacked chairs at teakwood tables, with mood lighting reminiscent of old oil lamps. Dine al fresco on the redwood deck and watch cavorting whales just offshore. Start with a spicy pesto grilled shrimp, chilled island gazpacho, or warm asparagus and crab salad. Entrée selections include a Hawaii sea bass, Colorado rack of lamb, pineapple-glazed chicken, bouillabaisse, and many more, most from $24–34.

Down by the beach, on a patio surrounded by a manicured coconut grove, is **The Beach House,** serving tropical libations, healthy fruit smoothies, burgers, and sandwiches for under $16 from 11:30 A.M.–4 P.M. Similarly, the **pool bar and café** offers light food and beverages 11:30–4 P.M.

From noon to midnight at the **lobby lounge** you'll find light appetizers, desserts, drinks, and complimentary coffee while you sit and gaze out over the courtyard from the patio. Nearby in the lobby and open 5–10 P.M. is the **Kai** sushi bar with the freshest of sushi.

Sansei

Located in the Kapalua Bay Shops is the exceptional **Sansei** seafood restaurant and sushi bar, 808/669-6286, which serves not only Japanese sushi, but also a whole variety of Pacific Rim food and drinks from the bar. Open daily 5:30–10 P.M. for dinner, and Thursday and Friday for a late-night dinner and laser karaoke from 10 P.M. until closing, which is usually around 2 A.M. For those who like to dine early, an early-bird special is offered 5:30–6 P.M. Sansei offers an extensive menu of sushi rolls and appetizers. Although traditional sushi (and sashimi) can be ordered, the Sansei has made its reputation by taking these Japanese morsels to a higher level with eclectic combinations of ingredients and sauces, as in the mango crab salad handroll with its spicy Thai vinaigrette sauce, and the Kapalua Butterfly, which is snapper, smoked salmon, crab, and veggies in a crisp panko batter roll with tangy ponzu sauce. An award-winning appetizer is the Asian rock shrimp cake, which is shrimp crusted with crispy noodles with ginger-lime-chili butter and cilantro pesto. The sushi and appetizers could certainly fill you up, but save room for an entrée. These delicacies include a special seafood pasta with tiger prawns, onion scallops, and Japanese noodles, a Szechwan-crusted ahi tuna, Peking duck breast with mushroom and potato risotto and foie gras demi-glaze, and Colorado lamb T-bone chop. Sushi rolls run $4–16, appetizers up to $13, and main entrées $16–24. The menu items are imaginative and the blends of flavors exceptional.

Jameson's Grill and Bar

Don't underestimate this excellent restaurant just because it's located between the golf clubhouse and tennis center. The Kapalua Bay Golf Course provides the backdrop, and the restaurant provides the filling, delicious food. The main room with its flagstone floor and open-beam ceiling is richly appointed with koa wood, and large windows frame a sweeping view of the super-green fairways of the golf course. Sit inside or out on the patio. Breakfast and lunch are mostly light and easy meals; the real treat comes in the evening from 5–10 P.M., when a more substantial dinner meal is served. Start with an appetizer such as stuffed mushrooms for $8.95 or seared sashimi for $12.95, and move on to a soup or one of the many fine salads. Entrées include fish of the day at market price, lemon pepper chicken for

$18.95, rack of lamb for $27.95, and New York strip steak for $25.95. Follow your meal with dessert or sip wine selected from an extensive list. All items can be ordered take-out. An excellent restaurant with a lovely setting at 200 Kapalua Drive. Call 808/669-5653 for reservations.

The Plantation House

Above Kapalua at the Plantation Golf Course Clubhouse, you'll find the lovely Plantation House Restaurant, 808/669-6299, open daily 8–11 A.M. for breakfast, 11 A.M.–3 P.M. for lunch, and 5:30–10 P.M. for dinner. Inside, the split-level floor, gabled roof, natural wood, fireplace, and carpeted and marbled floor add elegance, but the real beauty is the natural still life that pours through the floor-to-ceiling French doors. Kapalua lies at your feet and the West Maui Mountains rise behind. For breakfast, the extensive menu offers fare like a hearty rancher's breakfast of two eggs, toast, two scoops of rice or breakfast potatoes, grilled ham, bacon, or Portuguese sausage all for $8; or smoked salmon Benedict for $10. For lunch, start with pan-fried crab cakes served with basil pepper aioli for $8.50 or a Greek chicken salad for $11.50. A half-pound double-fisted Plantation House burger is available for $8 and a chicken breast sandwich for $9. The dinner menu tempts your palate with scallop skewers and prawn and pork pot stickers. The chef prepares pasta al giorno for $16, or tops it with scallops or shrimp for $21, and sautéed jumbo prawns with garlic mashed potatoes run $22. However, fish is the focus here, and one of the most popular of the many signature entrées is sautéed fish with braised asparagus and Alaskan snow crab meat. The food, with flavors and ingredients influenced by the Mediterranean, is a winner, and the views make it even more special.

Fleming's Restaurant

Fleming's "On the Greens at Kapalua" is the restaurant at the Village Golf Course clubhouse, 808/665-1000. As with the other clubhouse eateries at this resort, it has surprisingly good food, providing what can casually be referred to as golf gourmet. Breakfast, served 8 –11 A.M., is mostly eggs and griddle items. A lanai menu that's mostly *pu pu*, soup, salad, and sandwiches is served 11 A.M.–3 P.M. Dinner from 5 P.M. is definitely fine dining with a fancier twist. Start with crispy crab cakes, portobella mushroom ravioli, or Upcountry pear salad in the $7–12 range, and move on to such entrées as fish of the day, grilled pork chop, filet mignon Wellington, or pan-roasted rack of lamb that run mostly $20–29. Spiced with the flavors of the people who have migrated to the islands, your meal will be satisfying no matter your choice.

Honolua Store

Set next to the entrance of the Ritz-Carlton, this small general store also serves reasonably priced light meals and sandwiches. The breakfast menu, served 6–10 A.M., offers "The Hobo"—eggs, sausage, and rice for $3.95—or two pancakes for $2.95. Plate lunches, sandwiches, grilled items, and salads all run under $7 and are served 10 A.M.–3 P.M., or pick something out of the deli case or take away a box lunch. Sit at a table on the front porch and overlook the broad lawns and tall pine trees of the exclusive planned community of Kapalua. This is by far the cheapest place in the area to eat.

SHOPPING
Kapalua Shops

A cluster of exclusive shops service the resort, including **McInerny** with fine women's apparel, @Reyn's for islandwear, **Kapalua Kids** for the younger set, and **Kapalua Logo Shop** if you want to show off that you've at least been to the Kapalua Resort, since all items of clothing sport the butterfly logo. Visit **La Perle** for pearls, diamonds, and other fashionable jewels, and **South Seas Trading Post** for antiques, art, and more ethnic jewelry. For fine examples of Hawaiian quilts and other stitchery, try **Hawaiian Quilt Collection. Lahaina Galleries** has a wonderful collection of island and off-island artists on display, while the **Elizabeth Doyle Gallery** features art glass, and **W.H. Smith** has all your sundry supplies. For a bit more of an intellec-

tual stop, try **Kapalua Discovery Center** for a short historical, cultural, and natural-history lesson about the area; open 10 A.M.–5 P.M. daily, free. When you get hungry from all the shopping, stop into the **Sansei** restaurant and sushi bar for a taste of Japan and the Pacific with an eclectic twist. Adjacent to the Kapalua Bay hotel, these shops are open from 9 A.M. daily.

If you're here on Tuesday at 10:30 A.M., come and listen to slack-key guitar or ukulele and stories. On Thursdays 10–11 A.M., be sure to see the free ancient hula show, and on Fridays 10:30–11:30 A.M., you can participate in a hula lesson. Some Mondays and Wednesdays, crafts are taught, and Fridays at 9:45 A.M. a cultural history lesson is presented by the resort's Hawaiian Cultural Advisor. These shops are connected to those in Ka'anapali and Lahaina by the Holo Ka'a public transit shuttle.

Honolua Store

This well-stocked, reasonably priced general store, open daily 6 A.M.–8 P.M., is a rare find in this expensive neck of the woods. The shelves hold beer, wine, and liquors, basic food items from bananas to sweets, books and gifts, and even a smattering of sunglasses, shorts, hats, aloha shirts, and logo wear. Breakfast and lunch are dispensed from the deli in the back, and boxes of preinspected pineapples can be purchased here to be taken back to the Mainland. Built in 1929 and metamorphosed over the years, this shop has served the needs of this community for nearly as long as there has been a community here, and it functioned in more than one way as the center of village life until the village was eclipsed by the Kapalua Resort in the mid-1970s.

RECREATION
Golf

Kapalua's three golf courses combine to make one of the finest golfing opportunities in the state. The Bay Course is an ocean course that extends up the hill into the trees. The signature hole 5 is a challenge, with the fairway laid out around the curve of a bay. Pushing up against the surrounding pineapple fields, the Village

Course is a mountain course that offers vistas over the distant ocean. At more than 7,000 yards, the Plantation Course is the longest and is used by the PGA for professional championships. For information and tee times, call 808/669-8044. In addition, the new Kapalua Golf Academy, 808/669-6500, is the largest such instructional facility in the state, offering clinics and lessons. Outdoors are target greens, putting greens, wedge areas, bunkers, a short game area, and an 18-hole putting course.

Tennis

The Kapalua Resort boasts 20 plexipave courts in two tennis centers, representing the largest private tennis facility in the state. Both offer pro shops, equipment rental, clinics, lessons, and tournaments. Some courts are lighted so evening play is possible. Courts times run $10 per person for resort guests or $12 for others; call for reservations. The Tennis Garden, 808/669-5677, is located near the Bay Course clubhouse, while the Village Tennis Center, 808/665-0112, is ensconced near the water below the Ritz-Carlton.

Other Activities

Kapalua Dive Company, 808/669-3448 or 877/669-3448, www.kapaluadive.com, services guests at both the Kapalua Bay Hotel and the Ritz-Carlton. Aside from the gear it rents, this company offers lessons and various dives, which include shore dives, scooter dives, and a kayak dive. Also of interest is its kayak/snorkel trip that cruises the coast from Kapalua Bay to Honolua Bay.

Ironwood Ranch has the only riding opportunities on this side of the island, from an easy jaunt through the lower foothills to a more advanced ride up the mountain. Rides range

$80–110 for up to two hours. To reserve a spot and get information on where to meet, call the ranch at 808/669-4991.

Tours

Above the Kapalua Resort, **The Maunalei Arboretum** is open to tours. Within this private garden is a two-mile loop trail that takes you up to about 2,600 feet. This garden is the work of D. T. Fleming, a former Honolua Ranch manager, who collected a multitude of tropical plants from around the world. Hikes leave daily at 8 A.M. for the four-hour trip. Contact Maui Eco-adventures, 808/661-7720, to reserve your spot.

Kapalua is pineapple country, and what would be better than to take a walk through pineapple fields and learn about this sweet golden fruit, its production, and the pineapple industry as a whole? Sponsored by the Kapalua Nature Society, plantation tours are held weekdays except holidays from 9:30 A.M.–noon and again from 12:30–3 P.M. if there is enough interest and demand; $29 per person. Wear a hat, closed-toe shoes, and clothes that you don't mind getting a little dusty. Tours leave from the Kapalua Villas reception center; call 808/669-8088 for additional information and reservations.

Kapalua Art School

Located in the former plantation blacksmith shop at 800 Office Road, the Kapalua Art School is a community center open to residents and resort guests alike that offers a variety of classes on a rotating basis, including watercolor, drawing, weaving, ceramics, dance, and yoga. In operation since 1995, this school functions on a drop-in basis, and fees run about $30 for three-hour sessions. Call 808/665-0007 for information about what's currently being offered.

South Maui

Ma'alaea

Ma'alaea is a small community located in the southwestern corner of the Maui isthmus that is home to a small harbor, a handful of houses, a row of condominiums, several fine restaurants, the Maui Ocean Center aquarium, and a new and expanding shopping plaza. It sits on the edge of the huge and beautiful Ma'alaea Bay, often referred to as a whale's nursery because so many mother whales head here to birth and raise their young during their winter and spring stay in the islands. Until the advent of plane travel to and between the islands, Ma'alaea was a busy port for interisland steamer traffic, principally serving the Ma'alaea and Kihei areas. Constructed in its current configuration in 1952, **Ma'alaea Harbor** is a bite-size working port, one of two on the island where tour boats dock (the other being Lahaina Harbor). With the comings and goings of all types of craft, the harbor is colorful, picturesque, and always busy; and it has the dubious distinction of being the second windiest harbor in the world, with sustained winds averaging 25 knots. Upon entering the harbor, you are greeted by a small U.S. Coast Guard installation at the east end and

Pu'u Ola'a (Red Hill) dominates the South Maui coast.

SOUTH MAUI

To Wailuku

To Kahului

MOKULELE HWY.

KEALIA POND WILDLIFE REFUGE

Lahaina Pali Trail

Kealia Pond

311

HAYCRAFT PARK

31

MAUI OCEAN CENTER

Ma'alaea

Ma'alaea Beach

KEALIA BEACH PLAZA

To Lahaina

30

Ma'alaea Harbor

KIHEI WHARF

McGregor Point

MAI POINA 'OE IA'U BEACH COUNTY PARK

CAPTAIN VANCOUVER MONUMENT

Ma'alaea Bay

KALEPOLEPO BEACH PARK

PI'ILANI

MAUI RESEARCH AND TECHNOLOGY PARK

Best Place for Whale migration Sitting (Jan-April Peak time)

AZEKA PLACE SHOPPING CENTER

31

ELLEAIR MAUI GOLF CLUB

Kihei

To Kula

Nov—May Migration

KALAMA PARK

KAMA'OLE BEACHES COUNTY PARKS

HWY.

Maui Meadows

Keokea

KIHEI BOAT RAMP

37

MOKAPU BEACH PARK

ULUA BEACH PARK

WAILEA SHOPPING VILLAGE

WAILEA BEACH PARK

Wailea

POLO BEACH PARK

WAILEA GOLF COURSE

PALAUEA BEACH PARK

WAILEA ALANUI RD.

MAKENA LANDING

Makena Bay

KEAWALA'I CHURCH (1832)

Makena

Ulupalakua Ranch

MARINE LIFE CONSERVATION DISTRICT

Onouli Beach

Pu'u Ola'i

MAKENA GOLF COURSE

TEDESCHI WINERY

SEABIRD SANCTUARY

Oneloa Beach

31

Molokini Island

MAKENA ALANUI RD.

MAUI'S LAST VOLCANIC ERUPTION SITE (1790)

Kanahena

'Ahihi Bay

'AHIHI-KINA'U NATURAL AREA RESERVE

To Hana

'Alalakeiki Channel

Cape Kina'u

La Perouse Bay

Ancient Paved Road

0   3 mi

0   3 km

ROBERT NILSEN

Walk through the tunnel at the Maui Ocean Center, where you can see fish above, below, and to the side of you, and imagine yourself submersed in a coral reef.

Buzz's Wharf, a well-known restaurant, at the other. Between these two, you'll find restrooms and the Ma'alaea Activities booth at harborside, which can book all sea, land, and air tours and activities for you. Across the street from the Coast Guard Station is Ma'alaea Store (est. 1946), and tucked in beside it is the Shinto fishermen's shrine Ebesu Kotohira Jinsha, which was constructed in 1914 and rebuilt in 1999. Up above the shrine and store are the aquarium and new gaggle of shops. The condominiums line Hauoli Street, which culminates in Haycraft Park, the western end of Ma'alaea Beach. Outside the breakwater is Ma'alaea's only well-known surf spot, called Freight Trains by locals and Ma'alaea Pipeline by others for its fast break.

For decades, Ma'alaea was little more than a sleepy village and harbor. It's still small, but the influx of money and development is changing the face and character of the community. With greater traffic, Ma'alaea is busier and its visitors require more services. More than just a place to get on a snorkel boat or pass by on your way from Ka'anapali to Kihei, it's beginning to form an integrated identity all its own—a destination, not a byway. Luckily for those who live here, most changes are taking place up by the highway.

Maui's electric power generation plant sits outside of Ma'alaea. While not particularly conspicuous, you will recognize the towers that rise above the surrounding sugarcane fields along Route 31 as it descends down to the ocean east of the village as you approach the Kealia Pond Natural Wildlife Refuge. Two power-generation units have been built, with only one currently in operation. Another unit is being planned, perhaps in anticipation of future island growth.

SIGHTS
Maui Ocean Center
The most radical change for the community in years was the opening of the Maui Ocean Center. The Ocean Center is a large aquarium and marine park with several dozen indoor and outdoor displays and hands-on exhibits. Explore the realm of the reef in the Living Reef building, handle tide pool creatures at the Touch Pool, and learn

SOUTH MAUI

about the fascinating turtles, stingrays, and whales in their separate exhibits. As an added benefit during winter, whales can be seen cavorting and breaching in the bay beyond the harbor. Perhaps the most unique feature at the center is the Underwater Journey, where you walk through a four-inch-thick, 54-foot-long transparent acrylic tunnel in the 750,000-gallon "open ocean" tank, Hawaii's largest aquarium, which offers a 240-degree view of the waterlife. There are no trained animal shows here, only periodic feedings and presentations by ocean naturalists at various locations throughout the center. No matter what your focus, this will be an enjoyable and educational experience as you'll learn about Hawaii's unique marine culture; all animals are indigenous or endemic. A stop here could easily be a half-day affair, so when you get hungry, have a quick bite at the Reef Cafe snack bar, or try the Seascape Ma'alaea Restaurant for a more substantial lunch meal. Before leaving, pick up a memento of your day's visit at the gift shop. The Maui Ocean Center, 808/270-7000, www.mauioceancenter.com, is open daily 9 A.M.–5 P.M. (until 6 P.M. in summer); $19 adults, $13 children 3–12, $17 seniors. Audio guides are available in English and Japanese for an additional $2. If you're without transportation, ride the Holo Ka'a public transit shuttle from either the South Maui or West Maui areas, $5 one way to either section or $10 for a one-day systemwide pass.

The strong winds make thin Ma'alaea Beach less desirable for sunbathing than others on the island, but it's a windsurfer's dream. The beachcombing and strolling are quiet and productive.

Ma'alaea Beach

Consisting of three miles of windswept sand partially backed by Kealia Pond National Wildlife Refuge, Ma'alaea Beach has many points of access between Ma'alaea and Kihei along Route 31. The strong winds make this thin beach less desirable for sunbathing than others on the island, but it's a windsurfer's dream. The hard-packed sand is a natural track for joggers, which are profuse in the morning and afternoon. Few come here except locals to picnic, fish, or play games in the sand with kids. The beachcombing and

strolling are quiet and productive. From the Ma'alaea end, you can access the beach from Haycraft Park. If you're up by 6 A.M. you can see the Kihei canoe club practice at the Kihei end; they put their canoes in the water near the old Kihei wharf just across the road from Suda's Store.

Kealia Pond National Wildlife Refuge

Established in 1992, this refuge stretches between Ma'alaea and Kihei, mostly on the inland side of Route 31. Now set aside for stilts, coots, and other wildlife, this pond was once two productive fish ponds used by Hawaiians living around the bay. Aside from the stilt and coot, other birds and fowl that inhabit the pond are Hawaiian duck, black-crowned night heron, golden plover, and ruddy turnstone. Migratory waterfowl such as the pintail and shoveller visit the refuge, and hawksbill turtles come to shore to lay eggs. The refuge entranceway is off Mokulele Highway near mile marker 6, between Kihei and Kahului. A short walkway to the pond starts from the refuge headquarters, which is open weekdays 8 A.M.–4:30 P.M. Because of the birds' breeding and nesting season, it's perhaps best to visit from Aug.–April. As with most such refuges, this environment lies in a delicate balance and changes according to the season. With the winter rains and runoff the pond may increase in size to more than 400 acres; during periods of drought, parts of it may dry up all together, shrinking the size by over half and leaving a salty residue on exposed ground. One of Maui's first airstrips, the old Ma'alaea Airport used to occupy the flats near here.

PRACTICALITIES

Accommodations

There are no hotels in Ma'alaea. Condominiums stand one after another along the water east of the harbor. For rooms, check with the **Maalaea Bay Rentals** agency, 808/244-7012 or 800/367-

6084, fax 808/242-7476, www.maalaeabay.com. This agency has an office at the Hono Kai Resort, 280 Hauoli St., Ma'alaea, HI 96793, and handles more than 100 units in a majority of the condos along this road. All units are fully furnished with complete kitchens, TVs, telephones, and lanai; and each property has a pool and laundry facility. Rates run $125–225 from mid-December to the end of April, with substantial discounts for summer and fall; five-night minimum, 10 nights during the Christmas holidays. Rates are reduced by 10 percent for monthly stays.

Food

The award-winning **Waterfront Restaurant** at the Milowai Condo, 808/244-9028, has a well-deserved reputation and a great view of the harbor and bay. It's owned and operated by the Smith brothers, who work both the front and the kitchen. The Waterfront is open for lunch 10 A.M. –1:30 P.M. daily except Saturday and daily from 5 P.M. for dinner. Choose a horseshoe-shaped booth tucked around the room's perimeter or a table out on the deck with sea breezes and the setting sun, and order a bottle of wine from the extensive international list. For starters, consider the Caesar salad for $8.95, Pacific oysters on the half shell at $10.95, or imported French escargot for $8.95. Definitely order the Maine lobster chowder, a famous specialty, for $8.50. The entrée scampi is $24.95, medallions of tenderloin is $25.95, while rack of lamb in a Sichuan peppercorn sauce is $28.95. However, the best choice is the fresh island fish, priced daily, of which there might be 5–8 varieties available each night and which can be prepared in a variety of ways: Sicilian; à la meuniere in a white wine sauce with lemon; Bastille, which is imprisoned in angel hair potato and sautéed and topped with fresh scallions; Southwestern; Cajun; baked with crab stuffing; baked in parchment paper; or sautéed, broiled, baked, or poached. Save room for one of the prize-winning desserts. The Waterfront provides an excellent dining experience, from the fine service to the wonderful food, and is well worth the price. Free parking in designated spots in the Milowai lot.

Buzz's Wharf restaurant, 808/244-5426, open daily 11 A.M.–11 P.M., specializes in seafood. The waterfront atmosphere and second-story views are first rate. It's a favorite spot and often busy. *Pu pu* selections include steamed clams for $11.95, escargot on the shell for $8.95, and coconut panko shrimp for $11.95. The lunch menu offers an assortment of sandwiches for under $12, fish and chips for $13.95, and fish and meat plates. For dinner, try prawns Tahitian, the seafood medley, or a mouthwatering rib eye for $18–27. Enjoy a liter of house wine for $12 or cocktail for $6. End your meal with dessert followed by a stroll around the moonlit harbor.

Bamboo predominates in the tables, chairs, and room dividers of the **Ma'alaea Grill** at the Ma'alaea Harbor Village next to the Maui Ocean Center. Hardwood floors, old-style lighting and ceiling fans, and large French doors that let in the ocean breezes and let you look out over the harbor add to the ambiance. A full bar greets you as you enter this restaurant, and you can see into the kitchen through a plate-glass window on the way to your seat. Ma'alaea Grill is open for lunch 10:30 A.M.–3 P.M., dinner daily except Monday 5:30–9 P.M., and it has a simpler café menu from 3–5 P.M. Lunch is casual with salads, sandwiches, and several light entrées for under $10. Dinner is more formal and pricier, but expect larger portions and a touch more class. Try fried ahi stuffed calamari or tempura potato cake appetizer before moving on to a full entrée, like sautéed mahimahi, macadamia nut–crusted duckling, grilled jumbo shrimp, or *kiawe* grilled New York steak, all $14–23. Like its sister restaurants in Wailuku, Lahaina, and Makawao, the Ma'alaea Grill offers quality food at a decent price.

More casual is the **Blue Marlin** grill and bar, an open-air eatery located on the lower level of Ma'alaea Harbor Village and looking out over Ma'alaea Harbor. Hanging on the wall at the entrance is a stuffed blue marlin, a grander size approaching 1,200 pounds caught by one of the boats at the harbor. Not surprisingly, fish and seafood are the mainstay of the menu, but steaks, burgers, and sandwiches also make an appearance. Open from 11 A.M. for lunch and dinner, most entrées run $15–25.

The **Tradewinds Deli and Mart,** located at

the Maalaea Mermaid condo, carries groceries, drinks, and alcohol, creates deli sandwiches (from $3.99), and also rents snorkel equipment and boogie boards. Hours are Monday–Thursday 9 A.M.–8 P.M. and Friday 9 A.M.–9 P.M.

Located directly across from the Coast Guard station and open daily except Monday 8 A.M.–5 P.M., the **Ma'alaea Store** is where you have a much better chance of buying fishing tackle than you do a loaf of bread, but it does have some very limited groceries, snacks, and sundries.

Shopping

Following the opening of the Maui Ocean Center, the two-level **Ma'alaea Harbor Village** opened next to the aquarium, with a **Whalers General Store** for sundries and food items, **Moonbow Tropics** for tropical clothing, and an **Island Soap and Candle Works** store for scents and perfumes of the tropics. You can book your water tours with the ocean activities center, eat at two restaurants, or snack on ice cream and cookies at **Hula Cookies.** On the lower level is a **Maui Dive Shop.**

The **Pacific Whale Foundation** also has a store here where you can pick up logowear, books on whales and other marine subjects, look at the exhibit area, or garner information about water tours and educational programs run by the foundation. It's definitely worth a stop to see what this organization is offering. Next door is the Pacific Whale Foundation's new Ocean Science and Discovery Center, which conducts numerous classes, programs, video presentations, and activities for kids and adults alike throughout the week.

In a booth at the edge of the harbor is **Ma'alaea Activities Center,** 808/242-6982. Not only can the staff here book you on a fishing boat or other water excursion from this harbor, but they can also take care of all your activity needs for the entire island. Having been around since 1981, they know their business. Stop by 8 A.M.–4 P.M. daily.

At the far end of this triangular commercial area are a gas station, fast-food eatery, and the Maui Golf and Sports Park, open 10 A.M.–10 P.M. daily, where you can putt around a miniature golf course.

Kihei

Kihei (Shoulder Cloak) takes it on the chin whenever antidevelopment groups need an example at which to wag their fingers. From the 1960s to the 1980s, construction along both sides of Kihei Road, which runs the length of town, was unabated. Because there was no central planning for the development, mostly high-rise condos and a few hotels were built wherever they could be squeezed in: some lovely, some crass. Building continued in the 1990s, although at a slower pace and with more restrictions, and in the 2000s much of the new construction has been inland. There's hardly a spot left where you can get an unobstructed view of the beach as you drive along. That's the "slam" in a nutshell. The good news is that Kihei has so much to recommend it that if you refrain from fixating on this one regrettable feature, you'll thoroughly enjoy yourself, and save money, too.

The developers went hyper here because it's perfect as a tourist area. The weather can be counted on to be the best on all of Maui. Haleakala, looming just behind the town, catches rainclouds before they drench Kihei. Days of blue skies and sunshine are taken for granted. On the other side of the condos and hotels are gorgeous beaches, every one open to the public. Once on the beachside, the condos don't matter anymore. The views out to sea are unobstructed vistas of Lana'i, Kaho'olawe, Molokini, and West Maui, which gives the illusion of being a separate island. The buildings are even a buffer to the traffic noise! Many islanders make Kihei their home, so there is a feeling of real community here. It's quieter than Lahaina with not as much action; but for sun and surf activities, this place has it all.

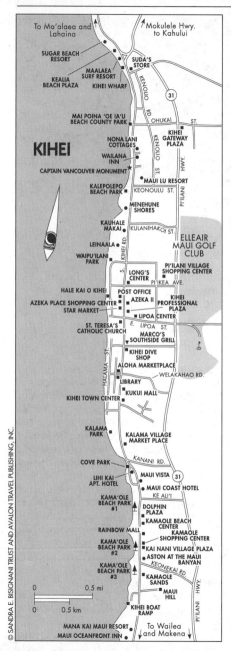

The six-mile stretch bordered by beach and mountain that makes up Kihei has always been an important landing spot on Maui. Hawaiian war canoes moored here many times during countless skirmishes over the years; later, Western navigators such as Captain George Vancouver found this stretch of beach a congenial anchorage. A totem pole across from the Maui Lu Resort marks the spot where Vancouver landed. During World War II, when a Japanese invasion was feared, Kihei was considered a likely spot for an amphibious attack. Overgrown pillboxes and rusting tank traps are still found along the beaches. Kihei is a natural site with mountain and ocean vistas. It's also great for beachcombing up toward Ma'alaea, but try to get there by morning because the afternoon wind is notorious for creating minor sandstorms.

Kihei's commercial sections are separated by residential areas. There is no one town center as such, although the highest concentration and greatest number of businesses are near the post office and the Azeka Place shopping centers. The new Maui Research and Technology Park has been built above the Elleair Maui Golf Club in Kihei, sprucing up the image of the area a little and bringing in some high-tech white-collar jobs at the same time, particularly with the creation of the Maui High Performance Computing Center. While only three shiny glass and steel office buildings have been built at this office park so far, land has been set aside for many more.

BEACHES

Mai Poina 'Oe Ia'u Beach County Park

On Kihei's northern fringe, this beach offers only limited paved parking, otherwise just along the road. Showers, tables, and restrooms front the long and narrow white-sand beach, which has good, safe swimming but is still plagued by strong winds by early afternoon. These trade winds are a delight for windsurfers and kiteboarders alike, and here you can see more than 100 sporting enthusiasts out trying the wind when conditions are optimal.

SOUTH MAUI

outrigger canoes ready for launch near the old Kihei Wharf

Kalepolepo Beach Park

Next to the Humpback Whale National Marine Sanctuary office, this park has a small beach that's good for kiddies. Centuries ago, the thriving community of Kalepolepo occupied this area of Kihei and farmed the three-acre royal fish pond **Koʻieʻie Loko Iʻa,** small but best preserved of the royal fish ponds on Maui. Remnants of its rock wall can still be seen arcing through the water. Now much reduced in size, the walls once stood higher than high tide and wider than two men abreast. It's estimated that more than 2,000 pounds of fish per year were harvested from these waters when it was a functioning fish pond in the late 1500s.

Waipuʻilani Park

Just south of Kalepolepo is this park with its narrow beach, broad lawn, tennis courts, smattering of coconut trees, great sunsets, and windsurfers in season. Rather infrequented, it's like a big greenway to the sea for the condos that front it. The shoreline for over one-half mile south has been set aside as a State Beach Preserve. Access to it is at the end of West Lipoa Street. Off

the coast here were three large fish ponds that have now all but disappeared.

Kalama Park

This park is more suited to family outings, athletic games, and enjoying the vista than it is for beach activities. Kalama has a large lawn ending in a breakwater, a small beach in summer, and none in winter. However, there are 36 acres of pavilions, tables, barbecue pits, volleyball, basketball, and tennis courts, a baseball diamond, a soccer field, and plenty of expanse to throw a frisbee. With its great views of Molokini and Haleakala, it is considered the best family park in the area. At its extreme southern end, just across the highway bridge, is the diminutive Cove Park, where locals put small boats in the water and others come to surf.

Kamaʻole I, II, and III

These beach parks, often referred to as Kam I, II, and III, are at the south end of town. All three have beautiful white sand, picnic tables, lifeguards, and all the amenities. The swimming and bodysurfing are good. At the north end of

Kam I is an area called Charley Young Beach. Snorkeling is good here and for beginners on the reef between II and III, where much coral and many colorful reef fish abound. Kama'ole III has a kids' playground. Shopping and dining are nearby.

Kihei Boat Ramp

Just south of Kama'ole III Beach is the Kihei Boat Ramp, used by many ocean activity companies in the area to launch boats and rafts.

ACCOMMODATIONS

The emphasis in Kihei is on condos. With keen competition among them, you can save some money while having a more homey vacation. Close to 100 condos, plus a smattering of vacation apartments, cottages, and even a few small hotel resorts, are all strung along Kihei Road. As always, you pay more for ocean views. Don't shy away from accommodations on the *mauka* side of Kihei Road. You have total access to the beach, some superior views of Haleakala, and you usually pay less money. The accommodations that follow are listed north to south. By and large, these places are located north of the Azeka Place shopping centers and south of Kalama beach park, leaving the central section of town for businesses and homes.

Hotels

Maui Lu Resort, 575 S. Kihei Rd., Kihei, HI 96753, 808/879-5881 or 800/922-7866, fax 808/879-4627, a 28-acre Aston-managed property at the north end of Kihei, attempts to preserve the feeling of old Hawaii with its emphasis on *ohana*. The Maui Lu is not designed as an ordinary hotel—it looks more like condo units—but none of the rooms have kitchens. Amenities here include an activities desk, tennis and volleyball courts, a Maui-shaped swimming pool, and two tiny pocket beaches. While three buildings are located next to the water, most rooms are located in the newer wings up the hill near the entrance lobby. Rooms are priced $108–180 during value season and $131–215 during regular season. All hotel-style rooms include TV, air-conditioning, refrigerator, and daily maid service.

The **Maui Coast Hotel,** 2259 S. Kihei Rd., Kihei, HI 96753, 808/874-6284 or 800/895-6284, fax 808/875-4731, www.mauicoasthotel.com, is Kihei's only true "high-rise" hotel. Completed in 1993 and renovated in 1999, the 265 rooms and suites here are bright and cheerful, blending Southwestern pastels and Hawaiian-style furniture. Adding to your comfort are standard amenities like remote-control color TV, air-conditioning and ceiling fans, complimentary in-wall safes, coffeemakers, refrigerators, slippers to pad around in, full bathrooms that include a jacuzzi bathtub, and a "who asked for one?" bathroom scale. A wet bar is in all the larger suites. Guests are also treated to morning coffee, and washers and dryers are on every other floor. This seven-story hotel offers two spas with whirlpools, a swimming pool, lighted guests-only tennis courts, Spices Restaurant, the Tradewinds poolside bar with nightly entertainment, sundries shop, and free parking. Rates are reasonably priced at $165–175 for a standard room, $195–350 for a suite, $20 each additional person, with discounted off-season and weekly rates. Rental car packages are also available, and a fifth night free is offered on some rooms. The Maui Coast Hotel, set back from busy Kihei Road, offers a small oasis of peace and tranquility with excellent rates for the amenities offered.

Best Western Maui Oceanfront Inn, 2980 S. Kihei Rd., 808/879-7744 or 800/263-3387, fax 808/874-0145, www.mauioceanfrontinn.com, is located at the entrance to Wailea. In 2000, this intimate complex was given a complete makeover including buildings, furnishings, and grounds, and reborn as a boutique hotel where low-rise, multiunit buildings run from the road down to the water. Each air-conditioned room and suite has a TV and entertainment center, air-conditioning and ceiling fans, in-room safe, and a small refrigerator. None has cooking facilities. Rates are $151 for a mountain-view room, $159 for garden-view, $215–231 for garden-view and oceanview suites, and $240 for oceanfront suites.

Condos and Cottages

One of the several condos at the far north end of Kihei, at the eastern end of Ma'alaea Beach, is **Sugar Beach Resort,** 145 N. Kihei Rd., 808/879-7765. All one- and two-bedroom units have full kitchens, ceiling fans and air-conditioning, TVs, and lanai, with guest-only tennis courts, swimming pool, spa, sauna, barbecue grills, sundries shop, sandwich shop, and activities desk on property. The activity desk can book you on virtually any land and sea excursion, while the sundry shop offers rental bikes, kayaks, snorkel gear, and beach equipment. All units are individually owned and decorated. Rates run about $125–195 for one-bedroom and $220–325 for two-bedroom suites, but these rates vary a bit according to the rental agency. Contact the following agents for rooms here and at other nearby condos: Condominium Rentals Hawaii, 808/879-2778 or 800/367-5242 Mainland, 800/663-2101 in Canada; Rainbow Rentals, 808/244-1688 or 800/451-5366; or Maui Condominium and Home Realty, 808/879-5445 or 800/451-5008.

The Polynesian-style roofs and dark wooden siding might draw you to the two-story, luxury **Maalaea Surf Resort,** 12 S. Kihei Rd., 808/879-1267 or 800/423-7953, fax 808/874-2884, but the fully furnished bright interiors, well-tended lawns, tennis courts, swimming pools, and white-sand beach will captivate you. Each unit has air-conditioning and daily maid service. One-bedroom suites run $205–230, and two-bedroom units are $277–350. A fifth night is offered free during their value season. This condo is near the intersection of Highways 31 and 311.

The first place south of Suda's Store is **Nona Lani Cottages,** 455 S. Kihei Rd., 808/879-2497 or 800/733-2688, www.nonalanicottages.com, owned and operated by Dave and Nona Kong. These eight clean and neat units on the *mauka* side of the road have full kitchens and baths, queen beds, and daybeds. Laundry facilities, public phones, hammocks, chaise lounges, and barbecues are on the premises, and each unit has a raised lanai with tables. Rates are $90 per night during low season, $15 per additional person and four-night minimum, and $99 per night during high season when there's a seven-night minimum stay. Weekly and monthly rates are available. These individual plantation-style units are about as down-home Hawaiian as you can get, a good place to come if you're looking for relaxation. The Nona Lani also has three rooms (no kitchens) in the main house, which run $65 and $75, respectively, for low- and high-season, three- and four-night minimum rental.

A few steps away is **Wailana Inn,** 14 Wailana Place near the Vancouver Monument, 808/874-3131 or 800/399-3885, fax 808/874-0454, www.wailanabeach.com, an apartment turned condo rental. This two-story building has less than a dozen units so it's quiet, and it's just a minute's walk to the beach. Each unit has a king or queen bed, kitchen or kitchenette, TV with DVD player, air-conditioning, and telephone. A sun deck with a hot tub is located on the roof, and there is a washer and dryer on premises for your use. Spacious enough, these units have been totally remodeled and run $140 per night for a room with kitchen and $100 for the kitchenettes.

Menehune Shores, 760 S. Kihei Rd., mailing address P.O. Box 1327, Kihei, HI 96753, 808/879-3428 or 800/558-9117, fax 808/879-5828, is a huge, family-oriented and moderately priced high-rise condo on the beach overlooking an ancient fish pond. The building is highlighted with replicas of Hawaiian petroglyphs. On the oceanside is a new swimming pool. The Menehune is used mostly by seniors, except during Christmas when families come. All units have an ocean view, and rates are $130–220 for one- to three-bedroom condos in high season, three-day minimum. Low-season rates are about 10 percent less, discounts are given for week-long and month-long stays, and special car/room packages can be arranged. Full kitchens with dishwashers, and washers and dryers are in each unit, which are individually owned, so furnishings vary. All units have recently been remodeled.

Kauhale Makai, 938 S. Kihei Rd., has fully furnished, individually decorated studios and suites that are a mixture of garden, mountain, and ocean view. All are clustered around a central courtyard garden and lawn. A swimming pool, kiddie pool, barbecues, putting green, and sauna are available, making it good for the family. Rates from $85–110 studio, $95–120 one bedroom, and $130–190 two bedroom, four-night minimum; weekly and monthly discounts given. All reservations are handled through Maui Condominium and Home Realty, P.O. Box 1840 Kihei, HI 96753, or call 808/879-5445 or 800/451-5008, fax 808/874-6144.

The boxy four-story **Leinaala** condos, 998 S. Kihei Rd., 808/879-2235 or 800/334-3305, may not attract everyone, but don't let the appearance fool you. Each of the 24 fully appointed units faces the beach across the lawns of the Waipu'ilani Park, and all are narrow units that run from the front of the building to the back so cooling breezes can waft right through. Set back from the road, this is a quiet spot where you can splash in the pool in peace. Winter rates are $135 and $180 for one- and two-bedroom units during high season. The best time for space is during the summer, when rates are $30–50 less; four nights minimum. Weekly and monthly rates can be adjusted and car rental packages arranged. Other reduced rates are available.

Off the main thoroughfare, **Hale Kai O Kihei,** 1310 Uluniu Rd., Kihei, HI 96753, www.hkokmaui.com, is a three-floor apartmentlike cinder block affair, simple and utilitarian, clean, well-kept, and cute for what it is—and it's recently been spruced up. Each furnished unit has a direct ocean view with a lanai that looks over the pool, garden, and beach. There is also shuffleboard, barbecue grills, and coin laundry, with maid service on request. Reasonable rates are $132 for a one-bedroom unit ($112 for low season) and $168 for two bedrooms ($135 low season); three nights minimum—15 percent discount for stays of one month or greater. For information, contact AA Oceanfront Condo Rental, 808/879-7288 or 800/457-7014, fax 808/879-7500.

The following condos are all south of Kalama Park. First is **Lihi Kai Cottages,** 2121 Ili'ili Rd., Kihei, HI 96753, 808/879-2335 or 800/544-4524, set across the road from the tiny Cove Park. These nine cottages are such a bargain that they're often booked by returning guests, particularly during winter. They're not plush, there's

no pool, and they've been around a while, but they're homey and clean, with little touches like banana trees growing on the property. Rates are $90 daily for 3–6 nights, $80 for seven or more nights; three nights minimum. Monthly rates are available on request, no credit cards accepted. For reservations, call or write well in advance c/o Manager, at the above address.

Maui Vista, 2191 S. Kihei Rd., 808/879-7966 or 800/535-0085, fax 808/874-5612, is a pleasing 10-acre condo complex on the *mauka* side of the main road that has units managed by Marc Resorts. Three swimming pools, six tennis courts, barbecue grills, and an activities desk are available to all guests. All studios and one- and two-bedroom suites have kitchens, are modern in their appointments, spacious in layout, have air conditioning, contain in-room washers and dryers, and have maid service. Studios run $169, one-bedroom suites $169–189, and two-bedroom suites $229–239, $20 less during "value" periods, $15 each extra person.

Stretching up from the road long and lean is **Aston at the Maui Banyan,** 2575 S. Kihei Rd., 808/875-0004 or 808/922-7866, fax 808/874-4035. Several multiple-unit buildings climb the hill, and set to the side are two patio areas with swimming pools, hot tubs, barbecue grills, and plenty of space to catch the sun. While there are some hotel rooms in this complex, most are one-, two-, and three-bedroom condo units with kitchens for $250–365 per night. All are pleasantly modern in decor, spacious, and have all needed amenities for a restful and relaxing vacation.

At **Kamaole Sands,** 2695 S. Kihei Rd., 808/874-8700 or 800/367-5004, fax 808/879-3273, all apartments come completely furnished with a full bath and kitchen, roomy living area, and lanai. Prices are $167–220 one bedroom, $252–335 two bedrooms, $366–410 three bedrooms, fifth night free; winter season rates slightly higher and rental car packages available. Stepping down the hillside, the Kamaole Sands is a full-service, family-oriented condo geared toward making the entire family comfortable. The Sandpiper Grill, situated poolside and for guests only, serves inexpensive breakfasts, lunches, and dinners on Friday featuring fresh island fish and pasta. One of the main features of the Kamaole Sands is its wonderful tennis courts, free to guests, with a tennis instructor to help you work on the fine points of your game. Here as well are a swimming pool, kid's pool, a jet spa, volleyball courts, and barbecue areas. The Kamaole Sands is bright, cheerful, and gives you a lot for your money.

If you want to rise above it all in Kihei, come to **Maui Hill,** 2881 S. Kihei Rd., 808/879-6321 or 800/922-7866, an upbeat Aston-managed condo with a Spanish motif. This condo resort sits high on a hill and commands a sweeping view of the entire area. The one-, two-, or three-bedroom suites are spacious, bright, and airy; all have ceiling fans and air-conditioning, cable TV, daily maid service, and full kitchens. A concierge service helps with your every need, and all sun and surf activities can be arranged at the activity desk. The grounds are secluded, beautifully maintained, and offer a pool with whale mosaic on the bottom, tennis courts, and spa. Regular-season rates are one bedroom from $280 (up to four people), two bedrooms from $365 (up to six people), and three bedrooms from $495 (up to eight people); *substantial* savings during low-season. A weekly complimentary mai tai party complete with games, singing, and door prizes is held for guests, along with a continental breakfast at 8 A.M. that offers an orientation on island activities. Guests can also enjoy a weekly afternoon lei-making class and a poolside scuba orientation several days per week.

At the very south end of Kihei is **Mana Kai Maui** oceanfront resort, 2960 S. Kihei Rd. On-site features include an activities desk, daily maid service, a sundries store, swimming pool, and the Five Palms oceanside restaurant and bar. Condo units have full kitchens, TV, private lanai, and ceiling fans. All hotel rooms, with outdoor access, air-conditioning, and refrigerators, are on the garden level. Winter rates run $116–140 for the hotel rooms, $210–247 for a one-bedroom, and $247–303 for a two-bedroom suite. Summer rates (until Dec. 15) are substantially cheaper, Christmas rates are 10 percent higher, and there is a 10 percent discount for stays of one month or more at any time of year. For rentals and information, contact Condominium Rentals Hawaii, 808/879-2778 or 800/367-5242 Mainland, 800/663-2101 Canada, fax 808/879-7825.

Rental Agencies

Numerous rental agencies handle condo units and rental homes in Kihei and South Maui. Several of these agencies are as follows:

Condominium Rentals Hawaii, 362 Huku Li'i Place, #204, Kihei, HI 96753, 808/879-2778 or 800/367-5242 Mainland, 800/663-2101 Canada, fax 808/879-7825, www.crhmaui.com, can arrange your stay in 10 condos in Kihei.

Kihei Maui Vacations, P.O. Box 1055, Kihei, HI 96753, 808/879-7581 or 888/568-6284, fax 808/879-2000, www.kmvmaui.com, has units in more than two dozen condos, mostly in Kihei, but a few in Ma'alaea and Wailea.

Maui Condominium and Home Realty, P.O. Box 1840, Kihei, HI 96753, 808/879-5445 or 800/451-5008, fax 808/874-6144, www.mauicondo.com, manages mostly economical to midrange units in Kihei.

Maui Resort Vacation Rentals, P.O. Box 1755, Kihei, HI 96753, 808/879-5973 or 800/441-3187, fax 808/879-1357, www.mauiresort4u.com, handles units in more than two dozen condos along the Kihei coast and also has a few rental homes.

AA Oceanfront Condo Rentals, 1279 S. Kihei Rd., Ste. 107, Kihei, HI 96753, 808/879-7288 or 800/488-6004, fax 808/879-7500, www.aaoceanfront.com, manages properties from north Kihei to Makena, economy to deluxe.

Kumulani Vacations and Realty, P.O. Box 1190, Kihei, HI 96753, 808/879-9272 or 800/367-2954, fax 808/874-0094, www.kumulani.com, handles rentals in 10 condos in Kihei and Wailea.

Bed-and-Breakfasts

At 815 Kumulani Drive in the quiet neighborhood of Maui Meadows is **Eva Villa,** tel/fax 808/874-6407 or 800/884-1845 Mainland and Canada, pounder@maui.net, www.maui.net/~pounder. Built with the clean lines of contemporary design, Eva Villa is set in a finely landscaped yard sporting an attractive koi pond. Here you'll find a studio and two-room apartment that overlook the swimming pool. In a separate structure is a small cottage with its own kitchen. All units have phones and TV, a small refrigerator and eating area, and a private entrance. Rates run $115–140. The roof-top deck, pool, and hot tub are open to all guests, and everyone is provided with a simple continental breakfast left in your room to have at your leisure.

A few blocks lower is **Anuhea Bed and Breakfast,** 3164 Mapu Place, 808/874-1490 or 800/206-4441, fax 808/874-8587, lodging @anuheamaui.com, www.anuheamaui.com. Owned and operated by Russell and Cherie Kolbo, Anuhea has three comfortable rooms in the upper floor with private bathrooms and air-conditioning and two garden-level rooms with fans that share a bath. Each room has a king-size bed, small refrigerator, and television. Everyone can share the living room, use the washer and dryer, as well as relax in the garden with its hot tub and hammock. A health-oriented breakfast of grains and eggs is served each morning on the lanai. The upper rooms run $115 per night, the garden rooms $105. No children under 12 years old please.

One block closer to the highway but still away from the noise of traffic is **Dreams Come True on Maui,** 3259 Akala Dr., 808/879-7099 or 877/782-9628, staymaui@aol.com, www.maui .net/~tcroly. Two rooms in the main house, situated off the garden and each with a private entrance and kitchenette, run $75–85 during low season and $10 more per night during high season, mid-December into spring; three- or four-night minimum stay. Out front, with a view down onto the coast, is a detached vacation cottage, which has a six-night minimum and rents for $650 per week.

FOOD

With few exceptions, restaurants listed as follows are all located at shopping centers in Kihei.

Inexpensive

At the north end, the first inexpensive eatery is **Suda's Snack Shop,** open Mon.–Sat.

6 A.M.–12:30 P.M., for burgers, plate lunches, and drinks. Adjacent to the Suda's Store, the snack shop is nothing special but is a good spot for a quick bite to eat.

Heat-flushed tourists hoping to chill out should head for **Stella Blue's Cafe,** located at Longs Shopping Center, 808/874-3779, open daily 7:30 A.M.–9 P.M. This is an economical place, good for the family, where the kids will love the selections and adults can still order a beer or wine. Breakfast, served 8–11 A.M., features a continental breakfast for $7.95, French toast for $6.95, and a "create your own" omelet starting at $5.95. Sandwiches, everything from a BLT to hot pastrami and turkey breast, average about $8.50. From the grill you can have a tuna melt, blues burger, grilled chicken, or Reuben for under $9.75. Dinners are more complete, with such offerings as spinach lasagna, scampi Provençale, baby back ribs, and charbroiled taro burger all for $8–20.

Kal Bi House, 808/874-8454, in a corner of Longs Shopping Center and open Wed.–Sun. 10:30 A.M.–9 P.M., offers a full range of Americanized Korean standards like barbecued short ribs, fried squid, noodles, stews, and small intestine soup, as well as plate lunches and combination plates, and a few Japanese dishes like chicken teriyaki. Most everything is under $12 except for the full-meal bulgogi for $24.99; takeout is available. This restaurant is basic but clean.

Azeka's Ribs and Snack Shop, at Azeka Makai next to Ace Hardware, is an institution and is very famous for its specially prepared (uncooked) ribs, perfect for a barbecue. Also available are plate lunches, burgers, sushi, and saimin. Open 7–3:30 (until 5 P.M. for ribs).

For Asian food that's still a bit out of the ordinary for most, try **Vietnamese Cuisine** restaurant in the Azeka Makai shopping center, 808/875-2088. A full range of dishes include pho ga or pho tai, chicken and beef soups; lau cai do bien, seafood combo soup; bun bo xao, sautéed lemongrass and beef over vermicelli noodles; com chien tom, shrimp fried rice; and plenty of dishes prepared in the wok.

Let the rich aroma of roasting coffee lure you to **The Coffee Store,** 808/875-4244, open daily 6 A.M.–10 P.M. at Azeka Mauka. Breakfast fare features quiche for $3.75 or a breakfast quesadilla for $6.95. Lunch selections, always served with crusty homemade bread, include a Caesar salad for $4.95—or $6.95 for the large size that can easily feed two—and sandwiches like tuna, turkey, or vegetarian for $5.50–6.50. Daily homemade soup for $3.95 including bread and coffee, stuffed quesadillas of all sorts for $4–6, and wraps complete the menu. Enjoy coffee drinks that range in price $1–2.50, along with hot and iced herbal teas, hot chocolate, and Italian cream sodas. A deli case is filled with luscious desserts sure to satisfy any sweet tooth, and, of course, you can purchase bulk coffee. You can dine inside or sit outside, especially in the evening to hobnob with local residents who come here to chat and enjoy a rich cup of coffee and snack or to check the Internet.

The fountain bar, jukebox, Formica tabletops, leatherette booths, distinctive color scheme, period decorations, and music peg **Peggy Sue,** at Azeka Mauka, 808/875-8944, as a classic, theme hamburger joint—with a modern twist. You can order your Big Bopper burger for $9.25 or the Earth Angel garden burger for $8.25, or sample one of the salads, sandwiches, hot dogs, or other menu items, mostly for under $11. No '50s joint worth its name would be without that cool summer favorite, so Peggy Sue serves ice cream, shakes, sundaes, and fountain drinks. Stop in for the nostalgia rush.

If you've been having too much fun and need a reviving cup of espresso, stop in at the **Kihei Caffe,** at Kalama Village Marketplace, 808/878-2230, open daily at 5 A.M., Sunday at 6 A.M., and enjoy your coffee along with an excellent assortment of sandwiches and baked goods. Order a complete breakfast of eggs, bacon, home fries, and biscuits with gravy for $6, or a giant raisin muffin for $2.75. Sandwiches, all under $6.50, are served on your choice of homemade bread—only cold sandwiches after 2 P.M. The café provides a few tables and stools inside and more outside, where you can watch the action on Kihei Road or across the road through Kama'ole Beach Park to the ocean.

Sushi Go, 808/875-8744, has a different concept than most Japanese restaurants. Chairs here are located around a bar that has a conveyor carrying ready-made sushi selections. Select what you want and pay for what you've eaten. All plates are color coded by price, so you should have a rough idea of where you stand when the bill comes. Wednesday 4–8 P.M. is an all-you-can-eat special for $22.99. Take-out platters are also available. Sushi Go is located in the Kukui Mall and open daily for lunch and dinner.

A few steps away is **Alexander's,** 808/874-0788, open 11 A.M.–9 P.M. This local long-term establishment is definitely a cut above most fast-food restaurants and has taken a few steps along the upscale, yuppie, health-conscious road. The menu offers fresh fish, shrimp, and chicken sandwiches for $6.50–7.75. Plate lunches for $10 or under, sides, salads, and drinks, as well as larger baskets for $16.25–19.95, are also on the menu. Full meals are served with coleslaw and french fries or rice. All deep frying is done in canola oil, but you can request broiling instead. You can't go wrong here. There's not much decor or atmosphere, but the food is delicious and makes a perfect take-out meal that can be enjoyed at the beach.

Sports Page Bar and Grill, at the Kamaole Beach Center, 808/879-0602, open 11 A.M.–midnight for cocktails and until 10 P.M. for food service, scores big with a full bar, a large-screen TV, and foosball and a pool table in the back. Order a mug of beer and a light snack like oyster shooters for $1.25 or teriyaki chicken breast strips for $7.95. The burger and sandwich menu goes all the way with a San Francisco '49er burger topped with bacon and cheese, a Chicago Cubs hot dog, or a Boston Celtics turkey sandwich, all for under $8.50. There's music some evenings, and a cover may be charged. Mostly a working man's bar, although visitors are certainly welcome, its walls are covered with sports pictures, pennants, and posters. Families and even the athletically challenged will be comfortable here.

Also at Kamaole Beach Center is **Hawaiian Moon's Deli and Natural Foods,** open Mon.–Sat. 8 A.M.–9 P.M., Sunday until 7 P.M. Stop for a healthy bite to eat (the hot bar and salad bar run $5.99 per pound), juice or espresso, or shop for groceries, vitamins, and bulk foods.

Also at the Kamaole Beach Center is **Maui**

Tacos, 808/879-5005, open daily 9 A.M.–9 P.M. and serving Mexican food with definite Hawaiian bump. Here you can get soft tacos, big burritos, chimichangas, enchiladas, and other typical Mexican treats for under $7.

Open 7:30–11 A.M., **Annie's Cafe and Deli** at Kai Nani Village Plaza serves smoothies, juices, coffees, and a variety of quick snack deli items, mostly for less than $8.

Moderate

Margarita's Beach Cantina, 101 N. Kihei Rd. in the Kealia Beach Plaza, 808/879-5275, open daily 11:30 A.M.–11:30 P.M., has a well-deserved reputation for good food at fair prices. Formerly vegetarian, it now serves a variety of meat and chicken dishes but still uses the finest ingredients, cold-pressed oils, and no lard or bacon in the bean dishes. The decor is classical Mexican with white stucco walls and tiled floors. There's an outdoor deck affording a great sunset view and sea breezes, or stop by for live music and dancing Friday 5–7 P.M. The *carta* offers taco salads for $11.95, combination plates for $11.95–16.95, money-saving daily fish specials, and live Maine lobster on Monday evenings. Most entrées are in the $12–15 range, with nothing more than $20. Look for reduced-price well drinks, beers, and margaritas during the 2:30–5 P.M. happy hour.

Restaurant Isana, 515 S. Kihei Rd., 808/874-5700, is open daily for the best Korean food in the area and also has Japanese sushi from 4–8 P.M. You can either sit at the sushi bar or have dinner cooked at your table. Upstairs is the bar, which has a karaoke sing-along after 10 P.M. Most dinners are in the $14–19 range.

While you can order hoagies, hot sandwiches, and calzone at **Shaka Sandwich and Pizza,** 808/874-0331, it's perhaps best known for pizza. New York–style thin crust, a Sicilian crust, and gourmet pizzas with various kinds of crusts are all available from $14 on up. Located behind Jack In The Box across from Star Market. Delivery is available.

With a grander scale and pleasing decor of vaulted ceilings, piano music in the evening, and inside and outside seating, **Marco's Southside Grill,** 1445 S. Kihei Rd., just across from Maui Dive Shop, 808/874-4041, is much different than its sister restaurant in Kahului, but it has a similar menu. Marco's serves fine Italian food all day long. Breakfast specialties are omelets, lunch brings deli and grill sandwiches, but dinner is finer dining. Pizza and all sorts of pasta are on the menu, but other entrées, like chicken parmigiano and ribeye steak, are good choices. Dinner entrées run mostly $13–19.

Although you can get appetizers, salads, sandwiches, burgers, shrimp, and chicken at **Tony Roma's,** at the Kukui Mall, 808/875-1104, Tony's is especially known for ribs, ribs, and more ribs. Prepared in several different ways, rib entrées run about $16, with most other entrées less. For those who want just a little extra, try the combo meals for $17–29. Open for lunch and dinner daily.

In the Rainbow Plaza, **The Thai Chef Restaurant,** 808/874-5605, offers you a full menu of tasty Thai food at reasonable prices. Like its sister restaurant in Lahaina, you can get appetizers like spring rolls for $7.50 or green papaya salad at $6.50, and various soups for around $10. Entrées include red, green, or yellow curries from $9–11, with noodle, rice, and seafood dishes up to $14. There's a hefty selection for vegetarians, and desserts run $2–3. Well maintained, Thai Chef has a casual decor.

In the Kihei Kalama Village you'll find **Pita Paradise,** 808/875-7679. Stuck in the back of the center, Pita Paradise offers a variety of pita items, served with roasted potatoes or rice pilaf, but also serves kebabs, pasta, and salad. Pita run mostly in the under $11 range, and most other items run $13–19. Open for lunch and dinner until 9:30 A.M.

Upstairs at the Rainbow Plaza is **Dean O's Maui Pizza Cafe,** 808/891-2200. Dean O's serves lunch of pizza and sandwiches before 5 P.M. and again after 9 P.M. Available 5 P.M.–9 P.M., dinner is pizza and pasta in small and large portions. Sandwiches include barbecue pork and chicken parmesan for around $9.50. Pizzas run $12.50–16.25, and pasta might be fettuccine or a Big Kahuna Bolognese. The full-service bar can take care of you for after-dinner drinks.

In the Kamaole Center, **Canton Chef,** 808/879-1988, offers the usual long list of choices from appetizers to meat and seafood dishes. Several spicy Sichuan items are on the menu to fire up your day. Most entrées are in the $7–13 range.

KKO Kai Ku Ono, 808/875-1007, a semi-sports bar casual dining place below Harlow's at Kai Nani Village Plaza, is open 8 A.M.–midnight with entertainment nightly. Grab a pizza and beer and cool off after a day at the beach with a game of pool or darts. A variety of *pu pu,* sandwiches, and pasta is available, as are heartier selections in the evening and a seafood bar until closing. Most items are under $15. The full bar will set you up with drinks, while you kick back and catch your favorite sporting event on one of the televisions.

Tucked into the rear of Kai Nani Village Plaza is **Ziziki's Restaurant and Bar,** 808/879-9330, where the flavors and textures of the Greek and Mediterranean dishes will excite your palate. Dinner only is served 5–10 P.M. and includes chicken souvlakia, spanakopita, moussaka Alaniki, and leg of lamb, all ranging $18–25. Other items are stuffed grape leaves for $8, Grecian village salad for $9, and several pasta dishes. If you're in doubt as to what would be tasty, try the A Taste of Greece platter, a sampling of several homemade entrées on the menu. Sit inside or out.

Expensive

Upstairs at the Kai Nani Village Plaza toward the south end of Kihei is **Harlow's,** 808/879-1954. Specializing in prime rib and seafood, Harlow's is open for dinner only from 5 P.M., offering most entrées for $22–36, including black angus prime rib, opakapaka macadamia nut, and braised brisket of beef. Located on the second floor, Harlow's also offers great sunset views.

Sansei seafood restaurant and sushi bar, at the Kihei Town Center, 808/879-0004, has the same excellent menu as the original restaurant in Kapalua. Entrées include shichimi-seared fresh Atlantic salmon, Sansei seafood pasta, and spicy crab-stuffed whole lobster tail, all ranging $16–24. More numerous are the appetizers, like tee duck egg roll, miso garlic prawns, and Japanese calamari salad. Sansei is best known for its innovative and exceedingly pleasing sushi, which

run $4–16. Sansei is open daily 5:30–10 for dinner and 10 P.M.–2 A.M. on Thursday, Friday, and Saturday for late-night dining and free karaoke.

Roy's Kihei Bar and Grill, at the new Pi'ilani Village Shopping Center, 808/891-1120, is a great addition to food options in town. Reservations are recommended and casual resortwear is preferred. Open 5:30–10 P.M. for dinner, Roy's Kihei has many of the same features as those at his other restaurants, like an open kitchen, a regular menu with specials that change nightly, and food that blends the flavors of Hawaii and Asia. Some regulars on the menu include hibachi teriyaki salmon and seared shrimp on a stick with wasabi cocktail sauce appetizer, poached D'anjou pear salad, and entrées like roasted macadamia nut mahimahi, "jade pesto" steamed seabass, herb-grilled chicken breast, and *kiawe* grilled rack of lamb. Specials of the night are just as inventive and usually greater in number. Save room for dessert.

Overlooking the beach, the casual **Five Palms** restaurant, located at the Mana Kai Maui Resort at the extreme south end of Kihei, 808/879-2607, is open for brunch daily 8 A.M.–2:30 P.M., with a *pu pu* menu and happy hour from 3–6 P.M. Dinner runs 5–9:30 P.M. Brunch includes the usual breakfast items such as eggs, omelets, and griddle fare, but also gives you the wider options of soups, salads, sandwiches, and some fish and meat dishes. Dinner is more romantic, and the kitchen turns it up a few notches. Start with a roasted artichoke, crispy Kahuku prawn, or hichimi-spiced and seared ahi appetizer. Move on to slow-roasted prime rib, Hawaiian seafood bouillabaisse, seared duck breast, oven-roasted lobster tail, or fresh fish, the specialty of the house. Appetizers are $8–13 while main entrées run $22–40, but you can come before the rush for the $20 early-bird special. Set so close to the water, the location and scenery are an integral part of the dining experience here.

Only steps from Wailea is the fine-dining restaurant called **Sarento's On The Beach,** 808/875-7555. Open for dinner only 5:30–10 P.M., with a full bar from 5 P.M., all parking is complimentary valet only because of limited space. The excellent reputation and proximity draw many guests from the resorts and condos of Wailea. The seating couldn't be better, with the restaurant set right on the beach, and it's the water and sparkling light off the waves rather than the interior decoration that draws your attention most. However, the interior's contemporary design and modern touches certainly render a warm and friendly atmosphere. The anticipation starts when guests walk past a glassed-in wine cooler on the way to their tables. Appetizers like grilled prawns and pancetta with fire-roasted sweet pepper sauce or mussels in garlic white wine parmesan sauce tempt the palate, which one of the fine salads will clear before the main entré. Main dishes might include baked potato ravioli, seafood "Fra Diavolo," osso bucco, swordfish "saltimbocco," grilled beef filet, or rack of lamb, and run $26–40. Whatever the choice, the flavors and tastes are sure to be impeccable. Sarento's sister restaurants are Nick's Fishmarket down the road at the Fairmont Kea Lani Maui in Wailea, and Aaron's Atop the Ala Moana and Sarento's Top of the "I," both in Honolulu.

ENTERTAINMENT

Kihei isn't exactly a hot spot when it comes to evening entertainment, although several venues do provide options. **Margarita's Beach Cantina** has live-band dancing on Friday evenings 5–7 P.M. Try **Tradewinds** poolside bar at the Maui Coast Hotel for nightly music in a relaxed setting. **Kahale Beach Club** at the Kihei Kalama Village Market Place, a local bar for people who work in the area, is a place that offers music and dancing on an occasional basis. To its front is the fun little bar **Life's a Beach,** which serves up evening entertainment along with burgers, sandwiches, salads, and *pu pu*. Next door is the intimate **La Creperie** café, the premier jazz venue in the area, with live music nightly 8 P.M.–1 A.M. A bit more upscale is **Bocalino** bistro in the Azeka Makai shopping center, where live music and dancing happens 10 P.M.–1 A.M. Up for Karaoke? Try the **Isana** restaurant after 10 P.M. Many of the restaurants in the area offer entertainment on a hit-and-miss basis, usually one artist with a guitar, a small dinner combo, or

some Hawaiian music. These acts are usually listed in the free tourist brochures.

Hapa's Brew Haus, 41 E. Lipoa St. in the Lipoa Center, is a big place that once brewed its own beer. Now it serves a variety of others' beers and offers a good-time atmosphere with games, entertainment, and dancing until the wee hours of the morning on its big dance floor. While the schedule changes monthly, local live bands often perform from about 9 P.M., and occasionally a big-name musician will stop by. Willie K has played here for years. On other nights, DJs spin the music. Different covers for different events.

The **Kukui Mall Theater** at the Kihei Town Center is the only movie theater on this side of the island. It's a four-screen theater with shows starting at about noon. Admission is $8 adults, $5 seniors and kids, and $5.50 matinee.

Into billiards? Visit **Dick's Place** at the Kamaole Shopping Center, on the second floor. Open 11 A.M.–midnight, Dick's also serves food and has a full bar.

SHOPPING

While driving the length of Kihei, you will find shopping centers, both large and small, strung along the entire coastal area like shells on a dime-store lei. At many you can buy food, clothing, sporting goods, picnic supplies, sundries, photo equipment, cosmetics, resortwear, ice cream, pizza, dinner, and liquor. You can also book activities, order a custom bikini, or just relax with an ice-cold beer while your partner satisfies his or her shopping addiction. In Kihei, you have more than ample opportunity to spend your hard-earned vacation money that would be a sin to take back home. Aloha!

North End Shopping

At the very north end of Kihei, as you approach from Wailuku or Lahaina, is the **Sugar Beach General Store,** with a small clutch of shops selling resortwear, snacks, and gifts. The activities company here can set you up for a fun afternoon or rent you a bicycle or water gear.

Suda's Store, 61 S. Kihei Rd., is a basic little market with limited food items, but with cold beer, fresh fish, and deli items. Open Monday–Friday 7:30 A.M.–5 P.M., Saturday until 4 P.M., and Sunday 8 A.M.–3 P.M., it sits along the *mauka* side, across from the Kihei Canoe Club. Locally grown produce is sold in the parking lot here from 1:30–5:30 P.M. on Monday, Wednesday, and Friday. A few minutes down the road from Suda's heading for Kihei, look for the **Nona Lana Cottages,** where you can pick up a fresh-flower lei for a reasonable price.

Set along Pi'ilani Highway (Route 31), the main thoroughfare above Kihei that parallels Kihei Road, is **Kihei Gateway Plaza.** Even with the **Aloha Gifts and Gallery** shop and **Maui Clothing Outlet** store, its perhaps most useful for its gas station, minimart, and video rental outlet.

Pi'ilani Village Shopping Center

The newest shopping center in town, and one of the largest, is set along Pi'ilani Highway at the corner of Pi'ikea. This is a big place with a little of everything for local residents and visitors. You can buy gas, clothing, food, and sundries. Several of the largest stores are **Roy's Kihei** restaurant for fine dining, **Hilo Hattie** for Hawaiian fashions and gifts, and a **Safeway** supermarket for groceries and a pharmacy. Aside from these, **Waldenbooks** has a good selection of books, **Blockbuster Video** has evening entertainment for rent, **ABC Stores** for sundries, **Flash Back Photo** for film, **Tropical Disk** for music, and the **Kihei-Wailea Medical Center** has an office here.

Longs Shopping Center

Located at 1215 S. Kihei Road, almost opposite the post office, this shopping center is dominated by a huge **Longs Drugs,** stocked with electronics, photo equipment and film developing, sundries, cosmetics, stationery, a pharmacy, and even sporting goods. Around the center you will find the **T-Shirt Factory** featuring all kinds of discounted wearable take-home gifts, and you can do everything from faxing to packing and shipping at **Mail Boxes Etc. American Savings Bank** is conveniently located here for all the shopping that you may be doing in this center and along the Kihei strip. A **farmers market** is held here in the parking lot every Saturday from 8 A.M.–noon.

Azeka Place

Adjacent to the post office is the Azeka Place Shopping Center, now also referred to as Azeka Makai, in what might be considered the center of town. Once filled with small boutique shops, you now mostly find small restaurants and fast-food eating establishments, as well as the **Kihei Ace Hardware** and **B&B Scuba.** Just down the street is a **Star Market** for all your grocery needs.

The Kihei **post office,** 1254 S. Kihei Rd., is open Monday–Friday 8:30 A.M.–4:30 P.M. and Saturday until 1 P.M.

Azeka Place II

This newer and larger shopping center is located just across the street from the original Azeka Place and is now also called Azeka Mauka. Featured here are **The Coffee Store,** a great place for a cup of coffee, a light lunch or late-night snack, or to check your email; **Cyber Surf Lounge** also for Internet access; and **Bank of Hawaii,** a full-service bank with ATMs. For vitamins, minerals, and supplements, try **General Nutrition Center,** and **Hula Hogs** rents motorcycles, which can be filled at the **gas station** at the corner. Started in 1950 as a one-store, mom-and-pop operation, the two Azeka Place shopping centers comprise more than 50 shops and make the largest shopping complex in South Maui.

Lipoa Center

Until Pi'ilani Village Shopping Center was built, the Lipoa Center was the only major shopping center not on the main drag. Lipoa Center is located a hop, skip, and a jump up Lipoa Street, just around the corner from Azeka Place II. Here you'll find a **First Hawaiian Bank, Kihei Professional Pharmacy, Shell gas station,** and **Gold's Gym.** Perhaps more of interest for the traveler are **Hapa's Brew Haus** for music and drinks and the **Lipoa Laundry Center,** a clean and modern full-service laundry that's open daily from 8 A.M. and Monday–Saturday until 9 P.M., Sunday 5 P.M.

Kukui Mall

At the Kukui Mall, across from Kalama Park, is the apparel store **Local Motion.** Tired of the beach, or just need to beat the heat? Stop at the multiscreen **Kukui Mall Theater.**

Across the street at the corner is the **Aloha Marketplace.** Once just a bunch of stalls under awnings and trees, it's now an open-air courtyard building ringed with stalls where you can shop daily 9 A.M.–9 P.M. for jewelry, clothing, carvings, and other touristy gifts.

Kihei Town Center

This small shopping center just south of the Kukui Mall offers a 24-hour **Foodland, Cyberbean** for drinks and Internet access, the **Rainbow Attic** consignment shop, and several eateries.

Kihei Kalama Village Market Place

Look for this bargain-filled, semi-open-air warren of stalls under a tall roof superstructure at 1945 S. Kihei Road, offering everything from tourist trinkets to fine art; clothes, crafts, and jewelry predominate. This is the best open-air market in South Maui and perhaps on the island. Around the periphery are other shops. Among them you will find **Serendipity,** a small, well-appointed boutique that displays imported items mainly from Malaysia and Brazil, and **Clementines** for one-of-a-kind women's clothing. Out front at the corner, **Maui Discount Activity World** will set you up with your day's activity. If you're hungry, you'll find all sorts of food options here as well.

Dolphin Shopping Plaza

This small, two-story plaza at 2395 S. Kihei Road includes **Boss Frogs,** where you can rent snorkel gear at a reasonable price, and **Hawaiian Island Cruisers** can provide you with a rental bike or moped. In the back are several small restaurants. Upstairs, you'll find **Kihei Chiropractic.**

Kamaole Beach Center

A small group of shops between Dolphin and Rainbow plazas, this center has **Honolulu Surf Company** clothing store for local fashions and **Snorkel Bob's** to pick up snorkel gear for the week. You can get groceries and deli food at **Hawaiian Moon's Natural Foods** or come by after a warm day on the beach for a cool beer at **The Sports Page Grill and Bar.**

Rainbow Mall

Yet another small mall just up the road at 2439 S. Kihei Road features **South Pacific Kayaks and Outfitters** and **Aloha Destination's Auntie Snorkel** for the sales and rental of snorkel gear, boogie boards, kayaks, and camping and hiking gear for very reasonable prices. Other shops in the mall are **Maui Custom Beachwear,** where you can buy off the rack or have a bikini made especially for you; **Haleakala Trading Company** for Hawaii-made gifts and souvenirs; **Premiere Video** for evening entertainment if you're staying in a condo; and **Topaz,** a fine jewelry and watch store. **Aloha Discount Liquor** is located at the back of the mall.

Kamaole Shopping Center

Last in this quick succession of small malls is the slightly larger Kamaole Shopping Center at 2463 S. Kihei Road. This mall has several inexpensive eateries and various clothing, souvenir, and sundries stores. From its two floors of shops you can buy baubles, beads, and some nicer pieces at **Unique Jewels;** tropical fashions at **Panama Jack's;** sunglasses at **Shades of Hawaii;** and liquor, gifts, and souvenirs at **Whalers General Store. Lappert's Aloha Ice Cream** sells island-made delights and fat-free yogurt. Also in the center is a **Maui Dive Shop,** a complete diving and water sports store offering rentals, swimwear, snorkels, cruises, and windsurfing lessons, and an **Ocean Activities Center** booth for booking water sports. **Postal Plus,** open Mon.–Sat. 9 A.M.–6 P.M., can take care of your stamp, box, and shipping needs, and offers computer connections, as does **Hale Imua Internet** next door.

Kai Nani Village Plaza

This small cluster of restaurants sits at the south end of Kihei. Aside from the eateries, you'll find the **Sunshine Mart** for sundries and food items.

Farmers Markets

A small farmers market is held in the parking lot in front of Suda's Store at 61 S. Kihei Road, every Monday, Wednesday, and Friday 1:30–5:30 P.M. Besides fresh produce, stalls sell shells, T-shirts, and knickknacks of all kinds. There is also a farmers market in the Longs Shopping Center every Saturday 8 A.M.–noon.

Food/Liquor Stores

Foodland, at Kihei Town Center (open 24 hours), **Star Market** (5 A.M.–2 A.M.) at 1310 S. Kihei Road, and **Safeway** (open 24 hours) at Pi'ilani Village Shopping Center, are full-service supermarkets with a complete liquor, wine, and beer selection.

Hawaiian Moon's Natural Foods at the Kamaole Beach Center is a small but full-service natural health-food store. Stop in for bulk foods, groceries, herbs, organic fruits and vegetables, vitamins, minerals and supplements, juices, bottled water, soy drinks, and beer. There's even a freezer case for ice cream and a deli case for take-out sandwiches.

At the very south end of Kihei are two small markets. Smaller and more basic, the **Sunshine Mart** is located at the Kai Nani Village Plaza. At Mana Kai Maui Resort, try **Keawakapu General Store** for groceries, sundries, snacks, and spirits. Open daily 7 A.M.–9 P.M.

At the Rainbow Mall, **Aloha Discount Liquor** has a good selection of liquor, imported beers, and wine.

RECREATION

Golf

Associated with the Maui Beach Hotel in Kahului, the only golf course in Kihei is **Elleair Maui Golf Club,** 808/874-0777. Set along Pi'ilani Highway, this course has been totally reworked over the past few years, so it now presents a new face. Young and open, there are good views over town to the coast. Greens fees are an economical $85. After a round of golf, stay for dinner or a drink at The Palm Restaurant at the clubhouse, open Tues.–Sun. 5–10 P.M.

Water Gear and Rentals

The **Maui Dive Shop,** 808/879-3388, has a main store and office at 1455 S. Kihei Road near the Star Market in Kihei and offers a full range of equipment, lessons, and rentals. Open daily 7:30 A.M.–9 P.M., it is one of the oldest and most respected companies in the business. Another location along this coast is at the Kamaole Shopping Center, 808/879-1533.

Dive and Sea Maui, 1975 S. Kihei Rd., 808/874-1952, is also a full-service dive shop offering dives, certification, air refills, equipment rentals, and dive/snorkel boat trips to Molokini Crater.

Snorkel Bob's, 808/879-7449, is easy to spot at the Kamaole Beach Center. Open daily 8 A.M.–5 P.M., Bob has some of the best deals around for some very good gear. The weekly prices can't be beat at $9–36 for snorkel gear and about the same for boogie boards. Daily rentals are available too, as are prescription lenses. You also get snorkel tips and Bob's semi-soggy underwater humor. Looking for an above-water activity? Bob can arrange that too.

Auntie Snorkel, 808/879-6263, located at the Rainbow Mall, rents snorkel gear, along with boogie boards, beach chairs, and even ice chests at prices that are among the lowest in the area.

Also at the Rainbow Mall, **South Pacific Kayaks and Outfitters,** 808/875-4848 or 800/776-2326, open daily 8 A.M.–4 P.M., offers half a dozen kayak options from a half-day introductory trip for $59 to an advanced explorer tour along the remote South Maui coastline for $89. The longer tours include lunch, and all have plenty of snorkeling opportunities as you glide in and out of tiny bays fashioned from jutting lava rock fingers. South Pacific Kayaks offers rentals of single kayaks at $30 and double kayaks at $40 per day. For those who love the land more, several hiking trips can also be arranged.

INFORMATION AND SERVICES

Information

The member organization South Maui Destination Association has some information about South Maui: hotels, B&Bs, restaurants, activities, shopping, services, real estate, and more. Contact the association at 101 N. Kihei Rd., Ste. 4, Kihei, HI 96753, 808/874-9400, fax 808/879-1283, info@southmauivacations.com, www.kihei.org. Their *Maui Guide* can be seen online at www.mauiguide.com.

Medical Services

For minor medical emergencies, try **Urgent Care Maui/Kihei Physicians,** 1325 S. Kihei Rd., Ste. 103, 808/879-7781, where doctors, a clinical lab, and X-rays are available from 6 A.M.–midnight daily. **Kihei-Wailea Medical Center,** 808/874-8100, in the Pi'ilani Village Shopping Center, has physicians, a pharmacy, physical therapy, and a clinical laboratory and is open Monday–Friday 8 A.M.–8 P.M., Saturday and Sunday until 5 P.M.

Chiropractic services are available at the **Chiropractic Clinic of Kihei,** 1847 S. Kihei Rd., 808/879-7246, which specializes in nonforce techniques, and **Kihei Chiropractic Center,** at the Dolphin Plaza, 808/879-0638. There's also **Kihei Acupuncture Clinic,** 1051 S. Kihei Rd., 808/874-0544, specializing in gentle needling techniques and offering a full selection of Chinese herbs.

Transportation

The **Holo Ka'a public transit shuttle** connects Kihei with Wailea and Makena to the south and west to the Maui Ocean Center in Ma'alaea, from where you can carry on to Lahaina, Ka'anapali, and Kapalua in West Maui. The shuttle runs daily approximately 9 A.M.–10 P.M. Fares are $1 point to point, $5 for Makena–Ma'alaea, and $10 for a one-day pass for the whole system.

Banks

There are several branch banks in Kihei. **Bank of Hawaii,** 808/879-5844, is at Azeka Place II; **First Hawaiian Bank,** 808/875-0055, is at the Lipoa Center; **American Savings Bank,** 808/879-1977, is at the Longs Center; **Hawaii National Bank,** 808/879-8877, is at 1325 S. Kihei Road; and **City Bank,** 808/891-8586, is at the Kukui Mall.

Post Offices

The main **post office** in Kihei is located at Azeka Place, 1254 S. Kihei Road. **Mail Boxes Etc.,** at Longs Shopping Center, open weekdays 8 A.M.–6 P.M., Saturday 9 A.M.–5 P.M., Sunday 10 A.M.–3 P.M., offers fax services, copies, notary, and packing and shipping.

Laundry

Lipoa Laundry Center at the Lipoa Center, 808/875-9266, is also a full-service laundry and dry cleaning establishment. Open 8 A.M.–8 P.M. with shorter hours on Sunday.

Library

The **Kihei Public library,** 808/875-6833, is across the street and down from the Kukui Mall. It has variable daily hours.

Wailea

Wailea (Waters of Lea) isn't for the hoi polloi. It's a deluxe resort area custom-tailored to fit the egos of the upper class like a pair of silk pajamas. This section of South Maui was barren and bleak until Alexander and Baldwin Co. decided to landscape it into an emerald 1,450-acre oasis of world-class golf courses and destination resorts. Every street light, palm tree, and potted plant is a deliberate accessory to the decor so that the overall feeling is soothing, pleasant, and in good taste. To dispel any notions of snootiness, the five sparkling beaches that front the resorts were left open to the public and even improved with better access, parking areas, showers, and picnic tables—a gracious gesture even if state law does require open access! You'll know when you leave Kihei and enter Wailea. The green, quiet, and wide tree-lined avenues give the impression of an upper-class residential suburb. Wailea is where you come when quality is the most important aspect of your vacation. The brilliant five-star resorts are first-rate architecturally, and the grounds are exquisite botanical jewel boxes.

Aside from the beaches, the two main attractions in Wailea are the fantastic golf and tennis opportunities. Three magnificent golf courses have been laid out on Haleakala's lower slopes, all open to the public. Tennis is great at the Wailea Tennis Club, and many of the hotels and condos have their own championship courts.

To keep up the quality, a few years ago Wailea Shopping Village was completely razed and rebuilt as The Shops at Wailea and in a fashion that would outdo even the fine upscale shops of Ka'anapali and Kapalua on the west end of the island.

Running along the water from one end of Wailea to the other is a 1.5-mile-long beach walk. This cement path cuts across all properties from the Renaissance Wailea Beach Resort to the Kea Lani, and like the beaches, it's open to the public. Used often in the early morning or late afternoon for exercise by walkers and joggers, it's a convenient way to get to the next beach or to the next resort for lunch or dinner. Even if you're not staying in the area, take a stroll down the path and have a look at the wonderfully landscaped gardens and resort properties here.

You can get to Wailea by coming straight down South Kihei Road through the strip of condos and shopping centers. To miss this area and make better time, take Pi'ilani Highway, Route 31. This route takes you up on the hillside, where you have some nice views out over the water and can watch Kihei slip by in a blur below. Where this highway stops, Wailea Ike Drive snakes down the hill to Wailea Alanui Drive and deposits you in the heart of Wailea at the new shopping center.

For greater information on Wailea, have a look at the website: www.wailea-resort.com.

Onward and Backward

If you turn your back to the sea and look toward Haleakala, you'll see its cool, green forests and peak wreathed in mysterious clouds. You'll want to run right over, but you can't get there from here! Outrageous as it may sound, you have to double back 18 miles to Kahului and then head up Route 37 for another 20 miles just to get to the exact same spot on Route 37 that you can easily see. Some maps show a neat little road that connects the Wailea/Makena area with Upcountry in a mere three-mile stretch, but it's a private 4WD road that's never open to the public because it traverses ranchland. If this appalling situation is ever rectified, you'll be able to travel easily to the Tedeschi Winery and continue on the "wrong way" to Hana, or go left to Kula and Upcountry. For now, however, happy motoring!

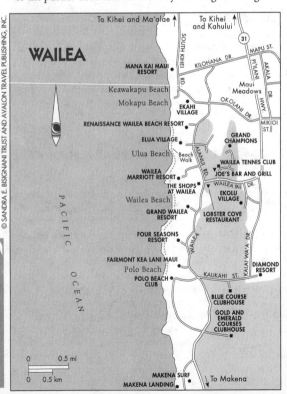

BEACHES

If you're not fortunate enough to be staying in Wailea, the best reason for coming here is its beaches. These little beauties are crescent moons of golden sand that usually end in lava outcroppings on both ends. This makes for sheltered, swimmable waters and good snorkeling and scuba. Many of the hotel guests in Wailea seem to hang around the hotel pools, maybe peacocking or just trying to get their money's worth, so the beaches are surprisingly uncrowded. The following beaches are listed from north to south.

Keawakapu

The first Wailea beach, almost a buffer between Kihei and Wailea, is just past the Mana Kai Resort. Turn left onto Kamala Place, or proceed straight on South Kihei Road until it dead-ends. Plenty of parking is available at both accesses, but no amenities are provided. Keawakapu is a lovely beach with a sandy bottom. Good swimming and fair snorkeling. There's also a beginner's dive spot offshore.

Mokapu and Ulua

These two beaches are shoulder to shoulder, separated only by a rock outcropping. Turn right off Wailea Alanui at the first turn past the Renaissance Wailea Beach Resort. The beach is clearly marked, and there's a parking area, showers, and restrooms. Being resort beaches, they're both particularly well-kept. Beautiful sand and protected waters are perfect for swimming. There's good snorkeling at the outcropping separating the beaches, or swim out to the first reef just in front of the rocks for excellent snorkeling.

Wailea Beach

The Outrigger, Grand Wailea, and Four Seasons resorts front this beach. One-half mile past The Shops at Wailea, turn right onto a clearly marked access road between the Grand Wailea and the Four Seasons; at the end of the drive there's good parking, as well as showers and toilets. A short but wide beach, Wailea offers good swimming and bodysurfing, but the snorkeling is only fair.

Polo Beach

Follow Wailea Alanui toward Makena. Turn right on Kaukahi Street just past the Fairmont Kea Lani Maui and right again at the clearly marked sign near the Polo Beach condo. Here also are paved parking, showers, and toilets. Polo Beach is good for swimming and sunbathing, with few tourists. There's excellent snorkeling in front of the rocks separating Polo from Wailea Beach— tremendous amounts of fish, and one of the easiest spots to get to.

LUXURY ACCOMMODATIONS

Renaissance Wailea Beach Resort

Always a beauty, the Renaissance Wailea, 3550 Wailea Alanui, Wailea, HI 96753, 808/879-4900 or 800/992-4532, fax 808/874-5370, www.renaissancehotels.com, is like a rich red cabernet that has aged superbly. The Renaissance is a superbly appointed resort with attention given to the most minute details of comfort and luxury. When you enter the main lobby, you're actually on the fifth floor; the ones below terrace down the mountainside to the golden sands of Mokapu Beach. The lobby has original artworks on the walls and a sweeping marble staircase leading down to the Palm Court Restaurant. A bubbling spa fashioned from lava rock is surrounded by vines and flowering trees; another spa contains three little pools and a gurgling fountain, so that while the therapeutic water soothes your muscles, the music of the fountain soothes your nerves. The impeccable grounds have grown into an actual botanical garden. And everywhere there is water, cascading over tiny waterfalls, tumbling in brooks, and reflecting the amazing green canopy in tranquil lagoons.

The 345 white-on-tan rooms are appointed with koa and rattan furniture. Beds are brightened with quilted pillows, and each room is accented with standing lamps, paintings of Hawaiian flora, an entertainment center with VCR and remote-control TV, wall safe, a glass-topped writing desk, even matching *happi* coats for an evening of lounging. Sliding doors lead to a lanai, where you can relax or enjoy a quiet in-room meal. The bathrooms are small but adequate, with double marble-topped sinks and a queen-size tub. The hotel features the very private Mokapu Beach Club, a detached low-rise wing complete with its own pool and daily continental breakfast, where the hotel's impeccable service rises yet higher with valet service and 24-hour concierge. Room rates are $345 terrace view, $400 garden view, $450 ocean view, and $600 Mokapu Beach Club; $40 each additional person over age 18. Suites run $1,050–4,000 for one and two bedrooms. Varying rates include a family plan, where children under 18 stay free if they're in their parents' room, and also a variety of golf and tennis packages.

You will enjoy the Palm Court, Hana Goin Japanese, and poolside Maui Onion restaurants, the lobby cocktail lounge, where there's live music nightly, and the Wailea Sunset Luau held three times weekly. The Renaissance offers valet parking, 24-hour room service, a business center, a fitness center, therapeutic massage and body care, the part-day Camp Wailea children's program, free daily newspaper, a small shopping arcade, a twice-weekly arts and crafts mini-fair, and a concierge desk to book you into every kind of outdoor Maui activity. The most amazing feature about the resort is its feeling of peace and tranquility. The Renaissance is part of the Marriott family of hotels.

Wailea Marriott Resort

The Wailea Marriott, an Outrigger Resort property branded with the Marriott name, is a class act, and since its remodel in 2000, its an even finer place. The entryway has been opened to let more light into the main building and reception area, and other public areas of the hotel have been reconfigured into new lounges and restaurants. The main lobby, supported by gigantic wooden beams, is still inviting with its informal setting and frames a wide panorama of the sea and Lana'i floating on the horizon. Walk out onto a stone-tiled portico and below, in a central courtyard ringed by palms, is a series of quiet lily ponds highlighted with red torch ginger and alive with serenading bullfrogs in the evening. Stroll the 22 meticulously landscaped acres and dip into one of the pools, take the kids to the new family pool with its waterslide and play

areas, or have a look at the Hawaiian fishermen's shrine near the shore. All rooms have been totally remodeled with simple and suitable furnishings and decorations, and throughout the property designs in the carpet, light fixtures, and other decorative features have been taken from Hawaiian mythology and symbolism.

The Wailea Marriott was the first large hotel property in Wailea. It has roots here. Not only that, but it makes the claim of being the "most Hawaiian hotel in Wailea." From the little touches to the large efforts, most would say that it is so. The hotel has established a position of Director of Hawaiian Culture and runs a Hawaiian cultural program called Ho'olokahi that not only educates the staff about its own Hawaiian heritage but also shares the Hawaiian culture with guests and brings the community to the hotel for cultural exchanges. The Hawaiian cultural program has a varied schedule of activities and workshops presented by knowledgeable Hawaiian elders and teachers. All you need to do to attend is sign up. Some activities are hula demonstrations and contests, lei making, and ukulele instruction. On Aloha Friday, arts and crafts are displayed and sold, and hula is performed in the hotel lobby. The resort also hosts a Hawaiian sailing canoe regatta, which is accompanied by numerous cultural activities and events. In addition, the restaurant Hula Moons is dedicated to Don Blanding, an early enthusiast of Hawaii and Hawaiian culture from the early 20th century, and it proudly displays some of Blanding's personal belongings and mementos of the times.

At least 80 percent of the resort's 521 rooms have ocean views, which in most cases are actually oceanfront. Rooms are coordinated with light pastel tones of green-on-tan and beige. All have a large entertainment center with remote-control TV and small refrigerator. Granite bathrooms are well-proportioned with a full bath and shower, sinks, and separate dressing area. Doors open to a terra cotta–floored lanai, flushed with sunshine and sea breezes, from where you have a private view of the Lahaina Roads. More amenities include room service, the Mandara Spa, a business center, a row of shops, self-service laundry, and complimentary valet parking in a covered parking lot. For children, the Cowabunga Kids Club fills the day with supervised activities for a nominal fee.

For food and entertainment, head to the newly redesigned lobby-level Hula Moons Restaurant or poolside Kumu Bar and Grill, pop into the new Mele Mele Lounge next to Hula Moons for a drink or *pu pu* while you chat or watch the sunset, or attend the award-winning lu'au and Polynesian show, "Wailea's Finest Luau," down by the water. Outings and activities can be arranged at the concierge desk in the lobby. Room rates run $325 for a standard garden room to $525 for a deluxe oceanfront room; suites are available at $650–1,500; $40 per extra person. Special family plans, room and car, honeymoon, golf, and other packages are available. The Wailea Marriott Resort is located at 3700 Wailea Alanui, Wailea, Maui, HI 96753, 808/879-1922 or 800/688-7444, fax 808/874-8331, www.outriggerwailea.com.

after Stay @ Hana

Grand Wailea Resort Hotel & Spa

A sublime interplay of cascading water, light diffused and brilliant, and the music of natural sound have been entwined with fine art, sculpted landscaping, and brilliant architecture to create the intangible quality of grandeur so apparent at the astounding Grand Wailea Resort Hotel & Spa, 3850 Wailea Alanui, Wailea, HI 96753, 808/875-1234 or 800/888-6100, fax 808/879-4077, www.grandwailearesort.com. On arrival the spume of a thunderous waterfall, misting a heroic sculpture of the warrior king, Kamehameha, is the tangible spirit of the grand hotel. Inside the towering reception atrium, the water and sculpture interplay continues. Hula dancers both male and female, some with arms outstretched to the sun, others in repose or in a stance of power, are the visual *mele* singing of the ancient times. A mermaid, bronzed, barebreasted, offers a triton shell of sweet water, and behind, sleek canoes float on a pond of blue. Ahead the glimmering sea, foaming surf, and wind-tossed palms dance to their immortal tune. Left and right, Fernando Botero's sculpted women—enormous, buxom, and seductive—lie in alluring repose.

In the garden, a formal fountain, surrounded by royal palms, is reflected in a rectangular pool inlaid with white and gold tile forming a giant hibiscus. The pool area surrounds a "volcano" and fronts Wailea beach. Here, a canyon river, complete with gentle current, glides you through a series of pools and past small grottoes where you can stop to enjoy a hot tub, swing like Tom Sawyer on a suspended rope, swim up to a bar for your favorite drink, or just slip along until you are deposited in the main pool. Waiting is the world's only water elevator, to lift you to the top again and again. Other meandering waterways and pools dot the property.

If Nero had the health and relaxation resources found at the hotel's Spa Grande, his fiddle playing would have vastly improved and Rome never would have burned. The magic begins as soon as you enter this marble-clad facility, the largest in the state and arguably the best equipped. Dip first into a Japanese *ofuro* that unjangles nerves and soothes muscles. From there, a cold dip to revitalize and then into the termé baths, followed by a cascading waterfall shower or jet rinse. Awaiting you are private massage rooms where you can choose a multitude of different massage, facial, and body treatments. Each room opens to the sea, whose eternal rhythm helps create complete relaxation.

The Grand Wailea is a huge complex of five separate wings and a tower, with 780 guest rooms. These rooms feature private lanai that look out over the water and flower gardens below, while inside they are sanctuaries of pure luxury. All are appointed in soothing earth tones with complete entertainment centers, a bar (some have mini refrigerators), in-room safes, and twice-daily maid service. Rates are $450–760 for standard rooms, and $1,575–2,000 for suites. Guests of the Napua Tower have concierge service and many special amenities. Rooms here run $800, suites $2,000–10,000. Numerous packages are offered.

For the dining and entertainment pleasure of its guests, the Grand Wailea has six restaurants, four bars and lounges, and one nightclub. To make a family visit perfect, **Camp Grande** holds court for children ages 5–12. Run by professionals, both day and evening camps feature movies, a preschool playroom, arts and crafts, a computer learning center, a videogame room, and a kids' restaurant. The Grand Wailea has Wailea's largest collection of resort shops, and if that's not enough, you are only a 10-minute walk from the Shops at Wailea next door. For those unfortunate enough to be in Hawaii on business, the hotel's business center is set up to take care of all equipment and service needs.

Scuba diving lessons, a catamaran sail, and other water activities and rentals are arranged by an outside concession on hotel property near the beach. Periodic tours of the grounds and hotel art are offered—worth some $30 million when collected; some now say it's worth $75 million. The garden tour is free and given Thursday at 10 A.M. and starts at the concierge desk; sign-up is required. Beginning from the Napua Gallery, the art tour is offered Tuesdays and Fridays at 10 A.M.; free to hotel guests, but $6.25 for nonguests. Finally, there is a nondenominational **chapel** that's used for weddings (the hotel does about 500 per year), a miniature cathedral with floor-to-ceiling stained-glass windows.

Four Seasons Resort Maui at Wailea

AAA five-diamond award winner the Four Seasons, 3900 Wailea Alanui, Wailea, Maui, HI 96753, 808/874-8000 or 800/334-6284, fax 808/874-6449, www.fourseasons.com/maui, situated on 15 acres at the south end of Wailea Beach, is oriented to the setting sun and opens itself up to the sweet sea breezes. Casually elegant, the open-air lobby is full of cushy chairs and couches, fountains, flowers, fans, and a grand staircase that glides down to the huge pool at beach level. On the way down, say "hello" to Ricky and Lucy, the hotel parakeets who make their home below the staircase. The pool and the colonnade of lobby pillars above it hint at a Romanesque architectural influence, yet the ambiance and colors of the hotel say island natural. Original artwork and reproductions hang throughout the lobby and hallways, while huge fossilized sea anemones are displayed on lobby tables, and birds and plants bring the outdoors inside. Countless little details make this resort pleasant and special.

The Four Seasons is a study of cream-on-cream, and this color scheme runs throughout the resort, offset by coral, almond, muted greens, and other pastels. Each large room has a bedroom and sitting area, an exceptionally large bath with separate shower and deep tub, a well-stocked wet bar, TV, room safe, and private lanai; 85 percent of the rooms have an ocean view and all have twice-daily room service. While air-conditioning is standard, rooms also have sliding screen doors or louvered French doors and overhead fans. Double rooms and suites are even more spacious, with the addition of a second bathroom and/or a dining area. Rates for the standard rooms run $335 for a mountain view up to $665 for a prime ocean view, $100 per extra person. Depending on the number of bedrooms and location, suites run $755–6,700. Rates on the Club Floor, which includes on-floor check-in, complimentary continental breakfast, afternoon tea, sunset cocktails and hors d'oeuvres, and a personal concierge, run $750–2,450, $160 per extra person. The club lounge on this floor also provides books, newspapers, magazines, and board games. Golf, family, room and car, romance, and two-island packages are also available.

Other resort amenities include three top-notch restaurants, a lobby lounge that has entertainment nightly except Sunday, five shops, a game room with a fine collection of surfing memorabilia, meeting rooms for conventions, complimentary valet parking, 24-hour room service, and an early-arrival/late-departure lounge where you can relax and enjoy the hotel services, store a small bag, or shower off the grit of travel. In addition, the supervised "Kids for all Seasons" program can keep your little ones ages 5–12 busy for all or part of the day, 9 A.M.–5 P.M., with games and activities. On site are two tennis courts and lawn croquet (for guests only); an expanded health club with exercise machines and a steam room that offers massage and personal training; and organized beach activities. Down by the beach, all beach chairs, cabanas, snorkel equipment (free rental for one hour), boogie boards, and the like are complimentary—added value for guests. These and most hotel amenities are included in the room charge. Although not cheap, you get a lot for your money and great service.

SOUTH MAUI

ROBERT NILSEN

courtyard pool and gardens at the Fairmont Kea Lani Maui

Fairmont Kea Lani Maui

While Aladdin napped and dreamed of high adventure, his genie was at work building a pleasure dome more splendid than the great Khan's Xanadu. The Fairmont Kea Lani Maui, 4100 Wailea Alanui, Wailea, HI 96753, 808/875-4100 or 800/441-1414, fax 808/875-1200, www.fairmont.com, is an alabaster fantasy bazaar where turrets and cupolas cover vaulted and coved ceilings suspended above towering pillars. Enter the central lobby, an open-air court with a bubbling fountain, completely sculpted and gilded; sultan's slippers would be appropriate here to pad around on the mosaic floors. One level down is the lounge, formal but comfortable, with giant shoji-like mirrors and sculpted harps and lyres embedded in the walls. A staircase leads down from there to a tranquil pool area fronting a wide sweep of grass and perpetual blue sea. Three restaurants, a deli, and a lounge bar service the food needs of the guests.

Lodging at the Kea Lani is in one-bedroom luxury suites with separate living area priced $339–629, or in opulent two- and three-bedroom villas set closer to the water and priced $1,400–2,400, with several room/car, room/meal, and romance packages as options. Enter the suites, very roomy at just under 900 square feet, to find a richly embossed carpet contrasting with white-on-white walls. These units sleep four. Double doors open to the master bedroom. The sitting room, formal but comfy, is appointed with puff-pillow chairs, a queen-size sleeper sofa, entertainment center, marble-topped tables, and a full bar with microwave and coffeemaker. All rooms are air-conditioned, but there are also ceiling fans. The bathroom, marble from floor to ceiling, features an oversize tub, two pedestal sinks, a huge stall shower, and cotton *yukata* for a day of lounging. The bi-level villas, sleeping 6–8, include more of the same but have greater floor space and more bedrooms. They are completely furnished with full and modern kitchens and laundry rooms. Outside each villa in its private courtyard is a plunge pool, slightly heated and perfect for two, and a gas barbecue.

The hotel's pool area is grand, just right for frolicking or for savoring an afternoon siesta. A free-form upper pool, boasting a swim-to bar, and serviced by the Polo Beach Grill, is connected to the lower pool by a 140-foot water slide. The lower area is family oriented with a

SOUTH MAUI

football-shaped children's pool, but escape is at hand at the casbah pool, inlaid with multihued tiles forming an entwined moon and sun around it; adults can shelter in Camelot-like tents providing shade and privacy or relax in one of two jet spas. Other amenities include a beach activities booth, an activities desk, in-house doctor's office, business center, complimentary fitness center, health and body spa, and a clutch of swank boutiques. The children have their own Keiki Lani children's program, open daily 9 A.M.–3 P.M., where children ages 5–12 are entertained with a mixture of fun and educational activities and even given lunch.

Destination Resorts Hawaii

This complex is made up of six separate villages that are scattered along the coast or up around the golf course. Check-in is handled at the Destination Resorts office on the lower level of The Shops at Wailea near the front. For those properties that have a peak season, it runs from mid-December to the end of April. Year-round and high-season rates are quoted; low-season rates will be approximately 10 percent cheaper. **Ekolu Village,** located near the Blue Course, has one- and two-bedroom condo units for $195–275. Also on the golf links, next to Wailea Tennis Club, is **Grand Champions,** with one-, two-, and three-bedroom units for $200–385. At the entrance to Wailea and with oceanfront and hillside units, **Ekahi Village** has studio, one-, and two-bedroom condos for $180–410. Tucked between the Renaissance and Outrigger hotels, **Elua Village** fronts Ulua Beach and has one-, two-, and three-bedroom condos ranging $295–825. Right on Polo Beach is **Polo Beach Club,** the only high-rise condo building in the bunch. Rates here are $350–515 for one- or two-bedroom units. The newest and perhaps the most exclusive is **Makena Surf,** on a private section of coast a short way down the road toward Makena. Here one-, two-, and three-bedroom units run $417–775.

All rates are based on double occupancy, with children 12 years and younger free; an additional $20 is assessed for each extra adult. Special golf, tennis, car, and romance packages are available.

There is a three- to five-night minimum stay, 10–14 nights during the Christmas–New Year's season. The fifth or seventh night is free depending on the village. An additional resort fee may be charged on check-in with each reservation. All units are plush and fully furnished, with kitchens, daily housekeeping service, a swimming pool or pools, barbecue grills, and some with tennis courts on the premises. All have gated entrances. The beach, two golf courses, and additional tennis courts are nearby. Amenities include concierge services; reservations for dinners and all air, land, and sea activities; and arrangements for rental vehicles and water equipment. For information and reservations, contact Destination Resorts Hawaii at 808/879-1595 or 800/367-5246, fax 808/874-3554, www.drhmaui.com.

Diamond Resort

Formerly a member-only resort, this condo property is now open to all but gets plenty of Japanese visitors. The Diamond Resort, 555 Kaukahi St., Wailea, HI 96753, 808/874-0500 or 800/800-0720, fax 808/874-8778, www.diamondresort.com, sits high above the Wailea Blue Golf Course and has a wonderful view over the ocean. The slate roof and stone exterior on the round portion of the main building make a wonderful first impression, and the pools and stream that cascade down between the buildings create a restful feeling. Let the resort's three restaurants fill your belly, the training center help you work out, and the spa soothe your muscles. The spa features Japanese *ofuro,* Scandinavian saunas, and various baths. The 72 large, air-conditioned, one-bedroom guest suites have ocean, partial-ocean, or garden views and come with kitchenettes, TV and VCRs, and lanai. Rates run $240–340 per night, with numerous packages available, and this includes daily maid service and complimentary spa use.

FOOD

At the Renaissance

The **Palm Court** is the main dining room at the Renaissance, a first-rate restaurant. Walk though the lobby and look over the rail to the partially open-air restaurant below. The Palm Court is open for breakfast 6–11 A.M. and for dinner nightly from 5:30 P.M. Breakfast is Mediterranean à la carte or American buffet. The evening menu offers a blend of East and West, featuring theme buffets and à la carte entrées ranging from pizza to porterhouse steak to prawns linguine, all $16–30.

The **Sunset Terrace** in the lobby is a delightful perch on which to have a drink and survey the grounds and beach below. Every evening brings a dramatic torch-lighting ceremony. The drums reverberate and the liquid melancholy of the conch trumpet sends a call for meditation at day's end. Drinks include the full complement of island specialties, and you can order wonderful gourmet-quality *pu pu* while listening to the sweet sounds of island music.

Maui Onion is a convenient snack-type restaurant at poolside that's open 11 A.M.–6 P.M. for light lunches. Burgers, sandwiches, salads, smoothies, and Maui onion rings, the specialty, are on the limited menu. Prices are reasonable, especially if you don't want to budge from your lounge chair.

Last but not least, **Hana Gion** offers Kyoto-style Japanese food daily except Tuesday and Thursday from 5:30–9 P.M. in a small and intimate restaurant off the lobby. The focus here is on teppanyaki and sushi, but the à la carte menu is an option. Not cheap, but memorable.

Wailea Marriott Resort

Serving contemporary Hawaiian cuisine is **Hula Moons Restaurant,** the Outrigger's main dining establishment. Open daily for breakfast buffet and à la carte or buffet dinner, this casual restaurant is on the lobby level next to the Mele Mele Lounge. While fish is the main focus here, many other entrées are also on the menu. Wednesday is a prime rib buffet, Friday a seafood buffet, and every night a well-stocked salad bar. The name Hula Moons derives from the writings of Don Blanding, Hawaii's poet laureate, who arrived by steamship in 1924, dead broke, and remained for more than 40 years, all the while singing the island's praises. A few of the poet's personal belongings are still displayed—all whispering of

the time when Hawaii was a distant land where only the rich and famous came to escape. Nice nostalgic touch.

Newly created next to Hula Moons, the **Mele Mele Lounge** serves tropical drinks and *pu pu* 11 A.M.–11 P.M. Low-lit, comfortable, full of bamboo and tropical designs, it serves as a place to relax, ponder your next outing, or just watch the sun set into the water beyond the garden. Open daily 11 A.M.–9 P.M., the **Kumu Bar and Grill** is a casual poolside eatery that serves light lunches and more substantial evening fare, accompanied by nightly music and hula. While appetizers and salads hold court during the day, in the evening seafood, steak, and ribs are the main offerings.

For the little ones, the **Wailele Snack Bar** is located next to the kids activity pool and serves a children's menu from 10 A.M.–4 P.M., with lots of goodies that are easy and fun to eat.

Grand Wailea Resort Hotel & Spa

The resort has an eclectic mix of restaurants, all landscaped around the central theme of water, art, and flowers, offering a variety of cuisines catering to all tastes and appetites. **The Grand Dining Room Maui** has perhaps the best seat in the house, overlooking the gardens and the sea. Open for breakfast only, both a daily buffet and à la carte menus are offered. A fun and informal restaurant is the open-air **Bistro Molokini**. Island fusion, with a dash of the health conscious, items include wood-fired pizza, light sandwiches, and grilled seafood dinners. Open 11:30 A.M.–9:30 P.M. **Cafe Kula,** open daily 6 A.M.–6 P.M., specializes in casual terrace dining. Here the freshest fruits, organic vegetables, and whole grains provide the foundation for most dishes. Enjoy salads and sandwiches, fruits, pastries, and desserts.

Humuhumunukunukuapua'a, the resort's signature restaurant, is a thatched-roof Polynesian restaurant afloat on its own lagoon complete with tropical fish in a huge aquarium. The specialties prepared at the Humu come from throughout the Pacific. *Pu pu* like coconut prawn or crispy crab and lobster shrimp cakes are great to nibble on while enjoying a special exotic drink. Entrées are delightful, with offerings like

Breakfast

SOUTH MAUI

pan-seared ahi, roasted duck breast, and vegetable coconut curry. Delectable but not cheap; entrées in the $22–30 range. Open Tuesday–Saturday 5:30–9 P.M. for dinner only, with nightly entertainment.

Perhaps the most elegant restaurant at the hotel is **Kincha,** serving superb Japanese cuisine. Enter over stepping stones past a replica of a golden tea kettle used by Toyotomi Hideyoshi, who was revered as both a great warrior and a master of the *chanoyu,* the tea ceremony. Follow the stones past stone lanterns that light your way over a humpbacked bridge. Inside a raised tatami area awaits, with sushi chefs ready to perform their magic, and private rooms are perfect for a refined full meal. Sushi and tempura are prominent on the menu. Entrées are Japanese favorites like hotategai, a broiled sea scallop and sake-broiled salmon, or seared Hawaiian snapper with Japanese spices and a lemon-miso butter sauce, with prices from $26 on up. Open Saturday–Monday, 6–9 P.M. only.

Four Seasons Resort

Located at the Four Seasons Resort, **Spago** restaurant is an experience in fine dining. Elegant but not stuffy, its windows open to let in sea breezes and moonlight. Start the experience with an appetizer such as spicy ahi tuna "poke" in sesame-miso cones, sautéed oysters with hot-sweet Chinese mustard, or local goat cheese with organic greens. Main delicacies include Chinois lamb chops grilled with Hunan eggplant and chili-mint vinaigrette, steamed Big Island moi fish with chili, ginger, and baby bok choy, roasted duck with wild huckleberries, star anise, and black pepper, and pan-seared scallops. This dinner-only restaurant has entrées in the $29–42 range. Reservations are recommended, and proper resort dress is required.

The casual **Pacific Grill** restaurant combines a large selection of foods from Asia and the West. The breakfast buffet is a long-established special, but an à la carte menu is also available. For dinner, some entrées are cooked in view of the guests. Pacific Rim entrée specialties include sautéed mahimahi, Hawaii salt-crusted rotisserie prime rib of beef, and a seafood stir-fry, most

$26–36. At the Pacific Grill, alohawear and activewear are the norm.

The remodeled and expanded **Ferraro's at Seaside** serves food throughout the day. For breakfast, you can choose from an à la carte menu or have coffee and something lighter from the coffee and pastry bar. For lunch, served 11 A.M.–4 P.M., light fare of salads, sandwiches, and pizza are good options. Light lunch is served from 4–6 P.M. when dinner starts. Dinner is more formal and features the new *kiawe* wood-burning oven. As Italian as Italian can be, Ferraro's throws in Italian music for free, Monday–Saturday. Start with an antipasti such as oven-baked clams and mussels, and move on to fresh black truffle alla parmagiana risotto, potato gnocchi with creamy Genovese pesto, sautéed veal scaloppini, or Maine lobster and Tuscan-style seafood stew, with most entrées in the $25–30 range. Set almost on the water, Ferraro's is a great place to watch the sunset.

Fairmont Kea Lani Maui

An elegant breakfast at the Kea Lani happens at the **Kea Lani Restaurant,** 808/879-7224, where you can order à la carte or dive into the full-scale buffet from 6:30–11 A.M. For a casual lunch or early dinner, with outdoor poolside seating from 11 A.M.–5 P.M., try the **Polo Beach Grill and Bar** for a light salad, sandwich, or kiawe-grilled burger. If you're in the pool, you can swim up to the bar until 7 P.M. for a cool-down drink.

For casual dining any time of day, visit the **Ciao Deli** rich with the smell of espresso, where the shelves hold homemade jellies, jams, chutney, peppercorn ketchup, and Italian olives. Choose fresh-baked bread, pastries, or a spicy focaccia from the bakery, pesto salad or a sandwich from the deli. For a sit-down lunch or dinner meal, try the outdoor trattoria **Caffe Ciao** across the walk, where you'll find hot and cold appetizers, sandwiches, and fresh island fish for lunch, and pizza from the wood-fired oven, pasta and risotto dishes, and other entrées like pesca alla Isolana, pollo alla Florentina, and ossobusso di Vitello in the evening, ranging $22–32.

The fine-dining restaurant at the Kea Lani is **Nick's Fishmarket,** which produces Hawaiian regional cuisine with an emphasis on fish and seafood. A selection of entrées includes roasted salmon, seafood paella, grilled ahi with cracked pepper, and seared swordfish with candied peanut crust. Expect entrées from $27–37 and quality to match. Open nightly 5:30–10 P.M., there is a dress code and reservations are highly recommended.

Diamond Resort

The two resort restaurants are the Taiko and the Le Gunji. With a Frank Lloyd Wright feel in the architecture and appointments, **Taiko** serves breakfast, lunch, and dinner nightly except Tuesday and is open 7–10 A.M., 11 A.M.–1:45 P.M., and 6–9 P.M. The day starts with a Japanese- or Western-style breakfast for $13; lunch includes sandwiches and burgers, or Japanese soba, udon, or other traditional dishes for less than $13. Dinner entrées, like teriyaki chicken, onaga shioyaki, and lobster daiyaki, run $21–35; a whole range of sushi is also available. The more intimate **Le Gunji** has limited seating of up to 16 people at 6 P.M. and 8 P.M. only; reservations are a necessity and a dress code is enforced. Choose from five set menus, ranging $50–70. Food is a unique blend of French cuisine prepared in a Japanese teppanyaki style. Call 808/874-0500 for reservations.

An independent establishment, **Capische?**, 808/879-8255, offers sophisticated Italian food evenings only 5:30–8:30 P.M., except Sunday. Seating is limited, so definitely call for reservations. The relatively small menu has sautéed calamari, quail saltimbocca, and seafood antipasti for appetizers and soups and salads for $8–16. Pasta and risotto like cioppino and shrimp carbonara run $28–30. Meat and fish entrées include seared scallops, crispy Pacific snapper, lamb osso bucco, and filet mignon for $29–35. This sophisticated restaurant has dishes that will certainly please. Capische?

Nonresort Restaurants

The following restaurants are located along the golf links in the area, except for Joe's, which is located at the Wailea Tennis Club.

On the 15th fairway of the Wailea Blue Course, just up from The Shops at Wailea, is the **Lobster Cove Restaurant,** 808/879-6677, a seafood restaurant that shares space with **Harry's Sushi Bar.** Appetizers include garlic clams for $10.95, sweet and sour crispy shrimp for $11.95, and lobster cakes for $11.95. These tasty treats would go well with the Caesar salad for $6.95. Entrées, limited but wonderful, might be seafood penne pasta for $20.95, blackened ribeye steak with king crab for $32, fresh island fish at market price, or a filet mignon for $25. Choose from an adequate wine list for a bottle to accompany your meal. You can order *pu pu* or make a meal from the offerings at Harry's. The choices of sushi are numerous and run mostly $4.25–7 per order and are double that for a plate of sashimi. Also consider such items as California rolls or bowls of noodles. These restaurants are open daily 5:30–10 P.M.

A little up the hill and across the road at the Wailea Tennis Club is **Joe's Bar and Grill,** 808/875-7767. Open for dinner every evening from 5:30–10 P.M., Joe's serves large and tasty portions of honest American, homestyle comfort food in a relaxing atmosphere. Joe's is set directly above the tennis courts in a wood-floored, open-beamed room, and cool breezes waft through the sliding-glass partitions. Chief schmoozer Joe Gannon is the other half to Haliimaile General Store restaurant's chef Beverly Gannon. While the ambiance and lighting set a welcome mood, the real treat is the food. Ahi carpaccio, Asian fried calamari, and Joe's gazpacho come first, with other appetizers and salads. Entrées include grilled thick-cut pork chop, pan-seared New York steak, and Joe's famous meatloaf, one of the best sellers; all range from $24–32. You know this is a family affair because Joe's daughter makes the mouth-watering desserts. The bar has a full range of beers and can make any mixed drink you desire. Martinis are specialties. Eat at Joe's, and have food the way you wish your mother used to make it.

At the Blue Golf Course clubhouse is **Mulligan's on the Blue** bar and pub restaurant, 808/874-1131. Mulligan's serves pancakes, corn beef and hash, an Irish breakfast, and other such dishes as breakfast for $7–11. Later in the day, a full pub menu of burgers, fish and chips, shepherd's pie, and many other items are available, as are tap beer and mixed drinks at the long bar. Long after the golfers are gone, the drinks continue to flow, and nearly every evening you can hear Hawaiian, contemporary, or Irish tunes until 1:30 A.M. Stop by for a pint, Paddy.

The **SeaWatch,** 808/875-8080, at the Emerald Golf Course clubhouse, looks out over the fairway, but the most outstanding feature of its location is the view over Molokini and Kaho'olawe. The SeaWatch serves Hawaiian regional cuisine, and many selections are prepared over a kiawe-wood grill. Breakfast and lunch are served 8 A.M.–3 P.M. and are mostly egg and other grill items, or salads and sandwiches. Dinner, served 6–10 P.M., is more refined, focusing on well-balanced flavors and ingredients. Start with chilled tiger prawns and brandied blue crab salad or a macadamia nut–crusted brie with pineapple relish on crostini. A sweet Kula organic green salad might complement your main entrée, which could be parmesan-crusted chicken breast on cappellini pasta, roasted rack of lamb, or miso-glazed tiger prawns. Fresh fish, prepared with a mango chutney macadamia crust, kiawe grilled, or peppered and sautéed, are all always fine choices. Entrées run $23–30. The servers are attentive, the service is professional, and dinner is enhanced by classical piano accompaniment.

At The Shops at Wailea

At the ocean end of this center are three fine-dining restaurants and one that's more casual; two upstairs and two down.

Tommy Bahama's, 808/875-9983, is casual yet sophisticated, open to the ocean breezes, a perfect spot for lunch or dinner or an evening drink at the bar. Its tropical colors and rattan furniture lend it an island feel, and these combined with evening entertainment create a relaxing and welcoming place.

At the other side on the upper level is **Ruth's Chris Steak House,** 808/874-8880. Just like its restaurant in Lahaina, the dark wood, table linens, crispness of dress and service, and huge wine rooms lend this restaurant a semiformal feeling. The emphasis here is meat, and you'll find it in many permutations from petit filets to ribeye, New York strip, and lamb chops, mostly $24–36. Potatoes, rice, and vegetables are ordered separately, but don't skimp on the mouth-watering desserts. Ruth's Chris has a huge selection of wines, one to go with any entrée. Reservations are definitely recommended, and resortwear is appropriate.

After having run a very successful operation in Lahaina for many years, **Longhi's,** 808/891-8883, opened a second restaurant here to great anticipation—and no one is disappointed. This spacious eatery with its classic black-and-white-checkered marble floor is open, airy, and has a full bar. Food is served from 8 A.M. (7:30 A.M. on weekends) until 10 P.M., and the emphasis is on pasta, seafood, and steak. Some of what you might find on the menu are mussels in marinara sauce, corned beef sandwich, Bolognaise rigatoni pasta, grilled New York steak, fresh island fish Veronique, prawns amaretto, or a simpler eggplant parmesan. Expect lunch sandwiches and pasta in the $8–16 range and dinner entrées mostly $27–30.

The most casual of the restaurants is **Cheeseburger, Mai Tais, & Rock N Roll,** 808/874-8990. With a tropical bar, lots of rattan, and hoards of knickknacks and other decorations hanging from the walls and ceiling, you know that Cheeseburger is a place to hang loose, enjoy your meal, or slowly sip one of those special mai tais. While the day starts with eggs, pancakes, and other griddle items, burgers, burgers, and more burgers are what it's really all about here. Of course, the cheeseburger and double cheeseburger are on the menu, but chicken, turkey, garden, and veggie burgers are all options, as are a calamari steak sandwich, various salads, and a few fish selections. Don't forget the sides. Most burgers and sandwiches run $8.25–10.

ENTERTAINMENT

Lu'au

Wailea has two lu'au that have been favorites of guests for years. At the Renaissance, the **Wailea Sunset Lu'au** shows Tuesday, Thursday, and Saturday from 5:30 P.M.; $70 adults, $33 kids 5–12, An open bar accompanies the island-style foods that include *poi, lomi lomi* salmon, and *kalua* pig. Entertainment by the Tihati company is a Polynesian revue of hula and drumming that ends in a fiery knife dance. If you don't go away full and with a smile on your face, it's your own fault. Call 808/891-7811 for reservations.

Wailea's Finest Lu'au is performed at oceanside by the Outrigger resort every Monday, Tuesday, Thursday, and Friday from 5–8 P.M.; $68 adults, $30 children 6–12. An *imu* ceremony and torch-lighting ceremony kick off the affairs. A sumptuous buffet dinner of Hawaiian favorites and hula show follow, and the night is finished by an enthralling fire knife dancer. To reserve, call 808/874-7831.

Music
If you haven't had enough fun on the Wailea beaches during the day, you can show off your best dance steps at the **Tsunami** nightclub at the Grand Wailea. This venue hops to Top 40 DJ music every Friday and Saturday 9:30 P.M.–1:30 A.M. Complimentary for resort guests, the cover for others is $10. For men, long pants are required with covered shoes; for the ladies, dressy resortwear is fine.

Easy-listening music is performed every evening at the **Sunset Terrace** lounge on the lobby level of the Renaissance Resort overlooking the gardens, and all hotels provide some venue for soft Hawaiian music, often with a little hula show included, like the **Kumu Bar** at the Outrigger Wailea, **Botero Lounge** at the Grand Wailea, or the lobby lounge at the Four Seasons.

RECREATION
Golf and Tennis
The 54 links to the Wailea golf course should not disappoint anyone. Studied and demanding, each offers its own challenges plus the beauty of the surrounding area. At more than 7,000 yards (from the gold tee), the Gold Course demands attention to natural and man-made obstacles and design. It's consistently rated one of the top courses in the state. Sharing a clubhouse, the Emerald Course is the most compact but perhaps provides the most stunning scenery. Much tamer, the old-

est of the three, and ranging the farthest, the Blue Course meanders like a lazy brook through the surrounding condominiums. Greens fees run between $115–135, club rentals $35, and the driving range $6; lessons are also available. For tee times, call 808/875-7450.

Aside from its award-winning golf courses, Wailea Resort sports an 11-court tennis facility, with one championship court that can seat nearly 1,000 fans. Court fees run $27 per hour for resort guests and $30 for nonguests. Private lessons, clinics, and round robins can be arranged, and equipment is rented. For information or court times, call 808/879-1958.

SHOPPING
The Shops at Wailea
Each major hotel in the resort has an arcade of shops for quick and easy purchases, but the real shopping opportunity in Wailea is at The Shops at Wailea, a new upscale, open-air shopping center with sophisticated shops that rivals any on the island. International retailers like **Louis Vuitton, Gucci, Tiffany & Co., Fendi,** and **Cartier** are here, as are local and national firms like **Banana Republic, Crazy Shirts, Reyn's** and **Martin & MacArthur.** Clothing stores make up a bulk of the shops, but jewelry shops, art galleries, camera shops, and sundry stores have also found a place here. Head to **Island Camera** or **Ritz Camera Center** for all your photographic needs, **Lapperts** for sweet ice cream treats, and set up island excursions at **Activity Warehouse.** Even the ubiquitous **ABC Stores** and **Whaler's General Store,** for such items as suntan lotion that you inadvertently left at home, gifts, and sweet treats, are a bit more upscale here than at other locations around the island.

As you might expect, there are a handful of art galleries in this center, including **Lahaina Galleries, Lassen Gallerie, Dolphin Gallery,** and **Wyland Galleries,** which each display many painted works by Hawaiian artists and others. **Ki'i Galleries** shows art glass; **Kela** hangs nature photographs, turned wooden bowls, and some impressionist paintings; and **Elan Vital Galleries** has totally unique jewels of vibrant, swirling, and flowing canvases of shimmering color. **Destination Resorts,** the management company for most of the condo units in Wailea, has its reservations office on the lower level.

Wednesday evenings at The Shops at Wailea are special. A "Festival of the Arts," called **Wailea on Wednesdays,** is held here 6:30–9:30 P.M. Taking after the Friday evening festivities in Lahaina, galleries at The Shops at Wailea have special showings, put out goodies and wine, and sometimes host artists for discussions and demonstrations, all while music is played in the central courtyard for the enjoyment of all who wander through. At times, other festivities and activities of the art world will also be hosted to create broader appeal for this event.

SERVICES

There are no banks or post offices in Wailea, but there are two ATMs at The Shops at Wailea. For money exchange or postal needs, ask for assistance from your hotel front desk, or use facilities up the road in Kihei.

Transportation

The **Wailea Resort Shuttle** is a complimentary jitney that stops at most major hotels, The Shops at Wailea, and golf clubhouses in Wailea about every 30 minutes. It operates 6:30 A.M.–8 P.M. Be sure to check with the driver about the last pickup times if you are out in the evening. With a little walking, this is a great way to hop from one beach to the next.

The **Holo Ka'a** public transit shuttle runs throughout the Makena, Wailea, and Kihei area seven times a day from 7 A.M.–7 P.M., with additional service several times a day up to Ma'alaea, and on to Lahaina, Ka'anaplai, and Kapalua. The one-way fare within South Maui is $1. It's $5 as far a Ma'alaea, and $10 for a daily pass throughout the system.

Makena

Just a skip south down the road is Makena Beach, but it's a world away from Wailea. This was a hippie enclave during the '60s and early '70s, and the freewheeling spirit of the times is still partially evident in the area, even though Makena is becoming more refined, sophisticated, and available to visitors. For one thing, "Little Makena" is a famous (unofficial) clothing-optional beach, but so what? You can skinny-dip in Connecticut. The police come in and sweep the area now and again, but mostly it's mellow, and they've been known to arrest nude sunbathers on Little Makena to make the point that Makena "ain't free no more." Rip-offs can be a problem, so lock your car, hide your camera, and don't leave anything of value. Be careful of the *kiawe* thorns when you park; they'll puncture a tire like a nail. What's really important is that Makena is *the last* pristine coastal stretch in this part of Maui that hasn't succumbed to undue development . . . yet. The Maui Prince Hotel and its adjacent golf course and tennis courts comprise the 1,600-acre Makena Resort. Carved from land that was used for generations to graze cattle, this resort is as yet much less developed than Wailea up the road but has great potential for expansion.

Aside from the sundries shop at the Maui Prince Hotel, there's nothing in the way of amenities past Wailea, so make sure to stock up on all supplies. In fact, there's nowhere to get *anything* past the hotel except for the lunch wagon that's usually parked across from the state park entrance. The road south of the Maui Prince Hotel to La Pérouse Bay is by and large fairly good with a decent surface. It does, however, narrow down to almost a single lane in spots, particularly where it slides past small coves. Drive carefully and defensively.

Makena Beach is magnificent for bodysurfing if you have experience, and for swimming, but only when the sea is calm. Whales frequent the area and come quite close to shore during the season. Turtles waddled on to Makena to lay their eggs in the warm sand until early in the 19th century, but too many people gathered the eggs and the turtles scrambled away forever. The

ROBERT NILSEN

Keawala'i Church, Makena, one of the oldest on the island

sunsets from **Pu'u Ola'i** (Red Hill), the cinder cone separating the big Makena beach from Oneuli Beach, are among the best on Maui; you can watch the sun sink down between Lana'i and West Maui. The silhouettes of pastel and gleaming colors are awe-inspiring. Oranges, russets, and every shade of purple reflect off the clouds that are caught here. Makena attracts all kinds: gawkers, burn-outs, adventurers, tourists, free spirits, and a lot of locals. It won't last long, so go and have a look now!

Keawala'i Church

This Congregational Church was established in 1832. The present stone structure was erected in 1855 and restored in 1952. Services are held every Sunday at 9:30 A.M. and 5 P.M., and many of the hymns and part of the sermon are still delivered in Hawaiian. Notice the three-foot-thick walls and the gravestones, many with a ceramic picture of the deceased. A parking lot, restrooms, and showers are across the road for the beach access, which is just down the road. Take Honoiki Road from the main highway, or come down the old coast road from Polo Beach past Makena Boat Landing. The church is almost at the road's dead end, beyond which is the Maui Prince Hotel property.

Small Beaches

You'll pass by the local **Palauea** and **Po'olenalena** beaches, via the coastal Old Makena Road, as you head toward Makena. There is no development here yet, no amenities, and usually few people, but good swimming and white, sloping sands. **Nahuna (Five Graves) Point** is just more than a mile past Polo. An old graveyard marks the entrance. Not the best for swimming, it's great for scuba and snorkeling because of the underwater ridges of lava and caves, and the fish and turtles that hang out there. A short distance farther on is the **Makena Boat Landing** (water, restrooms, showers), a launch site for kayakers and scuba divers. Makena Landing was a bustling port in the mid-1800s and a principal point for shipping goods and cattle from this end of the island to other major island seaports.

Oneuli, on the north side of Pu'u Ola'i, actually has a salt-and-pepper beach, with a tinge of red from the dirt of the hill. Turn down a rough dirt road for one-third mile. Not good for swimming, but good diving, unofficial camping, and

MAKENA

To Wailea

To Kahului

POLO BEACH PARK ■

WAILEA GOLF COURSE

WAILEA ALANUI RD.

Palauea Beach

Po'olenalena Beach

37

TEDESCHI WINERY ■

Makena Bay

MAKENA BOAT LANDING ■

KEAWALA'I CHURCH (1832) ★

Malu'aka Beach
MAUI PRINCE HOTEL ■

Makena

MAKENA GOLF COURSE

Oneuli Beach

MAKENA TENNIS CLUB ■

Ulupalakua Ranch ○

MOLOKINI ISLAND SEABIRD SANCTUARY

Little Makena Beach

▲ MAKENA STATE PARK

Molokini Island

Oneloa Beach (Big Makena)

Pu'u Ola'i (360 ft.) ▲

[ROUGH ROAD]

SITE OF MAUI'S LAST VOLCANIC ERUPTION (1790) ■

31

Kanahena

'Ahihi Bay

'AHIHI-KINA'U NATURAL AREA RESERVE

To Hana

MAKENA RD.

■ 1790 LAVA FLOW

■ MAKENA STABLES

Cape Kina'u

La Perouse Bay

Cape Hanamanioa

Hoapili (King's) Trail

Ancient Paved Road

Kanaio Beach

Keoneoia Beach

'Alalakeiki Channel

0 ___ 3 mi

0 ___ 3 km

© SANDRA E. BISIGNANI TRUST AND AVALON TRAVEL PUBLISHING, INC.

shore fishing. Open 5 A.M.–9 P.M.; no amenities and not many people. Signs warn you not to climb the hill—also from the Big Beach side—but obvious trails lead to the top and over its sides. The Maui Prince fronts **Malu'aka Beach.** There is public access from the end of the road near Keawala'i Church and from the end of a dead-end road just past the resort, that swings back toward the hotel.

Makena State Park

A few minutes past the Maui Prince Hotel, look for a *kaukau* wagon or fruit stand on the left, where you might pick up a snack before turning right onto the park access road. Negotiate the excessive speed bumps for a few hundred yards to the parking lot and a few portable toilets; a second beach access is a few hundred yards farther on. This is **Oneloa Beach,** generally called Big Beach or Makena Beach, a nice long, golden strand of fine sand that's open 5 A.M.–9 P.M. daily. Right leads you to **Pu'u Ola'i** (Earthquake Hill), a 360-foot cinder cone. When you cross over the point from Big Makena Beach you'll be on

Little Makena, a favorite clothing-optional beach for locals and tourists alike. You'll know that you're on the right beach by the bare bums. Both beaches are excellent for swimming (beware of currents in winter), bodysurfing, and superb snorkeling in front of the hill (sometimes called Red Hill because of its color), yet there is not much shade at either. With families and clothed sunbathers moving in (especially on weekends), Little Makena is no longer so remote or isolated. The beginning of the end may be in sight, although there is a loosely organized movement to retain this small sanctuary as a place for those who still wish to swim in the buff.

'Ahihi-Kina'u Natural Area Reserve

Look for the sign four miles past Polo Beach. Even this far down toward the end of the road—or perhaps because of it—this stretch of the coast is becoming a bit more populated, and fancy homes are popping up here and there. The jutting thumb of lava is **Cape Kina'u,** part of Maui's last lava flow, which occurred in 1790. Here you'll find a narrow beach, the small commu-

SOUTH MAUI

nity of Kanahena, and a desolate, tortured lava flow. Within the reserve, several walking trails, one to a natural aquarium pool, start at pullouts along the road and lead to the water. Start at pole no. 18 for the "fishbowl" or pole no. 24 for the "aquarium." Please stay on established paths and wear sturdy hiking shoes or boots. Dolphins often play off this point, and whales can be seen near shore during winter. Aside from the lava fields, 'Ahihi-Kina'u is also an underwater reserve, so the scuba and snorkeling are first-rate. The best way to proceed is along the reef toward the left, or along the reef to the right if you enter at La Pérouse Bay. Beware not to step on the many spiny urchins in the shallow water. If you do, vinegar or urine will help with the stinging.

La Pérouse Bay and Beyond

On the far side of Cape Kina'u is La Pérouse Bay, named after the French navigator Jean de François La Pérouse, first Westerner to land on Maui in May 1786. The bay is good for snorkelers and divers. The public road ends at the entrance to La Pérouse Bay, but with a 4WD you can get a distance down the rough track from here for good shore fishing and unofficial camp-

ing. If you walk farther around to the south you'll come across a string of pocket-size beaches, some with pebbles, others with sand. The currents can be tricky along here, so be careful. Beyond the bay, the 4WD road ends at a navigational light on the point, below which are a coral beach and several small coves.

Past the bay is a remnant of the **Hoapili Trail,** now part of the state Na Ala Hele trail system and still hikable for perhaps two miles. Two trailheads, both indicated by gates—the first through a metal fence, the second through a rock wall—are marked by signs and an area map. This trail, sometimes referred to as the "King's Trail," leads over a rough stone bed that was at one time trudged by royal tax collectors. While parts have recently been refurbished, notice the neat rock curb; this trail is still in very good condition after nearly 200 years. Along the way, a spur trail leads down to Kanaio Beach and the sea, where you get a view of Cape Hanamanioa and its Coast Guard navigational light. At the end of the refurbished section of this trail you reach Keoneoia Beach. Set just inland are many ancient house sites, *heiau,* and canoe sheds in very good condition, and other tangible remains are strewn

ROBERT NILSEN

Archaeological remains of an old Hawaiian village can be found near Kanaio Beach.

throughout this archaeological district and beyond to the east. Stay on the trail and leave everything as you find it! Beyond Keoneoia Beach is private land, over which a torturous 4WD road leads across and eventually up to Highway 31 between Ulupalakua and Kaupo. It could easily be a good day's hike exploring out this way, but remember that no help is available. Wear good shoes, bring a hat, and carry plenty of water, water, and more water.

ACCOMMODATIONS
Maui Prince Hotel

A gleaming wing-shaped building, understated and almost stark on the outside, the Maui Prince Hotel, 5400 Makena Alanui, Makena, HI 96753, 808/874-1111 or 800/321-6248, fax 808/879-8763, is a fabulous destination resort that opens into an enormous central courtyard, one of the most beautiful in Hawaii. Japanese in its architecture and its sense of beauty, the courtyard is a protected haven of cascading waters, black lava rock, stone lanterns, breeze-tossed palms, and raked Zen-like gardens. Lean over the hardwood rails of the balconies on each floor and soak in the visual pleasure of the landscape below, where from these balconies cascade flowers and ferns in sympathetic mimicry of Maui's waterfalls.

All 310 rooms have an alcove door, so you can open your front door yet still have privacy and allow the breeze to pass through. Oceanview and oceanfront rooms ranging $310–480 are beautifully accentuated in earth tones and light pastels. One-bedroom suites, priced $600 and $1,500, feature a giant living room, three lanai, a large-screen TV and VCR, and white terrycloth robes for lounging. The master bedroom has its own TV, listening center, and king-size bed. A nonsmoking wing is also available. The bathrooms have a separate commode and a separate shower and tub. The Prince also offers the very reasonable Prince Special that includes an oceanview room and midsize rental car priced only $350 per night per couple; other honeymoon, golf, tennis, and car packages are also available. For your food and entertainment needs, the Prince has three restaurants and one lounge at the hotel and one restaurant at the golf clubhouse.

The Maui Prince faces fantastic, secluded Malu'aka Beach, almost like a little bay, with two points of lava marking it as a safe spot for swimming and snorkeling. Sea turtles live on the south point and come up on the beach to nest and lay their eggs. To the left you can see Pu'u Ola'i, a red cinder cone that marks Makena. The pool area is made up of two circular pools—one for adults, the other a wading pool for kids—two whirlpools, cabanas, and a poolside snack bar. There's volleyball, croquet, and six plexipave tennis courts with a pro on staff, but the 36 holes of the Makena Golf Course are the main athletic attraction of the Prince. The concierge desk offers a variety of complimentary activities including a snorkel and scuba introduction, plus several fee activities. For the little ones, the Prince Keiki Club children's program can be arranged for healthy and supervised morning and/or afternoon activities. For the big people, see what the complimentary fitness center and spa can do for you. The boat *Kai Kanani* arrives each morning and will take you snorkeling to Molokini or arrange other activities throughout the island.

The Makena Resort **shuttle** runs on an on-demand basis for resort guests only and can take you to and fetch you from the Makena golf course and tennis courts and all facilities in the Wailea resort. Arrange your ride through the hotel concierge.

FOOD
At the Prince

The Prince has three restaurants. The fanciest restaurant is the **Prince Court,** featuring fine dining nightly for dinner only 6–9:30 P.M., except for the truly exceptional Sunday champagne brunch, which is served 9 A.M.–1:30 P.M. The evening fare is Hawaiian regional cuisine and then some. Start with appetizers like ginger duck pot stickers and Kona lobster summer rolls, or soups and salads that include Ma'alaea asparagus bisque and tomato and portabello mushroom salad. From the grill, entrées include Hawaiian fresh catch, butterflied lamb chops, and grilled Thai pork tenderloin, most for

$22–30. In addition, Friday night brings a prime rib and seafood buffet for $40, and the Sunday brunch runs $39. The room is subdued, elegant, and highlighted with snow-white tablecloths and sparkling crystal. The view is serene facing the courtyard or dramatic looking out to sea.

Hakone is a superb and traditional Japanese restaurant and sushi bar. Open Tuesday–Saturday 6–9 P.M., it serves complete dinners like sukiyaki, isaribi, shabu shabu, and haruyama for $36 and under, and it also serves sushi and sashimi, plus traditional *kaiseki* dinners for $45–58. A special Monday night dinner buffet is offered at $42, where you have your choice from a panoply of delightful dishes. In keeping with the tradition of Japan, the room is subdued and simple, with white shoji screens counterpointed by dark, open beams. The floor is black slate atop packed sand, a style from old Japan.

The main dining room, serving breakfast and lunch, is the more casual and affordable **Cafe Kiowai.** Located on the ground level, it opens to the courtyard and fish ponds. Breakfast brings a breakfast buffet or an à la carte menu of griddle items and eggs, while you can get salads, sandwiches, wraps, and pizza until 3 P.M.

For now, food and accommodations in Makena mean the Maui Prince. The only exceptions are the **Makena Clubhouse** restaurant at the golf course, which serves sandwiches and grilled items for lunch, mostly for under $12, and late afternoon *pu pu* until sunset.

For evening entertainment in Makena, the only option is the **Molokini Lounge** at the hotel. Live entertainment is performed nightly 6–10:30 P.M. with the addition of a hula show on Mondays, Wednesdays, and Fridays.

RECREATION

Because the Maui Prince Hotel is a destination resort, on-site recreation possibilities include the beach, beach activity booth, a sailing catamaran, and the swimming pool. Golf at **Makena Golf Course** and tennis at **Makena Tennis Club** are just across the road and offer world-class courts and links. The golf course offers 36 holes; greens fees for hotel guests run $125–150, with twilight rounds cheaper. The six-court tennis club has two lighted courts for night play. Lessons, matches, and rentals are handled at the pro shop. Court fees run $20 per hour for resort guests and $24 for nonguests.

Loading from the beach in front of the hotel, the *Kai Kanani* sailing catamaran takes passengers to Molokini (the shortest route) for a half day of fun, food, and snorkeling. The ship runs Tuesday–Saturday 7–11:30 A.M. for $79 per person.

Makena Stables offers trail rides through this dry, remote region at its location near the end of the road at La Pérouse Bay. Rides range from $120–195, and you must be at least 13 years old and weigh no more than 205 pounds. Call 808/879-0244 for the different rides available.

M

SOUTH MAUI

Upcountry

Upcountry is much more than a geographical area to the people who live there: It's a way of life, a frame of mind. You can see Upcountry from anywhere on Maui by lifting your gaze to the slopes of Haleakala. There are no actual boundaries, but this area is usually considered as running from Makawao in the north all the way around to Kahikinui Ranch in the south, and from below the cloud cover down to about the 1,500-foot level. It swathes the western slope of Haleakala like a large, green floral bib patterned by pasturelands and festooned with wild and cultivated flowers. In this rich soil and cool-to-moderate temperatures, cattle ranching and truck farming thrive. Up here, *paniolo* ride herd on the range of the enormous 35,000-acre Haleakala Ranch, spread mostly around Makawao, and the smaller but still siz-

able 23,000 acres of the Ulupalakua Ranch, which *is* the hills above Wailea and Makena.

While Makawao retains some of its real cowboy town image, it has become more sophisticated, with some exclusive shops, fine-dining restaurants, art galleries, and alternative healing practitioners. Pukalani, the largest town and expanding residential area, is a waystation for gas and supplies, and is pineapple country. Kula is Maui's flower basket. This area is one enormous garden, producing brilliant blooms and hearty vegetables. Polipoli Spring State Recreation Area is a forgotten wonderland of tall forests, a homogenized stand of trees from around the world. Tedeschi Winery in the south adds a classy touch to Upcountry—a place where you can taste wine and view the winemaking process. There are

Upcountry rangeland

plenty of commercial greenhouses and flower farms to visit all over Upcountry, but the best activity is a free Sunday drive along the mountain roads and farm lanes, just soaking in the scenery. The purple mists of mountain jacaranda and the heady fragrance of eucalyptus encircling a mountain pasture manicured by herds of cattle portray the soul of Upcountry.

Makawao

Makawao is proud of itself; it's not *like* a cowboy town, it *is* a cowboy town. Depending on the translation that you consult, Makawao means "Eye of the Dawn" or "Forest Beginning." Both are appropriate. Surrounding lowland fields of cane and pineapples give way to upland pastures rimmed with tall forests, as Haleakala's morning sun shoots lasers of light through the town. Makawao was settled in the late 19th century by Portuguese immigrants who started raising cattle on the upland slopes. It loped along as a *paniolo* town until World War II, when it received an infusion of life from a nearby military base below Kokomo. After the war, it settled back down and became a sleepy village again, where as many horses were tethered on the main street as cars were parked. Most of its false-front, one-story buildings are a half-century old, but their prototype is strictly "Dodge City, 1850." During the 1950s and '60s, Makawao started to decline into a bunch of worn-out old buildings. It earned a reputation for drinking, fighting, and cavorting cowboys, and for a period was derisively called "Macho-wao."

In the 1970s it began to revive. It had plenty to be proud of and a good history to fall back on. Makawao is *the* last real *paniolo* town on Maui and, with Kamuela on the Big Island, is one of the last two in the entire state. At the Oskie Rice Arena, it hosts the largest and most successful rodeo in Hawaii. Happening at the same time, the Paniolo Parade is a marvel of homespun humor, *aloha,* and an old-fashioned good time, when many people ride their horses to town, leaving them to graze in a public corral. They do business at stores operated by the same families for 50 years or more. Although many of the dry goods are country-oriented, a new breed of merchant has come to town. You can buy a wood stove, art glass, Asian medicine, homemade baked goods, designer jeans, contemporary painting, and espresso coffee all on one street. At its eateries you can have fresh fish, a steamy bowl of saimin, Italian pasta, a plate lunch, or a Mexican quesadilla. Artists of all mediums have found Makawao and the surrounding area fertile ground for their work, and the town has become a hotbed of alternative healing practitioners. Look on any bulletin board in town and you'll see a dozen fliers advertising formulas for better life, better health, reawakening of the spirit, Asian health therapies, and new-age, new-health concepts.

Everyone, old-timers and newcomers alike, agrees that Makawao must be preserved, and they work together to do so. They know that tourism is a financial lifeline, but they shudder at the thought of Makawao becoming an Upcountry Lahaina. It shouldn't. It's far enough off the track to keep the average tourist away but easy enough to reach and definitely interesting enough to make the side trip worthwhile.

The main artery to Makawao starts in Pa'ia. Turn right onto Baldwin Avenue, and from there it's about six miles uphill to Makawao. You can also branch off Route 37 (Haleakala Hwy.) in Pukalani onto Route 365, which will also lead you to the town. The back way reaches Makawao by branching off Route 36 through Ulumalu and Kokomo. Just where Route 36 turns into Route 360, there's a road that branches inland: This is Kaupakalua Road, Route 365. Take it through backcountry Maui, where horses graze around neat little houses and Haleakala looms above. At one Y intersection there's Hanzawa's Variety Store; continue on through Kokomo to Makawao. Notice the mixture of old and new houses—Maui's past and future in microcosm. Here, the neat little banana plantation on the outskirts of the

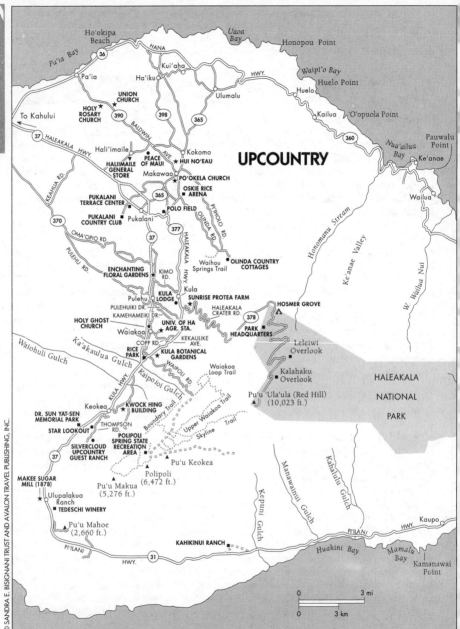

To Kahului

Ho'okipa Beach

Pa'ia Bay

36

HANA

Uaoa Bay

Honopou Point

Kui'aha

Ha'iku

Ulumalu

Waipi'o Bay

Huelo Point

Huelo

Kailua

O'opuola Point

Pauwalu Point

360

Nua'ailua Bay

Ke'anae

Wailua

Pa'ia

UNION CHURCH

HOLY ROSARY CHURCH

390

398

365

BALDWIN AVE.

Hali'imaile

37 HALEAKALA HWY.

KEAHUA RD.

KULA HWY.

HALIIMAILE GENERAL STORE

PEACE OF MAUI

Kokomo

HUI NO'EAU

Makawao

PO'OKELA CHURCH

OSKIE RICE ARENA

PUKALANI TERRACE CENTER

PUKALANI COUNTRY CLUB

365

POLO FIELD

PIIHOLO RD.

OLINDA RD.

UPCOUNTRY

Honomanu Stream

Ke'anae Valley

W. Wailua Nui

370

OMA'OPIO RD.

Pukalani

37

377

HALEAKALA HWY.

PUEHU RD.

ENCHANTING FLORAL GARDENS

Pulehu

KIMO RD.

Kula

Waihou Springs Trail

OLINDA COUNTRY COTTAGES

KULA LODGE

SUNRISE PROTEA FARM

PULEHUIKI DR.

HOLY GHOST CHURCH

KAMEHAMEIKI DR.

Waiakoa

UNIV. OF HA AGR. STA.

HALEAKALA CRATER RD.

378

HOSMER GROVE

PARK HEADQUARTERS

Leleiwi Overlook

Ka'akaulua Gulch

COPP RD.

KEKAULIKE AVE.

RICE PARK

KULA BOTANICAL GARDENS

Kalahaku Overlook

HALEAKALA

Waiohuli Gulch

Kaipo'oi Gulch

WAIPOU RD.

Waiakoa Loop Trail

Pu'u 'Ula'ula (Red Hill) (10,023 ft.)

NATIONAL

PARK

DR. SUN YAT-SEN MEMORIAL PARK

Keokea

KWOCK HING BUILDING

THOMPSON RD.

Boundary Trail

Upper Waiakoa Trail

Skyline Trail

Kahalulu Gulch

STAR LOOKOUT

SILVERCLOUD UPCOUNTRY GUEST RANCH

POLIPOLI SPRING STATE RECREATION AREA

37

Pu'u Keokea

MAKEE SUGAR MILL (1878)

Ulupalakua Ranch

TEDESCHI WINERY

Polipoli (6,472 ft.)

Pu'u Makua (5,276 ft.)

Manawainui Gulch

Kepuni Gulch

PI'ILANI HWY.

Kaupo

Pu'u Mahoe (2,660 ft.)

PI'ILANI

KAHIKINUI RANCH

Huakini Bay

Mamalu Bay

Kamanawai Point

31 HWY.

0   3 mi

0   3 km

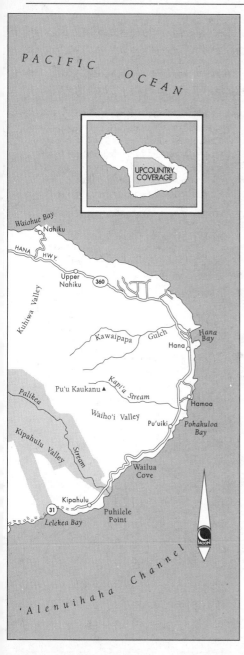

diminutive town says it all. Pass St. Joseph's Catholic Church and you've arrived through Makawao's back door. This is an excellent off-track route to take on your way to or from Hana. Alternately, you can also come up Kokomo Road, Route 398, through Haiku from the Hana Highway.

Events

Makawao has a tremendous rodeo season every year—2003 was the 48th annual. Most meets are sponsored by the Maui Roping Club. They start in the spring and culminate in the massive **Makawao Rodeo,** held over three days on the weekend nearest July 4. These events attract the best cowboys from around the state, with substantial prize money as reward. Both males and females try their luck in separate groupings. The numerous competitions include barrel racing, break-away, team, and calf roping, and bull and bronco riding. Organization of the event is headed by long-time resident Brendan Balthazar, who welcomes everyone to participate with only one rule: "Have fun, but maintain safety." General admission is $10, $5 for seniors and children; call 808/572-2076 for information. Every year the rodeo is accompanied by the fun-loving Paniolo Parade, which is in its 38th year.

The day-long **Upcountry Fair** happens at the Eddie Tam Center in mid-June. A real county event, you'll find all sorts of craft displays, games, ethnic dances, competitions, and food booths, as well as the 4-H judging and animal auction.

Upcountry plays **polo.** The Maui Polo Club, 808/877-7744, www.mauipolo.com, sponsors matches in the spring and fall. From Apr.–June, matches are held at the Haleakala Ranch polo arena, about one mile above Pukalani and just off Highway 377. The Sept.–Nov. matches take place above Makawao at the Olinda outdoor polo field next to Oskie Rice rodeo arena. All matches are held on Sundays at about 1 P.M. and admission runs $3 per person.

SIGHTS

Up From Pa'ia

En route on Baldwin Avenue (Route 390) you pass the Pa'ia **sugar mill,** a real-life Carl Sandburg poem. A smaller sister mill to the one at Pu'unene, it was until a few short years ago a green monster trimmed in bare lightbulbs at night, dripping with sounds of turning gears, cranes, and linkbelts, all surrounded by packed, rutted, oil-stained soil. Now it stands silent and unused, a testimony to better economic times. Farther along Baldwin Avenue sits **Holy Rosary Church** and its sculpture of Father Damien. The rendering of Damien is idealized, but the leper, who resembles a Calcutta beggar, has a face that conveys helplessness while at the same time faith and hope. It's worth a few minutes' stop. Coming next is **Makawao Union Church** (1916), and it's a beauty. Like a Tudor mansion made completely of stone with lovely stained-glass windows and a heavy slate roof, the entrance is framed by two tall and stately royal palms. Farther up is tiny **Rainbow County Park,** one of the few noncoastal parks on Maui. Set in the bend of the road, the grassy lawn here would be okay for a picnic.

At mile marker 5 along Baldwin Avenue, Hali'imaile Road turns to the south and leads

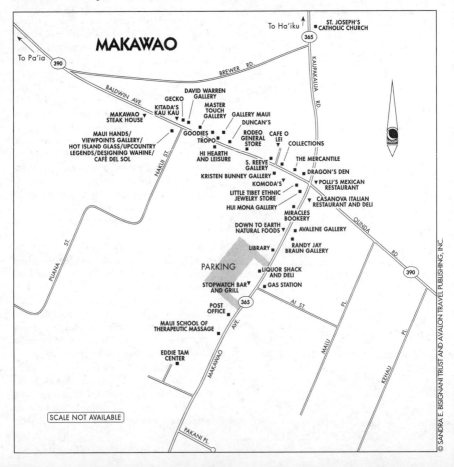

ROBERT NILSEN

Makawao Union Church

to the small pineapple town of **Hali'imaile.** This tiny community, a combination of old plantation town and new development, offers a wonderful restaurant, the Haliimaile General Store—well worth the drive—a farm-fresh pineapple and produce market, and a well-shaded county park that features picnic tables, ball fields, and lighted tennis courts.

Farther up the street is the **Hui No'eau Visual Arts Center,** 2841 Baldwin Ave., 808/572-6560, www.huinoeau.com, a local organization that features traditional and modern arts housed at Kaluanui, a mansion built in 1917 by the Baldwin family on their 10-acre estate. The member artisans and craftspeople produce everything from ceramics to *lau hala* weaving, and drawings to sculpture. The old house is home to the center office, gift gallery, and periodic shows, while the former stable and carriage house have become studios. Throughout the year classes, lectures, and exhibits are offered, along with an annual Christmas Fair featuring their creations. One of the best features of visiting Hui No'eau (Club of Skills) is the resplendent mansion. Built

in a neo-Spanish motif with red-tiled roof and light pink stucco exterior, Kaluanui sits among the manicured grounds that feature a reflection pond just in front of the portico. The gift shop and gallery are open daily 10 A.M.–4 P.M. (a $2 donation is suggested), and you'll often find someone around working in the studios.

Nearby Attractions

Take Olinda Road out of town. All along it custom-designed houses have been built. Look for **Po'okela Church,** a coral-block structure built in 1843. **Seabury Hall,** a private boarding school for grades 6–12, sits among trees above Makawao. In May, it hosts a day-long arts and crafts fair, with entertainment, food, games, and auctions. An annual event for nearly 30 years, it has become the best-known and best-subscribed crafts fair on the island. In four miles you pass **Rainbow Acres,** 808/573-8313. Open Tuesday and Thursday 9 A.M.–4 P.M., this nursery specializes in cacti and succulents. Then shortly you come to the Maui Bird Conservation Center and Maui Forest Bird Recovery Project office—neither open to the public. Near the top of Olinda, turn left onto Pi'iholo Road, which loops back down. Along it is **Aloha O Ka Aina,** 808/572-9440, a nursery specializing in ferns. Open Wednesday–Saturday 9 A.M.–4 P.M.

Hiking Trail

The **Waihou Spring Trail** is the easiest hiking access in the area, but in reality it is little more than a good walk. The trailhead is just below the intersection of Olinda Road and Pi'iholo Road. Running entirely through a forest canopy of pine and eucalyptus, this trail, flat and wide for most of its length, only narrows when it drops steeply down into a ravine as it gets close to the spring, which is now virtually always dry. The trail starts out by running through an experimental tree-growing area. Shortly you come to a T-intersection. Going right, you keep to the main trail; left brings you in a half-mile loop back to the main trail. From an overlook on the main path, the trail zigzags down to the boulder-strewn bottom of a narrow ravine, a cool and quiet sanctuary. Usually dry, a dripping curtain of water must cover the back wall during the rains. Neither strenuous nor lengthy, this one-mile hike is nonetheless good exercise.

PRACTICALITIES

Accommodations

Built in 1924 and used by a Portuguese family to raise 13 children, the plantation house **Hale Ho'okipa Inn,** 32 Pakani Place, 808/572-6698 or 877/572-6698, fax 808/573-2580, mauibnb@maui.net, www.maui-bed-and-breakfast-inn.com, has been turned into a lovely B&B. Not a modern rendition, this well-loved place has real-world, lived-in charm and is filled with comfortable period-style and antique furniture and furnishings and artwork by Hawaiian artists. Three rooms on one side of the house have their own private baths, while the two-bedroom suite on the other side shares a bath and has use of the big country kitchen. A continental breakfast with fruit from the garden is served each morning in the parlor. Rates run $95–125 per night for the rooms and $150–165

for the suite. The inn is within walking distance of town, not far beyond and above the highway from the Eddie Tam Center. For those who like to hike, the owner offers guided tours up into Haleakala or over to the West Maui Mountains for a reasonable fee.

Olinda Country Cottages and Inn, 2660 Olinda Rd., 808/572-1453 or 800/932-3435, fax 808/573-5326, olinda@mauibnbcottages.com, www.mauibnbcottages.com, is up above Makawao past mile marker 11. Located on an old protea farm at about 4,000 feet in elevation, and backed up against Haleakala Ranch, this B&B is secluded, spacious, and homey. The main house has two rooms upstairs and a suite below, with two separate cottages for plenty of privacy. The two bedrooms in the house have a private entrance and share a sitting room, and each has a private bath. Breakfast is provided each morning for these rooms. The downstairs suite and individual cottages are more like small homes with all the amenities. Because each has a kitchen, breakfast is served only the first morning. All have plenty of country-style furnishings and antiques, and the color and design work well. The bedrooms run $140 per night, the suite $140, and the cottages $195–245. The rooms and suite have a two-night minimum, the cottages three. No smoking is permitted inside, and no children under eight years old are allowed to stay here. Highly recommended for quiet and seclusion, yet close enough to get to a fine restaurant in town. With gregarious hosts and good value, the only drawback for some folks might be the windy road leading up to the B&B.

Down near Hali'imaile is **Peace of Maui** vacation rentals, 1290 Hali'imaile Rd., Makawao, HI 96768; 808/572-5045 or 888/475-5045, pom@maui.net, www.maui.net/~pom. Peace of Maui overlooks the broad pineapple fields of this agricultural region, and from the property you have views of the north coast, the West Maui Mountains, and the great mountainside sweep of Haleakala. Rooms in the main house are not extravagant but clean and serviceable at $40 single or $45 double. Guests share a bathroom, comfy living room and kitchen, and the outdoor patio with barbecue grill. A separate cottage across the yard sleeps 1–4 , has a bright and efficient kitchen, small living room with TV, a lanai, and washer and dryer. At $85 per night for two and $5 extra for an additional person, it's a bargain. Breakfast is not included because you have full use of the kitchen.

Food

Inexpensive: Kitada's Kau Kau Korner, 808/572-7241, makes the best saimin on Maui—according to all the locals. It's a town institution and located across from the Makawao Steak House in a small plantation-style wood-frame building. Very local, nothing fancy, it's open Monday–Saturday 6 A.M.–1:30 P.M. The sharp slap of the screen door announces your entry. Order at the counter, then pour yourself a glass of water and take a seat. The saimin is inexpensive, and there are also plate lunches, burgers, and sandwiches that mostly run less than $6.

Komoda's is a general store that has been in business for more than 80 years. It sells a little of everything, but the bakery is renowned far and wide. It's open 7 A.M.–5 P.M. except Tuesday and Sunday, and until 2 P.M. on Saturday. People line up outside to buy their cream puffs and home-made cookies, which are all gone by late morning.

Sheltered down a short alley behind the Reeve Gallery is **Café O'Lei,** 808/573-9065, which offers simple but filling soups, salads, and sandwiches daily for lunch 11 A.M.–4 P.M. Menu items run $6.25–8 and include a snow crab and avocado sandwich, vegetarian chili, and curry chicken salad. Courtyard seating is available.

Just down the street is **Duncan's Coffee Company,** 573-9075, open most days 6:30 A.M.–9 P.M. for coffee (by the cup or pound), sodas, juices, salads, bagels, and wraps, and ice cream. Duncan's makes a great pit stop in the morning for a pick-me-up or a rest stop later in the day.

If you need a break from looking at all the art and glass, head to the **Café del Sol,** 808/572-4877, in the courtyard behind Viewpoints Gallery. This little eatery is open Monday–Saturday until 11 A.M. for breakfast and 11 A.M.–5 P.M. for lunch. People come just for the coffee, but you can also get granola, lox and bagels, fresh pastries, and egg breakfasts, or hot or cold sandwiches that run mostly $5.50–8.25.

Moderate: At 1127 Makawao Avenue you'll find the **Stopwatch Sports Bar & Grill,** 808/572-1380. Open for lunch and dinner, a variety of inexpensive burgers and sandwiches are served along with more substantial steak, fried chicken, fish entrées, and evening specials. Most items on the menu are under $10. There's live entertainment and dancing on Friday and Saturday evenings, and the bar holds happy hour daily 4–7 P.M.

An excellent place to eat is **Polli's Mexican Restaurant,** 808/572-7808, open daily 11 A.M.–10 P.M. The sign, Come In and Eat or We'll Both Starve, greets you at the front. The meals are authentic Mexican, using the finest ingredients. Formerly vegetarian—they'll still prepare any menu item in a vegetarian manner—they use no lard or animal fat in their bean dishes. You can have full lunch dishes for under $10 or dinner entrées for $10–17. Margaritas are large and tasty, the cervezas cool and refreshing. Monday night is barbecue night; Tuesday is kid's night. Still down home, still wholesome meals, still a happening place, this is one of Makawao's favorites.

Makawao Steak House, 808/572-8711, near the bottom end of town, is open daily for dinner from 5:30 P.M., with early-bird specials until 6:30. Casual, with wooden tables, salad bar, and good fish selections, dinners run to around $26. The steak dishes, and especially the Monday night special prime rib, are the best, and it has one of the only standard salad bars in the area. The Makawao Steak House has been around a long time and maintains a good, solid reputation. Even if you're not up for a meal, you might consider stepping into the lounge for a drink.

Expensive: A surprising and delicious dining experience, the best restaurant in town is found at **Casanova Italian Restaurant and Deli,** 808/572-0220, located across from Polli's at the main intersection of town. The deli is open daily for breakfast and lunch 7:30 A.M.–6 P.M. The interior is utilitarian—a refrigerated case loaded with salads, chocolates, cheese, and juice, and a few tables for eating. A real gathering spot in the morning, breakfast brings waffles, omelets, and pastries; lunch is sandwiches and hot entrées. Order your meal at the counter. The best place to sit is on the front porch, where you can perch above the street and watch Makawao life go by. Upcountry-yuppie-elegant, Casanova's restaurant occupies the adjoining section of the building, open daily except Sunday, for lunch 11:30 A.M.–2 P.M. and nightly for dinner 5:30–9 P.M., featuring pizza, pasta, and other fine Italian cuisine. Of course, pasta is the staple, but meat, fish, and poultry entrées are also popular. While you wait, you can watch the pizza maker toss the dough before putting it in the wood-burning oven. Expect pasta and pizza entrées in the $12–16 range, others $20–24. While the food is as good as the deli fare next door, many come for the music and dancing, which starts around 9:45 P.M. and runs until 1 A.M. Wednesday–Saturday. Having a nightclub atmosphere, a large dance floor, and a first-class sound system, it draws people not only from Upcountry but also from Central and South Maui. Casual attire is fine, but remember, Upcountry gets cool at night, so you might need something to cover your arms and shoulders.

The **Haliimaile General Store,** 808/572-2666, open Mon.–Fri. 11 A.M.–2:30 P.M., and again 5:30–9:30 P.M., with a Sunday brunch 10 A.M.–2:30 P.M. and a mini-menu 2:30–5 P.M., serves elegant gourmet food to anyone lucky enough to find this Upcountry roadhouse. Located in Hali'imaile village along Hali'imaile Road between Baldwin Avenue and the Haleakala Highway, the restaurant is housed in what was this pineapple town's general store. Climb the steps to a wide veranda and enter to find the vintage utilitarian wood-floored interior transformed into an airy room with tropical fish hung from the ceiling, primitive ceramics and sculptures placed here and there, and original paintings of brilliant colors. It's as if the restaurant is part contemporary boutique and art gallery, and the old grocery shelves are filled with distinctive gift and gourmet food items. Choose a table in the casual front room, perch on a canvas chair at the copper-top bar in front of the open kitchen, or ask for a table in the back room, more formal with dark wood paneling, ceiling fans, track lighting, and floral displays. Master chef Beverly Gannon presents creative "Hawaiian regional cuisine with an American and international twist," while

her Irish husband, master schmoozer Joe Gannon, presents an equally magnificent Blarney Stone atmosphere! While the menu changes seasonally, a sampling of what you might expect includes appetizers like the sashimi Napoleon, Asian pear and duck taco, or Bev's crab dip served on boboli bread, all under $17. These are an experience in themselves but serve to prepare you for the main course to come. Entrées include *paniolo* barbecue ribs, coconut seafood curry, aged Midwest beef rib eye, rack of lamb Hunan style, or chili verde enchiladas, all of which range in price from $22–32. Save room for a masterful dessert created by pastry chef and daughter Teresa Gannon. Piña colada cheesecake anyone? The food is always healthy and fresh and the portions are plentiful. Whatever your choice, you'll leave with a full belly and a smile on your face. The setting is casual and alohawear is okay, but because of the elevation, long sleeves and pants might be in order. The Haliimaile General Store has been reborn, and its spirit lives on in this wonderful restaurant.

Food Markets

Down To Earth Natural Foods, 1169 Makawao Ave., 808/572-1488, open daily 8 A.M.–8 P.M., is a first-rate health food store that originated in Wailuku and later opened a branch here in Makawao. Inside you'll find shelves packed with minerals, vitamins, herbs, spices, and mostly organic fruits and vegetables. Bins hold bulk grains, pastas, honey, and nut butters, while a deli case holds sandwiches and drinks. You can even mix up a salad from the salad bar to take out, or choose a hot entrée from the food bar. At $6.49 per pound, the hot entrées are one of the best bargains in town for a meal. Down to Earth has a philosophy by which it operates: "To promote the living of a healthy lifestyle by eating a natural vegetarian diet; respect for all forms of life; and concern for the environment."

Rodeo General Store, 3661 Baldwin Ave., is a one-stop shop with a wide selection of natural foods, deli items, pastries, produce, fresh fish, wines, spirits, and cigars. Open 7 A.M.–10 P.M. daily. The **Liquor Shack and Deli,** 1143 Makawao Ave., provides plate lunches for about

$6.75 and a full range of liquid refreshments daily 9 A.M.–10:30 P.M.

In Hali'imaile, **Maui Fresh** is an outlet for Maui Pineapple Company. Available are fresh and canned pineapples and a variety of seasonal fruits and vegetables. A small plantation museum offers visitors a snapshot of the pineapple industry and the company operation. Open Monday–Friday, 10 A.M.–6 P.M., Saturday 9 A.M.–5 P.M., this store is located next to the plantation office along Hali'imaile Road and only a few steps from the Haliimaile General Store restaurant. This shop sponsors a flea market every first and third Saturday and an annual pineapple picnic in May for food, games, crafts, music, and plantation tours.

Art Galleries

The Courtyard of Makawao is a consortium of shops at 3620 Baldwin Avenue near the bottom end of town where you can dine, peruse fine art, collect country craft, or watch as glassblowers pursue alchemical art. In the reconstructed Makawao Theater building, **Maui Hands,** 808/572-5194, is open daily except Sunday 10 A.M.–6 P.M. This artists' "consignment shop" specializes in Maui-made art and crafts like semiprecious stone necklaces, sterling and gold jewelry, prints, bamboo work, raku pottery, primitive basketry, and even some T-shirts. **Viewpoints Gallery,** 808/572-5979, open daily 10 A.M.–6 P.M. (Sunday until 4 P.M.), is an artists' cooperative specializing in locally created paintings, sculptures, handicrafts, and jewelry. Most of the artists live in the area, and with enough notice they will come to meet you if time permits. This shop is a perfect place to spend an hour eyeing the contemporary art scene that is so vibrant in Upcountry. Every month brings a new exhibit. Outside is a pleasant courtyard, around which are several more shops.

In the back you will find artisans making magic at **Hot Island Glass,** 808/572-4527, open daily 9 A.M.–5 P.M., with glass being blown most days 10 A.M.–4 P.M. These very talented glassblowers turn molten glass into vases, platters, sea creatures, and some small items like paperweights. Just line up at their window and watch the artists

work. Incidental pieces run as cheap as $10, but the masterpieces go for several thousand. Don't worry about shipping or packing glass; they're also masters at packing so things don't break on the way home. In the back corner, **Upcountry Legends,** 808/572-3523, open daily 10 A.M.–6 P.M., Sunday 11 A.M.–5 P.M., sells hand-painted silk shirts, ladies apparel, sterling silver jewelry, huggable teddy bears and other stuffed animals, greeting cards, candles, and baskets.

For more fine art, painting, pottery, wood sculpture, and more, check out **David Warren Gallery** across from the Courtyard and the **Master Touch Gallery** for fine jewelry. Up the street a bit and behind Tropo is the small **Gallery Maui,** with a wide selection of art and wood furniture by island artists. Farther up Baldwin Avenue is the **Sherri Reeve Gallery,** where you'll find the inspiring watercolor florals of the artist. Nearly across the street, **Kristen Bunney Gallery** hangs paintings by the owner, displays woodwork, gifts, and jewelry by others, and sells Tibetan rugs. At the corner, you're sure to find something that catches your eye at the **Hui Mona Gallery** "art collective."

Although Baldwin Avenue has been the scene of most studios and shops, a few newer businesses have slowly begun to occupy buildings along Makawao Avenue. The **Randy Jay Braun Gallery,** 1156 Makawao Ave., displays Braun's photo art, plus plenty of art in other media, gifts, rugs, and wood crafts. Next door is **Avalene Gallery,** open Mon.–Sat. 10–6 P.M., where they have whimsical pottery sculpture on Smeltzer, paintings by Kasprzycki, and wood, metal, glass, and ceramic pieces by other fine island artists.

Shopping

Makawao is changing quickly, and nowhere is this more noticeable than in its local shops. The population is now made up of old-guard *paniolo,* yuppies, and alternative people. What a combo! Some unique and fascinating shops here can provide you with distinctive purchases.

When Mimi Merrill opened **Miracles Bookery,** 3682 Baldwin Ave., 808/572-2317, she put her heart, soul, and all of her resources into the place. Miracles Bookery specializes in books on new-age spiritualism, astrology, Tarot, self-discovery, children's classics, Hawaiiana, poetry, and "pre-loved" books. Miracles also has unique gift items: angels, petroglyph reproductions, candles, puzzles, Native American jewelry, bumper stickers with an attitude, posters, and music of all kinds from spiritual to rock. Open Monday, Thursday, and Sunday 8 A.M.–8 P.M., Wed.–Sat. until 9 P.M.

At the corner is the tiny **Little Tibet Ethnic Jewelry Store,** open Mon.–Sat. 10 A.M.–5 P.M., for brass and bronze jewelry and religious art and accouterments.

Collections Boutique, open daily until 6 P.M., Saturday until 4, imports items from throughout Asia: batiks from Bali, clothes from India, silk Hawaiian shirts, and jewelry, lotions, cosmetics, accessories, sunglasses, and handicrafts from various countries. Next door, **The Mercantile** also deals in women's fashions, as do several other shops along Baldwin Avenue.

HI Hearth and Leisure, 808/572-4569, has the largest line of wood-burning and gas stoves in Hawaii. That's right, stoves! Nights in the high country can get chilly, and on top of Haleakala it's downright cold. Here as well are barbecue grills, fireplaces, chimneys and accessories, a good selection of cutlery, and a large variety of hot sauces and rubs.

Listen for tinkling wind chimes to locate **Goodies,** open 9:30 A.M.–5:30 P.M., Sunday 10 A.M.–5 P.M., a boutique that looks like a spilled treasure chest. Crystals, silk and cotton casual and elegant clothing, dolls, children's wear, stuffed animals, locally crafted trays, and magic wands fill this shop. Just down the way, **Gecko** carries an eclectic collection of mostly imported gifts, some jewelry, and wearable accessories.

About the only shop in town for men's clothing is **Tropo,** where you can find shorts, polo shirts, aloha shirts, and even hats and ties. Open Monday–Saturday 10 A.M.–6 P.M., Sunday 11 A.M.–4 P.M.

At the front of The Courtyard of Makawao building is the **Designing Wahine** shop, where you can find kid's clothing, gifts, home decoration, and plenty of other nifty island-style gifts.

Down a narrow alley a few steps from the intersection of Baldwin and Makawao avenues is **The Dragon's Den Herb Store,** 808/572-2424, a shop stuffed full of Chinese herbs and medicines, minerals, crystals, teas, gifts, and books on Eastern healing arts. The **Dragon's Den Healing Center,** 808/572-5267, occupies the same building. Also in the alley is **Grace Health Clinic,** 808/572-6091, which specializes in chiropractic care, massage, and traditional Asian medicine, and half a dozen other health professionals. Check the bulletin board here for medical practices and community events. For an alternative practice, contact **Maui School of Therapeutic Massage,** 1043 Makawao Ave., 808/572-2277.

Pukalani

This waystation town, at the intersection of the Old Haleakala Highway and Route 365, is a good place to get gas and supplies for a driving trek through Kula or a trip up Haleakala. It's a rapidly growing community with many new housing developments around its periphery. There are no outstanding cultural or historical sights in Pukalani, but a fine golf course graces its southern edge. Across the street from the major shopping center is a large community park with ball fields, basketball courts, and a great swimming center with an Olympic-size swimming pool.

At the **Pukalani Terrace Center,** the largest shopping mall in Upcountry, are an **Ace Hardware, Foodland** grocery store (open 24 hours), **Paradise Video,** a **Bank of Hawaii** and **American Savings Bank,** both of which have ATMs, a **Maui Medical Group** clinic office, and a **post office.** In the corner of the mall, the full-service **Upcountry Laundry and Dry Cleaning** is open daily 8 A.M.–9 P.M. except Sunday, when it closes at 5 P.M. There are a variety of economical eateries here, including **Royal King's Garden** Chinese restaurant (no MSG) and **Ono Loco Food** mixed-plate shop, along with several fast-food places.

One of the best restaurants in the area is the

Pukalani Country Club Restaurant, 808/572-1325, open daily 7:30 A.M.–2 P.M. and 5–9 P.M. It has a salad bar and sandwiches but specializes in local and Hawaiian foods such as *kalua* pig and *lau lau* plates at reasonable prices. Most patrons are local people, so you know that they're doing something right. The only Upcountry golf course on Maui, **Pukalani Country Club,** offers 18 holes of inexpensive golf. In the bargain come spectacular views over the isthmus and up toward Haleakala. Turn south at the Pukalani Terrace Center and follow the road for four or five blocks to reach the golf course.

Farther up the road at the corner of Aewa Place is the **Cow Country Cafe,** 808/572-2395, in a faded pink and gray building. Open daily 7 A.M.–2 P.M. and again for dinner Wednesday–Sunday 5:30–9 P.M., the café has brought wholesome and unpretentious dining to Upcountry. Inside, wooden tables, bent-back chairs, a tiled counter, and a black-on-white Holstein motif set the ambiance in this American/island standard restaurant. The Cow Country Cafe is a perfect economical breakfast or lunch stop while touring Kula.

At the intersection of Makawao Avenue is the

Pukalani Superette, a well-stocked grocery store, especially for this neck of the woods, that's open Monday–Friday 6:30 A.M.–9 P.M. with shorter hours on the weekends. Down from the superette, going toward Makawao, is a second smaller shopping center, the **Pukalani Square,** where you'll find an **'Ohana Physicians** clinic, **Paradise Pharmacy,** the Maui **Nature Conservancy** office, and a **First Hawaiian Bank.**

Located at 112 Ho'opalua Drive, not far out of Pukalani on the way toward the lower Kula area, is the **Kula Hula Inn,** 808/572-9351 or 888/485-2466, fax 808/572-1132. This Christian B&B has three rooms in the main house and two separate units. The rooms have their own bathrooms, and one has a separate entrance and lanai. They rent for $90–130. For $125 you can get the three-room Suite Plumeria. The larger and more private two-bedroom Hula Moon Cottage with full bath and kitchen goes for $145. An extra $15 per person is added to the bill when there are more than two people in a unit. Breakfast is included daily except Sunday for all except the cottage, where it's optional for an additional charge. This is a secure gated property surrounded by a large lawn, so it's good for kids.

Kula

Kula (Open Country) could easily provide all of the ingredients for a full-course meal fit for a king. Its bounty is staggering: vegetables to make a splendid chef's salad, beef for the entrée, flowers to brighten the spirits, and wine to set the mood. Up here, soil, sun, and moisture create a garden symphony. Sweet Maui onions, cabbages, potatoes, tomatoes, apples, pineapples, lettuce, herbs, asparagus, and artichokes grow with abandon. Herefords and Black Angus graze in knee-deep fields of sweet green grass. Flowers are everywhere: Beds of proteas, camellias, carnations, roses, hydrangeas, and blooming peach and tangerine trees dot the countryside like daubs from van Gogh's brush. As you gain the heights along Kula's lanes, you look back on West Maui and a perfect view of the isthmus. You'll also enjoy wide-open spaces and rolling green hills

fringed with trees like a lion's mane. Above, the sky changes from brooding gray to blazing blue, then back again. During light rainy afternoons, when the sun streams in from the west, you could easily spot a rainbow on the hillside, as if sprouting from the rich green pastureland. Kula is a different Maui—quiet and serene.

Getting There

The fastest way is the route to Haleakala. Take Route 37 through Pukalani, turn onto Route 377, and when you see Kimo Road on your left and right, you're in Kula country. Following Route 37 a few miles past Pukalani gets you to the same area, only lower on the mountain slope. If you have the time, take the following scenic route. Back in Kahului start on Route 36 (Hana Highway), but shortly after you cross Dairy Road

M

look for a sign pointing to Pulehu-Oma'opio Road on your right. Take it! You'll wade through acres of sugarcane, and in six miles this road splits. You can take either because at the top they deposit you in the middle of things to see. Once the road forks, you'll pass some excellent examples of flower and truck farms. The cooperative vacuum cooling plant is in this neighborhood, a place where many farmers store their produce. Cross Route 37 (Kula Highway) and turn onto Lower Kula Road. Explore this road for a while before heading straight uphill via (Lower) Kimo Drive, Pulehuiki Drive, Kamehameiki Road, or Copp Road, which bring you through some absolutely beautiful countryside to Route 377.

SIGHTS

Botanical Gardens

Follow Route 377 south—it turns into Kekaulike Avenue after Haleakala Crater Road, Route 378, turns up the mountain. Look for the **Kula Botanical Gardens,** 808/878-1715, on your left just before the road meets again with Route 37. These privately owned gardens are open daily 9 A.M.–4 P.M.; be sure to start by 3 P.M. to give yourself enough time for a thorough walk-around. Admission is $5 adults, $1 children 6–12. Here are nearly six acres of identified tropical and semitropical plants on a self-guided tour. There is also a stream that runs through the property, a koi pond, and a small aviary. Some of the 2,000 different varieties of plants include protea, orchid, bromeliad, fuchsia, and ferns, and the native koa, *kukui,* and sandalwood. First opened to the public in 1971, the gardens are educational and will give names to many flowers and plants that you've observed around the island. It makes for a relaxing afternoon—a wonderful spot. Enter through the gift shop.

Located across from mile marker 10 on the Kula Highway, the privately owned **Enchanting Floral Gardens,** 808/878-2531, is newer and more commercial than Kula Botanical Garden, yet worthy of a look. Its eight acres are neatly laid out, with many of the 2,000 varieties of flowers and plants identified. Stroll down the path and be captivated by the abundance. Plan on taking

about an hour to see the entire lot. Open daily 9 A.M.–5 P.M.; entrance $5 adults, $1 children.

The University of Hawaii maintains an **agriculture experimental station** of 20 acres of flowers and other agricultural plants that change with the seasons. Located on Mauna Place above Route 37; open Monday–Thursday 7 A.M.–3:30 P.M. Check in with the station manager at the office—closed during the lunch hour. A self-guided tour map is available at the office. While there are experimental plots for other ornamental flowers, vegetables, and fruits, the main focus of this facility is hybridized protea for commercial production. Perhaps best from Oct.–May, it's more a stop for scholarly interest because you can find more showy plants at the botanical gardens and flower shops nearby.

Flower Shops

Upcountry Harvest, 808/878-2824 or 800/575-6470, www.upcountryharvest.com, sits next door to the Kula Lodge and is open daily 8 A.M.–5:30 P.M. Don't miss seeing the amazing fresh and dried flowers and arrangements. Here you can purchase a wide range of protea and other tropical flowers that can be shipped back home, or you can order off the Internet. Live or dried, these flowers are fantastic. Gift boxes starting at $45 are well worth the price. The salespeople are friendly and informative, and it's educational just to visit.

The **Sunrise Protea Farm,** 808/876-0200 or 800/222-2797, www.sunriseprotea.com, and gift shop is less than one-half mile up Haleakala Crater Road. The shop sells gift items, local Maui produce, homemade sweets, sandwiches, and fruit juices. In the flower shop you'll find fresh and dried flowers and arrangements that can be sent anywhere in the country; fresh bouquets from $50, dried arrangements from $42. An easy stop on the way back from Haleakala. Open daily 7:30 A.M.–4 P.M.

The nursery and flower shop **Proteas of Hawaii,** 808/878-2533 or 800/367-7768, www.hawaii-exotics.com, is located across the road from the University of Hawaii agricultural experimental station; hours are 8 A.M.–4:30 P.M. Fresh protea baskets, tropical bouquets, and individual flowers can be purchased and shipped anywhere. Prices start at about $40, or $20 for lei.

Polipoli Spring State Recreation Area

If you want quietude and mountain walks, come here, because few others do. Just past the Kula Botanical Gardens look for the park sign on your left leading up Waipoli Road. This 10-mile stretch is only partially paved; the first half zigzags steeply up the hill, and the second half, although fairly flat, is dirt and can be very rutted, rocky, or muddy. Hang gliders use this area, jumping off farther up and landing on the open grassy fields along the lower portion of this road. Hunting is also done in the forests here, and several trails lead off this road to prescribed hunting areas. As usual, the trip is worth it. Polipoli has an established forest of imported trees from around the world: eucalyptus, redwoods, cypress, ash, cedar, and sugi pines. Much of the area was planted in the 1920s by the state and in the 1930s by the Civilian Conservation Corps. These trees do well here because the park lies right in that band where moisture-laden clouds seem to hang around the mountain. There is a great network of trails in the immediate area and even one that leads up to the top of the mountain. One of the most popular is the Redwood Trail, which you can take to a shelter at the end. These trails are for hiking and mountain biking only—no motorcycles or horses.

At 6,200 feet, the camping area can be brisk at night. Camping is free, but permits are required and are available from the Division of State Parks, 54 S. High St., Rm. 101, Wailuku, HI 96793, 808/984-8109. Water, picnic tables, and outhouses are provided at the camping spot, which is a small, grassy area surrounded by tall eucalyptus trees. The cabin here is a spacious three-bedroom affair with bunks for up to 10 people. It starts at $45 per night for 1–4 people and goes up $5 per additional person. It's rustic, but all camping and cooking essentials are provided, including a wood-burning stove. If you want to get away from it all, this is your spot.

Hiking Trails

Most of these trails form a network through and around Polipoli Spring State Recreation Area and are all accessible from the camping area at 6,200 feet. **Redwood Trail,** 1.7 miles, passes through a magnificent stand of redwoods, past the ranger station and down to an old Civilian Conservation Corps camp at 5,300 feet where there's a rough old shelter. **Tie Trail,** one-half mile, joins Redwood Trail with **Plum Trail,** so named because of its numerous plum trees, which bear fruit during the summer. **Skyline Trail,** 6.5 miles, starts atop Haleakala at 9,750 feet, passing through the southwest rift and eventually joining the **Haleakala Ridge Trail,** 1.6 miles, at the 6,500-foot level, then descends through a series of switchbacks. You can join with the Plum Trail or continue to the shelter at the end. Both the Skyline and Ridge trails offer superb vistas of Maui.

Other trails throughout the area include **Polipoli,** 0.6 miles, passing through the famous forests of the area; **Boundary Trail,** four miles, leading from the Kula Forest Reserve to the ranger's cabin, passing numerous gulches still supporting native trees and shrubs; and **Waiohuli Trail,** descending the mountain to join Boundary Trail and overlooking Keokea and Kihei with a shelter at the end. **Waiakoa Trail,** seven miles, begins at the Kula Forest Reserve Access Road. It ascends Haleakala to the 7,800-foot level and then descends through a series of switchbacks, covering rugged territory and passing a natural cave shelter. It eventually meets up with the three-mile **Waiakoa Loop Trail.** All of these trails offer intimate forest views of native and introduced trees, and breathtaking views of the Maui coastline far below.

Other Sights

In the basement of the Kula Lodge, tucked away as if in a wine cellar, is the **Curtis Wilson Cost Gallery,** 808/878-6544 or 800/508-2278, www.costgallery.com. One of Maui's premier artists, Cost captures scenes reflecting the essence of Upcountry Maui; handles color, light, and shadow to perfection; and portrays the true pastoral nature of the area. This is traditional realism with a touch of imagination. Stop in and browse daily 8:30 A.M.–5 P.M., or visit his other shop on Front Street in Lahaina.

Holy Ghost Catholic Church, on Lower

ROBERT NILSEN

Built by Portuguese immigrants in 1897, Holy Ghost Catholic Church continues to serve this multiethnic community after more than a century of use.

Kula Road in Waiakoa, is an octagonal house of worship (Hawaii's only) raised in 1897 by the many Portuguese who worked the farms and ranches of Upcountry. It was rededicated in 1992 after extensive renovation and has many fine hand-carved and hand-painted statues and an elaborate altar that was sent by the king and queen of Portugal when the church was built. This church is worth a look, not only for the museum-quality woodwork inside, but also for the great view over the isthmus. In 1983, it was placed on the National Register of Historic Places.

Near the intersection of Highways 37 and 377 is **Rice Park,** a grassy wayside rest area that has a few picnic tables, bathrooms, and a public phone. From here, you get a good view over the lower mountain slope, the coast at Kihei and Wailea, and the isthmus.

In Waiakoa, there's a gas station; down on the main highway is the **post office.** Across the highway from there is a Montessori School, which hosts a Christmas Faire every year just before the holiday season.

Accommodations and Food

The **Kula Lodge,** RR 1, Box 475, Kula, HI 96790, 808/878-1535 or 800/233-1535, fax 808/878-2518, info@kulalodge.com, www.kulalodge.com, is on Route 377 just past Kimo Road and just before Haleakala Crater Road. Lodging here is in five detached chalets ranging $100–165; check-in is at the lodge restaurant. Two of the chalets have fireplaces with wood provided, four have lofts for extra guests, and all have lanai and excellent views of lower Maui. With their dark wood, carpets, and cathedral ceilings, they are almost contemporary in appearance. The Kula Lodge is a fine establishment with a wonderful location at 3,200 feet in elevation. Perhaps the only drawback is the clamor created when riders on the Haleakala downhill bike trips arrive in a large group for breakfast. Be up early so as not to be disturbed.

The lobby and dining area of the **Kula Lodge Restaurant,** 808/878-1535, are impressively rustic, with open beamwork and framing, dark wood, and stone. This building started as a private residence when it was built more than 50 years ago. The walls are covered with high-quality photos of Maui: windsurfers, silverswords, sunsets, cowboys, and horses. The large main dining room has giant plate-glass windows with a superlative view. Breakfast is served daily 6:30–11:15 A.M., lunch 11:45 A.M.–4:15 P.M., and dinner 4:45–9 P.M.; Sunday brunch runs 6:30 A.M.–noon. The menus are surprisingly large. Try Hawaiian buttermilk griddle cakes or vegetarian Benedict for breakfast, or a fresh fish sandwich or grilled chicken breast for lunch. Start dinner with miso oyster Rockefeller or a Kula farm green salad, and move on to a fresh fish, New York steak, or macadamia nut pesto pasta. The assortment of gourmet desserts includes a tasty mango pie, and one of these should round out your meal. There may be entertainment in the evenings. Before or after dinner, sit at the bar for a drink or warm yourself on the couches that front the stone fireplace.

Just up the road is **Kula Sandalwoods** restaurant, 808/878-3523, serving breakfast from about 7:30 and lunch until 2:30 P.M. or 3 P.M. Set on the hillside above the road, Kula Sandalwoods has a great view out over the isthmus. Breakfast might be eggs Benedict for $9.75, omelets for $8.95, or griddle items. Lunch is mostly burgers and sandwiches that run $8.50–9.75.

Kula View Bed & Breakfast, 808/878-6736, at 600 Holopuni Road below Highway 37, offers a room on the upper level of the home with private entrance, private lanai, and sweeping views of Upcountry and across the isthmus to the West Maui Mountains. Surrounded by two lush acres, peace is assured in your bright and cheery room appointed with queen-size bed, wicker furniture in a breakfast nook, and a shower; telephone and TV are available upon request. The rate is $85 per night, single or double occupancy, which includes a simple continental breakfast. Weekly discounts are available; cash and traveler's checks only. For reservations, contact host Susan Kauai at P.O. Box 322, Kula, HI 96790, sfkauai@mauigateway.com, www.kulaview.com.

In the tiny community of Waiakoa on Lower Kula Road you'll find **Morihara Store,** open daily 7 A.M.–8 P.M. for basic necessities. Across the street is the spacious but spartan **Cafe 808,** open daily 6 A.M.–8 P.M., serving down-home local food, with nothing on the menu more than $8.95.

CONTINUING SOUTH
Keokea

Continue south on Route 37 through the town of Keokea, where you'll find gas, a small selection of items at Henry Fong's and Ching's general stores, two rural churches, including St. John's Episcopal Church, and an excellent park for a picnic. At the far end of the village are **Keokea Gallery,** open Tues.–Sat. 9 A.M.–5 P.M., which displays modern art by Maui artists, and next door is **Grandma's Maui Coffee.** Grandma's is open every day, 7 A.M.–5 P.M. You can enjoy fresh pastries for

breakfast until 10 A.M. and sandwiches, taro burgers, and pies for lunch. The real treat, however, is the coffee, grown on the slope below and roasted in an old-fashioned, hand-crank, 115-year-old coffee machine in the shop. Stop in for a sip or take a package to go. Partway down Thompson Road south of town are the Thompson Ranch Riding Stables corral, Silvercloud Upcountry Guest Ranch bed-and-breakfast, and Star Lookout cottage.

For the diehard history buff, there is an old structure up above town that represents a link to the past, when Chinese workers inhabited the area in greater numbers than they do today. This is the **Kwock Hing Society Building** on Middle Road, a two-story green structure with cream trim that has signboards on either side of the front door that are carved with Chinese characters. A smaller plantation-style building sits to the side. Both have been well maintained. Here, local Chinese would congregate for all sorts of social purposes.

Almost as evidence of that Chinese connection is **Dr. Sun Yat-sen Memorial Park,** farther along the highway. A small triangular county park, here you'll find a statue to this famous Chinese physician/politician, two carved stone lions, and picnic tables. Dr. Sun Yat-Sen spent some of his younger years studying in Honolulu and also had a brother who lived on Maui. It seems that Dr. Sun's movement to overthrow the Manchu Dynasty, which ruled China until 1911, germinated here in Hawaii.

Tedeschi Winery

Past Keokea you'll know you're in ranch country. The road narrows and herds of cattle graze in pastures that seem like manicured gardens highlighting *panini* (prickly pear) cactus. You'll pass Ulupalakua Ranch office and store and then almost immediately come to the Tedeschi Winery tasting room on the left, 808/878-6058, www.mauiwine.com. Open for tastings daily 9 A.M.–5 P.M., the winery sells bottles of all its

> *Past Keokea you'll know you're in ranch country. The road narrows and herds of cattle graze in pastures that seem like manicured gardens highlighting* panini *cactus.*

wines and cushioned boxes for transporting them. Here, Emil Tedeschi and his partner Pardee Erdman, who also owns the 23,000-acre Ulupalakua Ranch, offer samples of their wines. This is one of two wineries in Hawaii, the only one on Maui. When Erdman bought the ranch and moved here in 1963, he noticed climatic similarities to the Napa Valley and knew that this country could grow decent wine grapes. Tedeschi comes from California, where his family has a small vineyard near Calistoga. The partners have worked on making their dream of Maui wine a reality since 1974.

It takes time and patience to grow grapes and turn out a vintage wine. While they waited for their carnelian grapes (a cabernet hybrid) to mature and be made into a sparkling wine, they fermented pineapple juice, which they call Maui Blanc. If you're expecting this to be a sickeningly sweet syrup, forget it. Maui Blanc is surprisingly dry and palatable. In 1984 the first scheduled release of the winery's carnelian sparkling wine, Maui Brut, celebrated the patience and craftsmanship of the vintners. Maui Blush, a zinfandel-like light-pink dinner wine, and Maui Nouveau, a young red wine that's no longer available, were then added to the list. Most recently, Plantation Red, a very dry, oaky, red wine; Maui Splash, a sweet dessert wine that is a combination of pineapple and passion fruit; the mellow Ulupalakua Red table wine; and the dry salmon-colored Rose Ranch Cuvée have made their debut. On occasion, special varietals are bottled. You can taste these wines at the white ranch house set among the tall, proud trees just off the highway, once visited by King Kalakaua in 1874.

From here, free tours run at 10:30 A.M. and 1:30 P.M. to the working winery buildings just a few steps away. Hugging the ground closer to the road is a 100-year-old plaster and coral building that used to be the winery's tasting room. Formerly, it served as the jailhouse of the old Rose Ranch owned by James Makee, a Maui pioneer sugarcane planter. Look for the 25-acre vineyard one mile before the tasting room on the ocean side of the highway. Tedeschi wines are available in restaurants and stores around the island and on the Internet.

Across the street are remains of the old **Makee Sugar Mill**. A few steps away is the Ulupalakua Ranch store and office and the ranch store and deli, which is open regular business hours. Hanging around the store like old plantation workers after a hard day's work are several carved and painted lifelike figures, representing various groups of people who have contributed to Maui's past. Sit down and say hello.

The ranch runs two-hour and four-hour **ATV Tours** over its property, either down close to the water or up on the mountain side. These rides give guests an unprecedented view of a sizable section of Maui that is normally off limits. For information, contact **Maui ATV Tours** at 808/878-2889.

At the end of April, an agricultural trade show called **The Ulupalakua Thing** gives growers and producers an opportunity to show their goods and hand out samples. Products grown and manufactured throughout the state are on display, making this the largest such agricultural event in Hawaii. The Ulupalakua Thing is held at the Ulupalakua Ranch on the grounds of the Tedeschi Winery.

Accommodations

A good place for groups and couples, the **Silvercloud Upcountry Guest Ranch,** 1373 Thompson Rd., Kula, HI 96790, 808/878-6101 or 800/532-1111, fax 808/878-2132, slvrcld@maui.net, www.silvercloudranch.com, is located just out of Keokea and lies just up the slope from the Thompson Ranch horse corral. This fine country accommodation has six rooms in the main house and five studios in an adjoining building. The cottage on the hillside up behind is very private and an excellent retreat for newlyweds. Appropriately ranch-style, all rooms are surrounded by pastureland, and at nearly 3,000 feet in elevation, have unobstructed views down on the green lower slopes of the mountain, Ma'alaea Bay, and West Maui. Rooms in the large well-appointed main house run $110–162, and everyone has access to the kitchen, living room, and dining room. Each bedroom has a private bath but no telephone, and the upstairs rooms have a balcony that overlooks the front lawn. The studios run $132 and $188, and come with a bath, kitchen, and private lanai. Renting for $195 per night, the cottage is a fully furnished unit with its own woodstove for heat. A full breakfast is included for all guests and is served on the back lanai of the main house, surrounded by a flower garden. There is a $15 surcharge for one-night stays. Rates increase about 10 percent from December 15 to the end of February.

Just down the road is the **Star Lookout,** tel/fax 907/346-8028, www.starlookout.com, a single cottage, semi-ranch-style "retreat" that's just right for a quiet and restful stay. This cottage has a kitchen, great views, and plenty of privacy, and rents for $150 per night, two nights minimum.

Haleakala National Park

Haleakala (House of the Sun) is spellbinding. Like seeing Niagara Falls or the Grand Canyon for the first time, it makes no difference how many people have come before you; it's still an undiminished, powerful, personal experience. What is perhaps the most profound aspect of this astounding spot is it grandeur and diversity. The arid volcanic mountaintop "crater" basin is grand in its immensity and that which draws the greatest number of visitors, but the park holds within its boundary numerous other climactic zones and geologic regions, which include frigid alpine peaks, sparsely vegetated upper mountain slopes, a thick and nearly undisturbed tropical forest valley, and a warm coastal littoral strip. Within these differing areas is a great biodiversity that in many respects is quite fragile and in great need of care and protection.

At just over 10,000 feet in elevation, Haleakala is one of the world's largest dormant volcanoes, composed of amazingly dense volcanic rock, almost like poured cement. Counting the 20,000 feet or so of it lying under the sea makes it one of the tallest mountains on earth. The park's boundaries encompass 30,183 variable acres, which stretch from Hosmer Grove on the west end to Kipahulu on the east. Of these, nearly 28,000 acres have wilderness status. The most impressive feature is the "crater" basin itself. It's 3,000 feet deep, 7.5 miles east to west, and 2.5 miles north to south, accounting for 19 square miles, with a circumference of 21 miles. A mini mountain range of nine prominent and additional smaller cinder cones marches across the basin floor. They look deceptively tiny from the observation area, but the tallest at about 600 feet is Pu'u O Maui.

In 1916, much of the mountaintop area of the present Haleakala National Park, along with a large portion of what is now Hawaii Volcanoes National Park, some 100 miles distant on the Big Island of Hawai'i, was created as Hawaii National Park. Kipahulu Valley was brought within the park boundary in 1951. The Maui and Hawai'i sections were split into separate entities in 1961 and Haleakala National Park was born. In 1969, the coastal Kipahulu section was added to the park, and in the late 1990s, 52 additional acres were added along the coast. An additional 2,000 acres were acquired in 2001 between 'Ohe'o and Kaupo, and this Ka'apahu section runs in a swath from the basin ridge down to the ocean.

The entire park is a nature preserve dedicated to Hawaii's quickly vanishing indigenous and endemic plants and animals, and it was recognized as an International Biosphere Reserve by the United Nations in 1980. Two of the endangered species at home here are the *nene,* the Hawaiian wild goose, and the *'ahinahina,* the a fantastically adapted yet fragile silversword plant. Within the park boundaries are six endangered bird species and perhaps 35 endangered plant species. To help mitigate the negative effects of large introduced animals, miles of fence has been raised and, over the years, thousands of goats, cattle, pigs, and other animals removed from the park.

Aside from the *nene,* other endangered birds within the park are the *pueo* (owl), often seen soaring above open scrubland hunting for rodents, and the *'ua'u* (petrel), which nests on cliffs at about 8,000 feet but spends much of its time at sea fishing for food. Common forest birds that might be seen in native stands of trees, such as at

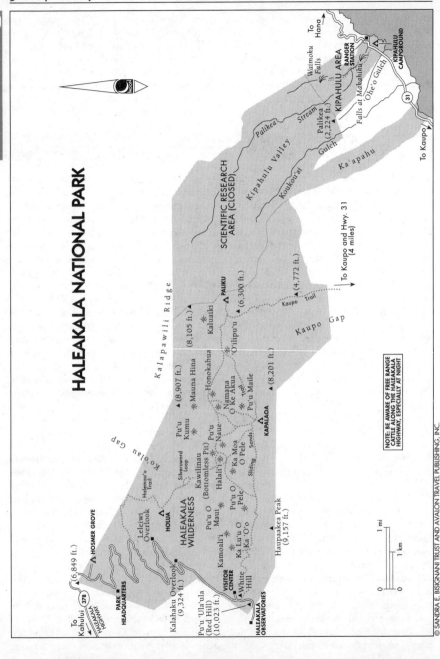

HALEAKALA NATIONAL PARK

To Hana

Waimoku Falls

KIPAHULU AREA

RANGER STATION

KIPAHULU CAMPGROUND

Palikea Stream

Falls at Makahiku

'Ohe'o Gulch

Palikea (2,224 ft.)

Kipahulu Valley

Koukou'ai Gulch

SCIENTIFIC RESEARCH AREA (CLOSED)

Ka'apahu

31

To Kaupo

To Kaupo and Hwy. 31 (4 miles)

▲ PAUKU (6,300 ft.)

(8,105 ft.)

Kaluaiki

'O'ilipu'u

(4,772 ft.)

Kaupo Trail

Kaupo Gap

Kalapawili Ridge

▲ (8,907 ft.)

Mauna Hina

Honokahua

Namana O Ke Akua

Pu'u Maile

▲ (8,201 ft.)

KAPALAOA ▲

Pu'u Naue

Halali'i

Ka Moa O Pele

Sliding Sands

Pu'u Kumu

Silversword Loop

Kawilinau (Bottomless Pit)

Pu'u O Maui

Pu'u O Pele

Ka Lu'u O Ka 'O'o

Kamoali'i

Halemau'u Trail

Leleiwi Overlook

▲ HOLUA

HALEAKALA WILDERNESS

Ko'olau Gap

Haupaakea Peak (9,157 ft.)

▲ HOSMER GROVE

(6,849 ft.)

To Kahului

378

HALEAKALA HIGHWAY

PARK HEADQUARTERS

VISITOR CENTER

Kalahaku Overlook (9,324 ft.)

Pu'u 'Ula'ula (Red Hill) (10,023 ft.)

White Hill

HALEAKALA OBSERVATORIES

NOTE: BE AWARE OF FREE RANGE CATTLE ALONG THE HALEAKALA HIGHWAY, ESPECIALLY AT NIGHT

1 mi

1 km

0

Hosmer Grove, are the red *'apapane* and *'i'iwi*, and the yellowish green *'amakihi* and *'alauahio*. Also common, but introduced species, and more often seen along the road or on land with some cover are the ring-necked pheasant and chukar. Perhaps 400 or so species of insects live within the park, and it's estimated that some 20 percent of these are found nowhere else than on Haleakala.

Note: A discussion of the Kipahulu section of the national park and its hiking and camping options is found in the Beyond Hana section of the East Maui Chapter.

Weather

As high as it is, Haleakala helps create its own weather. Sunshine warms air that rises up the mountainside. When this moisture-laden air pushes into a cooler strata, it creates a band of clouds that moisten the forest and create what is known as the cloud forest. These clouds often push up into the basin itself, gushing up through the Ko'olau and Kaupo gaps, sometimes obscuring the basin from view. When there are clouds, they retreat back down the mountainside in the cool of the evening, leaving the basin clear once again. As air temperature drops about three degrees for every 1,000 feet, the top may be more than 30 degrees cooler than the sunny beaches along the Kihei coast below. Haleakala also traps moisture from the trade winds, so the high mountain slopes above Hana get about 400 inches of rain per year, creating thick forest cover, while the slopes above Makena and farther around to Kaupo, mostly dry and scrubby, get only a dozen inches yearly. Average temperatures at the park headquarters run 52°F in winter and 59°F in summer, with minimum and maximum of 30°F and 80°F, respectively. Monthly rainfall averages 1–2.5 inches May–Oct. and 4.5–10 Nov.–Apr. at park headquarters. The average annual rainfall is slightly less at the summit, but substantially more at the east end of the basin and nearly 200 inches per year in the Kipahulu area and valley above. In

> *Haleakala is spellbinding. Like seeing Niagara Falls or the Grand Canyon for the first time, it makes no difference how many people have come before you; it's still an undiminished, powerful, personal experience.*

2001, Haleakala received snow that stayed for three days. It was the first snow in a decade.

The Experience

If you're after *the* Haleakala experience, you must see the sunrise or sunset. Both are magnificent and both perform their stupendous light show with astonishing speed. The sun, as it rises or sets, infuses the clouds with streaks, puffs, and bursts of dazzling pastels, at the same time backlighting and edging the basin in glorious golds and reds. If conditions are right, a rainbow may hang over the basin at sunset. Prepare for an emotional crescendo that will brim your eyes with tears at the majesty of it all. Engulfed by this magnificence, no one can remain unmoved. For this show of shows, the weather must be cooperative, and you may not be able to tell how it will be from down below. Misty, damp clouds can surround the basin, blocking out the sun, or pour into the basin, obscuring even it from view. Don't forget the wind. It's usually breezy at the top, which tends to drop the temperature even more, so wear appropriate clothing: jacket, hat, and gloves. The *Maui News* prints the hours of sunrise and sunset (on a daily basis) because they vary with the season, so make sure to check. The National Weather Service provides a daily weather recording at 808/877-5111. For more specific information, you can call the park headquarters at 808/572-4400 for a recorded message. Plan on taking a minimum of 90 minutes to arrive from Kahului, and to be safe, arrive at least 30 minutes before dawn or dusk, because even one minute is critical. For sunrise, the view from the edge of the basin is best. For sunset, hike up to the enclosure on top of Red Hill or sit just over the edge of the hill so you're out of the wind, on the west side of the parking lot.

Note: If you want to avoid downhill bikers and tourists, you can also get a great view from the Kalahaku Overlook. When you drive back down the mountain, shift into a low gear to control your speed to prevent riding the brakes.

"Crater" Facts

Haleakala was formed by flow upon flow of lava. Lava is the hottest natural substance on earth, and it can run like a swift, fiery river. Because of the high viscosity of its lava and the generally nonexplosive nature of the volcanoes in Hawaii, they form classic shield volcanoes. Primarily smooth pahoehoe in form, plenty of 'a'a is also found in the mountain's composition. You'll be hiking over both, but be especially careful on 'a'a because its jagged edges will cut you as quickly as coral. While most activity ceased long long ago, some volcanic activity has been suspected within the basin as recently as 800 years ago. The basin is primarily formed from erosion, not from caving in on itself—hence not a crater, per se. The erosion on Hawaii is quite accelerated due to carbonic acid buildup, a by-product of the quick decomposition of abundant plant life. The rocks break down into smaller particles of soil, which are then washed off the mountain by rain or blown off by wind. Natural drainage patterns form, and canyons begin to develop and slowly eat their way to the center. The two largest are

Ko'olau Gap at the upper end of the Ke'anae Valley in the north and **Kaupo Gap** in the south. These canyons, over time, moved their heads past each other to the center of the mountain, where they took several thousand feet off the summit. Following this great erosion, the mountain erupted time and again, forming a huge amphitheater-like basin, most often referred to as Haleakala Crater. Extra spilled into and filled up both major canyons, hence the solidified flow that appears today coming from both ends of the crater. For more information on Haleakala's volcanic history, see http://hvo.wr.usgs.gov/volcanoes/haleakala.

Some stones that you encounter while hiking will be very lightweight. They once held water and gases that evaporated. If you knock two together, they'll sound like crystal. Also, look out for Maui diamonds, a crystalline mineral called pyroxene.

The cinder cones in the basin are fascinating. They're volcanic vents with a high iron content. Climbing them violates park rules made to protect endangered plants and threatened insects that pollinate them. Notice the

ROBERT NILSEN

Haleakala's crater basin is one of the most awe inspiring sights on the island.

color of the compacted earth on the trails. It's obvious why you should remain on them. Plants like the *'ahinahina* (silversword) are shallow-rooted and live by condensing moisture on their leaves. Don't walk too close to them because you'll compact the earth around them and damage the roots. The ecosystem on Haleakala is very delicate, so please keep this in mind to better preserve its beauty for future generations.

SIGHTS

You'll start enjoying Haleakala long before you reach the top. Don't make the mistake of simply bolting up the mountain without taking time to enjoy what you're passing. Route 37 from Kahului takes you through Pukalani, the last big place to buy supplies. There it branches to clearly marked Route 377. In six miles the zigzag Route 378 or **Haleakala Highway** heads more steeply up the mountain. Along the way are forests of indigenous and introduced trees, including eucalyptus, beautifully flowering jacaranda, and stands of cactus. The vistas change rapidly from one vantage point to the next. Sometimes it's the green rolling hills of Ireland, and then instantly it's the tall, yellow grass of the plains. This is also cattle country, so don't be surprised to see herds grazing as you roll past or on the road itself. Before ranchers and farmers cleared this land, the entire mountainside from Pukalani all the way up to Hosmer Grove was native forest.

Headquarters

Admission to the park is $10 per car, $5 for bikers, hikers, and motorcycles, and is good for seven days; national park discount passes are honored. After paying your entrance fee, the first stopping point in the park is **Hosmer Grove Campground** (see Camping section), a short way down a secondary park road on your left. Proceed past this turnoff a few minutes and you'll arrive at **park headquarters,** elevation 7,000 feet, open daily 8 A.M.–4 P.M. Campers can get their permits here, and others will be happy to stop for all manner of brochures and information concerning the park, for water, or to use the toilet or pay phone. There are some *'ahinahina* outside, and a few *nene* can occasionally be seen wandering the area. After you pass the park headquarters, zig and zag a couple more times, there's parking for Halemau'u Trail (see Hikes section). Following are two overlooks, **Leleiwi** and **Kalahaku.** Both offer tremendous views and different perspectives on the basin. They shouldn't be missed, especially Kalahaku, where there are *'ahinahina* and the remnants of a travelers' lodge from the days when an expedition to Haleakala took two days.

Visitors Center

Near road's end is the visitors center, elevation 9,740 feet, approximately 10 miles up the mountain from headquarters and a half-hour drive. You get one of the best views into the basin from here. It's open from sunrise to 3 P.M. and contains a clear and concise display featuring the basic geology of Haleakala. Maps and books are available, and ranger talks are particularly informative, delving into geology, natural and cultural history, and legends pertaining to this great mountain. A 15–20-minute ranger talk takes place daily at 9:30 A.M., 10:30 A.M., and 11:30 A.M. at the summit above the visitors center. Various ranger-led hikes are also given, including the hike down Sliding Sands Trail and the Hosmer Grove forest walk. Additional interpretive talks and ranger-led hikes are conducted at the Kipahulu ranger station. Check with the park headquarters or the visitors center for times and days of programs. All horse rides into the basin and bike trips down the mountainside through the park start from the parking lot to the front of the visitors center. By 10 A.M., there will be lots of people at the top, so enjoy the time between when the bikers leave and the buses arrive. Before going farther, have a stop at the potty.

Bikes going down the mountain travel about 20–25 miles per hour, sometimes faster. If you're caught behind a string of bikes on your way down, just slow down and wait for them to pull over and let you pass.

HALEAKALA SPIRITUALITY

Although some doubt their authenticity, stories have led others to believe that certain *kahuna* brought their novitiates to Haleakala to perform final rites of initiation. Legends have said that intense power struggles took place atop the mountain between the healing practitioners, the *kahuna lapa'au*, and their rivals the *kahuna ana'ana*, the "black magic" sorcerers of old Hawaii. **Kawilinau,** a sulfur vent on the basin floor that's sometimes referred to as the "Bottomless Pit," was the site of an ancient battle between Pele and one of her siblings, and thus held tremendous significance for both schools of *kahuna*. Average Hawaiians did not live on Haleakala, but came now and again to quarry tool-stones. Only *kahuna* and their apprentices may have lived here for any length of time, as a sort of spiritual preparation and testing ground.

For some in the modern age, Haleakala is a power spot, a natural conductor of cosmic energy that attracts students of higher consciousness from around the world. They claim that it accelerates personal growth, and they compare it to remote mountain and desert areas in the Holy Lands. It is held that not only is there an energy configuration coming from the earth itself, but there is also a high focus of radiation coming from outside the atmosphere. Perhaps the mountain's mass accounts for the strange power ascribed to Haleakala as it sits like a mighty magnetic pyramid in the center of the North Pacific. No one is guaranteed a spiritual experience on Haleakala, but if you're at all sensitive, this is fertile ground.

HIKING AND CAMPING

Walks

One of the topside paths leads to **Pa Ka'oao** (White Hill). An easy quarter-mile hike will take you to the summit, and along the way you'll pass stone shelters and sleeping platforms from the days when Hawaiians came here to quarry the special tool-stone. It's a type of whitish slate that easily flakes but is so hard that when you strike two pieces together it rings almost like iron. Next comes **Pu'u 'Ula'ula** (Red Hill), the highest point on Maui at 10,023 feet. Atop is a glass-encased observation area (open 24 hours). This is where many people come to view the sunset. From here, if the day is crystal clear, you can see all of the main Hawaiian Islands except Kaua'i. To add some perspective to size and distance, it's 100 miles from the top of Haleakala to the volcanic peak Mauna Loa on the Big Island to the southeast. O'ahu is seldom seen and then only as a small bump on the horizon because it's some 140 miles away. Behind you on the slope below is **Maui Space Surveillance Complex,** a research facility with eight telescopes that's used by the University of Hawaii, and a satellite tracking station that's staffed by the U.S. Air Force. Closed to the public, tours of these facilities are no longer given. For more information, check www.ifa.hawaii.edu/haleakala in reference to the research site and www.maui.afmc.af.mil for the military site.

The easy **Hosmer Grove Nature Trail** leads you through a stand of introduced temperate zone trees planted in 1910 to see if any would be good for commercial lumber use. There are perhaps a dozen different species of trees here, and the walk should take a half hour or so over mostly level ground. Originally planted in separate areas, these trees and others have intermingled now. Here you will see Jeffrey pine, ponderosa pine, lodgepole pine, incense cedar, eucalyptus, Norway spruce, eastern red cedar, Douglas fir, and Japanese sugi. Several signs are posted along the trail to explain what the trees are and how the forest developed. This is a good spot to look for native birds.

Halfway up the hill and a completely different environment, a one-quarter-mile **nature walk** leads you from a parking lot to the Leleiwi Overlook. Along the way you find low shrubs and alpine plants rather than trees and thick vegetation. Views from the overlook into the crater basin are well worth the walk.

Various **ranger-led walks** are given during the week, leaving either from the visitors center or

ROBERT NILSEN

'Ahinahina, the endangered silversword plant, grows precariously in isolated spots within Haleakala.

from Hosmer Grove campground. On Mondays and Thursdays at 9 A.M., a naturalist leads a hike down into the Waikamoi cloud forest from Hosmer Grove, and on this hike you'll learn about trees, birds, and natural features of the area. This hike is three hours, three miles, and moderately strenuous. A ranger-led hike also goes down the Sliding Sands trail on a Cinder Desert Hike on Tuesdays and Fridays at 9 A.M. from the trailhead at the visitors center parking lot. The two-mile walk takes about two hours and is moderately strenuous.

Hikes

There are three major trails in Haleakala Wilderness Area (Halemau'u, Sliding Sands, and Kaupo) and several connecting trails—about 27 miles of trails in all. **Halemau'u Trail** starts at the 8,000-foot level along the road about three miles past the park headquarters. It descends quickly by way of switchbacks to the 6,600-foot level on the basin floor, offering expansive views of Ko'olau Gap

along the way. En route you'll pass Holua Cabin, Silversword Loop and Kawilinau sulfur vent (the "Bottomless Pit"—a mere 65 feet deep), and junctions with both the Sliding Sands and Kaupo trails before you reach Paliku Cabin. If you go out via the Sliding Sands Trial and visitors center, you shouldn't have any trouble hitching back to your car left at the Halemau'u trailhead.

Sliding Sands begins at the summit of Haleakala near the visitors center. This could be considered the main trail into the basin and gives you the best overall hike, with up-close views of cinder cones, lava flows, and unique vegetation. It joins the Halemau'u Trail more than one mile west of the Paliku Cabin. Near Kapalaoa Cabin, you can turn left to Kawilinau and exit via Halemau'u Trail, or circle around by way of other connecting trails and exit the way you came. Exiting the Halemau'u Trail is a good choice, but you'll have to hitch back to your car at the visitors center.

The **Kaupo Trail** is long and tough. It descends rapidly through the Kaupo Gap to the park boundary at 3,880 feet. Below 4,000 feet the lava is rough and the vegetation thick. It then crosses private land, which is no problem, and after a steep and rocky downhill grade along well-marked trails deposits you in the semi-ghost town of Kaupo, on the dry rugged southern slope of the mountain. You'll have to hitch west just to get to the scant traffic of Route 31, or head nine miles east to Kipahulu and its campground, and from there back along the Hana Road.

For those inclined, Pony Express offers horse tours into the basin. Hikers should also consider a day with the professional guide service Hike Maui. The guide's in-depth knowledge and commentary will make your trip not only more fulfilling, but enjoyably informative as well.

Hikers

Serious hikers or campers must have sturdy shoes, good warm clothes, raingear, plenty of water, down sleeping bags, and a serviceable tent (unless you've reserved one of the cabins). Hats and sunglasses are needed. Compasses are useless because of the high magnetism in the rock, but binoculars are particularly rewarding. No cook-fires are allowed in the basin, so you'll need a stove. Don't burn any dead wood because the soil needs all of the decomposing nutrients it can get. Water is usually available at all of the cabins within the basin, but the supply is limited and must be treated before use, so bring what you will need. This environment is particularly delicate. Stay on the established trails so you don't cause undue erosion. Leave rocks and especially plants alone. Don't walk too close to 'ahinahina or any other plants because you'll compact the soil. Leave your pets at home; ground-nesting birds here are easily disturbed. If nature calls, dig a very shallow hole, off the trail, and pack out your used toilet paper because the very dry conditions are not conducive to it biodegrading. Best is to use the pit toilets at the campsites if at all possible.

Camping

Camping is free with a necessary camping permit from park headquarters. The **Hosmer Grove campground,** named after Ralph Hosmer, is at the 6,800-foot level, just before park headquarters; the free camping here is limited to three nights and to 50 people, but there's generally room for all. There's water, pit toilets, picnic tables, grills, and a pavilion. While here take a stroll along the half-mile forest loop that threads its way through the grove of trees that Hosmer planted.

Kipahulu Campground is a primitive camping area on the coast near 'Ohe'o Stream. It's part of the park, but unless you're an intrepid hiker and descend all the way down the Kaupo Trail, you'll come to it via Hana.

There are cabins in the basin at **Holua, Kapalaoa,** and **Paliku,** each with twelve padded bunk beds and a pit toilet. Tent camping is allowed at Holua and Paliku. Cabins at any of these sites are extremely popular, and reservations must be sent in advance by mail at least three months ahead. Each cabin is reserved for one group of up to 12 people only. A lottery of the applicants chosen for sites keeps it fair for all. Environmental impact studies limit the number of campers to 25 per area per day. Camping is

limited to a total of three days per month, with no more than two consecutive days at each spot. Rates for cabin use are $40 for up to six persons and $80 to a maximum of 12 people. For complete details and reservation form, contact Haleakala National Park, P.O. Box 369, Makawao, HI 96768, 808/572-4400. If writing by mail, include the note "attn. cabins" on the outside of the envelope. Visit the park's website at www.nps.gov/hale.

Making Do

If you've come to Hawaii for sun and surf and you aren't prepared for alpine temperatures, you can still enjoy Haleakala. For a day trip, wear a windbreaker or jacket and your jogging suit or a sweater, if you've brought one. Make sure to wear socks, and even bring an extra pair as makeshift mittens. Use your dry beach towel to wrap around inside your sweater as extra insulation, and even consider taking your hotel blanket, which you can use Indian fashion. Make raingear from a large plastic garbage bag with holes cut for head and arms; this is also a good windbreaker. Take your beach hat, too. Don't worry about looking ridiculous in this get-up—you will! But you'll also keep warm! Remember that for every thousand feet you climb, the temperature drops three degrees Fahrenheit, so the summit is about 30 degrees cooler than at sea level. As the sun reaches its zenith, if there are no rain clouds, the basin floor will go from about 50°F to 80°F. It can flip-flop from hot to dismal and rainy several times in the same day. The nights may drop below freezing, with the coldest recorded temperature inside the basin a bone-chilling 14°F. Dawn and dusk are notorious for being bitter. Because of the altitude, be aware that the oxygen level will drop, and those with any impairing conditions should take precautions. The sun is ultra-strong atop the mountain, and even those with deep tans are subject to burning. Noses are particularly susceptible.

East Maui

The Road to Hana

On the long and winding road to Hana's door, most people's daydreams of paradise come true. A trip to Maui without a visit to Hana is like ordering a sundae without a cherry on top. The 50 miles from Kahului to Hana are some of the most remarkable in the world. The Hana Highway (Route 36) starts out innocently enough, passing Pa'ia. The inspiration for Pa'ia's gaily painted storefronts looks like it came from a jar of jelly beans. Next come some north-shore surfing beaches where windsurfers fly, doing amazing aquabatics. Soon there is a string of "rooster towns," so named because that's about all that seems to be stirring. Then Route 36 becomes Route 360, and at mile marker 3 the *real* Road to Hana begins.

The semiofficial count tallies more than 600 rollicking turns and 57 one-lane bridges, inducing everyone to slow down and soak up the sights of this glorious road. It's like passing through a tunnel cut from trees. The ocean winks with azure blue through sudden openings on your left. To the right, streams, waterfalls, and pools sit wreathed with jungle and wildflowers. Coconuts, guavas, mangos, and bananas grow everywhere on

ROBERT NILSEN +

windsurfing at Ho'okipa Beach

the mountainside. Fruit stands pop up now and again as you creep along. Then comes Ke'anae with its arboretum and taro farms, indicating that many ethnic Hawaiians still live along the road. There are places to camp, picnic, and swim, both in the ocean and in freshwater streams.

Along with you, every other car traveling the Hana Highway is on the road to take in the beauty that this coast has to offer. Nearly all visitors pass through, some stay a day or a week, while others take up residence. Islanders, mainlanders, and foreigners alike are enticed by the land, and under its spell they put down roots. George Harrison had a house a few miles down the coast in Nahiku, and Jim Nabors, Kris Kristofferson, and Carol Burnett maintain homes here.

Then you reach Hana itself, a remarkable town, the birthplace of the great Queen Ka'ahumanu. Past Hana, the road becomes even more rugged and besieged by jungle. It opens up again around 'Ohe'o Gulch. Here waterfalls cascade over stupendous cataracts, forming a series of pools until they reach the sea. Beyond is a rental car's no-man's land, where the passable road toughens and Haleakala shows its barren, volcanic face scarred by lava flows and covered by dryland forest.

PA'IA

Pa'ia (Noisy) was a bustling sugar town that took a nap. When it awoke, it had a set of whiskers and its vitality had flown away. At the beginning of the 19th century, many groups of ethnic field workers lived here, segregated in housing clusters called camps that stretched up Baldwin Avenue. Pa'ia was the main gateway for sugar on East Maui, and even a plantation railroad functioned here until about 30 years ago. During the 1930s, its population, at more than 10,000, was the largest on the island. Then fortunes shifted toward Kahului, and Pa'ia lost its dynamism—until recently. Pa'ia was resuscitated in the 1970s by an influx of paradise-seeking hippies, and then again in the '80s came another shot in the arm from windsurfers. These two groups have metamorphosed

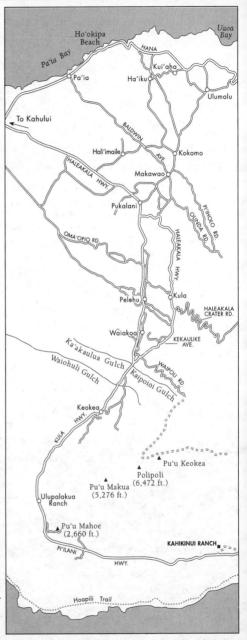

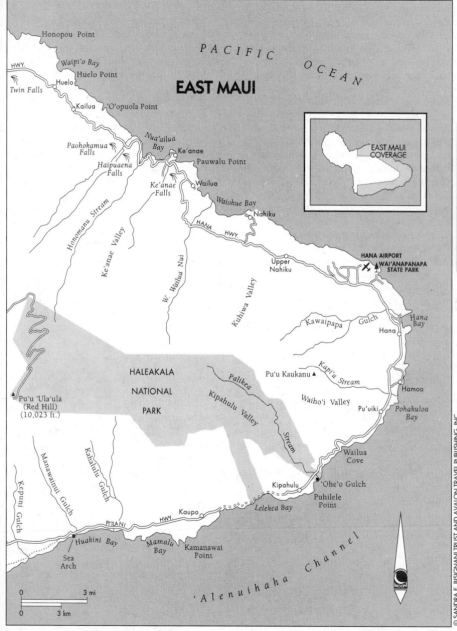

EAST MAUI

PACIFIC OCEAN

Honopou Point

Waipi'o Bay

Huelo Point

HWY.

Huelo

Twin Falls

Kailua

'O'opuola Point

Nua'ailua Bay

Ke'anae

Paohokamua Falls

Haipuaena Falls

Ke'anae Falls

Pauwalu Point

Wailua

Honomanu Stream

Ke'anae Valley

W. Wailua Nui

Waiohue Bay

Nahiku

HANA HWY.

EAST MAUI COVERAGE

Upper Nahiku

HANA AIRPORT

WAI'ANAPANAPA STATE PARK

Kuhiwa Valley

Kawaipapa Gulch

Hana Bay

Hana

HALEAKALA NATIONAL PARK

Pu'u 'Ula'ula (Red Hill) (10,023 ft.)

Palikea

Kipahulu Valley

Pu'u Kaukanu

Kapi'a Stream

Waiho'i Valley

Hamoa

Pu'uiki

Pohakuloa Bay

Manawainui Gulch

Kahalulu Gulch

Kepuni Gulch

Stream

Wailua Cove

Kipahulu

'Ohe'o Gulch

Puhilele Point

PI'ILANI HWY.

Kaupo

Lelekea Bay

Huakini Bay

Sea Arch

Mamalu Bay

Kamanawai Point

'Alenuihaha Channel

0   3 mi

0   3 km

MOON

EAST MAUI

into townsfolk and have pumped new life into
Pa'ia's old muscles. The practical shops catering
to the pragmatic needs of a plantation town
were replaced. The storefronts were painted
and spruced up. A new breed of merchants
with their eyes on passing tourists has taken
over. Now Pa'ia focuses on boutiques, crafts,
artwork, and food. It also has a golf course in
Spreckelsville, a high-end residential neighborhood to the west. Opened in 1925, this
well-kept private course, the Maui Country
Club, is the oldest functioning golf course on
the island. Since you've got to pass through on
your way to Hana, it serves as a great place not
only to top off your gas tank, but also to stop
for a bite and a browse. The prices are good
for just about everything, and the nearby village
of Ku'au boasts one of the island's best fish
restaurants. Pa'ia, under its heavy makeup, is
still a vintage example of what it always was—
a homey, serviceable, working town.

There is a large new public parking lot at
the west end of Pa'ia, across the highway from
the Maui Crafts Guild. Because Pa'ia is so
small, it's best to leave your car here and walk
around town.

Sights

A mile or so before you enter Pa'ia on the left is
Rinzai Zen Mission—reached by going through
H. P. Baldwin Park. The grounds are pleasant
and worth a look. **Mantokuji Buddhist Temple**
on the eastern outskirts of Pa'ia heralds the sun's
rising and setting by ringing its huge gong 18
times at dawn and dusk. Built in 1921, this temple is a fine example of a Zen mission structure
and perhaps the best representative on Maui.
The yearly *obon* festival is celebrated here with
ceremony and dance.

H.P. Baldwin Beach County Park is on
your left about seven miles past Kahului on
Route 36, just past Maui Country Club and
the well-to-do community of Spreckelsville.
This spacious park is good for swimming, shell-
collecting, and decent winter surfing. It has
full amenities. Unfortunately, hassles and rob-
beries have been known to occur—there are a
lot of "park at your own risk" signs. Be nice,
calm, and respectful. At the far western end of
this beach, with access through the community of Spreckelsville, is a protected spot that's
just fine for kids.

Ho'okipa Beach County Park is about 10

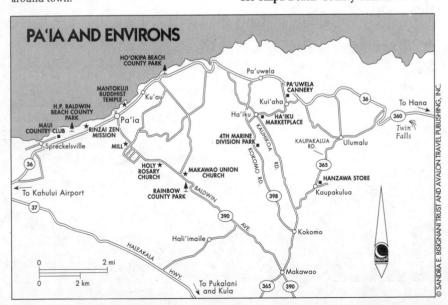

PA'IA AND ENVIRONS

© SANDRA E. BISIGNANI TRUST AND AVALON TRAVEL PUBLISHING, INC.

Still serving its congregation, Mantokuji Buddhist Temple continues to foster the beliefs brought to the islands by early Japanese immigrants.

minutes past Pa'ia. There's a high, grassy sand dune along the road, and the park is down below, where you'll enjoy full amenities—unofficial camping occurs. Swimming is advisable only on calm days because there are wicked currents. Primarily a surfing beach that is now regarded as one of the best sailboarding areas in Hawaii, this is home to the Aloha Classic, held yearly in October or November. The world's best sailboarders come here, trying to win the substantial prize money. Bring binoculars.

Accommodations

One of the few place to lodge in Pa'ia is at the **Nalu Kai Lodge,** 808/579-8009, located down the alley just off the T intersection where Baldwin Avenue meets the Hana Highway; ask for Myrna. This plain and simple two-story cement-block building offers clean, quiet, adequate rooms. Don't expect anything fancy, just the necessities; no TV and no telephones, linoleum floors, and fans in some rooms. Rates vary—Myrna bargains—but expect to spend about $40 for one night or $350 for a month. There are seven units, one double and six singles. Many people stay long-term.

Surfers and others looking for very inexpensive accommodations can find space in a house at 151 Hana Highway, only a few steps from the center of Pa'ia. Basically a house turned into a rental pad, where dorm beds go for $20 per day and a private room $40 per day. Call 808/579-8015 for more information.

Just east of Pa'ia, before you get to Ku'au, is **The Spyglass House,** 367 Hana Hwy., Paia, HI 96779, 808/579-8608 or 800/475-6695, relax@spyglass-maui.com, www.spyglassmaui.com. With rooms and suites, or combinations thereof, in three houses, it has plenty of options to choose from. Set nearly on the water with a hot tub in the yard, this is a restful, breezy, modern place with bright colors and a marine motif. Rooms in the main house run $120–150 per night, in the Dolphin House $90–120. Next door, the Blue Tile House has rooms and two suites for $90–250. Rentals for fewer than three nights are charged a $30 cleaning fee.

About a mile away in the tiny community of Ku'au is the **Kuau Plaza Condo,** 808/579-8080, fax 808/579-8533. Rooms have private baths and color televisions. Laundry facilities are located on premises. These rooms are nothing special, but they get you close to Maui's best surfing spots, and it's just a skip down the road from Pa'ia. Rooms and suites generally run $40–70 per night.

Fronting the beach next to Mama's Fish House is **The Inn at Mama's Fish House,** 799 Poho Place, Paia, HI 96779, 808/579-9764 or 800/860-4852, fax 808/579-8594, www.mamasfishhouse.com. Close to the action but not bothered by the hubbub of town, this is very much a tropical hideaway. Hidden by foliage from the restaurant and the neighbor houses, one-bedroom and two-bedroom units, each nicely furnished, come complete with a modern kitchen and entertainment center, air-conditioning, telephone, and lanai with gas grill. The one-bedroom unit runs $175 per night, while the larger units go for $350; three nights minimum.

For all sorts of vacation rentals in Pa'ia, the Northshore, and other areas of the island, contact **Ho'okipa Haven Vacation Services,** 808/579-8282 or 800/398-6284, fax 808/579-9953, info@hookipa.com, www.hookipa.com. This company has rental units from studios along a stream for $70 per night to luxury homes for more than $1,000 per night.

Food

There are more than a handful of restaurants in and around Pa'ia that cater to all type of palates. The following is a sampling, listed roughly from inexpensive to expensive.

Offering an alternative for the java jock is the easygoing **Anthony's Coffee,** on Baldwin Avenue, 808/579-8340, where you can get coffee by the cup or a pound to go. Come for breakfast and pastries or try a lunch sandwich or ice cream as you hang out and read the paper.

Picnic's, 30 Baldwin Ave., 808/579-8021, is open daily 7 A.M.–3 P.M. Breakfast and lunch offer everything from eggs and pancakes to plate lunches and vegetarian sandwiches, like the famous spinach nut burger, all under $8. The best options are boxed picnic lunches that add a special touch if you're heading to Hana. They start from the basic Upcountry Picnic, which includes sandwiches and sides at $8.50 per person, to the Holo Holo Pikiniki for four, with all the fixings for sandwiches, herb-roasted chicken, sides,

condiments, dessert, and even a tablecloth all in a Styrofoam ice chest for $52. Picnic's is one of the best stops along the Hana Road even for a quick espresso, cappuccino, or frozen yogurt. Or treat yourself with the fresh-baked pastries like macadamia nut sticky buns and the apple and papaya turnovers: worth the guilt!

The **Hokus Pokus,** 115 Baldwin Ave., 808/579-9144, open daily 3–9 P.M., is an extraordinary health-conscious restaurant that those into healthy food frequent. You won't come here for the decor, you'll come for the large portions of incredibly delicious food. Hokus Pokus serves only vegetarian food made with organic products and uses no meat; the food is mostly cholesterol-free. Standard menu items include hummus salad at $6.50, the tempeh burger for $5.95, tofu soft tacos for $9.50, curry veggies at $10.95, and polenta au gratin for $9.95; specials nightly. Luscious smoothies are priced at $3.25. Sit at one of the few tables inside, or call ahead for orders to go.

At the corner is the **Paia Fish Market,** 808/579-8030, a casual sit-down restaurant with picnic tables inside. Specializing in charbroiled fish, the menu also includes more than a dozen types of fish and seafood, all at market price, that can be prepared in one of four different manners. You can also have charbroiled chicken, blackened sashimi, seafood salad, or fresh fish to take home and prepare yourself. Open for lunch and dinner 11 A.M.–9:30 P.M., the menu also includes burgers, pasta, and fajitas. Most lunch and dinner plates run $7–15, but the fish entrées may be more expensive. This is a perennial favorite.

Cafe des Amis, 42 Baldwin Ave., 808/579-6323, is a small eatery featuring a mixture of French and Indian foods. On the menu are crepes, like spinach with feta, ham and gruyere, or roast vegetables, feta, and pesto for $6–8. Dinner entrées might include beef and mushroom, shrimp, or vegetable curries in the $9–12 range. Coffee, tea, smoothies, and lassi are available to drink, but you can bring your own bottle of wine if you like. Open 8:30 A.M.–8:30 P.M., you'll find Cafe des Amis an intimate place with energetic music and food that will delight your taste buds.

For a quick bite, you have **Charley's,** 808/579-

9453, a restaurant specializing in pizza, pasta, and sandwiches that's open 7 A.M. for breakfast, from 11:30 for lunch, and from 5 P.M. for dinner. Charley's is a gathering place for breakfast and has items like huevos rancheros for $7.95. For lunch, select a fish sandwich for $8.25 or burgers for around $9. Some dinner specials, like fettuccini Alfredo at about $15, are more pricey but still very reasonable. Soups, salads, and appetizers are priced equally well. In the back is a saloon with a long bar, booths, pool tables, and occasional live music. This is a big, rambling, amiable place, a town institution, where tourists and locals alike come for a pleasant time, and the bar is a good afternoon hangout for locals.

Across the street and also on the corner, a great place to people-watch or be watched is **Milagros Bar and Restaurant,** 808/579-8755. Milagros does burgers, sandwiches, and fish; eat inside or outside on the patio along the sidewalk. This is semi-Mexican fare with sandwiches and burgers in the $6–8 range and dinners like seafood enchiladas and grilled ahi burritos mostly $12–16. Milagros has a full bar so you can ease into the evening with a tropical margarita, south-of-the-border beer, glass of fine wine, or well drink.

Having moved up the street, reworked the menu, and created a whole new environment, **Jacques Northshore,** 808/579-8844, is now a festive, colorful, happening restaurant and bar with outdoor lanai seating under umbrellas and an indoor sushi bar. Whether it's meat or fish, Jacques serves the freshest. Lunch brings a long list of appetizers, many sandwiches, and a few main entrées all under $12, but perhaps the dinner menu is more memorable. Start with a pumpkin coconut soup with diced scallops or shiitake salmon shrimp coconut ravioli appetizer, or a fried tofu salad or salad Niçoise. Several pasta dishes are favorites, but entrées like fresh fish, oven-roasted pork, spicy peanut chicken, sautéed beef, or seafood curry are special. Dinner entrées run mostly $16–20. A lively place with food at a reasonable price make Jacques a winner.

Moana Bakery and Cafe, 71 Baldwin Ave., 808/579-9999, is another good choice. Food is served 8 A.M.–9 P.M., and baked goods are always available from the deli case. Breakfast is mostly egg dishes, griddle items, and saimin, while lunch choices include salads, sandwiches, and wraps. Dinner is more substantial, with dishes like island pesto pasta, chili-seared ahi, and medallions of filet mignon, $11–27. To top it off, there's live jazz or Hawaiian music on some evenings—no cover.

Mama's Fish House, 808/579-8488, where reservations are highly recommended, is just past Pa'ia in Ku'au and on the left heading toward Hana. Look for the turnoffs near the blinking yellow light; you'll see a vintage car with a sign for Mama's, a ship's flagpole, and a fishing boat marking the entranceway. There's plenty of off-road complimentary valet parking. Mama's, serving lunch 11 A.M.–2:30 P.M., cocktails and *pu pu* until dinner at 5 P.M., has earned the best reputation possible—it gets thumbs up from local people even though it is expensive. It's perhaps the best upscale beach shack on the island, set right on the water surrounded by coconut trees and tiki torches with outrigger canoes drawn up on the lawn out front. The fish is caught fresh daily, with some broiled over *kiawe,* while the vegetables come from local gardens and the herbs are Mama's own. Fish entrées run $30–39 for dinner, other items are $29–49. For a meal with the same special flavors but a bit easier on the pocketbook, stop by for lunch. Special Hawaiian touches, wonderful food, friendly professional service, and a great view of Maui's north shore add to the enjoyment of every meal. A terrific idea is to make reservations here for the evening's return trip from Hana.

For groceries and foodstuffs, try the following: **Mana Natural Foods,** 49 Baldwin Ave., 808/579-8078, open daily 8:30 A.M.–8:30 P.M., is a well-stocked health food store, one of the best on Maui, that's kind of funky and still not "modernized." Inside the old building you'll find shelves full of local organic produce, vitamins, grains, juices, bulk foods, and more. For takeout, try the salad bar for about $5 per pound or the hot entrée bar with items at various prices, or look for picnic items in the cooler. Outside, check out the great community bulletin board for what's selling and happening around Pa'ia and to find rental housing.

Just before Baldwin Avenue along the Hana Highway is **Nagata Store,** a general grocery store with a seafood department that's open Monday–Friday 6 A.M.–7 P.M., Saturday 6 A.M.–6 P.M., Sunday 6 A.M.–1 P.M.

The **Wine Cooler,** at the corner of Baldwin Ave. and the Hana Hwy., is a well-stocked bottle shop with a superb selection of wines, liquor, and ice-cold beer. Microbreweries are well represented. Open 11 A.M.–9:30 P.M. most days and until 10 P.M. on some days.

Shopping

Maui Crafts Guild, 43 Hana Hwy., P.O. Box 609, Pa'ia, HI 96779, 808/579-9697, www.mauicraftsguild.com, is on the left just as you enter Pa'ia. Open daily 9 A.M.–6 P.M., the Crafts Guild is one of the best art outlets in Hawaii. It's owned and operated by the artists themselves, now numbering more than two dozen, all of whom must pass a thorough jurying by present members. All artists must be islanders, and they must use natural materials found in Hawaii to create their work except for some specialized clay, fabrics, and printmaking paper. Items are tastefully displayed, and you'll find a wide variety of artwork and crafts, including pottery, prints, woodwork, stone art, bamboo work, fiber art, silk painting, and jewelry. Different artists staff the shop on different days, but business cards and phone numbers are available if you want to see more of something you like. Prices are reasonable, and this is an excellent place to make that one big purchase.

Along the Hana Highway before you get to Baldwin Avenue is **Paia Trading Co.,** a discovery shop open Monday–Friday 9 A.M.–5 P.M. with collectibles like glass, telephones, aloha shirts, lanterns, jewelry, license plates, oil lamps, flotation balls, old bottles, and a smattering of pottery and antique furniture. Next door is **Boutique II,** open daily 10 A.M.–6 P.M., Sunday to 4 P.M., filled with ladies' apparel and alohawear. **Nuage Bleu,** a boutique open daily 10 A.M.–5 P.M., features distinctive fashions and gift items, mostly for women. **Jaggers,** open daily 9 A.M.–5 P.M., carries alohawear, fancy dresses, replicas of vintage aloha shirts for men, and some umbrellas. **Maui Hands** is nearby and has prints, turned wood, and some

paper art pieces. Across the street is a shaved ice shop and **Sand and Sea,** primarily a sculpture gallery featuring dolphins.

Around the corner and open daily until 6 P.M. is **Paia Mercantile,** displaying a collection of quilts, wooden boxes, hand-blown glass, jewelry, and many more intriguing craft items. Nearby is the **Hemp House,** a shop that carries hemp clothing, bags, accessories, soap, smoking paraphernalia, and information on hemp fiber and its uses. Here too is **Moon Beam Tropics,** carrying women's sundresses, men's aloha shirts, shorts, T-shirts, and other islandwear. Walk along the opposite side of Baldwin Avenue for a half block and you'll find a drawerful of boutiques and fashion shops, including **Old Plantation Store** for Hawaiian gifts, crafts, and clothing; **Lotus Moon** for jewelry, **Neccesaries Boutique** antique and curio shop of "Hawaiian Bohemian Funk;" and **Mandala Ethnic Arts,** which carries furniture, clothing, gifts, statues, and alternative art from South and Southeast Asia. All are interesting shops and worth a peek.

A bit farther along Baldwin Avenue is a branch **Bank of Hawaii** building and quite a bit farther up the new **post office** and laundromat. For the windsurfer, look for boards and gear at **HT High Tech Surf Sports.** At this and other surf shops in town, you can dress yourself for the beach and get a board to ride over those waves.

Pa'ia has three **gas stations: 76,** which has made-to-order sandwiches at its minimart, a **Chevron,** and a newer **Shell** station on the west end of town with a mini-mart. These gas stations are the last places to fill your tank before reaching Hana. Next door to the 76 station is **Paia General Store** (open until 9 P.M.) for groceries, supplies, and sundries, with a take-out snack window called the **Paia Drive Inn** (6 A.M.–2 P.M.), where most "local food" is under $7. Next to that, in what was at one time the Lower Pa'ia Theater, is **Simmer** sailboard shop. Simmer sells clothing, boards, components, and accessories, does sail repair, and rents boards. Lessons can also be arranged. Across the street is the **Pa'ia Mercantile Shopping Complex,** a collection of little shops ranging from surfing equipment to beads and gifts.

Heading down the road to Hana you'll see a community center on your right, the Mantokuji Buddhist temple on your left, and a little farther on the **Kuau Market,** a convenience store to get snacks for the road that's open daily 6 A.M.–7 P.M. Just around the bend is **Mama's Fish House,** and shortly after Ho'okipa Beach, near mile marker 14 on the mountain side of the highway, you'll come across **Maui Grown Market and Deli.** Housed in a vintage corrugated roof plantation-style building with a porch out front, it carries mostly sandwiches, plate lunches, salads, smoothies, drinks, and packaged food items, with a limited supply of fresh produce. Lunch boxes are a specialty. Open daily 6:30 A.M.–6 P.M., this is the last place you'll see before you really start to wind your way down the Hana Highway. A public phone is out front. Aside from side trips to Ha'iku, Kui'aha, and Ulumalu, you'll have clear sailing down the road to Hana.

HA'IKU

Around mile marker 11, Ha'iku Road heads up the hill to the little community of Ha'iku. From Upcountry, follow Kokomo Road down the hill after turning off Route 365 below Makawao. Kokomo Road runs past the 4th Marine Division Park, a community park of athletic fields and a few picnic tables that was the site of the World War II 4th Marine Division camp. Ha'iku is an old cannery town, canning, boxing, and sending millions of pineapples and guavas to the world over the decades. After the cannery companies stopped production, their industrial buildings were renovated and turned into shops and studios, and have become, along with the Pa'uwela Cannery down the road, a center for artists and craftspeople. In the largest of the old cannery buildings, the pineapple cannery, now called **Ha'iku Marketplace,** you'll find among the many shops here a **True Value Hardware** store, the **Haleakala Bike Company** shop for sales and rental, **Haiku Video, Ha'iku Pharmacy, Ha'iku Laundromat, Postal Plus, Colleen's Bakeshop and Haiku Cannery Pizza,** and the **Ha'iku Grocery Store,** open daily and a good place to pick up supplies. For what's happening in and around town, check out the community bulletin board around the side. To the side of the huge parking lot in a separate building is **Hana Hou Cafe,** 808/575-2661, a wonderful local-style eatery that has indoor and patio seating with a take-out window with the same menu. And what's more, there's live music by the owner on Thursday, Friday, and Saturday evenings. The menu contains mostly plate lunches, but pasta, burgers, and full meal dinners are also available, and most items run $7–17.

Also at the main intersection is **Fukushima Store,** a mini-mart that's open daily 6:30 A.M.–8 P.M., Sunday until 5 P.M. Here too you'll find a community bulletin board. For a quick bite to eat, stop around the corner at **Haiku Gourmet Takeout and Deli,** a small place with only a few tables inside. Open 6 A.M.–8 P.M., you have your choice of breakfast items, deli salads, pastries, and sandwiches, and in the evening, more substantial entrées like prime rib, spicy chicken, and Thai veggie stir-fry for around $12. Across Ha'iku Road is the **post office,** and tucked behind it is **Ha'iku Town Center,** the second of the big remodeled cannery buildings that's been turned into space for other use. This was the guava cannery. Among other shops you'll find **The Hemp Stock,** a small shop dealing almost entirely with the numerous and various products made from the hemp plant. Stop by daily 10 A.M.–5 P.M. to see what great products they carry, most of it made in the studio in back. Check out what they have or order online at www.sativahempwear.com. Just up the line is **Veg Out,** 808/575-5320, a vegetarian restaurant open Monday–Friday 10:30 A.M.–7:30 P.M. and Saturday 11:30–6. Every Saturday from 8 A.M.–noon, you can find a **farmers market** in front of this center for local produce and crafts.

Ha'iku Road runs east, wending its way in and out of gulches, over bridges, and through thickly vegetated forests to the community of Kui'aha. This is a great way to see the back roads of lower mountain Maui. There are lots of roads in this area, and many people have settled here, carving out their little bit of paradise. An alternate road to Kuiaha from the Hana Highway starts just past mile marker 12. Look for West Kui'aha Road and make a right heading for the old

Pa'uwela Cannery, which is less than five minutes up the road. This huge tin can of a building has been divided into a honeycomb of studios and workshops housing fine artists, woodworkers, potters, T-shirt makers, and surfboard and sailboard makers. These artists and craftspeople come and go, so you're never sure just who will be occupying the studios. **Hawaiian Fish Prints Gallery** is one of these places. It's unique focus is making color prints from actual sea creatures. While here, be sure to stop at the **Pauwela Cafe** for a cold drink, hot coffee, salad, sandwich, or pastry. Sit inside or out. Open Monday–Saturday 7 A.M.–3 P.M., Sunday 8 A.M.–2 P.M. For other needs, try the small **Ohashi General Store** across and a bit up the street; open 8 A.M. to about 6 P.M.

Not situated along the coast but in the forest above Ulumalu is **Lanikai Farm,** P.O. Box 797, Ha'iku, HI 96708, 808/572-1111 or 800/484-2523, fax 808/572-3498, lanibb@maui.net, www.maui.net/~lanibb. This "Victorian-European style" newer home lies next to the Ko'olau Forest Reserve and is surrounded by tropical fruit trees. The guest rooms have private entrances, TVs, small refrigerators, and lanai, and there is use of the washer/dryer and barbecue grill. A scrumptious breakfast of European-style breads and fresh fruit is served every morning. Rates are $65 single, $70 double, or $100 for two rooms; two nights minimum. A studio rental without breakfast runs $80 or two rooms for $105. The athletically inclined might want to have a turn on the squash court on property.

Just down the road at 81 Lanikai Place is **Lanikai Vacation Rentals.** Set next to a stream and small waterfall, this property has two rental units. The Garden Suite is a quiet two-bedroom, two-bath unit with full kitchen that goes for $95 per night or $600 per week. Around back and more secluded is Hale Nahele, a one-room unit with a small kitchen and deck that overhangs the streambank. Perfect for a romantic couple, this unit runs $75 per night or $450 per week. Three nights minimum for either unit; cash or traveler's checks please. For information and reservations, contact Dharmo Feldmann, tel/fax 808/573-0750, lanikaivacations@maui.net, www.maui.net/~dharmo/lanikai.

THE ROAD BEGINS

The Road to Hana holds many spectacles and surprises, but one of the best is the road itself . . . it's a marvel! The road was hacked out from the coastline and completed in 1927, every inch by hand using pick and shovel. Crushed volcanic rock was the first surface material. Rebuilt and partially paved in 1962, only in 1982 was the road fully paved. Mother nature and man's machines have taken their toll on the road, and in the early '90s, the Hana Highway was widened and again resurfaced. Today it's smooth sailing, although stretches are periodically closed for repair. An ancient Hawaiian trail followed the same route for part of the way, but mostly people moved up and down this coastline by boat. What makes the scenery so special is that the road snakes along Maui's windward side. There's abundant vegetation and countless streams flowing from Haleakala, carving gorgeous valleys. There are a few scattered villages with a house or two that you hardly notice, and the beaches, although few, are empty. Mostly, however, it's the feeling that you get along this road. Nature is close and accessible, and it's so incredibly "South Sea island" that it almost seems artificial—but it isn't.

SIGHTS

Twin Falls

A favorite of locals, the trail to Twin Falls should take about 20–30 minutes. It's one of the first places to stop and enjoy along the road. Park near mile marker 2 just before the Ho'olawa Bridge. A metal gate marks the jeep trail. This is private property and people live back here, but everyone seems to use it as if it were open to all. There's even a fruit stand at the entrance and a sign along the jeep trail pointing to the falls. On the way, a couple of side trails go off to the left and down to the stream. Guavas grow in this area, and you might find ripe fruit at the right time of the year—there used to be a guava cannery in Ha'iku not far away. Before you get to an irrigation ditch, a small trail heads off to the left and leads to the stream and falls. The

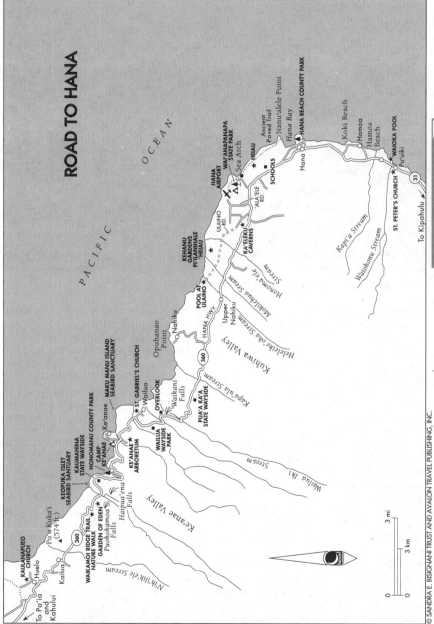

ROAD TO HANA

ROBERT NILSEN

Twin Falls makes a refreshing stop along the road to Hana.

first pool is fed by two falls that give the area its name. A trail to the right goes up to the top of the falls and on to a second falls a short distance above. There you'll have more privacy. If you continue on to the irrigation ditch, cross it, and enter a secondary ravine, the trail will lead you to another small falls.

Huelo

A few miles past the new bridge and pulloff for Twin Falls is Huelo. Huelo means "Famous Owl," a name given for the birds that used to inhabit trees in the area. In the 1840s, Huelo was a bustling sugar town surrounded by cane fields and even sustained a mill. Later, the area grew pineapples and then reverted to a quiet "rooster town." Now it's not a town at all anymore, just a collection of homes and hobie ranches, but it's still known for the **Kaulana-pueo Church,** built in 1853. This structure is made from coral that was hauled up block by block from Waipi'o Bay below and is reminiscent of New England architecture. It's still used on the second and fourth Sundays of each month at 10 A.M., and a peek through the

door will reveal a stark interior with straight-backed benches and a front platform. The pit on the ocean side of the church building was used to make the lime and mortar mix. Few bother to stop here, so it's quiet and offers good panoramas of the village and sea below. At the broad turnoff to Huelo, between mile markers 3 and 4, there's a public telephone and a row of mailboxes.

Kailua

The next tiny community is Kailua. Plenty of mountain apple trees flourish along this stretch. The multicolored trees are rainbow eucalyptus, introduced in the late 1800s from Australia and some of the most beautiful trees in Hawaii. Close by is a cousin, *Eucalyptus robusta,* which produces great timber, especially flooring, from its reddish-brown heartwood. This tree gets extremely hard once it dries because of its resins, so it must be milled immediately or you can do nothing with it. A few minutes beyond Kailua, notice a sudden difference in the humidity and in the phenomenal jungle growth that becomes even more pronounced.

TIPS FOR DRIVING THE ROAD TO HANA

You've got 30 miles of turns ahead when Route 36 (mile marker 22) becomes Route 360 (mile marker 0) and the fun begins. The Hana Highway has the reputation of being a "bad road," but this isn't true. It's narrow, with plenty of hairpin turns, but it's well banked, has clearly marked bridges, and there's frequent maintenance going on (which can slow you up). Years back, it was a harrowing experience. When mudslides blocked the road, drivers were known to swap their cars with those on the opposite side and carry on to where they were going. The road's reputation sets people up to expect an ordeal, so they make it one, and unfortunately, drive accordingly. Sometimes it seems as though tourists demand the road to be rugged, so that they can tell the folks back home that they, too, "survived the road to Hana." This popular slogan appears on T-shirts, copyrighted and sold by Hasegawa's famous store in Hana, and perpetuates this belief. You'll have no problem, though, and you'll see much more if you just take it easy.

Your speed will often drop below 10 miles per hour and will rarely exceed 25. Cloudbursts occur at any time, so be ready for slick roads. A heavy fall of fruit from roadside mango trees can also coat the road with slippery slime. Look as far up the road as possible, and don't allow yourself to be mesmerized by the 10 feet in front of your hood. If your tire dips off a rough shoulder, don't risk losing control by jerking the wheels back on immediately. Ride it for a while and either stop or wait for an even shoulder to come back on. Local people trying to make time will often ride your rear bumper, but generally they won't honk. Pull over and let them by when possible. Pulloffs on this road are not over-abundant, so be sure to choose your spot carefully. As a safety measure and courtesy to others, yield to all oncoming traffic at each bridge.

Driving from Kahului to Hana will take three hours, not counting some recommended stops. The greatest traffic flow is 10 A.M.–noon; returning "car trains" start by 3 P.M. and are heaviest around 5 P.M. Many white-knuckled drivers head for Hana as if it were a prized goal, without stopping along the way. This is ridiculous. The best sights are before and after Hana; the town itself is hardly worth the effort. Expect to spend a long day exploring the Hana Road. To go all the way to 'Ohe'o Stream and take in some sights, you'll have to leave your hotel at sunup and won't get back until sundown. If your budget can afford it, plan on staying the night in Hana (reservations definitely) and return the next day. This is a particularly good plan if you have an afternoon departing flight from Kahului Airport. Also, most tourists seem terrified of driving the road at night. Actually, it can be easier. There is far less traffic, road reflectors mark the center and sides like a runway, and you're warned of oncoming cars by their headlights. Those in the know make much better time after dark! In case of **emergency,** roadside telephones are located *makai* between mile markers 5 and 6, at the Halfway to Hana roadside stand, and at Pua'a Ka'a State Wayside. Less than 3,000 people live along the entire north coast of East Maui leading to and including Hana.

Waikamoi Ridge

This nature walk (mosquitoes!) is a good place to stretch your legs and learn about native and introduced trees and vegetation (some are labeled). The turnout, good for about half a dozen vehicles, is not clearly marked along the highway past mile marker 9, but look for a metal gate at roadside and picnic tables in a clearing above the road. The well-defined, gradual trail leads through tall stands of trees. You know that you're on the right path when you pass the signboard that says "Quiet, trees at work." This trail is about one mile long and takes less than an hour. On the way, you will get glimpses of the highway and stream below. For those never before exposed to a bamboo forest, it's most interesting when the wind rustles the trees so they knock together like natural percussion instruments. Picnic tables are available at the start and end of the trail. Tall mango trees tower over the upper picnic area. Return via the same trail or walk down the jeep path.

Back on the road, and at the next bridge, is excellent drinking water. There's a stone barrel with a pipe coming out, and local people come to fill jugs with what they call "living water." It doesn't always run in summer but most times can be counted on. About one-half mile beyond Waikamoi Ridge the road crosses another stream where there's limited parking. Walk along the stream a short way to this waterfalls. Although it may be slippery, you can go around the right side and up to another falls and cascade. Back on the road, you can see still other falls that are much farther up this valley.

Garden of Eden

This finely landscaped property is a private arboretum and botanical garden. Entrance $7.50; open daily 8 A.M.–3 P.M. Have a stroll here among the 26 acres of tropical trees and flowering bushes, more than 500 of which are labeled for easy identification, or walk out to the Puohokamoa Falls overlook, where you have a fine view down onto this graceful waterfall. There are restrooms here and a place to picnic, so make a stop on your way down the road.

Puohokamoa Falls

At mile marker 11, you'll find this nice pool and picnic table. A short trail will take you to the

pool and its 30-foot cliff, from which local kids jump off. You'll also find a trail near the falls, and if you go upstream about 100 yards you'll discover another invigorating pool with yet another waterfall. Swimming is great here, and the small crowd may be gone. If you hike downstream about one-half mile *through* the stream (no trail), you come to the top of a 200-foot falls from where you can peer over the edge. Be very conscious of water conditions and the dangers of being near the cliff edge.

Wayside Rest and Park

Less than two miles past Waikamoi Ridge are **Kaumahina State Wayside,** along the road, and the largely undeveloped **Honomanu County Park** down at Honomanu Bay. Some people camp here unofficially with splendid views out to sea overlooking the rugged coastline and the black-sand and rock beach of Honomanu Bay. Honomanu is not good for swimming because of strong currents but is good for surfing. Two dirt roads, one on either side of the stream, lead to it. There are no amenities at Honomanu, but Kaumahina has picnic tables and restrooms. From Kaumahina, you're rewarded with splendid

Ke'anae Peninsula, as seen from the highway, is one of the most productive taro-producing areas of the island.

views down the coast to the Keʻanae Peninsula. Slicing deep into the heart of the mountain, Honomanu Valley has 3,000-foot cliffs and 1,000-foot waterfalls.

Keʻanae

Running back about five miles toward the center of the mountain, Keʻanae Valley is the largest on the north side of Haleakala. It and the Kaupo Valley on the mountain's southern slope were filled in by lava flows or landslides, greatly reducing their original size.

Usually clearly marked on the right side of the highway—the sign at times has gone missing—will be the six-acre **Keʻanae Arboretum,** established in 1971. A hike through this facility will exemplify Hawaiian plant life in microcosm. There are two sections, one of ornamental tropical plants (identified) and the other of Hawaiian domestic plants. Toward the upper end of the arboretum are taro fields, and the hillsides above are covered with the natural rainforest vegetation. You can picnic along Piʻinaʻau Stream. Although the trail is hard to pick out, hardier hikers can continue for another mile or so through the rainforest; at the end of the trail is a pool and waterfall. Because there is a gate across the entrance to the arboretum (located at a sharp curve in the road), pull well off the road to park your car and walk in.

YMCA Camp Keanae, 808/248-8355, fax 808/248-8492, YMCACampKeanae@aol.com, is just before the arboretum. It looks exactly as its name implies, set on a gorgeous, grassy slope. There are three bunkhouses (you must provide your own bedding), two bathrooms with showers, a gymnasium, and for large groups only, a dining room and kitchen. Tent camping is allowed on the lawn; bring your own cooking gear. Arrival time is between 3 and 9 P.M., three-day maximum stay, $15 per person or $30 per family. Y members have reduced rates. Overlooking the entire area with views over the ocean are two cottages that sleep up to four and rent for $115 per unit. All accommodations and camping space are by reservation only.

Keʻanae Peninsula is a thumblike appendage of land formed by a lava flow that came down the hollowed-out valley from Haleakala Crater. Its rocky shoreline is a favorite of local fishermen, perhaps appropriate because *keʻanae* means "mullet." A fantastic lookout is here—look for a telephone pole with a tsunami loudspeaker atop it at mile marker 17, and pull off just there. Below you'll see neat little farms, mostly raising taro. Shortly before this lookout, and about 200 yards past the arboretum, a public road heads down into the peninsula, arcing around to a turnaround and parking area past the church. If you walk, park well off the roadway just as you get down the hill. About one mile, this stroll should take less than half an hour, but you may want to stop to chat. Most people living here are native Hawaiians. They still make poi the old-fashioned way: Listen for the distinctive thud of poi-pounding in the background. Although *kapu* signs abound, most people are friendly, and someone has even set up a fruit stand. If you visit, be aware that this is one of the last patches of ground owned by Hawaiians and tended in the old way. Be respectful, please. Notice the lava-rock missionary church. Built in 1860, **Lanikili ʻIhi ʻIhi O Lehowa O na Kaua Church** was rebuilt in 1969. Neat and clean, it has straight-back, hardwood pews and a pleasant altar inside. Services are held twice a month. The cemetery to the side is groomed with tropical flowers, while the grounds are rimmed by tall coconut trees. A ballpark and public telephone stand next to the church.

Fruit Stands

Past Keʻanae between mile markers 17 and 18 is the **Halfway to Hana** roadside refreshment stand, where you can buy banana bread, shave ice, ice cream, sandwiches, fruit, and something to drink. Notice the picture-perfect, idyllic watercress farm on your left.

Do yourself a favor and look for **Uncle Harry's Fruit Stand,** clearly marked on the left past the Keʻanae Peninsula just beyond the Keʻanae school. Unfortunately, this *kahuna*, who knew a great deal of the natural pharmacology of old Hawaii and was a living encyclopedia on herbs and all their healing properties, has passed away, but his spirit lives on.

Other fruit stands pop up now and again on

this road. It's just a down-home cottage industry. No definite times necessarily, just open when they are. Look for them as you pass, stop to refresh yourself, and leave a little for the local economy.

Wailua

At mile marker 18, you come to Wailua, a picturesque spot. Similar to Ke'anae, it too is covered in taro but not to as great an extent. Turn left here on Wailua Road and proceed to **St. Gabriel's Church.** Set at the back of the lawn to the side near the cemetery you'll find the **Miracle of Fatima Shrine,** so named because a freak storm in the 1860s washed up enough coral onto Wailua Beach that the church could be constructed by the Hawaiian congregation. There is a lovely and relatively easy-access waterfall nearby. Pass the church, turn right when you get to the bottom of the hill, and park by the large field. Look for a worn path (may be private, but no signs or hassle) that leads down to the falls. Look inland up the valley and you'll see a long sliver of a falls just below the roadway that clings to the *pali.* You can look down on this village and valley from several pulloffs and the Wailua Wayside Park, all past the Wailua Road turnoff along the Hana Highway.

Plenty of mountain apple trees flourish along the stretch to Kailua. The multi-colored trees are rainbow eucalyptus, introduced in the late 1800s from Australia and some of the most beautiful trees in Hawaii.

Wailua Wayside Park

Cut into the ridge directly along the roadway is the small parking lot of this tiny wayside park. Drive slowly and keep your eyes peeled because the sign comes up quickly and you have little time to signal your turn to get off the road. A short series of steps leads up under a canopy of overhanging *hao* tree branches to a flat, grassy area about 20 feet above the road. From here you have an expansive view down onto Wailua and up along the face of the *pali.* From the rear of the parking area, you can peer into the adjoining *mauka* valley, and when it rains you can see several waterfalls cascading down the valley walls inland. No facilities are available. From here,

you can see the Ke'anae Valley and Ko'olau Gap. Look closely. From this vantage point it is obvious how lava and rubble from the Haleakala basin poured down the mountain, filling this once deep-cut valley. A pulloff on the ocean side of the roadway about one-half mile farther provides you with perhaps a better view down into Wailua Valley.

Pua'a Ka'a State Wayside

This spot is about 14 miles before Hana. There's no camping, but there are a few picnic tables and restrooms. Across the road from the parking lot is a short path that leads to Kopili'ula and Waikani Falls. A very public place, it's not the best scenery along the road, and these are not the best pools for swimming.

Nahiku

The village, named after the Hawaiian version of the Pleiades, is reached by a steep but now paved three-mile road and has the dubious distinction of being one of the wettest spots along the coast. Turn near mile marker 25. The well-preserved and tiny village church near the bottom of the road was constructed in 1867 (renovated in 1993) and is just big enough for a handful of pews. You may see school kids playing ball in the yard next to the church, the only place in the community that's open and large enough. The turnaround at oceanside is where many locals come to shore-fish. Often during the summer, an extended family pod of dolphins enters Nahiku Bay in the afternoon to put on an impromptu performance of water acrobatics just for the joy of it. At one time Nahiku was a thriving Hawaiian village with thousands of inhabitants. Today it's home to only about 70 people. A few inhabitants are Hawaiian families, but mostly the people are wealthy Mainlanders seeking isolation. After a few large and attractive homes went up, the real estate agents changed the description from "desolate" to "secluded." What's the difference? About $1 million per house! In the early

1900s, this was the site of the Nahiku Rubber Co., the only commercial rubber plantation in the United States. Many rubber trees still line the road, although the venture collapsed in 1912 because the rubber was poor as a result of the overabundance of rainfall. Some people have augmented their incomes by growing *pakalolo* in the rainforest of this area; however, the alternative-lifestyle people who first came here and have settled in have discovered that there is just as much money to be made raising ornamental tropical flowers and have become real "flower children." Many have roadside stands along the Hana Highway, where payment for the flowers displayed is on the honor system. Leave what is requested—prices will be marked.

Near mile marker 29 in Upper Nahiku, you'll come upon **Nahiku Ti Gallery** for gifts and crafts, a pastry and refreshment shop, and a little stand selling baked breadfruit bread and smoked fish kebabs.

ACCOMMODATIONS

Several bed-and-breakfast establishments and similar accommodations lie along the road to Hana, many at or near Huelo. Only a few are listed as follows.

Surrounded by trees, bamboo, and wildflowers, **Halfway to Hana House,** P.O. Box 675, Haiku, HI 96708, 808/572-1176, fax 808/572-3609, gailp@maui.net, www.maui.net/~gailp, is a small and peaceful getaway with views over the lush north coast. As a one-studio apartment on the lower level of the house, there are no distracting noises. Its private entrance leads into a comfortable room with double bed and mini kitchen. In a separate room is the bath, and a breakfast patio is out the back. Breakfast of pastries and fruit from the property is waiting every morning if you desire. The room rate is $100 double with breakfast, $85 without; three nights minimum, 10 percent discount for a week or more. A kayak and scuba enthusiast, the owner can tell you about good ocean spots to visit.

Hono Hu'aka Tropical Plantation, P.O. Box 600, Haiku, HI 96708, 808/573-1391, fax 808/573-0141, info@retreatmaui.com, www.re-treatmaui.com, down behind Kaulanapueo Church on a 300-foot cliff above Waipi'o Bay, is a peaceful 38-acre retreat and alternative working plantation farm. This place retains a connection to the past in the guise of a *heiau* while it looks toward the peace and tranquility of the future. The property is dotted with tropical permaculture orchards and gardens, and the stream was blocked to form a naturally heart-shaped pond. Set amid bamboo, a globelike kiva meditation hall sits about the main house and office, below which is a heated swimming pool and spa. The two suites on the garden level of the house rent for $60 per night, or together for $110. The gazebo suite at poolside below the nine-sided office is often used by newlyweds; it runs $100. Overlooking much of the farm and surrounding forested hillsides, the bamboo octagons go for $75–85. Much more of an adventure is the two-story treehouse for $135. The cliff house, set on the precipice of the 300-foot *pali* next to a waterfall, with a commanding view of the bay, is yours for $150. High-season rates run about 20 percent more. Any stay less than three nights requires an additional housekeeping fee. Breakfast of organic fruits from the property, home-baked muffins and croissants, juice, and tea will be placed in your refrigerator for your first morning. After the first day, there is a nominal charge for breakfast if you desire to order it, but you can fix whatever you want because each unit is equipped with a kitchenette. Come, relax, refresh, and reinvigorate, or participate in one of the activities offered.

Also in the community of Huelo, with a spectacular view up the coast toward Hana, is **Huelo Point Lookout,** P.O. Box 790117, Paia, HI 96779, 808/573-0914 or 800/871-8645, fax 808/573-0227, dreamers@maui.net, www.maui.net/~dreamers. Here, the main house and three cottages are scattered around the acreage, which is finely landscaped with tropical trees and bushes. The rock-wall swimming pool is inviting, and a soak in the hot tub under a cloudless night sky befits a day on the island. Wake up to the sound of birds singing in the trees, have your breakfast on the lanai, and spend your day leisurely hanging out here or venture out to see the island sights. Once a fisherman's cottage, surrounded by banana trees and heliconia, the remodeled Star Cottage has an indoor/outdoor bathroom, a solarium, and a queen-size bed and double futon, $185–225. A bit smaller and with views of the mountain, Haleakala Cottage studio has a full kitchen and king-size bed in one room, $185–195. Outside is an enclosed shower and a covered lanai. The Rainbow Cottage is a newer building, renting for $275–345. Downstairs are the living room and kitchen; a 22-foot-tall wall of glass offers the best views of the coast from either floor. Make your way up the handmade wooden spiral staircase to the upstairs bedroom, where a king-size bed lies under a large skylight. Outside is your own private hot tub. The Sunrise Suite in the main house has a wall of sliding-glass doors that faces east for perfect sunrise views, its own kitchen, and a large bath. This suite rents for $345–360 per night, but the entire main house can also be rented for families or groups of up to eight people for $2,650–2,850 per week, one-week minimum. Cash or traveler's checks only; no credit cards accepted.

About one mile down a dirt road near Twin Falls is **Maluhia Hale B&B,** 808/572-2959, P.O. Box 687 Haiku, HI 96708, djg@maui.net, www.maui.net/~djg/cottage.htm. Off the main route, this 2.5-acre quiet and relaxing spot is enveloped by greenery, yet has the wide ocean vista spreading at your feet. A detached open-beam plantation-style cottage, dressed in white, with screened porch and a sitting room has a king-size bed, a nearly full kitchen, and a detached bathing room that has a clawfoot tub and shower; very commodious. The cottage can accommodate three. Light, open, and airy, it rents for $115 per night with breakfast, $20 for an extra person; two nights minimum.

Down at the end of the road is the **Tea House Cottage,** P.O. Box 335, Ha'iku, HI 96708, 808/572-5610, teahouse@maui.net, www.maui teahouse.com. This B&B is "off the grid," generating its own power by photovoltaic cells and collecting its own water. Quiet, with no distractions, from here you have broad views of the ocean. The one cottage has a Japanese feel, with a living room, kitchen, bedroom, and screened lanai; a few steps away is the redwood bathhouse. Art on the walls is by the owner/artist, and it complements the rattan furniture and oriental rugs. The room rate is $120 double or $105 single per night; two nights minimum, seventh night no charge. A daily breakfast is provided. A tunnel through the trees leads you to the house, and walkways run throughout the property, one to a small stupa built some 30 years ago by a Tibetan monk.

The lush and verdant grounds of the **Kailua Maui Gardens,** Box 790189, Paia, HI 96779, 808/572-9726, fax 808/572-3409, info@kailu-amauigardens.com, www.kailuamauigardens.com, is located in the tiny community of Kailua. Set amid a landscape of tropical trees and flowering plants are three cottages and one garden apartment, yet surprisingly each unit maintains a great deal of privacy. The swimming pool, two spas, and two barbecue grills are for everyone's use. With a full kitchen, queen-size bed, full-size futon, and twin bed on the porch, the Aloha Cottage is the largest, sleeps up to five, and goes for $120 for two nights or $110 for three or more. The Jungle Bungalow has a full kitchen and king-size bed; rates are $110 for two nights or $90 for three or more. Smallest is The Love Shack. More intimate yet very comfortable, it has a queen-size bed, and like the Jungle Bungalow, it has a private outdoor shower. It rents for $95 for two nights or $75 for three or more. With one bedroom, a full kitchen and sitting area, and its own entrance, the Garden Apartment is located below the main house but is completely separate and rents for $110 for two nights or $90 for three nights or more. Two nights minimum; weekly rates can be arranged. A continental breakfast is served each morning by the pool.

Hana

Hana is about as pretty a town as you'll find anywhere in Hawaii, but if you're expecting anything stupendous you'll be sadly disappointed. For most it will only be a quick stopover at a store or beach en route to 'Ohe'o Stream: The townsfolk refer to these people as "rent-a-car tourists." The lucky who stay in Hana, or those not worried about time, will find plenty to explore throughout the area. The town is built on rolling hills that descend to Hana Bay; much of the surrounding lands are given over to pasture, while trim cottages wearing flower corsages line the town's little lanes. Before the white man arrived, Hana was a stronghold that was conquered and reconquered by the kings of Maui and those of the north coast of the Big Island. The most strategic and historically laden spot is Ka'uiki Hill, the remnant of a cinder cone that dominates Hana Bay. This area is steeped in Hawaiian legend, and old stories relate that it was the demigod Maui's favorite spot. It's said that he transformed his daughter's lover into Ka'uiki Hill and turned her into the gentle rains that bathe it to this day.

Hana was already a plantation town in the mid-1800s when a hard-boiled sea captain named George Wilfong started producing sugar on his 60 acres there. Later, Danish brothers August and Oscar Unna came to run the plantation, and over the years the laborers came from the standard mixture of Hawaiian, Japanese, Chinese, Portuguese, Filipino, and even Puerto Rican stock. The *luna* were Scottish, German, or American. All have combined to become the people of Hana. After having grown to half a dozen plantations and producing for decades, sugar production faded out by the 1940s and Hana began to die, its population dipping below 500. Just then, San Francisco industrialist Paul Fagan purchased 14,000 acres of what was to become the **Hana Ranch.** Realizing that sugar was *pau,* he replanted his lands in *pangola* range grass and imported 300 Hereford cattle from another holding on Moloka'i. Their white faces staring back at you as you drive past are now a standard part of Hana's scenery. Today, Hana Ranch has about 3,000 acres and raises more than 2,000 head of cattle. Hana's population, at 1,850, is about 48 percent Hawaiian.

Fagan loved Hana and felt an obligation to and affection for its people. He also decided to retire here, and with enough money to materialize just about anything, he decided that Hana could best survive through limited tourism. He built the Ka'uiki Inn, later to become the Hotel Hana-Maui, which catered to millionaires, mostly his friends, and began operation in 1946. Fagan owned a baseball team, the San Francisco Seals, and brought them to Hana in 1946 for spring training. The community baseball field behind the hotel was made for them. This was a brilliant publicity move because sportswriters came along; becoming enchanted with Hana, they gave it a great deal of copy and were probably the first to publicize the phrase "Heavenly Hana." It wasn't long before tourists began arriving.

Unfortunately, the greatest heartbreak in modern Hana history occurred at just about the same time, on April 1, 1946. An earthquake in Alaska's Aleutian Islands sent huge tsunamis that raked the Hana coast. These destroyed hundreds of homes, wiping out entire villages and tragically sweeping away many people. Hana recovered but never forgot. Life went on, and the menfolk began working as *paniolo* on Fagan's spread and during roundup would drive the cattle through town and down to Hana Bay, where they were forced to swim to waiting barges. Other entire families went to work at the hotel, and so Hana lived again. It's this legacy of quietude and old-fashioned *aloha* that attracted people to Hana over the years. Everyone knows that Hana's future lies in its uniqueness and remoteness, and no one wants it to change. The people as well as the tourists know what they have here. What really makes Hana heavenly is similar to what's preached in Sunday school: Everyone wants to go there, but not everyone makes it.

Hana Festivals

As is the case in most Hawaiian towns, Hana has many local festivals and events. First in the year is the fireworks on New Year's Eve over Fagan's cross. In late March, the weekend **Taro Festival,** with its traditional ceremonies, games, music, authentic foods and a food market, arts and crafts exhibitions, and hula demonstrations, thrills everyone. People come from all over the state to watch and participate; make plans well in advance. Later in June or early July, the chil- dren of town get treated to the **Makeke,** a chil- dren's festival, when all sorts of games and cele- brations are held. For decades, Hana has had a tie with the great American sport of baseball. To honor this connection, a softball tournament is held over the Labor Day weekend, pitting fam- ilies and friends against one another in friendly but serious competition. As with all of the state, the **Aloha Festival** is celebrated with gusto. Pa- rades, lu'au, a fishing tournament, and many other activities are organized.

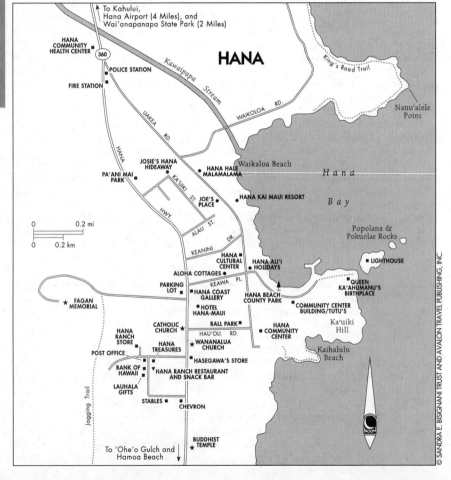

EAST MAUI

© SANDRA E. BISIGNANI TRUST AND AVALON TRAVEL PUBLISHING, INC.

SIGHTS

Hana Bay

Dominating the bay is the red-faced **Ka'uiki Hill.** Fierce battles raged here, especially between Maui chief Kahekili and Kalaniopu'u of Hawaii, just before the islands were united under Kamehameha. Kalaniopu'u held the natural fortress until Kahekili forced a capitulation by cutting off the water supply. It's believed that Kamehameha boarded Captain James Cook's ship after a lookout spotted it from this hill. More important, Queen Ka'ahumanu—Kamehameha's favorite and the Hawaiian *ali'i* most responsible for ending the old *kapu* system and leading Hawaii into the "new age"—was born in a cave here in 1768. Until very recent times fish-spotters sat atop the hill looking for telltale signs of large schools of fish.

To get there, simply follow Uakea Road when it splits from the Hana Road at the police station, and follow the signs to the bay. Take it right down to the pier and **Hana Beach County Park,** open 6 A.M.–10 P.M. Hana Beach has full amenities and the swimming is good. It's been a surfing spot for centuries, although the best breakers occur in the middle of the bay. Until the '40s, cane trains rode tracks from the fields above town out onto the pier, where the cut stalks were loaded onto boats to be taken to the mill for processing. To explore the base of Ka'uiki, look for a pathway to the right of the pier and follow it. Hana disappears immediately, and few tourists walk out this way. Walk for a few minutes until the lighthouse comes clearly into view. The footing is slightly difficult, but there are plenty of ironwoods to hang onto as the path hugs the mountainside. A few pockets of red-sand beach eroded from the cinder cone are below. A copper plaque erected in 1928 commemorates the spot of Ka'ahumanu's birth. Proceed straight ahead to the lighthouse sitting on a small island. To cross, you'll have to leap from one jagged rock to another. If this doesn't suit you, take your bathing suit and wade across a narrow sandy-bottomed channel. Stop for a few moments and check the wave action to avoid being hurled against the rocks. When you've got it timed, go for it! The view from up top is great.

Fagan Memorial

Across from the Hotel Hana-Maui, atop Lyon's hill, is a lava-stone cross erected to the memory of Paul Fagan, who died in 1960. The land is privately owned, but it's okay to drive or walk up there if there are no cattle in the pasture; inquire at the hotel first for a key to the gate if you want to drive. The road to the top starts at the hotel guest parking lot, and although it starts out fairly level, it gets deceptively steep toward the top. From atop the hill you get the most panoramic view of the entire Hana area. After a rain, magic mushrooms have been known to pop up in the "cow pies" in the pasture surrounding the cross.

Wananalua Church

Near the hotel is the Wananalua Congregational Church, built from coral blocks in 1838 and placed on the National Register of Historic Places in 1988. Sunday service is at 10 A.M. The missionaries deliberately and symbolically built it on top of an old *heiau,* where the pagan gods had been worshipped for centuries. It was the custom of chiefs to build *heiau* before entering battle, and this area is supposed by some to be a site of battle between forces of King Kamehameha I from the Big Island and Maui soldiers. Because Hana was always contested ground, dozens of minor *heiau* can be found throughout the region.

Across the street is the newer and lovely St. Mary's Catholic Church. Its wood construction and decorative detail contrast vividly with the plain, sturdy, rather unornamented Wananalua Church. Mass is celebrated Sunday 9 A.M., weekdays 7 A.M., and Saturday 4 P.M. Visitors welcome.

Hana Cultural Center

Located along Uakea Road on the right, kitty-corner from the Hana Bay entrance road, this center is open daily 10 A.M.–4 P.M. (but may open at noon on Sunday); $2 donation gladly accepted. Founded in 1971, the Hana Cultural Center, 808/248-8622, www.planet-hawaii.com/hana, occupies an unpretentious building (notice the

EAST MAUI

beautifully carved koa doors, however) on the grounds of the old courthouse and jail. The center houses fine examples of quiltwork: one, entitled "Aloha Kuuhae," was done by Rosaline Kelinoi, a Hana resident and the first woman voted into the state legislature. There are precontact stone implements, tapa cloth, and an extensive shell collection. Your donation entitles you to visit the courthouse and jail next door. Simple but functional, with bench and witness stand, it makes Andy of Mayberry look like big time. This tiny courthouse was used regularly 1871–1978 and is still used monthly for the same purpose. It's been placed on the Hawaii Register of Historic Places. The jail, "Hana Lockup," was also built in 1871 and finally renovated in 1997. The townsfolk knew whenever it held an inmate because he became the groundskeeper and the grass would suddenly be mowed.

In the ancient Hawaiian style and using traditional materials, a sleeping house, cook house, meeting house, and canoe shed have been constructed to the side and below the center to give you an idea of what types of buildings were used in Hawaii in the past. On the terrace below these structures is a small **ethnobotanical garden** of medicinal and agricultural native plants. Pick up a brochure about the plants inside the museum. Be sure to stop at the cultural center while in Hana to learn a bit about local history and culture.

Ka'eleku Caverns

One of Hana's unique adventures is spelunking. There are 50 known caves on Maui and 150 on the Big Island. Only a short section of the Thurston Lava Tube in Hawaii Volcanoes National Park and two to three others can be entered. Some 30,000 years old, Ka'eleku (Standing in the Dark) Cave near Kahanu Gardens in Hana is the only cave on Maui that's open to the public, and it's a beauty. This cave, like all others in Hawaii, is actually a lava tube 30–40 feet below the surface, so the cave follows the lay of the land up and down the mountainside. No matter what the temperature is outside, it's always a moderate 64–72°F inside. You enter through a skylight and make your way down the steps to the floor of the

cave, which once flowed with molten lava. Here you must let your eyes adjust to the darkness before proceeding downhill. As liquid lava surged through this tube it scored the walls, leaving striations. Here and there, you will also see benches and ledges along the sides, where lava cooled faster on the periphery than the middle. Some rubble has fallen from the ceiling or off the walls, creating small mounds, but the trail skirts or traverses these obstructions. You can walk upright all the way, no kneeling or crawling involved.

Other natural features that occur in this cave are lava stalactites and stalagmites, drip columns, a bowling alley–like channeling with gutters down both sides, ropy pahoehoe lava levees, clinkers of rough 'a'a, side loops, convergent channels, and over tubes. A very unusual feature found in certain portions of the cave, and perhaps peculiar to this cave alone, are delicate, filigreed grapelike botryoid clusters. And the colors, who would have thought? There is gray, blue, brown, gold, and copper—quite astounding. One of the mysteries of this cave is that the air flows in two different directions. Through the lower portion, the flow is downward and out a series of skylights; in the upper section, the air flows uphill, exiting at a yet undiscovered spot. Because this cave has only recently been open to visitors, it's still in pristine condition. Care must be taken not to touch delicate formations or accidentally crush or break anything fragile. "Cave softly and carry a big light" is the owner's motto.

Maui Cave Adventures, P.O. Box 40, Hana, HI 96713, 808/248-7308, info@mauicave.com, www.mauicave.com, is run by Chuck Thorne, and he can set you up with a tour. All tours are guided, very informative, and safe. Chuck is happy to share with you what he knows about this cave as well as other caves in the state. Check-in is at the kiosk at the cave entrance, located about one-half mile along Ulaino Road after turning off the Hana Highway. An informative schematic drawing of the cave, with explanation, is displayed at the parking lot. A hard hat, light, and drinks are provided. Wear long pants, closed-toe shoes, and a T-shirt—something that you don't mind getting a little dirty. If you have any interest in caving or have never even been underground before, you'll be glad you had a look at this one. A one-hour walking tour costs $29 per person, and adventurers must be at least seven years old. The two-hour "wild" tour is $69 per person, with an age requirement of 15 years old. Two-person minimum for tours to run. Contact the company (open 8 A.M.–8 P.M.) for information, advanced reservations, and departure times.

Kahanu Gardens

Turn off Hana Highway onto Ulaino Road and proceed toward the ocean. Here, the pavement soon gives way to a dirt track and leads about 1.5 miles to Kahanu Gardens, 808/248-8912, www.ntbg.org, located just past a shallow stream. The gardens are open Monday–Friday 10 A.M.–2 P.M., but may be closed at any time if, because of heavy rains, the stream (no bridge) is too high or moving too swiftly to cross. This 123-acre tropical garden runs down to the tortured lava coastline. Part of the National Tropical Botanical Garden system, the Kahanu Gardens contain a variety of domestic and imported tropical plants, including a huge native pandanus forest and large and varied collections of breadfruit and coconut trees. While

one of the purposes of the garden is to propagate and protect Hawaiian and Polynesian ethnobotanical plants, within its property is **Pi'ilanihale Heiau,** Hawaii's largest, with massive walls that rise more than 50 feet and a broad top that's twice as long as a football field and half that wide. A National Historical Landmark, this *heiau* is probably from the 14th century and possibly a royal compound associated with Pi'ilani, a Maui king from around 1500 who seems to have unified the island as one political unit. You may walk through on your own for $10. The walk is level, but leave yourself 1–1.5 hours for the tour.

Just before the Kahuna Gardens is the private **Hana Maui Tropical Botanical Garden,** a 10-acre site open daily 9 A.M.–5 P.M. for self-guided tours; $3 entrance fee.

Pool at Ulaino

Past Kahanu Gardens, Ulaino Road continues to roughen, crosses two more streams, passes several homesites carved out of the bush, and ends after more than a mile at a parking area near the ocean. This may not be drivable during heavy rains with a 2WD rental car but

Pi'ilanihale Heiau is the largest on the island and one of the most important for Maui history.

may be passable with a 4WD vehicle. Walk across the boulders that form the beach at the mouth of the stream and stay along the *pali* for 100 yards or so until you come upon what some people call Blue Pond or Blue Pool tucked behind some larger rocks. This hideaway is an old local favorite, a clothing-optional swimming spot where a waterfall drops fresh water into an oceanside pool. Not always blue, it's sometimes murky when water brings large amounts of sediment down from the hillside above. As always at pools, be aware of stones and branches that might come over the top and give you a knot on your noggin as a souvenir of your time in paradise.

Hana Airport

Less than a mile in toward town from Ulaino Road, on Ala'ele Road, a sign points left to Hana Airport, where **Pacific Wings,** 808/873-0877, schedules some flights. Most flights to Hana go through Kahului, although there are a few from Honolulu. Hotel Hana-Maui operates a shuttle between the airport and the hotel for its guests and will take others when not full. There is no public transportation in Hana, and only **Dollar Rent A Car,** 808/248-8237, can provide wheels for you, so make reservations *before* arriving in Hana. Their booth is open 8 A.M.–5 P.M. daily at the airport. Aside from the airline counters, there is only a public telephone and restrooms here at this tiny terminal.

Blue Hawaiian helicopters makes one run up the Hana coast that stops at the Hana Airport. Here, it connects with ground transportation by **Temptation Tours,** so you can go one way by air and the other by land, a fly-drive offering. Neither company has an office at the Hana Airport.

The real adventurer may want to take note that power hang-gliding flights are offered at the Hana Airport, but by appointment only. Contact Hang Gliding Maui, 808/572-6557, to arrange a 30- or 60-minute flight over the Hana Coast.

Wai'anapanapa State Park

Only three miles outside Hana, and down a road that's clearly marked along the highway at mile marker 32, this state park offers not only tent

and RV camping but also housekeeping cabins sleeping up to six. Set some distance from the beach and tenting area, the cabins offer hot water, electricity, a full kitchen, bathroom, bedrooms, and bedding, and rent for $45 per night for up to four people and $5 for each additional person. A deposit is required. They're very popular, so book far in advance by writing to the Division of State Parks or visiting its office at 54 S. High St., Rm. 101, Wailuku, HI 96793, 808/984-8109. The grassy camping area has picnic tables, water, showers, and restrooms. Even for those not camping, Wai'anapanapa is a "must stop." Pass the office to get to the beach park and its black-sand beach. The swimming is dangerous during heavy surf because the bottom drops off quickly, but on calm days it's mellow. The snorkeling is excellent, and it should be, because Wai'anapanapa means "Glistening Waters." Just offshore is a clearly visible natural stone bridge. Some very brave local kids come and jump off the rocks here—for the thrill, no doubt.

A short, well-marked trail leads to **Wai'anapanapa Caves.** The tunnel-like trail passes through a thicket of vines and *hau,* a bush used by the Hawaiians to mark an area as *kapu.* The two small caves are formed from lava. The water trapped inside is clear. These caves mark the site of a Hawaiian legend, in which a lovely princess named Popu'alaea fled from her cruel husband Ka'akae. He found her hiding here and killed her. Bringing a sense of truth to this legend, hordes of tiny red shrimp occupy these caves at certain times of the year, turning the waters red, which the Hawaiians take as a reminder of the poor slain princess.

Along the coastline here are remnants of an ancient paved Hawaiian trail known as the **King's Highway.** You can follow it for a short distance. To get to the section running north toward the airport, cross the black-sand beach and head up the far side. This trail is reasonably well maintained but fairly rugged because of lava and cinders and stays on or near the cliffs most of the way. This walk takes about two hours. A section of the trail also runs south past the cabins along the coast toward Hana. Along the way you'll pass small bays, lava cliffs, blowholes, and an old *heiau.* The vegetation is lush, and long fingers of black lava stretch out into cobalt-blue waters. Expect about a three-hour hike. Along this road to the state park and at various spots along the Hana Highway, you'll find small roadside stands with flowers or fruits for sale on the honor system.

BEACHES

Kaihalulu Beach

Named Kaihalulu (Roaring Sea) but also known as Red Sand Beach, this is a fascinating and secluded beach area. Follow Uakea Road past the turnoff to Hana Bay. Proceed ahead until you pass the public ballpark and tennis courts on your right and the community center on your left. The road dead-ends shortly. Head through the open lot between the community center and hotel property, where you pick up a worn path. Ahead is a Japanese cemetery with its distinctive headstones, some now being lost to wave erosion and a degrading shoreline. Below are pockets of red sand amid fingers of black lava washed by sky-blue water. There are many tide pools here. Stay close to the water and walk the shoreline path around Ka'uiki Head until you are obviously in the hollowed-out amphitheater of the red cinder cone. Pat the walls to feel how crumbly they are—the red "sand" is eroded cinder. The water in the cove is fantastically blue against the redness. There is another trail that leads over the edge of the cliff and *steeply* down to the beach, but unfortunately the walk down can be treacherous. This path clings to the side of a cliff, and the footing is made tough because of unstable and crumbly cinders. Grave accidents have occurred, and even locals often won't make the trip. Use the shoreline path.

Across the mouth of the bay are jagged fingers of stone, jutting up like castle parapets from a fairy kingdom, that keep the water safe for swimming. This is a favorite fishing spot for local people, and the snorkeling is good, too. The beach is best in the morning before 11 A.M.; afterward it can get hot if there's no wind and rough if the wind is from the north—remember the beach's name. The coarse red sand massages your feet, and there's a natural jacuzzi area

in foamy pools of water along the shore. This secluded beach is unofficially clothing optional, so if you're going to be upset by nude sunbathers, it may be better to head somewhere else.

Koki Beach

The beach is a mile or so out of town heading toward 'Ohe'o. Look for Haneo'o Road on your left with a sign directing you to Koki and Hamoa Beaches. Koki is only a few hundred yards on the left, at the first set of pullouts by the water. This beach is a mixture of white sand and red sand from the hill next to it. The riptides are fierce in here, so don't swim unless it's absolutely calm, but locals surf here when conditions are right—usually in summer. The winds can whip along here, too, even though at Hamoa Beach, less than a mile away, it can be dead calm. Koki is excellent for beachcombing and for a one-night unofficial bivouac.

A very special person named Smitty lived in a cave on the north side of the beach. A distinguished older man, he "dropped out" years back and came here to live a simple monk's existence. He kept the beach clean and saved several people from the riptide. He was a long-distance runner who would tack up a "thought for the day" on Hana's public bulletin board. People loved him and he loved them in return. In 1984 the roof of his cave collapsed and he was killed. When his body was recovered, he was in a kneeling position. At his funeral, all felt a loss, but there was no sadness because all were sure that Smitty had gone home.

Hamoa Beach

Follow this loop road a few minutes past Koki Beach to the other side of this small thumb of a peninsula to Hamoa Beach. Between Koki and Hamoa are the remnants of the extensive Haneo'o fish pond, part of which is still discernible. This entire area is an eroding cinder cone known as **Kaiwi O Pele** (the Bones of Pele). This is the spot where the swinish pig god, Kamapua'a, ravished her. Pele also fought a bitter battle with her sister here, who dashed Pele on the rocks, giving them their anatomical name. Out to sea is the diminutive 'Alau Island, a remnant left over by Maui after he finished fishing up the Hawaiian Islands.

You can tell that the gray-sand Hamoa Beach is no ordinary beach the minute you start walking down the paved walkway. This is the semiprivate beach of the Hotel Hana-Maui, but don't be intimidated, because no one can own the beach in Hawaii. Hamoa is terrific for swimming and snorkeling on calm days or bodysurfing or surfing on days when the wind is up a little. The hotel guests are shuttled here by buses throughout the day, so if you want this lovely beach to yourself arrive before midmorning and stay after late afternoon. There is a pavilion that the hotel uses as well as restrooms and showers for its guests, but there are public toilets as well.

ACCOMMODATIONS

Hotel Hana-Maui *Stay here 1st*

The legacy of Paul Fagan who built it in the late '40s, **Hotel Hana-Maui,** 808/248-8211 or 800/321-4262, fax 808/248-7202, www.hotel-hanamaui.com, is as close to a family-run hotel as you can get. Most personnel have either been there from the beginning or their jobs have passed to their family members, and the hotel has had fewer than 10 managers in the last 60 years. Guests love it that way, proven by an astonishing 80 percent in repeat visitors, most of whom feel as if they're staying with old friends. Unfortunately, the hotel suffered a downturn in the late '90s, but after a change of ownership in 2001, renovation of rooms and restaurants, and a new executive chef, it's on the upswing once again. The public areas in the hotel are done in muted beige and browns with touches of blues, greens, and other light colors. It's open and airy with flagstone floors and easy furniture of hardwood and colorful leather. The low-slung Bay Cottages cluster around the lawn, eight spa suites have been renovated below the main building, while the newer plantation-style Sea Ranch Cottages overlook the ocean on land that slopes down to the water. Rooms, all with their own lanai, surround the beautifully appointed grounds, where flowers add a splash of color to the green-on-green blanket of tropical plants and gently sloping lawn. All suites have a wet bar and large, comfortable sitting area with hardwood, bamboo, and coconut furniture and furnishings. The floors, a rich natural wood, are

Hotel Hana-Maui's Sea Ranch Cottages look out over the water and allow guests to relax in luxurious ranch-style accommodations.

ROBERT NILSEN

covered here and there with natural pandanus mats. The beds, all king-size or two twins, are covered with quilts, while overhead fans provide all the cooling necessary. These quilts, plus some of the wallpaper in the units and design details in other parts of the hotel, were inspired by traditional 18th- and 19th-century Hawaiian *kapa*, patterns. The guest-cottage rooms have king-size beds and freestanding armoires. The bathrooms, as large as most sitting rooms, are tiled with earth-tone ceramic. You use the walk-in shower or climb a step to immerse yourself in the huge tub, then open eye-level windows that frame a private mini-garden like an expressionist's still life.

The hotel staff adds an intangible quality of friendliness and *aloha*. In the main building, there is a library for use by guests, a few shops for clothes, necessities, and gifts, and a superb art gallery. The refurbished hotel restaurant is open for breakfast, lunch, and dinner, and the Paniolo Bar serves drinks from the late morning until 10 P.M. Thursday. Sunday bring a free hula show to the dining room at 7 P.M., and Thursday–Sunday 6:30–9:30 P.M., the soft lilt of Hawaiian music and song wafts through the house from the bar. Other facilities and activities include a wellness center, dedicated spa facilities, two heated swimming pools, a hot tub, tennis courts, superb horseback riding, a three-hole practice golf course, a croquet lawn, free bicycle use by guests, hikes to nearby sites, and daily transportation to the hotel's facilities on Hamoa Beach, where there is an attendant on duty and water gear to use. All activities are easily arranged by visiting the activities desk, which can be counted on to keep family and children happy with lei-making, swaying hula lessons, and other such interests. Free shuttle service is provided by the hotel throughout the area as well as to the airport for those arriving and leaving.

The Bay Cottages have rates starting at $295 for a garden-view suite and progress up to $365 for an oceanview suite. The Sea Ranch Cottages run $395–725 and include all activities and in-room snacks. For large families or groups, the plantation house, the former plantation manager's home, goes for $1,500 per night. From December 20 through January 5, holiday rates on all rooms are approximately 20 percent higher. There is a $50 extra charge for each additional adult in a room; kids 18 and younger stay free with existing bedding. The entire scene isn't stiff or fancy, but it is a memorable first-class experience!

Vacation Rentals

Joe's Place, 808/248-7033, is on Uakea Road not far from the entrance to the bay. A very modest but clean self-serve guesthouse, this is a home that's been split into eight guest rooms. Rooms for singles or doubles cost $45, $55 with a private bath. Also available is a room for $65 that can sleep three. Cash or traveler's checks only. Check-out time is at 10 A.M. and check-in is at 3 P.M. or as soon as your room is available. Reservations are held until 6 P.M. There's kitchen access, a communal TV room, daily towel change, and maid service on request at an extra charge. If no one is in the office, ring for assistance.

Located across from the Heavenly Hana Inn on the north end of town, **Hana Maui Vacation Rental,** P.O. Box 455, Hana HI, 96713, tel/fax 808/248-8087 or 800/991-2422, www.maui-hana.com, is a small place with three units. Neat, tidy, and inexpensive, one has a kitchen while the other two have only microwaves and mini-refrigerators. All have bedrooms separate from the cooking area, bathrooms with showers, and separate entrances. While not large, it's certainly adequate, and the price is right. The room with a kitchen runs $65 per night, with the microwave $55; maximum three guests per room.

Kulani's Hideaway, 808/248-8234, has two units that rent for $65 double occupancy that are conveniently located on the road down to the state park. While nothing special, they are comfortable and each has a bedroom, bathroom, and a small kitchen.

Adjacent to the Hana Cultural Center, the **Aloha Cottages,** P.O. Box 205, Hana, HI 96713, 808/248-8420, are owned and operated by Zenzo and Fusae Nakamura and are the best bargain in town. The studio and cottages are meticulously clean, well built, and sparsely appointed. For $65–95, $10–25 per additional guest, you get two bedrooms and bath, a full kitchen, living

EAST MAUI

room, linoleum floors throughout, a deck, and outdoor grills, but no television or phones. Mrs. Nakamura is very friendly and provides daily maid service. In season, fruit trees on the property provide free fruit to guests.

Josie's Hana Hideaway, P.O. Box 265, Hana HI, 96713, 808/248-8418 or 808/248-7727, offers two spartan rooms in the rear of her house and one up at the front. Each large and comfy unit (the front unit is smaller than the ones behind) has a bedroom/sitting room with a kitchenette in the corner, color TV by the queen bed, a full bathroom, and a separate entrance. If you want, you can prepare your meal in the kitchenette on the upper lanai. No breakfast is served. The daily room rate is $75 single or $85 double, $10 for an extra person, and five- and seven-day rates are available. Owner Josie Diego also rents the one-bedroom house next door for $125 per night and a cabin behind it for $95 per night. Aside from these, Josie also rents five other houses and cottages in town from 1–3 bedrooms that range from $100–150 per night. No credit cards or personal checks are accepted. To find Josie's, turn off the Hana Highway onto Ka'uiki Street, near Pa'ani Mai Park, and go down to the bend in the road.

Located on the road that leads to the airport, **Tradewinds Cottages,** P.O. Box 385, Hana, HI 96713, 808/248-8980 or 800/327-8097, twt@maui.net, www.hanamaui.net, rents two detached houses set in a tropical flower garden that have full kitchens and bathrooms, queen-size beds and sleeper sofas, color TVs, ceiling fans, and a hot tub on each desk. The Tradewinds Cottage runs $145 per night, maximum of six, while the smaller Hana Cabana is $120 per night, maximum of four; $10 each additional person after the first couple. No meals are provided, but you can pick fruit from the trees on property when it's ripe. In addition, the owner has a new rental house in town with an unobstructed view over the bay, where rooms go for $135–$210, depending on the number needed.

A magnificent place on the lower road into town, **Hana Hale Malamalama,** P.O. Box 374, Hana, HI 96713, 808/248-7718, hana-hale@maui.net, www.hanahale.com, overlooks an ancient, rebuilt fish pond. This is a culturally significant site, and numerous artifacts have been found here. Great care has been taken to aesthetically landscape the property so that the buildings seem to fit in as if they've been here for years. Four buildings make up the compound. Set next to the pond, the Royal Lodge is a two-floor, 1,800-square-foot house made in the Philippines of hardwood, transported here, and reconstructed. Upstairs is the Royal Suite; downstairs, the Garden Suite. Up on the bluff are the two-story Tree House Cottage, Poolside Bungalow, and Banana Cabana. The Royal Suite runs $225 and the Garden Suite $125, but these two can be rented together as a complete unit. The Poolside Bungalow is $160, the Tree House Cottage $175, and the Banana Cottage runs $150. There is a two-night minimum for all units, and a continental breakfast comes with each. This is a perfect place for a honeymoon or for a couple who just wants a little luxury and class without spending an arm and a leg. Two units next door are also rented, the Bamboo Inn Suite at $150 and the two-story, two-bedroom Bamboo Inn Villa for $200. Call John Romain for reservations.

Hana Accommodations, 808/248-7868 or 800/228-4262, fax 808/248-8240, info@hana-maui.com, www.hana-maui.com, rents two private houses and two studios on the lush, tropical Hana coast just beyond town near Waioka Pool. Your choices include a three-bedroom, one-bathroom house with a full kitchen that can sleep up to eight for $150 and sits on its own property. Next door is a two-bedroom cottage with a full kitchen and an outdoor shower in the garden for $120. Located in the garden, the smaller units are both cozy studios for up to two people, one with an efficiency kitchen and the other with only a few cooking appliances, that run $76–95. Rates drop slightly after four days. Contact Tom Nunn for reservations.

Hana Ali'i Holidays, P.O. Box 536, Hana, HI 96713, 808/248-7742 or 800/548-0478, fax 808/248-8595, info@hanaalii.com, www.hanaalii.com, a second and larger agency in Hana, rents everything from a seaside cottage to large plantation homes scattered throughout the Hana area, offering more than a dozen homes, cottages, and studios to choose from. One of the smallest is the Hauoli Lio Cottage, which is situated on a horse ranch and perfect for two at $80 per night. At the other end are Hale Kilohana, which is a two-story, three-bedroom island house with all amenities, and only a short walk to Hamoa beach, for $250 per night, and the Hamoa Beach house, also a two-story affair with three bedrooms, that rents for $300 per night or $100 more with a detached studio. All others, oceanfront, secluded, budget, fall in between, and several can be rented together for larger groups. Weekly and monthly rentals are also available. Some units are nonsmoking, some have a minimum of two nights' stay. Contact Duke; he'll set you up with something that's just right for your needs. He runs a quality business with quality homes.

Hamoa Bay House and Bungalow, P.O. Box 773, Hana, HI 96713, 808/248-7884 or fax 808/248-7047, hamoabay@maui.net, www.hamoabay.com, sits in a copse of trees and bamboo just off the Hana Highway above Hamoa Beach. Inspired by the architecture of Bali, two stone lions holding umbrellas greet you at the driveway. The main house and a second-story studio in the back are both for rent. The main house has two bedrooms, while the upstairs unit has a living room/bedroom. Both have full kitchens and baths, plus ceiling fans, TVs, phones, and barbecues. The studio has a hot tub/shower on the screened porch, while the house has an outdoor shower. Laundry facilities are available. Either makes a fine romantic getaway. Rates for the house are $250 for two or $350 for four, with a three-night minimum. For the upstairs studio, it's $195 per night, with a three-night minimum. Cash, personal and traveler's checks only; no credit cards. No smoking, and no children under 14.

Hana Oceanfront Cottages, P.O. Box 843 Hana, HI 96713, 808/248-7558 or 877/871-2055, dansandi@maui.net, www.hanaocean-frontcottages.com, sits above and overlooks Hamoa Beach. The downstairs one-bedroom suite in the main house is a large 1,100-square-foot unit with Hawaiian decoration fronted by a covered lanai. It rents for $195 per night. The Hamoa Beach Cottage is a separate unit, also large and also in Hawaiian decor, that goes for $235 per night. Each has a complete kitchen and all necessities, a gas grill, an entertainment center, and a outdoor showers; two nights minimum.

Beyond Hamoa Beach is Waioka Pool. High above the highway near this pool, with a million-dollar view out over the ocean, is the new **Hana's Heaven** vacation rental, P.O. Box 1006, Hana, HI 96713, 808/248-8854 or 888/205-3030, www.hanasheaven.com, great for a sunrise because it faces east. Hana's Heaven is one studio unit, bright, clean, and cheery, with a full kitchen, tiled bathroom, washer and dryer, and screened porch. Huge picture windows front the unit for the best views. This studio runs $150 per night for a couple and $20 extra for each additional person. For information and reservations, contact the owners who live on property.

Set high above the west end of town, the luxurious vacation rental **Ekena,** P.O. Box 728, Hana HI 96713, tel/fax 808/248-7047, ekena@maui.net, www.maui.net/~ekena, is owned and operated by Robin and Gaylord Gaffney. The upper and lower floors are separate, but only one level is rented at a time—unless the entire building is desired—so you won't be disturbed by anyone. So spacious are these units that each floor could be rented by two couples, one on each end, who want to share the cost and enjoy each others' company. Both floors have large living rooms, fully equipped kitchens, two master bedrooms, and spacious bathrooms. Ekena is a wonderful pole building with a huge deck and spectacular views both down to the coast and up the mountainside. Because it sits high up the hill, it is almost always graced with trade winds, so even if it's dead calm in town it may be breezy up there. At the upper end of the vacation rental bracket, it's not cheap, but it's good value for the money. The Jasmine level with one bedroom goes for $185 per night, two bedrooms $250. The Sea Breeze level is $350. Both together for up to eight guests run $600 per night. Three nights minimum, no kids younger than 14. For information and reservations, contact T. Isetorp.

The second most famous Hana accommodation, the **Heavenly Hana Inn,** P.O. Box 790, Hana, HI 96713, tel/fax 808/248-8442, hanainn@maui.net, www.heavenlyhanainn.com, resembles a Japanese *ryokan*. It's located within the bamboo fence, just past the schools on the way into town. Walk through the formal garden and remove your shoes on entering the open-beamed main dining hall. Skylights brighten this central dining area. The inn is homey and delightful, and tea and meditation rooms flank the front entrance, adding a sense of tranquility. Having undergone renovations, the inn is more beautiful than ever in its simplicity. A variety of woods give warmth to the living areas, shoji screens hide what need not always be present, and the decoration is perfectly authentic. The three suites seem like little apartments broken up into sections by shoji screens. Each has a sleeping room, bathroom with soaking tub, a sitting room with television but no telephone, and its own private entrance. One suite has a second bedroom. No children under age 15 and no smoking is allowed inside. Special gourmet breakfasts are served at $15 per person with at least one week prior notice, and lunch or tea service can also be accommodated upon request with advance notice. These suites run $185-250 per night, with a two-night minimum.

Hana Kai Maui Resort

These resort condos, the only condo rentals in town at 1533 Uakea Road, and AAA approved, are all well maintained and offer a lot for the money. Because there are only 16 rental units on property, you know this is an intimate place. Rates are studios $125-145, deluxe one-bedrooms $145-195; fifth night free, and weekly and monthly rates available. All have private lanai with exemplary views of the bay, maid service, laundry facilities, and barbecues, but no phone or television. The views couldn't be better because the grounds, laid out in a lovely garden highlighting the interplay of black lava rock and multihued blooms, step down the mountainside to Popolana Beach on Hana Bay. For additional information, contact: P.O. Box 38, Hana, HI 96713, 808/248-8426 or 800/346-2772, fax 808/248-7482, hanakai@maui.net, www.hanakaimaui.com.

FOOD

Hotel Hana-Maui

As far as dining out goes, there's little to choose from in Hana. The Hotel Hana-Maui main dining room offers breakfast, lunch, and dinner. Prices vary according to your choice of options, but expect to spend $10-15 for breakfast and lunch and $24-37 for a dinner entrée. Reservations are highly recommended; call 808/248-8211. Light food and appetizers are also served at the Paniolo Bar 2:30-9 P.M. The bar menu includes such items as paniolo baby back ribs, Hana cobb salad, teriyaki burger, and furikake shoestring fries. Served 7:30-10:30 A.M., breakfast is all manner of fresh fruits and juices, hot pastries, eggs Benedict, pancakes, and omelets. Lunch, served 11:30 A.M.-2:30 P.M., includes hoisin-orange glazed duck salad, steamed pork and vegetable gyoza, plus a variety of burgers and sandwiches. Special dinner menus are prepared daily, but you can begin with ahi sashimi, Hana breadfruit cakes, or shiitake mushroom soup, and then move on to an assortment of grilled, seared, or roasted chicken and seafood, or locally grown beef and lamb, all basted in a variety of sauces. Desserts are too tempting to resist. Dinner is served 6-9 P.M.

If you're going the Hamoa Beach for the day, the hotel can prepare a picnic lunch for you at $18.50 per person. Make reservations at the activities desk in the hotel lobby.

Entertainment at the hotel—and that, quite frankly, is it for the whole town—is an informal hula and Hawaiian music shows put on by local families during dinner on Thursday and Sunday at 7 P.M. Aside from that, music is performed Thursday-Sunday at the Paniolo Bar, usually by one or two local musicians on ukulele and/or guitar, who fill the entire building with good cheer and melodious song before and after dinner. The Paniolo Bar is open daily 11:30 A.M.-10:30 P.M. For alternate entertainment, try the frequent evening baseball games at the ballpark behind the hotel.

Hana Ranch Restaurant

The Hana Ranch Restaurant, 808/248-8255, serves very tasty meals, but it can be stampeded by ravenous tourists heading up or down the Hana Road. Reservations are recommended. Seating is inside or on the lanai under a timber framework. A buffet lunch is served daily 11 A.M.–3 P.M. Dinner is served Friday and Saturday evenings 5:30–8:30 P.M., and Wednesday is pizza night. The dinner menu includes appetizers like crispy crab cakes and homemade onion rings. Follow this with your choice of salad and an entrée, which might include fish chowder, grilled salmon, and baby back pork ribs, mostly in the $17–23 range. A short wine list is available, or you can choose some other drink or beer from the bar. A notch or two below the hotel restaurant, the food here is tasty, filling, and decently priced. Besides the Hotel Hana-Maui, the Hana Ranch Restaurant is the only place in Hana to have an evening meal. The outside take-out window is open 6:30 A.M.–7 P.M. for plate lunches, burgers, sandwiches, and saimin, but is only open until 4 P.M. on nights that the restaurant serves dinner inside. Shaded picnic tables are to the side.

Tu Tu's

Tu Tu's Snack Shop, open Mon.–Sat. 8 A.M.–4 P.M. at the community center building fronting the beach, offers window service and a few tables on the porch. Eggs, *loco moco,* French toast, and other breakfast items are all under $4.50, sandwiches to $4, and plate lunches under $6.50. Other items include salads, saimin, hamburgers, drinks, and ice cream. This building, which has bathrooms, was donated to the community by Mrs. Fagan, the wife of Paul Fagan, the original owner of the Hotel Hana-Maui.

SHOPPING
Hasegawa's General Store

In the ranks of general stores, Hasegawa's would be commander-in-chief. This institution, run by Harry Hasegawa, had been in the family for 80 years before it burned to the ground in the fall of 1990. While your gas tank was being filled, you could buy anything from a cane knife to a computer disk. There were rows of food items, dry goods, and a hardware and parts store out back. Cold beer, film, blue jeans, and picnic supplies—somehow it was all crammed in there. Everybody went to Hasegawa's, and it was a treat just to browse and people-watch. Now revived and housed in the old movie theater building, this store still serves the community and visitors that sustained it for so long. It's just as packed as ever, has the only one-day film processing in town, and its only ATM. Open Monday–Saturday 7 A.M.–7 P.M., Sunday 8 A.M.–6 P.M.; 808/248-8231.

Hana Ranch Store

From the Hana Road, make the first right past St. Mary's Catholic Church and go up to the top of the hill to find the Hana Ranch Store, 808/248-8261, open daily 7 A.M.–7 P.M., a general store with an emphasis on foodstuffs. It carries a supply of imported beers, a wide selection of food items, film, videos, and some gifts. The bulletin board here gives you a good idea of what's currently happening in town.

In the small complex next to the Hana Ranch Restaurant, look for **Hana Treasures,** open Mon.–Fri. 9 A.M.–4 P.M., Saturday and Sunday until 3 P.M. The small shop features airbrushed T-shirts by Hana artists, an assortment of Hawaiian gifts and souvenirs, particularly those made in the Hana area, and a display case of silver necklaces, bracelets, and rings. Also in this complex look for **Lauhala Gifts,** the small flower shop, gift, and craft store across the way.

Hana Coast Gallery

Located at Hotel Hana-Maui, this gallery displays an excellent collection of fine art by Hawaiian residents. Not only is the work of very high quality, but the whole gallery is set up in a way that's conducive to show off each piece to its fullest. The list is long, but some of what you'll find here is watercolors, turned wood bowls, Asian brush paintings, bronze sculpture, woodblock prints, jewelry, basketry, and wood furniture. The gallery, 808/248-8636, is open daily 9 A.M.–5 P.M.

ACTIVITIES

Hana-Maui Sea Sports

Arranged through the Hotel Hana-Maui activities desk or by calling 808/248-7711, this kayak adventure heads to Hana Bay for a two-hour session and can take as many as eight people. Kayak and snorkel tours are given at 9:30 A.M. and 2 P.M.; $79 per person, half price under age 12. They'll even snap pictures underwater for you as you snorkel and print them before you leave.

Horseback Riding

Horseback rides are given at the Hana Ranch Stables. A one-hour trail ride, either along the coast or in the upper pastures, leaves at various times throughout the day, and a two-hour ride goes at 9 A.M. on Tuesdays and Thursdays. The short rides cost $50 per person, the longer ride $90, and riders must be at least seven years old. Private rides can also be arranged.

Jogging Trail

A walking, jogging, bicycling trail is maintained on Hana Ranch property, on what was the narrow-gauge sugarcane railroad bed. The trail runs for a bit more than two miles and starts partway up the path to the Fagan Memorial. Walk south. The trail meets the highway near where Haneo'o Road turns down to Koki Beach.

Power Hang Gliding

The only commercial ultralight motorized paragliding on the island runs out of the Hana Airport, and only then by appointment. **Hang Gliding Maui,** 808/572-6557, offers tandem flights that run 30–60 minutes for $115–190. This open-cockpit, slow-speed tour gets you as close to a bird's-eye view of the area as is possible.

SERVICES

Medical Services

Along the Hana Road at the Y intersection, clearly marked on the right just as you enter town, is

Hana Community Health Center, 808/248-8294. Open weekdays 8:30 A.M.–4:30 P.M. Walk-in, nonemergency treatment is available. For emergencies, use the phone at the hospital entrance or dial 911.

Police Station

The police station is at the Y intersection between Hana Highway and Uakea Road, just as you enter town. For emergencies call 911; otherwise, 808/248-8311.

Bank, Post Office, and Library

The Bank of Hawaii, 808/248-8015, is open Monday–Thursday 3–4:30 P.M., Friday 3–6 P.M.; cash advances on Visa and MasterCard can be made there. For an ATM, go to Hasegawa's store.

The **post office** is open weekdays 8 A.M.–4:30 P.M.; a community bulletin board is posted outside. Both are next door to the Hana Ranch Restaurant. The excellent Hana school/public **library,** 808/248-7714, is located at the new Hana School on the western edge of town; open Monday, Tuesday, and Friday 8 A.M.–4 P.M. (from 9 A.M. on Tuesday), Wednesday and Thursday 11 A.M.–7 P.M.

Gas

There is one gas station in town. The Chevron station next to the horse stables is open daily 7:30 A.M.–6:30 P.M. It has a public bathroom and telephone. Gas in Hana is expensive, about $.40 per gallon higher than elsewhere on the island. Be sure to fill up before leaving town because the nearest gas station west is in Pa'ia; going south around the bottom, the closest is in Keokea in Upcountry.

Car Rental

Located at the airport, **Dollar Rent A Car,** 808/248-8237, is the only show in town. It's best to call in advance to ensure a reservation. Cars may be available on short notice during low season, but don't count on it. If you're staying at the Hotel Hana-Maui, the activity desk there can also help arrange this service.

Beyond Hana

About one-half mile south of Hana is mile marker 51. From there, the mile markers decrease in number as you continue around the south coast back to Kahului. Now you're getting into adventure. The first sign is that the road becomes narrower, then the twists and turns begin again. After 'Ohe'o Gulch, a few miles are still unpaved, which is followed by a long stretch that's nothing more than a patchwork quilt of filled potholes. You know you're in a rural area with not much traffic when you come across the sign "Caution: Baby Pigs Crossing." There is one phone, no gas, only a fruit or flower stand or two, and one store until you reach Ulupalakua Ranch. Although the road is good for most of the year, during heavy rains sections do still wash out and become impassable. The fainthearted should turn back, but those with gumption are in for a treat. There are roadside waterfalls, thick luscious forests, cascading streams filling a series of pools, pocket-size ranches, a hero's grave, tiny plantation communities, some forgotten towns, isolated homesteads, million-dollar retirement retreats, and desolate scrubby ranchland. If you persevere all the way, you pop out at the Tedeschi Winery,

where you can reward yourself with a glass of bubbly before returning to civilization.

Waioka Pool

A myth-legend says Waioka Pool, also referred to by some as Venus Pool, was once used exclusively by Hawaiian royalty. At the Waiohonu bridge just past mile marker 48, cross over the fence and hike (public-access trail) through the fields above the river to its mouth. There you'll find a series of waterfalls below the bridge and a freshwater pool scoured out of the solid rock walls of this water course. Used by Hawaiian royalty during centuries past, it's now a refreshing, usually solitary, place for a swim or to sunbathe on the smooth rocks. Be safe and stay out of the ocean because the surf, which can be just over the narrow sandbar, is strong. At certain times of the year you may see giant turtles just off the rocks a short way farther down the coast. In the fields above and to the north of Waiohino Stream are the remains of an old sugar mill and part of the King's Highway, a paved pathway that once ran along the coast. In 2002, Hana Ranch set aside 41 acres of the oceanfront property running north from the

EAST MAUI

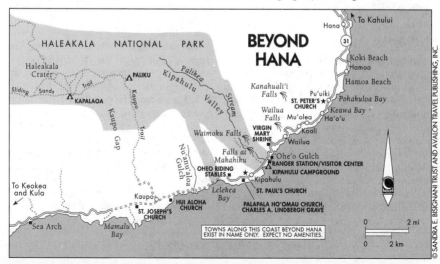

© SANDRA E. BISIGNANI TRUST AND AVALON TRAVEL PUBLISHING, INC.

stream as a "perpetual conservation easement" that cannot be developed in the future but may still be grazed by ranch cattle. Just down the road in Pu'uiki is the refurbished **St. Peter's Church** (1859).

Wailua Falls

About six miles after leaving Hana, Wailua and Kanahuali'i Falls tumble over steep lava *pali,* filling the air with a watery mist and filling their pools below. They're just outside your car door, and a minute's effort will take you to the mossy grotto at the base. There's room to park. If not for 'Ohe'o up ahead, this would be a great picnic spot, but wait! Sometimes roadside artists park here, and basket makers or fruit sellers ply their trade. Check out the taro fields that have been created on the ocean side of the road. If you are going back toward Hana on this road, you will see another falls high above Wailua Falls on the mountain above. In a few minutes, about one-half mile before you enter the park, you pass a little shrine cut into the mountain. This is the **Virgin by the Roadside.** It's usually draped with a fresh lei.

A myth-legend says Waioka Pool, also referred to by some as Venus Pool, was once used exclusively by Hawaiian royalty. It's now a refreshing, usually solitary, place for a swim or to sunbathe on the smooth rocks.

KIPAHULU

This is where the enormous **Kipahulu Valley** meets the sea. It's also the coastal boundary of Haleakala National Park. Most of this valley, about one-third of the national park area, is off limits to the public, set aside as a biological preserve. Palikea Stream starts way up on Haleakala and steps its way through the valley, leaving footprints of waterfalls and pools until it spends itself in the sea. The area was named the Seven Sacred Pools by some unknown publicity person in the late '40s. The area should have been held sacred, but it wasn't. Everything was right here. You can feel the tremendous power of nature: bubbling waters, Haleakala red and regal in the background,

and the sea pounding away. Hawaiians lived here—there are remains of housing sites—but the numerous *heiau* that you might expect seem to be missing. Besides that, there aren't seven pools—there are a few dozen! The name "Seven Sacred Pools" is falling into disfavor because it is inaccurate. Local people and the National Park Service prefer the proper name Kipahulu, Pools of 'Ohe'o, and 'Ohe'o Gulch, instead. In the late '90s, 52 acres were added to the park near the pools, including additional shoreline and the Kanekauila Heiau.

Visitors Center

About 10 miles out of Hana you'll come to a large cement arched bridge (excellent view) and then a parking area to your left with a ranger's station/visitors center, restrooms, and public telephone. Pay your $10 entrance fee at the visitors center. From the visitors center lanai you can see the Big island looming on the horizon on a clear day. Information on the Kipahulu district of the national park, area trails and their conditions, the native Hawaiian people who lived in the area and their lifestyle, and the natural resources of the district are all well explained by displays inside. The center also stocks a selection of books about the area. A small bulletin board outside displays other information. The center is open daily 9 A.M.–5 P.M. The rangers are friendly and informative, so before doing any exploring stop in and ask about trail conditions. They know a tremendous amount of natural history concerning the area and can inform you about the few dangers in the area, such as the flash flooding that occurs in the pools. Interpretive talks are given at the ranger station daily at 12:30, 1:30, 2:30, and 3:30 every afternoon, and occasional cultural programs are offered every Thursday. Call the ranger station, 808/248-7375, for information. You can hike the trail by yourself, but ranger-led hikes are also given. A short one-mile hike goes to the Bamboo Forest daily except Saturday at 9:30 A.M. Those intending to hike or camp should bring their own water. Most people go to the easily accessible lower pools, but a stiff hike up the mountain takes you to the upper pools, a bamboo forest, and a fantastic waterfall; 99 percent of park visitors are gone by sundown. From the parking lot, a short dirt track leads down to the large, grassy camping area.

The Lower Pools

Head along the clearly marked **Kuloa Point Loop Trail** from the parking area to the flat, grass-covered peninsula. The winds are heavy here as they enter the mouth of the valley from the sea. A series of pools to choose from is off to your left. It's delightful to lie in the last one and look out to the sea crunching the shore just a few yards away. Move upstream for the best swimming in the largest of the lower pools. Be careful, though, because you'll have to do some fairly difficult rock climbing. The best route is along the right-hand side as you face up the valley. Once you're satiated, head back up to the road along the path on the left-hand side and

ROBERT NILSEN

relaxing at the lower pools

above the riverbank. This trail will take you back to the ranger station, or you can walk up to the arch bridge that you crossed when arriving, one of the best vantage points from which to look up and down this amazing valley. This trail is a half-mile loop from the ranger station. From near the point, the **Kahakai Trail** runs along the coast to the campground.

Waterfalls

Few people head for the waterfalls, buat those who do will be delighted. The trail is called **Waimoku Falls Trail,** and it begins at the ranger station. The falls at Makahiku are one-half mile uphill, and Waimoku Falls is two miles distant. The toughest part is at the beginning as you huff-puff your way uphill. Soon, the trail brings you to an overlook, from where you can see the lace-like **Falls at Makahiku** as it plummets 181 feet to the rugged valley floor below. A short way beyond this is a shorter second falls, where the pool has undercut the opposite bank and the water then cascades down through a narrow gorge and series of stepped pools. During summer, guava and other fruit drops to the ground, creating a pungent or downright smelly fragrance along the trail. The path continues over two new metal bridges that cross more cascades and pools, and then zigzag up the opposite bank. After passing some enormous mango trees, you head through a high jungle area. Suddenly you're in an extremely dense bamboo forest—an incredible experience in itself. The trail is well cut as you pass through the green darkness of this stand. If the wind is blowing, the bamboo will sing a mournful song for you. Here you get the first glimpse of the waterfall—a tease of what's ahead. This trail gets somewhat sloppy and slippery in sections, and about one-quarter mile of boardwalk had been built over small streams and the worst of the soggy ground. Emerge into more mangos and thimbleberries and there's the creek again. Turn left and follow the creek, without crossing yet, and the trail will become distinct again. There's a wooden walkway, and then, eureka!—Waimoku Falls. It cascades over the *pali* and is so high that you have to strain your neck back as far as it will go. It's more than a waterfall; it's silver filigree. You can stand in the shallow pool below surrounded by a sheer rock amphitheater. The sunlight dances in this area and tiny rainbows appear and disappear. If you are there during the rains, you may see more than one extra waterfall coming off the cliff above.

One word of warning: As at all such waterfalls on the islands, where the pool beckons to slack the heat and the surrounding scenery is so captivating, rocks and boulders periodically dislodge from the *pali* above and tumble into the pool below. How else have the boulders in the pool below gotten to where they are? Usually, although not always, these falling rocks are accompanied by sounds of rock striking rock. Always keep an ear out for danger and an eye upward. At popular and oft-visited waterfalls, warning signs are posted to warn you of such dangers and to keep you out of harm's way. Know the dangers and heed the warnings.

Camping

Kipahulu is part of Haleakala National Park, and camping is free (obtain permit at the visitors center) in designated sites only for a three-day limit. No backcountry camping or camping along the streams is allowed. Groups of more than 12 should obtain permits from the park superintendent at Park Headquarters, P.O. Box 369, Makawao, HI 96768, 808/572-9306. The campground (maximum 100) is primitive and mostly empty, except for holiday weekends, when they can be packed. From the parking lot follow the camping sign and continue down the hill on the rutted dirt track. Bear right to a large, grassy area overlooking the sea, where signs warn you not to disturb an archaeological area. Notice how spongy the grass is here. Move to the trees to escape the wind. Here are clean outhouses, a few picnic tables and barbecue grills, but no potable water, so make sure to bring plenty of your own to drink.

BEYOND 'OHE'O GULCH

Some of Route 31 beyond 'Ohe'o is genuinely rugged and makes the car companies cry. But it can be driven, and even the tourist vans make it part of their regular route. Be aware, however,

that rough weather can bring landslides; the road may be closed by a locked gate with access available only for official business and local residents. Check the bulletin board at the ranger station for road conditions! If the road is closed, a sign in Hana will warn you of this condition. In 1.5 miles you come to the well-kept clapboard **St. Paul's Church,** which sits right next to the highway. Services are conducted here twice a month. To its side are the smokestack and ruins of the long-silenced sugar mill that once processed cane from this area. A little farther along and down a side road is **Palapala Ho'omau Church** (founded 1864) and its tiny cemetery, where Charles Lindbergh and Sam Pryor are buried. People, especially those who are old enough to remember the "Lone Eagle's" historic flight, are drawn here like pilgrims. The public is not really encouraged to visit, but the human tide cannot be stopped. If you go, please follow all of the directions posted. Right next to the church cemetery is the tiny **Kipahulu Lighthouse Point County Park,** which sits on the edge of the cliff overlooking the frothy ocean below. Several trees and picnic tables provide a quiet and shaded place for a bite to eat and a rest. Up the road is Samuel F. Pryor's Kipahulu Ranch. Mr. Pryor was a vice president of Pan Am and a close chum of Lindbergh's. It was he who encouraged Lindbergh to spend his last years in Hana.

Kipahulu Ranch has seen other amazing men. Last century a Japanese samurai named Sentaro Ishii lived here. He was enormous, especially for a Japanese of that day, more than six feet tall. He came in search of work, and at the age of 61 married Kehele, a local girl. He lived in Kipahulu until he died at the age of 102.

Past Sam Pryor's place is **Oheo Riding Stables,** up a long driveway from the road. From here two rides a day are taken through the lush vegetation to spots overlooking Makahiku and Waimoku Falls, both in the national park. About three hours are spent in the saddle; six guests maximum per ride.

A few dozen yards past the Kukuiula Bridge is a great spot for a view of the coastline and the roadway carved into the side of the hill. Park near the bridge and walk up the road to take pictures. Past here the road really begins to get rugged and narrow, but only about eight miles remain partially unpaved. If the road is dry, continue cautiously; if it's been raining hard, consider turning back. At the Kalena Bridge, a couple of miles ahead, the road designation changes to Pi'ilani Highway, Route 31.

Kaupo

The vistas open up at the beginning of the Kaupo Gap just when you pass **Hui Aloha Church.** Built in 1859, this church sits on a level, grassy spot below the road near the sea. Depending on the weather and how long since it was last graded, the road down may be very rough and impassable except with a 4WD vehicle. Eight miles from 'Ohe'o, the village of **Kaupo** and the Kaupo Store follow Hui Aloha Church. Kaupo means Landing at Night and may refer to travelers from other islands who landed by canoe at night on this south shore of Maui. Both the coastline and inland areas of Kaupo sustained substantial Hawaiian communities for hundreds of years.

After so many years of erratic hours and unpredictable closures, Kaupo Store once again has regular hours, Monday–Saturday 10 A.M.–5 P.M. A real anachronism, the store serves double duty as unofficial dusty museum and convenience store. Along with the antiques hanging on the walls and filling the shelves (not for sale), the store stocks cold juices and beer, ice cream, candy, and chips—mostly snacks and traveling food—but it also has a few gifts.

Only a few families live in Kaupo, old ones who ranch and new ones trying to live independently. During decades past, Kaupo Store, which was established in the mid-1920s, was the center of this community. If only the walls could talk, what stories they would tell. Kaupo Store is the last of a chain of stores that once stretched all the way from Ke'anae and were owned by the Soon Family. Nick Soon was kind of a modern-day wizard. He lived in Kaupo, and among his exploits he assembled a car and truck brought piecemeal on a barge, built the first electric generator in the area, and even made from scratch a model airplane that flew. He was the son of an indentured Chinese laborer.

A short distance past Kaupo is **St. Joseph's Church.** Built in 1862, it was renovated in 1991. Services are held on the fifth Sunday of the month, so only a few times per year. In 2002, this church hosted a wedding, the first in 47 years! The abandoned rectory stands to the side.

Once you get to the Kaupo Gap, the tropical vegetation suddenly stops and the landscape is barren and dry for most of the year. Here Haleakala's rain shadow creates an environment of yellow grassland dotted with volcanic rock. Everywhere are *ahu,* usually three stacked stones, that people have left as personal prayers and wishes to the gods. Just after Kaupo, the dirt road becomes a beat-up patchwork that wheels along past range land and ranches with the ocean far below. When the road dips to the ocean, you are in Kaupo Ranch. Near the mouth of the deepest valley to slit this side of the island, you'll find a pebble beach that seems to stretch a mile. At mile marker 32, look down to the coast and see two rough volcanic peninsulas. On the westernmost sits a *heiau.* A short way beyond, before the road dips down the hillside, is a pulloff where you can walk out on a bluff and overlook these peninsulas. A good but distant view of these peninsulas is also possible from another pulloff near mile marker 29. Near here, looking west, is a good spot to view a sea arch, and by mile marker 28 you get a good look at the bottom end of one of the mountainside's deepest gulches. Beyond that, the road gains elevation and the landscape becomes more arid except for the green carpet of trees high up on the mountainside. From there, you can look down on Maui's last lava flow and La Pérouse Bay. Near mile marker 23, the new road surface starts, and before the road tucks back into the trees you get great views of the coast. Be aware of free-range cattle, which can be in the middle of the road around any turn, all the way along this road through Kaupo. Enjoy the road, because in a few minutes you'll be back in the civilized world.

Lana'i

Lana'i (Day of Conquest), in the long, dark past of Hawaiian legend-history, was a sad, desolate, and secluded place inhabited by man-eating spirits and fiendish blood-curdling ghouls. It was redeemed by spoiled but tough Prince Kaulula'au, exiled there by his kingly father, Kaka'alaneo of Maui. Kaulula'au proved to be not only brave, but wily too; he cleared Lana'i of its spirits through trickery and opened the way for human habitation. Lana'i was for many generations a burial ground for the *ali'i* and therefore filled with sacred *mana* and *kapu* to commoners. Later, reports of its inhospitable shores filled the logs of old sailing vessels. In foul weather, captains navigated desperately to avoid its infamously treacherous waters, whose melancholy

whitecaps still outline Shipwreck Beach and give credence to its name.

Most people visiting the Hawaiian Islands view Lana'i from Lahaina on West Maui but never actually set foot on this lovely, quiet island. For two centuries, first hunters and then lovers of the humpback whale have come to peer across the waters of the 'Au'au Channel, better known as the Lahaina Roads, in search of these magnificent giants. Lana'i is a victim of its own reputation. Most visitors were informed by even longtime residents that Lana'i, nicknamed The

Picture-perfect Hulopo'e Bay has the best beach on Lana'i.

ROBERT NILSEN

Pineapple Island, was a dull place covered in one large pineapple plantation: endless rows of the porcupine plants, sliced and organized by a labyrinth of roads, contoured and planted by improbable-looking machines, and tended by mostly Filipino workers in wide-brimmed hats and goggles. It's true that Lana'i had the largest pineapple plantation in the world, 15,000 cultivated acres, which accounted for about 90 percent of U.S. production, but production stopped in the mid-1990s and the carpet of pineapples is gone. The remnants of these fields are still obvious in the swirls of grass as you approach the island by air. Now only about 100 acres remain in cultivation out by the airport—as a testimony to a bygone era—and these fruits are raised for local consumption only. All other pineapples on the island are raised by local gardeners. But the island has 74,000 acres that remain untouched and perfect for exceptional outdoor experiences,

ranging from golf to mountain biking to snorkeling.

Because of its past reputation as a place where almost no one went and recent shift from pineapple production to tourism that caters to the well-to-do who want their peace and quiet, Lana'i is once again becoming known as the "Secluded Island."

The people of Lana'i live in one of the most fortuitously chosen spots for a working village in the world: Lana'i City. All but about two dozen of the island's 3,200 permanent residents make their homes here. Nestled near the ridge of mountains in the northeast corner of the Palawai Basin, **Lana'i City** (elev. 1,600 feet) is sheltered, cooled, and characterized by a mature and extensive grove of Cook pines planted in the early 1900s by the practical New Zealand naturalist George Munro. This evergreen canopy creates a parklike atmosphere about town while reaching

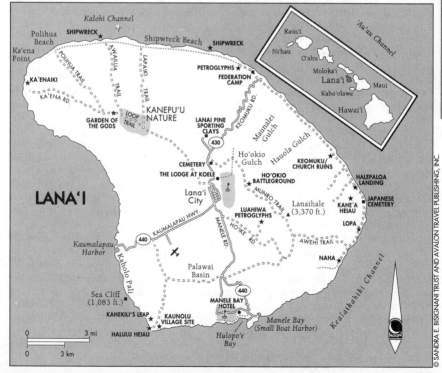

tall green fingers to the clouds. A mountainous spine tickles drizzle from the water-bloated bellies of passing clouds for the thirsty, red, sunburned plains of Lana'i below. The trees, like the bristled hair of an annoyed cat, line the **Munro Trail** as it climbs Lana'ihale, the highest spot on the island (3,370 feet). The Munro Trail's magnificent panoramas encompass sweeping views of no less than five of the eight major islands as it snakes along the mountain ridge, narrowing at times to the width of the road itself.

Maunalei Gulch, a vast precipitous valley, visible from "The Trail," was the site of a last-ditch effort of Lana'i warriors to repel an invasion by the warrior king of the Big Island at the turn of the 18th century. Now its craggy arms provide refuge to mouflon sheep as they execute death-defying leaps from one rocky ripple to the next. On the valley floors roam axis deer, and, until recently, on the northwest grasslands were the remnants of an experimental herd of pronghorn antelope brought from Montana in 1959. After saturating yourself with the glories of Lana'i from the heights, descend and follow a well-paved road from Lana'i City to the southern tip of the island. Here, **Manele** and **Hulopo'e** bays sit side by side. Manele is a favorite spot of small sailing craft that have braved the channel from Lahaina. Hulopo'e Bay, just next door, is as salubrious a spot as you hope to find. It offers camping and all that's expected of a warm, sandy, palm-lined beach. With its virtually untouched underwater marine park, Hulopo'e is regarded as one of the premier snorkeling spots in the entire island chain.

You can hike or drive a 4WD vehicle to **Kaunolu,** one of the best-preserved ancient Hawaiian village sites. Kamehameha the Great came to this ruggedly masculine shore to fish and frolic his summers away with his favorite cronies. Here, Kahekili leaped from a sea cliff to the ice-blue waters below and challenged all other warriors to prove their loyalty to Kamehameha by following his example and hurtling themselves off what today is known as **Kahekili's Leap.**

You can quickly span a century by heading for the southeast corner of Lana'i and its three abandoned villages of **Lopa, Naha,** and **Keomuku.** Here legends abound. *Kahuna* curses still guard a grove of coconut trees, which are purported to refuse to let you down if you climb for their nuts without offering the proper prayers. Here also are the remnants of a sugar train believed to have caused its cane enterprise to fail because the rocks of a nearby *heiau* were disturbed and used in its track bed. Nearby, a decaying abandoned Hawaiian church, the only remnant of the town of Keomuku, insists on being photographed.

You can head north along the east shore to **Shipwreck Beach,** where the rusting hulk of a ship, along with timbers and planks from the great wooden square-riggers of days gone by, lie along the beach, attesting to the authenticity of its name. Shipwreck Beach is a shore-stroller's paradise, a real beachcomber's boutique. Also along here are some thought-provoking **petroglyphs.** Other petroglyphs are found on a hillside overlooking the former "pine" fields of the Palawai Basin.

If you hunger for a totally private beach, head to the northwest corner of the island. En route, you'll pass through a scarce remnant of Hawaiian dryland forest at **Kanepu'u Preserve** and a fantastic area of ancient cataclysm aptly called **The Garden of the Gods.** This raw, baked area of monolithic rocks and tortured earth turns incredible shades of purple, red, magenta, and yellow as the sun plays on it from different angles. If you're hot and dusty and aching for a dip, continue north to trail's end, where the desolation of the garden suddenly gives way to the gleaming brightness of virtually unvisited **Polihua Beach.**

After these daily excursions, return to the green serenity of Lana'i City. Even if you're only spending a few days here, you'll be made to feel like you're staying with old friends. You won't have to worry about bringing your dancing shoes, but if you've had enough hustle and bustle and yearn to stroll in quietude, sit by a crackling fire, and look up at a crystal-clear sky, head for Lana'i. Your jangled nerves and ruffled spirit will be glad you did.

ROBERT NILSEN

The south and west shores of Lana'i are characterized by sheer cliffs that drop into deep blue water.

THE LAND

The sunburned face of Lana'i seems parched but relaxed as it rises in a gentle, steady arc from sea level. When viewed from the air it looks like an irregularly shaped kidney bean. The sixth largest of the eight main islands, Lana'i is roughly 140 square miles, measuring 18 miles north to south and 13 miles east to west at its longest points, with 47 miles of coastline. A classic single-shield volcano, at one time Lana'i was probably connected to Maui, Moloka'i, and Kaho'olawe as a single huge island when the sea level was much lower. Its rounded features appear more benign than the violent creases of its closest island neighbors; this characteristic earned it the unflattering appellation of "Hump." More lyrical scholars, however, claim the real meaning has been lost to the ages or may in fact mean "Day of Conquest," but Lana'i does look like a hump when viewed from a distance at sea.

Its topography is simple. A rugged mountain ridge runs northwest to southeast through the eastern half of the island, and much of its length is traversed by the Munro Trail. The highest peak is Lana'ihale (3,370 feet). This area is creased by precipitous gulches on its windward side: The two deepest are Maunalei and Hauola at more than 2,000 feet. The topography tapers off steadily as it reaches the sea to the east. Beaches stretch from the white sands of Polihua, past Shipwreck Beach in the north, terminating at the salt-and-pepper sands of Naha on the east. Beyond a short section of sea cliff lie the beautiful rainbow arches of Manele and Hulopo'e in the south. Marine fossils found at the 1,000-foot mark and even higher in the mountains indicate its slow rise from the sea.

Until 1993, Palawai, Lana'i's central basin, was completely cultivated in manicured, whorled fields of pineapple. Before pineapple production, Palawai was covered in cactus, cattle were grazed, and some wheat was grown. Now it's nearly all gone fallow in tall grass. The southwest and west coasts have phenomenal sea cliffs accessible only by boat. Some of the most majestic are the **Kaholo Pali,** which run south from Kaumalapau Harbor, reaching their most amazing ruggedness before Kaunolu Bay. At many spots along this stretch the sea lies more than 1,500 feet below. Starting at Lana'i City in the center, a half hour of driving in any direction presents a choice of this varied and fascinating geography.

Climate

The daily temperatures are quite balmy, especially at sea level, but it can get blisteringly hot in the basin and on the leeward side, so be sure to carry plenty of water when hiking or four-wheel-driving. At 1,600 feet, Lana'i City gets refreshingly cool in the evenings and early mornings, but a light jacket or sweater is adequate, although thin-blooded residents bundle up. While it's sunny most days, fog rolls into town occasionally, evoking an ethereal, mysterious feel and sense of magic. The average summer temperature along the coast of Lana'i is about 80°F while the average winter temperature is about 70°F. It can be as much as 10 degrees cooler in Lana'i City.

Water

Lying in the rain shadow of the West Maui Mountains, even Lana'i's windward side receives only 40 inches of rainfall per year. The central basins and leeward shores taper off to a scant 12 inches, not bad for pineapples and sun worshippers. Lana'i has always been short of water, but wells now help satisfy the needs of the residents. Its scruffy vegetation and red-baked earth are responsible for its inhospitable reputation. There are no rivers, and the few streams, found mostly in the gulches of the windward mountains, carry water only when the rains come and are otherwise dry. Most ventures at colonizing Lana'i, both in ancient and modern times, were kept to a minimum because of this water shortage. The famous

Cook pines of Lana'i City, along with other introduced greenery, greatly helped the barrenness of the landscape and provided a watershed. They tickle the underside of and drink water from the clouds that graze the highland ridge. But the rust-red earth remains unchanged, and if you get it onto your clothes, it'll remain there as a permanent souvenir.

FLORA AND FAUNA

Most of Lana'i's flora and fauna have been introduced. In fact, the Cook pine and the regal mouflon sheep were a man-made attempt to improve the natural, often barren habitat. These species have adapted so well that they now symbolize Lana'i, as the ubiquitous pineapple once did. Besides the mouflon, Lana'i boasts axis deer and a few feral goats. A wide variety of introduced game birds include the Rio Grande turkey, ring-necked pheasant, and an assortment of quail, francolins, and doves. Like the other Hawaiian islands, Lana'i, unfortunately, is home to native birds that are headed for extinction. Along the Munro Trail and on the windward coast you pass through forests of Cook pines, tall eucalyptus stands, shaggy ironwoods, native koa, and silver oaks. Everywhere, dazzling colors and fragrances are provided by Lana'i's flowers.

Flowers

Although Lana'i's official flower is the *kauna'oa,* it's not really a flower, but an airplant that grows wild. It's easily found along the beach at Keomuku. It grows in conjunction with *pohuehue,* a pinkish red, perennial seashore morning glory. Native to Hawaii, the *pohuehue* grows in large numbers along Lana'i's seashore. It's easy to spot,

LANA'I CITY TEMPERATURE AND RAINFALL						
	Jan.	March	May	June	Sept.	Nov.
High	70	71	75	80	80	72
Low	60	60	62	65	65	62
Rainfall	3	3	2	0	2	4

Note: Temperature is in degrees Fahrenheit; rainfall in inches.

and when you see a yellow-orange vinelike air-plant growing with it, you've found Lana'i's *kauna'oa*, which is traditionally fashioned into lei. The medicinal *'ilima*, used to help asthma sufferers, is found in large numbers in Lana'i's open fields. Its flat, open yellow flower is about one inch in diameter and grows on a waist-high shrub. Two other flowers considered by some to be pests are the purple *koali* morning glory and the miniature red and yellow flowering lantana, known for its unpleasant odor. Both are abundant on the trail to the Garden of the Gods.

Cook Pines

These pines were discovered by Captain Cook in the South Pacific, and some say that the first were brought here by Captain Vancouver as a future supply of ship masts. Imported in great numbers by George Munro, they adapted well to Lana'i and helped considerably to attract moisture and provide a firm watershed. Exquisitely ornamental, they can also be grown in containers. Their perfect cone shape makes them a natural Christmas tree, used as such in Hawaii; some are even shipped to the Mainland for this purpose.

Endemic Birds

The list of native birds still found on Lana'i gets smaller every year, and those still on the list are rarely seen. The *'amakihi* is about five inches long with yellowish green plumage. The males deliver a high-sounding tweet and a trilling call. Vegetarians, these birds live mostly on grasses and lichen, building their nests in the uppermost branches of tall trees. Some people believe that the *'amakihi* is already extinct on Lana'i.

The *'ua'u* or Hawaiian petrel is a large bird with a 36-inch wingspan. Its head and back are shades of black with a white underbelly. This "fisherbird" lives on squid and crustaceans, which it regurgitates to its chicks. Unfortunately, the Hawaiian petrel nests on the ground, sometimes laying its eggs under rocks or in burrows, which makes it easy prey for predators. Its call is reported to sound like a small yapping dog.

The *'apapane* is abundant on the other main islands but dwindling rapidly on Lana'i. It's a chubby red-bodied bird about five inches long with a black bill, legs, wingtips, and tail feathers. It's quick, flitty, and has a wide variety of calls and songs from beautiful warbles to mechanical buzzes. Its feathers were sought by Hawaiians to produce distinctive ornate featherwork.

Axis Deer

This shy and beautiful creature came to Lana'i via Moloka'i, where the first specimens arrived in 1868 as a gift from the Hawaiian consul in Hong Kong. Its native home is the parkland forests of India and Sri Lanka. The coats of most axis deer are golden tan with rows of round lifetime spots, along with a black stripe down the back and a white belly. They stand 3–4 feet at the shoulder, with bucks weighing an average of 160 pounds and does about 110. The bucks have an exquisite set of symmetrical antlers that always form a perfect three points. The antlers can stand 30 inches high and more than 20 inches across, making them coveted trophies. Does are antlerless and give birth to one fawn, usually between November and February, but Hawaii's congenial weather makes for good fawn survival anytime of the year. Axis deer on Lana'i can be spotted anywhere from the lowland *kiawe* forests to the higher rainforests along the Munro Trail. Careful and proper hunting management should keep the population stable for many generations. The meat from axis deer is reported to have a unique flavor, different from Mainland venison—one of the finest tasting of all wild game.

Mouflon Sheep

Another name for these wild mountain sheep is Mediterranean or European bighorn. One of only six species of wild sheep in the world, mouflon are native to the islands of Sardinia and Corsica, whose climates are quite similar to Hawaii's. They have been introduced throughout Europe, Africa, and North America. Although genetically similar to domestic sheep, they are much more shy, lack a woolly coat, and only infrequently give birth to twins. Both rams and ewes are a similar tannish brown, with a snow-white rump, which is all that most people get to see of these always-alert creatures as they quickly and expertly head for cover. Rams weigh about

125 pounds (ewes a bit less) and produce a spectacular set of recurved horns. They need little water to survive, going for long periods on only the moisture in green plants. On Lana'i they are found along the northwest coast in the grasslands and in the dry *kiawe* forests.

HISTORY

Kaka'alaneo peered across the mist-shrouded channel between West Maui and Lana'i and couldn't believe his eyes. Night after night, the campfire of his son Kaulula'au burned, sending its faint but miraculous signal. Could it be that the boy was still alive? Kaulula'au had been given every advantage of his noble birth, but still the prince had proved to be unmanageable. King Kaka'alaneo had even ordered all children born on the same day as his son to be sent to Lahaina, where they would grow up as his son's friends and playmates. Spoiled rotten, young Kaulula'au had terrorized Lahaina with his pranks and one day went too far: He destroyed a new planting of breadfruit. Even the chief's son could not trample the social order and endanger the livelihood of the people. So finally the old *kahuna* had to step in. Justice was hard and swift: Kaulula'au must be banished to the terrible island of Lana'i, where the man-eating spirits dwelled. There he would meet his fate, and no one expected him to live. But weeks had passed and Kaulula'au's nightly fires still burned. Could it be some ghoulish trick? Kaka'alaneo sent a canoe of men to investigate. They returned with incredible news. The boy was fine! All the spirits were banished! Kaulula'au had cleansed the island of its evil fiends and opened it up for the people to come and settle.

Oral History

In fact, it's recorded in the Hawaiian oral genealogical tradition that a young Kaulula'au did open Lana'i to significant numbers of inhabitants in approximately 1400. Lana'i passed through the next few hundred years as a satellite of Maui, accepting the larger island's social, religious, and political dictates. During this period, Lana'i supported about 3,000 people, who lived by growing taro and fishing. Most inhabited the eastern shore facing Maui, but old home sites show that the population became established well enough to homestead the entire island. Lana'i was caught up in the Hawaiian wars that raged in the last two decades of the 1700s and was ravaged and pillaged in 1778 by the warriors of Kalaniopu'u, aging king of the Big Island. These hard times marked a decline in Lana'i's population; accounts by Western sea captains who passed by even a few years later noted that the island looked desolate, with no large villages evident.

Lana'i began to recover and saw a small boost in population when Kamehameha the Great established his summer residence at Kaunolu on the southern shore. This kept Lana'i vibrant for a few years at the beginning of the 19th century, but it began to fade soon thereafter. The decline continued until only a handful of Hawaiians remained by the 20th century. The old order ended completely when one of the last traditional *kanaka,* a man named Ohua, hid the traditional fish god, Hunihi, and died shortly thereafter in his grass hut in the year 1900.

Early Foreign Influences

No one knows his name for sure, but all historians agree that a Chinese man tried his luck at raising sugarcane on Lana'i in 1802. He brought boiling pots and rollers to Naha on the east coast, but after a year of hard luck gave up and moved on. About 100 years later a large commercial sugar enterprise was attempted in the same area. This time the sugar company even built a narrow-gauge railroad to carry the cane. A story goes that after disrupting a local *heiau* to make ballast for the rail line, the water in the area, never in great abundance to begin with, went brackish. Again sugar was foiled.

In 1854 a small band of Mormon elders tried to colonize Lana'i by starting a "City of Joseph" at Palawai Basin. This began the career of one of Hawaii's strangest, most unfathomable yet charismatic early leaders. Walter Murray Gibson came to Palawai to start an idyllic settlement for the Latter-day Saints. He energetically set to work improving the land with funds from Utah and the hard work of the other Mormon settlers. The only fly in Gibson's grand ointment occurred when the Mormon Church discovered that the acres of Palawai were not registered to the church at all but to Walter Murray Gibson himself! He was excommunicated and the bilked settlers relocated. Gibson went on to have one of the strangest political careers in Hawaiian history, including championing native rights and enjoying unbelievable influence at the royal Hawaiian court as Prime Minister to King Kalakaua. His land at Palawai passed on to his daughter, who became possessed by the one evil spirit Kaulula'au failed to eradicate: She tried to raise sugarcane, but was fated, like the rest, to fail.

A few other attempts proved uneconomical, and Lana'i languished. The last big attempt at cattle raising produced The Ranch, part of whose lands make up the Cavendish Golf Course in Lana'i City. This enterprise did have one bright note. A New Zealander named George Munro was hired as the manager. He imported all manner of seeds and cuttings in his attempt to foliate the island and create a watershed. The Ranch failed, but Munro's legacy of Cook pines stands as a proud testament to this amateur horticulturist.

The Coming of Pineapples

The purchase of Lana'i in 1922 was one of the niftiest real estate deals in modern history. James D. Dole, the most enterprising of the pineapple pioneers, bought the island—lock, stock, and barrel—from the Baldwins, an old missionary family, for $1.1 million. That comes to only $12 per acre, although many of those acres were fairly scruffy, not to mention Lana'i's bad economical track record. Dole had come from Boston at the turn of the 20th century to figure out how to can pineapple profitably. Dole did such a remarkable job of marketing the "golden fruit" on the Mainland that in a few short years, Midwestern Americans who'd never even heard of pineapples before were buying cans of it regularly from the shelves of country grocery stores. In 1922, Jim Dole needed more land for his expanding pineapple fields, and the arid basin of Palawai seemed perfect.

Lana'i Plantation was an oligarchy during the early years, with the plantation manager as king.

One of the most famous of these characters was H. Broomfield Brown, who ran Lana'i Plantation in the '30s. He kept watch over the fields from his house through a telescope. If anyone loafed, he'd ride out into the fields to confront the offender. Mr. Brown personally "eyeballed" every new visitor to Lana'i: All prostitutes, gamblers, and deadbeats were turned back at the pier. An anti-litter fanatic, he'd even reprimand anyone who trashed the streets of Lana'i City.

During the labor strikes of the 1960s, workers' grievances were voiced, and Lana'i began to function as a more fair enterprise. With pineapple well established on the world market, Lana'i finally had a firm economic base. From a few thousand fruits in the early days, the flow at its peak reached a million fruits per day during the height of the season. They were shipped from the man-made port at Kaumalapau, which was specially built in 1926 to accommodate Lana'i's "pines."

Crushed Pineapples

At its height, Lana'i had 18,000 acres of pineapples under production (15,000 acres for most of its heyday). These acres made up the largest single pineapple plantation in the world. Virtually the entire island was operated by the Dole Co., whose name had become synonymous with pineapples. In one way or another, everyone on Lana'i owed their livelihood to pineapples, from the worker who twisted his ankle in a pine field to the technician at the community hospital who X-rayed it. Now, all has changed and only a few plots remain, mostly for use by the hotels.

Foreign production, especially in the Philippines, has greatly increased, and the Lana'i pineapple industry has folded. As acreage was taken out of pineapple production, and as the population of the island and number of visitors have increased, the company has experimented, without much success, with raising various organic vegetables, grains, and cattle to diversify the island's economy. This seems to be a pet project of the owner, and the hope is to make the economy of Lana'i more locally sustainable and less dependent on imports from the other islands and the Mainland.

Changing Lana'i

Most are amazed that George Munro's pines still shelter a tight-knit community that has remained untouched for so long. But all that's changing, and changing quickly. Two new hideaway luxury hotels have risen, and they're beauties. The coming of these resorts has brought the most profound changes to Lana'i since James Dole arrived at the turn of the 20th century. Castle and Cooke, practically speaking, owns the island—98 percent of it anyway. David Murdoch is the CEO and owner of Castle and Cooke, and the hotels are his babies. He developed them and the two golf courses and continues to develop residential lots (up to 700 in the next 10 years) through a permutation of companies that is now called the Lana'i Company. This company employs a staff of about 1,200 or so, more than all the workers needed to tend the pineapple fields, which was just over 500 people. The hotels have brought an alternative job market, new life to the downtown area, and a housing spurt. One fact was undeniable concerning Lana'i: If you wanted to make a living you either had to work the pineapple fields or leave. Now that has changed. To stop the disenfranchisement of the local people, which was generally the case with rapid development, the Lana'i Company has built several new housing projects, which have come with a promise. Local people, according to seniority with the company and length of residence on Lana'i, had first choice. One group of houses is multiple-family, geared to the entry-level buyer, and the second is single-family homes. Million-dollar homes are also starting to pop up above town and now begin to line the fairways of the new golf courses. This isn't all heart on the part of the Lana'i Company. It wants to ensure that the hotels will have a steady and contented workforce to keep them running without a hitch and to make the whole venture economically viable.

Downtown Lana'i is inadequate. It couldn't possibly handle the hotel guests and all of the new workers and their families who have moved to the island. Old buildings have been refurbished, some torn down and replaced, with more upscale businesses taking their place. The tired little shops in town are on Lana'i Company property, most with month-to-month leases. The Lana'i Company again promises to be fair, but like the rest of Lana'i, they'll have a choice: progress or perish. Most islanders are optimistic, keeping an open mind and adopting a wait-and-see attitude concerning the inevitable changes and the promises that have been made for a better life, but so far it looks promising.

THE PEOPLE

Lana'i is characterized by the incredible mix of racial strains so common in Hawaii—Filipino, Japanese, Hawaiian, Chinese, and Caucasian. It is unique, however, in that 60 percent of its people are Filipino. The Filipinos, some recent immigrants, were solicited by Castle and Cooke to work as laborers on the pineapple plantation. Mostly single young men, the majority Ilocano, some may have come to join relatives already on Lana'i. Here they learned English and from Lana'i they spread out. As workers they were perfect: industrious and quiet. At night you wonder where they all are. Because of the tremendous shortage of eligible women, most workers stay home or fish or have a beer in the backyard with buddies. And on Sundays, there is the illegal (officially nonexistent) cockfight. For high living, everyone heads for Maui or O'ahu.

The next largest racial groups are Japanese (14 percent), Hawaiian (12 percent), and whites (11 percent). The Japanese started as the field workers before the Filipinos, but now, along with the whites, are Lana'i's professionals and middle management. The races coexist, but there are still unseen social strata. There's even a small Chinese population (1 percent), who continue their traditional role as shopkeepers. Finally, about 2 percent fall into the "mixed" category, with many of these Filipino-Hawaiian.

Community

Lana'i has a strong sense of community and uniqueness that keeps the people close. For example, during a bitter three-month strike in 1964, the entire community rallied and all suffered equally: laborers, shopkeepers, and management. All who remember say that it brought out the best in the island tradition of *aloha*. If you really want to meet Lana'ians, just sit in the park in the center of Lana'i City for an hour or two. You'll notice a lot of old-timers, who seem to be very healthy. You could easily strike up a conversation with some of them.

Other Faces

It once might have struck you that most of the people you saw around Lana'i were men. That in itself was a social comment about Lana'i, where men worked the fields and women stayed at home in their traditional roles, nurturing and trying to add to the pleasantries of life. Now you will see more and more women about, many who work at the hotels. You might notice that there are no famous crafts of Lana'i and few artists working commercially. This is not to say there is no art on Lana'i, but the visitor rarely sees it until they stop at the Lana'i Art Center in town. One reason that Lana'i produces so little commercial art is that it's a workers' island with virtually no unemployment, so everyone is busy making a living. Old-timers are known to make superb fishing poles, nets, and even their own horseshoes. The island ladies are excellent seamstresses and, with the rising interest in hula, make lovely lei from the beautiful *kauna'oa*, Lana'i's flower. If you turn your attention to the young people of Lana'i, you'll see the statewide problem of babies having babies. Although the situation is getting better, teenage parents are still not uncommon. Young guys customize their cars, although there's no place to go. If as a young person you wish to remain on Lana'i, then in almost every case your future will be tied to the Lana'i Company. If you have other aspirations, it's "goodbai to Lana'i." These islanders are some of the most easygoing and relaxed people you'll encounter in Hawaii, but with the electronic age extending its long arms of communication, even here they're not nearly as "backwater" as you might think.

Events

All official holidays are honored and celebrated. As anywhere in the state, Lana'i celebrates special events in its own unique way, and each ethnic group has festivities that the whole island participates in. Some community events include **Community Kite Flying** day, held at Lana'i City in March. **May Day** is important throughout the state, and events here take place at Lana'i High School. The **Fourth of July** (or another day in early July) brings the **Pineapple Festival** to Hulopo'e Beach on Lana'i, when all the town gathers to enjoy music, crafts, demonstrations, and, of course, lots of pineapple. A farmers market is held for produce and home-baked goods, and a cooking contest is conducted for amateurs and professionals alike. To cap off the event, fireworks light the night sky. As everywhere in the state, **Aloha Festivals** happens on the island with a parade and other activities.

SPORTS AND RECREATION

No question that Lana'i's forte is its natural unspoiled setting and great outdoors. Traffic jams, neon lights, blaring discos, shopping boutiques, and all that jazz just don't exist here. The action is swimming, hiking, snorkeling, fishing, horseback riding, and some hunting. Tennis and golf round off the activities. Lana'i is the place to revitalize your spirits. You want to get up with the birds, greet the sun, stretch, and soak up the good life.

Camping

The only official camping permitted to nonresidents is located at Hulopo'e Bay, administered by

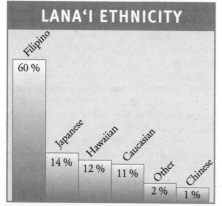

LANA'I ETHNICITY

Filipino 60 %

Japanese 14 %

Hawaiian 12 %

Caucasian 11 %

Other 2 %

Chinese 1 %

the Lana'i Company. Reservations for one of the six official campsites on the grass up from the beach are a must, although unbelievably there's usually a good chance of getting a space. Lana'i Company officials state that they try to accommodate any overflow unreserved visitors, but don't count on it. Because Lana'i is largely privately owned by Castle and Cooke, the parent company of the Lana'i Company, you really have no recourse but to play by their rules. It seems they want to hold visitors to a minimum and keep strict tabs on the ones that do arrive.

Nonetheless, the campsites at Hulopo'e Bay are great. Lining the idyllic beach, they're far enough apart to afford some privacy. The showers are designed so that the pipes, just below the surface, are solar heated. This means a good hot shower during daylight and early evening. Campsite use is limited to six nights, and you must be 18 years of age or older to make an application. The fee includes a one-time $5 registration, plus $5 per person per night. For reservations write to the Lana'i Company, P.O. Box 310, Lanai City, Lanai, HI 96763, attn. Camping, or call 808/565-3982. Permits, if not mailed in advance, are picked up at the Lana'i Company office, and payment of fees are made to the ranger at the camp site. If visiting on the spur of the moment from a neighboring island, it's advisable to call ahead.

Note: While hiking or four-wheel-driving the back roads of Lana'i, especially along Naha, Shipwreck, and Polihua beaches, a multitude of picture-perfect camping spots will present themselves, but they can be used only by Lana'i residents, although there's little supervision. A one-night bivouac would probably go undetected. No other island allows unofficial camping, and unless it can be statistically shown that potential visitors are being turned away, it seems unlikely that the Lana'i Company will change its policies. If you're one of the unlucky ones who have been turned down, contact parent company Castle and Cooke with your protest: 650 Iwilei Rd., Honolulu, HI 96817, 808/548-4811.

Hiking and Jogging

All of the paved roads and many of the gravel roads in Lana'i City are decent for walking and jogging. Although the traffic is not heavy, be careful if you're on the roadway.

One trail on the island has been marked, the **Koloiki Ridge Trail.** Pick up a map at either of the resort front desks. Start at the rear of the Lodge at Koele and head up through the golf course into a tall stand of pine trees. Cross under the power lines and into Hulopo'e Valley, where an abandoned road heads up to the Munro Trail. Once there, turn right and head south, walking into and out of Kukui Gulch, until you round an eroded "moonscape" on your right. A short way farther, turn left down an old jeep trail for perhaps 5–10 minutes. Head through a tunnel in the trees to the flat, open Koloiki lookout. From here, you can look down into Naio and Maunalei gulches and out toward Maui and Moloka'i. This trail is about five mile round-trip and should take at least three hours. An organized group hike also does this route for $15 per person, and on the way you get treated to historical and cultural anecdotes about the island. Contact the concierge for details.

Shorter and easier is **Fisherman's Trail,** a 1.5-mile one-way shoreline trail that runs from Hulopo'e Bay, below the Manele Bay Hotel, west to the end of the golf course. A project of the State Na Ala Hele trail system, this was once part of an ancient trail that circled the island.

Snorkel and Scuba

Lana'i, especially around Manele/Hulopo'e Bay, has some of the best snorkeling and scuba in Hawaii. If you don't have your own equipment, and you're not a guest at one of the hotels, you could buy gear from Pine Isle or Richards stores or rent from the Adventure Lana'i Ecocentre. If you're the adventurous sort, you can dive for spiny lobsters off Shipwreck, but make absolutely sure to check the surf conditions because it can be super-treacherous. It would be best to go with a local person.

Trilogy Ocean Sports, 808/565-2387 or 888/628-4800, www.sailtrilogy.com, operates a catamaran and a rigid-bottom inflatable raft from Manele Boat Harbor for several sailing and snorkel options. The four-hour snorkel/sail

($110) leaves Mondays, Wednesdays, and Fridays at 8:45 A.M., and Saturdays at 10 A.M. A scuba adventure runs at the same time and on the same days for $159–169, or there is the option of an early morning scuba dive at Cathedrals, one of the island's best dive sites, for $95. Rafting tours for scuba divers run three days a week for $130, while the four-hour Sunday raft adventure runs $125. For those who don't care to start from a boat, beach dives are also offered daily at Hulopo'e Beach for $65–75. Book directly or through the concierge desk at the Manele Bay Hotel or at the Lodge at Koele.

Trilogy, in the business for years, has worked out all the kinks, and their boat, crew, and services are truly state-of-the-art. No matter how many times they make the trip, they never seem to forget that it's a new and exciting adventure for you, and they go out of their way to be helpful, upbeat, and caring without being intrusive. The catamaran's aft is set up for easy entry and exit, with steps going down to the water level. Just make like a seal and slither in and out! If the winds are up, the captain will be happy to set sail as they head toward Kahekili's Leap and other famous Lana'i landmarks. The experience is not just underwater, but also in the magnificent views of this pristine island that hasn't changed much since the days of the Polynesian explorers. On morning sails, you return in the early afternoon with plenty of time left for more sightseeing or just relaxing. For those on Trilogy boats coming from Lahaina, the company has a pavilion at Manele Harbor that's used to feed their guests and from where they are taken to Hulopo'e Bay to snorkel and swim or tour the island by van.

Spinning Dolphin Charters, 808/565-6613, owned and operated by Capt. Jeff Menze, a longtime Lana'i resident, will take you fishing (children welcome), snorkeling, and whale-watching in season; six person maximum. Captain Jeff is a commercial fisherman and master diver who knows all of the best spots in Lana'i's waters. Offered are whole-day and half-day adventures, special off-the-beaten-path dives, and private boat charters. Rates run $400 for a half-day trip to $800 for a full-day trip.

The **Kila Kila** also offers sunset cruises, whale-watch trips in season, and full- and half-day fishing expeditions for $825–1,200 (for up to six people). Contact either hotel concierge for reservations.

Swimming

Lana'i City has a fine swimming pool. Located in town near the high school, it's open to the public during summer, usually 10:30 A.M.–5 P.M. daily except Wednesday and on a limited schedule during other seasons. Each of the two resorts has its own swimming pool and spa—for use by registered guests only. By far the best swimming beach on Lana'i is at Hulopo'e Bay, but a few other spots for a dip can be found along the coast from Shipwreck Beach to Naha.

Other Outdoor Adventures

An independent company that caters largely to hotel guests, **Adventure Lana'i Ecocentre,** P.O. Box 1394, Lanai City, HI 96763, 808/565-7373, www.adventurelanai.com, can take you along the north coast of Lana'i on a kayak/snorkel trip, on a 4WD expedition of the highlights around the island, biking down to Shipwreck Beach, a shore dive for scuba enthusiasts, or on several other outings on the island. Half-day outings cost $79 per person, the scuba trip is $129. Guided tours and introduction are provided, and private tours can be arranged. Rentals can be accommodated. Adventure Lana'i has camping gear, kayaks, mountain bikes, and snorkel gear at competitive prices. See your hotel concierge or arrange reservations directly.

Hotel Lanai rents mountain bicycles for $24 on a day-by-day basis, 7 A.M.–7 P.M. If you are staying at the Lodge at Koele, check with the concierge about their rental bicycles and accompanying picnic backpack.

Tennis and Golf

You can play **tennis** at two lighted courts at the Lana'i School from 7 A.M.–8:30 P.M. They have rubberized surfaces called royal duck and are fairly well maintained—definitely okay for a fun game. The Lodge at Koele and the Manele Bay

Hotel have plexipave courts, and their use is complimentary for hotel guests but $25 per hour for nonguests. The six courts at Manele Bay are newer than the three at the Lodge and in better condition. Equipment rental (rackets and ball machines), court times, and fees can be arranged at the pro shops or through the concierge desks. Private lessons and clinics are available.

Golfers will be delighted to follow their balls around **Cavendish Golf Course** on the outskirts of Lana'i City. This nine-hole, 3,058-yard, par-36 course (use the blue tees the first time around, the white tees if you want to go a second nine holes) is set among Cook pines and has been challenging local residents since the 1930s. It's free to all, but visitors to the island are requested to leave a donation for maintenance at the first tee, which, unless you're familiar with the course, could be a bit hard to find. Ask—it's straight up from the clubhouse. Even this unassuming community course has a signature hole with some difficulty. It's the ninth hole, and its green is about

50 feet higher than the tee, plus you must golf through a narrow opening in the trees to reach the green. You'll find this course at the end of Nani Street.

The **Experience at Koele,** 808/565-4653, a Greg Norman–designed course, won the *Fortune Magazine* Best New Golf Course of 1991 award. This magnificent course, set in the mountains above the Lodge, offers not only challenging links but also a fantastic series of views of Moloka'i and Maui on a shimmering canvas of sea. With four sets of tees ranging from forward to tournament, the course yardage varies accordingly from 5,425–7,014 yards. The course also boasts the only bent-grass greens in the state. Two of the finest holes are the number 8, par four, which cascades 250 feet from ridgetop to glen below, and the short but maximum water-challenged number 9.

The **Challenge at Manele,** 808/565-2222, designed by the legendary Jack Nicklaus, officially opened on Christmas Day 1993. Employing the five-tee concept, the par-72 course

The unique eighth hole at the Experience at Koele drops from ridge to valley.

LANA'I GOLF AND TENNIS

Golf Course	Par	Yards	Fees	Cart	Clubs
Cavendish Golf Course	36	3,058	Donation	None	None
The Challenge at Manele 808/565-2222	72	7,039	$205 nonguest $165 hotel guest	Incl.	$50
The Experience at Ko'ele 808/565-4653	72	7,014	$205 nonguest $165 hotel guest	Incl.	$50

Tennis Court	No. of courts	Lighted
The Lodge at Ko'ele Tennis Courts	3	Yes
Manele Bay Hotel Tennis Center	6	No
Lana'i School (Lana'i City)	2	Yes

ranges in length 5,024–7,039 yards. This course is set above the cliff edge, along the sparkling ocean at the Manele Bay Hotel. Three of the main holes, including the signature number 12, par-three hole, demand a tee shot over the greatest water hazard in the world, the wide Pacific.

Horseback Riding

The Stables at Koele, 808/565-4424, open daily and just a few minutes from the Lodge at Koele, offers a variety of mounted excursions. Trail rides run 1–3 hours for $50–110. Three- and four-hour trail rides with lunch are $110–140. Private rides can be arranged for $75–260, as can a full-day ride to the top of the mountain for $400 or a sunset ride for $150. Other rides are available, including a 10-minute children's pony ride and a carriage ride through town for $75. Lana'i enjoys a ranching heritage that goes back to the 1870s. Many of the trails you'll be following date from those early days. Riders must be in good health, weigh less than 250 pounds, and be at least nine years old and stand four foot, six inches tall—except for the pony rides. Everyone must wear long pants and close-toed shoes. Safety helmets will be provided for all riders.

Hunting

The first cliché you hear about Lana'i is that it's one big pineapple plantation. The second is that it's a hunter's paradise. The first was true, and the second still is. Both private and public hunting are allowed. Because virtually all of Lana'i is privately owned, about two-thirds of the island is set aside as a private reserve, and one-third is leased to the state for public hunting and is co-operatively managed.

The big-game action for public hunting is provided by mouflon sheep and axis deer. Various days are open for hunting game birds, which include ring-necked and green pheasant; Gambel's, Japanese, and California quail; wild turkey; and a variety of doves, francolins, and partridges. The public hunting area is restricted to the northwest corner of the island. Brochures detailing all necessary information can be obtained free of charge by writing to the Department of Land and Natural Resources, 1151 Punchbowl St., Honolulu, HI 96813. Contact Derwin Kwon at the Lana'i regional office, P.O. Box 732, 911 Fraser Ave., Lanai City, HI 96763, 808/565-7916. Licenses are required ($20 residents, $105 nonresidents) and can be purchased by mail from the Department of Land and Natural Resources or picked up in person at the office on Lana'i.

Public archery hunting of mouflon sheep is restricted to the last Saturday in July and first Saturday in August. The muzzleloader rifle season occurs on the second and third Saturday in August, and for rifles, shotguns, and bows and arrows for the nine following Saturdays. Tags are required and hunters are restricted by public drawing. Regular season for axis deer (rifle, shot-gun, and bows) opens on the nine consecutive Saturdays starting from the third Saturday in March; it's also restricted by public drawing. Muzzleloader season is the two Saturdays before that, and archery season for axis deer is the two Saturdays and days in between preceding the muzzleloader season. Bag limits are one mou-flon ram and one buck.

On the private land, only axis deer are hunted. Hunting is done year-round, although the best trophy season is May–November. Hunting dates must be mutually agreed upon by the hunter and the rangers because there are a limited number of rangers and this is a three-day process, although the hunt is only one long day affair. Write 3–6 months in ad-vance for best results. The rate is $275 per day for a regular hunting permit or $50 for an archery hunting permit that is good until the Hawaiian hunting license expires. Guide ser-vice is not officially mandatory, but you must prove that you have hunted Lana'i before and are intimately knowledgeable about its terrain, hunting areas, and procedures. If not, you *must* acquire the services of a guide. Guide service is $750 per day, which includes a per-mit and all necessities, except lodging and meals, from airport pickup to shipping the trophy. For all hunters, a Hawaii state hunting license and a hunter safety card are required. For full details, write to Gary Onuma, Chief Ranger, The Lana'i Company, Game Man-agement, P.O. Box 310, Lanai City, HI 96763, 808/565-3981, fax 808/565-3984.

Sporting Clays

An outgrowth of hunting, sporting clays is a sport that helps develop and maintain your hand-eye coordination. Shooting is done from different stations around a course, and the ob-ject is to hit a small, round clay disk. Different from trap or skeet shooting, sporting clays relies on moving targets that mimic different animal and bird movements, hopping along the ground like a rabbit, springing off the ground like a quail, or flying high like a pheasant. Here you can have all the enjoyment of hitting a tar-get without the guilt of killing a living animal. **Lana'i Pine Sporting Clays,** 808/563-4600, is a high-tech operation that services both be-ginners and advanced shooters. To satisfy every-one's needs, there are skeet and trap ranges here as well and an airgun station for kids. Several shooting competitions are held here every year, including the Hawaii Pacific Open Ducks Un-limited Shoot in October.

Register at the pro shop and pick up your needed supplies and accessories there. A paved path connects each of the 14 stations; take a golf cart or walk the course. The basic package, including 100 targets, gun rental, cartridges, eye and ear protection, and safety vest, runs $145 per person; $85 for 50 targets. For ex-perienced shooters, guns, cartridges, targets, and carts can be rented separately, and you may use your own gun. Instruction is also given for beginners at $75; private lessons are avail-able. Pull!

Archery

Set up next to Lana'i Pine Sporting Clays is the newer **Lana'i Pine Archery** course, 808/565-3800. With 12 targets set 15 and 35 yards from the firing line, this is enough to give everyone a challenge. Open 9:15 A.M.–2:30 P.M. daily, the pro shop will set you up with all the needed equipment for your ability. Instruction runs $45, and course use for those who already know how to shoot is $35 or $25 with your own gear.

Fishing

Spinning Dolphin Charters, 808/565-6613, operates a fishing boat out of Lana'i for full- or half-day charters from 1–6 people. Similarly, the *Kila Kila* also offers fishing expeditions.

One of the island's greatest pastimes is the relaxing sport of fishing. Any day in Lana'i City Park, you'll find plenty of old-timers to ask where the fish are biting. If you have the right approach and use the right smile, they just might tell you. Generally, the best fish-ing and easiest access on the island is at Ship-wreck Beach running west toward Polihua. Near the lighthouse ruins is good for *papio* and *ulua,* the latter running to 50 pounds.

Many of the local fishermen use throw-nets to catch the smaller fish such as *manini,* preferred especially by Lana'i's elders. Throw-netting takes skill usually learned from childhood, but don't be afraid to try even if you throw what the locals call a "banana" or one that looks like Maui (a little head and a big body). They might snicker, but if you laugh too, you'll make a friend.

Mostly you'll fish with rod and reel using frozen squid or crab, available at Lana'i's general stores. Bring a net bag or suitable container. This is the best beachcombing on the island, and it's also excellent diving for spiny lobster. There is good shore fishing (especially for *awa*) and easy accessibility at Kaumalapau Harbor, from where the pineapples used to be shipped and where the supplies for the island now come. There is also superb offshore fishing at Kaunolu, Kamehameha's favorite angling spot on the south shore. You can catch *aku* and *kawakawa,* but to be really successful you'll need a boat. Finally, Manele Hulopo'e Marine Life Conservation Park has limited fishing, but as the name implies, it's a conservation district, so be sure to follow the rules prominently posted at Manele Bay.

GETTING THERE
By Air
Hawaiian Airlines, 800/882-8811 on Lana'i, 800/367-5320 Mainland and Canada, flies to Lana'i. It currently has a direct daily early morning flight from Honolulu that returns via Moloka'i. The daily afternoon flight from Honolulu comes through Moloka'i, returning directly to Honolulu. Morning and afternoon flights to Kahului go via Moloka'i and/or Honolulu.

Daily flights are available to and from Lana'i by **Island Air,** 800/652-6541 on Lana'i or 800/323-3345 elsewhere. Using some jets and some turboprops, Island Air flies to and from Honolulu seven times daily, with twice-daily flights between Lana'i and Kahului, Maui.

Based in Kahului, the small commuter and tour operator **Pacific Wings,** 888/575-4546, also flies regularly scheduled flights to and from Lana'i twice daily on weekdays with an abbreviated schedule on weekends. Flights also connect Lana'i twice a day direct to Honolulu.

Lana'i Airport is a practical little strip about four miles southwest of Lana'i City, out near the remaining pineapple fields. The pleasing new terminal offers a departure lounge, gift shop, bathrooms, and public phones. If you are staying at any of the three hotels, a shuttle will transport you into town and drop you at the appropriate place for a $10 use fee. Complimentary airport pickup can also be arranged with Dollar Rent A Car if you rent from them. Otherwise, Rabaca's Limousine Service, 808/565-6670, rabaca@aloha.net, can shuttle you into town for $5 per seat or $10 minimum for ride.

By Boat
The passenger ferry *Expeditions,* 808/661-3756 on Maui or 800/695-2624 on Lana'i and elsewhere, www.go-lanai.com, plies daily between Lahaina and Manele Bay. This shuttle offers speedy and convenient alternative transportation to the island. The crossing takes less than one hour, and the ferry leaves Manele Bay at 8 A.M., 10:30 A.M., 2 P.M., 4:30 P.M., and 6:45 P.M. From Lahaina's public loading pier, ferries leave at 6:45 A.M., 9:15 A.M., 12:45 P.M., 3:15 P.M., and 5:45 P.M. The adult fare is $25 one-way while children 2–11 are $20; *kama'aina* rates are available. It's best to reserve a place. Luggage is taken free of charge, except for a $20 fee for bicycles. Because only two bikes are permitted on each ferry, be sure to let the company know well ahead of time so your bike can go with you. Ground transportation on Lana'i from the pier at Manele Bay is provided by Lana'i City Service, which will take you up to Lana'i City for $20 round-trip or $10 round-trip to the Manele Bay Hotel. An added perk of this trip is that you will see dolphins from the boat most of the year, and there's good whale-watching during the winter.

GETTING AROUND
Shuttle and Limousine Service
No public bus service operates on Lana'i, but **Lana'i City Service,** 808/565-7227, operates a free airport shuttle service during their business

ROBERT NILSEN

Expeditions makes several daily crossings to Lana'i from Lahaina, Maui, making this an easy and convenient trip.

hours (7 A.M.–7 P.M.) if you're renting a vehicle from them. Lana'i City Service also meets all ferries at the pier at Manele Bay and shuttles passengers to Manele Bay Hotel for $10 round-trip or up to Lana'i City for $20 round-trip.

Otherwise, shuttle service is handled by **Rabaca's Limousine Service,** 808/565-6670, rabaca@aloha.net. To/from the airport or anywhere in and around Lana'i City, the charge is $5 per seat, and from Lana'i City to Manele Bay Hotel or the pier at Manele Harbor it's $10 per seat; two-seat minimum on all rides. Rabaca has three stretch limos that are available 24 hours a day. Itineraries are set by the guest.

Lana'i Resort Shuttle

A shuttle service is offered for guests of the two big resorts and Hotel Lanai. This shuttle runs daily 7 A.M.–11 P.M. every hour during the day and every 30 minutes on the hour and half hour in the evening, and picks up passengers at the front of each hotel. A connecting shuttle runs to and from the airport, $10 per person round-trip, meeting all arriving and departing planes.

Car Rental

For a car—or better yet, a jeep—try **Lana'i City**

Service, Dollar Rent A Car, 1036 Lana'i Ave. in Lana'i City, 808/565-7227. You'll be outfitted with wheels and given a drive guide with information about road conditions and where you're allowed and not allowed to drive with their vehicles. Pay heed! Make sure to tell them your plans, especially if you're heading for a remote area. Lana'i City Service is a subsidiary of Trilogy Excursions and has a franchise with Dollar Rent A Car. It rents compacts for $59.99 per day, full-size cars for $79.99, eight-passenger minivans for $129.99, and 4WD Jeep Wranglers for $129.99 per day; all prices are exclusive of tax. Ask about weekly, monthly, and *kama'aina* rates. No insurance is available for vehicles rented on Lana'i, except for no-fault insurance, which is required by law. Lana'i City Service offers free shuttle service to and from the airport if you rent with them. This service operates only during their regular business hours, 7 A.M.–7 P.M. If you need to be at the airport before they start in the morning or after they close in the evening, there will be a $10 pickup charge if you drop off the vehicle at the airport. A fee of $20 is charged for picking up a vehicle left at the ferry pier.

Lana'i City Service has the only gas station on the island, and it's open daily 7 A.M.–7 P.M.

With the few roads on the island, you won't be using much gas, but you'll have to fill the tank up on a rental vehicle when you return it. The price of gas varies but is usually $.50 per gallon more expensive on Lana'i than the average price on Maui.

Using a 4WD Rental

With only 30 miles of paved road on Lana'i and rental cars firmly restricted to these, there is no real reason to rent one unless you are here just to golf. The *real* adventure spots of Lana'i require a 4WD vehicle, which on Lana'i is actually useful and not just a yuppie showpiece because mind-boggling spots on Lana'i are reachable only on foot or by 4WD. Unfortunately, even the inveterate hiker will have a tough time because the best trailheads are quite a distance from town, and you'll spend as much time getting to them as hiking the actual trails.

Many people who have little or no experience driving 4WDs are under the slap-happy belief that they are unstoppable. Oh, would that it were true! They do indeed get stuck, and it's usually miserable getting them unstuck. The rental agency will give you up-to-the-minute information on the road conditions and a fairly accurate map for navigation. It tends to be a bit conservative on where they advise you to take their vehicles, but the staff also live on the island and are accustomed to driving off-road, which balances out their conservative estimates. Also, remember that road conditions change rapidly: A hard rain on the Munro Trail can change it from a flower-lined path to a nasty quagmire, or wind might lay a tree across a beach road. Keep your eye on the weather, and if in doubt, don't push your luck. If you get stuck, you'll not only ruin your outing and have to hike back to town, but you'll also be charged for a service call, which can be astronomical, especially if it's deemed to be a result of your negligence. Most of your dirt road driving will be in 2WD, but certain sections of some roads and other roads during inclement weather will require 4WD. Only on the rarest occasion will you need low-range gearing.

Jeep Tours

Personalized, escorted jeep tours on the island can be arranged through **Rabaca's Limousine Service,** 808/565-6670, rabaca@aloha.net. Let them know your preferences and they'll tailor a tour for you. The rate is $50 per hour with a maximum of four passengers. There is a two-hour minimum, but it usually takes at least three hours to get to some place on the island, have a look around, and get back. If you are unsure about driving dirt roads or may not want to rent a jeep for the out-of-the-way places, leave the driving to the professionals. It can be a good deal. You can also inquire here about kayaking, mountain biking, hiking, photography, fishing, and hunting options. Rabaca can either arrange this for you or send you in the right direction to match your needs.

Hitchhiking

Hitching is legal in Maui County, and that includes Lana'i. Islanders are friendly and quite good about giving you a lift. Lana'i, however, is a workers' island, and the traffic is really skimpy during the day. You can only reasonably expect to get a ride from Lana'i City to the airport or to Manele Bay because both are on paved roads and frequented by normal island traffic, or to Shipwreck Beach on the weekends. There is only a very slim chance of picking up a ride farther afield, toward the Garden of the Gods or Keomuku, for example, so definitely don't count on it.

INFORMATION AND SERVICES

The following phone numbers may be useful as you visit Lana'i: Emergency: 911; police, 808/565-6428; weather and surf conditions, 808/565-6033; Lana'i City Service gas station, 808/565-7227; Department of Land and Natural Resources, 808/565-7916; Lana'i Airport, 808/565-6757; Lana'i Community Hospital 24-hour emergency service, 808/565-6411; Lana'i Family Health Center, 808/565-6423

Information

For general information about Lana'i, and activities and services on the island, contact Destination Lana'i, P.O. Box 700, Lanai City, HI 96763, 808/565-7600 or 800/947-4774, fax 808/565-9316, dlanai@aloha.net, www.visitlanai.net.

Additionally, maps, brochures, and pamphlets on all aspects of staying on Lana'i are available free from the Lana'i Company, P.O. Box 310, Lanai City, HI 96763, 808/565-3000.

For an up-close look at local news and what's happening in the community, have a look at the monthly *Lana'i Times* newspaper.

Banks

Try full-service **First Hawaiian Bank,** in Lana'i City, 808/565-6969, for your banking needs. **Bank of Hawaii,** 808/565-6426, also has a branch here. Banks are open Monday–Thursday 8:30 A.M.–3 P.M. (4:30 P.M. for Bank of Hawaii) and Friday until 6 P.M., but they may be closed for lunch. Both have ATMs outside their offices for after-hours banking. All major businesses on the island accept traveler's checks, and many now also accept credit cards.

Post Office

The Lana'i post office, 808/565-6517, at its new location on Jacaranda Street, just a few steps off the city park, is open weekdays 9 A.M.–4 P.M. and Saturday 10 A.M.–noon. You can find boxes and padded mailers for your beachcombing treasures at the two general stores in town.

Library

Located at 6th Street and Fraser Avenue next to the school, the public library is open Tuesday, Thursday, and Friday 8 A.M.–4 P.M., Wednesday 1–8 P.M., and Saturday 11 A.M.–4 P.M.

Cinema

On the corner of Lana'i Avenue and 7th Street, Lana'i Playhouse, 808/565-7500, is the only theater on the island; it runs current-release movies. Open Friday–Tuesday; tickets run $7 adults, $4.50 kids and seniors.

Laundry

Located on the north side of Dole Park in the middle of Lana'i City, the only laundromat on the island is open every day from "morning until nighttime": 5 A.M.–8:30 P.M. Bring coins.

Lana'i City

Lana'i City would be more aptly described and sound more appealing if it were called Lana'i Village. A utilitarian town, it was built in the 1920s by Dole Pineapple Company. The architecture, field-worker plain, has definitely gained character in the last 70 years. It's an excellent spot for a town, sitting at 1,600 feet in the shadow of Lana'ihale, the island's tallest peak. George Munro's Cook pines have matured and now give the entire town a green, shaded, parklike atmosphere. It's cool and breezy—a great place to launch from in the morning and a welcome spot to return to at night. Most visitors head out of town to the more spectacular sights and never take the chance to explore the back streets.

As you might expect, most houses are square boxes with corrugated roofs, but each has its own personality. Painted every color of the rainbow, they'd be garish in any other place, but here they break the monotony and seem to work. The people of Lana'i used to make their living from the land and can still work wonders with it. Around many homes are colorful flowerbeds, green gardens bursting with vegetables, fruit trees, and flowering shrubs. When you look down the half-dirt, broken-pavement roads at a line of these houses, you can't help feeling that a certain nobility exists here. The houses are mud-spattered where the rain splashes red earth against them, but inside you know they're sparkling clean. Many of these narrow lanes are one-way streets—watch for signs!

The modern suburban homes that line the few blocks at the extreme south end of town are mostly from the late 1980s and early '90s. Most of these belong to Lana'i's miniature middle class and would fit unnoticed in any up-and-coming neighborhood on another island. On the north

LANA'I CITY

To Garden of the Gods and Polihua Beach

To Shipwreck Beach

TENNIS COURTS

STABLES
430

THE LODGE AT KOELE

THE EXPERIENCE AT KOELE GOLF COURSE

KEOMUKU RD.

CAVENDISH GOLF COURSE

DETAIL

THEATER
BANK

KOELE AVE.

LANA'I FAMILY STORE

OKAMOTO REALTY

TANIGAWA'S

DESTINATION LANA'I

LANA'I AVE.

7TH ST.

D O L E   P A R K

8TH

BANK

PETRO'S

PINE ISLE MARKET

RICHARD'S SHOPPING CENTER

3RD

FRASER

HOUSTON

IIMA

GAY

4TH AVE.

5TH

JACARANDA AVE.

KOELE AVE.

LANA'I AVE.

NANI AVE.

MAHANA AVE.

HALE O LANA'I

6TH ST.

LIBRARY

COFFEE WORKS

POST OFFICE

CLINIC

HEART OF LANA'I

SCHOOL

LOCAL GENTRY

LAUNDROMAT

LANAI ART PROGRAM

BLUE GINGER CAFE

GIFTS WITH ALOHA

HOSPITAL

DOLE   PARK

8TH ST.

HOTEL LANA'I

GYM

ADVENTURE LANA'I COMPANY

PELE'S OTHER GARDEN

SEE DETAIL

PUUANI PL.

KAUNA'OA

TENNIS COURTS

POOL

POLICE

INTERNATIONAL FOOD AND CLOTHING

9TH

DLNR

10TH

LANAI CITY SERVICE

DOLLAR RENT A CAR

11TH

DREAMS COME TRUE

QUEENS

PALAWAI

OUAPA

AHA

MANA

LANAI COMPANY CENTRAL SERVICES

12TH

13TH

AKAHI ST.

HALE MOE

AKOLU

0   0.25 mi

0   0.25 km

FIRE STATION

AKOLU

440

To Airport

KAUMALAPAU HWY.

MANELE RD.

To Manele Bay

LANA'I

edge of town are a few new apartments and multifamily buildings that were put up in the mid-1990s. On the slope above town, set along the golf course fairways, are the more recent townhouses and luxury homes that will, over the years, become more predominant if development goes as planned. Similarly, a luxury home development is growing along the golf fairways to the side of Manele Bay Hotel.

Around Town

Lana'i City streets running east-west are numerical starting with 3rd Street and running to 13th Street; the streets running north-south have alphabetical first letters and include Fraser, Gay, Houston, Ilima, Jacaranda, Ko'ele, and Lana'i avenues, with a few more streets beyond this central grid. If you manage to get lost in Lana'i City you should seriously consider never leaving home.

If you sit on the steps of Hotel Lanai and peer across its huge front yard, you can scrutinize the heart of downtown Lana'i City. Off to your right are offices, the community hospital and health center sitting squat and solid. In front of them, forming a type of town square, is Dole Park, where old-timers come to sit and young mothers bring their kids for some fresh air. No one in Lana'i City rushes to do anything. Look around and you'll discover a real fountain of youth: The many octogenarians walk with a spring in their step. Years of hard work without being hyper or anxious is why they say they're still around. The park is surrounded by commercial Lana'i. There's nowhere to *go* except over to the schoolyard to play some tennis or to Cavendish Golf Course for a round of nine holes. Lana'i City has a movie theater, and its now showing pictures once again. You can plop yourself at the Blue Ginger Cafe or Tanigawa's for coffee or stay in the park if you're in the mood to strike up a conversation—it shouldn't take long.

Meander down Lana'i Avenue past a complex of former agricultural buildings and shops. Once full of heavy equipment, this is where Lana'i showed its raw plantation muscle. Part of it has now been tamed and is the site of a new senior citizen's housing complex. Beyond the commercial buildings on both sides of the downtown park are the rows of plantation houses, now with newer subdivisions farther to each end. Do yourself a favor: Get out of your rental car and walk around town for at least 30 minutes. You'll experience one of the most unique villages in America.

ACCOMMODATIONS
Hotel Lanai

Being the only hotel on the island until 1990, you'd think the lack of competition would have made Hotel Lanai arrogant, indifferent, and expensive. On the contrary: It is delightful. The hotel has gone through a few cosmetic changes since it was built in 1923 as a guest lodge, then called The Clubhouse, primarily for visiting executives of Dole Pineapple Co., the progeny of which still owns it. Its architecture is simple plantation-style Hawaiiana, and its setting among the tall Cook pines fronted by a large lawn is refreshingly rustic. With a corrugated iron roof, board and batten walls inside and out, wooden floors, and two wings connected by a long, enclosed veranda, it looks like the main building at a Boy Scout camp—but don't be fooled. The 10 remodeled rooms may not be plush, but they are cozy as can be, and four open onto the front lanai. All have been painted in lively colors and are immaculate with refurbished private baths. All have pine dressers and tables, lamps, area rugs, and ceiling fans, and patchwork quilts like grandma used to make cover each comfortable bed. Original artwork, done specifically for the hotel by island artist Denise Henning, graces the rooms and public areas.

Room rates are $98–115, which includes a complimentary continental breakfast from 7–9:30 A.M. of pastries from the kitchen, juice, and coffee. A newly renovated cottage to the side of the main building, at one time the caretaker's house, has its own living room and bath with tub. It rents for $150. One added benefit is that guests of the hotel have signing privileges for meals, golf, and gift shop items at both the Lodge at Koele and at the Manele Bay Hotel. Contact Hotel Lanai at P.O. Box 630520, Lanai

ROBERT NILSEN

Hotel Lanai was the only hotel on the island until the two new luxury hotels were built in the 1990s.

City, HI 96763, 808/565-7211 or 800/795-7211 (7 A.M.–8 P.M. local time), fax 808/565-6450, www.hotellanai.com.

The hotel has the only in-town bar, where guests and islanders alike have a quiet beer and twilight chat. The dining room, which occupies the center of the hotel, is paneled in knotty pine boards and lined with hunting trophies. So if you're lured by the quiet simplicity of Lana'i and wish to avail yourself of one of the last family-style inns of Hawaii, stay at the lovely little Hotel Lanai.

The Lodge at Koele

A stately row of Cook pines bids welcome as they line the red-brick driveway leading to this grand manor house perched in genteel quietude just a 15-minute walk from downtown Lana'i City. An upland country hotel befitting this area of trees and cool summers, it's gracefully done in neo-Victorian style. Here, a huge pineapple mural painted above the front entrance greets everyone upon arrival. The name for this section of the island, Ko'ele, means dark sugarcane. The Lodge at Koele, P.O. Box 310, Lanai City, HI 96763, 808/565-7300 or 800/321-4666, www.lodgeatkoele.com, with its encircling veranda and sweep of broad lawn, exudes gracious relaxation. You enter into the Great Hall, where the back ceiling is a translucent skylight through which the sun casts diffused beams onto the formal Victorian parlor below. Encircled by a rich koa balcony, the Great Hall holds two immense fireplaces, the largest in Hawaii. Parlor settings of velvet chairs, cushy couches, wicker lounges, credenzas covered in flowers and ferns, and lustrous end tables are perfect for a lazy afternoon of perusing the newspapers and magazines of the world or listening to soft island music every evening. At each corner of the spacious Great Hall is a hexagonal room of beveled windows: one for dining; one for music; one a library; and the last a game room with backgammon, chess, and dominoes. Afternoon tea by reservation is served in the tea room or on the terrace.

Out front is a croquet pitch, to the side a lawn bowling green. Out back through glass French doors are two more croquet lawns, the swimming pool and fitness/healing center, gazebo and reservoir, Japanese strolling garden, orchid house, palm and fruit gardens, and an executive putting green—a professionally designed "miniature" but real golf course. Here, with putter and a glass of chilled champagne and chocolate-dipped strawberries, you can test your skill against tiny sand traps, puddle-size water traps, and challenging Chihuahua-inspired doglegs both left and right.

Walk along the wide, covered veranda past a row of rocking chairs to the two wings off the Great Hall, where you will find the 102 guest rooms, which range in price from $375 for a garden view to $3,000 for the best suite. A renewal project of the entire property was completed in 2000. Once inside, you can take the brass-doored elevator, but you should climb instead the sweeping wooden staircases bearing carved pineapples, the symbol of hospitality, and walk the broad hardwood hall hung with the works of island artists (ask the concierge for an art list for the hotel), letting period wall lamps light your way. Rooms are furnished in a combination of wicker and heavy knotty pine, with a four-poster bed—each topped with a carved pineapple—covered by a downy quilt, while billowy printed curtains flutter past a window seat. Along with this early-1900s charm comes a full entertainment center, in-room safe, and wet bar. Each room has its own lanai with tile floor and wooden furniture. The bathroom, perhaps blue- or black-on-white marble, features a sink and deep soaking tub with old-fashioned brass knobs, and separate commode. Each room also has multiple phones, ceiling fans, and even umbrellas to borrow and walking sticks for an afternoon foray into the surrounding hills.

An unexpected favorite for many guests is the hotel's Visiting Artist Program. Started in 1992, this ongoing cultural event brings writers, musicians, chefs, poets, filmmakers, and a whole host of other creative people to the hotel for free informal gatherings and presentations about one weekend a month. Two in-house restaurants are here to serve the guests. You can find sundries (and film developing) at the hotel shop, open 8 A.M.–9 P.M. All hotel and island activities, including croquet, tennis, golf, hunting, horseback riding, jeep tours, sporting clays, and beach and boating activities, as well as Internet connection, can be arranged by the concierge. There is regular and frequent shuttle service to meet all arriving and departing planes, to and from Lana'i City, Hotel Lanai, and to Manele Bay Hotel.

The Manele Bay Hotel

Although it's located overlooking Manele Bay, this hotel property is dealt with here because it's the only other hotel accommodation on the island.

Glass doors curved in a traditional Roman arch sympathize with the surging Pacific as you enter the seaside 250-room Manele Bay Hotel, P.O. Box 310, Lanai City, HI 96763, 808/565-7700 or 800/321-4666, www.manelebayhotel.com, fashioned in a fusion of Mediterranean, Asian, and Hawaiian design and motif. The open reception area, all marble and glass, with cushy chairs and couches, a huge colorful rug, and carved elephant tusks, holds two massive murals of Lana'i and the wide Pacific dotted with islands. Heroic paintings depict pioneering Polynesians in a double-hulled canoe sighting the Hawaiian Islands and the rascal Prince Kaulula'au, redeemer of Lana'i, standing triumphantly on a windswept beach after banishing the vexatious specters of Lana'i. The lower lobby in contrast has a decidedly Asian feel, with hints of Hawaii. High on the upper walls are painted huge murals depicting Chinese scenes. Below, salubrious chairs and cushions invite you to relax, Asian-style adornments please the eye, and a huge Hawaiian-theme chandelier provides light. For an elegant evening, order a drink or come to hear the evening entertainment at the Hale Aheahe Lounge. The hotel library is a genial room filled with leather-bound tomes, globes, and models of sailing ships. Overhead, the recessed wooden ceiling has been painted with various emblems of Hawaii; the floor is the intricate paisley of tasseled Persian carpets. Sit in a highbacked chair just near the balcony and enjoy the vantage point overlooking Hulopo'e Court below.

From the main reception area, descend a grand staircase and pass a formidable lava rock wall draped with the purples and pinks of living bougainvillea. Here is the grand cloverleaf pool encircled by a marble apron, open for use 24 hours a day. On the lawn below the pool lies an archeological site. Nearby, the newly renovated hotel spa is complete with steam rooms, saunas, and professional staff. The fitness machines and free weights have been moved to one of the open but covered patios. The formal gardens, two on the east and three on the west, and each with its own theme, are tranquil oases where rivulets drop into koi ponds surrounded by patches of broad-leafed taro and swaying stands of bamboo. It's a marvelous setting, but perhaps the best outdoor feature of all is the unobstructed natural beauty of Hulopo'e Bay.

The hotel rooms and suites are mainly in wings east and west. East rooms bear marine names derived from the sea; the west rooms are named after flowers. These oversize guest rooms ranging in price $375–525, designed with Mediterranean and Asian themes, offer four-poster mahogany beds covered with thick quilts, wicker lounge chairs, wet bars, and user-friendly entertainment centers. Marble-tiled bathroom features extra-deep soaking tubs, double sinks and vanity, separate commodes, and glass-enclosed shower stalls big enough for two. Each room has its own private lanai that either overlooks one of the gorgeous gardens or offers an ocean panorama. The hotel also offers several suites that range in price $725–2,200. A typical midrange suite offers a formal parlor and separate master bedroom with a dressing room attached. On the Butler Floor, someone will pack and unpack clothing, draw a hot bath, pour cold champagne, make dinner reservations, and act as your personal liaison at the hotel.

The hotel also offers valet parking, tennis courts, a beach kiosk, a children's program, a gift shop, three restaurants, and a cocktail lounge, where music is performed nightly 5:30–9:30 P.M. Saturdays and Sundays are special with *keiki* hula dancers who come to perform their special magic in the Hulopo'e Court. Another treat is to walk a few minutes to the hotel's **Lana'i Conference Center,** where the antechamber holds museum-quality artifacts. In glass cases, you will find stone implements ranging from *'ulu maika,* Hawaiian bowling stones similar to Italian boccie, to *poho kukui* (*kukui* nut oil lamps). Most of these implements, including a petroglyph stone, have been gathered from Lana'i. There is also an impressive replica of a Hawaiian double-hulled canoe.

B&Bs and Vacation Rentals

For a more homey stay on the Pineapple Island, try one of the few bed-and-breakfast inns or vacation rentals on Lana'i, all of which are in Lana'i City. These places offer a substantially cheaper alternative to staying on Lana'i than the resorts, and they get you into the community.

Dreams Come True, 808/565-6961 or 800/566-6961, fax 808/565-7056, hunter @aloha.net, www.dreamscometruelanai.com, is a guesthouse in the oldest part of town at 12th Street and Lana'i Avenue. Four rooms in this comfortable plantation house are rented to guests, each with its own bathroom (Italian marble and whirlpool tub) and use of the common room and full kitchen. Decent size for the island, one room has two queen beds, two have one queen bed, and the fourth has two singles. An expanded continental breakfast, with fresh-squeezed lilikoi juice, is served each morning. The rate is $98.50 single or double per night; $35 extra for a child in the same room as parents, or $380 for the entire house. In-house massage can be arranged by appointment only; the owners sell their handmade jewelry; and 4WD vehicles can be rented (inquire as to rates). Find out more about these properties by contacting the owners, Michael and Susan Hunter.

Hale Moe, on the south side of town at 502 Akolu St., P.O. Box 196, Lanai City, HI 96763, 808/565-9520, www.staylanai.com, rents three rooms, each with a bathroom, or the entire house. Usually no breakfast is served, but guests can use the kitchen. Two rooms go for $80 and the third is $90. The whole house can be rented for $300.

Several fully equipped houses can be rented from Phylis McOmber, 808/565-6071. One is a two-story affair that can sleep up to eight; the others sleep 5–6 persons. Call for rates.

Hale O Lana'i, 808/247-3637, fax 808/235-2644, hibeach@lava.net, www.hibeach.com, is a newer two-bedroom, two-bath house on 4th Street and Lana'i Avenue that has all the amenities for a fine vacation stay. It rents for $115–135 per night, two nights minimum; or $685 on a weekly basis.

Aside from these, try Dolores Fabrao, 808/565-6134, who rents rooms in the family house, 538 Akahi St., for $50 single, $60 double. She also has a larger room that's often used by hunting groups; $25 per person with four or more.

Rental Agents

Okamoto Realty, 730 Lana'i Ave., #112, P.O. Box 630552, Lana'i City, HI 96763, 808/565-7519, fax 808/565-6106, was Lana'i's first house rental agency, and it handles upscale property. Although the number of houses in its listing varies, you're likely to find three-bedroom affairs at $150–175 per night for up to seven people or a four-bedroom, three-bath cedar house for $495 per night that will sleep 10. All houses are completely furnished, including linens and kitchen utensils, and most have washer/dryer and TV. Houses are rented by the day (with a two-night minimum), week, or month.

Handling some vacation rental properties on the island is **Lana'i Realty,** P.O. Box 676, Lanai City, HI 96763, 808/565-6597 or 800/943-0989. They have homes for $100–145 per night with a two-night minimum.

RESTAURANTS

Aside from the resort hotels, Lana'i City is the only place on the island where you can dine, shop, and take care of business. The food situation on Lana'i used to be discouraging. Most everything had to be brought in by barge, and the fresh produce, fish, and meat was at a premium. People surely ate differently at home, but in the two tiny restaurants open to travelers, the fare was restricted to the "two-scoop rice and teri beef" variety, with fried noodles and Spam as the pièce de résistance. But, the times they are a-changin'! Now there are more options from which to choose and more culinary variety.

By far the best restaurant in town is **Henry Clay's Rotisserie** at the Hotel Lanai, 808/565-7211; open for dinner daily 5:30–9 P.M. Set just off the entry porch is the barrel-vaulted dining room; guests are also seated in the adjacent back room and bar and on the back patio. Evening appetizers run the gamut from oyster shooters at $1.75 apiece to Cajun shrimp for $10.95. A soup or salad prepares the way for an entrée, be it eggplant creole and angel hair pasta for $18.95, "Louisiana style" barbecue ribs for $19.95, rotisserie roasted whole chicken for $25.95, or either fresh catch and roasted free-range venison loin at a daily quote. Gourmet pizzas are also served, and don't forget the homemade desserts. This is down-home country cooking with a Cajun twist and island influence. Have a look through the glass window into the kitchen to see the large commercial rotisserie full of chicken and other meat. Order a variety of beers or a glass of wine with your meal or simply stop by the bar for a drink from 5:30 P.M. until closing.

The banging screen doors announce your presence as you enter the plantation-era wainscoted **Blue Ginger Cafe,** 808/565-6363, open daily 6 A.M.–2 P.M. and 3–9 P.M., which could actually be called chic for Lana'i. Upon entering, baked goods let you know that not long ago it was Dahang's Bakery, a Lana'i institution whose motto, "Mo betta grind ova hea," has also survived. It offers a full breakfast menu with choices like two eggs with sausage for $4.75, along with plenty of side orders, and fresh pastries. Plate lunches are $6.50 or so, while a bowl of saimin goes for $2.95. Burgers, sandwiches, pizza, and ice cream are also on the menu at comparable prices. Varying nightly, dinner specials, served with rice "toss" salad or macaroni salad, run $8–16. Eat inside or on the front veranda, where you can see everything there is to see in Lana'i City. If you *really* like it here, take home one of their T-shirts. Look for the blue roof.

An authentic workers' restaurant, **Tanigawa's,** open daily except Wednesday for breakfast and lunch 6:30 A.M.–1 P.M., is one of those places that you must visit at least for morning coffee. Totally down-home, but a pure cultural experience, you can also get hot cakes, omelets, burgers, and plate lunches, most for under $7. Arrive before 7 A.M., when many of the older people come to "talk story." Just one look around at the crinkled faces will reveal the tough but sweet spirit of Lana'i.

For a healthy, quick, light meal, try **Pele's Other Garden,** 8th St. and Houston Ave., 808/565-9628. This deli and pizzeria is open Monday–Saturday 9 A.M.–3 P.M. for lunch and 5–9 P.M. for dinner. Eat in or take out. Try a turkey, veggie wrap, or other sandwich for $8 or less, or a hot entrée, like a cheese quesadilla or grilled chicken breast, for $4.50–7.99. More substantial dinner entées run $13–19. Individual or family-size pizzas run $7–22, or choose a salad or something else from the deli case, which also holds gourmet meats, olives, and cheeses. Be sure to check the special board because you never know what scrumptious delicacy will be offered each day.

Occupying the old Akamai Trading Company shop is **Petro's,** 808/565-6622, serving pizza and sub sandwiches. Open 10 A.M.–8 P.M., Petro's serves pizza by the slice or you can "build your own."

The **Coffee Works,** 604 Ilima St., 808/565-6962, offers espresso, latte, or cappuccino, herb tea, or refreshing ice cream. Open Monday–Friday 6 A.M.–6 P.M., Saturday until 5 P.M., and Sunday until 1 P.M.

Hotel Restaurants

In harmony with the rest of the Lodge at Koele, the dining rooms are impeccably furnished. Serving all day, **The Terrace,** set in a section off the Great Hall and the more casual of the two restaurants, looks out over the exotic gardens, while the separate dinner-only Formal Dining Room lends itself to evening attire—jackets required. Breakfast selections at The Terrace include continental breakfast, eggs Benedict, and sweet rice waffles with *lilikoi*-coconut chutney. At midday satisfy your hunger with light fare. Dinner, like the other daily fare, is made from the freshest island ingredients. Choose standards like roasted veal chop, braised short ribs, grilled fresh prawns on pasta, or a superbly prepared catch of the day.

In the **Formal Dining Room** you'll have a grand dining experience. It always gets rave reviews form diners who are into serious eating. Once again, the freshest island ingredients are used to prepare each meal that leaves the kitchen. Not only are they sumptuous, but they are also presented in a pleasing manner. All of this elegance doesn't come cheap, however. Expect prices in the $40–50 range for an entrée, which includes butter-braised Maine lobster, seared Hawaiian snapper, and herb-crusted rack of Colorado lamb.

The **Clubhouse** at the Experience at Koele golf course is open daily 10:30 A.M.–3:30 P.M., serving excellent soups, sandwiches, and salads at reasonable prices. Everyone is welcome, and the standing room only lets you know that the food is very good. Try a Korean barbecued beef sandwich, Caesar salad, or one of the many pasta dishes for $7–13. Indoor or outdoor seating is available, with a great view of the 18th green.

The master chef at the Manele Bay Hotel's formal **Ihilani Restaurant** offers a prix fixe menu nightly, along with a complete menu of à la carte suggestions. Expect most entrées in the $32–44 range, with the six-course prix fixe menu at $100 per person. The Ihilani serves dinner only Tuesday–Saturday 6–9:30 P.M.—jackets recommended. Begin with ravioli of Hawaiian goat cheese in a sauce of cilantro and sun-dried tomatoes or gratinée of South Pacific blue prawns. Second courses can be Mediterranean antipasto or Provençale saffron lobster fish soup. Entrées include lavender honey–glazed Muscovy duck breast, grilled catch of the day, and baked onaga and citrus in a sea salt crust. All of this, with a superb view of the bay and beach, is magnifique!

The less formal but still extremely elegant **Hulopo'e Court** offers breakfast and dinner of contemporary Hawaiian regional cuisine, with prices similar to the Ihilani. This is perhaps the best breakfast spot on the island. Begin the day with a continental breakfast, choose all manner of traditional favorites from the breakfast buffet, or make an à la carte selection. Dinner begin with appetizers like crispy fried calamari and cilantro hummus. Soups and salads introduce the entrées, like smoked chicken penne pasta, Hawaiian seafood stew, tarragon-crusted center-cut pork chop, and pan-seared mahimahi. An excellent selection of domestic and imported beer and wine completes the meal.

The least formal dining setting is poolside at **The Pool Grille,** an al fresco restaurant serving

LANA'I

lunch and afternoon snacks 11 A.M.–5 P.M. daily. Start with an appetizer such as a chicken quesadilla or cocktail of Pacific shrimp. Lighter appetites will enjoy main-course salads, including marinated grilled vegetables, Cobb salad, or seafood salad. The sandwich board features a good old-fashioned club, a grilled beef burger, or a hot dog. Special offerings are Hawaiian favorites like grilled fresh catch or a steamy bowl of savory saimin.

Overlooking the pool, the **Hale Aheahe Lounge** is open every evening 5–11, serves appetizers until 10 P.M., and has sweet sounds of soft piano music playing until 9:30 P.M.

One must not forget the **Clubhouse Restaurant** at the Challenge at Manele golf course, which has superb underwater scene murals painted on its walls by John Wulbrandt. The view from here is perhaps the best on the property, overlooking both the hotel and bay, with Haleakala on Maui in the background, particularly on a night when the full moon is rising early. Food is served daily 11 A.M.–3 P.M., dinner Thursday–Sunday 6–9 P.M. Small plates are the theme here. Some selections on this hot and cold *pu pu* menu are shrimp satay, spiced lamb, and grilled *ahi* with white bean cassoulet, all for under $15 a plate.

SHOPPING

Except for the clutch of shops at the Lodge at Koele and Manele Bay Hotel, and the gift shop at the airport, shopping on Lana'i means shopping in Lana'i City. Be aware that all but a few shops are closed on Sunday, and remember that some shops in town may close their doors for an hour or longer at midday for a siesta.

The two grocery stores in town are fairly well stocked with basics. The markets are almost next door to each other. **Pine Isle Market,** 808/565-6488, run by Kerry Honda and open 7 A.M.–10 P.M. every day except Sunday, is Lana'i's closest equivalent to a supermarket, although it also carries hardware and general merchandise. It has a good community bulletin board outside. **Richards Shopping Center,** 808/565-6047, is open Monday–Saturday 8:30 A.M.–5:30 P.M. A

small grocery and sundries store, it supplies all your basic camping, fishing, and general merchandise needs, including clothing and medicines, some groceries, liquor, and odds and ends.

Around the corner is **International Food and Clothing Center,** 808/565-6433, where you can pick up not only things to eat, but also hardware and hunting supplies. They have their own butcher, but not much in the way of clothing anymore. This is an old-fashioned general store, definitely a local place; open weekdays 8 A.M.–6 P.M., until 1:30 on Sunday, closed Saturday. On the next street over are a couple of small new shops that sell CDs and tapes and a few snacks. On the far side of the city park is the **Lana'i Family Store,** 808/565-6485, for video rentals and furniture.

Gifts With Aloha, 808/565-6589, a shop that carries art and craft items from local and other Hawaii residents, is just down the road. Some items include cloth and clothing, jewelry, quilts, and candles. You should be able to find something for that special occasion here, Mon.–Sat. 9:30 A.M.–6 P.M. Behind Gifts With Aloha is **The Local Gentry,** 808/565-9130, a clothing boutique for women that's open Monday–Friday 10 A.M.–6 P.M. and Saturday until 5 P.M.

Nearby is the **Lana'i Art Program** gallery, 808/565-7503, open daily at irregular hours because it's staffed by volunteers, which has taken the spirit of the Zimbabwe saying "If you can walk, you can dance," and changed it into "If you've got life, you've got art." This co-op of local Lana'i citizens has created a nonprofit organization dedicated to developing the artistic talents of its members and has a strong kids program. Classes, chaired by guest artists, are periodically offered in photography, woodworking, Japanese doll-making, fabric-making, drama and cultural arts, painting, glass, ceramics, and pen and ink drawing. The showroom offers purchases such as hand-dyed silk scarves, stenciled T-shirts, naturally dyed incidental bags, notecards, and lovely pareu for women. Pottery and silk painting seem to predominate. The work is always changing, but you are sure to find a distinctive island memento that couldn't be more genuine. All are welcome, resident or not, so you can drop in on a workshop, pay for your supplies, and create your own art.

Now in a bright yellow plantation-era house at 758 Queen Street, behind Hotel Lanai, **Heart of Lana'i Art Gallery,** 808/565-6678, features watercolors of island scenes by Denise Henning, wooden bowls and ukuleles by Cyrus Keanini, and oil paintings by Macauio Pascual and Pam Andelin. The works are casually displayed but of top quality. With no fixed hours, it's best to call ahead to be sure that the gallery is open. Tues-day–Saturday 2:30–4:30 P.M., Denise hosts an afternoon tea, not only to open her gallery but also to invite special island *kapuna* to talk story. Reservations are requested.

Are you looking for fresh food to cook yourself? Try the **farmers market** at Dole Park, Saturday morning 7–9 A.M. For snacks and sundries, you can also try the Lana'i Plantation Store at the Lana'i City Service gas station. For last-minute souvenirs, have a look at the **airport gift shop** in the terminal building.

Exploring Lana'i

MUNRO TRAIL

The highlight of visiting Lana'i is climbing the Munro Trail to its highest point, Lana'ihale (3,370 feet), locally called **The Hale.** As soon as you set foot on Lana'i, the silhouette of this razorback ridge with its bristling coat of Cook pines demands your attention. Set off for The Hale and you're soon engulfed in its cool stands of pines, eucalyptus, and ironwoods, all colored with ferns and wildflowers. George Munro, a New Zealander hired as the manager of the Lana'i Ranch a short time before Jim Dole's arrival, is responsible for this lovely flora. With a pouch full of seeds and clippings from his native New Zealand, he trudged all over Lana'i planting, in an attempt to foliate the island and create a permanent watershed. Driven by that basic and primordial human desire to see things grow, he climbed The Hale time and again to renew and nurture his leafy progeny. Now, all benefit from his labors.

The Trail

There are two basic ways to go to The Hale, by foot or 4WD. Some local people go on horseback. Head out of town on Keomuku Road toward Shipwreck Beach. It's preferable to start in the morning; cloud cover is common by early afternoon. At mile marker 1, still on the Lana'i City side of the mountains, take the first major road to the right. The sign here should read Cemetery Road. In about one-quarter mile the road comes to a Y intersection—go left. You immediately start climbing and pass through a forested area. Continue and the road forks; again bear left. Always stay on the more obviously traveled road, and don't be fooled by the shortcuts that have been constructed for water drainage. The side roads may look muddy or be overgrown, and it's obvious which is the main one. Robert Frost would be disappointed.

As you climb, you pass a profusion of gulches, great red wounds cut into Lana'i's windward

on the Munro Trail

side. First comes deep and brooding **Maunalei (Mountain Lei) Gulch,** from where Lana'i draws its water through a series of tunnels bored through the mountains. It's flanked by **Ko'oLana'i Trail,** a rugged and dangerous footpath leading all the way to the coast. Past the communication towers is **Ho'okio Gulch,** a battleground where Lana'i's warriors were vanquished in 1778 by Kalaniopu'u and his ferocious fighters from the Big Island. All that remains are a few room-size notches cut into the walls where the warriors slept and piled stones to be hurled at the invaders. After Ho'okio Gulch, a trail bears left, bringing you to the gaping mouth of **Hauola Gulch,** more than 2,000 feet deep. Keep your eyes peeled for axis deer, which seem to defy gravity and manage to cling and forage along the most unlikely and precipitous cliffs. Be very careful of your footing—even skilled Lana'i hunters have fallen to their deaths in this area.

The jeep trail narrows on the ridge to little more than 10 feet across. On one side are the wild gulches, on the other the whorling fingerprints of the former pineapple fields. At one point along the way, there's even a picnic table with a view down the west side at one of the short pulloffs. Along the trail, in season, you can munch strawberries, common guavas, and as many thimbleberries as you can handle. At the crest of The Hale, let your eyes pan the horizon to see all of the main islands of Hawaii, except for Kaua'i and Ni'ihau. Rising from the height-caused mirage of a still sea is the hazy specter of O'ahu to the north, with Moloka'i and Maui clearly visible just 10 miles distant. Haleakala, Maui's magical mountain, has a dominant presence viewed from The Hale. Sweep right to see Kaho'olawe, bleak and barren, its body shattered by years of bombs, a victim of controversial war games now ended, that with great volunteer help is slowly on the mend. Eighty miles southeast of Kaho'olawe is the Big Island, its mammoth peaks, Mauna Loa and Mauna Kea, looming like ethereal islands floating in the clouds.

Just past the final lookout is a sign for **Awehi Trail,** which leads left to Naha on the beach. It's extremely rough, and a drive down would definitely require 4WD in compound low gear. Access to this road is not permitted by the rental car company, so you'll have to walk if you want to explore this route. Follow the main road down this dusty decline and take either Ho'ike Road, which flattens out and joins with Route 440 just south of Lana'i City, or head straight ahead and join the highway near where it heads down the hill to Manele Bay. If you have time for only one outing on Lana'i or funds budgeted for only one day of 4WD rental, make sure to treat yourself to the unforgettable Munro Trail.

HEADING SOUTH

Joseph Kali'ihananui was the last of the free Hawaiian farmers to work the land of Lana'i. His great-grandson, Lloyd Cockett, lived in Lana'i City until a few years ago. Joseph made his home in the arid but fertile Palawai Basin, which was later bought by Jim Dole and turned into the heart of the pineapple plantation. Just south of Lana'i City on Route 440 (Manele Road), the Palawai Basin is the crater of the extinct single volcano of which Lana'i is formed. Joseph farmed sweet potatoes, which he traded for fish. He gathered his water in barrels from the dew that formed on his roof and from a trickling spring. His lands supported a few cattle among its now-extinct heavy stands of cactus. Here, too, Walter Murray Gibson attempted to begin a Mormon colony, which he later aborted, supposedly because of his outrage over the idea of polygamy. Nothing noteworthy remains of this colony, but on a hillside overlooking Palawai are the Luahiwa Petroglyphs.

Luahiwa Petroglyphs

Heading south on Manele Road, look to your left for six tall pine trees and the back side of a stop sign at Ho'ike Road. Ho'ike Road was once paved but has now disintegrated into gravel. Parenthetically, during the pineapple days, major roads that ran through the pineapple fields were paved in order to keep the big trucks running from field to warehouse even when rains made the fields slick with mud. These roads were lines with stone, quarried and set in place by Korean stone masons in the early 1900s. While the rows of pineapples are gone, whorls of grass still grow in the fields. A telltale sign that these fields were recently cultivated are the ever-present bits and pieces of black plastic irrigation pipe and weed cloth that can be seen here and throughout the Palawai basin, an ugly remnant of the plantation days that will be around for years.

After turning left onto Ho'ike, head straight down the road about one mile. When the road comes up a low rise, turn left and follow this secondary road, keeping the ditch on your right. Proceed about one-half mile until you come to a silver water pipe about 12 inches in diameter. Follow this pipe, heading back toward Lana'i City, jogging right up onto the dike, crossing the pipe, and continue on the upper road about three-tenths mile to rocks on your right at the base of the hill.

Scamper up the hill to the boulders on which appear the petroglyphs. Once brownish black and covered in lichen, their appearance has changed somewhat following an accidental grass fire, which, oddly enough, exposed additional petroglyphs in a ravine to the south that had not been remembered by island residents. Their natural arrangement resembles an oversize Japanese rock garden. Dotted on the hillside are sisal plants that look like bouquets of giant green swords. As you climb to the rocks be very careful of your footing because the ground is crumbly and the vegetation slippery. The boulders cover a three-acre area; most of the petroglyphs are found on the south faces of the rocks. Some are hieroglyphics of symbolic circles, others are picture stories complete with canoes gliding under unfurled sails. Dogs snarl with their jaws agape, while enigmatic triangular stickmen try to tell their stories from the past. Equestrians gallop, showing that these stone picture-books were done even after the coming of the white man. The Luahiwa Petroglyphs are a very special spot where the ancient Hawaiians still sing their tales across the gulf of time. Unfortunately, some modern graffiti now mars the stones.

Hulopo'e and Manele Bays

Proceed south on Route 440 to Lana'i's most salubrious spots, the twin bays of Manele and Hulopo'e. At the crest of the hill, just past the milepost, you can look down on the white, inviting sands of Hulopo'e to the right and the rockier small-boat harbor of Manele on the left. The island straight ahead is Kaho'olawe, and on very clear days you might be able to glimpse the peaks of Hawai'i's Mauna Loa and Mauna Kea. Years and years ago, Manele was the site of an ancient Hawaiian village, and it was the principal port for the island until the current commercial harbor was built at Kaumalapa'u. **Manele Bay** is a picture-perfect anchorage where a dozen or so small boats and yachts are tied up on any given day. Ferries from Maui drop off passengers here, and tour boats also tie up here. In the trees overlooking the harbor are a few picnic tables and a public bathroom. Manele and Hulopo'e are a Marine Life Conservation District, with the rules for fishing and diving prominently displayed on a large bulletin board at the entrance to Manele. Because of this, the area is superb for snorkeling, and you can often see a pod of spinner dolphins playing in the water. The tidepools here are also past of this marine reserve and can provide great fun and exploration. No boats are allowed within Hulopo'e Bay except for Hawaiian outrigger canoes, and you may see the canoe club using the bay for practice.

Hulopo'e Bay offers gentle waves and soothing, crystal-clear water. The beach is a beautiful expanse of white sand fringed by palms with a mingling of large boulders that really set it off. Aside from the day-use picnic areas with lawns and grills, this is Lana'i's official camping area, and six sites are available. All are well spaced, each with a picnic table and fire pit. A series of shower stalls made of brown plywood provides solar-heated water and just enough privacy, allowing your head and legs to protrude. After refreshing yourself you can fish from the rock promontories on both sides of the bay, or explore the tide pools on the left side of the bay out near the point. It's difficult to find a more wholesome and gentle spot anywhere in Hawaii. For the more adventurous, walk the path that skirts the headland around to Flat Rock, where you have a direct view out to Pu'upehe Rock. Easily seen on top of this pinnacle are the remains of a fishing **heiau.** Some snorkel tours bring their guests to dive just below this headland. Alternately, take the Na Ala Hele Fisherman's Trail from the beach and along the shore below the hotel and golf course to the farthest fairway.

Kaumalapa'u Harbor

A side trip to Kaumalapa'u Harbor might be in order. This man-made facility, which used to ship more than a million pineapples a day during peak harvest, was the only one of its kind in the world. Activity is now way down, with only one ferry a week on Thursday to deliver supplies, yet it is still Lana'i's lifeline for off-island goods. As you've probably already rented a vehicle, you might as well cover these few paved miles from Lana'i City on Route 440 just to have a quick look. En route you pass Lana'i's odoriferous garbage dump, which is a real eyesore. Hold your nose and try not to notice. The harbor facility is no-nonsense commercial, but the coastline is reasonably spectacular, with a glimpse of the island's dramatic sea cliffs. Also, this area has super-easy access to some decent fishing, right off the pier. An added bonus for making the trek to this lonely area is that it is one of the best places on Lana'i from which to view the sunset, and you usually have it all to yourself.

KAUNOLU: KAMEHAMEHA'S GETAWAY

At the southwestern tip of Lana'i is Kaunolu Bay, a point where currents from both sides of the island converge. At one time, this vibrant fishing village surrounded Halulu Heiau, Lana'i's most important religious spot, and a sacred refuge where the downtrodden were protected by the temple priests who could intercede with the benevolent gods. Halulu Heiau is perhaps named after the man-eating bird Halulu from Tahiti, one of the legendary birds that guided Polynesians from the south to the Hawaiian islands. Kamehameha the Great would escape Lahaina's blistering summers and come to these fertile fishing waters with his loyal warriors. Some proved their valor to their great chief by diving from Kahekili's Leap, a man-made opening in the rocks 60 feet above the sea.

The remains of more than 80 house sites and a smattering of petroglyphs dot the area. The last inhabitant was Ohua, elder brother of Joseph Kali'ihananui, who lived in a grass hut just east of Kaunolu in Mamaki Bay. Ohua was entrusted by Kamehameha V to hide the *heiau* fish-god, Kuniki; old accounts by the area's natives say that he died because of mishandling this stone god. The natural power still emanating from Kaunolu is obvious, and you can't help feeling the energy that drew the Hawaiians to this sacred spot.

Getting There

Proceed south on Manele Road from Lana'i City through Palawai Basin until it makes a hard bend to the left. Here, a sign points you to Manele Bay. Do not go left to Manele, but proceed straight and stay on the once-paved pineapple road. The rental car company doesn't allow their vehicles on this and most other former plantation roads, but you can hike. Head straight through the old pineapple fields until you come upon two orange pipes (like fire hydrants) on the left and right. Turn left here onto a rather small road. Follow the road left to a sign that actually says Kaunolu. This dirt track starts off innocently enough as it begins its plunge toward the sea, and you pass two abandoned dryland farms along the way that once experimented with herbs and vegetables that didn't require much water. Only two miles long, the local folks consider it the roughest road on the island. It *is* a bone-cruncher, so take it super slow if you are in a vehicle. Plot your progress against the lighthouse on the coast. This road is not maintained. Because of natural erosion; it may be too rugged for any vehicle to pass. This area is excellent for spotting axis deer and wild turkeys. The deer are nourished by *haole koa,* a green bush with a brown seed pod that you see growing along the road. This natural feed also supports cattle but is not good for horses, causing the hair on their tails to fall out.

Kaunolu

The village site lies at the end of a long, dry gulch that terminates at a rocky beach, suitable in times past as a canoe anchorage. This entire area is a mecca for archaeologists and anthropologists. The most famous was the eminent Dr. Kenneth Emory of the Bishop Museum; he filed an extensive research report on the area in the 1920s. A more recent research team covered the area in the mid-1990s. In response to its importance, Kaunolu has been designated an Archaeological Interpretive Park and been given the status of a National Historical Landmark. At its terminus, the road splits left and right. Go right to reach a large *kiawe* tree with a picnic table under it. Just in front of you is a large pile of nondescript rocks purported to be the ruined foundation of Kamehameha's house. Numerous other stone remnants dot the slope on both sides of the gulch. Unbelievably, this sacred area is sometimes trashed by disrespectful and ignorant picnickers. Hurricane 'Iwa also had a hand in changing the face of Kaunolu, as its tremendous force hit this area head on and even drove large boulders from the sea onto the land. As you look around, the ones that have a whitish appearance were washed up on shore by the fury of 'Iwa.

The villagers of Kaunolu lived mostly on the east bank and had to keep an ever-watchful eye on nature because the bone-dry gulch could suddenly be engulfed by flash floods. In the center of the gulch, about 100 yards inland, was Pa'ao, the area's freshwater well. Pa'ao was *kapu* to menstruating women, and it was believed that if the *kapu* was broken, the well would dry up. It served the village for centuries, but it's totally obliterated now. In 1895 a Mr. Hayselden tried to erect a windmill over it, destroying the native caulking and causing the well to turn brackish—an example of Lana'i's precious water being tampered with by outsiders, causing disastrous results.

The Sites

Climb down the east bank and cross the rocky beach. The first well-laid wall close to the beach on the west bank is the remains of a canoe shed. Proceed inland and climb the rocky bank to the remains of Halulu Heiau. Just below in the undergrowth is where the well was located. The *heiau* site has a commanding view of the area, best described by the words of Dr. Emory himself:

The point on which it is located is surrounded on three sides by cliffs and on the north rises the magnificent cliff of Palikaholo, terminating in Kahilikalani crag, a thousand feet above the sea. The ocean swell entering Kolokolo Cave causes a rumbling like thunder, as if under the heiau. From every point in the village the *heiau* dominates the landscape.

As you climb the west bank, notice that the mortarless walls are laid up for more than 30 feet. If you have a keen eye you'll notice a perfectly square fire pit right in the center of the *heiau*.

This area still has treasures that have never been catalogued. For example, you might chance upon a Hawaiian lamp, as big and perfectly round as a basketball, with an orange-size hole in the middle where *kukui* nut oil was burned. Old records indicate that Kuniki, the temple idol, still lying here face down no more than a few hundred yards away. If you happen to discover an artifact, do not remove it under any circumstance. Follow the advice of the late Lloyd Cockett, a *kapuna* of Lana'i, who said, "I wouldn't take the rock because we Hawaiians don't steal from the land. Special rocks you don't touch."

Kahekili's Leap

Once you've explored the *heiau*, you'll be drawn toward the sea cliff. **Kane'apua Rock,** a giant towerlike chunk, sits just offshore at the end of the cliff. Below in the tide pool are basin-like depressions in the rock-salt evaporation pools, the bottoms still showing some white residue. Follow the cliff face along the natural wall obstructing your view to the west. You'll see a break in the wall about 15 feet wide with a flat rock platform. From here, **Shark Island,** which closely resembles a shark fin, is perfectly framed. This opening is Kahekili's Leap, perhaps named after a Lana'i chief, not the famous chief of Maui. Here, Kamehameha's warriors proved their courage by executing death-defying leaps into only 12 feet of water and clearing a 15-foot protruding rock shelf. Scholars also believe that Kamehameha punished his warriors for petty offenses by sentencing them to make the jump. Today, daredevils plunge from the cliff for fun in a yearly cliff-diving competition. Kahekili's Leap is a perfect background for a photo. Below, the sea surges in unreal aquamarine colors. Off to the right is Kolokolo Cave, above which is another, even more daring leap at 90 feet. Evidence suggests that Kolokolo is linked to Kaunolu Gulch by a lava tube that has been sealed and lost.

Petroglyphs

To find the petroglyphs, walk directly inland from Kane'apua Rock, using it as your point of reference. On a large pile of rocks are stick figures, mostly with a bird-head motif. Some heads even look like a mason's hammer. This entire area has a masculine feeling to it. There aren't the usual swaying palms and gentle, sandy beaches. With the stones and rugged sea cliffs, you get the feeling that a warrior king would enjoy this spot. For their enjoyment, the vacationing chiefs often played *konane,* and a few stone boards can still be found from this game of Hawaiian checkers. Throughout the area is *pili* grass, used by the Hawaiians to thatch their homes. Children would pick one blade and hold it in their fingers while reciting *"E pili e, e pili e, 'au hea ku'u hale."* The *pili* grass would then spin around in their fingers and point in the direction of home. Pick some *pili* and try it yourself before leaving this wondrous, powerful area.

Here, Kamehameha's warriors proved their courage by executing death-defying leaps into only 12 feet of water and clearing a 15-foot protruding rock shelf. Today, daredevils plunge from the cliff for fun in a yearly cliff-diving competition.

THE EAST COAST: KEOMUKU AND NAHA

Until the 20th century, most of Lana'i's inhabitants lived in the villages of the now-deserted east coast. Before the coming of Westerners, 2,000 or so Hawaiians lived along these shores, fishing and raising taro. It was as if they wanted to keep Maui in sight so they didn't feel so isolated. Numerous *heiau* from this period still mark the ancient sites. The first white men also tried to make a go of Lana'i along this stretch. The Maunalei Sugar Co.

tried to raise sugarcane on the flat plains of Naha but failed and pulled up stakes in 1901—the last time this entire coastline was populated to any extent even though some cattle ranching was done here following the demise of the sugar plantation. Today, the ancient *heiau* and a decaying church in Keomuku are the last vestiges of habitation, holding out against the ever-encroaching jungle. You can follow a jeep trail along this coast and get a fleeting glimpse of times past.

The shallow coastline that wraps around the north and east coast of Lana'i opposes the shallow south coast of Moloka'i. Although many fewer than on that coast of Moloka'i, most ancient fish ponds of Lana'i were located here, and their remnants can still be seen. Because of the shallow nature of the water and its rocky bottom, swimming is not particularly good along most of this coast except for a few isolated sandy spots. In fact, the water cannot be seen well from the road most of the way to Naha because of the growth of trees and bushes along the beach. Numerous pullouts and shore access roads have been created, however, so you can get to the water. Unfortunately, inconsiderate visitors have left these pullouts a bit trashy with junk tossed to the ground rather than taken out.

Getting There

Approach Keomuku and Naha from one of two directions. The most straightforward is from north to south. Follow Keomuku Road from Lana'i City until it turns to dirt and branches right (south) at the coast, about one-half hour. This road meanders for about 12 miles all the way to Naha, another 30–60 minutes. Although the road is partially gravel and packed sand and not that rugged, you will need a 4WD in spots. Watch for washouts and fallen trees. Because of storm wash or flooding from the hills, this road is sometimes closed to traffic and not safe to traverse. The road is paralleled by a much smoother beach route partway along the coast, but it can only be used at low tide. Many small roads connect the two, so you can hop back and forth between them every 200–300 yards. Consider three tips: (1) If you take the beach road, you can make good time and have a smooth ride, but could sail past most of the sights because you won't know when to hop back on the inland road; (2) dry sand can easily bog down even a 4WD vehicle, making an expensive rescue mission for a tow truck, so be wise and only drive where sand is hard-packed; and (3) be careful of the *kiawe* trees because the tough, inch-long thorns can puncture tires as easily as nails.

The other alternative is to take Awehi Trail, a rugged jeep track, about halfway between Lopa and Naha. This route is not open to rental jeeps, but you can hike it. This trail leads up the mountain to the Munro Trail, but because of its ruggedness it's best to take it down from The Hale instead of up. A good long day would take you along the Munro Trail, down Awehi Trail, then north along the coast back to Keomuku Road. If you came south along the coast, it would be better to retrace your steps instead of heading up Awehi. When you think you've suffered enough, remember that this trail and others were carved out by Juan Torqueza. He trailblazed alone on his bulldozer, unsupervised, and without benefit of survey.

Keomuku Village

There isn't much to see in Keomuku Village other than an abandoned Hawaiian church. This village was the site of the Maunalei Sugar Co. The town was pretty much abandoned after 1901 when the sugar company ceased operations, but a ranching operation did utilize this area until midcentury. Most all of the decaying buildings were razed in the early 1970s. A few hundred yards north and south of the town site are examples of some original fish ponds. They're tough to see because they're overgrown with mangrove, but a close observation gives you an idea of how extensive they once were. The **Hawaiian church** is worth a stop, and it almost pleads to be photographed. From outside, you can see how frail it is, so if you go in, tread lightly. The altar area, a podium with a little bench, remains. A banner on the fading blue-green walls reads *"Ualanaano Je-hova Kalanakila Malamalama,* October 4, 1903." Only the soft wind sounds where once strong voices sang vibrant hymns of praise.

A few hundred yards south of the church is a walking trail. Follow it inland to **Kahe'a Heiau** and a smattering of petroglyphs. This is the *heiau* disturbed by the sugarcane train; its desecration was believed to have caused the sweet water of Keomuku to turn brackish. The people of Keomuku learned to survive on the brackish water and kept a special jug of fresh water for visitors.

Heading South

Farther south a Japanese cemetery and monument were erected for the deceased workers who built **Halepaloa Landing,** from where the cane was shipped. Today, only rotting timbers and stonework remain, but the pier offers an excellent vantage point for viewing Maui, and it's a good spot to fish.

The road continues past **Lopa,** ending at **Naha.** Both were sites of ancient fish ponds; the one at Naha can still be discerned at low tide. On the way, you'll pass several roads heading inland that lead to hunting areas. You also pass a few coconut groves. Legend says that one of these was cursed by a *kahuna*—if you climb a tree to get a coconut you will not be able to come down. Luckily, most tourists have already been cursed by "midriff bulge" and can't climb the tree in the first place. When you get to Naha, check out the remnants of the paved Hawaiian walking trail before slowly heading back from this decaying historical area.

SHIPWRECK BEACH

Heading over the mountains from Lana'i City to Kaiolohia Beach (Shipwreck Beach) offers you a rewarding scenario: an intriguing destination point with fantastic scenery and splendid panoramas on the way. Head north from Lana'i City on Keomuku Road. In less than 10 minutes you crest the mountains, and if you're lucky the sky will be clear and you'll be able to see the phenomenon that guided ancient navigators to land: the halo of dark brooding clouds over Maui and Moloka'i, a sure sign of landfall. Shorten your

ROBERT NILSEN

Abandoned on Lana'i's north reef, this ship is the destination of many island kayak adventures.

gaze and look at the terrain in the immediate vicinity. Here, in the gulches and gullies, wounded earth bleeds red while offering patches of swaying grass and wildflowers. It looks like the canyons of Arizona have been dragged to the rim of the sea. As you wiggle your way down Keomuku Road, look left to see the decaying hull of a World War II oiler sitting on the shallow reef almost completely out of the water. Made of concrete, this ship has not rusted apart like others that have foundered here, but it too is slowly disintegrating. Curiously, this ship was deliberately beached here when it apparently outlived its usefulness. For most, this derelict is the destination point on Shipwreck Beach.

As you continue down the road, little piles of stones, usually three, sit atop a boulder. Although most are from modern times, these are called *ahu,* a traditional Hawaiian offering to ensure good fortune while traveling. Under no circumstances should you disturb them. Farther down, the lush grasses of the mountain slope disappear, and the scrub bush takes over. The pavement ends and the dirt road forks left (west) to Shipwreck Beach or straight ahead (south) toward the abandoned town of Naha. If

you turn left you'll be on an adequate sandy road, flanked on both sides by thorny, tire-puncturing *kiawe* trees. In less than a mile is a large, open area to your right. If you're into unofficial camping, this isn't a bad spot for a one-night bivouac—the trees here provide privacy and an excellent windbreak against the constant strong ocean breezes. About two miles down the road is Federation Camp, actually the remains of a tiny village of unpretentious beach shacks built by Lana'i's workers as getaways and fishing cabins. Charming in their humbleness and simplicity, they're made mostly from recycled timbers and boards that have washed ashore. Some have been worked on quite diligently and skillfully and are actual little homes, but somehow the rougher ones are more attractive. You can drive past the cabins for a few hundred yards to park and begin your walk.

Petroglyphs

Near the very end of the road is a cabin that a local comedian has named the "Lana'i Hilton." Park your car to the end of the sand road and walk a short way up the coast to a cement base for a long-since-gone lighthouse. Look closely and you can see that two workers of days gone by, John Kapau and Kam Chee, put their names and initials in the wet cement of this foundation on November 28, 1929. Behind the cement block, arrows point you to "The Bird Man of Lana'i Petroglyphs." Of all the petroglyphs on Lana'i, these are the easiest to find; trail-marking rocks have been painted white by Lana'i's Boy Scouts. Running almost directly inland, follow them for a couple hundred yards to a large rock bearing the admonition Do Not Deface. Climb down the path into a small gully and look with a keen eye—the rock carvings are small, most only about one foot tall. Little childlike stick figures, some have intriguing bird heads whose symbolic meaning has been lost. Dog or other animal figures are also found here as well as a larger two-foot-high figure on a rock on the opposite side of the wash.

Hiking the Beach

The trail along the beach goes for eight long, hot miles to Polihua Beach. That trip should be done separately, but at least walk as far as the ship, about a mile from the end of the road. The area has some of the best beachcombing in Hawaii; no telling what you might find. The most sought-after treasures are glass floats that have bobbed for thousands of miles across the Pacific, strays from Japanese fishnets. You might even see a modern ship washed onto the reef, like the Canadian yacht that went aground in spring 1984. Navigational equipment has improved, but Shipwreck Beach can *still* be a nightmare to any captain caught in its turbulent whitecaps and long, ragged coral fingers. This area is particularly good for lobsters and shore-fishing, and you can swim in shallow sandy-bottom pools to refresh yourself as you hike.

Just inland of the beach and west of the end of the road is an overgrown section of an old trail that once connected villages along this coast, now nearly lost among the *kiawe* trees and buried under sand. Named the Kaiolohia-Kahue Trail and part of the state's Na Ala Hele trail system, it awaits

funding to be restored for its cultural significance and as an alternate means of access to this area.

Try to time your return car trip over the mountain for sundown. The tortuous terrain, stark in black and white shadows, is awe-inspiring. The larger rocks are giant sentinels: It's easy to feel the power and attraction they held for the ancient Hawaiians. As you climb the road on the windward side with its barren and beaten terrain, the feelings of mystery and mystique attributed to spiritual Lana'i are obvious. You come over the top and suddenly see the plateau—manicured, rolling, soft, and verdant—and the few lights of Lana'i City beckoning.

THE GARDEN OF THE GODS AND POLIHUA

The most ruggedly beautiful, barren, and inhospitable section of Lana'i is out at the north end. After passing through a broad stretch of former pineapple fields, you come to Kanepu'u Preserve, the island's only nature reserve and best example of dryland forest. Just as you pop out the far side of the preserve, you reach Keahi Kawelo, the appropriately named Garden of the Gods. Waiting is a fantasia of otherworldly landscapes—barren red earth, convulsed ancient lava flows, tortured pinnacles of stone, and psychedelic striations of vibrating colors, especially moving at sunrise and sunset. Little-traveled trails lead to Ka'ena (The Heat) Point, a wasteland dominated by sea cliffs where adulterous Hawaiian wives were sent into exile for a short time in 1837. Close by is Lana'i's largest *heiau*, dubbed Ka'enaiki, so isolated and forgotten that its real name and function were lost even to Hawaiian natives by the middle of the 19th century. After a blistering, sun-baked, 4WD drubbing, you emerge at the coast on Polihua, a totally secluded, white-sand beach where sea turtles once came to bury their eggs in the natural incubator of its soft, warm sands (Polihua means "eggs in bosom").

Getting There

Lana'i doesn't hand over its treasures easily, but they're worth pursuing. To get to the Garden of the Gods, head past the Lodge at Koele, and turn left onto the road that runs between the tennis courts and the riding stable. After about one minute, there's an intersection where you should turn right. Follow this road through former pineapple fields, keeping the prominent ridge on your right. Proceed for about 20 minutes until you pass through the Kanepu'u dryland forest preserve. Disregard the roads to the right and the left. Once out the back side of the preserve, you soon begin to see large boulders sitting atop packed red earth, the signal that you're entering the Garden of the Gods. It's about another hot half hour drive down to Polihua Beach, and on the way you'll find a marker on the left for Ka'ena Road, which leads to magnificent sea cliffs and Ka'enaiki Heiau. Basically, you're heading toward the western tip of Moloka'i, which you can keep in your sights in the distance across the channel. Have no illusions about this road. It's long and bumpy, but if you want a beach to yourself, persevere. Definitely do not attempt the lower reaches of this road without 4WD.

Kanepu'u Preserve

Straddling the road leading to the Garden of the Gods, this 590-acre preserve is the best remaining example of dryland forest on Lana'i and a sampling of what covered much of the lower leeward slopes of the Hawaiian Islands before the coming of humans. In this forest you'll find *olopua,* a native olive tree; *lama,* a native ebony; *na'u,* Hawaiian gardenia; the *'iliahi* sandalwood tree; and numerous other plant varieties, 49 species of which are found only in Hawaii, as well as many species of birds. Over the centuries, these dryland forests were reduced in size by fire, introduced animals, and the spread of non-native weeds and trees. Erosion control measures, such as the planting of native shrubs and seeds, have been implemented to cover bare spots and fill contour scars. Under the care of The Nature Conservancy and local conservation groups, this forest and others like it are being protected.

As you pass through this preserve, stop at the self-guided loop trail to get a close-up look at some of the trees in the forest. It's about a 15-minute walk over level ground, if you stop and read the posted signs. Overlooking this trail and set on a nearby rise is Kanepu'u (Kane's Hill) Heiau.

Guided hikes through the preserve are occasionally offered. For more information about these hikes or for general information about the preserve, try 808/565-7430.

The Garden of the Gods

There, a shocking assault on your senses, is the bleak, red, burnt earth, devoid of vegetation, heralding the beginning of the garden—a Hawaiian Badlands. The flowers here are made of rock, the shrubs are the twisted crusts of lava, and trees are baked minarets of stone, all subtle shades of orange, purple, and sulfurous yellow. Although most is obviously created by natural erosion, some piles of stone are just as obviously erected by man. The jeep trail has been sucked down by erosion and the garden surrounds you. The beginning seems most dramatic, but much more spreads out before you as you proceed down the hill. Stop often to climb a likely outcropping and get a sweeping view. While you can't see Lana'i's coastline from here, you do have a nice view of Moloka'i across the channel. The wind rakes these badlands and the silence penetrates to your soul. Although eons have passed, you can feel the cataclysmic violence that created this haunting and delicate beauty. The Garden of the Gods is perhaps best in the late afternoon when slanting sunlight enriches colors and casts shadows that create depth and mood.

Polihua Beach

After leaving the Garden of the Gods, you can bear left to lonely **Ka'ena Point,** where you'll find Lana'i's largest *heiau,* a brooding setting full of weird power vibrations. Straight ahead, the trail takes you down to the coast. Abruptly the road becomes smooth and flat. Like a mirage too bright for your eyes, an arch is cut into the green jungle, framing white sand and moving blue ocean. As you face the beach, to the right it's flat, expansive, and the sands are white, but the winds are heavy; if you hiked eight miles, you'd reach Shipwreck Beach. A few shade trees edge the sand so you can get out of the heat. More interesting is the view to the left, which has a series of lonely little coves. The sand is brown and coarse, and large black lava boulders are marbled with purplish gray rock embedded in long, faulted seams. Polihua is not just a destination point where you come for a quick look. It takes so much effort coming and going that you should plan on having a picnic and a relaxing afternoon before heading back through the Garden of the Gods and its perfectly scheduled sunset light show.

Moloka'i

Moloka'i is a sanctuary, a human time capsule where the pendulum swings inexorably forward, but more slowly than in the rest of Hawaii. It has always been so. In ancient times, Moloka'i was known as Pule O'o, "Powerful Prayer," where its supreme chiefs protected their small underpopulated refuge, not through legions of warriors but through the chants of their *kahuna*. This powerful, ancient mysticism, handed down directly from the goddess Pahulu, was known and respected throughout the archipelago. Its *mana* was the oldest and strongest in Hawaii, and its practitioners were venerated by nobility and commoners alike—they had the ability to "pray you to death." The entire island was a haven, a refuge for the vanquished and *kapu*-breakers of all the islands. It's still so today, beckoning to determined escapees from the rat race!

The blazing lights of supermodern Honolulu can easily be seen from the west end of Moloka'i, while Moloka'i as viewed from O'ahu is fleeting and ephemeral, appearing and disappearing on the horizon. The island is home to the largest number of Hawaiians. In effect it is a tribal homeland: More than 3,000 of the island's 7,400 inhabitants have more than 50 percent Hawaiian blood and, except for Ni'ihau, it's the only island where they are the majority. The 1920s Hawaiian Homes Act allowed *kuleana* of 40 acres to anyone with more than 50 percent Hawaiian ancestry. *Kuleana* owners form the grassroots organizations that fight for Hawaiian rights and battle the colossal forces of rabid developers who have threatened Moloka'i for decades.

Kalaupapa Peninsula and the steep cliff that separates it from the rest of Moloka'i

Moloka'i has had several sobriquets through the years. Many decades ago, it was know as the Lonely Isle, undoubtedly because so many leprosy patients were dumped on its shore. These individuals were truly lonely people, sent away from family, friends, and loved ones, abandoned by society to the netherworld of the kingdom. Perhaps in an effort to shift its image to a positive one, Moloka'i became know as the Friendly Isle because of the nature of its inhabitants, a characteristic that they certainly still exhibit today. Within the last couple of decades, and coinciding with the resurgence of a popular interest in the Hawaiian culture, people began to call Moloka'i the Most Hawaiian Island because it has the largest percentage of Hawaiian residents for its population, aside from the private island of Ni'ihau. Most recently, and in a bid to play up its natural potential as a place to come and play outdoors, officials in the tourism business have given to Moloka'i the phrase Hawaiian by Nature. Most Hawaiians know the monikers Friendly Isle and Most Hawaiian Isle. Time will tell if its new name will stick.

Kaunakakai and West

Kaunakakai, the island's main town, once looked like a Hollywood sound stage where Jesse James or Wyatt Earp would feel right at home. The town is flat, with few trees, and three blocks long. Ala Malama, its main shopping street, is lined with false-front stores; pickup trucks are parked in front where horses and buggies ought to be. To the west are the prairie-like plains of Moloka'i, some sections irrigated and now planted in profitable crops. The northern section of the island contains **Pala'au State Park,** where a campsite is always easily found, and **Phallic Rock,** a natural shrine where island women came to pray for fertility. Most of the west end is owned by the mammoth 54,000-acre **Molokai Ranch.** Part of its lands supports several thousand head of cattle and herds of axis deer imported from India in 1867.

The 40-acre *kuleana* are here on the uplands beyond the airport, as well as abandoned Dole and Del Monte pineapple fields. The once-thriving pineapple company town of **Kualapu'u** is now a semi-ghost town since Del Monte pulled up stakes in 1985, and coffee is now grown on some of the fields. This area attracts its scattered Filipino workers mostly on weekends, when they come to unofficially test their best cocks in the pit. Look for the small A-frame shelters in yards here that house these creatures. Dole shut down the pineapple fields around **Maunaloa** in 1975, after which the town took a swift nose dive into neglect. Having recently undergone a massive facelift, Maunaloa is holding on as the Molokai Ranch is expanding its operations to include more tourism-related activities.

On the western shore is the **Kaluakoi Resort,** perched above the island's best beach. Here, 6,700 acres sold by the Molokai Ranch to the Louisiana Land and Exploration Company, later sold to another concern, and most recently bought back by the ranch, are *slowly* being developed as homesites, but so far houses are only scattered here and there. This area, rich with the finest archaeological sites on the island, is a hotbed of contention between developers and preservationists. The Kaluakoi Resort with its golf course and the low Polynesian-style architecture of its hotel and condominiums that blend well with the surroundings was pointed to as a well-planned development, but unfortunately it has gone through economic trouble and fallen on hard times.

The East Coastal Road

Highway 450 is a magnificent coastal road running east from Kaunakakai to Halawa Valley. A slow drive along this bucolic country thoroughfare rewards you with easily accessible beach parks, glimpses of fish ponds, *heiau,* wildlife sanctuaries, and small one-room churches strung along the road like rosary beads. Almost every mile has a historical site, like the **Smith and Bronte Landing Site** where two pioneers of trans-Pacific flight ignominiously alighted in a mangrove swamp, and **Paikalani Taro Patch,** the only one from which Kamehameha V would eat poi.

On Moloka'i's eastern tip is **Halawa Valley,**

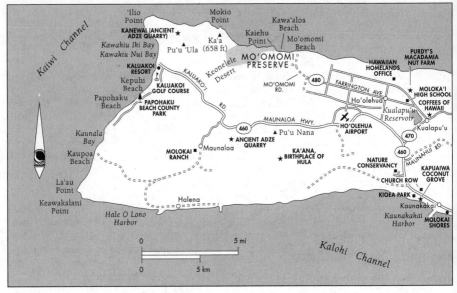

a real gem accessible by car. This pristine gorge has two lovely waterfalls and their pools, and a beach park where the valley meets the sea. Most of the population of Halawa moved out in 1946 after a 30-foot tsunami washed their homes away and mangled their taro fields, leaving a thick, salty residue. Today only a handful of those from the old families and a few alternative lifestylers live in the valley among the overgrown stone walls that once marked the boundaries of manicured and prosperous family gardens. On Pu'u O Hoku Ranch property is **Kalanikaula,** the sacred *kukui* grove of Lanikaula, Moloka'i's most powerful *kahuna* of the classic period. This grove was planted at his death and became the most sacred spot on Moloka'i.

The Windward Coast

Kalaupapa (Flat Leaf) is a lonely peninsula formed by lava flow from the 400-foot-high Kauhako Crater, the highest spot on this relatively flat nub of land. Kalaupapa colony for leprosy patients, completely separated from the world by a hostile, pounding surf and a precipitous 1,600-foot *pali,* is a modern story of human dignity. Kalaupapa, and Kalawao before it, was a dispossessed settlement of dispossessed people where the unfortunate victims of leprosy were banished to die. Here humanity reached its lowest ebb of hopelessness, violence, and depravity, until one tiny flicker of light arrived in 1873—Joseph de Veuster, a Belgian priest known throughout Hawaii as Father Damien. In the greatest example of pure *aloha* yet established on Hawaii, he became his brothers' keeper. Tours of Kalaupapa operated by well-informed residents are enlightening and educational.

East of Kalaupapa along the windward (northeast) coast is a series of amazingly steep and isolated valleys. The inhabitants moved out at the beginning of the 20th century, except for one pioneering family that returned some years ago to carve out a home. Well beyond the farthest reaches of the last road, this emerald-green primeval world awaits. The *pali* here mark the tallest sea cliffs in the world (although some dispute this designation), with an "average incline of more than 55 degrees." Many spots are far steeper. About halfway down the coast near Umilehi Point, the cliffs

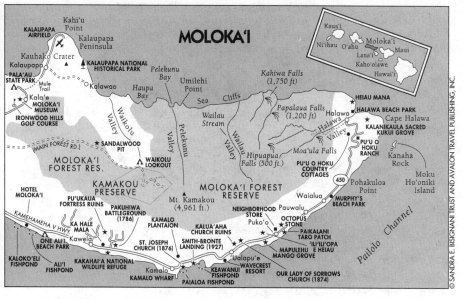

are at their highest at 3,300 feet. Farther to the east and diving headfirst out of a hanging valley is the thin sliver of **Kahiwa (Sacred One) Falls,** the highest in Hawaii at 1,750 feet. You get here only by helicopter excursion or by boat in the calmer summer months. For now, Moloka'i remains a sanctuary, reminiscent of the Hawaii of simpler times. Around it the storm of modernity rages, but still the "Friendly Island" awaits those willing to venture off the beaten track.

THE LAND

With 260 square miles, Moloka'i is the fifth largest Hawaiian island. Its northwestern tip, at 'Ilio Point, is a mere 22 miles from O'ahu's eastern tip, Makapu'u Point. Resembling a jogging shoe, Moloka'i is about 38 miles from heel to toe and 10 miles from laces to sole, totaling 166,425 acres, with just over 88 miles of coastline. Most of the arable land on the island is owned by the 54,000-acre Molokai Ranch, primarily on the western end, and the 14,000-acre Pu'u O Hoku Ranch on the eastern end. Moloka'i was formed by three dis-

tinct shield volcanoes. Two linked together to form Moloka'i proper, and a later and much smaller eruption formed the flat Kalaupapa Peninsula.

Physical Features

Although Moloka'i is rather small, it has a great deal of geographical diversity. Western Moloka'i is dry with rolling hills, natural pastures, and a maximum elevation of only 1,381 feet. The eastern sector of the island has heavy rainfall. The tallest sea cliffs in the world, and craggy, narrow valleys perpetually covered in a velvet cloak of green plants edge its northern front. Viewed from the sea it looks like a 2,000-foot vertical wall from surf to clouds, with tortuously deep chasms along the coastline. Mount Kamakou is the highest peak on Moloka'i, at 4,961 feet, and lying below it on the south shore is a narrow littoral of farms and fields. Moloka'i's south shore is also worthy of note as it has about 28 miles of reef, the state's only continuous barrier reef. The south-central area is relatively swampy, while the west and especially northwest coasts around Mo'omomi have rolling sand dunes. Papohaku Beach, on the

ROBERT NILSEN

The mountains of east Moloka'i have been carved into deep valleys.

west end of Moloka'i, is one of the most massive white-sand beaches in Hawaii. A controversy was raised when it was discovered that huge amounts of sand were dredged from this area and hauled to O'ahu; the Molokai Ranch was pressured and the dredging ceased. A hefty section of land in the north-central area is a state forest where new species of trees are planted on an experimental basis. The 240-acre Pala'au State Park is in this cool upland forested area.

Man-Made Marvels

Two man-made features on Moloka'i are engineering marvels. One is the series of 62 ancient fish ponds strung along the south shore like pearls on a string—best seen from the air as you approach the island by plane. The outlines of dozens can still be seen, but the most amazing is the enormous **Keawanui Pond,** covering 54 acres and surrounded by a three-foot-tall, 2,000-foot-long wall. It's on the National Register of Historic Places. The other is the modern **Kualapu'u Reservoir** completed in 1969. The world's largest rubber-lined reservoir, it can hold 1.4 billion gallons of water. Part of its engineer-

ing dramatics is the Moloka'i Tunnel, which feeds it with water from the eastern valleys. The tunnel is eight feet tall, eight feet wide, and almost 27,000 feet (five miles) long.

Climate

The average island daytime maximum temperature runs 75–85°F (24–29°C), winter to summer. The yearly average rainfall is 27 inches; the east receives a much greater percentage than the west.

FLORA AND FAUNA

Land animals on Moloka'i were brought by humans: pigs, goats, axis deer, and cattle. The earliest arrival still extant in the wild is the *pua'a* (pig). Moloka'i's pigs live in the upper wetland forests of the northeast, but they can actually thrive anywhere. Hunters say the meat from pigs that have lived in the lower dry forest is superior to those that acquire the muddy taste of ferns from the wetter upland areas. Pigs on Moloka'i are hunted mostly with the use of dogs, who pin them by the ears and snout while the hunter approaches on foot and skewers them with a long knife.

MOLOKA'I

MOLOKA'I TEMPERATURE AND RAINFALL

	Jan.	March	May	June	Sept.	Nov.
High	79	79	81	82	82	80
Low	61	63	68	70	68	63
Rain	4	3	0	0	0	2

Note: Temperature is in degrees Fahrenheit; rainfall is in inches.

Offspring from a pair of **goats** left by Captain Cook on the island of Ni'ihau spread to all the islands; they were very well adapted to life on Moloka'i. Originally from the arid Mediterranean, goats could live well without any surface water, a condition quite prevalent over most of Moloka'i. They're found primarily in the mountainous area of the northeast.

The last free-roaming arrivals to Moloka'i were **axis deer.** Moloka'i's deer came from the upper reaches of the Ganges River, sent to Kamehameha V by Dr. William Hillebrand while on a botanical trip to India in 1867. Kamehameha V sent some of the first specimens to Moloka'i, where they prospered. Today they are found mostly on western Moloka'i, although some travel the south coast to the east.

Birdlife

A few of Hawaii's endemic birds can be spotted by a determined observer at various locales around Moloka'i. They include the Hawaiian petrel *('ua'u);* Hawaiian coot *('alae ke'oke'o),* prominent in Hawaiian mythology; Hawaiian stilt *(ae'o),* a wading bird with ridiculous stick legs that protects its young by feigning wing injury and luring predators away from the nest; and the Hawaiian owl *(pueo),* a bird that helps in its own demise by being easily approached. Moloka'i has a substantial number of introduced game birds that attract hunters throughout the year.

The nonprofit organization **Nene O Moloka'i** operates a facility that breeds, releases, and monitors the state bird, the *nene.* Located about four miles east of Kaunakakai, it offers free tours daily at 9 A.M., but you must make an appointment to visit. To learn more about these friendly geese, call

808/553-5992 or visit the organization's website at www.aloha.net/~nene.

Flora

The *kukui* or candlenut tree is common to all of the Hawaiian Islands; along with being the official state tree, its tiny white blossom is Moloka'i's flower. The *kukui,* introduced centuries ago by the early Polynesians, grows on lower mountain slopes and can easily be distinguished by its pale green leaves. Low and dry, the western end of Moloka'i is typified by shrubby bushes and gnarled trees. Only in the windy desertlike Mo'omomi sand dune area does hearty native shore vegetation still survive. In the upper reaches of the north shore valleys, the vegetation is as rich, diverse, and luxuriant as the wet areas of the other islands.

Conservation Controversy

It has long been established and regretted that introduced animals and plants have destroyed Hawaii's delicate natural balance, leading to the extinction of many of its rare native species. Several well-meaning groups and organizations are doing their best to preserve Hawaii habitat, but they don't always agree on the methods employed. Feral pigs, indiscriminate in their relentless hunt for food, are ecological nightmares that virtually bulldoze the rainforest floor into fetid pools and gouged earth, where mosquitoes and other introduced species thrive while driving out the natives. Moloka'i's magnificent Kamakou Preserve, Upper Pelekunu Valley, and the central Moloka'i ridges are some of the last remaining pockets of natural habitat on the island. The Kamakou Preserve, 2,774 pristine acres, is covered, like the others, in 'ohi'a forest, prime habitat for the almost-extinct *oloma'o* (Moloka'i thrush), *kakawahie* (creeper), and the hearty but beleaguered *'apapane* and *'amakihi*. No one disagrees that the wild boar must be managed to protect these areas, but they do not agree on *how* they should be managed. The Nature Conservancy in its dedication to preserving the rainforest backed a policy to snare the wild boar, maintaining that this was the best possible way of eliminating these pests while placing the forest under the least amount of stress. In opposition to the practice of snaring is Pono, a local organization of native Moloka'i hunters that maintains snaring pigs is inhumane, causing the animals to starve to death or to die slowly from strangulation. Pono also abhors the wasting of the meat and the indiscriminate killing of sows.

Aside from the **Kamakou Preserve,** the Nature Conservancy also maintains 5,759 acres of the upper Pelekunu Valley on the remote north coast of the island, where there is no public access. There is access, however, to the **Mo'omomi Preserve,** a 921-acre area of sand dunes west of Mo'omomi Beach that is safe harbor for several species of endangered coastal plants, seabirds, and green sea turtles. You can walk in on your own, but the Nature Conservancy conducts guided hikes once a month into the Kamakou and Mo'omomi preserves. These hikes run $10 for members and $25 for nonmembers (who then become members for one year). If you wish to attend, call well in advance for dates and to reserve your spot; 808/553-5236. For more information, log onto the organization's website at www.tnc.org.

HISTORY

The oral chant *"Moloka'i nui a Hina . . ."* ("Great Moloka'i, child of Hina") refers to Moloka'i as the island-child of the goddess Hina and the god Wakea, male progenitor of all the islands; Papa, Wakea's first wife, left him in anger as a result of this unfaithfulness. Hina's cave, just above Kalua'aha on the southeast coast, can still be visited and has been revered as a sacred spot for countless centuries. Another ancient spot, Halawa Valley, on the eastern tip of Moloka'i, is considered one of the oldest settlements in Hawaii. As research continues, settlement dates are pushed farther back, but for now scholars agree that early wayfarers from the Marquesas Islands settled Halawa in the mid-7th century.

Moloka'i, from earliest times, was revered and feared as a center for mysticism and sorcery. In fact, an ancient name for the island is Moloka'i Pule O'o (Moloka'i of the Potent Prayers). **'Ili'ili'opae Heiau** was renowned for its powerful priests, whose incantations were mingled with the screams of human sacrifice. Commoners avoided 'Ili'ili'opae, and even powerful *kahuna* could not escape its terrible power. One, Kamalo, lost his sons as sacrifices at the *heiau* for their desecration of the temple drum. Kamalo sought revenge by invoking the help of his personal god, the terrible shark deity Kauhuhu. After the proper prayers and offerings, Kauhuhu sent a flash flood to wipe out Mapulehu Valley where 'Ili'ili'opae was located. All perished except for Kamalo and his family, who were protected by a sacred fence around their home.

This tradition of mysticism reached its apex with the famous Lanikaula, "Prophet of Moloka'i." During the 16th century, Lanikaula lived near Halawa Valley and practiced his arts, handed down by the goddess Pahulu, who predated even Pele. Pahulu was the goddess responsible for the "old ocean highway," which passed between Moloka'i and Lana'i and led to Kahiki, lost homeland of all the islanders. Lanikaula practiced his sorcery in the utmost secrecy and even buried his excrement on an offshore island so that a rival *kahuna* could not find and burn it, which would surely cause his death. Hawaiian oral history does not say why Palo, a sorcerer from Lana'i and a friend of Lanikaula, came to spy on Lanikaula and observed him hiding his excrement. Palo burned it in the sacred fires, and Lanikaula knew that his end was near. Lanikaula ordered his sons to bury him in a hidden grave so that his enemies could not find his bones and use their *mana* to control his spirit. To further hide his remains, he had a *kukui* grove planted over his body. **Kalanikaula** (Sacred Grove of Lanikaula) is still visible today.

Incursions from Outside

Captain James Cook first spotted Moloka'i on November 26, 1778, but because it looked bleak and uninhabited, he decided to bypass it. It wasn't until eight years later that Capt. George Dixon sighted the island and decided to land. Very little was recorded in his ship's log about this first encounter, and Moloka'i slipped from the attention of the Western world until Protestant missionaries arrived at Kalua'aha in 1832 and reported the native population at approximately 6,000.

In 1790, Kamehameha the Great came from the Big Island as a suitor seeking the hand of Keopuolani, a chieftess of Moloka'i. Within five years he returned again, but this time there was no merrymaking: He came as a conquering chief on his thrust westward to capture O'ahu. His war canoes landed at Pakuhiwa Battleground, a bay just a few miles east of Kaunakakai between Kawela and Kamalo; it's said that warriors lined the shores for more than four miles. The grossly outnumbered warriors of Moloka'i fought desperately, but even the incantations of their *kahuna* were no match for Kamehameha and his warriors. Inflamed with recent victory and infused with the power of their horrible war-god Ku ("of the Maggot-dripping Mouth"), they slaughtered the Moloka'i warriors and threw their broken bodies into a sea so filled with sharks that their feeding frenzy made the waters appear to boil. Thus subdued, Moloka'i slipped into obscurity once again as its people turned to a quiet life of farming and fishing.

Molokai Ranch

Moloka'i remained almost unchanged until the 1850s. The Great Mahele of 1848 provided for private ownership of land, and giant tracts were formed into the Molokai Ranch. About 1850, German immigrant Rudolph Meyer came to Moloka'i and married a high chieftess named Dorcas Kalama Waha. Together they had 11 children, with whose aid he turned the vast lands of the Molokai Ranch into productive pastureland. A man of indomitable spirit, Meyer held public office on Moloka'i and became the island's unofficial patriarch. He managed Molokai Ranch for the original owner, Kamehameha V, and remained manager until his death in 1897, by which time the ranch was owned by the Bishop Estate. In 1875, Charles Bishop had bought half of the 70,000 acres of Molokai Ranch, and his wife, Bernice, a Kamehameha descendant, inherited the remainder. In 1898, the Molokai Ranch was sold to businessmen in Honolulu for $251,000. This consortium formed the American Sugar Co., but after a few plantings the available water on Moloka'i turned brackish, and once again Molokai Ranch was sold. Charles Cooke bought controlling interest from the other businessmen in 1908 and remained in control of the ranch until 1988, when it was sold to Brierly Investments, a business concern from New Zealand.

Changing Times

Very little happened for a decade after Charles Cooke bought the Molokai Ranch from his partners. Moloka'i did become famous for its honey production, supplying a huge amount to the world up until World War I. During the 1920s, political and economic forces greatly changed Moloka'i. In 1921, Congress passed the **Hawaiian Homes Act,** which set aside 43,000 acres on the island for people who had at least 50 percent Hawaiian blood. By this time, however, all agriculturally productive land in Hawaii had already been claimed. The land given to the Hawaiians was very poor and lacked adequate water. Many Hawaiians had long since left the land and were raised in towns and cities. Now out of touch with the simple life of the taro patch, they found it very difficult to readjust. To prevent the Hawaiians from selling their claims and losing the land forever, the Hawaiian Homes Act provided that the land be leased to them for 99 years. Making a go of these 40-acre *(kuleana)* parcels was so difficult that successful homesteaders were called "Moloka'i Miracles."

In 1923 Libby Corporation leased land from Molokai Ranch at Kaluako'i and went into pineapple production; Del Monte followed suit in 1927 at Kualapu'u. Both built company towns and imported Japanese and Filipino field laborers, swelling Moloka'i's population and stabilizing the economy. Many of the native Hawaiians subleased their *kuleana* tracts to the pineapple growers, and the Hawaiian Homes Act seemed to backfire. Instead of the homesteaders working their own farms, they were given monthly checks and lured into a life of complacency. Those who grew little more than family plots became, in effect, permanent tenants on their own property. Much more importantly, they lost the psychological advantage of controlling their own future and regaining their pride, as envisioned in the Hawaiian Homes Act.

Modern Times

For the next 50 years life was quiet. The pineapples grew, providing security. Another large ranch, **Pu'u O Hoku** (Hill of Stars) was formed on the eastern tip of the island. It was originally owned by Paul Fagan, the amazing San Francisco entrepreneur who later developed the Hana Ranch on Maui. In 1955, Fagan sold Pu'u O Hoku to George Murphy, a Canadian industrialist, for a meager $300,000. The ranch, under Murphy, became famous for beautiful white Charolais cattle, a breed originating in France.

In the late 1960s, things started quietly happening on Moloka'i. The Molokai Ranch sold 6,700 acres to the Kaluakoi Corp., which they controlled along with the Louisiana Land and Exploration Company. In 1969 the long-awaited Moloka'i reservoir was completed at Kualapu'u; finally west Moloka'i had plenty of water. Shortly after Moloka'i's water problem appeared to be finally under control, Dole Corp. bought out Libby in 1972, lost millions in the next few years, and shut down its pineapple production at Maunaloa in 1975. By 1977 the acreage sold to the Kaluakoi Corp. started to be developed, and the Molokai Sheraton (later called the Kaluakoi Hotel, but now closed) opened along with lowrise condominiums and 270 fee-simple home sites ranging 5–43 acres. Plans then for this area included two more resorts, additional condominiums, shopping facilities, bridle paths, and an airstrip (it's only 20 minutes to Honolulu). Lo and behold, it seemed that sleepy old Moloka'i with the tiny Hawaiian Homes farms was now prime real estate and worth a fortune.

To complicate the picture even further, Del Monte shut down its operations in 1982, throwing more people out of work. In 1986 it did resume planting 250-acre tracts, but now all of the pineapple is gone. Recently, coffee has been put into production near the old pineapple town of Kualapu'u, some experimental plots of fruits and vegetables have been planted, and the Molokai Ranch has brought in sheep and cattle. After Brierly Investments bought the Molokai Ranch, other changes started to take place, including a total facelift for the town of Maunaloa and greater emphasis on tourism for a slice of the ranch's income. These new avenues of diversification are still in their infant stages but might possibly lead to greater economic strength and stability. In 2002, Molokai Ranch bought back the acreage it sold in the 1960s, and it remains to be seen if other changes will happen on the west end. Moloka'i is in a period of flux in other ways. There is great tension between developers, who are viewed as carpetbaggers interested only in a fast buck, and those who consider themselves the last remnants of a lost race holding on desperately to what little they have left.

ECONOMY

If it weren't for a pitifully bad economy, Moloka'i would have no economy at all. At one time the workers on the pineapple plantations had good, steady incomes and the high hopes of the working class. With all of the pineapple jobs gone, Moloka'i was transformed from an island with virtually no unemployment to a hard-luck community with a high rate of people on welfare. With the start of the coffee plantation, this bleak economic situation lessened somewhat, but the more recent downturn in tourism has dealt the island a blow. Inexplicably, Moloka'i also has the highest utility rates in Hawaii. Some say this is because the utility company built a modern biomass plant and didn't have enough biomass to keep it operating, so the people were stuck with the fuel tab. The present situation is even more ludicrous when you consider that politically Moloka'i is part of Maui County. It is lumped together with Ka'anapali on Maui's western coast, one of Hawaii's poshest and wealthiest areas, where most people are recent arrivals from the Mainland. This amounts to almost no political/economic voice for grassroots Moloka'i.

Agriculture

The word that is now bandied about is "diversified" agriculture. What this means is not pinning all hope on one crop like the ill-fated pineapple, but planting a potpourri of crops. Attempts at diversification are evident as you travel around Moloka'i, and many fields are set off by long rows of tall trees as windbreaks. Fields of corn, wheat, fruits, nuts, and coffee are just west of Kaunakakai; many small farmers are trying truck farming by raising a variety of garden vegetables that they hope to sell to the massive hotel food industry in Honolulu. Watermelon, bell pepper, onions, and herbs are perhaps the most well known, and one farm—some say the largest in the state—grows sweet potatoes. Maui Community College, part of the University of Hawai'i system, also has some acreage here for experimentation in raising native trees. The problem is not in production, but transportation. Moloka'i raises excellent crops, but not enough established transport exists for the perishable vegetables. A barge service, running on a loose twice-weekly schedule, is the only link to the market. The lack of proper storage facilities on Moloka'i makes it tough to compete in the hotel food business, which requires the freshest produce. Unfortunately, vegetables don't wait well in the heat for late barges.

Development

When development was new, a debate raged between those in favor of tourist development, which they said would save Moloka'i, and grassroots organizations, which insisted that unchecked tourism development would despoil Moloka'i and give no real benefit to the people. A main character in the debate was the Kaluakoi Corp., which wanted to build condos and sell more home lots. It claimed that this, coupled with a few more resorts, would bring in jobs. The people know that they will be relegated to service jobs (maids and waiters), while all the management jobs go to outsiders. Most islanders felt that only rich people from the Mainland could afford million-dollar homes and condos and that eventually they will become disenfranchised on their own island. Claims were that outsiders have no feeling for the 'aina (land) and would destroy important cultural sites whenever growth dictates. While quieted much over the years, this issue is only barely under the surface and erupts quickly when any talk of development is in the winds.

Some years back the Kaluakoi Corp. hired an "independent" research team to investigate the area around Kawakiu Iki Bay, known to be an ancient adze quarry. After weeks of study, this Maui-based research team reported that Kawakiu was of

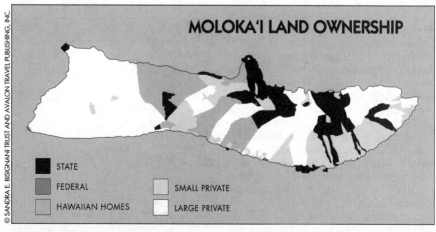

MOLOKA'I LAND OWNERSHIP

- STATE
- FEDERAL
- HAWAIIAN HOMES
- SMALL PRIVATE
- LARGE PRIVATE

MOLOKA'I

"minor importance." Hawaii's academic sector went wild. The Society of Hawaiian Archaeology dispatched its own team under Dr. Patrick Kirch, who stated that Kawakiu was one of the richest archaeological areas in Hawaii. In one day they discovered six sites missed by the "independent" research team and stated that a rank amateur could find artifacts by merely scraping away some of the surface. Reasonable voices call for moderation. Both sides agree Moloka'i must grow, but the growth must be controlled, and the people of Moloka'i must be represented and included as beneficiaries.

THE PEOPLE

Aside from the tiny island of Ni'ihau, Moloka'i has the largest percentage of Hawaiian population, perhaps partly because of relatively small commercial development on the island throughout its history, which did not bring in large numbers of ethnic workers. Although sugar was tried early on with some success, it never grew to vast size, and the pineapple production on the island was also limited. Only ranching has really persevered, and this doesn't require any large number of laborers. More recently, with the slow development of tourism, white-collar workers have filtered into the workforce, and there has been a small increase in tourism-related jobs. Local Hawaiians make up 48 percent of Moloka'i's population; 21 percent are Filipino, 18 percent Caucasian, 9 percent Japanese, 1 percent Chinese, and 3 percent various other groups.

Moloka'i is obviously experiencing a class struggle. The social problems hinge on the economy—the collapse of pineapple cultivation and the move toward tourism. The average income on Moloka'i is quite low, and the people are not consumer-oriented. Tourism, especially getaway condos, brings in the affluent. This creates friction; the have-nots don't know their situation until the haves come in and remind them. Today, most people hunt a little, fish, and have small gardens. Some are small-time *pakalolo* growers who get over the hard spots by making a few dollars from some back-

yard plants. There is no organized crime on Moloka'i. The worst you might run into is a group of local kids drinking on a weekend in one of their favorite spots. It's a territorial thing. If you come into their vicinity, they might feel that their turf is being invaded, and you could be in for some hassles. All this could add up to a bitter situation except that the true nature of most of the people is to be helpful and friendly. Just be sensitive to smiles and frowns and give people their space.

Ethnic Identity

An underground link exists between Moloka'i and other Hawaiian communities such as Waianae on O'ahu. Moloka'i is unusual in that it is still Hawaiian in population and influence, with continuing culturally based outlooks that remain unacceptable to Western views. Ethnic Hawaiians are again becoming proud of their culture and heritage, as well as politically aware and sophisticated, and are just now entering the political arena.

Social problems on Moloka'i relate directly to teenage boredom and hostility in the schools, fueled by a heavy drinking and drug scene. A disproportionate rate of teen pregnancy is a direct by-product. The traditional educational approach is failing.

Ho'oponopono is a fascinating family problem-solving technique still very much employed on Moloka'i. The process is like "peeling the onion,"

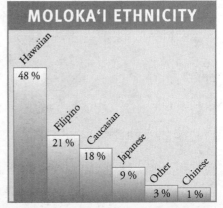

MOLOKA'I ETHNICITY

Hawaiian 48 %
Filipino 21 %
Caucasian 18 %
Japanese 9 %
Other 3 %
Chinese 1 %

where a mediator, usually a respected *kapuna,* tries to get to the heart of a problem. Similar to group therapy, it's a closed family ordeal, never open to outsiders, and lasts until all emotions are out in the open and all concerned feel "clean."

FESTIVALS AND EVENTS

Like all of the other islands, Moloka'i celebrates all federal and state holidays and major events. In addition to these, specific events have particular importance on this island. A few of these follow.

January

The day-long **Makahiki Festival,** held at Kaunakakai Park, includes food, arts, crafts, and games in a revived version of the ancient Hawaiian Olympics.

May

Music, song, and hula contests are the focus of the day at the **Moloka'i Ka Hula Piko,** held at Papohaku Beach Park on the west end of Moloka'i. This event, which includes craft and art demonstrations and Hawaiian foods, is held to honor the birth of hula, traditionally held to have been on top of Ka'ana Hill above Maunaloa.

July

The annual **Moloka'i to O'ahu Paddleboard Race,** a 32-mile paddle race on longboards, runs across Kaiwi Channel from Papohaku Beach to Maunaloa Beach Park in Hawaii Kai on O'ahu.

September

The **Wahine O Ke Kai Outrigger Canoe Race** for women takes off at the end of September in Hawaiian-style canoes from the remote Hale O Lono Beach on Moloka'i's west end to Kahanamoku Beach in Waikiki. In crossing, the teams must navigate the always-rough Kaiwi Channel.

October

The **Moloka'i Hoe Outrigger Canoe Race** is the men's version of this canoe contest, which also starts from Hale O Lono Beach and races to Kahanamoku Beach on O'ahu.

SPORTS AND RECREATION

Because Moloka'i is a great place to get away from it all, you would expect an outdoor extravaganza. In fact, Moloka'i is a "good news, bad news" island when it comes to recreation, especially in the water. Moloka'i has few excellent beaches, with the two best, Halawa and Papohaku, on opposite ends of the island; Papohaku Beach on the west end is treacherous during the winter but generally good the rest of the year. Surfers and windsurfers will be disappointed with Moloka'i except at a few locales at the right time of year, while bathers, sun worshippers, and families will love the few small, secluded beaches with gentle waves located mostly on the south shore.

Moloka'i has a small population and plenty of undeveloped "outback" land. This *should* add up to great hiking and camping, but the land is mostly privately owned, camping spots are few, and you need permission or must enter with an organized activity company for most of the trails. However, those bold enough to venture into the outback on open trails will virtually have it to themselves. Moloka'i has tame, family-oriented beach parks along its southern shores, superb hunting and fishing, two golf courses, and a handful of tennis courts. Couple this with clean air, no industrial pollution, no city noise, and a deliciously casual atmosphere, and you wind up with the epitome of relaxation.

Camping

The best camping on Moloka'i is at **Pala'au State Park** at the end of Route 470, in the cool mountains overlooking Kalaupapa Peninsula. It's also the site of Moloka'i's famous Phallic Rock. Here you'll find pavilions, grills, picnic tables, and fresh water. What you won't find are crowds; in fact, most likely you'll have the entire area to yourself. The camping here is free, but you need a permit, good for seven days, from the park headquarters office in Kalae, 808/567-6923, or from the Division of State Parks in Wailuku on Maui, 808/984-8109.

Camping is permitted for two days at **Waikolu Lookout** in the Moloka'i Forest Reserve, but you'll have to follow a tough dirt road (Main

Forest Road) for 10 miles to get to it. Bring your own water because none is available there. A free permit must be obtained from the Division of Forestry and Wildlife, 54 S. High St., Wailuku, HI 96793, 808/984-8100, or if you write, allow at least a week.

County park, seaside camping is allowed at **One Ali'i Park,** just east of Kaunakakai, and at **Papohaku Beach Park,** on the west end. These parks have full facilities. Papohaku is isolated and quiet, but because of its location and easy access just off the highway, One Ali'i is often noisy. Also, you are a target here for any rip-off artists. A county permit is required and available from County Parks and Recreation at the Mitchell Pauole Center in Kaunakakai, 808/553-3204, open Mon.–Fri. 8 A.M.–4 P.M.; fees are $3 per day for adults, $.50 for children under age 17. Camping is limited to three consecutive days and a total of 15 days per year.

Until renovation is completed, camping is not permitted at the Hawaiian Home Lands' **Kioea Park,** one mile west of Kaunakakai, the site of one of the most amazing royal coconut groves in Hawaii.

Hiking

Moloka'i should be a hiker's paradise, and there are a few well-maintained and easily accessible trails, but others cross private land, skirt guarded *pakalolo* patches, are poorly maintained, and/or are tough to follow. This section provides a general overview of some hiking possibilities available on Moloka'i.

One of the most exciting hassle-free trails descends the *pali* to the **Kalaupapa Peninsula.** You follow the well-maintained mule trail down, and except for some "road apples" left by the mules, it's a totally enjoyable experience suitable for in-shape hikers. Because this trail is within the boundary of the National Historical Park, you *must* have a reservation with the guide company to descend this trail and tour the peninsula.

Another excellent trail is at **Halawa Valley,** following Halawa Stream to cascading Moaula Falls, where you can take a refreshing dip if the famous *mo'o*, a mythical lizard said to live in

the pool, is in the right mood. This trail is strenuous enough to be worthwhile and thrilling enough to be memorable. Halawa Valley is one of the most ancient populated sites in the islands, and many remnants of the past still dot the floor of the valley. In years past, anyone could walk up into Halawa Valley; however, because of abuse, disrespect, degradation of the land, and a few lawsuits, it was closed to the public for two years. It has been opened again, and you can go in with a group booked by the Molokai Ranch Outfitters Center, 808/552-2791. These trips run daily at 9:30 A.M. for $75 per person, and each guide not only shows you the way but also gives you a private historical and cultural lesson on the way. Call for reservations and all particulars. Some valley residents are willing to guide the curious for about $20, and, while you are not supposed to go in without permission because it is private land, some people do make the trip in by themselves. If you know the way and go in by yourself, leave a donation ($5 should be sufficient) at the flower stand by the wooden bridge over the stream in appreciation for those in the valley who maintain the trail.

Moloka'i Forest Reserve, which you can reach by driving about 10 miles over the rugged Main Forest Road (passable by 4WD only in the dry season), has fine hiking. On the way you'll find the Sandalwood Measuring Pit and just at the reserve boundary the Waikolu Lookout. The hale and hearty who push on for several more miles will find themselves in the Nature Conservancy's **Kamakou Preserve** overlooking Pelekunu and Wailau, two fabulous and enchanted valleys of the north coast.

The Molokai Ranch offers the greatest number of diverse and unique cultural hiking tours across its land at the west end of the island. For schedules, times, and fees, call the Ranch Outfitters Center at 808/552-2791 or 888/729-0059.

For guided hiking tours to other parts of the island, try the services of Eddie Tanaka, 808/558-8396, a Moloka'i native who knows all of the good trails, or either of the outdoor adventure companies, Molokai Outdoors, 808/553-4477, or Molokai Rentals and Tours, 808/553-5663.

Beaches

East End: The beaches of Moloka'i have their own temperament, ranging from moody and rebellious to sweet and docile. Heading east from Kaunakakai along Route 450 takes you past a string of beaches that vary from poor to excellent. Much of this underbelly of Moloka'i is fringed by a protective coral reef that keeps the water flat, shallow, and at some spots murky. This area was ideal for fish ponds but leaves a lot to be desired as far as beaches are concerned. The farther east you go, the better the beaches become. The first one you come to is at **One Ali'i Park,** about four miles east of Kaunakakai. Here you'll find a picnic area, campsites, good fishing, and family-class swimming where the kids can frolic with no danger from the sea. Next you pass **Kakahai'a Beach Park,** but perhaps the best beach along the road is **Murphy's Beach** at mile marker 20. **Halawa Bay,** on Moloka'i's far east end, is the best all-around beach on the island. It's swimmable year-round, but be extra careful during the winter. The bay protects the beach for a good distance; beyond its reach the breakers are excellent for surfing. The snorkeling and fishing are good to very good.

West End: The people of Moloka'i favor the isolated beaches on the northwest section of the island. **Mo'omomi Beach** is one of the best and features good swimming in summer, fair surfing, and pleasurable snorkeling along its sandy, rocky bottom. You have to drive over a very rutted dirt road to get there. Although car rental agencies are against it, you can make it, but only in dry weather. From Mo'omomi you can walk west along the shore and find your own secluded spot in a series of small and large beaches. Very few visitors go south from Maunaloa town, but it is possible and rewarding for those seeking a secluded area. As you enter Maunaloa town a crushed coral track goes off to your right. Follow it through Molokai Ranch land and down the hill to **Hale O Lono Harbor,** start of an Outrigger Canoe Race. The swimming is only fair, but the fantasy feeling of a deserted island is pervasive. **Kepuhi Beach** just below the Kaluakoi Hotel is excellent, and **Papohaku Beach** beyond the headland farther to the south is renowned for its vast expanse of sand. Unfortunately, both are treacherous in the winter, with giant swells and heavy rips, which make them a favorite for surfers. Anyone not accustomed to strong sea conditions should limit themselves to sunning and wading only to the ankles. During the rest of the year, this area is fairly good for swimming, sometimes becoming like a lake in the summer, but still exhibits areas of undertow and shore break. Stay on the safe side and limit yourself to walks along the sand. About one-half mile north of Kepuhi Beach is an ideal spot named **Kawakiu Beach,** good for swimming, depending on tide conditions, secluded sunbathing, and unofficial camping. This area is well established as an archaeological site, and access to the beach was a hard-fought controversy between the people of Moloka'i and the Molokai Ranch.

Snorkel and Scuba

Some charter fishing boats arrange scuba and snorkeling excursions, but scuba and snorkeling on Moloka'i are just offshore, and you don't need a boat to get to it. Beginners will feel safe at **One Ali'i Park,** where the sea conditions are mild, although the snorkeling is mediocre. The best underwater area is the string of beaches heading east past mile marker 18 on Route 450, and especially at mile marker 20. Mo'omomi Beach on the northwest shore is very good, and Kawakiu Beach out on the west end is good around the rocks, but stay away during winter. For those staying at Molokai Ranch, Halena and Kolo beaches along the south coast also offer decent snorkeling.

Moloka'i Fish and Dive in Kaunakakai, 808/553-5926, is a full-service snorkel shop. It has very good rental rates at $9 a set per day and can give you directions to the best spots.

Bill Kapuni's Snorkel and Dive Adventure, P.O. Box 1962, Kaunakakai, HI 96748, 808/553-9867, cpgroup@aloha.net, www.molokai.com/kapuni, is an excellent way to enjoy Moloka'i's underwater spectacle. Owner Bill Kapuni, a native Hawaiian, is intimately familiar with both the marine life you will encounter and the Hawaiian myths and legends of his heritage. Bill's trips, including complimentary snacks, are $65 for snorkeling and $95 for a two-tank dive. Bill offers professional PADI instruction and has a compressor to fill tanks for certified divers. Other water activities can be accommodated. All trips operate on a Boston Whaler, six-person maximum.

Ma'a Hawaii, Moloka'i Action Adventures

Walter Naki knows Moloka'i—its mountains, seas, shores, trails, flowers, trees, and birds. His one-man action-adventure company, Ma'a Hawaii, P.O. Box 1269, Kaunakakai, HI 96748, 808/558-8184, loosely translates as "used to, accustomed to, or familiar with." A native Hawaiian raised on the island and versed in its myths and mysteries, Walter has won the Hawaiian decathlon five times and has won renown in statewide spearfishing and free-diving contests. If it has to do with the outdoors, Walter does it. Walter's north shore boat trip is his number-one activity. He's one of the few who takes guests to the "backside" of the island. The boat goes summer or winter—summer is best—but only when the water is safe, and the trip costs $100 per person. In summer, the water on the north shore is a bit choppy, but there is no surf so you can get close to shore and land, swim, and hike in Wailua Valley. In winter, the water is smoother, but there are larger—sometimes immense—swells, and it's not possible to land or even get very close to the shore because of the strong surf.

Walter is a certified boat captain as well as a certified scuba diver. For a scuba trip, you must bring your own gear. Deep-sea fishing excursions, kayaking, whale-watching, snorkeling, spear fishing, and reef fishing tours are also available on request. Walter can arrange other activities, such as hunting for axis deer, wild boar, or goats on private land, which costs $200 per day for bow hunters (you supply the equipment) and $300 per day for rifle hunters (two hunters per day only, Walter suppies the guns and ammunition). Hiking and "camera safaris" over many of the same hunting trails cost $50 for a half day (up to six people only) and are often guided by Walter's friend Eddie Tanaka; call 808/558-8396. Walter is a great guide, but he is definitely "fo real," absolutely genuine with no glitz or glamour.

He will do everything he can to make your day safe and enjoyable, even stopping at his friend's taro patch to give you a glimpse of preserved island life. If you seek a unique experience where you can touch the spirit of Moloka'i, travel for a day with Walter Naki.

Kayaking

The Molokai Ranch **Outfitters Center,** 808/552-2791 or 888/729-0059, runs a rather tame but thoroughly fun kayak tour along the south shore inside the reef for $65, or $45 if you are a guest at the ranch.

If you want to take off on your own or be guided through the placid reef, try **Moloka'i Outdoors,** 808/553-4477. Guided trips run $78 for the coastline tour and $45 for the sunset tour. Single and double rental kayaks are available at $10 per hour or $25 per day, or $15 per hour or $40 per day, respectively. See them at Hotel Moloka'i.

Molokai Rentals and Tours, 808/553-5663, offers a morning kayak tour along the south shore for $45, as well as rents kayaks for those who care to go on their own. Daily rentals run $25 for a single and $40 for a tandem.

Sailing

Moloka'i is nearly devoid of charter sailboats; however, for those who like to feel the salty sea breeze in their hair, hear the snap of a full-furled sail, or enjoy the sunset from the deck of a sailing ship, try an excursion with **Moloka'i Charters,** P.O. Box 1207, Kaunakakai, HI 96748, 808/553-5852. The only charter sailing ship on the island is its 42-foot sloop *Satan's Doll,* berthed at the Kaunakakai wharf. Tours offered are a two-hour sunset sail for $40 and a full-day sail to Lana'i for swimming and snorkeling for $90. In season, whale-watching tours are also run for $50. Four-person minimum; priced per person.

Surfing

The best surfing that's easily accessible is out on the east end past mile marker 20. Pohakuloa Point has excellent breaks, which continue eastward to Halawa Bay. Mo'omomi Beach has decent breaks, as does Kepuhi Beach in front of Kaluakoi Resort (also good for windsurfing) and Papohaku farther down; Kawakiu's huge waves during the winter are suitable only for experts. For gear and accessories, stop at **Molokai Surf** along the highway in Kaunakakai. If you need to rent a surfboard, try **Moloka'i Outdoors,** 808/553-4477, or **Molokai Rentals and Tours,** 808/553-5663.

Horseback and Mule Rides

The **Molokai Ranch,** 808/552-2791, offers a variety of rides over its lands for ranch guests and nonguests. Included are a *paniolo* roundup for $80 and three different trail rides for $80–125. An inexpensive, tame wagon ride around part of the property is also an option.

On the far eastern tip of the island, **Pu'u O Hoku Ranch,** 800/558-8109, offers several trail rides through its working ranch, which range from a one-hour ride for $50 to a full-day waterfall excursion for $145. Other specialized rides are also offered, like a beach ride for $120 and an early morning sunrise ride for $80. These rides let you see scenery that is generally not open to others than those who work on the ranch.

Coupled with a tour of the Kalaupapa settlement, the **Molokai Mule Ride,** P.O. Box 200, Kualapuu, HI 96757, 808/567-6088 or 800/567-7550, muleman@aloha.net, www.muleride.com, runs tours from topside down to the peninsula. The well-trained mules will transport you round-trip down and up the 1,600-foot *pali* face, negotiating the switchbacks with ease. The ride each way is about 90 minutes. Conducted 8 A.M.–3:30 P.M. daily except Sunday, this tour is $150 per person and includes the ground tour of the settlement and lunch; add $9 per person (minimum two) if you need transportation from the Moloka'i Airport if you're flying in for the day for the tour. No riders who weigh more than 240 pounds, please; all must be at least 16 years old and in good physical shape. Molokai Mule Ride can also arrange the ground tour for you ($40) if you desire to hike down the hill, or a fly-in from Ho'olehua Airport to the peninsula and ground tour for $119. Other options are the ground tour and a fly-in from either Maui for $224 or Honolulu for $215.

Biking

For the only sales and repair of bikes on Moloka'i, and for guided bike tours of Pu'u O Hoku ranchland way out on the eastern tip of the island, see **Moloka'i Bicycle,** 808/553-3931 or 800/709-2453, www.bikehawaii.com/molokaibicycle. Open Monday, Tuesday, and Thursday 3–6 P.M. and Saturday 9 A.M.–2 P.M., this bike shop is located in a warehouse-type building at 80 Mohala Street, just up from the highway. It hardly looks like a bike shop, so keep your eyes peeled. Moloka'i Bicycle has the largest rental pool on the island, aside from those at the Mokola'i Ranch. Rental rates are regular mountain bikes, $15 per day or $70 per week; mountain bikes with front suspension, $20 per day or $85 per week; road bikes, $24 per day or $100 per week. Bicycle drop-off is possible around the island for a small fee. Guided-ride rates run $65 per person (minimum two) for three- to five-hour rides and $45 per person for one- to three-hour rides. Call 808/553-5740 for reservations.

Molokai Ranch offers several levels of bike riding over numerous courses across their ranch land. Half- and full-day guided tours are run for $35 and $80, respectively, and traverse a great deal of the rugged ranch land. These courses offer trails for the beginner to the advanced rider. A night ride is also an option. Renting bikes from the Outfitters Center is $20 per day or $30 for full suspension. For information, call 808/552-2791.

Moloka'i Outdoors, 808/553-4477, located at Hotel Moloka'i, rents bikes for $27 per day and mopeds for $25 per day. **Molokai Rentals and Tours,** 808/553-5663, has mountains bikes for $20 per day.

Golf

Moloka'i's two golf courses are as different as custom-made and rental clubs. When the **Kaluakoi Golf Course** opened in 1977, it was a picture-perfect beauty that would challenge any top pro. Laid out by master links designer Ted Robinson and located out at the Kaluakoi Resort at the extreme west end of the island, this par-72 wound through a dry but beautiful setting, including five holes strung right along the beach.

MOLOKA'I GOLF AND TENNIS

Golf Course	Par	Yards	Fees	Cart	Clubs
Ironwood Hills Golf Course	34	3,088	$18/9 holes	$7 (9 holes)	$8
808/567-6000			(18 holes)	$3 (pullcart)	$25
Kaluakoi Golf Course	36	3,138	$20/9 holes	$10	$10
808/552-0255			$35/18 holes	$5 (pullcart)	

Tennis Court Town	Location	No. of Courts	Lighted
Kaunakakai	Community Center	2	Yes
Ho'olehua	Moloka'i High School	2	Yes

Unfortunately, years of decline finally caused the course to close, but after being purchased by the Molokai Ranch, the first nine holes reopened in 2002 with plans for eventually opening the rest of the course. Although still in need of much work, the front nine are playable, and greens fees run $20 for nine or $35 if you want to go around twice. For tee times, call the pro shop at 808/552-0255.

Moloka'i's other golf course is the homey **Ironwood Hills Golf Course,** 808/567-6000, originally built for pineapple company executives. Open 7 A.M.–5 P.M. daily, this rarely used but well-maintained mountain course is nine holes, par 34, and 3,088 yards long. Pay the affordable greens fee to the office manager or to a groundskeeper who will come around as you play; $18 for nine holes or $25 if you want to loop the course twice. Twilight rates, club rental, riding and hand carts are also available. The course is located up in the hills in Kala'e at 1,200 feet in elevation, just before the Meyer Sugar Mill—look for the sign. Ironwood Hills is turning from a frog to a prince. Recent work has concentrated on improving the grounds. Even today there is no pro shop or snack shop available—all these will come in time—and only a small trailer as an office.

Tennis

Public courts are available at Moloka'i High School in Ho'olehua and at the Community Center in Kaunakakai, but you may have to reserve a spot with the office in the Mitchell Pauole Center next door for the courts in town. Condo tennis courts are reserved for guests only. Two courts are available at the **Ke Nani Kai Condos,** at the Kaluakoi Resort, and two courts are at the **Wavecrest Condo** east of Kaunakakai on Route 450.

Fishing

The Penguin Banks of Moloka'i are some of the most fertile waters in Hawaii. Private boats as well as the commercial fishing fleets out of O'ahu come here to try their luck. Trolling produces excellent game fish such as marlin, mahimahi, *ahi* (a favorite with sashimi lovers), and *ono,* with its reputation of being the best-tasting fish in Hawaii. Bottom fishing, usually with live bait, yields *onaga* and *uku,* a gray snapper favored by local people. Moloka'i's shoreline, especially along the south and west, offers great bait-casting for *ulua* and *'ama 'ama. Ulua* is an excellent eating fish, and with a variance in weight from 15–110 pounds, it can be a real whopper to catch from shore. Squidding, *limu* gathering, and torch-fishing are all quite popular and productive along the south shore, especially around the old fish pond sites. These remnants of Hawaii's one-time vibrant aquaculture still produce mullet, the *ali'i*s favorite; an occasional Samoan crab; the less desirable, introduced tilapia; and the better-left-alone barracuda.

The *Alyce C.,* 808/558-8377, www.worldwidefishing.com/hawaii/b225/index.html, is a

31-foot, fully equipped diesel-powered fishing boat, owned and operated by Captain Joe Reich, who can take you for full- ($400), three-quarter ($350), or half-day ($300) charters and offers whale-watching tours in season.

Fun Hogs Hawaii, 808/567-6789, www.molokai-rentals.com/funhogs also offers half- or full-day fishing excursions, as well as two-hour sunset cruises, and whale-watching trips in season. This company will also take a group body-boarding, give instruction, and provide gear. Charters for other purposes are welcome.

The **Moloka'i Fish and Dive Co.,** 808/553-5926, www.molokaifishanddive.com, also arranges deep-sea charters as well as excursions and shoreline sailing.

Hunting

Public hunting lands on Moloka'i are open to anyone with a valid state hunting license. Wild goats and pigs can be hunted in various hunting units year-round on weekends and state holidays, except when bird hunting is in effect. Bag limits are two animals per day. Hunting game birds (ring-necked pheasants, various quails and doves, wild turkeys, partridges, and francolins) is open on public lands from the first Saturday in November to the third Sunday in January. A special dove season runs late January through March. For full information, license, and fees, contact the Division of Forestry and Wildlife, P.O. Box 347, Kaunakakai, HI 96748, 808/533-1745.

Some of the best hunting on Moloka'i is on the private lands of the 54,000-acre **Molokai Ranch.** The ranch now has Hawaiian Kine Hunting coordinate its hunting operation. Call 808/336-0095 and speak with Joey Joao about all the particulars. From Jan.–Sept., hunting is open for axis deer only, and the rate is $650 per day without guide and $400 per day extra for guide service. Following state rules and regulations, game bird hunting is also offered on the ranch during regular state hunting season. The fee then is $100 per day without a guide and $300 per day extra with guide service. All hunters must be in possession of a Hawaii state hunting license. Ecological conditions may affect hunting at certain times of the year.

Land Tours

Only a few limited tours are offered on Moloka'i. Mostly, it's you and your rental car. **Moloka'i Off-road Tours and Taxi,** 808/553-3369, offers a six-hour narrated tour ($59) by air-conditioned van, which hits many of the highlights of the island. They can also tailor a tour to your needs; reservations are required.

Air Tours

An amazing way to see Moloka'i—particularly its north coast—is by helicopter. This method is admittedly expensive, but dollar for dollar it is *the* most exciting way of touring and can get you places that no other means can. A handful of companies operate mostly from Maui and include overflights of Moloka'i. Although a helicopter trip will put a big hole in your budget, most agree they are among the most memorable experiences of their trip. Try **Air Maui,** 808/877-7005; **Sunshine Helicopters,** 808/871-0722; and **Blue Hawaiian Helicopters,** 808/871-8844.

If you are lucky, your regularly scheduled flight from Kahului to Ho'olehua will also fly along the north coast and give you a glimpse, although not real close, of this spectacular line of *pali* and valley.

Activity Desk/Rentals

The **Moloka'i Outdoors** activity desk, 808/553-4477 or 877/553-4477, outdoors@aloha.net, www.molokai-outdoors.com, basically handles everything. The staff members here are well versed on what recreational possibilities are available on the island, and they go out of their way to make it happen for you. From them you can rent bikes and kayaks, snorkel gear, surfboards and windsurfing equipment, camping gear, and a host of accessories. They can guide you on a bike tour of the coffee plantation, kayak tour inside the fringe reef, or teach you how to surf or windsurf. This company can set you up with any of the other activity providers on the island, connect you with activities on other islands, shuttle you to and from the airport, and as a travel agency, can arrange transportation, lodging, and car rental. Contact them for all of your island activity needs. Open Monday–Saturday 8 A.M.–6 P.M., Saturday until 5 P.M.

Molokai Rentals and Tours, 808/553-5663 or 800/553-9071, also offers numerous options for rental equipment, rental cars, arranges kayak, hiking, and bike tours, other island activities, accommodation, and travel to and from the island.

SHOPPING

Coming to Moloka'i to shop is like going to Waikiki and hoping to find a grass shack on a deserted beach. Moloka'i has only a handful of shops where you can buy locally produced crafts and Hawaiiana. Far and away, most of Moloka'i's shopping is centered **along Ala Malama Street** in downtown Kaunakakai—all three blocks of it! Here you'll find the island's only health food store, two very good food markets, and a clutch of souvenir shops. Away from Kaunakakai the pickin's get mighty slim. Heading west you'll find the **Kualapu'u General Store** off Route 470 on the way to Kalaupapa, and a sundries store and gift shop in Kaluakoi Hotel on the far west end. The Maunaloa Road (Route 460) basically ends in Maunaloa town. Go there!

The best and most interesting shop, **The Big Wind Kite Factory,** is in town and is worth a visit in its own right. It's accompanied by the **Plantation Gallery,** an intriguing souvenir shop of Hawaiian and imported items. Heading east from Kaunakakai is another shoppers' wasteland with only the sundries store at the Molokai Shores condo, the gift shop at Hotel Molokai, and the Puko'o Neighborhood Store for anything to buy.

ACCOMMODATIONS AND FOOD

One quick overview can paint, in broad strokes, the picture of where accommodations are located and where food can be found on Moloka'i. While seemingly enough for visitors, places to stay are not numerous. The main town of Kaunakakai has one fine renovated and refurbished island-style hotel and one condominium. To the east is another condominium, and in this eastern section of the island are the bulk of its vacation rentals, cottages, and B&Bs, not surprising since the greatest number of people live in Kaunakakai and along the southeast coastline. The west end has the upper-end accommodations. Opened some 30 years ago as a top-notch hideaway resort, the Kaluakoi Hotel (now closed) and Golf Club (reopened) had many good years and then gradually began a slide into disrepair. Within the resort are three mid- to upscale condominiums. Up the hill in Maunaloa are the newest and most unusual accommodation options on the island. The Molokai Ranch started a high-end camping/activity experience several years ago that, through its ups and downs, has been a great experience for those lucky enough to have made the trek. In 1999, the ranch opened the lodge, and it is now the most luxuriant accommodation on the island. Built in retro island ranch style, this operation is a gem.

Food is another item all together. Kaunakakai has a handful of small eateries, mostly geared toward the local population, but the best of the bunch is the restaurant at Hotel Moloka'i. To the east of town, there is only one place to eat: the Neighborhood Store in Puko'o. After years of successful operation, the Kualapu'u Cookhouse, headquarters of "The Slow Food Chain," closed. Now Kamuela's Cookhouse has taken its place. Places to eat at the west end are few and far between. The Kaluakoi Hotel restaurants closed when the hotel ceased operation, so those staying at the resort condos and vacation homes must go into Kaunakakai or up the hill to Maunaloa if they want to eat out. There are three options: In the lodge are the upscale Maunaloa Room and the Paniolo Lounge; the local-style Paniolo Cafe is in the theater building in town. Those who stay at the ranch camps are provided food on site.

GETTING THERE

Only Hawaiian Airline, Island Air, and Pacific Wings have regularly scheduled flights to Ho'olehua Airport on Moloka'i. Molokai Air Shuttle, Commercial Flyer, and Paragon Air also fly to the island, but on an on-call or charter basis. Pacific Wings, Molokai Air Shuttle, and Commercial Flyer also fly to Kalaupapa, to connect with tours of the peninsula.

Hawaiian Airlines, 808/567-6510 on Moloka'i, 800/882-8811 in Hawaii, or 800/367-5320 Mainland, has daily flights each way connecting Moloka'i and Honolulu. Weekend morning flights from Honolulu and afternoon flights to Honolulu go through Lana'i. Flights to all other cities in Hawaii go through Honolulu.

Island Air, 808/567-6115 or 800/652-6541 Hawaii, 800/323-3345 Mainland, offers flights connecting Moloka'i with O'ahu and Maui. There are nine daily flights to/from Honolulu 6:25 A.M.–8 P.M. Morning and afternoon flights connect Moloka'i to Kahului, Maui.

Pacific Wings, 800/867-6814, connects Moloka'i with Kahului and Honolulu once a day, using eight-seat, twin-engine Cessna 402C aircraft. It also has morning and afternoon flights between Honolulu and Kalaupapa Peninsula.

Molokai Air Shuttle, 808/567-6847 Moloka'i or 808/545-4988 O'ahu, flies a Piper Aztec to/from Honolulu and Moloka'i for $69.95 round-trip or $39.95 one way. This is not a scheduled route: You call and let them know when you want to fly and they will tell you what's available that day. Molokai Air Shuttle offers a great fare; however, arrival/departure in Honolulu is along Lagoon Drive, which is on the opposite side of the runways from the main terminal building, so it's not convenient for connecting flights but is fine if you're just being picked up in the city. Molokai Air Shuttle also flies unscheduled flights from Honolulu to Kalaupapa for $49 one way and to Lana'i for $175 one way.

Commercial Flyer, 888/266-3597 or 808/833-8014 in Honolulu, also does non-scheduled flights from Honolulu to topside Moloka'i and to Kalaupapa. Rates are $70 round-trip and $40 one way to Ho'oluhua and $110 round-trip to Kalaupapa. Call to see what is flying when.

Paragon Air, 808/244-3356 on Maui or 866/946-4744 Mainland, also does on-demand flights between Moloka'i and Honolulu, plus islandwide air charters in small aircraft to any island destination.

Moloka'i Airport

The **Ho'olehua Airport** has a small terminal with an open-air baggage claim area to the far right, check-in counters next to that, and the waiting lounge on the left side. In the baggage claim area, Dollar and Budget have rental car booths, and each has a base yard a few steps away across the public parking lot out front. There is no public transportation on Moloka'i, but two companies offer taxi service. Also at the terminal you'll find a snack bar run by the Moloka'i Coffee Company, toilets, and public telephones in the baggage claim area and in the lobby. Pick up a loaf of excellent Moloka'i bread, the best souvenir available, or a lei from the small gift shop. Tourist brochures are available from a rack in the arrival area. On your way out of the airport, you are greeted first thing with the sign "Aloha. Slow Down. This is Moloka'i."

By Sea

The Maui Princess used to sail daily between Kaunakakai and Lahaina, but for economic reasons the service was stopped in 1997, affecting many businesses on Moloka'i. Island Marine, 808/667-6165 or 800/275-6969, www.molokaiferry.com, the company that operates this ship, started ferry operation again in 2001 with the refurbished and faster *Moloka'i Princess,* which is able to make the crossing in about one hour and 15 minutes. Although the schedule is subject to change, the yacht runs daily, leaving Kaunakakai at 5:45 A.M. and 3:30 P.M., returning from Lahaina at 7:30 A.M. and 5:15 P.M. The fares are $40 one way for adults and $20 for kids. Also offered are several day tour packages to Moloka'i from Maui. The cruise/car and cruise/van tour packages run $139 per person.

GETTING AROUND
Car Rental

Moloka'i offers a limited choice of car rental agencies, so make reservations to avoid being disappointed. Rental car booths at the air terminal close after the last flight of the day has arrived. Rental car companies on Moloka'i dislike their cars being used on dirt roads (there are plenty) and strongly warn against it. Sedans, economy through full-size, are the most numerous, but SUVs, small trucks, minivans, and full-size vans are also available in limited numbers. **Dollar Rent A Car,** 808/567-6156 or 800/800-4000, provides professional and friendly service; **Budget Rent A Car,** 808/567-6877 or 800/527-7000, is another option. These two companies have booths and base yards only at the airport. Pick up a copy of the *Molokai Drive Guide* magazine for maps and useful information on sights and activities.

The local company called **Island Kine Auto Rental,** P.O. Box 1018, Kaunakakai, HI 96748, 808/553-5242 or 866/527-7368, fax 808/553-3880, info@molokai-car-rental.com, www.molokai-car-rental.com, is located in Kaunakakai. Its slant is to rent the kind of vehicle that the big companies don't and to be competitive in pricing with the kind they do. It has a sizable fleet of two- and four-door sedans, 4WDs, 10- and 15-passenger vans, and pickups, all used but well maintained. Although these cars can be taken off paved roads, a cleaning fee may be tacked onto your bill depending on how much time is involved in putting the vehicle back in service. Let them know what kind of car you need and for how long, and they'll let you know what the rate will be. They even do a courtesy pickup at the airport or pier and give you a brief introduction of what's to see and do on the island. Island Kine gives personalized service, treats you well, and offers competitive rates.

Also offering a few rental vehicles at competitive rates is **Molokai Rentals and Tours,** 808/553-5663 or 800/553-9071, www.molokai-rentals.com.

There are only three **gas stations** on the island: two in Kaunakakai and one in Maunaloa. Fill your tank before turning in your rental car because there is not a station at or near the airport. Gas prices are generally $.40–50 higher on Moloka'i than on Maui.

Public Transportation

No public bus transportation services Moloka'i.

Moloka'i Off-road Tours and Taxi, 808/553-3369, does transfers to and from the airport 8 A.M.–6 P.M. for $7 per person ($8 after hours), minimum of three passengers. Alternately, **Molokai Outdoors,** 808/553-4477, also offers shuttle service between the airport and Kaunakakai for $22.50. Shuttle service to other parts of the island, as well as off-road touring, are options for both of these companies.

Hitchhiking

The old thumb gives fair to good results on Moloka'i. Most islanders say they prefer to pick up hitchhikers who are making an effort by walking along, instead of lounging by the side of the road. It shows that you don't have a car but do have some pride. Getting a ride to or from Kaunakakai and the airport is usually fairly easy. To other destinations, it's more problematic.

INFORMATION AND SERVICES

Telephone numbers for service agencies that you might find useful: emergency, 911; police, 808/553-5355; County Parks and Recreation, 808/553-3204; Division of Forestry, 808/553-1745; Hawaiian Homelands, 808/560-6104; Kaunakakai post office, 808/553-5845.

Information

The **Moloka'i Visitors Association** (MVA), 808/553-3876 or 800/800-6367 Mainland and Canada, mva@aloha.net, www.molokai-hawaii.com, can help with every aspect of your trip to Moloka'i. From their office at the Kamo'i Professional Center, they dispense up-to-the-minute information on accommodations, transportation, dining, activities, and services, and some brochures and island maps. The MVA should be your first contact if you are contemplating a visit to Moloka'i. Open Monday–Friday 8:30 A.M.–4:30 P.M.

For additional general information about the island, try the websites www.molokai-aloha.com, www.molokai.com, and www.visitmolokai.com.

Medical Services

Moloka'i is a small place with a small population, so there is not as much available here in the way of medical treatment as on Maui or the other larger islands. Yet Moloka'i has Moloka'i General Hospital, 808/553-5331, which is located at the end of Home 'Olu Street just above Ala Malama Avenue in Kaunakakai. There are half a dozen doctors on the island and half as many dentists. Try Molikai Drugs, 808/553-5790, in the Kamo'i Professional Center, one block off the main drag, for prescription drugs, first-aid items, potions, lotions, and sundries. Open Monday–Saturday 8:45 A.M.–5:45 P.M.

Banks

There are two banks on the island, both in downtown Kaunakakai and each open Monday–Thursday 8:30 A.M.–4 P.M., Friday until 6 P.M. Each has an ATM. They are Bank of Hawaii, 808/553-3273, and American Savings Bank, 808/553-3263.

Library

The Moloka'i Public Library (1937), 808/553-1765, is located next to the government buildings at the west end of Kaunakakai. Hours are Tuesday, Thursday, and Friday 10 A.M.–5 P.M. and Monday and Wednesday 12:30–8 P.M.

Newspapers

For a local look at what's happening on the island of Moloka'i, check out either of the island's two newspapers. The larger and more mainstream is *The Dispatch* (www.aloha.net/~mkkdisp), published in Maunaloa, while the more humble *Mokokai Advertiser-News* (www.molokaiadvertisernews.com) is published in Kaunakakai by solar power.

Laundry

Across from the Moloka'i Drive Inn, the Ohana Laundromat is open daily 6 A.M.–9 P.M. There is also a small laundromat behind Outpost Natural Foods, open daily 7 A.M.–9 P.M.

Kaunakakai

No matter where you're headed on the island, you have to pass through Kaunakakai (Beach Landing), the tiny port town and economic and government center that is Moloka'i's hub. An hour spent walking the three blocks of Ala Malama Street, the main drag, and its side streets gives you a good feeling for what's happening. If you need to do any banking, mailing, or shopping for staples, Kaunakakai's the place. Hikers, campers, and even day-trippers should get all they need here because shops, both east and west, are few and far between and mostly understocked. Evenings are quiet here, with no neon or glamour and no traffic lights, and that's just the way that people want to keep it.

SIGHTS

Head toward the water and you'll see **Kaunakakai wharf** stretching out into the shallow harbor for one-half mile. Not a natural harbor, the approach to the wharf had to be cleared through coral. Townsfolk like to drive their cars onto the causeway, but it's much better to walk out. On the landing are the harbor office, public toilets, boat moorings, and a boat launch. The ferry from Lahaina pulls into port here, the twice-weekly barge to the island stops here, and the few private and commercial sailing and fishing boats are tied up at its moorings. Fishing from the wharf isn't great, but it's handy and you never can tell. If you decide to stroll out, look for the raised platform surrounded by stone west of the approach road that was the site of Lot Kamehameha's summer house, "Malama" (circa 1864). Lot Kamehameha was King Kamehameha V, the last of the direct line of Kamehameha rulers. This site and the adjacent land is now part of the as-yet-undeveloped Malama Cultural Park, which only has restrooms, parking, and access to the water. To its side is the Moloka'i Voyaging Canoe Society building.

MOLOKA'I

Kapuaiwa Coconut Grove

A five-minute drive or a 20-minute walk west brings you to this 11-acre royal coconut grove planted in the 1860s for Kamehameha V, or Kapuaiwa to his friends. Kapuaiwa Coconut Grove was originally built because there were seven pools here in which the *ali'i* would bathe, and the grove was planted to provide shade and seclusion. The grove also symbolically provided the king with food for the duration of his life. The grove has diminished from the 1,000 trees originally planted, but more than enough remain to give a sense of grandeur to the spot. Royal coconut palms are some of the tallest of the species, and besides providing nuts, they served as natural beacons pinpointing the spot inhabited by royalty. These that remain are more than 80 feet tall. After years of becoming overgrown, this parklike grove is slowly being renovated and brought back into more beautiful shape. Mostly you'll have it to yourself. Pay heed to the signs warning of falling coconuts. An aerial bombardment of hefty five-pounders will rudely customize the hood of your rental car. Definitely do not walk around under the palms if the wind is up.

Church Row

Sin has no chance against the formidable defensive line of churches standing altar to altar along the road across from Kapuaiwa Coconut Grove. A grant from Hawaiian Homelands provides that a church can be built on this stretch of land to any congregation that includes a minimum number of Hawaiian-blooded parishioners. The churches are basically one-room affairs that wait quietly until Sunday morning, when worshippers come from all over the island. Let there be no doubt: Old Satan would find no customers around here, as all spiritual loopholes are covered by one denomination or another. Visitors are always welcome, so come join in. Be wary of this stretch of road, though, because all services seem to let out at the same time on Sunday morning, causing a minuscule traffic jam.

In-Town Parks

Right in the center of town is the Mitchell Pauole Center, which has the police, fire, county, and parks and recreation offices. Directly across the street is the Kaunakakai Ball Park; behind it are the community tennis courts and swimming

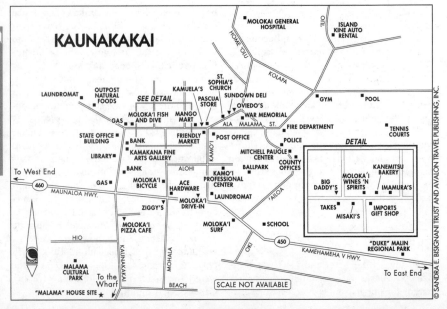

pool and more open spaces for athletic games. Adjoining this county land, but with access from the highway, is the new "Duke" Malin Regional Park, which has additional ball fields, restrooms, and a pavilion with picnic tables.

Classic Fish Ponds

Moloka'i is known for its fish ponds, which were a unique and highly advanced form of aquaculture prevalent from at least the early 13th century. Because of an abundance of shallow, flat waters along its southern shore, Moloka'i was able to support a network of these ponds numbering more than five dozen during their heyday. Built and tended by the commoners for the royal *ali'i,* they provided succulent fish that could easily be rounded up at any time for a meal or impromptu feast. The ponds were formed in a likely spot by erecting a wall of stone or coral. It was necessary to choose an area that had just the right tides to keep the water circulating, but not so strong as to destroy the encircling walls. Openings were left in the wall for this purpose. **Kaloko'eli Pond** is about two miles east of Kaunakakai along Route 450. Easily seen from the road, it's an excellent example of the classic fish pond. You can proceed a few more minutes east until you come to a coconut grove just one-half mile before One Ali'i Beach Park. Stop here for a sweeping view of **Ali'i Fishpond,** another fine example.

ACCOMMODATIONS

Besides camping, Kaunakakai has only two places to stay. Head here for adequate accommodations if you want to save money.

Molokai Shores, a Marc Resorts Hawaii management property, 808/553-5954 or 800/535-0085, fax 808/533-3241, www.marcresorts.com, only 1.5 miles east of downtown Kaunakakai, has full kitchens, large living rooms, and separate bedrooms. The white walls contrasting with the dark brown floors are hung with tasteful prints. Plenty of lounge furniture is provided, along with a table for outside dining and barbecues. The upper floor of the three-story building offers an open-beam ceiling including a full loft. Some units have an extra bedroom built into the loft. All units look out over the ocean. The grounds are very well kept, quiet, and restful. The swimming pool fronts the gentle but unswimmable beach, and nearby is a classic fish pond still in good shape. Architecturally, it's pragmatic and neat but not beautiful. Rates are $155 one-bedroom oceanfront, $199 two-bedroom oceanfront; $15 for each additional person.

The 45-room **Hotel Moloka'i,** P.O. Box 1020, Kaunakakai, HI 96748, 808/553-5347, fax 808/553-5047, www.hotelmolokai.com, was built in 1966 by an architect (Mr. Roberts) and a group of guys who wanted a place to vacation. Enamored with the South Seas, they wanted to give his hotel a Polynesian village atmosphere—and succeeded. The buildings are two-story, semi-A-frames constructed largely with redwood from the American Northwest, with sway-backed roofs covered with split-wood shingles that fit snugly in a coconut grove next to the water. The upstairs units are larger and more airy than the downstairs studios, but both feature lanai, phone, TV, a small refrigerator, and daily housekeeping service. This hotel had its heyday before the big resort and the big money came to the island. After a change of ownership in 1998, Hotel Moloka'i was closed for extensive room renovation and landscaping. By the beginning of 1999, the hotel was once again entertaining guests and has again become a happening place on the island. In a way, it's a throwback to the casual and slower '60s.

Not only tourists come looking for this slice of Hawaii, but also Hawaiian residents come to visit. Hotel Moloka'i was always known for good dining, weekend live entertainment, a well-appointed gift shop, a swimming pool, and a poolside bar, and it now continues that tradition. The restaurant and bar are open daily, and rooms run $85–140. For the convenience of guests, there is an on-site laundry facility and the island's most comprehensive activities desk. Hotel Moloka'i is located just before mile marker 2, east of town. The only drawback is that the hotel is located next to the highway, but overall traffic noise is not much of a concern. Hotel Molokai is a great choice. For current information on dining and room availability, contact Hotel

Moloka'i directly or Castle Resorts and Hotels, 800/272-5275 in Hawaii, 800/367-5004 Mainland and Canada.

FOOD

Like the hotel scene, Moloka'i has only a handful of places to eat, but among these are veritable institutions that if missed make your trip to Moloka'i incomplete. The following are all located on Kaunakakai's main street or just a minute away. Just ask anyone where they are.

Inexpensive: The **Kanemitsu Bakery,** 808/553-5855, has been in business for more than 70 years and is still run by the same family. The bakery is renowned for its numerous varieties of Moloka'i breads. Mrs. Kanemitsu's cookies are scrumptious, and anyone contemplating a picnic or a day hike should load up. The bakery is open 5:30 A.M.–6:30 P.M.; closed Tuesday. At the front counter you can order a sandwich made from bread that is baked in the back, and none are more than $4. There's a lunch counter too, where you can get eggs, pancakes, omelets, and local Hawaiian foods, open 5:30–11:30 A.M. daily except Tuesday. Kanemitsu Bakery is known far and wide for its "hot bread." In fact, this is one thing that you had to bring back for family and friends if you made a trip to Moloka'i. Fresh-baked hot bread is available from the bakery only from 10 P.M.–3 A.M. Go down the alley next to Imamura's to reach the bakery's back door. If the door isn't open, you may have to bang on it. Tell the person how many loaves you want and they'll be brought to the door. It's perhaps best to check out the price of bread during the day.

Big Daddy's, 808/553-5841, serves a variety of inexpensive Filipino food, in addition to the eggs and omelets for breakfast, local-style plate lunches for lunch, and ice cream. Next door is Big Daddy's Market for a limited selection of groceries, some prepared foods, and a few true Filipino delicacies like balut. The restaurant is open Monday–Friday until 4 P.M., the market daily 7:30 A.M.–10 P.M.

Sister restaurant to Kamuela's Cookhouse in Kualapu'u, **Kamuela's in Kaunakakai,** 808/553-4286, serves wholesome inexpensive down-home

cooking to happy customers in a clean, friendly, family-oriented environment. Breakfast is mostly standard American, like eggs, omelets, and corn beef hash, while lunch and dinner bring sandwiches and burgers, mostly in the $4–7 range. Open daily from 7 A.M.–3 P.M. and Monday–Saturday 5–9 P.M. The art on the wall is by a local artist.

Oviedo's Lunch Counter, 808/553-5014, in the last building on the left across from the war memorial, is a strictly Filipino restaurant where every item on the menu is only about $7.75. Choose from ethnic selections like pork adobo, chicken papaya, tripe stew, sweet and sour ribs, pig's feet, mongo beans, and eggplant pimakbet. Oviedo's is small and run-down but clean. The decor is worn linoleum floors and Formica tables. Basically a take-out place, there are a few tables inside if you care to eat there.

Next door to Oviedo's is the **Sundown Deli,** 808/553-3713. Making reasonably priced sandwiches for about $5, salads, and soups in a shop that's hardly big enough to turn around in, this place is establishing a fine reputation. Open Monday–Saturday 7 A.M.–4 P.M.; order at the counter or call your order in to pick up.

Outpost Natural Foods, 808/553-3377, serves wholesome, healthy, nutritious quick foods from its inside window Monday–Friday 10 A.M.–3 P.M. Here you can find various sandwiches for less than $6, burritos for up to $4.25, salads, veggie and tempeh burgers for around $5, and the daily lunch specials for under $6. This is the best vegetarian food on the island. In addition, there is an assortment of fresh juices and smoothies. While there, pick up any groceries you'll need for your time on the island.

Kamo'i Snack 'N Go is in the Kamo'i Professional Center. Stop here for Dave's ice cream, candies, cold drinks, and other snacks. Open daily until 9 P.M.

The **Moloka'i Drive-In,** 808/553-5655, open daily 6 A.M.–10 P.M., is along Kamehameha V Highway in a green, flat-roofed building that has the look of the '60s. You order from the window and then take your meal to eat under an awning, or step into the air-conditioned inside to find a few tables. Breakfast offers omelets, eggs,

Spam, bacon, or ham along with sides of rice, hashbrowns, or toast for under $5. Lunch is chili dogs, nachos, subs, fish, shrimp, plate lunches, and chicken burgers, with a special featured every day. The drive-in is actually tasteful, bright, and clean. It's a local place with decent food and very affordable prices, but you won't find food for the health-conscious here. It would make a great stop for a picnic lunch to go, especially if you're heading to Halawa and points east.

Ziggy's, 10 Mohala St., 808/553-8166, is split into two halves: one, the restaurant, the other, a sports bar and pool room. The restaurant half is open Monday–Thursday 6 A.M.–9 P.M., Friday and Saturday until 10 P.M., while the bar is open 11 A.M.–11 P.M., and Friday and Saturday until 2 A.M. While not memorable, the food here is standard American with a heavy dash of local "grind." Breakfasts can be griddle items, omelets, and corn beef and hash. For lunch and dinner, you can choose meals like kalbi ribs, mahimahi, hamburger steak, burgers, and nightly specials for $7–15.

Moderate: Don't let the name **Moloka'i Pizza Cafe,** 808/553-3288, fool you! Although this bright and cheery air-conditioned restaurant makes designer pizza, the emphasis is on *café.* Located wharfside of the town's main intersection, this eatery is open daily 10 A.M.–10 P.M. (until 11 P.M. on Friday and Saturday, from 11 A.M. on Sunday). The café does food with a flare. Pizzas come in three sizes and range in price from a Moloka'i small for $9.50 up to their giant Big Island with everything including green peppers, onions, sausage, beef, and bacon for $23.50. Sandwiches can be an Italian sub laden with turkey, ham, and roast beef, or a plump fresh-baked pocket sandwich. Hearty appetites will enjoy meals like pasta in marinara sauce, barbecued spare ribs (great!), or the fresh catch. Order it! Caught in these waters, the fish comes in the back door, is filleted, cooked, and served to you as fresh as it can be. Wednesday, Thursday, and Sunday specials are Mexican, Hawaiian *laulau,* and prime rib. Desserts too! The Moloka'i Pizza Cafe delivers—perfect for anyone staying in a condo. Take-out is also available.

The **Hotel Moloka'i Restaurant,** 808/553-5347, is the fanciest place in town and the best restaurant on the island east of Maunaloa. Located right on the water, it has a superb location. Breakfast, lunch, and dinner are served every day of the week, and there are always specials. Breakfasts are a mixture of standard American and island treats, while lunch is mostly salads and sandwiches with a few plate entrées. The kitchen shines best at dinner, when you can order such items as fresh catch of the day, coconut shrimp, *paniolo*-style pork ribs, or misoyaki charbroiled chicken breast, all for less than $20 an entrée. Friday and Saturday nights only there is a prime rib special. This is tasty food at good value. Entertainment happens on the weekends, when local and off-island bands play live dance music into the night, but a special tradition and authentic treat are the songs sung by local ladies from 4–6 P.M. on Aloha Friday. Aloha Friday is also a special at the bar, which is one of three on the island.

SHOPPING

Moloka'i Fish and Dive, in downtown Kaunakakai, 808/553-5926, sounds very practical, and it is, but it has a good selection of souvenirs, T-shirts and fashions, books (including a couple written by shop owner James Brocker), maps of Moloka'i, island music, jewelry, a good assortment of film, along with its fishing, hunting, and camping equipment. Basically, they stock a little bit of everything. They can give you detailed information about fishing and water sports on Moloka'i, arrange island tours, and rent some water gear like snorkel sets, boogie boards, or a rod and reel. Open Monday–Saturday 8 A.M.–6 P.M., Sunday until 2 P.M.

Moloka'i Island Creations, connected to Moloka'i Fish and Dive and open the same hours, features authentic Moloka'i designs on ladies' blouses, tank tops, and T-shirts. It also has original Moloka'i glassware, china, and porcelain, along with Hawaiian cards and notebooks. Fashions also include pareu, children's alohawear, shorts, hats, aloha shirts, **mu'umu'u,** swimwear, a good selection of jewelry, and a rack of cosmetics and perfumes in island scents.

Imamura's, open daily except Sunday 8:30 A.M.–5:30 P.M. and Sunday until noon, is a very friendly down-home shop that sells everything from flip-flops to fishnets. It also specializes in lei-making needles and has a great selection of inexpensive luggage. The shelves hold beach mats and hats, T-shirts, pots and pans, and kitchen utensils. The sales staff are all friendly and slow-paced; when you return, they'll smile a welcome.

Across the street is the newer **Imports Gift Shop,** which has an assortment of clothing, gifts, souvenirs, postcards, and a few snacks. Open Monday–Saturday until 9 P.M. and Sunday until 4 P.M.

Moloka'i Mango, open Mon.–Sat. 9 A.M.–7:30 P.M., is a place to find entertainment for the evening as well as packaged foods and some household supplies. There is no movie theater in Kaunakakai, but since 1998 there has been one in Maunaloa. People who want to watch a big-screen show must now travel to the west end for it—and they do. If not, rent your movie here.

For those who are into wholesome health food, **Outpost Natural Foods,** 70 Makaena Place across from the government buildings, 808/553-3377, is the only store of its kind on Moloka'i, but it's excellent. It's open Monday–Friday 9 A.M.–6 P.M., Sunday 10 A.M.–5 P.M.; closed Saturday. The fruits and vegetables are locally and organically grown as much as possible. Along with the usual assortment of health foods, you'll find bulk grains, granola, nuts, and dried fruits. The jam-packed shelves also hold rennetless cheese, fresh yogurt, nondairy ice cream, vitamins, minerals, supplements, and a good selection of herbs, oils, spices, and natural health care products. If you can't find what you need, ask Dennis, the owner, or the general manager on duty. The juice bar, open weekdays only 10 A.M.–3 P.M., is a great place for a healthy lunch and cold drink.

For general shopping along Ala Malama Street, the **Friendly Market,** open Mon.–Fri, 8:30 A.M.–8:30 P.M., Saturday to 6:30 P.M., is by far the best-stocked grocery store on Moloka'i.

There's a community bulletin board outside. It might list cars for sale, Hawaiian genealogies, or fund-raising sushi sales. Have a look!

Just down the street, **Takes Variety Store,** which also carries hardware and general merchandise, is open daily except Saturday. **Misaki's Groceries and Dry Goods** a few steps farther along sells just about everything in food and general merchandise that you'll require. Open daily from 8:30 A.M. but closes at noon on Sunday.

For that special evening, try **Moloka'i Wines 'N Spirits,** 808/553-5009, open daily until late evening, which has a very good selection of vintage wines, beer, and liquor, as well as gourmet treats. Although not the only place on Moloka'i that sells wine and beer, it is the only shop on the island with such selection. For a limited supply of drinks, candy, and other snacks, try **Pascua Store.**

On the second floor of the Moloka'i Center across from the library is **Kamakana Fine Arts Gallery,** 808/553-8520, www.kamakana-gallery.com. This gallery is the only such art gallery on the island and one of the best such gallery/gift shops in the state. The gallery is an important forum for the approximately 140 Moloka'i island artists to display their work, which includes hand-painted, "quilt design" paper, turned wooden bowls, exquisite pencil drawings, cloth quilts, photographs, alohawear, jewelry, and ukulele. The gallery is open Monday–Friday 9:30 A.M.–5:30 P.M., Saturday until 2 P.M. Stop in and support Moloka'i artists or at least just peruse what's being shown. You'll certainly find something that pleases.

Moloka'i Drugs, 808/553-5790, open daily 8:45 A.M.–5:45 P.M., closed Sunday, is the only full-service pharmacy and drugstore on the island. Don't let the name fool you, because it sells much more than potions and drugs. You can buy anything from sunglasses to film, watches, toys, baby food, small appliances, and garden supplies. It has the best selection of film on Moloka'i, with a very good selection of books, especially Hawaiiana. Film processing, including slides, takes 48 hours. It's located in the small Kamo'i Professional Center, one street back from the main drag.

Moloka'i Surf, open daily except Sunday 9 A.M.–6 P.M. in its shop along the highway, has bathing suits, sandals, T-shirts, shorts, alohawear, and surfing gear.

If you're in town on Saturday morning, be sure to have a look at the **farmers market,** held 7 A.M.–noon on the sidewalk in front of the bank buildings, for local produce and craft items.

The two full-service gas station and mechanic shops on the island are **Rawlin's Chevron Service,** 808/553-3214, at the corner of the highway and the wharf road; and **Kalama Service,** 808/553-5586, one block up. Larger and newer, Rawlins is generally open later and is the only one open on Sundays.

East to Halawa Valley

The east end of Moloka'i, from Kaunakakai to Halawa Valley, was historically the most densely populated area of the island. At almost every milepost is an historical site or point of interest, many dating from precontact times. A string of tiny churches attests to the coming of the missionaries in the mid-1800s, and a crash-landing site was an inauspicious harbinger of the deluge of Mainlanders bound for Hawaii in the 20th century. This entire stretch of Route 450 is almost entirely undeveloped, and the classical sites such as *heiau,* listening stones, and old battlegrounds are difficult to find, although just a stone's throw from the road. The local people like it this way because most would rather see the south shore of Moloka'i remain unchanged. A determined traveler might locate the sites, but unless you have local help, it will mean hours tramping around in marshes or on hillsides with no guarantee of satisfaction. Some sites such as **'Ili'ili'opae Heiau** are on private land and require permission to visit. It's as if the spirits of the ancient *kahuna* protect this area.

SIGHTS

It's a toss-up whether the best part about heading out to the east end of Moloka'i is the road itself or the reward of Halawa Valley at the end. Only 30 miles long, it takes 90 minutes to drive. The road slips and slides around corners, bends around huge boulders, and dips down here and there into coves and inlets. Out on the far end, the cliff face and protruding stones have been painted white so that you can avoid an accident, especially at night. Sometimes the ocean and

road are so close that spray splatters your windshield. Suddenly you'll round a bend to see an idyllic house surrounded by palm trees with a gaily painted boat gently rocking in a protected miniature cove. Behind is a valley of verdant hills with colors so vibrant they shimmer. You negotiate a hairpin curve, and there are Lana'i and Maui, black on the horizon, contrasted against the waves as they come crashing in foamy white and blue. Down the road chugs a pickup truck full of local people. They wave you a "hang loose" as their sincere smiles light up your already glorious day. Out in one of the innumerable bays are snorkelers, while beyond the reef, surfers glide in exhilarating solitude.

The local people think of the road as "their road." Why not? They use it as a sidewalk, playground, and extension of their backyards. Dogs snooze on it, while the rumps of grazing stock are only inches away from your fender. The speed limit is 35, but go slower and enjoy it more. The mile markers stop at mile 17, then four miles farther you come to the best part. Here, the well-tended two-lane highway with the yellow stripe plays out. The road gets old and bumpy, but the scenery gets much more spectacular. It's about nine miles from where the bumpy part begins until you reach the overlook at Halawa Valley. Come with a full tank of gas, plenty of drinking water, a picnic lunch, and your sense of wonder.

One Ali'i Beach Park

A few minutes east of Kaunakakai, the road brings you to a stand of perhaps 80 coconut palms, a place where you can get a view of one of the string of fish ponds that are famous in this

M

MOLOKA'I

ROBERT NILSEN

the mouth of Halawa Valley and its bay

area. One Ali'i Beach Park, only a few minutes farther along near mile marker 3, is actually split into two units. Although this park is open for camping, it's too close to the road, not well shaded, and a bit too overused to be comfortable. The swimming here is only fair for those who like a challenging surf, but excellent for families with little children who want calm waters. Restrooms and showers are available, and the grounds are generally in good shape. Those not camping here would find it pleasant enough for a short stop, but it's nothing compared with what's farther east along the road.

View from the Heights

About two minutes past One Ali'i, Makanui Road (the sign says Kawela Plantation I) leads up the hillside on the *mauka* side of the road. A two-minute ride up this road exposes the beginnings of a high-end residential development. As you gain height (one of the only roads that allows you to do so), you'll have an excellent view of the coastline with a panorama of the fish ponds below and Lana'i and Maui floating on the sea. Beyond this road are two others just like it, lead-

ing into a largely undeveloped subdivision with much the same overview.

Kawela

The Kawela area was a scene of tragedy and triumph in Moloka'i's history. Here was **Pakuhiwa,** the battleground where Kamehameha I totally vanquished the warriors of Moloka'i on his way to conquering O'ahu. In nearby Kawela Gulch are the remains of **Pu'ukaua,** the fortress that Kamehameha overran. The fortress oddly doubled as a *pu'uhonua,* a temple of refuge, where the defeated could find sanctuary. Once the battle had been joined, and the outcome was inevitable, the vanquished could find peace and solace in the very area that they had so recently defended.

Today the area offers refuge as **Kakahai'a Beach County Park** and across the highway, the **Kakahai'a National Wildlife Refuge.** The beach park is not used heavily: It, too, is close to the road. This is also an excellent area for coconut trees, with many nuts lying on the ground for the taking. The refuge is an area where birdwatchers can still be captivated by the sight of rare endemic birds.

Kamalo to Puko'o

This six-mile stretch is loaded with historical sites. Kamalo is one of Moloka'i's natural harbors and was used for centuries before most of the island commerce moved to Kaunakakai. In the late 1800s, **Kamalo Wharf** was the island's principal landing site—turn off the highway at mile marker 10, just at the bend on the road. There may be some fishing shacks here and outrigger canoes from a local club. Tracks once ran out on the wood and stone "mall" to help unload ships. Only remnants of this pier remain. From here, turn around and have a look at the mountains. You'll be facing the highest point on the island.

Saint Joseph Church, next in line, was built in 1876 by Father Damien and restored in 1995. It's small, no more than 16 by 30 feet, and very basic. Inside is a small wooden altar adorned with flowers. A picture of Father Damien and one of St. Joseph adorn the walls. Outside is a black metal sculpture of Damien and a small graveyard. It is said that Father Damien purposefully located the church here, to offer the Hawaiians an alternative to giving offerings at Pu'ili Heiau, which lies just inland.

One mile or so past St. Joseph's is the **Smith and Bronte Landing Site.** These two aviators safely crash-landed their plane here on July 14, 1927, completing the first trans-Pacific civilian flight in just over 25 hours. All you can see is a mangrove swamp, but it's not hard to imagine the relief of the men as they set foot even on soggy land after crossing the Pacific. They started a trend that would bring more than six million people a year to the islands. A mile or beyond that is **Keawanui Fishpond.** At 54 acres and with a 2,000-foot-long wall, it is the largest on the island. The Wavecrest Resort Condominium is nearby at mile marker 13, and just before you reach it you pass a shrimp farm on the ocean side of the highway.

Before Puko'o are three noteworthy sites. **Kalua'aha Church** looks like a fortress with its tiny slit windows and three-foot-thick plastered walls and buttresses. Built in 1844 by the Protestant missionaries Reverend and Mrs. Hitchcock, it was the first Christian church on Moloka'i and is considered by some to be the most significant building on the island. Used for worship until the 1940s, it has since fallen into disuse. In 1967, the bell and steeple came down, the roof is caving in, and the rest is mostly in ruins. While parishioners had repair plans, it is doubtful that the structure can be saved without major rehabilitation.

Our Lady of Sorrows Church, another built by Father Damien in 1874 and rebuilt in 1966, is next. Inside are beautiful pen-and-ink drawings of the Stations of the Cross imported from Holland. Mass is held on Sunday at 7:15 A.M. Across the street is a fine example of a fish pond.

Following on the ocean side is the deep shade of the **Mapulehu Mango Grove,** one of the largest in the world with more than 2,000 trees and 32 varieties. Planted by the Hawaiian Sugar Co. in the 1930s in an attempt to diversify, but now owned by the Bishop Estate, the trees came from all over the world, including Brazil, India, and Formosa. Unfortunately, most of the United States was not educated about eating exotic fruits, so the mangos rotted on the tree unpicked, and the grove became overgrown. While mangos are now well known and these trees still produce prodigiously, it seems that the cost would be too high to trim this grove back into shape to make it economical. So the grove still stands unused and uncared for. To compound matters, the Mediterranean fruit fly has become a problem.

Then comes **'Ili'ili'opae Heiau,** one of Hawaii's most famous human-sacrifice temples, and a university of sorcery, as it were, where *kahuna* from other islands were tutored. All of the wooden structures on the 286-by-87-foot stone platform have long since disappeared. Legend holds that all of the stone was carried across the island from Wailau Valley and perfectly fitted in one night of amazing work. Legend also holds that the sorcerers of 'Ili'ili'opae once sacrificed two sons of a local *kahuna* for some childish misbehavior at the temple. Outraged, he appealed to a powerful shark-god for justice. The god sent a flash flood to wipe out the evil sorcerers, washing them into the sea, where the shark-god and other sharks he had called for the feast waited to devour them. Because the temple is now on private land, it is necessary to receive permission to visit it.

MOLOKA'I

This *heiau* is now on the National Register of Historic Places.

At Puko'o, near mile marker 16, is the private **Mana'e Canoe Club** with its well-tended lawns and tiny inlets. There have been controversies about public access to the beach on the bay across from the canoe club, which has been the norm for generations. The situation culminated in public protests and walks to the beach. There is, however, public access to the old wharf area directly west of the canoe club, but this spot is only fair for swimming. There is also beach access on the east side of this lagoon, where there is better swimming.

Just past Puko'o is the **octopus stone,** a large stone painted white next to the road. It is believed that this stone signifies a cave inhabited by a mythical octopus and that it still retains magical powers. Across the road are the remains of **Paikalani Taro Patch,** reputed to have been three acres in size. Said to have been constructed by Pi'ilani, king of Maui, both Kamehameha I and Kamehameha V got taro to make poi from it.

More East End Beaches

Waialua Beach, also called Peabody Beach, almost at mile marker 19, is one of the best beaches on the island for swimming, snorkeling, and beginner surfing. A freshwater stream entering the ocean is convenient for rinsing off. Two minutes past mile marker 19 is a sand and coral beach where you can walk knee-deep out to the reef. At high tide, it's chest high.

Just before mile marker 20, a stone fish pond perimeter wall has been restored to near its original form, with a six-foot-wide flat top, outlet gate, and shrine to the fish deity. A grassroots restoration project, this is perhaps the best example of what a functioning fish pond looked like in centuries past. Slowly, others along the coast are also being restored with community involvement.

Mile Marker 20 Beach, known locally as Murphy's Beach, with its strand of white sand and protected lagoon, is the main beach on the east end. Pull off at a handy spot and enjoy the great snorkeling, although the swimming is only mediocre. It's very safe and perfect for a family

outing. Just past the beach there is a pulloff parking area on a rock point. At times, local youngsters come here to jump off the rocks into the water. In and out of another bay, you come to Pohakuloa, also called Rock Point, a well-known surf spot.

Note: All of these beaches are sand, but once you reach the water much of the bottom is sharp coral. Wear a pair of reef walkers or old sneakers. You do not want to go out there barefoot!

On to Halawa Valley

Past Puko'o, the road gets spectacular. Many blow-your-horn turns pop up as you wend around the cliff face following the natural roll of the coastline. Coming in rapid succession are incredibly beautiful bays and tiny one-blanket beaches, where solitude and sunbathing are perfect. Be careful of surf conditions! Some of the fruitful valleys behind them are still cultivated in taro. Offshore is the crescent of **Moku Ho'oniki Island,** now a seabird sanctuary but used at times during World War II for bombing practice. The road swerves inland, climbing the hills through pastureland to the 14,000 acres of **Pu'u O Hoku Ranch.** The ranch office at mile marker 25 doubles as the tiny Last Chance Store, which sells drinks, candy, and other snacks for the day until midafternoon. As you pass through the pasture on your way to the valley, you can see the famous and sacred *kukui* grove where Lanikaula, one of the most powerful sorcerers of Moloka'i, is buried on the highest hill ahead of you and on the oceanside. The different-looking cattle grazing these hilly pastures are Brangus, a cross between Angus and Brahman, imported by Pu'u O Hoku (Hill of Stars) Ranch and now flourishing on these choice pasturelands. In addition to cattle and horses, the ranch has about five organic acres planted in several varieties of *awa,* papaya, bananas, and vegetables. The road comes to a hairpin turn where it feels like you'll be airborne. Before you is the magnificent chasm of Halawa Valley with its famous waterfalls sparkling against the green of the valley's jungle walls. Hundreds of feet below, frothy aquamarine breakers roll into the bay.

Halawa Valley and Bay

This choice valley, rich in soil and watered by Halawa Stream, is believed to be the first permanent settlement on Moloka'i, dating from around A.D. 650. Your first glimpse is from an overlook along the road, from which you get a spectacular panorama across the half-mile valley to Lamaloa Head forming its north wall, and westward, deep into its two-mile cleft, where lies Moaula Falls. Many people are so overwhelmed when they gaze from the overlook into Halawa that they don't really look around. Turn to your right and walk only 15 yards directly away from Halawa. This view gives a totally different perspective of a deep-V valley and the pounding surf of its rugged beach—so different from the gently arcing haven of Halawa Bay. For centuries, Halawa's farmers carved geometric terraces for taro fields until a tsunami of gigantic proportions inundated the valley in 1946 and left a plant-killing deposit of salt. Most people pulled out and left their homes and gardens to be reclaimed by the jungle.

ROBERT NILSEN

Moa'ula Falls, Halawa Valley

Follow the winding paved road into the valley until you see Ierusalema Hou Church (1948). Go a little farther to the beach park pavilion, park your car, and walk out to the beach. Here you have a choice of bathing in the cool freshwater stream or in the surf of the protected bay. Alternately, take the road past the church. It curves to the right, crosses Halawa Stream, and continues to the opposite side of the bay. Don't venture out past the mouth of the bay because the currents can be treacherous. This area is great for snorkeling and fishing and is one of the good surfing beaches on Moloka'i.

Halawa Bay is a beach park, but it's not well maintained. Near the pavilion are toilet facilities and a few dilapidated picnic tables, but no official overnight camping is allowed and the water is not potable. People do bivouac for a night on Pu'u O Hoku Ranch land at the north end of Halawa Bay under a canopy of ironwood trees, but it's frowned upon. Be aware that this area attracts rip-offs, and it's not safe to leave your gear unattended.

Near the bridge over the stream is a flower farm, which runs the **Tea in the Valley** botanical tour. Offered at 10 A.M. and 2 P.M., the cost for the farm tour is $15 adults, $10 kids. This tour can be combined with a guided hike to Moa'ula Falls. For information, call 808/658-0117.

Moa'ula Falls

One of *the* best walks on Moloka'i, mosquitoes notwithstanding, is to the famous 250-foot Moa'ula (Red Chicken) Falls. Halawa Stream can be a trickle or torrent, depending on recent rains. If Moa'ula Falls is gushing, the stream too will be roaring. The entire area up toward the falls harbors the remains of countless terraces, rock walls, taro patches, and home sites. Leave everything as you find it. Groves of *kamani* trees mark the sites where *ali'i* were buried; their tall trunks at one time were used by Hawaiian fishermen and later by sailors as a landmark. Legend recalls that a female lizard, a *mo'o*, lives in the gorgeous pool at the bottom of the falls. Sometimes she craves a body and will drag a swimmer down to her watery lair. The only way to determine her mood is to place a *ti* leaf (abundant in the area) in the pool. If it floats, you're safe, but if it sinks, the lady lizard wants company—permanently! Minor gods who live in the rocks above Moa'ula Falls pool want to get into the act too. They'll drop tiny rocks on your head unless you make an offering (a penny under a *ti* leaf will do). Above Moa'ula Falls you can see **Upper Moa'ula Falls,** and in the next valley to the side the cascading brilliance of 500-foot **Hipuapua Falls.** For some years the trail to these waterfalls was closed because it goes across private property. You can once again gain access through a guided tour, by going with a resident of the valley, or if you are a guest of the Pu'u O Hoku Ranch cottages or lodge.

ACCOMMODATIONS AND FOOD

First down the line is **Ka Hale Mala,** just less than five miles east of Kaunakakai on Kamakana Place. This vacation rental is the ground floor of a family house, set amid a tropical garden. Here you have a large living room, full kitchen and bath, and a laundry room, plus use of snorkel gear. Rates are $70 without breakfast or $80 with. For more information, contact Cheryl or Chuck Corbiell, P.O. Box 1582, Kaunakakai, HI 96748, 808/553-9009, cpgroup@aloha.net, www.molokai-bnb.com.

Depending on your point of view, the **Wavecrest Resort** is either a secluded hideaway or stuck out in the sticks away from all the action. It's east of Kaunakakai on Route 450 just at mile marker 13. You'll find *no* hustle, bustle, anxiety, nightlife, or restaurants, and only basic supplies at the Wavecrest general store at the entrance. This condominium sits on five well-tended acres fronting a lovely-to-look-at lagoon that isn't good for swimming. It catches the morning sun and looks directly across the Pailolo Channel to Ka'anapali on Maui. Enjoy a putting green, shuffleboard court, newly refurbished swimming pool, and two lighted tennis courts free to guests. Be aware that there are no phones in any of the units. For those who need to call, there are two pay phones at the front office. In each unit is a fully furnished kitchen, spacious living room, ceiling fan, televi-

sion, and lanai. A laundry room is located on each floor for guest use. Even if you feel that you're too far from town, remember that nothing is going on there anyway. Another attraction is that local fishermen may put in just next to the Wavecrest and sell their fish for unbeatable prices. Guests can barbecue on gas grills. Rates are one-bedroom ocean or garden view $70, one-bedroom oceanfront $80, two-bedroom oceanfront $135; $15 per extra person. Car/condo packages are also available. Attractive monthly and low-season discounts are available. Call Friendly Isle Realty, 808/553-3666 or 800/600-4158, fax 808/553-3867, www.molokairesorts.com, which manages numerous other units in each of the condominiums on the island and also several homes on the west end and along the beaches on the east end.

Kamalo Plantation, HC 01, Box 300, Kaunakakai, HI 96748, tel/fax 808/558-8236, kamaloplantation@aloha.net, www.molokai.com /kamalo, is a five-acre tropical garden, where Glenn and Akiko Foster welcome guests. About 10 miles east of Kaunakakai, and across from Father Damien's St. Joseph Church, Kamalo Plantation is surrounded by well-vegetated grounds and even has a *heiau* on the property. The Fosters can accommodate you in a fully contained private studio cottage with king-size bed, full kitchen, indoor and outdoor showers, and deck for $85, two-night minimum. The cottage is secluded on the property and has a sitting area, necessary cooking appliances, an outside deck, and a barbecue grill in its own little gazebo. The tropical decor makes this comfy cottage a home away from home. A breakfast of fruit and baked breads and a tour of the grounds are part of the price. A fine place, perfect for a quiet getaway. The Fosters also have the **Moanui Beach House** for rent across from the beach at mile marker 20. This renovated A-frame sits up on the hillside overlooking a horse pasture and the water. With two bedrooms, 1.5 baths, and a full kitchen, this house is just right for a small family and goes for $140 double occupancy, with $20 for each additional person, three-night minimum.

Just past the Puko'o Neighborhood Store,

going east, is a casual oceanfront house with two bedrooms and two baths, a full kitchen, and only steps from the water. This cute little place runs $180 per night, three-night minimum. This and a half dozen other homes and cottages nearby on the east end that generally run $125–330 per night with a three-night minimum, plus one big house on Papohaku Beach, and condo units at different properties across the island, are handled by Swenson Real Estate, P.O. Box 1979, Kaunakakai, HI 96748, 808/553-3648 or 800/558-3648, fax 808/553-3783, rent@island-realestate.com, http://molokai-vacation-rental.com.

Some distance farther is the **Waialua Beach House,** 808/599-3838 or 888/579-9400, fax 808/537-2322, hawaiibeachhouse@hotmail.com, www.hawaiibeachhouse.org, a three-bedroom, two-bath, oceanfront home with all the conveniences. This island-style house sleeps up to six and runs $165 per night, three nights minimum, $1,055 per week, with an $85 cleaning fee.

At the far eastern end of the island, overlooking the lands of Pu'u O Hoku Ranch, P.O. Box 1889, Kaunakakai, HI 96748, 808/558-8109, fax 808/558-8100, hoku@aloha.net, www.puuohoku.com, is **Pu'u O Hoku Country Cottages.** Check in at the ranch office along the highway at mile marker 25. If you're looking for a place to really be away, this is it. The spacious Sunrise Cottage, once a guest cottage at the ranch manager's residence, is a large two-bedroom house that has been renovated but is still charming in its simplicity. It has a living room with a wall of glass, dining room, and full kitchen. Each of the two bedrooms has a private bath. With a couch and a bed in the living room, it can sleep six. You are on your own for food, but there is a television and a telephone. Feel free to use the swimming pool at the main lodge up the hill. Facing east and unencumbered by ambient light, it's just right for sunrise and star gazing. The rental rate is $125 per night for two, $20 for each extra person, or $750 per week.

Up the hill, the lodge is also available for group rental and would make a great place for a conference or retreat. The lodge has 11 bedrooms, seven bathrooms, a huge main room, and an industrial kitchen. Originally built for Paul Fagan, who later built Hotel Hana-Maui, this lodge will house up to 23 individuals and is surrounded by acres of lawn and trees. The rate for the lodge is $1,000 per night. Set in a small grove of trees at the edge of the pasture on the oceanside of the office is the Grove Cottage. Nearly twice as large as the Sunrise Cottage, this house has four bedrooms, three bathrooms, a full kitchen, and a large living room with a fireplace, as well as a television and telephone. For the Grove Cottage, the rental rate is $125 per night for two people, $165 for four, or $990 per week. Two nights minimum for any unit.

The only place to find food on this end of the island is the **Neighborhood Store N Counter,** 808/558-8498, in Puko'o. This convenience store carries basic necessities. Connected is a lunch window that serves breakfasts and lunches, such as sandwiches for $4 and plate lunches for $6–7. The store is open 8 A.M.–6 P.M. daily, and the lunch window has the same hours except that it's closed on Wednesday.

Middle Moloka'i and Kalaupapa

As you head west from Kaunakakai on Route 460 toward Ho'olehua Airport you pass fields planted in various crops. These are Moloka'i's attempt at diversified agriculture since the demise of pineapple. The cultivated fields give way to hundreds of acres filled with what seems like skeletons of dead trees. It's as if some eerie specter stalked the land and devoured their spirits. Farther along and just before a bridge, the **Main Forest Road** intersects, posted for 4WD vehicles but navigable in a standard car only during dry weather and if the road has been graded. As much as the traction of a 4WD, in spots you need the clearance of a high-profile truck or jeep to get through the ruts and puddles. This road is no joke. It's a long way for help and costly for a tow. This track leads to the Sandalwood Measuring Pit, a depression in the ground that is a permanent reminder of the furious and foolhardy trading of two centuries ago. Farther on is the Kamakou Preserve, a largely intact region of native trees and wildlife. Here too along little-used trails are spectacular views of the lost valleys of Moloka'i's inaccessible northeast shore.

West on Route 460, another branch road, Route 470, heads north through Kualapu'u, Del Monte's diminished pineapple town, to road's end at Pala'au State Park, Moloka'i's best camping area and home to the famous Phallic Rock. Near the state park entrance is the lookout for **Kalaupapa Peninsula** and the beginning of the mule trail, which switchbacks down more than 1,600 feet to the humbling and uplifting experience of Kalaupapa.

MAIN FOREST ROAD

Head west on Route 460 from Kaunakakai, and just before mile marker 4 turn right before the bridge. After a few hundred yards you pass the Homelani Cemetery. Here, a red dirt road called Main Forest or Maunahui Road heads into the mountains. Your car rental agency will tell you that this road is impassable except in a 4WD, and they're right—if it's raining or has rained re-

cently! But, even if it's dry, this road is rough. Follow the rutted road up into the hills and you'll soon be in a deep forest of 'ohi'a, pine, eucalyptus, and giant ferns thriving since their planting in the early 1900s. The cool, pleasant air mixes with rich earthy smells of the forest. At 5.5 miles you enter the Moloka'i Forest Preserve. At just under six miles there's a bend to the right. Proceed a few hundred yards, and on your left is a wood shop with turned wood bowls for sale! Ignore many small roads branching off.

After nine miles is the **Sandalwood Measuring Pit** (Lua Moku 'Iliahi), or Pit of the Sandalwood Ship, a depression in the ground in the shape of a ship's hull. Now bordered by a green pipe fence, it's not very spectacular, and this is a long way to go over a rough road to see a shallow hole in the ground, but the Sandalwood Pit is a permanent reminder of the days of mindless exploitation in Hawaii when money and possessions were more important than the land or the people. Hawaiian chiefs had the pit dug to measure the amount of sandalwood necessary to fill the hold of a ship. They traded the aromatic wood to Yankee captains for baubles, whiskey, guns, manufactured goods, and tools. The traders carried the wood to China, where they made huge profits. The trading was so lucrative that the men of entire villages were forced into the hills to collect it, even to the point where the taro fields were neglected and famine gnawed at the door. It only took a few years to denude the mountains of their copious stands of sandalwood, which is even more incredible when you consider that all of the work was done by hand and all of the wood was carried to the waiting ships on the coast using the *maka'ainana* as beasts of burden.

Travel past the Sandalwood Pit (beware of the mud) for about one mile, and you'll come to **Waikolu (Three Waters) Overlook.** From here you can peer down into the pristine valley 3,700 feet below. If rains have been recent, hundreds of waterfalls spread their lace as they fall to the green jungle. The water here seeps into the ground, which soaks it up like a huge, dripping sponge. Father Damien tapped a spring at the bottom end of this valley to supply fresh water to his flock at Kalawao. A water tunnel, bored into the valley, collects the water and conducts it for more than five miles until it reaches the 1.4 billion-gallon Kualapu'u Reservoir. Drive to this area only on a clear day because the rain will not only get you stuck in mud but also obscure your view with heavy cloud cover. Camping is allowed at the overlook park. Get your free permit from the Division of Forestry and Wildlife office in Wailuku, on Maui, before you come.

Past the Waikolu Overlook is the Kamakou Reserve. **Hanalilolilo Trail** begins not far from Waikolu Lookout and winds through high mountain forests of 'ohi'a. Hiking trails through this area are poorly marked, poorly maintained, and strenuous—great qualifications for those who crave solitude and adventure. Alternately, continue walking the 4WD road into the preserve. After about 4.5 miles, at a spot where the road makes a sharp right turn, the **Pepe'opae Trail** heads into the Pepe'opae Bog over a boardwalk, ending after 1.5 miles at the Pelekunu Lookout, where you are rewarded with a breathtaking view into Pelekunu Valley. Pelekunu means "smelly" (due to no sunshine). Don't let the name fool you, though. Hawaiians lived happily and well in this remote, north shore valley for centuries. Time, aided by wind and rain, has turned the 3,300-foot sea cliffs of Pelekunu into some of the tallest in the world. Today, Pelekunu is more remote and isolated than ever. There are no permanent residents, although islanders come sporadically to camp in the summer, when the waters are calm enough to land on the coast.

The 2,774-acre **Kamakou Preserve,** established by the Nature Conservancy of Hawaii in 1982, seeks to preserve this unique forest area, home to five species of endangered Hawaiian birds, two of which are endemic only to Moloka'i. There are 250 species of Hawaiian plants and ferns, 219 of which grow nowhere else in the world. Even a few clusters of sandalwood trees are tenaciously trying to make a comeback. The land was donated by the Molokai Ranch, which controls the water rights. Most trails have been mapped, and hunting is en-

couraged throughout most of the area. Up-to-the-minute information and maps are available from the preserve manager by writing to P.O. Box 220, Kualapuu, HI 96757, 808/553-5236.

KUALAPU'U AND KALA'E

Kualapu'u was a vibrant town when pineapple was king and Del Monte was headquartered here. Now, coffee is king and some of the town's former vibrancy has resurfaced. The coffee plantation produces about one-half million pounds of unroasted coffee beans per year, second only in the state to the much larger Kaua'i Coffee company on Kaua'i. It is the only town where you can find basic supplies and a post office on the way to Kalaupapa.

Right at the turnoff onto Farrington Avenue is the restored Plantation Store and an adjacent espresso bar. Displayed in the store are many attractive gifts, arts, and crafts done by Moloka'i and other island residents. The lunch counter has pastries, sandwiches, and various coffee (free samples) and juice drinks. This is now coffee country, so pick up a bag of Mululani Estate or Muleskinner coffee at the store or try a cup at the lunch counter. Both are open Monday–Friday 7 A.M.–4 P.M., Saturday from 8 A.M., and Sunday from 10 A.M.

Walking tours are given at the 500-acre **Coffees of Hawaii** coffee plantation that take you through the fields for an up-close look at the coffee plants, then head to the mill and roasting room to see what happens to the beans once they're picked. These 45- to 60-minute tours are generally offered Monday–Friday 9:30 A.M. and 11:30 A.M. and cost $7 per person; 24-hour advance reservations requested. For more information, contact the plantation at 808/567-9241 or 800/709-2326, www.molokaicoffee.com.

A minute down Farrington Avenue you'll come to the **Kualapu'u Market,** open daily 8:30 A.M.–6 P.M. except Sunday. Here you'll find a selection of foodstuffs, fresh produce and beef, and general merchandise.

Across the road from the market is the **Kamuela's Cookhouse,** the only restaurant in town. Open 7 A.M.–3 P.M., Kamuela's offers simple food in an unpretentious environment. Most choices are eggs, griddle items, lunch plates, and burgers. Order at the counter and sit either inside at one of the few tables or outside at the picnic table under the canopy.

Notice also the world's largest rubber-lined reservoir across the highway from town. Holding 1.4 billion gallons, its water comes via a five-mile-long, eight-foot-round tunnel from the water-filled valleys to the east.

Purdy's Macadamia Nut Farm

A few miles west of Kualapu'u, on Lihi Pali Avenue, is **Purdy's Na Hua 'O Ka Aina Farm,** www.molokai.com/eatnuts. A former airline employee, Mr. Purdy grew up just down the road. When the airline pulled out of Moloka'i, he decided to stay home, become a farmer, and teach people about the exquisite macadamia nut. His farm has 50 trees that are about 80 years old. These trees still produce nuts prodigiously and continuously for 10 months of the year—Sept.–June—with nuts at all different stages of maturity on the tree at one time. When mature, nuts fall to the ground. Harvested from the ground, they are taken to be cracked and either kept raw or roasted and lightly salted. This one-acre grove of trees is farmed naturally, but Mr. Purdy has put in about 250 trees at another location on the island that are fertilized and treated with pesticides. Purdy's is the only mac nut farm on Moloka'i, and his yield is about 250–300 pounds of unshelled nuts per tree, as opposed to the 150–200 pounds on the thousand-acre farms of the Big Island. Visit the shop at the farm, where Mr. Purdy tells everyone about the trees. Have a go at cracking one of the nuts, and have a taste of its rich fruit. Bags of nuts are sold at his gift shop—a little treat to yourself for the road—and can be mailed anywhere in the country. Free admission; open Tuesday–Friday 9:30 A.M.–3:30 P.M. and Saturday 10 A.M.–2 P.M.

Moloka'i Museum and Cultural Center

Along Route 470, two miles past Kualapu'u in the village of Kala'e, you'll discover the old R. W. Meyer Sugar Mill, now part of the Moloka'i

COCKFIGHTING

A hold-over from the more spirited days of the plantation-era, cockfighting is a notorious, semi-clandestine, and entirely enjoyable pastime of (mostly) older Filipino men. Moloka'i's Filipino population has long been known for cockfighting, an illegal activity, but no law prevents raising the fighting birds. Keep your eyes peeled as you travel the island's byways for encampments of these birds, often enclosed by a tall cyclone fence topped with nasty-looking barbed wire. Inside are row after row of tiny A-frames, like the pup tents of a brigade of GIs on bivouac. Restrained by leashes just long enough to prevent mortal combat are the prized fighting machines. These glorious roosters, displaying their feathers while clawing the earth, challenge each other with quite a show of devil-may-care bravado. While not unique to Moloka'i, it somehow seems more prevalent here.

Museum and Cultural Center, 808/567-6436. Open Monday–Saturday 10 A.M.–2 P.M., the self-guided mill tour is $2.50 adults, $1 students 5–18, which includes the cultural center building with its displays, gift and book shop, and historical video. Proceeds go into a fund to construct a new museum building. Built in 1878, the restored mill (1988) is on the National Register of Historic Places. It is in functioning order and clearly shows the stages of creating sugar from cane. As the smallest commercial mill in the state, it was used only until 1889, and it ground cane from 30 nearby upland acres. The museum and cultural center focus on preserving and demonstrating Hawaiian arts and handicrafts like quilting, *lau hala* weaving, wood carving, plus demonstrations of lei-making and hula. The idea is to share and revive the arts of Hawaii, especially those of Moloka'i, in this interpretive center. As an outgrowth, the center is used as the Elderhostel campus for Moloka'i. In August, the annual Moloka'i music and dance festival takes place at the center. Hula is performed, local musicians play, and the whole community turns out.

Just beyond the center is the Meyer cemetery. You can enter, but be respectful. Rudolph Meyer, his wife, and children are buried here. Up in among the trees above the mill is the Meyer home, which is not open to the public. Partially restored in 1973, it's now in disrepair. Perhaps one day it will be restored again and preserved as another tangible link to the family that helped shape the history and economy of the island. The three acres that the cultural center sits on were graciously donated by the Meyer family. Aside from sugarcane, coffee, vegetables, fruits, and dairy cattle were raised on Meyer land, and the present Meyer Ranch still occupies a large tract of the surrounding upland area.

A minute or two past the sugar mill in a bucolic scene of highland fields of knee-deep grass is the tiny community of Kala'e.

Pala'au State Park

A few minutes past Kala'e are the stables for Molokai Mule Rides, which take you down to Kalaupapa. Even if you're not planning on taking a mule ride, make sure to stop and check out the beauty of the countryside surrounding the mule stables. Follow the road until it ends at the parking lot for Pala'au State Park.

In the lot, two signs direct you to the Phallic Rock and to the Kalaupapa Overlook (which is not the beginning of the trail down to the peninsula). Pala'au State Park offers the best camping on Moloka'i, although it's quite a distance from the beach. Follow the signs from the parking lot for about 200 yards to **Phallic Rock** (Kauleo Nanahoa), one of the best examples of such a stone in the state. Nanahoa, the male fertility god inhabiting the anatomical rock, has been performing like a champ and hasn't had a "headache" in centuries! Legend says that Nanahoa lived nearby and one day sat to admire a beautiful young girl who was looking at her reflection in a pool. Kawahua, Nanahoa's wife, became so jealous when she saw her husband leering that she attacked the young girl by yanking on her hair. Nanahoa became outraged in turn and struck his wife, who rolled over a nearby cliff and turned to stone. Nanahoa also turned to stone in the shape of an erect penis, and there he

sits pointing skyward to this day. Barren women have come here to spend the night and pray for fertility. At the base of the rock is a tiny pool the size of a small bowl that collects rainwater. The women would sit here hoping to absorb the child-giving *mana* of the rock. You can still see offerings and of course graffiti.

Return to the parking lot and follow the signs to **Kalaupapa Overlook.** Jutting 1,600 feet below, almost like an afterthought, is the peninsula of Kalaupapa, which was the home of the lost lepers of Hawaii, picked for its remoteness and inaccessibility. The almost-vertical *pali* served as a natural barrier to the outside world. If you look to your right you'll see the mule trail switchbacking down the cliff. Look to the southeast sector of the peninsula to see the almost perfectly round **Kauhako Crater,** remnant of the separate volcano that formed Kalaupapa.

THE KALAUPAPA EXPERIENCE

No one knew how the dreaded disease came to the Hawaiian Islands, but they did know that if you were contaminated by it your life would be misery. Leprosy has caused fear in the hearts of humans since biblical times, and King Kamehameha V and his advisors were no exception. All they knew was that those with the disease had to be isolated. Kalawao Cove, on the southeast shore of Kalaupapa Peninsula, was regarded as the most isolated spot in the entire kingdom. So, starting in 1866, the lepers of Hawaii were sent to Kalawao to die. Through crude diagnostic testing, anyone who had a suspicious skin discoloration, ulcer, or even bad sunburn was rounded up and sent to Kalawao. The islanders soon learned that once someone was sent, there was no return. So the afflicted hid. Bounty hunters roamed the countryside. Babies, toddlers, teenagers, wives, grandfathers—none were immune to the bounty hunters. They hounded, captured, and sometimes killed anyone who had any sort of skin ailment. The captives were torn from their families and villages and loaded on a ship. No one would come near them on board, and they sometimes sat open to the elements in a cage. They were allowed only one small tin box of possessions. As the ship anchored in the always choppy bay at Kalawao, the cage was opened and the victims were tossed overboard, followed by a few sealed barrels of food and clothing that had been collected by merciful Christians. Those too weak or sick or young drowned; the unlucky made it to shore. While it wasn't always this way, at times the crew waited nervously with loaded muskets in case any of those on shore attempted to board the ship.

Hell on Earth

Waiting for the newcomers were the forsaken. Abandoned by king, country, family, friends, and apparently the Lord himself, some became like animals—beasts of prey. Young girls with hardly a blemish were raped by reeking, deformed men in rags. Old men were bludgeoned, their tin boxes ripped from their hands. Children and babies cried and begged for food. The arrivals made rude dwellings of sticks and stones, while others lived in caves or on the beach open to the elements. Finally, the conscience of the kingdom was stirred, and while the old dumping ground of Kalawao was not abandoned, new patients were mostly exiled to the more hospitable Kalaupapa side of the peninsula, just a mile or so to the west.

The Move to Kalaupapa

Those sent to Kalaupapa were treated more mercifully. Missionary groups provided food and rudimentary clothing, and *kokua* (helpers) provided aid. An attempt was made to end the lawlessness and depravity and to provide some semblance of civilized society. Still, the leprosy patients were kept separate, and for the most part lived outdoors or in very rude huts. They could never come in direct contact with the *kokua* or anyone else who came to the peninsula. Many *kokua*, horrified by Kalaupapa, left on the next available boat. With little medical attention, death was still the only release from Kalaupapa.

Light in Hell

It was by accident or miracle that Joseph de Veuster, **Father Damien**, a Catholic priest, came from Belgium to Hawaii. His brother, also a priest, was supposed to come, but he became ill

Father Damien just weeks before his death from Hansen's disease

and Father Damien came in his place. Damien spent several years on the Big Island of Hawai'i, building churches and learning the language and ways of the people, before he came to Kalaupapa in 1873. What he saw touched his heart. He was different from the rest, having come with a sense of mission to help those with the disease and bring them hope and dignity. The other missionaries saw Kalaupapa not as a place to live, but to die. Damien saw these people as children of God who had the right to live and be comforted. When they hid under a bush at his approach, he picked them up and stood them on their feet. He carried water all day long to the sick and dying. He bathed their wounds and built them shelters with his own two hands. When clothes or food or materials ran short, he walked topside and begged for more. Other church groups were against him, and the government gave him little aid, but he persevered. Damien scraped together some lumber and fashioned a

COURTESY OF HAWAII STATE ARCHIVE

MOLOKA'I

flume pipe to carry water to his people, who were still dying mainly from pneumonia and tuberculosis brought on by neglect. Damien worked long days alone, until he dropped exhausted at night.

Father Damien modified **St. Philomena Church,** a structure that was originally built in Honolulu by Brother Bertrant in 1872 and shipped to Moloka'i in segments. Father Damien invited his flock inside, but those grossly afflicted could not control their mouths, so spittle would drip to the floor. They were ashamed to soil the church, so Damien cut squares in the floor through which they could spit onto the ground. Slowly a light began to shine in the hearts of the shunned residents, and the authorities began to take notice. Conditions began to improve, but there were those who resented Damien. Robert Louis Stevenson visited the settlement, and after meeting Damien wrote an open letter that ended ". . . he is my father." Damien of course eventually contracted leprosy, but by the time he died in 1889 at age 49, he knew his people would be cared for. In 1936, Damien's native Belgium asked that his remains be returned. He was exhumed and his remains sent home, but a memorial still stands where he was interred at Kalaupapa. After lengthy squabbles with the Belgian government, Father Damien's right hand was returned to Kalaupapa in 1995 and has been reinterred as a religious relic. In 1995, he was beatified by Pope John Paul II. Several books have been written about Damien's life; perhaps the best of the bunch is *Holy Man, Father Damien of Molokai,* by Gavan Daws, while numerous others have been written about life at Kalaupapa as a leprosy patient.

The Light Grows Brighter

Brother Dutton, who arrived in 1886, and Mother Marianne Cope, a Franciscan nun from Syracuse, New York, who came in 1888 with two other Sisters of Saint Francis, carried on Damien's work. In addition, many missionary groups sent volunteers to help at the colony. Thereafter the people of Kalaupapa were treated with dignity and given a sense of hope. In 1873, the same year that Damien arrived at Kalaupapa,

Father Damien's grave at Kalawao, next to St. Philomena Church

Norwegian physician Gerhard Hansen isolated the bacteria that causes leprosy, and shortly thereafter the official name of the malady became Hansen's disease. By the turn of the 20th century, adequate medical care and good living conditions were provided to the patients at Kalaupapa. Still, many died, mostly from complications. Families could not visit members confined to Kalaupapa unless they were near death, and any children born to the patients—who were now starting to marry—were whisked away at birth and adopted, or given to family members on the outside. Even until the 1940s, people were still sent to Kalaupapa because of skin ailments that were never really diagnosed as leprosy. Many of these indeed did show signs of the disease, but there is always the haunting thought that they may have contracted it after arrival at the colony.

In the mid-1940s sulfa drugs were found to arrest most cases of Hansen's disease, and the prognosis for a normal life improved. By the 1960s further breakthroughs made Hansen's disease noncontagious, and in 1969 the quarantine on patients was eliminated. Patients at Kalaupapa were then free to leave and return to their homes. No new patients were admitted, but most, already living in the only home they'd ever known, opted to stay. In total over the years, about 8,000 unfortunate individuals were exiled to this forgotten spit of land. Almost as if it were an accident of fate designed to expunge evidence of the damning past, the community hospital along with all its records burned to the ground in the early '90s. No help was afforded by the local fire truck, which was unable to be started.

Nonetheless, medical treatment continues and all needed care is still provided. The community of resident patients numbers less than 45 today (down from a high of about 1,800 in 1917)—the average age is about 70—and state caretakers and federal employees in the community now outnumber patients. In all of Hawaii today, there are about 450 people registered with Hansen's disease; all but those at Kalaupapa live at home with their families. Each year on average, about 18 new cases are diagnosed in the state. Still the number of patients continues to drop as the old-

timers die. In 1980, Kalaupapa and adjoining lands were designated Kalaupapa National Historical Park, jointly administered by the state Department of Health, but the residents are assured lifetime occupancy and free care.

The Kalaupapa Peninsula and its three adjoining valleys are technically a separate county within the state structure called Kalawao. There is a sheriff but no elected officials, but residents can and do vote in state and national elections. Of this area, 12 acres have been designated parkland, about 500 are Hawaiian Homelands, and the rest is state property. In the past, much of the peninsula was fenced off as rangeland for cattle, but more recently the cattle and goats have pretty much destroyed the native vegetation, which is now overgrown by alien species.

Getting There

It shouldn't be a matter of *if* you go to Kalaupapa, but *how* you go. You have choices. You can fly, walk, or ride a mule. No matter how you go, you *cannot* walk around Kalaupapa unescorted. You *must* take an official tour, and children under 16 are not allowed. If you're going by mule, arrangements are made for you by the company, but if you're walking down or flying in, you have to call ahead to Richard Marks at **Damien Tours,** 808/567-6171, and he will give you an exact place and time to meet once down on the peninsula. Typically, this is a 9:45 A.M. pickup at the Kalaupapa Airport for those who fly in, followed by a 10 A.M. pickup at the bottom end corral for those who hike or ride the mules down. Damien Tours charges $32 for a fascinating, four-hour tour conducted by one of the residents. Definitely worth the money; the insight you get from the resident tour guide is priceless and unique. No food or beverages, except water, are available to visitors, so make sure to bring your own.

"I'd rather be riding a mule on Moloka'i" is an eye-catching T-shirt sported by some who have been lucky enough to have made the descent to Kalaupapa aboard the sure-footed mules of the **Molokai Mule Ride.** The well-trained mules will transport you down the 1,600-foot *pali*, expertly negotiating 26 hairpin switchbacks on the trail to the bottom. After your tour of the settlement, these gutsy animals carry you right back up so you too can buy your T-shirt and claim your ride-completion certificate. You are on the mule about 90 minutes each way. Operating daily except Sunday from 8 A.M., this tour runs $150 and includes the ground tour of the settlement and lunch. No riders weighing more than 240 pounds, please; you must be at least 16 years old and in good physical shape. For reservations, call 808/567-6088 or 800/567-7550.

If you're **hiking** to Kalaupapa, follow the mule trail cut by Manuel Farinha in 1886 and renovated in the late 1990s. Go about 200 yards past the stables and look for a road to the right. Follow this track down past pasture land to the trailhead, where there is a small metal building with an odd, faded sign that reads Advance Technology Center Hawaii USA, near an old overgrown observation point for the peninsula. The 3.8-mile, 90-minute trail going down the steep north face of the *pali* is well maintained and only mildly strenuous. You should be in good physical condition to hike it, however, because it can take a toll on your knees going down and requires strength and endurance on the way up. It may be preferable to leave before the mules do in the morning (around 8:15 A.M.), but in any case give yourself enough time to make it to the bottom before the tour pickup at 10 A.M. The trail will be rutted and muddy in spots, and you'll have to step around the road apples, so wear hiking boots if possible, sneakers at a minimum. A zigzag of 26 turns (they're numbered) gets you down to the bottom, and one long zag will bring you to the beach and the mule corral beyond. There is no swimming at this beach, which is pending status as a turtle sanctuary and is an area where monk seals have been known to give birth.

You can **fly** directly from Ho'olehua, top side Moloka'i, walk down and fly up, or fly both ways from Honolulu or Kahului, Maui. From topside to Kalaupapa with Molokai Air Shuttle, 808/567-6847, will run $49.90 one way. A round-trip flight from Honolulu to Kalaupapa (with one leg that goes through Ho'oluhua) via Pacific Wings runs about $140. For information and reservations, contact Pacific Wings, 800/867-6814 or 888/575-4546. Commercial Flyer,

888/266-3597 or 808/833-8014 in Honolulu, makes a Honolulu–Kalaupapa round-trip for $110. Paragon Air, 808/244-3356 on Maui or 866/946-4744 elsewhere, offers round-trip charter flights from both Kahului and Kapalua, Maui, for $210, which includes your airfare, tour fee, and a simple lunch. All flights get you to Kalaupapa in time for the start of your tour and pick you up when your tours ends at about 3 P.M. for your return flight. If you want to fly in, you must still arrange for the ground tour through Damien Tours (or be sponsored by someone who lives in Kalaupapa) before you will be sold a ticket. If you decide to fly, notice the breakers at the end of the runway sending spray high into the air. The pilots time their takeoffs to miss the spray!

The Tour

Damien Tours will pick you up by bus either at the airport or at the mule corral. From there, you start your tour by a drive into the main Kalaupapa settlement, where all residents live, and where the hospital, park service office, post office, several churches, and pier are located. Driving past the old visitors center, you arrive at the pier. Although many supplies come by plane, a ferry comes once a year to bring bulkier goods. Across from the pier is the remodeled St. Francis Church and next to it, the unassuming Father Damien Memorial Hall, a mini-museum dedicated to Father Damien, Brother Dutton, and Sister Marianne Cope. Both can be visited if time permits. The tour then takes you past the remains of the old burnt hospital and the Bishop Home, a residence for female patients, to a stop at the new visitors center. This new center has displays of the settlement and a few books and other items for sale.

From there, you head over the flank of Pu'u 'Uao (405 feet), the highest point on the peninsula, to the old Kalawao settlement site for a stop at St. Philomena Church. This is perhaps the most moving part of the tour because the church and its cemetery are about the only physical remains of the works of Father Damien. During Father Damien's time, there were nearly 300 mostly small and humble buildings in Kalawao, many of which were constructed with the help of this holy man. Lunch is at Judd Park nearby, located next to where the first leprosy hospital stood, and from this bluff you have a great view overlooking the precipitous north Moloka'i coast. Pu'u 'Uao was the volcanic caldera out of which lava flowed to create the Kalaupapa Peninsula. Its crater top contains a small lake about the size of a baseball infield that is said to be more than 800 feet deep. On your return, you'll pass several graveyards that line the road to the airport, the last resting place to the thousands of victims who were cruelly treated by their disease and the society in which they lived.

Moloka'i's West End

Long before contact with the Europeans, the west end of Moloka'i was famous throughout the Hawaiian Islands. The culture centered on Maunaloa, the ancient volcanic mountain that formed the land. On its slopes the goddess Laka learned the hula from her sister and spread its joyous undulations to all of the other islands. Not far from the birthplace of the hula is Kaluako'i, one of the two most important adze quarries in old Hawaii. Without these stone tools, no canoes, bowls, or everyday items could have been fashioned. Voyagers came from every major island to trade for this dense, hard stone. With all of this coming and going, the always-small population of Moloka'i needed godly protection. Not far away at Kalaipahoa, the "poison wood" sorcery gods of Moloka'i lived in a grove that supposedly sprouted to maturity in one night. With talismans made from this magical grove, Moloka'i kept invading warriors at bay for centuries.

Most of the island's flat, usable land is out that way. The thrust west began with the founding of the Molokai Ranch, whose 54,000 acres make up about 50 percent of the good farm and range land on the island and about one-third of the island. The ranch was owned in the 19th century by Kamehameha V, and after his death it was sold to private interests, who began the successful raising of Santa Gertrudis cattle imported from the famous Texas King Ranch. The ranch still employs a few *paniolo*. Today, anywhere between 6,000–10,000 head of Brahman and Brangus cattle roam ranch land, with about 80 horses to do the work.

THE NORTHWEST

The northwest section of Moloka'i, centered at **Ho'olehua,** is where the Hawaiian Home Land parcels are located. The entire area has a feeling of heartland America, and if you ignore the coastline in the background you could easily imagine yourself in the rolling hills of Missouri. Don't expect a town at Ho'olehua. All that's there is a little post office and a government office.

Mo'omomi Beach

The real destination is Mo'omomi Beach. Follow Route 460 until it branches north at Route 480 one mile east of the airport. Follow Route 480 until it turns left onto Farrington Avenue in Ho'olehua, and continue for about four miles until it turns into a red dirt road. This road can be extremely rutted, even tipping your car at a precarious angle. Be advised! Continue for 10–15 minutes, veer right, and shortly you come to a Hawaii Home Lands recreational pavilion. When the bottom section of this road washes out, traffic is directed onto a secondary road called Anahaki Road, which also takes you to the pavilion at the beach. Below you is Mo'omomi Beach. This area is a favorite with local people, who come here to swim, fish, and surf. The swells are good only in winter, but the beach becomes rocky at that time of year. The tides bring the sand in by April and the swimming until is good November. Unofficial camping is probably okay on this grassy area, and a toilet and water are available at the pavilion.

Mo'omomi Beach goes back to Hawaiian legend. Besides the mythical lizards that inhabited this area, a great shark-god was born here. The mother was a woman who became impregnated by the gods. Her husband was angry that her child would be from the spirit world, so he directed her to come and sit on a large rock down by the beach. She went into labor and began to cry. A tear, holding a tiny fish, rolled down her cheek and fell into the sea and became the powerful shark-god. The rock on which his mother sat is the large black one just to the right of the beach.

If you feel adventurous, you can head west along the shore, where you come to tiny beaches that you have entirely to yourself. Farther on is the isolated and much larger **Kawa'aloa Beach** and bay. Because this area is so isolated, be extremely careful of surf conditions. Inland from Kawa'alo and to the west is **Keonelele,** a miniature desert strip of sand dunes. The wind whips through this region and pushes the sand into rows. Geologists haunt this area trying to piece together Moloka'i's geological history. The Hawaiians used Keonelele as a burial site, and strange footprints found in the soft sandstone supposedly foretold the coming of white men. Today, Keonelele is totally deserted; although small, it gives the impression of a vast wasteland. A 921-acre plot west of Kaiehu Point, including much of the Keonelele area, is now overseen by the Nature Conservancy as the **Mo'omomi Preserve.** This coastal ecosystem, mostly unaltered over the centuries, safeguards 22 native plant species—four of which are endangered—that do well in this harsh, wind-blown environment. The Hawaiian green sea turtle also frequents these sands, making this preserve a sanctuary for this creature. Although the Hawaiian owl, plover, and numerous sea birds visit this distant stretch of shore, numerous birds that used to live here are now extinct, leaving only their bones in the sand to tell of their presence here. Within the preserve, use only the beach or the marked trails and 4WD roads.

> *Geologists haunt Kawa'aloa Beach trying to piece together Moloka'i's geological history. The Hawaiians used Keonelele as a burial site, and strange footprints found in the soft sandstone supposedly foretold the coming of white men.*

Papohaku Beach

The best attraction in the area doesn't have a price tag. Papohaku Beach is the giant expanse of white sand running south from the Kaluakoi Resort. The sands here are so expansive that some was dredged and taken to O'ahu in the 1950s. During the winter a great deal of sand is stripped away and large lava boulders and outcroppings are exposed. Every spring and summer the tides carry the sand back and deposit it on the enormous beach. Camping is permitted at the **Papohaku County Beach Park** just past the resort. Pick up your permit at the Mitchell Pauole Center in Kaunakakai, 808/553-3204, before you come all the way out here. Here you'll find a large, grassy play area, toilets, showers, picnic tables, grills for cooking, and a virtually empty beach. A sign on the road past the park tells you to watch out for deer. This road runs through a huge Papohaku Ranch lands home development area, with several beach access roads and parking areas that lead to other spots along this huge expanse of beach.

The last beach access at the end of the paved road leads to a secluded and protected small bay and fine sand beach that is even safe during winter when other beach areas are not. Locals refer to this beach as Dixie Maru Beach because a fishing boat of that name once sunk in the bay. The Kaupoa Trail starts from the south end of this beach and runs into Molokai Ranch lands—about a 30- to 40-minute walk.

One of the attractions of Moloka'i is its remoteness. Here the sky is clear, and at night the stars are brilliant. Yet, even here you know that you're not too far from the crush of humanity because directly across the Kaiwi Channel you can clearly see the glow of Honolulu, Wailua, and Kaneohe shimmering in the distance, and, closer at hand, the more muted lights of Maunaloa on the hill above.

MOLOKA'I

Kawakiu Beach

This secluded and pristine beach on the far northwestern corner of Moloka'i was an item of controversy between the developers of the Kaluakoi Corp. and the grassroots activists of Moloka'i. For years access to the beach was restricted, and the Kaluakoi Corp., which then owned the land, planned to develop the area. It was known that the area was very important during precontact times and rich in unexplored archaeological sites. The company hired a supposed team of "experts," who studied the site for months and finally claimed that the area had no significant archaeological importance. Their findings were hooted at by local people and by scholars from various institutions who knew better. This controversy resulted in Kawakiu Beach being opened to the public with plans of turning it into a beach park; the archaeological sites will be preserved.

The swimming at Kawakiu is excellent, with the sandy bottom tapering off slowly. To get there go to the Paniolo Hale Condo at Kaluakoi Resort and park at the end of the dirt road that heads toward the sea, past the last paved parking lot of the condo. Walk across the golf course fairway to the beach. Follow it north for three-quarters mile, dodging the tide until you come to the very private Kawakiu Beach—definitely not recommended during periods of high surf, when swimming would be too dangerous anyway. No rules or prying eyes here, so if you would like to swim au naturel, this is the place. If you have lots of time and energy, walk on farther to the smaller and rocky but more private Kawakiu Iki Beach, or farther on to the ancient adze quarry and abandoned Coast Guard station on 'Ilio Point. The hike is mildly strenuous, but Kawakiu is definitely worth it.

Practicalities

Much of the west end of Moloka'i is the Kaluakoi Resort. This complex includes three resort condominiums, the Kaluakoi Golf Course, private home sites, and Papohaku Beach. After years of decline, the Kaluakoi Hotel closed its doors in 2001. Although the hotel no longer accepts guests, several of its shops are still doing business. You'll find the small **A Touch of Molokai** clothing shop, along with the **West End Sundries** store, which sells snacks, magazines, and liquor. The **Laughing Gecko** shop stocks antiques, art, jewelry, Hawaiiana, and locally designed T-shirts made on Moloka'i.

Some of the units at the resort complex, collectively called the **Kaluakoi Villas,** 1131 Kaluako'i Rd., Maunaloa, HI 96770, 808/552-2721 or 800/367-5004 mainland, are managed by the Castle Group. Each studio, suite, and cottage has been tastefully decorated and includes a color TV, lanai, kitchen or kitchenette, and guests can use the hotel swimming pool. Rates range $135–155 for a studio, $160–190 for a one-bedroom suite, and $240 for the ocean cottages on the golf course; fourth night is free.

Built in 1981, the **Ke Nani Kai** condos, a Marc Resorts Hawaii management property, P.O. Box 289, Maunaloa, HI 96770, 808/552-2761, or 800/535-0085, fax 808/553-3241, www.marcresorts.com, are *mauka* of the road leading to the Kaluakoi Hotel. They cost $155–169 for one of the fully furnished one-bedroom apartments; two bedrooms rent at $189–209. All apartments are large and in excellent condition. On property are a swimming pool and two tennis courts, and you're only a few steps away from the Kaluakoi golf course.

Newer yet, **Paniolo Hale,** P.O. Box 190, Maunaloa, HI 96770, 808/552-2731 or 800/367-2984, fax 808/552-2288, stay@paniolohaleresort.com, www.paniolohaleresort.com, is another condo complex set in the trees surrounded by fairways. These buildings have more style than others on the area, and the whole complex is a little classier. The swimming pool, paddle tennis, and barbecue grill are for the use of all guests. Maid service is provided for stays of one week or longer, and each unit has a washer and dryer. Garden and ocean studios run $95–155, $115–230 for one bedroom, and $145–265 for two bedrooms; three-night minimum except over the Christmas holiday season, when it's one week. Two-bedroom units have a hot tub and enclosed lanai.

MAUNALOA AND THE SOUTHWEST COAST

According to legend, the hilltop area Ka'ana above Maunaloa was the first place in the islands that the Hawaiians received hula instruction. Today, there are many *hula halau* on Moloka'i, and the yearly Moloka'i Hula Ka Piko festival is held down the hill at Papohaku State Park to honor this ancient music and dance form.

Most people heading east-west between Kaunakakai and the Kaluakoi Resort never used to make it into Maunaloa town because Route 460 splits just east of Maunaloa, and Kaluako'i Road heads north toward the Kaluakoi Resort and away from the town. Until recently, with the pineapples gone and few visitors, the town barely hung on. Built in 1923, Maunaloa was a wonderful example of a plantation town. It was a little patch of humble workers' houses carved into a field. In front you were likely to see a tethered horse, a boat, or glass fishing floats hanging from the lanai. Overhead you could see a kite flying—a sign that you had arrived in Maunaloa. The townsfolk were friendly, and if you were looking for conversation or a taste of Hawaiian history, the old-timers hanging around under the shaded lean-to near the post office were just the ticket.

But the winds of change have started to blow in Maunaloa and the force increases. The Molokai Ranch, which owns the town, has instituted a new grand development scheme to completely "rejuvenate" the town. Most of the old homes, many falling apart and maybe uninsurable, have been torn down and have been replaced by new, similar-style homes. Bunched together away from the downtown area, these homes are set closer together than the old houses were. They are affordable for many and well below the state average. Local people have been given first choice, and many have taken the deal. Additionally, streets have been paved and new ones laid out. A new sewer system and water reservoir have been installed, along with other segments of a modern infrastructure. While several of the old standby commercial establishments have remained, like the post office, general store, church, and *The Dispatch* newspaper office, the town has gotten a

ROBERT NILSEN

the Big Wind Kite Factory

new face. A movie theater, local-style eatery, gas station, ranch activities center, and the ranch lodge with its rooms, restaurant, and bar have been built. An open-air "museum" features several renovated old buildings moved from other locations in town, and the Maunaloa Cultural Park is a spot where community events are staged. Future plans include more business establishments and new residential areas for custom homes, but only time will tell when those wil actually appear. With all these changes, there is certain to be some disagreement about their effect. Many people take a wait-and-see attitude, but others who live and/or work in town seem to think that the changes are for the better.

The only public shore access on this corner of the island is **Hale O Lono** harbor and beach. Turn just after the ranch outfitter and follow Mokia Street past the ranch lodge south out of town and keep to the major track of crushed coral. This road runs for a couple of miles down to the harbor. Hale O Lono is an old harbor that services the ranch, a few commercial boats related to the ranch, and the occasional passing ship. From here, the sand of Papohaku Beach was shipped to O'ahu in the 1950s. With its small but fine white-sand beach, Hale O Lono is the launch point for the annual Bankoh Moloka'i outrigger canoe championship races to Waikiki.

If you are staying at the Molokai Ranch, other spots along the coast might be of interest. About one mile east of Hale O Lono is **Halena Beach,** where there is an old Boy Scout camp and pavilion. East of there down the coastal dirt track is **Kolo Beach,** a fine, long strand that sports the dilapidated **Kolo Wharf** at its far end. Kolo Wharf was where Moloka'i once shipped its pineapples. Now only naked pilings stand to mark the spot. On the far western end of the island is **Kaupoa Beach,** a once distant and secluded old-time favorite of island residents that is now the site of a modern-day camp.

Molokai Ranch Accommodations

The only place to stay in Maunaloa is at the Molokai Ranch, but you don't just sleep there; you also find food and activities. Accommodations are either in the lodge or at Kaupoa Camp,

located at Kaupoa Beach, a perfect white-sand double crescent at the extreme west end, a place that's good for swimming and tidepooling, with an occasional monk seal on the beach or dolphin in the bay. Kaupoa Camp has 40 two-bedroom "tentalows." Wood-frame structures covered with heavy canvas, all are set up on wooden platforms that hold umbrella-covered patio tables, chairs, and benches. Inside are comfortable queen beds, a chest of drawers, and a chair. Set off to the side of the lanai is a composting toilet and half-roof shower that uses solar energy to heat the water. Electricity in each camp is powered by solar batteries; no televisions or phones. All this is done to impact the environment as little as possible. This is rustic simplicity—but luxurious camping. Rates are $275–295 per day, with reduced rates for children and *kama'aina*. These prices include a hearty morning breakfast served at an open-air pavilion on site, daily maid service, and transportation within the ranch; lunches run $12 and dinners $25.

In 2000, The Lodge at Molokai Ranch, now the **Sheraton Molokai Lodge,** 100 Maunaloa Hwy., Maunaloa, HI 96770, 808/552-2741 or 877/726-4656, fax 808/552-2773, www.sheraton-molokai.com, opened for the greater pleasure and comfort of those visiting the ranch who desired more than the rustic Kaupoa Camp had to offer. This two-story, 22-room lodge reflects the days of the 1920s and '30s, with its early ranch decor and Hawaiiana tourist memorabilia. It's a Hawaiian ranch lodge in the true sense of the word, with a central hall flanked by wings of bedroom suites. In the main hall, you can easily make yourself comfortable as you sit back on a fine leather coach or wicker chair in front of the warming stone fireplace beneath the high ceiling that rises above you on the shoulders of rough-hewn timber posts and beams. Deep-patterned tropical foliage fabric covers the furniture and pillows, and artwork reflecting earlier years of tropical Hawaii, the golden glow of table lamps, rustic accessories, and a chandelier made from deer horn fill the room. Relax to the live entertainment every evening or grab a book from the upstairs library and sit yourself down in one of the second-floor nooks that overlook this hall. The bedrooms are as salubrious, also done in the decor of days past, but with all modern amenities. Room rates are $360–425. For anyone staying at the ranch needing transportation to and from the airport, there is an additional $20 fee. The lodge also has a restaurant, bar with billiard table, fitness center, massage service at the spa, an outdoor swimming pool, and the island's only elevator. A wide variety of activities on ranch property and along the coast are offered through the Outfitters Center.

Food

Maunaloa Room is the lodge's restaurant, serving the island's most upscale cuisine, with a superb vista over ranchland and a view of O'ahu and the lights of Honolulu at night (so near, yet so far!). This is Moloka'i cuisine, gourmet ranch food. When the temperature is warm and balmy, sit outside on the verandah; when it cools down in the evening, move to one of the tables inside. Open for breakfast, Sunday brunch, and dinner, the lounge takes care of guests for lunch. Try an appetizer like salt-fried Molokai shrimp or "kahlua" duck lumpia, and entrées such as saffron-scented Pacific snapper, center-cut New York steak, and lemongrass-mango breast of chicken for $20–28. The **Paniolo Lounge** offers an easygoing atmosphere, whether sitting on a rawhide bar stool or at a table along the lanai. This full-service bar also offers lunch 10 A.M.–4 P.M. and *pu pu* from then until 9 P.M. for light evening fare. for those staying at Kaupoa Camp, all three meals of the day are served at the camp pavilion, with plenty of salads and greens and main dishes like New York steak, fresh fish, and chicken breast.

A few steps away in the theater building, the **Paniolo Cafe** serves inexpensive local food and is open daily 11 A.M.–7:30 P.M. This is the only other option in town and the only nonranch restaurant on the west end of the island.

Activities and Recreation

There was a theater is Maunaloa until the mid-1970s, after which the only one on the island was in Kaunakakai. When that one closed, the island was without until the new **Maunaloa Town Cinemas,** 808/552-2707, was built in 1997. This triplex theater shows first-run movies and draws people not only from Maunaloa but also from Kaluako'i and Kaunakakai. Tickets run $6.50 adults, $4 children and seniors.

For outdoor adventure, you must go to the Molokai Ranch **Outfitters Center,** 808/552-2791 or 888/729-0059, where all sorts of outdoor activities can be arranged. If you're staying at one of the camps, activities are arranged through the camp staff. These activities include horseback riding (corral roundup and trail rides), ocean kayaking, full or half-day mountain-biking tours, cultural walks, a wagon ride, archery and sporting clay shooting, whale-watching in season, arts and crafts, and a children's program; all equipment is provided. A separate charge is made for each activity; mostly $30–90 apiece. Those staying at the ranch get priority for activities, but anyone may participate. For those not staying at the ranch, the rates are somewhat higher. While at the Outfitters Center, choose a souvenir at the logo shop or have a peek at the mini-museum for a survey of the island's history and culture and a small display of photos and artifacts. The Outfitter Center is open daily 7 A.M.–7 P.M.

Shopping

A good reason to make the trek to Maunaloa is to visit the **Big Wind Kite Factory,** 808/552-2364, www.molokai.com/kites, open Mon.–Sat. 8:30 A.M.–5 P.M., Sunday 10 A.M.–2 P.M., owned and operated by Jonathan Socher and his wife Daphne. The hand-crafted kites and windsocks from this down-home cottage industry are the same ones that sell at outlets around the state. All are made on the premises by Jonathan, Daphane, son Zach, and a few workers, who come up with designs like butterflies, rainbow stars, and hula girls in *ti*-leaf skirts—ask for a free factory tour. Jonathan will give you a lesson in the park next door on any of the kites, including the stunt ones. They make beautiful, easily transportable gifts that'll last for years. The shop is ablaze with

M

MOLOKA'I

beautiful colors, as if you've walked into the heart of a flower. This is a happy store. The Big Wind Kite Factory is *the* most interesting shop on Moloka'i.

In the second half of this building, **The Plantation Gallery** sells a variety of crafts by local artists—Hawaiian quilt pillowcases, Pacific isle shell jewelry, scrimshaw (on deerhorn), earrings, bracelets, boxes, bamboo xylophones, and other wood objects. Part of the boutique has batiks, Balinese masks, wood carvings, quilts, and sarongs; especially nice are carved mirror frames of storks, birds, and flowers. And if you just can't live without a blowgun from Irian Jaya, this is the place. Here too you'll find perhaps the island's best selections of books on Hawaii, postcards, and a selection of T-shirts, Hawaiian shirts, and sarongs. After you've run through a million tourist shops and are sick of the shell lei, come here to find something truly unique.

Maunaloa General Store, 808/552-2346, is open Monday–Saturday 8 A.M.–6 P.M. It's a well-stocked store where you can pick up anything you'll need if you'll be staying in one of the condos at Kaluako'i. You can buy liquor, wine, beer, canned goods, meats, and vegetables.

Across from the theater and tucked into the side of the general store is the west end's only **gas station.** The price of gas here is virtually no different than anywhere else on the island. Open Monday–Friday 7 A.M.–1 P.M. and Saturday 10 A.M.–2 P.M., this station also carries drinks, sundries, and has an ATM. There is no bank in Maunaloa.

Kahoʻolawe

The island of Kahoʻolawe (the Carrying Away—as if by currents), known as Kanaloa in ancient days, is clearly visible from many points along Mauiʻs south shore. From Lahaina and Maʻalaea, the outline of Kahoʻolawe on the horizon resembles the back and dorsal fin of a whale half out of the water, ready to dive. In fact, many whales and dolphins do congregate around the island in summer to calve their young and mate for the coming year. Until recently Kahoʻolawe was a target island, uninhabited except for a band of wild goats that refused to be killed off.

Kahoʻolawe was a sacred island born to Wakea and Papa, the two great mythical progenitors of Hawaii. The birth went badly and almost killed Papa, and it hasnʻt been any easier for her ill-omened child ever since. Kahoʻolawe became synonymous with Kanaloa, the man-god. Kanaloa was especially revered by the *kahuna*

anaʻana, the "black sorcerers" of old Hawaii. Kanaloa, much like Lucifer, was driven from heaven by Kane, the god of light. Kanaloa held dominion over all poisonous things and ruled in the land of the dead from his power spot here on Kahoʻolawe. Kanaloa was also revered as the god of voyaging by early Polynesians and as such held an important place in their cast of deities.

For years, a long, bitter feud raged between the U.S. Navy, which wanted to keep the island as a bombing range, and Protect Kahoʻolawe Ohana, a Hawaiian native-rights organization, which wanted the sacred island returned to the people. The Navy finally agreed to stop bombing and returned the island to the state of Hawaii, bringing the Ohana one step closer to its goal. However, Kahoʻolawe remains closed to outside visitors, who must be content to view it from across the water.

ROBERT NILSEN

Kahoʻolawe

The Land

Kaho'olawe is 11 miles long and six miles wide, with 29 miles of coastline. Its 45 square miles make it the seventh largest of the main Hawaiian islands, larger only than Ni'ihau, and its mean elevation of about 600 feet is lower than all of the other islands except for that small, private enclave. The tallest hill, Moa'ulanui, is in the eastern section at 1,477 feet. Across the shallow Luamakika Crater is the nearly-as-tall hill Moa'ulaniki, at 1,444 feet. There are no natural lakes or ponds on the island, and all streams except for one or two are seasonal. Be-

cause Kaho'olawe lies in Maui's rain shadow (it's six miles across to South Maui), it receives only about 25 inches of rain per year.

The land is covered by sparse vegetation and is cut by ravines and gulches. Much of the island, particularly the south and east coasts, is ringed by steep *pali*, but the land slides off more gradually to the north and west. There are few beaches on the island, but the best are at the west end between Honokoa Bay and Honokanai'a Bay (some references say Hanakanaea Bay). Also known as Smuggler Cove, Honokanai'a Bay is said to be the site of a treasure buried on the beach in 1880

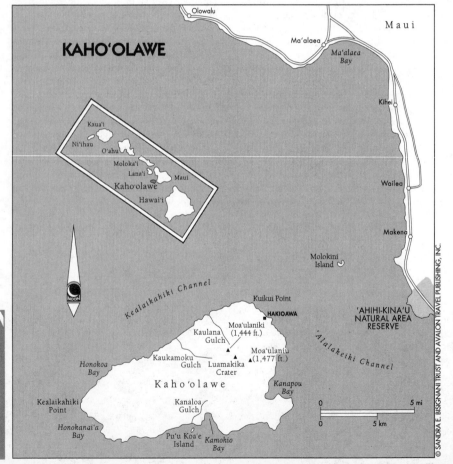

and as yet unclaimed. Kealaikahiki (the Way to Foreign Lands) Point is the island's western tip, and this rock was said to be used as a beacon during centuries past for canoe travelers to and from the island to the south.

Kaho'olawe's official color is gray and its plant is the *hinahina*, a low, spreading beach heliotrope with narrow silvery-gray leaves and small, white flowers.

HISTORY

It's perfectly clear that small families of Hawaiians lived on Kaho'olawe for countless generations and that religious rites were carried out by many visiting *kahuna* over the centuries, but mostly Kaho'olawe was left alone. There are scores of archaeological sites and remnants of *heiau* all over the bomb-cratered face of Kaho'olawe, perhaps from as early as A.D. 1150. Most of these sites are close to water near the area known as Hakioawa in the northeast corner of the island, but a few others have been discovered inland. One site of archaeological interest is an adze quarry, located up top and said to be the second largest in the state.

In the early 1800s, Kaho'olawe was used as a place of banishment for criminals. It was a harsh sentence because the island had little food and less water. Yet, many survived and some managed to raid the nearby islands of Maui and Lana'i for food and women! The first attempt at sheep ranching was started in 1858 but was not successful. This was followed by a second venture, which also proved largely unproductive because of the great numbers of wild goats that had by that time established themselves on the island. By the turn of the 20th century, Kaho'olawe was already overgrazed, and a great deal of its bare topsoil was blown away into the sea.

In 1917, Angus MacPhee, a cattleman, leased Kaho'olawe from the territorial government for $200 per year. The lease would run until 1954 with a renewal option, if by 1921 MacPhee could show reasonable progress in taming the island. Harry Baldwin bought into the **Kaho'olawe Ranch** in 1922, and with his money and MacPhee's know-how, Kaho'olawe turned a neat profit. Within a few years Kaho'olawe Ranch cattle were being shipped regularly to markets on Maui. MacPhee did more than anyone to reclaim the land. He got rid of many of the goats and introduced horses and game birds. While the island supported indigenous vegetation such as 'ohi'a, mountain apples, and even Hawaiian cotton and tobacco, MacPhee planted eucalyptus and range grass from Australia, which caught on well and stopped much of the erosion. Gardens were planted around the homestead and the soil proved to be clean and fertile.

The Navy Arrives

In 1939, with the threat of war on the horizon, MacPhee and Baldwin, stimulated by patriotism, offered a small tip of Kaho'olawe's southern shore to the U.S. Army as an artillery range. One day after the attack on Pearl Harbor, the U.S. Navy seized all of Kaho'olawe "to further the war effort" and evicted MacPhee, immediately disenfranchising the Kaho'olawe Ranch. During World War II, the Navy praised Kaho'olawe as being *the* most important factor in winning the Pacific War. The island was supposed to be returned after the war, but when the lease ran out in 1954 the island was appropriated by presidential decree for use solely by the military. No compensation was ever given to MacPhee or his family. Throughout its military stewardship, Kaho'olawe became the most bombarded piece of real estate on the face of the earth. The U.S. government held the island until the fall of 1990.

The Protect Kaho'olawe Ohana

Founded in 1976, the Protect Kaho'olawe Ohana (PKO) is an extended group favoring traditional values based on *aloha 'aina* (love of the land), which is the primary binding force for all Hawaiians. They would like the island to return to Hawaiian Lands inventory, with the *kahu* (stewardship) in the hands of native Hawaiians. The point driven home by the PKO is that the military has totally ignored and belittled native Hawaiian values, which are now beginning to be asserted. They maintain that Kaho'olawe is not a barren wasteland, but a vibrant part of their history and religion.

KAHO'OLAWE

Kaho'olawe was placed on the National Register of Historic Sites in 1981.

In a formal agreement with the PKO and the state of Hawaii in 1980, the U.S. Navy granted legal access to the island for four days per month. The PKO built a *halau* (longhouse), and members used the time on Kaho'olawe to dedicate themselves to religious, cultural, and social pursuits. The Ohana look to Kaho'olawe as their *pu'uhonua* (refuge), where they gain strength and knowledge from each other and the *'aina*. Hopefully, Kaho'olawe's future as a sacred island is now secure.

Changing Hands

In 1990, then-president George Bush, Sr. issued an order to immediately halt the bombing of Kaho'olawe, and at the same time established a congressional commission to create the terms and conditions for returning the island to the state. At that time, Ka Lahui Hawaii, the Native Nation of Hawaii, founded in Hilo in 1987, demanded that the island, as "totally ceded lands," be given to them as part of their sovereign nation. The PKO, in a more moderate stance, suggested "land banking" the island under the control of the state or federal government until the United States recognizes the sovereignty of the Ka Lahui Hawaii. In the meantime, the PKO continues to lobby for exclusive rights to the stewardship of Kaho'olawe. On May 7, 1994, Kaho'olawe was returned to the state of Hawaii.

Transition

With the transfer of the island back to state protection, Kaho'olawe has become an "island reserve." The U.S. Congress dedicated $400 million over a 10-year period toward cleaning the island of scrap and unexploded ordnance and for the rejuvenation of the environment. What appeared to be a huge amount of money soon turned out to be woefully inadequate for the task and only enough

It's perfectly clear that small families of Hawaiians lived on Kaho'olawe for countless generations and that religious rites were carried out by many visiting kahuna over the centuries, but mostly Kaho'olawe was left alone.

to start the process of making the island safe and healthy. The Kaho'olawe Island Reserve Commission (KIRC) was established by state law to oversee and manage this effort. The reserve includes the island of Kaho'olawe plus the waters surrounding it to a distance of two miles. This total area is one of restricted access.

Now that the goats are gone and some of the ordnance cleaned up, the greatest problem seems to be erosion. While vegetation has a hold in some valleys and clings to spots where goats could not feed, much of the soil covering the island's plateau and gentle slopes has been blown off, exposing red, hardpan earth. Much work has been done; various approaches have been tried to establish grasses and other plants, and dams of grasses have been placed to prevent dirt from washing down gullies to the sea. Still, much more needs to be done. Introduced species are overtaking the dwindling native plants, and field mice are swiftly eating native seeds. Two other serious problems that must be overcome are the remaining unexploded ordnance, which is both expensive and risky to remove and dispose of, and the perpetual lack of water. While the ordnance cleanup effort continues by the military, Mother Nature must be coaxed to help out with water. With similar natural conditions as those of South Maui, the island gets only minimal rain each year. Freshwater comes from rain catching, and few streams ever run.

The only habitation sites on Kaho'olawe are the traditional structures put up by the PKO near Hakioawa and the military installation on the west end of the island. There is currently virtually no infrastructure on the island except for a few rutted dirt roads. Over the years, several thousand people have visited the island, mostly to help with the cleanup efforts or to participate in religious and cultural activities. Kaho'olawe might become a great cultural resource, a place where Hawaiians could go to practice age-old traditions in a sympathetic environment, but it probably will never be a place for any large-scale habitation.

Although exact plans for the future are still undecided, it seems most likely that the island will be kept out of the hands of developers and open to visitors for cultural purposes if the risk factor finally drops low enough. How the island will be managed and what status it will eventually attain is still to be determined.

The Book on Kaho'olawe

Inez MacPhee Ashdown lived on the island with her father and was a driving force in establishing the homestead. She has written a book, *Recollections of Kaho'olawe,* that chronicles the events from 1917 until the military takeover and is rife with myths, legends, and historical facts about Kaho'olawe.

Information

Only a lucky few set foot on Kaho'olawe. For information about current happenings relating to this tortured island, log on to the PKO's website: www.kahoolawe.org. Alternately, try that of the KIRC at www.state.hi.us/kirc (or www.hawaii.gov/kirc), or the Navy information site at www.efdpac.navfac.navy.mil/news/kaho/hp1.htm. To contact the PKO, write: P.O. Box 152, Honolulu, HI 96810. For the KIRC: 811 Kolu St., Ste. 201, Wailuku, HI 96793, 808/243-5020 or 800/468-4644, administrator@kirc.state.hi.us.

Resources

Hawaiian Glossary

The list on the following pages gives you a "taste" of Hawaiian and provides a basic vocabulary of words in common usage that you are likely to hear. Becoming familiar with them is not a strict necessity, but they will definitely enhance your experience and make talking with local people more congenial. Many islanders spice their speech with certain words, especially when they're speaking "pidgin," and you too can use them just as soon as you feel comfortable. You might even discover some Hawaiian words that are so perfectly expressive they'll become regular parts of your vocabulary. Many Hawaiian words have been absorbed into the English dictionary. The definitions given are not exhaustive, but are generally considered the most common.

Words marked with an asterisk (*) are used commonly throughout the islands.

'a'a*—rough clinker lava. 'A'a has become the correct geological term to describe this type of lava found anywhere in the world.

'ae—yes

ahupua'a—pie-shaped land divisions running from mountain to sea that were governed by *konohiki,* local *ali'i* who owed their allegiance to a reigning chief

aikane—friend; pal; buddy

'aina—land; the binding spirit to all Hawaiians. Love of the land is paramount in traditional Hawaiian beliefs.

akamai—smart; clever; wise

akua—a god, or simply "divine"

ali'i*—a Hawaiian chief or noble

aloha*—the most common greeting in the islands; can mean both hello and good-bye, welcome and farewell. It can also mean romantic love, affection, or best wishes.

'a'ole—no

'aumakua—a personal or family god, often an ancestral spirit

auwe—alas; ouch! When a great chief or loved one died, it was a traditional wail of mourning.

'awa,—also known as *kava,* a mildly intoxicating traditional drink made from the juice of chewed *'awa* root, spat into a bowl, and used in religious ceremonies

halakahiki—pineapple

hale*—house or building; often combined with other words to name a specific place, such as Haleakala (House of the Sun), or Hale Pa'i at Lahainaluna, meaning Printing House

hana*—work; combined with *pau* means end of work or quitting time

hanai—literally "to feed." Part of the true *aloha* spirit. A *hanai* is a permanent guest, or an adopted family member, usually an old person or a child. This is an enduring cultural phenomenon in Hawaii, in which a child from one family (perhaps that of a brother or sister, and quite often one's grandchild) is raised as one's own without formal adoption.

haole*—a word that at one time meant foreigner, but which now means a white person or Caucasian

hapa*—half, as in a mixed-blooded person being referred to as *hapa haole*

hapai*—pregnant; used by all ethnic groups when a *keiki* is on the way

haupia*—a coconut custard dessert often served at a lu'au

heiau*—A platform made of skillfully fitted rocks, upon which temporary structures were built as temples and offerings made to the gods.

holomu*—an ankle-length dress that is much more fitted than a mu'umu'u, and which is often worn on formal occasions

hono—bay, as in Honolulu (Sheltered Bay)

honu—green sea turtle; endangered

ho'oilo—traditional Hawaiian winter that began in November

ho'olaulea—any happy event, but especially a family outing or picnic

ho'omalimali*—sweet talk; flattery

huhu*—angry; irritated

*hui******—a group; meeting; society. Often used to refer to Chinese businesspeople or family members who pool their money to get businesses started.

hukilau—traditional shoreline fish-gathering in which everyone lends a hand to *huki* (pull) the huge net. Anyone taking part shares in the *lau* (food). It is much more like a party than hard work, and if you're lucky you'll be able to take part in one.

*hula******—a native Hawaiian dance in which the rhythm of the islands is captured by swaying hips and stories told by lyrically moving hands. A *halau* is a group or school of hula.

huli huli—barbecue, as in *huli huli* chicken

i'a—fish in general. *I'a maka* is raw fish.

*imu******—underground oven filled with hot rocks and used for baking. The main cooking method featured at a lu'au, used to steam-bake pork and other succulent dishes. The tending of the *imu* was traditionally for men only.

ipo—sweetheart; lover; girl- or boyfriend

kahili—a tall pole topped with feathers, resembling a huge feather duster. It was used by an *ali'i* to announce his or her presence.

*kahuna******—priest; sorcerer; doctor; skillful person. In old Hawaii *kahuna* had tremendous power, which they used for both good and evil. The *kahuna ana'ana* was a feared individual who practiced "black magic" and could pray a person to death, while the *kahuna lapa'au* was a medical practitioner bringing aid and comfort to the people.

kai—the sea. Many businesses and hotels employ *kai* as part of their name.

kalua—means roasted underground in an *imu*. A favorite island food is *kalua* pork.

*kama'aina******—a child of the land; an old-timer; a longtime island resident of any ethnic background; a resident of Hawaii or native son or daughter. Hotels and airlines often offer discounts called *"kama'aina* rates" to anyone who can prove island residency.

kanaka—man or commoner; later used to distinguish a Hawaiian from other races. Tone of voice can make it a derisive expression.

*kane******—means man, but actually used to signify a relationship such as husband or boyfriend. Written on a lavatory door it means "men's room."

*kapu******—forbidden; taboo; keep out; do not touch

*kaukau******—slang word meaning food or chow; grub. Some of the best food in Hawaii comes from the *kaukau* wagons, trucks that sell plate lunches and other morsels.

kauwa—a landless, untouchable caste once confined to living on reservations. Members of this caste were often used as human sacrifices at *heiau*. Calling someone *kauwa* is still a grave insult.

kava—(see *'awa*)

*keiki******—child or children; used by all ethnic groups. "Have you hugged your *keiki* today?"

kiawe—an algaroba tree from South America commonly found in Hawaii along the shore. It grows a nasty long thorn that can easily puncture a tire. Legend has it that the trees were introduced to the islands by a misguided missionary who hoped the thorns would coerce natives into wearing shoes. Actually, they are good for fuel, as fodder for hogs and cattle, and for reforestation, none of which you'll appreciate if you step on one of the thorns or flatten a tire on your rental car!

*ko'ala******—any food that has been broiled or barbecued

kokua—help. As in "Your *kokua* is needed to keep Hawaii free from litter."

*kona wind******—a muggy subtropical wind that blows from the south and hits the leeward side of the islands. It usually brings sticky hot weather and one of the few times when air-conditioning will be appreciated.

konane—a traditional Hawaiian game, similar to checkers, played with pebbles on a large flat stone used as a board

ko'olau—windward side of the island

kukui—a candlenut tree whose pods are polished and then strung together to make a beautiful lei. Traditionally the oil-rich nuts were strung on the rib of a coconut leaf and used as a candle.

kuleana—homesite; the old homestead; small farms. Especially used to describe the small spreads on Hawaiian Homelands on Moloka'i.

Kumulipo*—ancient Hawaiian genealogical chant that records the pantheon of gods, creation, and the beginning of humankind

kupuna—a grandparent or old-timer; usually means someone who has gained wisdom. The statewide school system now invites *kupuna* to talk to the children about the old ways and methods.

la—the sun. Often combined with other words to be more descriptive, such as *La*haina (Merciless Sun) or Haleaka*la* (House of the Sun).

lanai*—veranda or porch. You'll pay more for a hotel room if it has a lanai with an ocean view.

lani—sky or the heavens

lau hala*—traditional Hawaiian weaving of mats, hats, etc., from the prepared fronds of the pandanus (screw pine)

lei*—a traditional garland of flowers or vines. One of Hawaii's most beautiful customs. Given at any auspicious occasion, but especially when arriving or leaving Hawaii.

lele—the stone altar at a *heiau*

limu—edible seaweed of various types. Gathered from the shoreline, it makes an excellent salad. It's used to garnish many island dishes and is a favorite at lu'au.

lomi lomi—traditional Hawaiian massage; also, raw salmon made into a vinegared salad with chopped onion and spices

lua*—the toilet; the head; the bathroom

luakini—a human-sacrifice temple. Introduced to Hawaii in the 13th century at Waha'ula Heiau on the Big Island.

lu'au*—a Hawaiian feast featuring poi, *imu*-baked pork, and other traditional foods. Good ones provide some of the best gastronomic delights in the world.

luna—foreman or overseer in the plantation fields. They were often mounted on horseback and were renowned for either their fairness or their cruelty. Representing the middle class, they served as a buffer between plantation workers and white plantation owners.

mahalo*—thank you. *Mahalo nui* means "big thanks" or "thank you very much."

mahele—division. The "Great Mahele" of 1848 changed Hawaii forever when the traditional common lands were broken up into privately owned plots.

mahimahi*—a favorite eating fish. Often called a dolphin, but a mahimahi is a true fish, not a cetacean.

mahu—a homosexual; often used derisively like "fag" or "queer"

maile—a fragrant vine used in traditional lei. It looks ordinary but smells delightful.

maka'ainana—a commoner; a person "belonging" to the *'aina* (land), who supported the *ali'i* by fishing and farming and as a warrior

makai*—toward the sea; used by most islanders when giving directions

make—dead; deceased

malihini*—what you are if you have just arrived: a newcomer; a tenderfoot; a recent arrival

malo—the native Hawaiian loincloth. Never worn anymore except at festivals or pageants.

mana*—power from the spirit world; innate energy of all things animate or inanimate; the grace of god. Mana could be passed on from one person to another, or even stolen. Great care was taken to protect the *ali'i* from having their *mana* defiled. Commoners were required to lie flat on the ground and cover their faces whenever a great *ali'i* approached. *Kahuna* were often employed in the regaining or transference of *mana*.

manini—stingy; tight; a Hawaiianized word taken from the name of Don Francisco *Marin*, who was instrumental in bringing many fruits and plants to Hawaii. He was known for never sharing any of the bounty from his substantial gardens on Vineyard Street in Honolulu; therefore, his name came to mean "stingy."

manuahi—free; gratis; extra

mauka*—toward the mountains; used by most islanders when giving directions

mauna—mountain. Often combined with other words to be more descriptive, such as Mauna Kea (White Mountain)

mele—a song or chant in the Hawaiian oral tradition that records the history and genealogies of the *ali'i*

Menehune—the legendary "little people" of Hawaii. Like leprechauns, they are said to shun humans and possess magical powers.

moa—chicken; fowl

moana*—the ocean; the sea. Many businesses and hotels as well as places have *moana* as part of their name.

moe—sleep

mo'olelo—ancient tales kept alive by the oral tradition and recited only by day

mu'umu'u*—a "Mother Hubbard," an ankle-length dress with a high neckline introduced by the missionaries to cover the nakedness of the Hawaiians. It has become fashionable attire for almost any occasion in Hawaii.

nani—beautiful

nui—big; great; large; as in *mahalo nui* (thank you very much)

'ohana—a family; the fundamental social division; extended family. Now often used to denote a social organization with grassroots overtones.

'okolehau—literally "iron bottom"; a traditional booze made from *ti* root. *'Okole* means "rear end" and *hau* means "iron," which was descriptive of the huge blubber pots in which *'okolehau* was made. Also, if you drink too much it'll surely knock you on your *'okole*.

oli—chant not done to a musical accompaniment

ono*—delicious; delightful; the best. *Ono ono* means "extra or absolutely delicious."

'opihi—a shellfish or limpet that clings to rocks and is gathered as one of the islands' favorite *pu pu*. Custom dictates that you never remove all of the *'opihi* from a rock; some are always left to grow for future generations.

'opu—belly; stomach

pahoehoe*—smooth, ropy lava that looks like burnt pancake batter. It is now the correct geological term used to describe this type of lava found anywhere in the world.

pakalolo—"crazy smoke"; grass; smoke; dope; marijuana

pake—a Chinese person. Can be derisive, de-

pending on the tone in which it is used. It is a bastardization of the Chinese word meaning "uncle."

pali*—a cliff; precipice. Hawaii's geology makes them quite common. The most famous are the *pali* of Oahu where a major battle was fought.

paniolo*—a Hawaiian cowboy. Derived from the Spanish *espa-ol*. The first cowboys brought to Hawaii during the early 19th century were Mexicans from California.

papale—hat. Except for the feathered helmets of the *ali'i* warriors of old Hawaii, hats were generally not worn. However, once the islanders saw their practical uses and how fashionable they were, they began weaving them from various materials and quickly became experts at manufacture and design.

pa'u—long split skirt often worn by women when horseback riding. In the 1800s, an island treat was watching *pa'u* riders in their beautiful dresses at Kapi'olani Park in Honolulu. The tradition is carried on today at many of Hawaii's rodeos.

pau*—finished; done; completed. Often combined into *pau hana*, which means end of work or quitting time.

pilau—stink; bad smell; stench

pilikia—trouble of any kind, big or small; bad times

poi*—a glutinous paste made from the pounded corm of taro, which ferments slightly and has a light sour taste. Purplish in color, it's a staple at lu'au, where it is called "one-, two-, or three-finger" poi, depending upon its thickness.

pono—righteous or excellent

pua—flower

puka*—a hole of any size. *Puka* is used by all island residents, whether talking about a pinhole in a rubber boat or a tunnel through a mountain.

punalua—a traditional practice, before the missionaries arrived, of sharing mates. Western seamen took advantage of it, leading to the spread of contagious diseases and eventual rapid decline of the Hawaiian people.

pune'e*—bed; narrow couch. Used by all ethnic

groups. To recline on a *pune'e* on a breezy lanai is a true island treat.

pu pu*—an appetizer; a snack; hors d'oeuvres; can be anything from cheese and crackers to sushi. Oftentimes, bars or nightclubs offer them free.

pupule—crazy; nuts; out of your mind

pu'u—hill, as in Pu'u 'Ula'ula (Red Hill)

tapa*—a traditional paper cloth made from beaten bark. Intricate designs were stamped in using beaters, and natural dyes added color. The tradition was lost for many years but is now making a comeback, and provides some of the most beautiful folk art in the islands. Also called Kapa.

taro*—the staple of old Hawaii. A plant with a distinctive broad leaf that produces a starchy root. It was brought by the first Polynesians and was grown on magnificently irrigated plantations. According to the oral tradition, the life-giving properties of taro hold mystical significance for Hawaiians, since it was created by the gods at about the same time as humans.

ti—a broad-leafed plant that was used for many purposes, from plates to hula skirts. Especially used to wrap religious offerings presented at the *heiau*.

tutu*—grandmother; granny; older woman. Used by all as a term of respect and endearment.

ukulele*—*uku* means "flea" and *lele* means "jumping," so literally "jumping flea"—the way the Hawaiians perceived the quick finger movements used on the banjo-like Portuguese folk instrument called a *cavaquinho*. The ukulele quickly became synonymous with the islands.

wahine*—young woman; female; girl; wife. Used by all ethnic groups. When written on a lavatory door it means "women's room."

wai—fresh water; drinking water

wela—hot. *Wela kahao* is a "hot time" or "making whoopee."

wiki*—quickly; fast; in a hurry. Often seen as *wiki wiki* (very fast), as in "Wiki Wiki Messenger Service."

Useful Phrases

Aloha ahiahi—Good evening

Aloha au ia 'oe—I love you

Aloha kakahiaka—Good morning

Aloha nui loa—much love; fondest regards

Hau'oli la hanau—Happy birthday

Hau'oli makahiki hou—Happy New Year

Komo mai—please come in; enter; welcome

Mele kalikimaka—Merry Christmas

'Okole maluna—bottoms up; salute; cheers; kampai

Suggested Reading

Many publishers print books on Hawaii. Following are a few that focus on Hawaiian topics: **University of Hawai'i Press,** www.uhpress.hawaii.edu, has the best overall general list of titles on Hawaii. The **Bishop Museum Press,** www.bishopmuseum.org/bishop/press, puts out many scholarly works on Hawaiiana, as does **Kamehameha Schools Press,** www.ksbe.edu/newsroom/kspress. Also good, with a more general-interest list, are **Bess Press,** www.bess-press.com; **Mutual Publishing,** www.mutual publishing.com; and **Petroglyph Press,** www.basicallybooks.com. A website specifically oriented toward books on Hawaii, Hawaiian music, and other things Hawaiian is **Hawaii Books** at www.hawaiibooks.com.

Astronomy

Bryan, E.H. *Stars over Hawaii.* Hilo, HI: Petroglyph Press, 1977. An introduction to astronomy, with information about the constellations and charts featuring the stars filling the night sky in Hawaii, by month. A excellent primer.

Rhoads, Samuel. *The Sky Tonight—A Guided Tour of the Stars over Hawaii.* Honolulu: Bishop Museum, 1993. Four pages per month of star charts—one each for the horizon in every cardinal direction. Exceptional!

Cooking

Alexander, Agnes. *How to Use Hawaiian Fruit.* Hilo, HI: Petroglyph Press, 1984. A slim volume of recipes using delicious and different Hawaiian fruits.

Beeman, Judy, and Martin Beeman. *Joys of Hawaiian Cooking.* Hilo, HI: Petroglyph Press, 1977. A collection of favorite recipes from Big Island chefs.

Choy, Sam. *Cooking from the Heart with Sam Choy.* Honolulu: Mutual Publishing, 1995. This beautiful, hand-bound cookbook contains many color photos by Douglas Peebles.

Fukuda, Sachi. *Pupus, An Island Tradition.* Honolulu: Bess Press, 1995.

Margah, Irish, and Elvira Monroe. *Hawaii, Cooking with Aloha.* San Carlos, CA: Wide World, 1984. Island recipes, as well as hints on decor.

Rizzuto, Shirley. *Fish Dishes of the Pacific—from the Fishwife.* Honolulu: Hawaii Fishing News, 1986. Features recipes using all the fish commonly caught in Hawaiian waters (husband Jim Rizzuto is the author of *Fishing, Hawaiian Style*).

Culture

Dudley, Michael Kioni. *Man, Gods, and Nature.* Honolulu: Na Kane O Ka Malo Press, 1990. An examination of the philosophical underpinnings of Hawaiian beliefs and their interconnected reality.

Hartwell, Jay. *Na Mamo: Hawaiian People Today.* Honolulu: Ai Pohaku Press, 1996. Profiles 12 people practicing Hawaiian traditions in the modern world.

Heyerdahl, Thor. *American Indians in the Pacific.* London: Allen and Unwin Ltd., 1952. Theoretical and anthropological accounts of the influence on Polynesia of the Indians along the Pacific coast of North and South America. Although no longer in print, this book is fascinating reading, presenting unsubstantiated yet intriguing theories.

Kamehameha Schools Press. *Life in Early Hawai'i: The Ahupua'a.* 3rd ed. Honolulu:

Kamehameha Schools Press, 1994. Written for schoolchildren to better understand the basic organization of old Hawaiian land use and its function, this slim volume is a good primer for people of any age who wish to understand this fundamental societal fixture.

Kirch, Patrick V. *Feathered Gods and Fishhooks: An Introduction to Hawaiian Archaeology and Prehistory.* Honolulu: University of Hawai'i Press, 1997. This scholarly, lavishly illustrated, yet very readable book gives new insight into the development of precontact Hawaiian civilization. It focuses on the sites and major settlements of old Hawai'i and chronicles the main cultural developments while weaving in the social climate that contributed to change. A very worthwhile read.

Fauna

Boom, Robert. *Hawaiian Seashells.* Honolulu: Waikiki Aquarium, 1972. Photos by Jerry Kringle. A collection of 137 seashells found in Hawaiian waters, featuring many found nowhere else on earth. Broken into categories with accompanying text including common and scientific names, physical descriptions, and likely habitats. A must-read for shell collectors.

Carpenter, Blyth, and Russell Carpenter. *Fish Watching in Hawaii.* San Mateo, CA: Natural World Press, 1981. A color guide to many of the reef fish found in Hawaii and often spotted by snorkelers. If you're interested in the fish that you'll be looking at, this guide will be very helpful.

Fielding, Ann, and Ed Robinson. *An Underwater Guide to Hawai'i.* Honolulu: University of Hawai'i Press, 1987. If you've ever had a desire to snorkel/scuba the living reef waters of Hawaii and to be familiar with what you're seeing, get this small but fact-packed book. The amazing array of marine life found throughout the archipelago is captured in

glossy photos with accompanying informative text. Both the scientific and common names of specimens are given. This book will enrich your underwater experience and serve as an easily understood reference guide for many years.

Goodson, Gar. *The Many-Splendored Fishes of Hawaii.* Stanford, CA: Stanford University Press, 1985. This small but thorough "fish-watchers" book includes entries on some deep-sea fish.

Hawaiian Audubon Society. *Hawaii's Birds.* 5th ed. Honolulu: Hawaii Audubon Society, 1997. Excellent bird book, giving description, range, voice, and habits of the more than 100 species. Slim volume; good for carrying while hiking.

Hobson, Edmund, and E. H. Chave. *Hawaiian Reef Animals.* Honolulu: University of Hawai'i Press, 1987. Colorful photos and descriptions of the fish, invertebrates, turtles, and seals that call Hawaiian reefs their home.

Kay, Alison, and Olive Schoenberg-Dole. *Shells of Hawai'i.* Honolulu: University of Hawai'i Press, 1991. Color photos and tips on where to look.

Mahaney, Casey. *Hawaiian Reef Fish, The Identification Book.* Thailand: Planet Ocean Publishing, 1993. A spiral-bound reference work featuring many color photos and descriptions of common reef fish found in Hawaiian waters.

Nickerson, Roy. *Brother Whale, A Pacific Whale-watcher's Log.* San Francisco: Chronicle Books, 1977. Introduces the average person to the life of earth's greatest mammals. Provides historical accounts, photos, and tips on whale-watching. Well-written, descriptive, and the best "first time" book on whales.

Pratt, Douglas. *A Field Guide to the Birds of Hawaii and the Tropical Pacific.* Princeton,

NJ: Princeton University Press, 1987. Useful field guide for novice and expert bird-watchers, covering Hawaii as well as other Pacific Island groups.

Tomich, P. Quentin. *Mammals in Hawai'i.* Honolulu: Bishop Museum Press, 1986. Quintessential scholarly text on all mammal species in Hawaii, with description of distribution and historical references. Lengthy bibliography.

van Riper, Charles, and Sandra van Riper. *A Field Guide to the Mammals of Hawaii.* Honolulu: Oriental Publishing. A guide to the surprising number of mammals introduced into Hawaii. Full-color pages document description, uses, tendencies, and habitat. Small and thin, this book makes a worthwhile addition to any serious hiker's backpack.

Flora

Kepler, Angela. *Hawaiian Heritage Plants.* Honolulu: University of Hawai'i Press, 1998. A treatise on 32 utilitarian plants used by the early Hawaiians.

Kepler, Angela. *Hawai'i's Floral Splendor.* Honolulu: Mutual Publishing, 1997. A general reference to flowers of Hawaii.

Kepler, Angela. *Tropicals of Hawaii.* Honolulu: Mutual Publishing, 1989. This small-format book features many color photos of nonnative flowers.

Kuck, Lorraine, and Richard Togg. *Hawaiian Flowers and Flowering Trees.* Rutland, VT: Tuttle, 1960. A classic, although out-of-print, field guide to tropical and subtropical flora illustrated in watercolor. Succinct descriptions of Hawaiian plants and flowers with a brief history of their places of origin and their introduction to Hawaii.

Merrill, Elmer. *Plant Life of the Pacific World.* Rutland, VT: Tuttle, 1983. This is the defin-

itive book for anyone planning a botanical tour to the entire Pacific Basin. Originally published in the 1930s, it remains a tremendous work, worth tracking down through out-of-print book services.

Miyano, Leland. *Hawai'i, A Floral Paradise.* Honolulu: Mutual Publishing, 1995. Photographed by Douglas Peebles, this large-format book is filled with informative text and beautiful color shots of tropical flowers commonly seen in Hawaii.

Miyano, Leland. *A Pocket Guide to Hawai'i's Flowers.* Honolulu: Mutual Publishing, 2001. A small guide to readily seen flowers in the state. Good for the backpack or back pocket.

Sohmer, S. H., and R. Gustafson. *Plants and Flowers of Hawai'i.* Honolulu: University of Hawai'i Press, 1987. The authors cover the vegetation zones of Hawaii, from mountains to coast, introducing you to the wide and varied floral biology of the islands. They give a good introduction to the history and unique evolution of Hawaiian plantlife. Beautiful color plates are accompanied by clear and concise plant descriptions, with the scientific and common Hawaiian names listed.

Teho, Fortunato. *Plants of Hawaii—How to Grow Them.* Hilo, HI: Petroglyph Press, 1992. A small but useful book for those who want their backyards to bloom into tropical paradises.

Wagner, Warren L., Derral R. Herbst, and H. S. Sohmer. *Manual of the Flowering Plants of Hawai'i,* revised edition, vol. 2. Honolulu: University of Hawai'i Press in association with Bishop Museum Press, 1999. Considered the scholarly Bible for Hawaii's botanical world.

Valier, Kathy. *Ferns of Hawaii.* Honolulu: University of Hawai'i Press, 1995. One of the few books that treat the state's ferns as a single subject.

Health

Gutmanis, June. *Kahuna La'au Lapa'au,* revised edition. Honolulu: Island Heritage, 2001. Text on Hawaiian herbal medicines: diseases, treatments, and medicinal plants, with illustrations.

McBride, L. R. *Practical Folk Medicine of Hawaii.* Hilo, HI: Petroglyph Press, 1975. An illustrated guide to Hawaii's medicinal plants as used by the *kahuna lapa'au* (medical healers). Includes a thorough section on ailments, diagnosis, and the proper folk remedy. Illustrated by the author, a renowned botanical researcher and former ranger at Hawaii Volcanoes National Park.

Wilkerson, James A., M.D., ed. *Medicine for Mountaineering and Other Wilderness.* 4th ed. Seattle: The Mountaineers, 1992. Don't let the title fool you. Although the book focuses on specific health problems that may be encountered while mountaineering, it is the best first-aid and general health guide available today. Written by doctors for the layperson to use until help arrives, it is jam-packed with easily understandable techniques and procedures. For those planning extended hikes, it is a must.

History

Apple, Russell A. *Trails: From Steppingstones to Kerbstones.* Honolulu: Bishop Museum Press, 1965. This "Special Publication #53" is a special-interest archaeological survey focusing on trails, roadways, footpaths, and highways and how they were designed and maintained throughout the years. Many "royal highways" from precontact Hawaii are cited.

Ashdown, Inez MacPhee. *Kaho'olawe.* Honolulu: Topgallant Publishing, 1979. The tortured story of the lonely island of Kaho'olawe by a member of the family who owned the island until it was turned into a military bombing target during World War II. It's also a first-person account of life on the island.

Barnes, Phil. *A Concise History of the Hawaiian Islands.* Hilo, HI: Petroglyph Press, 1999. An easy-to-read examination of the main currents of Hawaiian history and its major players, focusing on the important factors in shaping the social, economic, and political trends of the islands.

Cameron, Roderick. *The Golden Haze.* New York: World Publishing, 1964. An account of Captain James Cook's voyages of discovery throughout the South Seas. Uses original diaries and journals for an "on-the-spot" reconstruction of this great seafaring adventure.

Cox, J. Halley, and Edward Stasack. *Hawaiian Petroglyphs.* Honolulu: Bishop Museum Press, 1970. The most thorough examination of petroglyph sites throughout the islands.

Daws, Gavan. *Shoal of Time, A History of the Hawaiian Islands.* Honolulu: University of Hawai'i Press, 1974. A highly readable history of Hawaii dating from its "discovery" by the Western world to its acceptance as the 50th state. Good insight into the psychological makeup of influential characters who helped form Hawaii's past.

Dorrance, William H., and Francis S. Morgan. *Sugar Islands: The 165-Year Story of Sugar in Hawai'i.* Honolulu: Mutual Publishing, 2000. An overall sketch of the sugar industry in Hawaii from inception to decline, with data on many individual plantations and mills around the islands. Definitely a story from the industry's point of view.

Finney, Ben, and James D. Houston. *Surfing, A History of the Ancient Hawaiian Sport.* Los Angeles: Pomegranate, 1996. Features many early etchings and old photos of Hawaiian surfers practicing their native sport.

Fornander, Abraham. *An Account of the Polynesian Race; Its Origins and Migrations, and the Ancient History of the Hawaiian People to the*

Times of Kamehameha I. Rutland, VT: C.E. Tuttle Co., 1969. This is a reprint of a three-volume opus originally published 1878–1885. It is still one of the best sources of information on Hawaiian myth and legend.

Free, David. *Vignettes of Old Hawaii.* Honolulu: Crossroads Press, 1994. A collection of short essays on a variety of subjects.

Fuchs, Lawrence. *Hawaii Pono.* Honolulu: Bess Press, 1961. A detailed, scholarly work presenting an overview of Hawaii's history, based on ethnic and sociological interpretations. Encompasses most socioethnological groups from native Hawaiians to modern entrepreneurs. This book is a must for obtaining some social historical background.

Handy, E. S., and Elizabeth Handy. *Native Planters in Old Hawaii.* Honolulu: Bishop Museum Press, 1972. A superbly written, easily understood scholarly work on the intimate relationship of precontact Hawaiians and the *aina* (land). Much more than its title implies, this book should be read by anyone seriously interested in Polynesian Hawaii.

Ii, John Papa. *Fragments of Hawaiian History.* Honolulu: Bishop Museum, 1959. Hawaii's history under Kamehameha I as told by a Hawaiian who actually experienced it.

Joesting, Edward. *Hawaii: An Uncommon History.* New York: W.W. Norton Co., 1978. A truly uncommon history told in a series of vignettes relating to the lives and personalities of the first Caucasians in Hawaii, Hawaiian nobility, sea captains, writers, and adventurers. Brings history to life. Absolutely excellent!

Kamakau, S. M. *Ruling Chiefs of Hawaii,* revised edition. Honolulu: Kamehameha Schools Press, 1992.

Lili'uokalani. *Hawaii's Story by Hawaii's Queen,* reprint. Honolulu: Mutual Publishing, 1990.

Originally written in 1898, this moving personal account recounts Hawai'i's inevitable move from monarchy to U.S. Territory by its last queen, Lili'uokalani. The facts can be found in other histories, but none provides the emotion or point of view expressed by Hawaii's deposed monarch. This is a must-read to get the whole picture.

McBride, Likeke. *Petroglyphs of Hawaii.* Hilo, HI: Petroglyph Press, 1997. A revised and updated guide to petroglyphs found in the Hawaiian Islands. A basic introduction to these old Hawaiian picture stories.

Nickerson, Roy. *Lahaina, Royal Capital of Hawaii.* Honolulu: Hawaiian Service, 1978. The story of Lahaina from whaling days to present, spiced with ample photographs.

Takaki, Ronald. *Pau Hana: Plantation Life and Labor in Hawaii.* Honolulu: University of Hawai'i Press, 1983. The story of immigrant labor and the sugar industry in Hawaii until the 1920s from the worker's perspective.

Introductory

Carroll, Rick, and Marcie Carroll, eds. *Hawai'i: True Stories of the Island Spirit.* San Francisco: Travelers' Tales, Inc., 1999. A collection of stories by a variety of authors that were chosen to elicit the essence of Hawaii and Hawaiian experiences. A great read.

Cohen, David, and Rick Smolan. *A Day in the Life of Hawaii.* New York: Workman, 1984. On December 2, 1983, 50 of the world's top photojournalists were invited to Hawaii to photograph the variety of daily life on the islands. The photos are excellently reproduced and accompanied by a minimum of text.

Day, A. G., and C. Stroven. *A Hawaiian Reader,* reprint. Honolulu: Mutual Publishing, 1984. A poignant compilation of essays, diary entries, and fictitious writings originally published in

1959 that takes you from the death of Captain Cook through the "statehood services."

Department of Geography, University of Hawai'i, Hilo. *Atlas of Hawai'i.* 3rd ed. Honolulu: University of Hawai'i Press, 1998. Much more than an atlas filled with reference maps, this book also contains commentary on the natural environment, culture, and sociology; a gazetteer; and statistical tables. Actually a mini-encyclopedia on Hawai'i.

Michener, James A. *Hawaii.* New York: Random House, 1959. Michener's fictionalized historical novel has done more to inform *and* misinform readers about Hawaii than any other book ever written. A great tale with plenty of local color and information, but read it for pleasure, not facts.

Piercy, LaRue. *Hawaii This and That.* Honolulu: Mutual Publishing, 1994. Illustrated by Scot Ebanez. A 60-page book filled with one-sentence facts and oddities about all manner of things Hawaiian. Informative, amazing, and fun to read.

Steele, R. Thomas: *The Hawaiian Shirt: Its Art and History.* New York: Abbeville Press, 1984.

Language

Elbert, Samuel. *Spoken Hawaiian.* Honolulu: University of Hawai'i Press, 1970. Progressive conversational lessons.

Elbert, Samuel, and Mary Pukui. *Hawaiian Dictionary.* Honolulu: University of Hawai'i Press, 1986. The best dictionary available on the Hawaiian language. The *Pocket Hawaiian Dictionary* is a less expensive, condensed version of this dictionary and adequate for most travelers with a general interest in the language.

Pukui, Mary Kawena, Samuel Elbert, and Esther T. Mookini. *Place Names of Hawaii.* Honolulu: University of Hawai'i Press, 1974. The most current and comprehensive listing of Hawaiian and foreign place names in the state, giving pronunciation, spelling, meaning, and location.

Schutz, Albert J. *All About Hawaiian.* Honolulu: University of Hawai'i Press, 1995. A brief primer on Hawaiian pronunciation, grammar, and vocabulary. A solid introduction.

Mythology and Legends

Beckwith, Martha. *Hawaiian Mythology,* reprint. Honolulu: University of Hawai'i Press, 1976. More than 60 years after its original printing in 1940, this work remains the definitive text on Hawaiian mythology. Beckwith compiled this book from many sources, giving exhaustive cross-references to genealogies and legends expressed in the oral tradition. If you are only going to read one book on Hawaii's folklore, this should be it.

Beckwith, Martha. *The Kumulipo,* reprint. Honolulu: University of Hawai'i Press, 1972. Translation of the Hawaiian creation chant, originally published in 1951.

Colum, Padraic. *Legends of Hawaii.* New Haven, CT: Yale University Press, 1937. Selected legends of old Hawaii, reinterpreted but closely based on the originals.

Elbert, S. H., ed. *Hawaiian Antiquities and Folklore.* Honolulu: University of Hawai'i Press, 1959. Illustrated by Jean Charlot. A selection of the main legends from Abraham Fornander's great work, *An Account of the Polynesian Race.*

Kalakaua, His Hawaiian Majesty, King David. *The Legends and Myths of Hawaii.* Edited by R. M. Daggett, with a foreword by Glen Grant. Honolulu: Mutual Publishing, 1990. Originally published in 1888, Hawaii's own

King Kalakaua draws on his scholarly and formidable knowledge of the classic oral tradition to bring alive ancient tales from pre-contact Hawaii. A powerful yet somewhat Victorian voice from Hawaii's past speaks clearly and boldly, especially about the intimate role of pre-Christian religion in the lives of the Hawaiian people.

Melville, Leinanai. *Children of the Rainbow.* Wheaton, IL: Theosophical Publishing, 1969. A book on higher spiritual consciousness attuned to nature, which was the basic belief of pre-Christian Hawaii. The appendix contains illustrations of mystical symbols used by the *kahuna.* An enlightening book in many ways.

Pukui, Mary Kawena, and Caroline Curtis. *Hawaii Island Legends.* Honolulu: The Kamehameha Schools Press, 1996. Hawaiian tales and legends for youngsters.

Pukui, Mary Kawena, and Caroline Curtis. *Tales of the Menehune.* Honolulu: The Kamehameha Schools Press, 1960. Compilation of legends relating to Hawaii's "little people."

Pukui, Mary Kawena, and Caroline Curtis. *The Waters of Kane and other Hawaiian Legends.* Honolulu: The Kamehameha Schools Press, 1994. Tales and legends for adolescents.

Thrum, Thomas. *Hawaiian Folk Tales,* reprint. Chicago: McClurg and Co., 1950. A collection of Hawaiian tales originally printed in 1907 from the oral tradition as told to the author from various sources.

Westervelt, W. D. *Hawaiian Legends of Volcanoes,* reprint. Boston: Ellis Press, 1991. A small book originally printed in 1916 concerning the volcanic legends of Hawaii and how they related to the fledgling field of volcanism in the early 1900s. The vintage photos alone are worth a look.

Natural Sciences and Geography

Carlquist, Sherwin. *Hawaii: A Natural History.* National Tropical Botanical Garden, 1984. Definitive account of Hawaii's natural history.

Hazlett, Richard, and Donald Hyndman. *Roadside Geology of Hawai'i.* Missoula, MT: Mountain Press Publishing, 1996. Begins with a general discussion of the geology of the Hawaiian Islands, followed by a road guide to the individual islands offering descriptions of easily seen features. A great book to have in the car as you tour the islands.

Hubbard, Douglass, and Gordon Macdonald. *Volcanoes of the National Parks of Hawaii,* reprint. Volcanoes, HI: Hawaii Natural History Association, 1989. The volcanology of Hawaii, documenting the major lava flows and their geological effect on the state; originally printed in 1982.

Kay, E. Alison, comp. *A Natural History of the Hawaiian Islands.* Honolulu: University of Hawai'i Press, 1994. A selection of concise articles by experts in the fields of volcanism, oceanography, meteorology, and biology. An excellent reference source.

Macdonald, Gorden, Agatin Abbott, and Frank Peterson. *Volcanoes in the Sea.* Honolulu: University of Hawai'i Press, 1983. The best reference to Hawaiian geology. Well-explained for easy understanding. Illustrated.

Periodicals

Hawaii Magazine. 3 Burroughs, Irvine, CA 92618. This magazine covers the Hawaiian islands like a tropical breeze. Feature articles on all aspects of life in the islands, with special departments on travel, events, exhibits, and restaurant reviews. Up-to-the-minute information, and a fine read.

Naturist Society Magazine. P.O. Box 132, Oshkosh, WI 54920. This excellent magazine not only *uncovers* bathing-suit-optional beaches throughout the islands, giving tips for naturalists visiting Hawaii, but also provides reports on local politics, environment, and conservation measures from the health-conscious nudist point of view. A fine publication.

Pictorials

La Brucherie, Roger. *Hawaiian World, Hawaiian Heart.* Pine Valley, CA: Imagenes Press, 1989.

Political Science

Bell, Roger. *Last Among Equals: Hawaiian Statehood and American Politics.* Honolulu: University of Hawai'i Press, 1984. Documents Hawaii's long and rocky road to statehood, tracing political partisanship, racism, and social change.

Sports and Recreation

Alford, John, D. *Mountain Biking the Hawaiian Islands.* Ohana Publishing, 1997. Good off-road biking guide to the main Hawaiian islands.

Ambrose, Greg. *Surfer's Guide to Hawai'i.* Honolulu: Bess Press, 1991. Island-by-island guide to surfing spots.

Ball, Stuart. *The Hiker's Guide to the Hawaiian Islands.* Honolulu: University of Hawai'i Press, 2000. This excellent guide includes 44 hikes on each of the four main islands. Ball has also written *The Hikers Guide to O'ahu.*

Cagala, George. *Hawaii: A Camping Guide.* Boston: Hunter Publishing, 1994. Useful.

Chisholm, Craig. *Hawaiian Hiking Trails.* Lake Oswego, OR: Fernglen Press, 1999. Also *Oahu Hiking Trails.*

Cisco, Dan. *Hawai'i Sports.* Honolulu: University of Hawai'i Press, 1999. A compendium of popular and little-known sporting events and figures, with facts, tidbits, and statistical information. Go here first for a general overview.

Lueras, Leonard. *Surfing, the Ultimate Pleasure.* Honolulu: Emphasis International, 1984. One of the most brilliant books ever written on surfing.

McMahon, Richard. *Camping Hawai'i: A Complete Guide.* Honolulu: University of Hawai'i Press, 1997. This book has all you need to know about camping in Hawaii, with descriptions of different campsites.

Morey, Kathy. *Oahu Trails.* Berkeley, CA: Wilderness Press, 1997. Morey's books are specialized, detailed hiker's guides to Hawaii's outdoors. Complete with useful maps, historical references, official procedures, and plants and animals encountered along the way. If you're focused on hiking, these are the best guides to take along. *Maui Trails, Kauai Trails,* and *Hawaii Trails* are also available.

Rosenberg, Steve. *Diving Hawaii.* Locust Valley, NY: Aqua Quest, 1990. Describes diving locations on the major islands as well as the marine life divers are likely to see. Includes many color photos.

Smith, Robert. *Hawaii's Best Hiking Trails.* Kula, Maui, HI: Hawaiian Outdoor Adventures, 1991. Other guides by this author include *Hiking Oahu, Hiking Maui, Hiking Hawaii,* and *Hiking Kauai.*

Sutherland, Audrey. *Paddling Hawai'i,* revised edition. Honolulu: University of Hawai'i Press, 1998. All you need to know about sea kayaking in Hawaiian waters.

Wallin, Doug. *Diving & Snorkeling Guide to the Hawaiian Islands.* 2nd ed. Houston: Pisces Books, 1991. A guide offering brief descriptions of diving locations on the four major islands.

Travel

Clark, John. *Beaches of O'ahu.* Honolulu: University of Hawai'i Press, 1997. Definitive guide to beaches, including many off the beaten path. Features maps and black-and-white photos. Also *Beaches of the Big Island, Beaches of Kaua'i and Ni'ihau,* and *Beaches of Maui County.*

Stanley, David. *Moon Handbooks South Pacific.* 8th ed. Emeryville, CA: Avalon Travel Publishing, 2004. The model on which all travel guides should be based. Simply the best book in the world for travel throughout the South Pacific.

Internet Resources

The following websites have information about Maui County and the state of Hawaii that may be useful in preparation for a trip to the islands and for general interest.

www.co.maui.hi.us
The official website of Maui County. Includes, among other items, information on city government, the county-sponsored bus system, and a calendar of events.

www.go-hawaii.com
This official site of the Hawaii Visitors and Convention Bureau, the state-run tourism organization, has information about all of the major Hawaiian islands: transportation, accommodations, eating, activities, shopping, Hawaiian products, an events calendar, a travel planner and resource guide for a host of topics, as well as information about meetings, conventions, and the organization itself.

www.visitmaui.com
The official site of the Maui Visitors Bureau, a branch of the Hawaii Visitors and Convention Bureau, has much the same information as the previous website but specific to the island of Maui. A very useful resource. Tourist information specific to Molokaʻi and Lanaʻi, can be found at the following sites: **www.molokai-hawaii.com** and **www.visit-lanai.net.**

www.bestplaceshawaii.com
Produced and maintained by H&S Publishing, this first-rate commercial site has general and specific information about all major Hawaiian islands, a vacation planner, and suggestions for things to do and places to see. For a nongovernment site, this is a great place to start a search for tourist information about the state or any of its major islands. One of dozens of sites on the Internet

with a focus on Hawaii tourism-related information.

www.alternative-hawaii.com
Alternative source for eco-friendly general information and links to specific businesses, with some cultural, historical, and events information.

www.hawaiiecotourism.org
Official Hawaii Ecotourism Association website. Lists goals, members, and activities, and provides links to member organizations and related ecotourism groups.

http://calendar.gohawaii.com
For events of all sorts happening throughout the state, visit the calendar of events listing on the Hawaii Visitors Bureau website. Information can be accessed by island, date, or type.

www.state.hi.us/sfca/culturecalendar.html
This site of the State Foundation of Culture and the Arts features a calendar of arts and cultural events, activities, and programs held throughout the state. Information is available by island and type.

www.hawaiianair.com, www.alohaairlines.com, www.pacificwings.com
These websites for Hawaiian Airlines, Aloha Airlines, and Pacific Wings list virtually all regularly scheduled commercial air links throughout the state.

www.mele.com
Check out the Hawaiian music scene at Hawaiian Music Island, one of the largest music websites that focuses on Hawaiian music, books, and videos related to Hawaiian music and culture, concert schedules, Hawaiian music awards, and links to music compa-

nies and musicians. Others with broad listings and general interest information are Nahenahenet, **www.nahenahe.net;** and Hawaiian Music Guide, **www.hawaii-music.com.**

www.uhpress.hawaii.edu

This University of Hawai'i Press website has the best overall list of titles for books published on Hawaiian themes and topics. Other publishers to check for substantial lists of books on Hawaiiana are the Bishop Museum Press, **www.bishopmuseum.org/bishop/press;** Kamehameha Schools Press, **www.ksbe.edu /newsroom/kspress;** Bess Press, **www.bess-press.com;** Mutual Publishing, **www.mutu-alpublishing.com;** and Petrogylph Press, **www.basicallybooks.com.**

www.hawaiimuseums.org

This site is dedicated to the promotion of museums and cultural attractions in the state of Hawaii with links to member sites on each of the islands. A member organization.

www.mauinews.com

Website of Maui's largest newspaper, *Maui News*. It has a concentration of news coverage about Maui yet covers major news from the Neighbor Islands.

www.oha.org

Official site for the state-mandated organization that deals with native Hawaii-related affairs.

www.kalahui.org

Site for the oldest and largest organization of native Hawaiians who are advocating for sovereignty. Several dozen independent native Hawaiian rights organizations are pushing for various degrees of sovereignty or independence for native Hawaiian people. The major groups are as follows: Nation of Hawai'i, **www.hawaii-nation.org;** Reinstated Hawaiian Government, **www.rein-stated.org;** Kingdom of Hawaii, **www.free hawaii.org;** (another) Kingdom of Hawaii, **www.pixi.com/~kingdom;** and the Hawaiian Kingdom, **www.hawaiiankingdom.org.**

Index

Beaches

G

H

Hiking

Parks

Snorkeling

Acknowledgments

Since the passing of J. D. Bisignani, the original author of *Moon Handbooks Maui*, I have taken on the great task of revising this book and others in his series of guides to Hawaii. Joe, you have been an inspiration to me and have laid a solid foundation for the present revision. I pray that I'm able to shoulder the responsibility. Even though you are gone, you've been with me with each word. To you, my good friend, a big thank you.

As always, the staff at Avalon Travel Publishing has been professional in every way. A sincere thank you to everyone.

The following individuals require special thanks for their assistance in the revision of this book. Henry Nakahodo, Tom and Janice Fairbanks, Jim Heine, Candy Aluli, Kaui Dickson, Luana Pa'ahana, Nancy Brown, Jamie Mosley, Suzie Duro, Sherry Barbier, Nancy Daniels, Elizabeth Marquez, Ellen Unterman, David Sayre, Shelley Drake, Bea Wolfe, Cherrie Attix, Henry Clay Richardson, Michele Lee, Kirk Hansen, Maria Arceneaux, Keala, Haunani Vieira, Eric Dixson, Randy Coon, Jim Coon, Virginia DiPiazza, Steve and Barbara Schonely, Kathy Lane, and my wife, Linda Nilsen. A sincere *Mahalo* to you all.

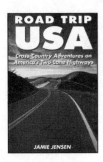

Hana Hotel 1st. → slow down (1 week)
Pg 80 (Hana)   massage (Buy lotions)
vist ① Kaihalulu Beach   Beach
2 Beaches ② Wai'anapaapa hot tub!
              Beach   Read a book
                         Hike/Day Trip on West?
                         Kayak lessons?

(Peak is Jan - AP)
Stay NOV - MAY ~ During Whales migration
Shops @ Wailia (not @ Hotel → too $ pricey) Shop Before get to Resort!
Wailia @ least 4 days ~ Spa (Buy lotion)
(stay during whale   use pools extensively
  week) →   Tennis courts

Kanapali Hotel "most Human" ~ shoping
Shoping

                                    ~ also in Lunar New Year
Pg 68 "Whale Month in February ~ Return of the   Pg 68
Whaling tours/Annual Whale Day Event   Humpback

www.maui.com   (Fridays Art Night in
Rainforest Day Hike   Lahina 213 1222)

261 Maui Ocean Center @ Ma'alaea Bay (mother whales
     "Ocean walk" tunnel   give birth in
                                         Bay!

Whale Celebration in February

Shop in the begining for : Swim suit, jewerly, clothes, Quilt
                    (imagine item in home ~ where put?)

www.bestplaceshawaii
March/April ~
ARTMAUI → Schaefer International Gallery
          Castle theater?
          (808) 242 7469

U.S.~Metric Conversion

1 inch = 2.54 centimeters (cm)
1 foot = .304 meters (m)
1 yard = 0.914 meters
1 mile = 1.6093 kilometers (km)
1 km = .6214 miles
1 fathom = 1.8288 m
1 chain = 20.1168 m
1 furlong = 201.168 m
1 acre = .4047 hectares
1 sq km = 100 hectares
1 sq mile = 2.59 square km
1 ounce = 28.35 grams
1 pound = .4536 kilograms
1 short ton = .90718 metric ton
1 short ton = 2000 pounds
1 long ton = 1.016 metric tons
1 long ton = 2240 pounds
1 metric ton = 1000 kilograms
1 quart = .94635 liters
1 US gallon = 3.7854 liters
1 Imperial gallon = 4.5459 liters
1 nautical mile = 1.852 km

To compute Celsius temperatures, subtract 32 from Fahrenheit and divide by 1.8. To go the other way, multiply Celsius by 1.8 and add 32.

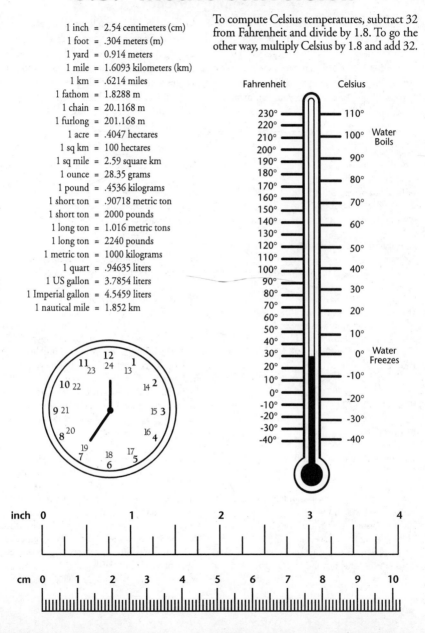

Keeping Current

Although we strive to produce the most up-to-date guidebook humanly possible, change is unavoidable. Between the time this book goes to print and the moment you read it, a handful of the businesses noted in these pages will undoubtedly change prices, move, or even close their doors forever. Other worthy attractions will open for the first time. If you have a favorite gem you'd like to see included in the next edition, or see anything that needs updating, clarification, or correction, please drop us a line. Send your comments via email to atpfeedback@avalonpub.com, or use the address below.

Moon Handbooks Maui
Avalon Travel Publishing
1400 65th Street, Suite 250
Emeryville, CA 94608, USA
www.moon.com

Editor and Series Manager: Kevin McLain
Copy Editor: Ginjer L. Clarke
Graphics and Production Coordinator:
    Justin Marler
Cover Designer: Kari Gim
Interior Designers: Amber Pirker, Alvaro
    Villanueva, Kelly Pendragon
Map Editor: Naomi Adler Dancis
Cartographers: Kat Kalamaras, Mike Morgenfeld
Indexer: Judy Hunt

ISBN: 1-56691-501-5
ISSN: 1099-8772

Printing History
1st Edition—1986
7th Edition—February 2004
5 4 3 2 1

Avalon Travel Publishing is a division of Avalon Publishing Group, Inc.

Some photos and illustrations are used by permission and are the property of the original copyright owners.

Front cover photo: © Dave Fleetham
Table of contents photos: Robert Nilsen

Printed in the USA by Malloy